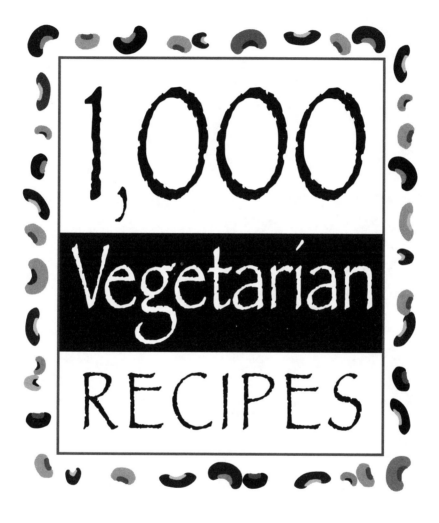

1,000
Vegetarian
RECIPES

1,000 Vegetarian RECIPES

Carol Gelles

Macmillan•USA

MACMILLAN

A Simon & Schuster Macmillan Company

1633 Broadway

New York, NY 10019

MACMILLAN is a registered trademark of
Macmillan, Inc.

A catalogue record is available from the Library
of Congress.

ISBN: 0-02-542965-5

Manufactured in the United States of America

10 9 8 7 6 5 4 3

DESIGN BY C&T DESIGNS

Dedicated to

my mother and father

for their extraordinary love and support

In memory of

Marshall T. Meyer

whose spirituality touched so many lives

Contents

One Thousand Recipes: An Odyssey   2

What Should Be the Focus of This Book?   *2*
To Whom Should This Book Be Directed?   *3*
Vegetarianism and Health   *4*
Yields and Number of Servings   *6*
Meals in Minutes   *7*
Cooking from Scratch—or Not   *7*
The Well-Stocked Pantry   *9*
Shopping for Recipe Ingredients   *12*
About Ingredients   *13*
Breakfast Choices   *19*
Brown Bagging It   *19*
Planning a Menu: Timing Is Everything   *20*
Company's Coming   *21*
  Elegant Dinner to Impress the Boss   *22*
  Caribbean-Spanish-African Cuisine   *24*
  Chinese Cuisine   *25*
  Eastern European Cuisine   *27*
  French Cuisine   *28*
  Greek Cuisine   *30*
  Indian Cuisine   *31*
  Italian Cuisine   *32*
  Japanese Cuisine   *34*
  Mexican and Southwest Cuisine   *35*
  Middle Eastern Cuisine   *37*
  Hearty Meals   *39*
  Last-Minute Meals   *40*
The Fat Content of Recipes in This Book   *43*
Mail Order Sources   *43*

Appetizers   44

Spreads   *46*
Dips   *63*
Finger and Toothpick Foods   *67*
First Courses   *79*
Snacks   *85*

Soups   92

Vegetable Soups   *93*
Heartier Grain and/or Bean Soups   *121*
Cold Soups   *130*

Entrees   136

Grains and Beans   *139*
Vegetables   *163*
Entree Strudels   *177*
Pasta, Pizza, Noodles, and Dumplings   *18*
Eggs, Cheese, and Dairy   *208*
Quiches and Savory Tarts   *211*
Tofu, Tempeh, Seitan, and Textured
  Vegetable Protein (TVP)   *217*

Side Dishes   228

Vegetables   *232*
Grains   *300*
Beans   *331*

Salads   336

Vegetable Salads   *339*
Fruit and Vegetable Salads   *365*
Grain and Bean Salads   *372*
Fruit Salads   *387*
Dressings   *391*

Breads   394

Quick Breads   *395*
Biscuits and Scones   *403*
Muffins   *408*
Yeast Breads   *413*
Flavored Breads and Toasts   *427*
Crackers   *429*

Breakfast, Brunch, Lunch   432

Pancakes   *434*
Waffles   *439*
French Toast   *442*
Blintzes   *445*
Cereal   *446*
Eggs   *447*
Sandwiches   *455*
Turnovers   *464*

Condiments, Sauces, Relishes, and Jams   468

Condiments   *470*
Sauces and Marinades   *473*
Relishes   *484*
Chutney   *486*
Flavored Butters, Jams, and Fruit and
   Vegetable Butters   *489*
Miscellaneous Stuff   *494*

Desserts   498

Yeast-Based Desserts   *500*
Cakes and Tortes   *503*
Icings, Fillings, and Frostings   *515*
Pies and Tarts   *517*
Strudel   *528*
Cheesecakes   *530*
Cookies   *532*
Fruit Desserts   *540*
Mousses, Puddings, and Custards   *547*
Sorbets   *550*
Crepes and Sauces   *552*

Beverages   556

Coffee   *557*
Tea   *558*
Fruit Drinks   *559*
Blender Fruit Shakes   *561*
Party Drinks   *564*

Index   567

Acknowledgments

To Justin Schwartz and Macmillan Publishing USA, who had faith in my abilities to accomplish this project, and to Judith Weber, without whom this book may have been written by someone else. Thank you both.

To my family and friends who tasted and tasted and tasted and tasted and tasted.

One Thousand Recipes:
An Odyssey

When colleagues would hear that the project I was working on was called *1,000 Vegetarian Recipes*, they would echo with a groan, "One *thousand* recipes?!"

I must have felt the same way when I started this book, since I'd go to sleep and dream about signing contracts to write books with titles like *1,000 Ways to Soft Skin*, *1,000 Ways to Clean Pots*, and *1,000 Ways to Knit Socks*. Invariably I'd wake up saying, "One *thousand* ways?!" You don't have to be Freud to figure out this was a daunting project.

But I dug in and started cooking. I'd cook anything and everything, and every possible variation to anything and everything, because, after all, I had a *thousand* recipes to create. As I worked at making interesting and delicious recipes, I watched the "finished" pile grow ever taller. Suddenly I panicked that I couldn't possibly get all the recipes I wanted to create into a book with *only* a thousand recipes.

As I continued cooking and testing and experimenting, two major questions came up along the way: how "healthy" should the recipes be, and what aspects of vegetarianism should they address?

What Should Be the Focus of This Book?

Should all the recipes be "healthy"? Many recipes well suited to vegetarianism include some or even a lot of fat, sugar, and/or sodium (salt). Should I exclude all recipes that are not "healthy"? After giving this subject serious consideration, I realized that the title is not *1,000 Low-Fat/Low-Sodium/Sugar-Free Vegetarian Recipes*. On the other hand, I felt that if I were to live up to an annotated title it should be *1,000 Really Great-Tasting Vegetarian Recipes*. To fulfill this objective I've used fat, sugar, and/or salt in recipes that truly need them, but I've tried to use the minimum amount necessary to achieve the best flavor and texture.

My approach is one of moderation. Most recipes that use fat for cooking use only about 1½ teaspoons or less of oil, butter, or margarine per serving. I've tried to balance flavor with health considerations. If you are on a very low-fat diet, many of these recipes will still contain too much fat for you; however, in recipes with sautéed ingredients you can reduce the fat content by half if you cook in a nonstick skillet. (I chose to test these recipes with common household equipment, rather than specialized items such as nonstick skillets.)

Similarly, the recipes in this book are probably too salty for people who are limiting their sodium intake, since I lightly salt most recipes. If you are watching your sodium intake, you can easily just omit salt wherever called for, except in yeast products, where salt actually has a chemical significance in retarding rising times. Also, be sure to buy salt-free bouillon or make homemade salt-free broth. If, on the other hand, you have a "normal" American palate, you may want to add extra salt to most recipes—just taste before you serve (you may even decide to double the amount of salt called for).

As for sugar, you can experiment by reducing the amount called for in the recipes. For items like fruit salads the sugar content can generally be changed without problems, but drastic cutbacks of sugar in baked products may cause an unfavorable change, not just in taste but in texture, too. I've developed these recipes to a point where I think the sugar content is already lower than that of conventional recipes for the same food; the success of further cutbacks depends on your own palate.

TO WHOM SHOULD THIS BOOK BE DIRECTED?

A vegetarian, by definition, is a person who does not eat the flesh of anything that was previously living. However, there are varying degrees of vegetarianism:

Pesco-Lacto-Ovo: Technically not vegetarians, they do not eat meat, but do eat fish, eggs, and dairy products.

Lacto-Ovo: People in this category do not eat meat, but do eat eggs and dairy products.

Lacto: Lacto vegetarians do not eat meat or eggs, but do eat dairy products.

Ovo: This type does not eat meat or dairy products but does eat eggs.

Vegan or Strict Vegetarian: Vegans do not eat meat, dairy products, or eggs, and may or may not use honey or other animal by-products.

Fructarian: Adherents of this very extreme form of vegetarianism eat only fruit. It is very difficult to fulfill all nutritional needs when on this diet.

Since this is a vegetarian cookbook, I decided against recipes that call for fish, but I have included eggs and dairy products (since the title is not *1,000 Vegan Recipes*). I believe this book contains enough egg-free and dairy-free recipes to be of value even to the vegan. To make it easier to identify recipes that fall into each category, each recipe has been coded to indicate which type of vegetarian it is suited for:

[LO] = Lacto-Ovo

[L] = Lacto

[O] = Ovo

[V] = Vegan

Some recipes containing eggs and/or dairy products have been given "V" codes because there are suggestions for non-lacto/ovo substitutions. For example, a "V" is given for recipes containing butter with the suggestion of using margarine as a substitute. Or if the lacto/ovo ingredient is optional, the recipe is given a "V." When a vegan recipe variation follows a lacto/ovo recipe, the variation is marked separately with a "V" for easy reference.

VEGETARIANISM AND HEALTH

Some people choose vegetarianism because of the health benefits. In fact, many of the conditions that can be prevented or treated by diet can be met by the vegetarian way of life.

Vitamins and Minerals

It's easy to miss out on many important nutrients when you follow a fast-food lifestyle. A Danish and coffee for breakfast; burger or sandwich for lunch; and meat and potatoes for dinner usually means you're not eating nearly enough fruits, vegetables, or fiber during the day. By switching to a vegetarian diet—which is based on vegetables, fruits, grains, and beans—you'll find yourself easily meeting the recommended 5 fruits and vegetables per day. It's important to keep in mind that variety is not only the spice of life, but also ensures that you will get the wide range of vitamins, minerals, and fiber you need.

Fat and Cholesterol

For a long time, cholesterol was considered the major dietary villain in heart disease. Now we've learned that avoiding saturated fats as well as reducing total fats is also important in a heart-healthy diet. Refer to page 43 for information on the fat content of recipes in this book.

While many oil companies have ingrained in the public the idea that polyunsaturated fats are desirable, the good news is that monounsaturated fats are even better. So what does this mean?

Here's a quick chemistry lesson to help define these terms. Fats are made up of very long chains of carbons (hydrogens and oxygens are also attached, but they don't count in determining saturation). These carbons (c) are held together in chains by covalent bonds and can be linked by one or more bonds in the following ways:

- Monounsaturated fats have one double bond between the carbons in the chain (c-c-c-c-c-c=c-c-c-c).

- Polyunsaturated fats have more than one double bond between the carbons in the chain (c=c-c-c=c-c-c=c-c-c).

- Saturated fats have no double bonds between the carbons in the chain (c-c-c-c-c-c-c-c-c-c).

For our purposes, polyunsaturated fats mean oils made from almost any plant source; the exceptions are coconut and palm oils, which are saturated fats. Canola and safflower oils are particularly high in double bonds and therefore particularly healthy choices, although any vegetable oil is fine.

Olive oil is monounsaturated, and current scientific findings show this to be the healthiest oil of all.

Butter, lard, suet, and other animal fats are saturated and therefore should be used only sparingly.

The simple truth is: there is *no* cholesterol in any vegetable, fruit, nut, grain, or bean. Cholesterol is found only in animal products. So if you are a strict vegetarian (vegan), you have automatically eliminated all cholesterol from your diet. If you are a lacto-ovo vegetarian, remember that eggs, butter, and cheese are animal products and you will still have to watch out for cholesterol (and fat). When using eggs, try to substitute extra whites for the yolks (two egg whites can be used as a whole egg; for example, make a two-egg omelet or scrambled eggs with 1 whole egg and 2 whites). When choosing cheeses, look for the lower-fat or nonfat varieties; use high-fat cheese only occasionally. Select low-fat or nonfat dairy products instead of whole-milk ones. The recipes in this book that call for milk, yogurt, or cottage cheese will work regardless of which type you select (although no-fat yogurt dishes will be slightly tangier than when prepared with regular or low-fat yogurt). I find fat-free sour cream and cheeses to be unacceptable in texture and flavor, but if you enjoy them, then by all means use them in these recipes.

Cheese and eggs are not the only culprits. Americans have a decided taste for fatty foods. Fried vegetables are still fatty foods, perhaps less fatty than chicken fried with the skin on, but fatty nevertheless. Butter is still butter, and if you use plenty of it on bread or vegetables or in cooking, you're still not improving your nutritional profile.

Per Ounce:	*Saturated Fat mgs*	*Calories*	*Cholesterol gm*	*Fat gm*	*Sodium mgs*
Beans, kidney	36	0	.1	0	.6
Beef, cooked	63	24	3.0	1.1	22
Cheese					
American	91	25	7.1	9.0	395
Blue	99	21	8.1	8.3	395
Brie	95	30	7.3	7.9	178
Cheddar	113	30	9.4	5.9	176
Cottage (4%)	30	4	1.3	.8	115
Cottage (1%)	21	1	.3	.2	115
Cream	6	100	31.0	10.0	85
Chicken breast, skinless	46	24	1	.3	21
Chicken (with skin)	66	30	3.8	1.1	22
Egg	42	122	2.8	.9	36
Fish					
Salmon	51	20	2.3	.3	16
Shrimp	28	55	.3	.1	63
Sole	33	19	.4	.1	30
Tuna (in oil)	56	5	2.3	.4	100
Tuna (in water)	32	5	.5	0	17
Lamb	83	27	5.9	2.5	20

YIELDS AND NUMBER OF SERVINGS

Some cookbooks provide recipes that always yield the same number of servings. I have intentionally prepared some recipes in large batches because I believe that if you're putting a lot of effort into preparing a recipe, it's nice to have leftovers to use in the next day or two or freeze for the future. You'll find this to be especially true in the soup chapter. I also include some larger-yield recipes to allow for company. If you are not fond of leftovers of any kind, just check the yield of the recipe before you choose a menu.

I've included both the yield and the number of servings because the number of people each recipe will serve may vary depending on your menu. For example, if you've chosen to serve lasagne with a salad, that may be enough for 8 people; on the other hand, if you are serving appetizers, soup, bread, and dessert with the lasagne and salad, that same lasagne may then be enough for 12 people. Another consideration is who are you serving. If your household consists of two adults and two teenage sons, a lasagne may only serve 4 to 6 people. You probably know how many people in your family 3 cups of rice will serve—it may be more or less than the number I have suggested.

MEALS IN MINUTES

Vegetarian cooking tends to conjure up images of earth mothers slaving hours over a hot (wood-burning) stove. In fact, some ingredients, such as whole grains and beans, do require relatively long cooking times (more than an hour). But the idea that they require lots of work is a fallacy. I don't think putting some ingredients into a pot and leaving it to simmer, basically unattended, is much more work than throwing ingredients into a pot and letting it simmer just a few minutes. The difference is *planning*. Longer-cooking soups or stews are not intended to become a spur-of-the-moment dinner for unexpected company. But there are many dishes based on items you should have on hand (see "The Well-Stocked Pantry," pages 9–11) that can be made almost in the blink of an eye (less than half an hour).

When you need a quick meal, try one based on these staples, each of which takes less than 20 minutes to cook (see also "Last-Minute Meals," pages 40–42):

Beans (canned)	Pasta
Bulgur	Polenta (instant)
Couscous	Quinoa
Kasha	Rice (white)
Millet	Rizcouz

COOKING FROM SCRATCH—OR NOT

I certainly prefer to cook everything from scratch, given enough time. However, enough time is a rare commodity nowadays. Many of the recipes in this book use ingredients that require longer-than-convenient cooking times. These include beans, recipes that use vegetable broth as a base, and longer-cooking grains. In some instances, turning to prepared products is a perfectly fine solution, in others it's not.

Beans: The advantage to cooking dried beans from scratch is that you have a much wider variety of beans to choose from. Besides the common ones available in the supermarket, health food and gourmet stores carry many more interesting varieties, such as rattlesnake beans, scarlet runners, appaloosas, Swedish brown beans, and dozens (probably hundreds, possibly thousands) more. You can also order interesting varieties by mail (see "Mail Order Sources," page xxx). Furthermore, beans cooked from scratch are not salted, which is not the case for canned.

Choosing canned beans over home-cooked can be fine in many cases. I have found that the quality of canned beans varies from brand to brand (the brands I like best, in order of preference, are S&W, Green Giant, and Goya). An acceptable canned bean should be tender but not mushy, should not have much (if any) sludge at the bottom of the can, and certainly should not taste tinny. The distinct advantage of having beans ready for a last-minute meal can override the disadvantages. (For more about beans, see pages 13–14.)

Broth: Broth adds to the complexity of flavor of many recipes. There's no doubt in my mind that good homemade vegetable broth is superior to any prepared broth or bouillon (and there are recipes for good homemade broth on pages 93–95). However, just because you don't have any on hand doesn't mean you have to skip a recipe that calls for broth. Vegetable broth or bouillon can be purchased in several forms: frozen or jarred stock is available in gourmet stores or by mail order; canned stock (from Swanson) can be found in the supermarket; bouillon cubes (from many manufacturers) and powdered stock is sold in packets or jars in some supermarkets and all health food stores. All of these can be used with excellent results as part of other recipes. Bear in mind that stock, broth, or bouillon that is only just okay when tasted alone may be perfectly fine as part of a bean soup or stew or curry. Like beans, you may have to try a few brands until you find one that is acceptable to you. The one that I use is Knorr. (For more on broth, see pages 93–95.)

Grain: Although some instant grains (such as couscous, rizcous, grits, and instant polenta) cook up quite well, most grains just have to be cooked the old-fashioned, more or less time-consuming way. I find instant rice to be a totally unacceptable substitute for the "real" thing—which in fact takes less than half an hour to cook. My strategy for "instant" grains is to cook a batch of slower cooking grains and use it for two or three different recipes. Many of the recipes that call for grains don't start from scratch, but rather call for grain that is already cooked. This allows you to use grain that you have cooked in advance and just reheat for that particular dish.

Baked Goods: The term *from scratch* is most frequently applied to baked goods. I think homemade cakes, bread, muffins, and so on are great (and I have two or three chapters chock-full of delicious recipes for them), but being a realist, I know that baking from scratch tends to be relegated to holidays and special occasions. Because baked goods keep so well in the freezer, I find it easy to have something homemade on hand. Whenever I bake anything I just freeze the leftovers. I may freeze a loaf or two of bread (sliced before freezing); muffins left from a batch I served a few of; and things I have left over when I bake for company.

Cooking from scratch or at the last minute is best accomplished if you keep a good supply of staples on hand. This brings us to the next section.

The Well~Stocked Pantry

Ideally, a well-stocked pantry (refrigerator included) will have everything in it that you need to prepare some, or even many, recipes without having to run to the market. This doesn't mean you should have every item you'd ever need to cook any recipe, just the basics that allow preparation of last-minute recipes, enough to be able to "throw together" a meal for unexpected company or when you just didn't make it to the supermarket.

This is a lot less complicated than you might imagine. The majority of ingredients used in these (and almost any) vegetarian recipes are staples, many of them shelf-stable (items that don't require refrigeration, or at least not until opening). These include grains, beans, and pastas. I've divided the pantry into two sections: one includes basics that I feel most households should have on hand at all times, the second includes optional ingredients. The optional list is more likely to depend on your preferences and/or lifestyle. For example, if you're vegan the dairy suggestions would not be for you; if you never bake, you probably don't need yeast, baking powder, or baking soda, but flour is good to have on hand for sauces and breading; whether to stock canned or dried beans depends on which you prefer to cook with. My own pantry includes all items on both lists (and then some).

Basic Pantry Items

Staples

Baking powder

Baking soda

Beverages (coffee and/or tea and/or other beverages)

Bread crumbs

Canned vegetables (at least 1 can each)

corn kernels (8- or 11-ounce can)

tomatoes

    paste (6-ounce can)

    sauce (8-ounce can)

    whole peeled (14$^1/_2$-ounce can)

Cornstarch

Flour (all-purpose and whole wheat)

Grains (barley, bulgur or couscous, oatmeal, and white and brown rice)

Honey

Legumes (beans), dry and/or canned (at least two types) preferably all of the following:

black beans

chickpeas

kidney beans

lentils

lima beans

split peas (yellow or green)

Mustard (Dijon and spicy brown or yellow)

Nuts (walnuts and/or pecans)

Oil (vegetable and olive)

Basic Pantry Items

Pasta (at least two shapes, preferably one long and one small)

Raisins (light or dark)

Rice (brown, white, Jasmine or basmati)

Salt

Soy milk (especially for vegan cooking)

Soy sauce

Sugar (granulated and light brown or dark brown)

Tabasco or other hot pepper sauce

Tofu (Silken tofu is sold in aseptic cartons and can be stored for long periods of time in the refrigerator until opening; once opened it should be used within a few days. Fresh tofu should be purchased as needed but shouldn't be stored too long.)

Vanilla extract

Vegetable bouillon, broth or stock

Vinegar (red wine and distilled white and/or cider)

Wine, red and/or white (You can stock cooking wine—which is wine with added salt—or you can just save any leftover wine from dinner or parties.)

Worcestershire sauce, anchovy-free

Herbs and Spices

Fresh

gingerroot
parsley (curly or flat leaf)

Dried

basil
bay leaves
oregano
rosemary
tarragon
thyme

Ground

black pepper (or whole peppercorns ground in a pepper mill)
cinnamon
chili powder
curry powder
ginger
paprika
red pepper

Fresh Produce (one or more of each)

Apples

Bell peppers (green or red)

Carrots

Celery

Garlic

Lemon

Lettuce (romaine and/or iceburg)

Onions (yellow)

Oranges

Potatoes

Scallions (aka green onion)

Tomatoes

Frozen Produce

Broth, vegetable (homemade or store-bought, if not using bouillon)

Corn

Orange and/or apple juice concentrate

Peas

Spinach, chopped

Dairy Products (for Lacto or Lacto-Ovo Vegetarians)

Butter (or margarine)

Eggs

Milk

Parmesan cheese (grated or whole)

Yogurt (unflavored)

OPTIONAL PANTRY ITEMS

Staples

Capers

Chilies (canned)

Chutney

Flour, rye

Fruit, dried (apricots and/or prunes)

Grains
 cornmeal
 kasha or millet
 quinoa
 wheat berries (whole grain wheat)

Hoisin sauce

Jam or jelly (whatever is your favorite)

Ketchup (catsup)

Mirin (rice wine) or sherry

Molasses

Mushrooms, imported dried

Mustard, honey

Nuts (almonds, peanuts, and/or pine nuts)

Olives (ripe black and/or stuffed green)

Peanut butter

Rice, wild and arborio

Roasted red peppers or pimientos

Salsa

Sesame oil (and/or chili oil)

Tomatoes, sun-dried (dried and/or oil-
 marinated)

Vinegar, balsamic

Wheat germ

Herbs and Spices

Fresh
 basil
 cilantro (aka fresh coriander, Chinese
  parsley)
 dill

Dried
 caraway seeds
 cinnamon sticks
 cloves
 mustard (ground)
 peppercorns
 red pepper flakes
 sesame seeds

Ground
 allspice
 cloves
 coriander
 cumin
 nutmeg
 turmeric

Fresh Produce

Cucumbers

Leeks

Mushrooms (white or wild)

Onions (red and/or mild such as Vidalia,
 Spanish, Bermuda)

Parsnips

Salad greens (endive and/or leaf lettuce
 and/or watercress)

Shallots

Zucchini

Dairy Products (for Lacto or Lacto-Ovo Vegetarians)

Buttermilk

Cheddar cheese

Mozzarella cheese

Swiss or Jarlsburg cheese

SHOPPING FOR RECIPE INGREDIENTS

I prefer to write my recipes using very specific amounts of ingredients. So, for example, the recipes here will call for 1 cup chopped onion instead of 1 medium onion, chopped. I believe that this method eliminates the need to guess; what, exactly, is a medium onion? On the other hand, it does leave the problem of guessing: How many whole onions will make up the 1 cup chopped? The next table will help eliminate that problem.

SHOPPING GUIDE

Item	Amount needed	To equal
Almonds, whole	4 ounces	1 cup chopped
Apple	1 medium (4 ounces)	1 cup chopped or diced
	1 large (5$^1/_3$ ounces)	1 cup shredded
Asparagus	5 medium (3$^1/_2$ ounces)	1 cup cut
Broccoli	2 medium stalks (9 ounces)	1 cup florets
Cabbage	1 wedge (3 ounces)	1 cup chopped
	1 wedge (2 ounces)	1 cup shredded
Carrot	1 large (6 ounces)	1 cup sliced
		1 cup shredded
		1 cup chopped
Cauliflower	$^1/_4$ small head (4 ounces)	1 cup florets
Celery	2 medium stalks (4 ounces)	1 cup sliced
	1 large + 1 medium stalk	1 cup chopped
Cucumber	$^3/_4$ medium (6 ounces)	1 cup sliced or chopped
Eggplant	$^1/_4$ small (3$^1/_2$ ounces)	1 cup cubed
Green beans	1 $^1/_4$ cups whole	1 cup cut (1-inch pieces)
Mushrooms, white	4 medium (3 ounces)	1 cup sliced or chopped
Onion	1 medium (4 ounces)	1 cup chopped
	1 large (7 ounces)	1 cup finely chopped
Peach	1 medium (6 ounces)	1 cup sliced
Pear	1 medium (5 ounces)	1 cup sliced
Pecan halves	4 to 4$^1/_4$ ounces	1 cup chopped
Pepper, bell	1 small (4$^1/_2$ ounces)	1 cup chopped or diced

Item	Amount needed	To equal
Potato	1 medium (5$^1/_2$ ounces)	1 cup cubed
	1 medium (4$^3/_4$ ounces)	1 cup shredded
Tomato	1 medium (6 ounces)	1 cup diced or chopped
Walnuts, shelled	4 ounces	1 cup chopped
Zucchini	1 small (3$^1/_2$ ounces)	1 cup sliced
	1 small (4$^1/_2$ ounces)	1 cup shredded

ABOUT INGREDIENTS

Beans: Many of the recipes in this book use beans. They're very nutritious (full of fiber and other good stuff), delicious, and filling. On the down side, you need time to cook them. On the up side, there are many brands of canned beans that are extremely good. So, if time is a problem for you, shop around and keep a variety of canned beans in your pantry. I like to keep chickpeas, kidney beans, and black beans as a minimum. Pinto, cannellini, small white beans, black-eyed peas, butter beans, fava beans, and pink beans are also available (some more readily than others). Caution: Don't use canned lima beans for dried, since they are very different creatures.

The advantage to cooking beans from scratch is that you have a much wider variety of beans from which to choose. Besides the common ones available in the supermarket, health food and gourmet stores carry many interesting beans. You can also mail order interesting varieties (see "Mail Order Sources," page 43).

If gas is a problem for you, you can purchase a product called Beano in health food stores and pharmacies. Just place a few drops on your food and you should be able to eat beans to your heart's delight (and I mean that literally as well as figuratively).

The following chart provides complete information on the stovetop cooking method for beans. I've tried to include all the beans you are likely to encounter.

For more information on beans, see also "Soy Products" (pages 17–18).

INSTRUCTIONS FOR STOVETOP COOKING OF BEANS

1. Rinse the beans and discard any debris.

2. For each cup of beans, add 4 cups of water and soak overnight, or until the interior of the bean is uniform in color when cut in half with a sharp knife. Or quick-soak by bringing the water and beans to a boil, reduce heat and simmer 2 minutes, and let stand 1 hour, or until the interior of the bean is uniform in color when cut in half with a sharp knife.

3. Drain, discard the soaking water.

4. Place 4 cups of fresh water and the soaked beans in a 2-quart saucepan and bring to a boil. Reduce the heat and simmer, covered loosely, for the suggested cooking time given below.

5. Start checking for doneness at the lower cooking time.

Type of Bean	*Cooking Time*
Adzuki	$3/4$ to $1^1/2$ hours
Black	1 to $1^1/2$ hours
Black-eyed peas	$3/4$ to $1^1/2$ hours
Cannellini	1 to $1^1/2$ hours
Chickpeas	2 to 3 hours
Fava (peel after cooking)	2 to 3 hours
Great Northern	1 to 2 hours
Kidney	1 to 2 hours
Lentils	$1/2$ to 1 hour
Lima (baby)	$3/4$ to $1^1/2$ hours
Lima (large)	1 to $1^1/2$ hours
Mung	$3/4$ to 1 hour
Navy (small white)	1 to 2 hours
Pink	1 to 2 hours
Pinto	1 to 2 hours
Roman (cranberry)	1 to 2 hours
Soy	$2^1/2$ to $3^1/2$ hours

Broth: See pages 8, 93–95.

Dairy Products: I'm intentionally not very specific about what type of dairy products to use in these recipes since I think it's perfectly acceptable to choose to use reduced-fat, skim, whole (full fat), or lactose-reduced products according to your own dietary needs. Recipes will call for milk or unflavored yogurt or cottage cheese and then you can feel free to use whatever you have on hand. Recipes with a ♥ symbol assume that you have chosen fat-free dairy items. Do bear in mind, however, that choosing skim milk over whole milk will yield a slightly less rich finished dish.

If you are vegan or are watching your cholesterol, just substitute margarine wherever butter is called for. I'm not extremely familiar with lower-fat margarine so I can't be sure that the results (especially in baked products) will be exactly the same as with regular margarine.

Eggs: All eggs used in this book are "large." If you are cholesterol-conscious, you can try substituting Egg Beaters or similar products where beaten eggs are called for, but I can't guarantee the results. Another strategy is to substitute 2 egg whites for 1 whole egg.

Fruits and Vegetables: Unless otherwise specified, you can assume that any fruit or vegetable called for in a recipe is fresh, not canned or frozen. For example, "1 cup chopped tomatoes" means fresh tomatoes. If canned tomatoes are called for, the recipe will say "One 8½-ounce can tomatoes, drained and chopped." Some processed fruits and vegetables can be used interchangeably with fresh and some cannot.

Frozen unsweetened fruit such as strawberries, raspberries, blueberries, cranberries, and peaches can be used in cooked or baked dishes instead of fresh. Measure when frozen, then if the recipe specifies thawed, thaw before adding to the recipe. Because canned fruits are sweetened, I don't find them suitable substitutions for fresh. For dishes such as salads, where the fruits are used raw, fresh is always best.

I always use fresh lemon (and lime) juice because I find that the juice available in bottles, plastic lemons, or the freezer tastes too artificial. If you can't keep fresh lemons around all the time, buy a batch, squeeze them, then freeze the juice in 1-tablespoon blocks in an ice cube tray. Once frozen, you can empty the tray into a plastic bag. That way you can always have "fresh" lemon juice on hand (and while you're at it, you may want to grate some rind and freeze it, too). I find frozen or refrigerated orange juice to be acceptable to use in any recipe calling for orange juice.

Frozen vegetables can also be substituted for fresh, although it's hard to maintain an al dente (tender-crisp) texture once a vegetable has been frozen. As with fruit, measure the vegetables while frozen, then thaw before cooking, unless otherwise specified (such as chopped spinach, which has to be thawed and drained before measuring). Canned vegetables (with the exception of beans and corn) change in flavor and consistency too much to be suitable substitutions for fresh vegetables. Information about specific vegetables can be found in the chapter on side dishes (pages 228–335).

Grains: See pages 300–302.

Herbs: When a recipe calls for a chopped herb (such as chopped parsley) I use fresh herbs. The recipes specify whether the herbs called for are fresh or dried. If you want to prepare a recipe that calls for fresh herbs and you don't have any on hand, the general rule of thumb is to substitute ¼ to ⅓ as much dried herbs as fresh (for example, 3 tablespoons chopped fresh parsley = 2 teaspoons to 1 tablespoon dried parsley).

Fresh herbs are great to perk up any dish. The nice thing about them is they can easily be grown from seeds in window boxes, and (except for basil, parsley, cilantro, and dill), you don't need too much to flavor a dish, so small plants should suffice.

If you don't want to grow them, many supermarkets now carry fresh herbs in the produce department. I always keep fresh parsley and dill on hand in the refrigerator. (They last a fair amount of time if stored moist in plastic bags.) If you don't use them very often, you can buy a bunch, chop it, then freeze it. I find that frozen fresh herbs are better than dried. When basil and cilantro are available, I keep them on hand too.

Oil

Oils do more than just lubricate pans. They definitely add flavor and seriously improve the texture of many dishes. Oils range from almost flavorless to extremely flavorful. Not all dishes need highly flavorful oil and, in that case, any vegetable oil that you prefer is the right choice (they can be mixed oils such as Wesson or Crisco, or specific oils such as canola, peanut, or corn). When olive or another highly flavored oil is called for in a recipe, it's because the flavor adds something special. Because oil goes rancid, it's best stored in the refrigerator if you do not use it too frequently. You can tell if your oil has gone rancid by smelling it. Vegetable oil should not have any distinct odor; if it smells like turpentine, you should get rid of it. Olive oil should smell fruity when fresh; if it smells like turpentine, it's rancid.

Olive Oil: There are basically three grades of olive oil available to the consumer: extra virgin, virgin, and pure (or regular). Extra virgin, the finest grade, comes from the first pressing of the olives. A good extra virgin olive oil should be slightly fruity and have peppery afterbite. Virgin olive oil is from the second pressing and is slightly less flavorful than the extra virgin.

Pure olive oil is from the third pressing. It's not uncommon that whatever oil is left in the olives is extracted with the assistance of chemicals. Regular olive oil is the least flavorful of the three grades and to my mind tends to be heavy and oily-tasting.

Although there are only three grades of olive oil, there are many other factors that can go into choosing the one you prefer. Olives are grown in different parts of the world; Italy, Greece, Spain, France, and the United States are large producers. Like grapes for wine, olives from each country taste different since soil and weather conditions differ. In addition to differences of nationality, prices differ vastly from one oil to the next. It's hard to predict which oil you will prefer, since personal preference is the determining factor in which oil you will enjoy the most.

I think it's acceptable to use virgin olive oil or regular olive oil in cooking, but in salads and other dishes where the olive oil is not cooked, try to choose extra virgin. Personally, I use extra virgin olive oil for all purposes. The brand that I usually use is Colavita. It has a pleasant fruity flavor, and it's much more reasonably priced than many of the high-quality oils.

Some people are not fond of olive oil. Before you make a definitive decision, I suggest you first try a better grade of olive oil. I used to think that olive oil was too heavy and oily, then I tasted a good extra virgin olive oil and have been happily using it ever since. If you still don't like olive oil, then feel free to substitute vegetable oil whenever olive oil is called for.

Vegetable Oil: I usually use canola oil because I find the flavor neutral, and nutritionally it's very high in polyunsaturated fat. If you prefer, any mixed vegetable oil will do. You can also use corn, peanut, safflower, or whatever flavors you like.

Sesame Oil: There are two types of sesame oil. One (usually cold-pressed) is light yellow in color and can be used as vegetable oil. The second is found in the Asian department of supermarkets or gourmet stores. This oil is deep amber in color and very strongly flavored. When recipes call for sesame oil, I am referring to the Asian type.

Chili Oil: Chili oil is very spicy and is to be used sparingly. Like sesame oil, it is usually sold with Asian ingredients rather than with vegetable oils. If you like spicy food, you can substitute chili oil for some of the sesame oil in a recipe.

Flavored Oils: Flavored oil can refer to two different categories: oils made from nuts (such as walnuts, almonds, or hazelnuts), which naturally lend their flavor to the oil, or those oils infused with flavors, such as garlic oil, basil oil, or herb-infused oils. Both types add a depth of flavor to the dishes in which they are used.

Salt: Bear in mind that salt reacts with certain foods, specifically whole grains and beans, both of which should always be cooked in unsalted liquids. Salt toughens the skin and impedes with the absorption of liquids. Beans cooked in salted (or acid) liquid will not soften properly. Whole grains cooked in salted liquid require a longer cooking time and will not absorb the normal amount of liquid.

I also recommend adding salt to foods *after* cooking because they will retain a saltier taste than foods made with the same amount of salt added earlier in the cooking process, thereby allowing you to use less salt in your food.

Soy Products

Soybeans: Soybeans cooked from dried are very versatile and have a lovely flavor. Soybeans and soybean products are an excellent source of protein in the vegetarian diet. The dried beans tend to require long cooking times (about 3 hours) and are not available in cans.

Bean Curd (Tofu): See page 217.

Miso: Miso is fermented soybean paste, sometimes combined with grains such as barley or rice. This paste has a strong flavor that is somewhat bitter and salty.

Seitan: See page 217.

Soy Flour: Soy flour is made from ground (heat-treated) soybeans. This flour can be used in baked goods to add protein to the final product.

Soy Milk: Soy milk is liquid extracted from soaked soybeans. Many commercial soybean milk products contain added oil, sugar, and other ingredients. Check the labels to see what a particular soy milk contains.

Soy Nuts: Roasted soy nuts are crunchy and are frequently used in trail mix or other snack foods.

Soy Sauce and Tamari: Soy sauce is a flavoring agent used throughout the Far East. Made from a combination of soybeans, wheat, and salt, it is allowed to ferment in vats for at least 18 months (some commercial soy sauces are fermented for shorter periods of time), then pressed to extract the liquids.

Chinese soy sauce (such as LaChoy) tends to be darker and saltier than Japanese soy sauce (such as Kikkoman). There are also darker and sweeter soy sauces available in Asian markets. Unless otherwise specified, the recipes in this book were prepared using Japanese soy sauce.

Real tamari is different from soy sauce in that it is a by-product of miso and is thicker and stronger than soy sauce. However, it's not uncommon for tamari sold in this country to be soy sauce.

Soy Sprouts: Soy sprouts are used as a fresh vegetable (see page 238 for more information).

Tempeh: See page 217.

Textured Vegetable Protein (TVP): See page 217.

Vinegars

All vinegars are dilute acids made from fermented fruits, malt, or other alcohols. By interchanging one type of vinegar for another you will alter the flavor of the recipe you are preparing. Since some vinegars are more tart than others, the proportions of vinegar to oil or sugar will have to be changed when you change vinegar types. Following are the most commonly available vinegars.

Balsamic vinegar: This dark brown wine vinegar is made from very sweet grapes and aged in wooden barrels; a good balsamic vinegar is very mellow and slightly sweet. Unfortunately, the quality of balsamic vinegar usually matches the price—cheap ones are generally sour and harsh; the smoother ones are more expensive. Because of the smoothness, it's easy to dress a salad with just balsamic vinegar and little or no oil—a real plus for dieters.

Cider Vinegar: Made from apples and golden in color, cider vinegar tastes fruitier than distilled white vinegar.

Distilled White Vinegar: Clear in color, distilled white vinegar is fermented from grain alcohol and does not have a very specific flavor, but rather just a tanginess.

Flavored Vinegar: Flavored vinegars are usually made from a base of distilled or white wine vinegar to which other flavors are added. Common flavorings are garlic, herbs, or fruits such as raspberries.

Rice Vinegar: Rice vinegar, available in the Asian section of supermarkets or in Asian groceries, is clear in color and somewhat sweet.

Wine Vinegar: Made from wine grapes, this vinegar, like wine, can be mellow or coarse and sharp. Try different brands until you find one you like; it doesn't have to be expensive. Red wine vinegar is the most common one, but white wine, champagne, and sherry vinegars are also available.

BREAKFAST CHOICES

Breakfast for the lacto-ovo vegetarian looks pretty much like everyone else's (except for the ham, bacon, or sausage—and there are even pretty good vegetarian sausages available now). Eggs, hot or cold cereal, pancakes, waffles, French toast, bread (or muffins or scones) with or without cheeses are all perfect breakfast choices.

For the vegan, hot or cold cereal with rice or soy milk (or even juice) is a good breakfast. Peanut butter and jelly happens to be a favorite in my household. Although muffins, pancakes, and waffles are usually made with milk and/or eggs, they can be made suitable for vegan breakfasts, too (see pages 437, 446).

BROWN BAGGING IT

Bringing lunch to work or packing it for school can be the most challenging meal, especially for vegans, since many people don't have facilities to heat food. Following are some ideas that may be helpful.

Sandwiches are the traditional American lunch, and being a vegetarian doesn't rule out the sandwich option. You can always serve up cheese, plain or fancy, depending on what breads and which cheeses you choose. American, Swiss, or Muenster cheese on whole wheat is pretty basic, but you can then spruce it up by adding interesting vegetables, or put it in a pita or on French or Italian bread. Or use one of the wonderful homemade breads you baked. More interesting cheeses, such as smoked Gouda, Brie, jalapeño Monterey Jack, or any blue cheese, will add luster to any sandwich.

In addition to cheese there are many other sandwich fillings. You needn't limit yourself to the ones in the sandwich chapter—many of the spreads in the appetizer chapter make excellent sandwich fillers. Spreads can also be packed in plastic containers, and bring crackers or pita bread as dippers. Assorted vegetables also make good sandwich fillers.

To round out a sandwich lunch, pack some cut-up vegetables (maybe an occasional snack bag of chips) and a piece of fruit for dessert (or an occasional cookie).

Following are some sample menus for this type of lunch.

SANDWICHES MADE FROM APPETIZER SPREADS

Schmear Kaese (page 47) or Ratatouille Spread (page 55) on pumpernickel

Hummus (page 57) or Baba Ganoujh (page 54) in pita bread

Beany Caponata (page 56) or Vegetable Savory Cheesecake (page 48) on whole wheat

Brandied Mushroom Spread (page 60) or Garlic-Herb Spread (page 46) on baguette

Guacamole (page 56) or Stilton Marscapone (page 50) on five-grain bread

If you have a microwave or stove available at lunchtime, soup is a perfect lunch, especially hearty, thick, beany soups. Even if you don't have heating facilities, if you invest in a good thermos you can have soup ready any time you are. Round out the lunch with a crusty roll or slice of whole grain bread, a piece of cheese if desired, salad, and piece of fruit. Quiches also reheat quite well and make nice lunches along with salad.

Lighter Fare

Pack a yogurt and some crunchy cereal, such as granola (homemade, page 446, or store-bought), Grape Nuts, or Bran Buds, or some trail mix (homemade, page 89, or store-bought) to sprinkle on top. Fresh fruit completes this easy lunch or snack. Or substitute a scoop of cottage cheese for the yogurt for a similar light lunch.

PLANNING A MENU: TIMING IS EVERYTHING

Whether it's an everyday meal or an "event" where you're hoping to impress the guests, timing can be a challenge for even the most accomplished cook, and positively daunting for the beginner.

There are two goals to accomplish as a host or hostess: have all the food ready and warm at the same time for each course, and having enough time out of the kitchen to spend with your guests. To accomplish these goals, try to plan menus with no more than one item that needs to be prepared at the last minute. It also helps to set the table early in the day and to select serving platters well in advance. You can even set up ahead of time some of the foods that will hold up (for example, you can put the cookies or cakes onto serving plates early in the day, then cover and/ or refrigerate until serving time).

Since this book is divided into chapters that conform to the different courses of a meal, you can just pick one or two recipes from each chapter that interests you that evening. The easiest menus to organize and the ones that will harmonize best are those based on a theme.

I've put together an "exchange list" system: pick one or more recipes from each course; all the recipes in a category are compatible combinations. A good rule of thumb is not to duplicate ingredients in a single meal (if you've got your heart set on asparagus as an appetizer, for instance, don't use them in the soup or the main or side dishes). Be sure to check the number of servings while planning your menu, since not all recipes in this book serve the same number of people (you may have some leftovers from one course or another).

All salads can be prepared ahead of time. Cut up and measure the ingredients and place in a bowl or plastic bag (if you are using raw onion or scallion in the salad, you may want to cut them up and store them separately from the rest of the salad,) and refrigerate until serving time. The dressings can be prepared in a small bowl ahead of time too. Just before serving, add the dressing to the salad and toss.

Remember, too, that desserts and breads are pretty universally appreciated. You probably won't receive too many complaints about a chocolate cake or cookies or fruit salad, no matter what the theme of the meal.

COMPANY'S COMING

Entertaining can be nerve-racking for all but the most experienced cook. Planning a menu for company can be further complicated by the fact that some (perhaps even most) of the guests are not vegetarians and may not be too excited about the forthcoming vegetarian meal. In these cases, I usually go for vegetarian dishes that are universally familiar entrees, even though they're meatless. This usually translates into Italian or other "ethnic" foods. An even easier route is to invite guests for brunch. Quiches, soufflés, waffles, or French toast are all perfect brunch foods that almost everyone would be happy to eat.

Occasionally you want to really show off, whether for your boss; for friends, family, or future in-laws; or just because you feel like it.

When I'm *really* tap dancing up a storm, I don't skip a single course; I'll make several appetizers as well as a first course. I also add two additional courses to an already overdone menu. The first is the intermezzo, which is used as a palate cleanser. It's a very small portion of homemade (you can also use store-bought) sorbet served between soup and main course. The other "extra" is the after-dessert course. For this I offer cognac or an after-dinner liqueur, along with Caramelized Grapes (page 547) or Chocolate-Dipped Strawberries (or dried fruit), or chocolate truffles or other chocolates (store-bought). Since I have the luxury of owning an espresso maker, I also offer that or cappuccino or an after-dinner liqueur-laced coffee (page 558). I'm frequently tempted to offer Alka Seltzer as a very last course, but that might lead people to worry about the quality of the foods they've just consumed.

Elegant Dinner to Impress the Boss

APPETIZERS AND FIRST COURSES

Red Pepper and Sun-Dried Tomato Dip (page 64)

Artichoke and Parmesan Dip (page 66)

Vegetable Savory Cheesecake (page 48)

Stilton Marscapone (page 50)

Poor Man's Caviar (page 53)

Onion Timbales (page 270) with
Curried Tomato–Red Pepper Sauce (page 271)

Croustades (pages 78–79)

Sautéed Julienned Vegetables (page 80)

Artichokes with Raspberry Vinaigrette (page 84) or
Lemon Garlic Mayonnaise (page 84)

SOUPS

Spring Vegetable (page 96)

Creamy Tomato and Leek (page 99)

Lettuce and Pea (page 106)

Peppery Potato-Fennel (page 114)

Leek and Wild Rice (page 126)

ENTREES

Green and White Lasagne (page 197)

Pasta Puttanesca (page 190)

Eggplant Rollatini (page 172)

Roquefort Soufflé (page 208)

Ragout of Wild Mushrooms (page 173)

Mushrooms Stroganoff (page 173)

SIDE DISHES

Asparagus with Walnuts and Browned Butter (page 236)

Parslied Carrots (page 248)

Creamy Parmesan Green Beans (page 260)

Lemon Wild and White Rice (page 321)

Fiddlehead Ferns with Wild Rice (page 321)

SALADS

Caesar (page 340)

Mixed Greens with Grilled Mushrooms (page 343)

Mixed Greens with Vegetable Threads (page 342)

Tomato, Endive, and Hearts of Palm (page 351)

Arugula with Fresh Figs and Feta Cheese (page 367)

Endive and Radicchio with Fresh Raspberries (page 368)

Wild Rice with Apples and Walnuts (page 378)

DESSERTS

Chocolate Cherry Loaf (page 504)

Easy Apple Tart (page 523)

Strawberry Shortcake (page 503)

Buttermilk Mocha Cake (page 512)

Assorted Tartlets (pages 525–27)

Lemon Squares (page 538)

Summer Brunch Fruit Salad (page 390)

Caribbean-Spanish-African Cuisine

This may at first seem an odd pairing of cuisines; however, the Caribbean has many cultures that reflect the cuisines of their neighbors and their immigrants. So in the Caribbean you will find islands with French, Indonesian, and Indian cuisines in addition to the Spanish and African ones.

APPETIZERS AND FIRST COURSES

Black Bean Spread (page 58)

SOUPS

Peanut (page 119)

Curried Sweet Potato–Mango (page 115)

Caribbean Carrot (page 113)

Curried Yellow Pepper (page 103)

Portuguese Vegetable (page 105)

ENTREES

Rice and Black Beans (page 141)

Cilantro Rice and Black Beans (page 141)

Creole Red Beans and Rice (page 142)

Cauliflower and Black Bean Stew (page 140)

Black Bean Picadillo (page 225)

SIDE DISHES

Green Beans with Chickpeas in Groundnut Sauce (page 262)

Creole Okra with Corn (page 269)

Baked Plantains (page 278)

Tostones (page 279)

Coconut Rice (page 315)

Saffron Rice (page 315)

Spanish Rice (page 317)

SALADS

Spanish Restaurant (page 340)

Cilantro Cucumber (page 354)

Tropical Wheat Berry (page 373)

Bulgur with Sofrito Dressing (page 374)

Spanish Rice (page 376)

Black Bean and Tomato (page 385)

RELISHES

Fresh Pineapple Salsa (page 481)

Cilantro Two-Onion Relish (page 484)

Green Tomato–Pineapple Chutney (page 487)

DESSERTS

Dried Apricot Cake (page 509)

Sweet Potato–Apple Cake (page 508)

Coconut-Pineapple Cake (page 510)

Rum Flan (page 550)

Kiwi-Pineapple Sorbet (page 552)

Frozen Piña Colada Mousse Tarts (page 524)

Chinese Cuisine

Although I usually suggest staying away from food that has to be cooked at the last minute, Chinese meals are the exception to that rule for entertaining. Since Chinese dishes are quickly stir-fried, they don't require too much time in the kitchen—assuming that you have cut up all the vegetables earlier in the day and have the sauces measured out and stirred together long before the company arrives. Don't forget to include plain (white or brown) rice in your menu plan, if appropriate.

APPETIZERS AND FIRST COURSES

Crispy Noodles (page 85)

Egg Rolls (page 77)

Mini Vegetable Dumplings (page 76)

SOUPS

Mandarin (page 107)

Chinese Cabbage (page 108)

Hot and Sour (page 108)

ENTREES

Szechuan Broccoli (page 179)

Almond Ding Vegetables (page 180)

Mu Shoo Vegetables (page 219)

Tofu in Brown Sauce (page 218)

Szechuan Shredded Vegetables with Pressed Tofu (page 217)

SIDE DISHES

Sesame Asparagus (page 237)

Szechuan Asparagus with Water Chestnuts (page 238)

Hoisin Sprouts with Cloud Ears (page 239)

Stir-Fried Bok Choy (page 241)

Spicy Green Beans with Shallots (page 260)

Fried Rice (page 318)

RELISHES

Oriental Dipping Sauce (page 482)

DESSERTS

Sorbet (pages 550–52)

Wonton Cookies (page 537)

Eastern European Cuisine

This cuisine includes that of Russia, Hungary, Germany, Poland, and other countries in that region. Although much of these cuisines is based on meat dishes, the vegetarian versions (such as Mushrooms Stroganoff, page 173, and Mushrooms Paprikash, page 174) don't sacrifice any of the flavor of the traditional meat dishes.

APPETIZERS AND FIRST COURSES

Schmear Kaese (page 47)

Strudel Bites (page 74)

SOUPS

Buttermilk Broccoli (page 119)

Borscht (page 131)

Schav (page 131)

ENTREES

Baby Limas and Barley (page 150)

Barley-Stuffed Peppers (page 161)

Sweet and Sour Stuffed Cabbage (page 166)

Mushrooms Stroganoff (page 173)

Mushrooms Paprikash with Dumplings (page 174)

Any main-dish strudel (pages 177–78)

SIDE DISHES

Sweet and Sour Beets (page 240)

Braised Red Cabbage with Apples (page 247)

Creamed Spinach (page 288)

Paprikash Rice (page 316)

Barley with Mushrooms (page 304)

Noodles with Sour Cream and Apple Sauce (page 331)

Noodle Pudding (page 330)

Kasha Varnishkas (page 306)

Pureed Lima Beans with Dill (page 334)

Beet-Horseradish Sauce (page 485)

SALADS

Marinated Chickpea (page 386)

Red Radish (page 353)

Wilted Cucumber (page 354)

Dilled Cucumber (page 356)

Red Cabbage Apple (page 366)

DESSERTS

Strudel (pages 528–30)

"Vedding" Cake (page 508)

Raspberry-Apricot Tart (page 522)

Apple Squares (page 539)

Cheesecake (pages 530–32)

French Cuisine

The French, though known for having one of the premier cuisines in the world, are not serious vegetarians—most entrees are meat-based. However, the French are masters when it comes to egg dishes: quiches, soufflés, and omelets are all French inventions.

APPETIZERS AND FIRST COURSES

Herbed Chèvre (page 49)

Sun-Dried Tomatoes and Goat Cheese on Sliced Baguette (page 49)

Carrot Pâté (page 61)

Croustades (pages 78, 79)

Leeks and Roasted Red Peppers Vinaigrette (page 80)

Onion Timbales with Red Pepper–Tomato Sauce (pages 270–71)

SOUPS

Sherried or French Onion (pages 101, 102)

Creamy Cauliflower-Asparagus (page 110)

Vichyssoise (page 114)

Creamy French Lentil (page 128)

French Lentil-Vegetable (page 129)

ENTREES

Ragout of Wild Mushrooms (page 173)

Roquefort Soufflé (page 208)

Any quiche (pages 211–12)

Spaghetti Squash Provençal (page 165)

SIDE DISHES

Asparagus with Lemon Butter (page 236)

Leeks Provençal (page 266)

Ratatouille (page 257)

Spinach-Herb Timbales (page 288)

Parslied Rice (page 315)

Yellow Potatoes with Red Swiss Chard, Rosemary,
and Garlic (page 285)

Wheat Berries Provençal (page 327)

SALADS

Baby Spinach (page 345)

Salad Greens with Baked Goat Cheese (page 346)

Watercress and Romaine with Roquefort Dressing (page 348)

DESSERTS

Little Apple Turnovers (page 527)

Crepes Suzette (page 552)

Apple Strawberry Tart (page 524)

Lemon Meringue Tartlets (page 525)

Raspberry-Apricot Tart (page 522)

Greek Cuisine

Greek cuisine is part of that healthy-cooking region now referred to as Mediterranean cuisine. The oil used is usually olive (now considered heart healthy); they also cook with lots of beans. An important part of the Greek meal is *meze* (appetizers). Unlike our appetizers, where you may serve none or only one per meal (unless you're having a big party), the Greeks will always have many on hand to munch on before the meal. Those *meze* that weren't eaten before the meal then become the side dishes (which is why there are many appetizer suggestions and almost no side dish suggestions).

APPETIZERS AND FIRST COURSES

Greek Cucumber Salad (page 50)

Chopped Tomato and Olive Spread (page 51)

Sue Levy's Eggplant Spread (page 53)

Yellow Split Pea Puree (page 59)

Greek Potato Pancakes (page 70)

Dolmas (page 72)

Couscous-Stuffed Grape Leaves (page 73)

SOUPS

Spinach Avgolemono (page 103)

Lentil-Escarole (page 127)

ENTREES

Spanakopita (page 176)

Mediterranean Eggplant (page 169)

Roasted Eggplant and Red Pepper Tart (page 214)

Moussaka (page 149)

SIDE DISHES

Sautéed Cucumbers with Tarragon (page 255)

Sautéed Young Zucchini (page 289)

Lentils in Tomato Sauce (page 334)

SALADS

Greek (page 341)

Spinach with Goat Cheese Dressing (page 344)

Tomato and Feta Cheese (page 351)

DESSERTS

Raspberry–Cream Cheese Cake (page 507)

Lemon-Scented Angel Food Cake (page 514)

Honey Couscous Pudding (page 549)

Honey Apple-Fig Tart (page 525)

Indian Cuisine

Since a large portion of the Indian population is vegetarian because of religious beliefs, Indian cuisine is a natural for vegetarian cooks. But (as with Mexican cuisine) I survey my guests to make sure they enjoy this type of cooking before I plan my menu.

APPETIZERS AND FIRST COURSES

Samosas (page 74)

Spicy Chickpea Wafers (page 86)

SOUPS

Mulligatawny (page 104)

Split Pea Dal (page 123)

Curried Yellow Pepper (page 103)

Senegalese (page 104)

ENTREES

Curried Chickpeas and Kale (page 147)

Mixed Vegetable Curry (page 181)

Indonesian Vegetable Stew (page 164)

Saag Paneer (page 182)

SIDE DISHES

Batter-Fried Cauliflower (page 251)

Green Beans with Chickpeas in Groundnut Sauce (page 262)

Curried Okra with Green Beans (page 270)

Curried Zucchini and Fennel (page 290)

Coconut Rice (page 315)

Yellow Indian Rice (page 316)

SALADS

Gado Gado (page 224)

Spanish Restaurant (page 340)

Curried Millet (page 380)

RELISHES

Chutney (any one, pages 486–88)

Cilantro Chutney Sauce (page 483)

Raita (page 496)

Tomato Raita (page 496)

DESSERTS

Cranberry-Pear Chutney Tart (page 522)

Italian Cuisine

Italian cooking is great for company because, in addition to being a popular cuisine, it's usually easy to prepare, with many do-ahead dishes. Pasta is simplest of all; although it requires cooking at meal times, most sauces can be prepared well in advance, then all that is required to make a simple yet satisfying meal is a salad and some crusty bread. Lasagne, cannelloni, or manicotti can be prepared well in advance and then just popped in the oven at the appropriate time. Not only is pasta easy, it can also be elegant. You will certainly impress even the fussiest of guests with a very simple but sumptuous dish such as Tortellini with Wild Mushroom Sauce (page 195).

APPETIZERS AND FIRST COURSES

Caponata (page 55)

Beany Caponata (page 56)

Broncaccia (page 68)

Fried Zucchini Sticks (page 68)

Garlicky Parmesan Stuffed Mushrooms (page 83)

Old-Fashioned Stuffed Mushrooms (page 82)

Stuffed Artichokes, Italian-Style (page 84)

Mozzarella en Carrozza (page 69)

Spinach-Rice-Cheese Balls (page 75)

Polenta with Gorgonzola Cheese Sauce (page 81)

Crostini (page 427)

SOUPS

Minestrone (page 96)

Escarole-Bean (page 127)

Vegetable Chickpea (page 129)

Lentil-Escarole (page 127)

ENTREES

Any pasta (pages 185–99)

Stewed Garbanzo Beans with Zuc-Quinoa (page 151)

Any risotto (pages 156–59)

Gnocchi (pages 203–4)

Eggplant Rollatini (page 172)

Eggplant or Grilled Vegetable Parmesan (pages 170, 171)

SIDE DISHES

Sautéed Broccoli with Garlic (page 242)

Braised Fennel (page 258)

Sautéed Escarole (page 263)

Pesto Vegetables (page 291)

Italian-Style Green Beans and Fennel (page 260)

Basil-Garlic Spaghetti Squash (page 294)

Polenta (page 307)

Quinoa Italiano (page 314)

Garbanzo Beans with Escarole (page 333)

SALADS

Gelles Family (page 339)

Caesar Salad (page 340)

Antipasto (page 341)

Tomato-Mozzarella (page 351)

Grilled Vegetable and Bread (page 352)

Cucumber Fennel (page 354)

Pasta (page 381)

Marinated Chickpea (page 386)

DESSERTS

Cornmeal Sandies (page 533)

Orange Polenta Pudding (page 549)

Strawberries with Zabaglione (page 542)

Anisette Raspberry Sorbet (page 550)

Japanese Cuisine

The Japanese cook with a delicate hand and subtle flavors. Although seafood and beef play a large part in the Japanese diet, the few recipes we have here are truly gems.

APPETIZERS AND FIRST COURSES

Tempura (page 180; can also be an entree)

SOUPS

Miso (page 121)

Spring Vegetable (page 96)

ENTREE

Sukiyaki (page 218)

SIDE DISHES

Teriyaki Grilled Vegetables (page 234)

Sugar Snap Sauté (page 273)

Wheat Berries with Gingered Eggplant (page 328)

SALADS

Wilted Sprout and Watercress (page 362)

Asian Millet (page 380)

DESSERTS

Sorbet (pages 550–52)

Yin and Yang Soup (page 133)

- -

Mexican and Southwest Cuisine

Mexican menus are extremely easy to plan for vegetarians because many Mexican recipes center around beans or cheese. The only drawback (as with Indian cuisine) is that a number of people wouldn't even consider tasting it. If I'm having only a few guests, before I plan my menu I ask them whether they enjoy this cuisine. It's good party fare, especially for that big football game or other casual party.

APPETIZERS AND FIRST COURSES

Guacamole (page 56)

Salsa (pages 479–81)

Nachos (page 67)

Chili con Queso (page 66)

Homemade Tortilla Chips (page 86)

Black Bean Spread (page 58)

Southwest Corn and Black Bean Dip (page 66)

· SOUPS

Southwest Salsa (page 97)

Tortilla (page 100)

Tomato, Corn, and Spinach (page 99)

ENTREES

Cauliflower and Black Bean Stew (page 140)

Southwestern Stew (page 140)

Mexicali Stew (page 142)

Chili (page 154)

Black Bean Chili (page 155)

Black Bean Tostadas (page 153)

Brown Rice and Black Bean Burritos (page 154)

Fajitas (page 163)

Tamale Pie (page 223)

SIDE DISHES

Grilled Vegetables (page 233)

Jalapeño Carrots (page 248)

Tex-Mex Corn Pudding (page 253)

Chili Fried Okra (page 269)

Chili Rice with Tomatillos (page 317)

Barbecue Rice with Beans and Corn (page 319)

Chili Millet with Peppers (page 311)

Mexican Millet (page 311)

Frijoles (page 331)

Refried Beans (page 332)

SALADS

South of the Border (page 348)

Tomato-Avocado (page 351)

Corn and Black Bean (page 384)

RELISHES

Easy Salsa (page 479)

Salsa Ranchero (page 480)

Salsa Verde (page 480)

Pico de Gallo (page 484)

Tomatillo Corn Relish (page 485)

DESSERTS

Rum Flan (page 550)

Lemon Squares (page 538)

Bourbon Broiled Pineapple (page 541)

Middle Eastern Cuisine

It's easy to find vegetarian cuisine in the Middle East, especially considering the arid climate that is not conducive to grazing land for cattle. Chickpeas and eggplant appear in many, many recipes for foods native to this area.

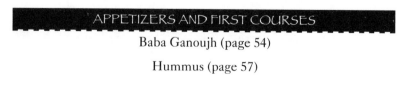

APPETIZERS AND FIRST COURSES

Baba Ganoujh (page 54)

Hummus (page 57)

SOUPS

Mushroom-Barley (page 126)

Lentil-Cauliflower (page 128)

ENTREES

Moroccan Vegetables with Couscous (page 145)

Eggplant with Butter Beans and Plums (page 146)

Couscous with Vegetable Sauce and Chickpeas (page 152)

Turkish Stuffed Eggplant (page 168)

SIDE DISHES

Cauliflower with Parsley and Lemon (page 250)

Sautéed Young Zucchini (page 289)

Stuffed Young Eggplants (page 256)

Tomato Bulgur with Eggplant (page 324)

Couscous with Golden Fruit and Vegetables (page 326)

Spiced Couscous and Diced Vegetables (page 327)

SALADS

Parsley (page 344)

Tomato-Scallion (page 350)

Israeli (page 356)

Moroccan Carrot (page 356)

Tabouli (page 373)

Couscous with Oranges (page 376)

DESSERTS

Cheese Tart (page 524)

Honey Apple-Fig Tart (page 525)

Poached Pears in Wine and Lime (page 544)

Plum Upside Down Cake (page 506)

Cheesecake (pages 530–32)

Hearty Meals

These dishes are perfect for those cold winter nights when you are looking for a hearty dinner.

APPETIZERS AND FIRST COURSES

Party Cheese Log (page 49)

Garlic Pea Puree (page 58)

Creamy Mushroom Pâté (page 59)

SOUPS

Randy's Vegetable (page 96)

Tomato–Cheddar Cheese (page 100)

Manhattan-Style Vegetable Chowder (page 109)

Corn Chowder (page 110)

Cream of Corn Soup (page 119)

Parsnip-Carrot (page 112)

Crunchy Broccoli-Cheddar (page 118)

Split Pea and Barley (page 123)

ENTREES

Rattlesnake Stew (page 139)

Lentil and Mushroom Stew (page 148)

Three-Cheese Macaroni and Cheese (page 216)

Vegetable Lasagne (page 196)

Black Bean–Polenta Pie (page 155)

Lentil Shepherd's Pie (page 147)

SIDE DISHES

Braised Brussels Sprouts (page 244)

Winter Vegetables for a Crowd (page 245)

Cauliflower in Cheese Sauce (page 250)

Baked Stuffed Onions (page 272)

Barbecue Rice with Beans and Corn (page 319)

Orange-Almond Millet (page 312)

Savory Noodle Pudding (page 330)

Grits with Cheese (page 308)

Baked Beans (page 332)

Barbecue Beans (page 332)

SALADS

Garden Vegetable (page 349)

Coleslaw (page 360)

Potato (pages 363–65)

Three-Bean (page 385)

Wheat Berry-Vegetable (page 372)

Brown Rice and Lentil (page 377)

Macaroni and Bean (page 382)

DESSERTS

Peanut Butter Cake (page 505)

Apple Gingerbread (page 511)

Carrot Cake (page 510)

Coconut Parsnip Layer Cake (page 511)

Apple Pie (page 520)

Oatmeal Raisin Cookies (page 532)

Apple Crisp (page 546)

Last-Minute Meals

Everyone needs to throw together a fast meal now and then. These are just a few of the "quick" items you'll find in the recipe sections. Don't hesitate to buy prepared foods to help with a last-minute meal. Some sure timesavers now widely available are vegetables already cut up; use these for appetizers with either homemade dips or prepared salad dressings for dip. You can also purchase prepared salads, soups, and desserts.

APPETIZERS AND FIRST COURSES

Honey-Mustard Dip (page 64)

Chutney Dip (page 64)

Nachos (page 67)

Hummus (page 57)

SOUPS

Spring Vegetable (page 96)

Zucchini Leek (page 106)

Crimini Mushroom and Green Bean (page 107)

ENTREES

Any omelet (pages 450–52)

Frittata (page 453)

Piperade (page 453)

Szechuan Broccoli (page 179)

Springtime Pasta (page 191)

Pasta with Olives, Garlic, and Pine Nuts (page 189)

Noodles with Peanut or Sesame Sauce (page 205)

SIDE DISHES

Sautéed Broccoli with Garlic (page 242)

Asparagus with Lemon Butter (page 236)

Parslied Carrots (page 248)

Cauliflower Polonaise (page 250)

Garlic Green Beans (page 259)

Sautéed Wild Mushrooms and Peas (page 268)

A Trio of Sautéed Peppers (page 277)

Zucchini with Shiitake Mushrooms (page 290)

Sautéed Tomatoes (page 296)

Minted Peas (page 275)

Parslied Boiling Potatoes (page 281)

Bulgur with Summer Squash (page 324)

Bulgur with Celery (page 325)

Couscous with Eggplant (page 326)

Pureed Lima Beans with Dill (page 334)

Barbecue Beans (page 332)

SALADS

Gelles Family (page 339)

Spinach and Mushroom (pages 344, 345)

Broccoli (page 357)

Creamy Couscous (page 375)

Spinach, Strawberry, and Nectarine (page 369)

Three-Bean (page 385)

DESSERTS

Easy Apple Tart (page 523)

Little Apple Turnovers (page 527)

Fruit Salad (pages 387–90)

The Fat Content of Recipes in This Book

Although this was not intended to be a book of low fat recipes, as explained earlier, I've used the minimum amount of fat necessary to create the flavor and textures I was looking for in these recipes. If you are watching the grams of fat in your diet, I have included a heart symbol, following the recipe title, which indicates recipes that I consider to be relatively low in fat. Initially, I chose a figure of 6 grams or less of fat, per serving, to qualify the recipe for a ♥. But when I came to certain chapters, such as Breads, I realized that a single value does not really apply to each type of dish. Six grams of fat may be a lot for a bread or beverage, but not for an entree or salad. Therefore here are the values which I have chosen the codes to represent; each number represents the maximum grams of fat per recipe in that chapter: Appetizers 4; Soups 4; Entrees 6; Side Dishes 4; Salads 4; Breads 3; Breakfast, Brunch, Lunch 4; Condiments, Sauces, Relishes, and Jams 4; Desserts 6; Beverages 2.

These codes are only approximations of the amount of fat, and I am making the assumption that if you are watching the fat in your diet you will be using any lower-fat option in the recipe (i.e., if there is milk in the recipe, I am assuming that you will use skim milk). I am also assuming that you will be eating the smaller serving size (if the recipe says serves 6 to 8, I based my calculations on 8 servings, not 6).

Mail Order Sources

Arrowhead Mills
P.O. Box 2059
Hereford, TX 79045
Primarily grains, some beans

Dean and DeLuca
560 Broadway
New York, NY 11101
Gourmet foods, grains, beans, coffees, equipment, books

Eden Foods
701 Tecumseh Road
Clinton, MI 49236
Beans, grains

Harvest Direct
Vegetarian Lifestyle
P.O. Box 4514
Decider, IL 62525-4514
Textured Vegetable Protein (TVP), vegetable burgers, pastas, books, equipment, Fantastic Foods products, vegetable broth

Williams-Sonoma
Mail Order Department
P.O. Box 7456
San Francisco, CA 94120-7456
Jarred vegetable stock, gourmet foods, equipment, books

Spreads

Garlic-Herb Spread   46

Schmear Kaese   47

Sun-Dried Tomato
Cheesecake   47

Roquefort Cheesecake   48

Vegetable Savory
Cheesecake   48

Herbed Chèvre   49

Party Cheese Log   49

Sun-Dried Tomato and Goat
Cheese on Sliced Baguette   49

Stilton Marscapone   50

Greek Cucumber Salad   50

Roasted Garlic   51

Chopped Tomato and
Olive Spread   51

Olive Caviar   52

Zucchini-Olive Caviar   52

Poor Man's Caviar   53

Grilled Eggplant Spread   53

Sue Levy's Eggplant Spread   53

Baba Ganoujh   54

Eggplant with Balsamic
Vinegar   54

Ratatouille Spread   55

Caponata   55

Beany Caponata   56

Guacamole   56

Hummus   57

Vegetable Hummus   57

Black Bean Hummus   58

Black Bean Spread   58

Garlic Pea Puree   58

Yellow Split Pea Puree   59

Creamy Mushroom
Pâté   59

Brandied Mushroom
Spread   60

Mushroom–Water
Chestnut Spread   60

Carrot Pâté   61

Tricolor Curried Pâté   62

Dips

Roasted Garlic Dip   63

Chutney Dip   64

Honey-Mustard Dip   64

Avocado Yogurt Dip   64

Red Pepper and Sun-Dried
Tomato Dip   64

Yogurt-Horseradish Dip   65

Caramelized Onion and
Sun-Dried Tomato Dip   65

Southwest Corn and
Black Bean Dip   66

Artichoke and
Parmesan Dip   66

Chili con Queso   66

Swiss Cheese Fondue   67

Finger and Toothpick Foods

Nachos   67

Nachos Grande   68

Mozzarella Bites   68

Fried Zucchini Sticks   68

Tempeh Fingers   69

Mozzarella en Carrozza   69

Traditional Latkes
(Potato Pancakes)   70

Greek Potato Pancakes   70

Corn and Scallion-Potato
Pancakes   71

Corn Latkes   71

Sweet Potato Pancakes   72

Dolmas   72

Couscous-Stuffed
Grape Leaves   73

Strudel Bites   74

Samosas   74

Spinach-Rice-
Cheese Balls   75

Mini Vegetable
Dumplings   76

Baked Brie and
Sun-Dried Tomatoes   76

Egg Rolls   77

Croustade Cups   78

Mushroom Croustades   78

Asparagus Croustades   79

First Courses

Leeks and Roasted Red
Peppers Vinaigrette   80

Sautéed Julienned
Vegetables   80

Polenta with Gorgonzola
Cheese Sauce   81

Old-Fashioned Stuffed
Mushrooms   82

Stilton Stuffed
Mushrooms   82

Garlicky Parmesan
Stuffed Mushrooms   83

Artichokes with Curried
  Mayonnaise   83

Stuffed Artichokes,
  Italian-Style   84

Artichokes with Lemon-
  Garlic Mayonnaise   84

Artichokes with Raspberry
  Vinaigrette   84

Stuffed Eggs   85

Snacks

Crispy Noodles   85

Spicy Chickpea
  Wafers   86

Spicy Garlicky Olives   86

Homemade Tortilla
  Chips   86

Sweet Potato Chips   87

Chili Peanuts   87

Mole Almonds   88

Hoisin Walnuts   88

Trail Mix   89

Roasted Chestnuts   89

Chili Popcorn   90

Spicy Seasoned
  Popcorn   90

Italian Popcorn   91

Appetizers tend to be a "company" or special-occasion dinner item. I don't recall any family I know serving appetizers before dinner on a regular basis, but that doesn't mean you should ignore the recipes in this chapter until you're expecting company. They actually make good little meals on their own. Many of the spreads are excellent lunch choices (such as hummus, baba ganoujh, or poor man's caviar) and a series of appetizers makes a very satisfying vegetarian meal.

Appetizers fall into a number of different categories, and the sections of this chapter reflect this: spreads, dips, finger and toothpick foods, first courses, and snacks. Choose your appetizer to fit the mood of the meal. If you've chosen an ethnic motif, find appetizers from that culture to serve as an appetizer. If you're having a Super Bowl party with casual food, dips and snacks may be the right foods to have first. Look at the menu planning section (pages 21–42) if you need help choosing the right appetizer for your meal.

SPREADS

Spreads are always popular at parties; guests love to eat them, and they're easy for the host or hostess because they can be prepared ahead of time. Spreads are also great to have on hand to use as sandwich fillings, or serve a number of different spreads as a main course, similar to a typical Israeli or Ethiopian meal. You will find additional spreads in the sandwich section of the Breakfast, Brunch, Lunch chapter, and occasionally as a variation of a main or side dish. Any of them make good appetizers. Another way to use spreads is for canapés, spread on crackers or bread, or piped through a pastry bag for an even more interesting presentation.

Choose interesting breads and crackers to serve with your spreads. Try Garlic Pita Points (page 430) or Nice and Crunchy, Crisp and Seedy Homemade Crackers (page 429).

Cheese Spreads

You can tailor these spreads to fit your needs. If you are not concerned about fat intake, or if you're making these for company and want a rich spread, choose cream cheese as the base. If you are watching fat intake, there are now many low-fat and no-fat soft cheeses available (you may not like the first one you taste, but keep trying different brands until you find one that suits you). Lower-fat products tend to be tangier and less smooth than their high-fat relatives. If you find you can't stand no-fat cheese, don't despair; you may like 1% or 2% fat and you'll still be better off than if you'd used whole milk or high-fat products. Another alternative to cream cheese is yogurt cheese (page 496), and again, you can use whole milk, low-fat, or fat-free yogurt. Finally, if you are vegan, there are now many tofu cream cheese substitutes available (one pretty good product is Tofutti's "Better than Cream Cheese").

Most of these recipes are made in a food processor, but if you don't own one, you can just soften the cheese, finely chop the ingredients, and stir them together with a spoon.

GARLIC-HERB SPREAD

Makes: 1 cup; serves: 16

This cheese mixture is available in the supermarket, sold under brand names such as Boursin or Allouette. It's easy and less expensive to make at home. Prepare the recipe with the recommended 2 cloves of garlic and let stand overnight so the flavors can meld. Taste it the next day and if you want a more garlicky flavor, add more garlic at that time.

One 8-ounce package whipped cream cheese or plain cream cheese, softened
2 or more cloves garlic, put through a garlic press
½ teaspoon dried marjoram or oregano
½ teaspoon dried thyme

1. In a medium bowl, stir together the cream cheese, garlic, marjoram, and thyme.

Variations: Thin with ¼ cup heavy cream to make a dip for vegetables.

Stuffed Celery: Fill the hollow center of celery stalks with this mixture, then cut into 1-inch pieces.

SCHMEAR KAESE

L

Makes: 1¹/₂ cups; serves: 8 to 10

This dish is officially known as liptauer—a Hungarian cheese spread—but in my family we call it Schmear Kaese (which is literally "spread cheese" in Yiddish or German, I'm not sure which). As a kid I would never even taste it because it has too many "yucky" things in it, like anchovies (for which I substitute sun-dried tomatoes), capers, and Parmesan cheese. Now I love it, and even my dad thinks this version tastes relatively authentic. Both he and my mom asked why I hadn't used anchovies—I had to remind them that anchovies aren't vegetarian. This spread is especially good served on pumpernickel bread or bagels.

³/₄ cup whipped or small-curd cottage cheese
¹/₃ cup butter or margarine, softened
¹/₄ cup grated Parmesan cheese
2 oil-marinated sun-dried tomato halves
2 teaspoons grated onion
2 teaspoons capers, drained
2 teaspoons Dijon mustard
2 teaspoons paprika
2 teaspoons caraway seeds

1. Place all the ingredients in a food processor container fitted with a steel blade. Process until smooth.

2. Chill at least 2 hours to allow the flavors to blend.

Variation: Use the white and green portions of 1 scallion, cut into pieces, instead of the grated onion.

Savory Cheesecakes

Although these are called cheesecakes, they're really just fancy cheese spreads. They're all very rich and can feed quite a few people. Serve them as spreads with thin slices of whole grain or pumpernickel bread, or with crackers or toasts. Or place thin slices on individual plates and serve as a pâté.

SUN-DRIED TOMATO CHEESECAKE

⊡

Makes: one 9-inch cheesecake; serves: 18 to 24

1 tablespoon grated Parmesan cheese
One 8-ounce package feta cheese
16 oil-marinated sun-dried tomato halves
¹/₃ cup sliced scallions (white part only)
3 cloves garlic, minced
Three 8-ounce packages cream cheese, softened
3 eggs

1. Preheat oven to 325°F. Grease a 9-inch springform pan. Dust with the Parmesan cheese.

2. Place the feta cheese in a food processor container fitted with a steel blade; cover and process until smooth. Add the sun-dried tomatoes, scallions, and garlic. Cover and process until finely chopped.

3. In a large bowl, beat the cream cheese until fluffy. Beat in the eggs, one at a time, beating after each addition. Beat in the feta mixture. Pour into prepared pan.

4. Place cheesecake pan in a larger pan filled with hot water 1¹/₂ inches deep. Bake 50 minutes in the water bath. Remove from oven and cool.

Variation: Pesto Cheesecake: Omit the sun-dried tomatoes and garlic; add ¹/₂ cup basil pesto (page 476) or cilantro pesto (page 476) when you add the scallions.

ROQUEFORT CHEESECAKE

Makes: one 9-inch cheesecake; serves: 18 to 24

1 tablespoon grated Parmesan cheese
½ cup walnuts
1½ cups crumbled Roquefort cheese
    (1 pound)
¼ cup chopped onions
2 cloves garlic, minced
Three 8-ounce packages cream cheese,
    softened
3 eggs

1. Preheat oven to 325°F. Grease a 9-inch springform pan. Dust with the Parmesan cheese.

2. Place walnuts in a food processor container fitted with a steel blade and process until finely chopped. Add the Roquefort, onions, and garlic. Process until fairly smooth.

3. In a large bowl, beat the cream cheese until fluffy. Beat in the eggs, one at a time, beating after each addition. Beat in the cheese-walnut mixture. Pour into prepared pan.

4. Place cheesecake pan in a larger pan filled with hot water 1½ inches deep. Bake 50 minutes in the water bath. Remove from oven and cool.

Variation: Substitute Stilton or Gorgonzola for the Roquefort.

VEGETABLE SAVORY CHEESECAKE

Makes: one 9-inch cheesecake; serves: 18 to 24

1 tablespoon plain bread crumbs
1 tablespoon vegetable oil
1 cup coarsely shredded zucchini
1 cup coarsely shredded carrots
¼ cup finely chopped red bell peppers
Two 8-ounce packages cream cheese,
    softened
2 eggs
½ cup sour cream
½ cup grated Parmesan cheese
½ cup chopped fresh parsley
4 cloves garlic, minced
¼ teaspoon dried thyme

1. Preheat oven to 350°F. Grease an 8-inch springform pan. Dust with bread crumbs.

2. In a large skillet, heat the oil over medium heat. Add the zucchini, carrots, and bell peppers. Cook, stirring until softened, about 3 minutes. Let cool.

3. In a large bowl, beat the cream cheese until fluffy. Beat in the eggs, one at a time, beating after each addition. Beat in the sour cream, Parmesan cheese, parsley, garlic, thyme, and vegetable mixture. Pour into prepared pan.

4. Place cheesecake pan in a larger pan filled with hot water 1½ inches deep. Bake 50 minutes in the water bath. Remove from oven and cool.

Variation: Substitute ⅓ cup chopped fresh basil for the parsley.

HERBED CHÈVRE

— L —

Makes: about 16 slices; serves: 8 to 16

Serve these slices on dense pumpernickel (I use a square presliced loaf called Wild's bread, which may not be available nationwide) or crackers. You can also serve them as canapés, perhaps on a slice of French bread, with a basil leaf on top.

3 tablespoons olive oil
1 teaspoon finely chopped fresh rosemary
1 teaspoon finely chopped fresh thyme
1 teaspoon finely chopped fresh oregano
1 clove garlic, sliced paper thin
One 8-ounce log chèvre (goat cheese)

1. In a 9-inch pie plate, stir together the oil, rosemary, thyme, oregano, and garlic.

2. Slice the cheese into $1/4$-inch-thick rounds. Place them into the oil mixture, then turn over to coat both sides with the oil and herbs. Let stand at least 1 hour.

Variation: Add 2 tablespoons chopped oil-marinated sun-dried tomatoes to the oil mixture.

PARTY CHEESE LOG

— L —

Makes: one (8-inch) cheese log; serves: 8 to 10

This technically may not be a spread, but it's close enough. This cheese mix improves if it sits a day or two before serving.

Half 8-ounce package cream cheese, softened (4 ounces)
$1/2$ cup port wine–Cheddar cheese
$1/2$ cup blue cheese
2 teaspoons grated onions
$1/2$ teaspoon anchovy-free Worcestershire sauce
$1/2$ cup chopped pecans

1. In a medium bowl, stir together all the ingredients until completely combined.

2. Form into an 8-inch log and roll in pecans. Chill.

Variation: Roll in chopped fresh parsley instead of pecans.

SUN-DRIED TOMATO AND GOAT CHEESE ON SLICED BAGUETTE

— L —

Makes: $1/2$ cup spread, 20 canapés; serves: 6 to 8

These can be served as canapés, or serve the cheese as a spread with bread slices on the side.

$1/3$ cup soft goat cheese (such as Montrachet)
$1/3$ cup minced oil-marinated sun-dried tomatoes
2 teaspoons olive oil
1 clove garlic, minced
20 thin slices French baguette
20 small fresh basil leaves

1. In a medium bowl, stir together the cheese, tomatoes, olive oil, and garlic.

2. Spread on bread. Top each slice with a basil leaf.

Variation: Stir 3 tablespoons chopped fresh basil into the cheese.

STILTON MARSCAPONE

Makes: 1³/₄ cups; serves: 6 to 10

Ripe Stilton looks slightly yellow, so if the cheese looks ivory it's probably underripe and not especially delicious. If you're having a really big party, you can buy a half wheel of Stilton, scoop out the cheese from the center, mix it with the Marscapone (2 parts Stilton to 1 part Marscapone), and then spoon the spread back into the hollowed-out wheel. Serve this incredibly fabulous spread with French bread or baguette slices.

1 ½ cups crumbled ripe Stilton cheese
¾ cup Marscapone cheese

1. In a medium bowl, mash the Stilton with a fork. Add the Marscapone and mash until fairly smooth and completely combined.

Variation: You can use Roquefort or Danish blue cheese instead of the Stilton.

GREEK CUCUMBER SALAD

Makes: 1 cup; serves: 4 to 6

I tasted a wonderful cucumber spread while out to lunch at a Greek restaurant and tried to duplicate it while the flavor was still fresh in my mind. This is especially tasty served with Toasted Pita (page 428).

½ cup crumbled feta cheese
½ 8-ounce package cream cheese, softened (4 ounces)
⅓ cup sour cream
½ cup finely chopped, seeded cucumber
1 tablespoon thinly sliced scallions (green part only)
⅛ teaspoon pepper

1. Place the feta, cream cheese, and sour cream into a blender or a food processor container fitted with a steel blade. Process until smooth.

2. Spoon into a medium bowl. Stir in cucumber, scallions, and pepper.

Variation: Add ¼ cup chopped radish when you add the cucumber.

Vegetable Spreads

ROASTED GARLIC

— [V][♥] —

Makes: 2 heads of garlic; serves: 4 to 8

Serve these whole heads of garlic with French bread slices or crackers. Guests lift roasted cloves out of the garlic head and spread them on crackers.

2 heads garlic
2 teaspoons olive oil, divided

1. Preheat oven to 275°F.

2. Slice the papery tops off the garlic heads (remove just enough so that the tops of the cloves are exposed). Discard most of the outer paper.

3. Cut four 12 × 12-inch squares of aluminum foil; stack two squares of foil. Place one garlic head in the center of the foil stack. Drizzle 1 teaspoon of olive oil over the exposed garlic cloves. Gather the edges of the foil over the garlic head and press to seal. Repeat with the second stack of foil, head of garlic, and remaining oil.

4. Bake 1 hour. Open the foil packets and bake 30 minutes longer or until the garlic cloves are very tender when pricked with the tines of a fork. Serve warm or cool.

CHOPPED TOMATO AND OLIVE SPREAD

— [V][♥] —

Makes: 1 cup; serves: 4 to 6

The consistency here is somewhere between a salsa and a spread; you really need to spoon it on bread or crackers rather than spread it. Although you can use an ordinary canned black olive in this recipe, I prefer to make the extra effort (and expense) to find imported olives, since the spread really gets its character from the type of olive that you choose.

1 cup finely diced tomatoes
1/4 cup chopped black (kalamata) olives
2 cloves garlic, minced
1 teaspoon fresh lemon juice
1 teaspoon olive oil
1/8 teaspoon salt

1. In a medium bowl, stir together all the ingredients. Let stand at least one hour to let the flavors meld.

Variation: Add 1 tablespoon chopped fresh parsley or basil.

OLIVE CAVIAR

Makes: 1¹/₄ cups; serves: 6 to 8

I tasted a spread similar to this at a restaurant in Fort Lauderdale. I think theirs was less olivey and more eggplanty. For a subtler flavor, sauté the garlic when you cook the eggplant, instead of adding the raw garlic to the spread.

2 tablespoons olive oil
1 cup finely chopped eggplant, unpeeled
1 tablespoon water
One 16-ounce can pitted ripe olives, drained (1¹/₂ cups olives)
2 tablespoons chopped pine nuts (pignoli)
2 teaspoons chopped capers
1 teaspoon red wine vinegar
2 cloves garlic, minced
¹/₈ teaspoon salt, or to taste

1. In a small skillet, heat the oil over medium-high heat. Add the eggplant; cook, stirring, until oil is absorbed, about 3 minutes. Add the water; cook, stirring, until eggplant is tender, about 3 minutes longer.

2. Place the eggplant and remaining ingredients in a food processor container fitted with a steel blade and process until smooth.

Variation: Substitute green stuffed olives for ¹/₂ cup of the black olives.

ZUCCHINI-OLIVE CAVIAR

Makes: 1²/₃ cups; serves: 4 to 8

Serve this with simple crackers, such as water biscuits, or with toasted French bread slices.

2 tablespoons olive oil
1 cup finely chopped zucchini
¹/₂ cup chopped onions
¹/₂ cup finely chopped green bell peppers
2 cloves garlic, minced
¹/₂ cup finely chopped, peeled, and seeded tomatoes
¹/₂ cup finely chopped pimiento-stuffed green olives
¹/₃ cup chopped fresh parsley
2 teaspoons fresh lemon juice
2 teaspoons chopped capers
¹/₂ teaspoon dried basil
¹/₈ teaspoon salt, or to taste
¹/₈ teaspoon ground red pepper

1. In a large skillet, heat the oil over medium-high heat. Add the zucchini, onion, bell pepper, and garlic. Cook, stirring, until softened, about 4 minutes.

2. Add the remaining ingredients; cook, stirring, until any liquids evaporate, about 5 minutes. Let stand at least 2 hours; preferably refrigerate overnight to allow the flavors to meld.

Variation: Substitute yellow squash for the zucchini. Add chopped black olives in addition to the green olives, if desired.

Poor Man's Caviar

— [V] —

Makes: 1¹/₂ cups; serves: 6 to 8

You can bake or microwave (page 255) the eggplant for an equally good result.

1 small eggplant (¾ pound), cooked until very tender
3 tablespoons olive oil
²/₃ cup chopped onions
½ cup finely chopped green bell peppers
2 cloves garlic, minced
1 cup chopped tomatoes
½ teaspoon sugar
½ teaspoon salt, or to taste
1½ tablespoons fresh lemon juice

1. Cut the eggplant in half and scrape the flesh from the skin, discarding the skin. Chop the eggplant very finely, until almost a puree.

2. In a large skillet, heat the oil over medium heat. Add the onions, peppers, and garlic; cook, stirring, until the vegetables are tender, about 4 minutes.

3. Stir in the eggplant, tomatoes, sugar, and salt. Bring to a boil. Reduce heat and simmer, covered, 30 minutes, stirring occasionally.

4. Stir in lemon juice. Chill.

Variation: Use red bell peppers instead of green.

Grilled Eggplant Spread

— [V] [♥] —

Makes: 1¹/₂ cups; serves: 6 to 8

This spread, which is similar to baba ganoujh, makes an excellent sandwich filler, especially on pita with salad on top.

2 cups grilled sliced eggplant (page 232)
1 recipe Tahini Dressing (page 392)
⅛ teaspoon salt
⅛ teaspoon ground red pepper

1. Place all the ingredients in a food processor container fitted with a steel blade. Cover and process until smooth.

Sue Levy's Eggplant Spread

— [V] [♥] —

Makes: 1³/₄ cups; serves: 8 to 12

Sue Levy said her mother made an excellent and easy eggplant spread, and she was happy to share the recipe with me. She serves this with pita bread.

1 medium eggplant (1½ pounds)
2 tablespoons extra virgin olive oil
2 tablespoons grated onion
1 tablespoon fresh lemon juice
¼ teaspoon salt, or to taste
¼ teaspoon pepper

1. Place the whole eggplant on a grill or under a broiler. Cook, turning about every 5 minutes, until charred all over (about 20 minutes total).

2. Let cool, cut eggplant in half, then scoop the flesh from the skin. Discard the skin and drain the flesh in a strainer for 10 minutes. Discard the liquid.

3. Chop the eggplant finely. Place in a medium-sized bowl. Stir in the oil, onion, lemon juice, salt, and pepper. Cool. Let stand 1 hour to allow flavors to meld.

Variation: Stir in ¹/₃ cup chopped fresh parsley or mint.

BABA GANOUJH

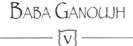

Makes: 1 1/4 cups; serves: 4 to 6 as a spread or 3 to 4 as a sandwich filling

In the Middle East you're likely to find this as a sandwich filler in a pita bread; here, it's usually served as a dip, with pita bread on the side. This version is fairly smooth; perhaps a more traditional version is the variation where you chop rather than puree the spread.

1 medium eggplant (1 pound)
1/4 cup lightly packed fresh parsley leaves
3 tablespoons fresh lemon juice
3 tablespoons tahini (sesame paste)
2 cloves garlic, minced

1. Place the whole eggplant on a grill or under a broiler. Cook, turning about every 5 minutes, until charred all over (about 20 minutes total).

2. Cut the eggplant in half, scoop out the flesh, and discard the skin. Let cool.

3. Place the eggplant, parsley, lemon juice, tahini, and garlic in a food processor container fitted with a steel blade. Process until the parsley is finely chopped. Let stand at least one hour for the flavors to meld.

Variation: Instead of using a food processor, finely chop the eggplant, then stir in the remaining ingredients.

EGGPLANT WITH BALSAMIC VINEGAR

Makes: 2 cups; serves: 8 to 12

This spread has a spicy afterbite that is quite deceiving, since you don't taste the pepper at all when you first eat the spread. Of course, you can tone down the pepper or omit it completely, if you like.

1 medium eggplant (1 1/2 pounds)
1/4 cup lightly packed fresh parsley leaves
2 tablespoons extra virgin olive oil
2 tablespoons balsamic vinegar
1 clove garlic, minced
1/2 teaspoon salt, or to taste
1/4 teaspoon ground red pepper

1. Place the whole eggplant on a grill or under a broiler. Cook, turning about every 5 minutes, until charred all over (about 20 minutes total).

2. Let cool, cut the eggplant in half, then scoop the flesh from the skin. Discard the skin and drain the flesh in a strainer for 10 minutes. Discard the liquid.

3. Put the eggplant, parsley, oil, vinegar, garlic, salt, and pepper in a food processor container fitted with a steel blade. Process until the parsley is finely chopped. Chill.

Variation: Add 1/4 cup chopped, sautéed green bell pepper to the processor with the eggplant.

RATATOUILLE SPREAD

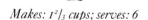

Makes: 1 1/3 cups; serves: 6 to 8

I like to serve this spread at room temperature (not chilled) with thinly sliced pumpernickel. The spread is rather thick and benefits nicely from an extra tablespoon or two of olive oil (if you don't mind adding the fat and calories).

2 tablespoons olive oil
1/2 cup chopped onions
1/3 cup chopped green bell peppers
1 clove garlic, minced
2 cups diced eggplant
1/2 cup diced zucchini
1/3 cup water
2 tablespoons tomato paste
1 tablespoon dry vermouth
1/4 cup lightly packed fresh parsley sprigs
2 teaspoons capers
1 teaspoon red wine vinegar
1/8 teaspoon salt, or to taste

1. In a large skillet, heat the oil over medium-high heat. Add the onions, bell peppers, and garlic. Cook, stirring, until softened, about 3 minutes.

2. Add the eggplant; cook, stirring until softened, about 4 minutes. Add the zucchini, water, tomato paste, and vermouth. Cook 5 minutes or until liquid has evaporated.

3. Place eggplant mixture, parsley, capers, vinegar, and salt in a food processor container fitted with a steel blade. Cover and process until pureed. Cool to room temperature.

Variation: Omit step 3 (including any ingredients added in this step) and serve warm, as a potato topper.

CAPONATA

Makes: 1 2/3 cups; serves: 6

This Italian appetizer can be purchased, canned, in the supermarket, but I think this version is much better.

2 tablespoons olive oil
1/2 cup chopped onions
1/2 cup chopped celery
3 cloves garlic, minced
2 cups diced eggplant
1/2 cup tomato sauce
1/4 cup water
2 tablespoons chopped oil-marinated sun-dried tomatoes
2 tablespoons red wine vinegar
1 tablespoon chopped capers
1 teaspoon dried basil
1 teaspoon sugar
1/4 teaspoon salt

1. In a large skillet, heat the oil over medium heat. Add the onions, celery, and garlic; cook, stirring, until the vegetables are tender, about 3 minutes. Add the eggplant; cook, stirring, until softened, about 4 minutes.

2. Stir in the tomato sauce, water, sun-dried tomatoes, vinegar, capers, basil, sugar, and salt. Bring to a boil. Reduce heat and simmer, covered, 30 minutes, stirring occasionally.

3. Chill.

BEANY CAPONATA

Makes: 2¹/₂ cups; serves: 8 to 10

In Baltimore, celebrating Jesse Weissman's graduation from Johns Hopkins, we had dinner at a local restaurant that had a delicious spread and soft breadsticks on the table. This is as close as I can remember the spread to taste, although my friend Paula (Jesse's mom) said my version was even better.

2 tablespoons olive oil
²/₃ cup chopped onions
¹/₃ cup chopped celery
3 cloves garlic, minced
1¹/₂ cups diced eggplant
One 8¹/₄-ounce can whole peeled tomatoes
1 cup cooked chickpeas (cooked from dry; or canned, drained)
¹/₄ cup water
1 tablespoons red wine vinegar
1 tablespoon capers
1 teaspoon dried basil
1 teaspoon sugar
¹/₂ cup pimiento-stuffed olives

1. In a large skillet, heat the oil over medium heat. Add the onions, celery, and garlic; cook, stirring, until the vegetables are tender, about 3 minutes. Add the eggplant; cook, stirring, until softened, about 4 minutes. Add the tomatoes with liquid and break up with the back of a spoon.

2. Stir in chickpeas, water, vinegar, capers, basil, and sugar. Bring to a boil. Reduce heat and simmer, uncovered, 30 minutes, stirring occasionally. Cool.

3. Place the mixture and olives in a food processor container fitted with a steel blade. Cover and process until finely chopped. Chill.

Variation: For a more eggplanty spread, increase eggplant to 2 cups and decrease the chickpeas to ³/₄ cup.

GUACAMOLE

Makes: 1 cup; serves: 2 to 4

This is a very basic recipe. I usually prepare it with all the variations when serving it as a dip. When using it as an ingredient for other Mexican dishes such as Burritos (page 154), I use the plain recipe below. People like to eat lots of guacamole, so you may want to double the recipe. I prefer to use Haas avocados, but if they aren't available any avocado will do.

1 cup avocado pulp (1 small to medium avocado)
2 tablespoons fresh lime juice
2 tablespoons chopped scallions (white and green parts)
1 tablespoon sour cream
2 cloves garlic, minced
¹/₂ fresh or marinated jalapeño pepper, seeded and minced

1. In a medium bowl, mash the avocado with a fork until smooth or slightly chunky (as you prefer). Add the remaining ingredients.

Variation: Add ¹/₂ cup chopped seeded tomatoes and/or 2 to 4 tablespoons chopped fresh cilantro.

Hummus

You will find this popular spread throughout the Middle East. Israelis serve it spread thinly over the bottom of a salad plate, drizzled with olive oil and with a few drops of hot sauce. The plate is garnished with olives and pepperonici (Italian pickled peppers), and warm pita bread is served to lap up the hummus—yum. They also serve it as a sandwich filler (see page 455). For a party, you may just want to serve the hummus with pita wedges for dipping/spreading.

HUMMUS

Makes: 1 1/2 cups; serves: 3 to 4 as a spread or 6 to 8 as a dip

1 1/2 cups cooked chickpeas (cooked from dry; or canned, drained)
3 tablespoons tahini (sesame paste)
3 tablespoons fresh lemon juice
2 tablespoons vegetable oil
1 tablespoon olive oil
2 cloves garlic, minced
1/4 teaspoon ground cumin
1/8 teaspoon salt, or to taste

1. Place all the ingredients in a food processor container fitted with a steel blade. Cover and process until pureed.

Variation: Add 1/4 cup chopped scallions and Tabasco to taste.

VEGETABLE HUMMUS

Makes: 1 2/3 cups; serves: 3 to 4 as a spread or 6 to 8 as a dip

1/3 cup finely shredded carrots
1/3 cup lightly packed fresh parsley leaves
1/4 cup sliced scallions (white and green parts)
1 1/2 cups cooked chickpeas (cooked from dry; or canned, drained)
1/4 cup tahini (sesame paste)
3 tablespoons fresh lemon juice
2 tablespoons extra virgin olive oil
2 cloves garlic, minced
1/4 teaspoon salt, or to taste
1/8 teaspoon ground red pepper

1. Place the carrots, parsley leaves, and scallions in a food processor container fitted with a steel blade. Cover and process until finely chopped.

2. Add the remaining ingredients. Cover and process until smooth.

Variation: Add 1/4 cup finely chopped green bell peppers when you add the carrots.

BLACK BEAN HUMMUS

Makes: 1³/4 cups; serves: 6 to 8

1 1/2 cups cooked black beans (cooked from
   dry; or canned, drained)
1/3 cup tahini (sesame paste)
1/4 cup fresh lime juice
3 tablespoons extra virgin olive oil
2 cloves garlic, minced
1/4 cup thinly sliced scallions (white and green
   parts)
1/4 teaspoon ground cumin

1. Place the beans, tahini, lime juice, olive oil, and garlic in a food processor container fitted with a steel blade. Cover and process until pureed.

2. Add the scallions and cumin; cover and process until just combined.

Variation: Add 1/4 cup chopped fresh cilantro and Tabasco to taste.

BLACK BEAN SPREAD

Makes: 1¹/3 cups; serves: 6 to 10

There are many excellent prepared salsas available in the supermarket that will be fine for this spread, or you can opt to use homemade salsa (page 479–81).

1 1/2 cups cooked black beans (cooked from
   dry; or canned, drained)
1/3 cup sliced leeks (white and light green
   parts only)
1/3 cup salsa
4 sprigs fresh cilantro
1/2 teaspoon ground cumin

1. Place all the ingredients in a food processor container fitted with a steel blade. Cover and process until smooth.

Variation: Add fresh chopped or canned jalapeño peppers to taste.

GARLIC PEA PUREE

Makes: 1³/4 cups; serves: 8 to 12

Serve these with Crostini (page 427) or other crispy crackers; melba toast is also a good accompaniment.

1 cup water
1/3 cup split green peas, rinsed
6 cloves garlic
1 cup green peas (fresh, cooked; or frozen,
   thawed)
1 tablespoon olive oil
1 tablespoon fresh lemon juice
1/4 teaspoon salt, or to taste
1/3 cup finely chopped, seeded tomatoes

1. In a 1-quart saucepan, bring the water to a boil. Add the split peas and garlic. Return to a boil. Reduce heat and simmer, covered, 1¹/2 hours.

2. Place the pea mixture, green peas, oil, lemon juice, and salt in a food processor container fitted with a steel blade. Cover and process until smooth. Add tomatoes and pulse once or twice to combine.

Variation: Add 1/3 cup chopped roasted red peppers when you add the tomatoes.

YELLOW SPLIT PEA PUREE

[V]

Makes: 2³/4 cups; serves: 12 to 20

Serve this puree at room temperature with Garlic Pita Points (see page 430). This recipe makes a large batch, but I enjoy it so much that I don't mind keeping it around for lunch or snacking.

2½ cups water
1 cup yellow split peas, rinsed
¾ cup sliced onions
6 tablespoons fresh lemon juice, divided
3 cloves garlic
⅓ cup extra virgin olive oil
⅓ cup finely chopped red onions
½ teaspoon salt, or to taste

1. In a 1½-quart saucepan, bring the water to a boil over high heat. Add the split peas, sliced onions, and ¼ cup of the lemon juice. Return to a boil. Reduce heat and simmer, covered, 1½ to 2 hours or until the beans are almost completely dissolved and the liquid has been absorbed. Check for doneness at 1½ hours, and frequently thereafter. You will have to stir the split peas often during the last 15 to 20 minutes so they do not start to burn on the bottom.

2. Place the pea mixture along with the garlic and remaining 2 tablespoons of lemon juice in a food processor container fitted with a steel blade. Cover and process until smooth.

3. Place puree in a medium bowl and stir in the olive oil, red onions, and salt. Let cool.

Variation: Use green split peas instead of yellow.

Pâté

CREAMY MUSHROOM PÂTÉ

[L]

Makes: 1²/3 cups; serves: 6 to 8

Because the delicate flavor of this spread is easily lost, I like to serve it with bread rather than crackers. You can certainly make this spread ahead of time—just refrigerate it until one hour before serving so that it is softened and more spreadable.

2 tablespoons butter or margarine
3 tablespoons minced shallots
2 cups finely chopped wild mushrooms (shiitake, porcini, portobello, or any that you like)
½ cup chopped fresh parsley
¼ teaspoon dried savory or thyme
One 8-ounce package cream cheese
3 tablespoons heavy cream

1. Melt the butter or margarine in a medium skillet over medium-high heat.

2. Add the shallots; cook, stirring, until softened, about 1 minute. Add the mushrooms; cook, stirring until softened, about 5 minutes. If liquid has seeped from the mushrooms, continue cooking until all the liquid has evaporated. Stir in the parsley and savory; cook, stirring, 30 seconds.

3. Remove from heat. Stir in the cream cheese, 1 ounce at a time, until melted and completely combined. Stir in heavy cream.

4. Chill.

Variation: Mushroom Tartlets: Spoon a rounded teaspoonful of the spread into baked mini tartlet shells. Makes about 40.

BRANDIED MUSHROOM SPREAD

Makes: generous 3/4 cup; serves: 4 to 8

This is reminiscent of liver pâté, but without the cholesterol.

1 tablespoon butter or margarine
2 tablespoons minced shallots
3 cups coarsely chopped mushrooms
2 tablespoons brandy
2 tablespoons chopped fresh parsley
8 Ritz crackers, crumbled
1/4 teaspoon salt
1/8 teaspoon pepper

1. In a medium skillet, melt the butter or margarine over medium-high heat.

2. Add the shallots; cook, stirring, until softened, about 1 minute. Add the mushrooms; cook, stirring, until softened, about 4 minutes. Add the brandy and parsley; cook, stirring occasionally, until liquid is evaporated, about 3 minutes.

3. Place mushroom mixture in a food processor container fitted with a steel blade. Add the crackers, salt, and pepper. Cover and process until smooth. Chill.

Variation: Add such fresh herbs as thyme or tarragon when you add the parsley.

MUSHROOM–WATER CHESTNUT SPREAD

V

Makes: 1 1/4 cups; serves: 6 to 8

The water chestnuts give this spread a mysterious crunch.

1 recipe Sautéed Mushrooms with Water Chestnuts (page 267)
15 crumbled Ritz crackers (or similar, such as Towne crackers)
1 teaspoon soy sauce

1. When the mushrooms and water chestnuts are finished cooking, place them in a food processor container fitted with a steel blade. Cover and process until smooth.

2. Add the crumbled crackers and soy sauce. Cover and blend until pureed.

Variation: Omit the water chestnuts for a smoother spread.

CARROT PÂTÉ

Makes: 1 loaf; serves: 8 to 10

Once you've unmolded your pâté, you may want to garnish the top with slices of carrot and/or mushrooms arranged to look like flowers, with sprigs of dill or parsley for leaves. To serve, you can slice the loaf, or leave it whole and place a knife (and lots of good whole grain bread) near it and let guests take as much as they want.

3 tablespoons vegetable oil
½ cup finely chopped onions
¾ cup finely chopped mushrooms
6 cups coarsely shredded carrots (about 1½ pounds)
¼ cup chopped fresh parsley
1 cup cooked cannellini or small white beans (cooked from dry; or canned, drained)
½ cup vegetable broth (pages 93–95)
3 egg whites
¼ cup fresh snipped dill
1 tablespoon tomato paste
1 tablespoon firmly packed light brown or dark brown sugar
½ teaspoon salt, or to taste
¼ teaspoon pepper

1. Preheat oven to 300°F. Grease an 8½ × 3⅝ × 2⅝-inch loaf pan. Line bottom and sides with waxed paper and grease again. Set aside.

2. In a large skillet, heat the oil. Add the onions; cook, stirring, until softened, about 2 minutes. Add the mushrooms; cook, stirring, until softened, about 3 minutes. Add the carrots and parsley; cook, stirring, until softened, about 3 minutes.

3. Place the beans, broth, egg whites, dill, tomato paste, sugar, salt, and pepper in a food processor container fitted with a steel blade. Cover and process until smooth. Add the vegetable mixture, cover, and process until smooth. Spoon into prepared pan.

4. Place loaf pan in a larger pan filled with hot water 1 inch deep. Bake 1 hour 20 minutes in the water bath, or until a knife inserted in center comes out clean.

5. Weight down the pâté by placing a second loaf pan, filled with water, on the pâté. Place in refrigerator at least 4 hours.

6. Remove the weight, turn pâté onto serving plate, and carefully peel off the waxed paper.

Variation: Substitute 3 cups coarsely shredded parsnip for 3 cups of the carrots.

TRICOLOR CURRIED PÂTÉ

Makes: 1 loaf; serves: 16

For an attractive presentation, place a few slices of carrot on the bottom of the loaf pan before spreading the first layer of spinach.

1½ cups sliced carrots

1½ tablespoons vegetable oil

1½ cups chopped onions

2 cloves garlic, minced

1¾ cups cannellini beans (cooked from dry; or canned, drained)

½ cup water

3 egg whites

3 tablespoons all-purpose flour

1 teaspoon salt

Three 10-ounce packages frozen chopped spinach, thawed and squeezed to drain thoroughly

1 teaspoon ground coriander

¾ teaspoon ground ginger

½ teaspoon cumin seeds

¼ teaspoon ground red pepper

One 10-ounce package frozen cauliflower, thawed and drained

1½ teaspoons curry powder

¼ teaspoon ground turmeric

1. Preheat the oven to 350°F. Thoroughly grease a 9 × 5 × 2½-inch loaf pan. Line bottom and sides with waxed paper and grease again. Set aside.

2. Cook the carrots in boiling water 2 minutes, or until just slightly cooked. Drain and set aside.

3. In a medium skillet, heat the oil over medium-high heat. Add the onions and garlic; cook, stirring, until softened, about 3 minutes.

4. Place the onion and garlic mixture in a food processor container fitted with a steel blade.

Add the cannellini beans, water, egg whites, flour, and salt to the container. Cover and process until the mixture is pureed.

5. Place 2 cups of the cannellini mixture in a large bowl. Add the spinach and mix until thoroughly combined. Stir in the coriander, ginger, cumin seeds, and red pepper.

6. Add the cauliflower, curry powder, and turmeric to the cannellini mixture remaining in the processor. Cover and process until finely chopped.

7. Spoon one third of the spinach mixture into the prepared pan. Top with all the carrot slices. Spoon half the remaining spinach mixture over the carrots. Top with the cauliflower mixture, then with the remaining spinach mixture.

8. Bake for 1¼ hours. Place a foil-wrapped brick, or a second loaf pan weighed down with cans or other heavy objects, on top of the loaf.

9. Refrigerate until chilled completely. Remove the weight, turn pâté onto a serving platter, and carefully peel off the waxed paper.

DIPS

Back in the 1950s—when the perfect host or hostess was serving onion dip with chips, pigs in blankets, and those famous cocktail meatballs prepared in a sauce of equal parts grape jelly and ketchup—crudités (at that time known simply as raw vegetables) consisted of carrot and celery sticks and cucumber slices. That was all, unless you were daring and included a cherry tomato or two. Nowadays, in addition to becoming more creative and health conscious about our dips, we serve them with a variety of interesting vegetables (called crudités, to be chic), taking the experience light years beyond the original concept of chip and dip.

Because we've become aware of the need to cut back on fat intake, most of these dips are made with yogurt, which replaces at least some of the traditional sour cream and/or mayonnaise. However, since yogurt is more watery than the fattier bases, I frequently add some mayonnaise and/or sour cream to improve the texture of the dip. After much consideration and soul searching, I've decided to include some old-fashioned sour cream and chip dips hidden among the healthier ones, but you can substitute yogurt for sour cream in these, too.

Some of the dippers I like to use (in addition to celery and carrot sticks, cucumber slices, and an occasional cherry tomato) are:

> raw or blanched broccoli or cauliflower florets
>
> rutabaga sticks
>
> zucchini sticks
>
> jícama sticks
>
> Jerusalem artichoke rounds
>
> Belgian endive leaves
>
> radishes (whole red or white), or daikon sticks
>
> whole button mushrooms

> red, yellow, orange, green, and/or purple bell pepper slices
>
> snow peas
>
> kohlrabi sticks

Presentation of the dip can also be more interesting than just a simple bowl. Be creative. Hollow out a small bread and fill it with dip. Or create bowls out of vegetables. Cut the tops off of bell peppers and discard the seeds, or scoop out the inside of a large tomato. Cooked artichokes or heads of cabbage or cauliflower can be carved to make room for dips.

In addition to the dips found in this section, sauces and some salad dressings make terrific substitutes; any type of hollandaise, for example, is good as a vegetable dip. Salsa and other Mexican sauces make perfect dips with tortilla chips.

ROASTED GARLIC DIP

Makes: 1¼ cups; serves: 8 to 12

In addition to serving this as a dip for crudités, it makes an excellent sauce for chilled, blanched asparagus. If you find the garlic flavor too subtle, just add more to taste.

½ cup mayonnaise
½ cup unflavored yogurt
3 tablespoons mashed roasted garlic cloves (page 51)
2 tablespoons milk
¼ teaspoon anchovy-free Worcestershire sauce
⅛ teaspoon Tabasco

1. In a medium bowl, stir together all the ingredients.

Variations: Omit milk for a thicker dip. Use additional mashed roasted garlic for a stronger garlic flavor.

CHUTNEY DIP

Makes: 1¹/₃ cups; serves: 8 to 12

This dip is especially good with vegetable chips (sold in stores as Terra chips or taro chips). I use any type of homemade chutney (see pages 486–88) for this dip, but commercially available chutney, such as Major Grey's mango chutney, is fine too.

1 cup unflavored yogurt
¹/₃ cup sour cream
2 tablespoons chopped chutney
¼ teaspoon curry powder
¼ teaspoon ground ginger
¼ teaspoon ground coriander
¼ teaspoon ground cardamom
⅛ teaspoon ground red pepper

1. In a medium bowl, stir together all the ingredients.

Variation: Use additional yogurt instead of sour cream for a lower-fat version.

HONEY-MUSTARD DIP

Makes: ³/₄ cup; serves: 4 to 6

This is one of those dips that also makes a great sauce for chilled vegetables to be served as an appetizer. You can find honey mustard in the supermarket.

½ cup unflavored yogurt
3 tablespoons mayonnaise
3 tablespoons honey mustard

1. In a medium bowl, stir together all the ingredients.

Variations: Stir in additional honey mustard for a more intense flavor.

Asparagus with Honey-Mustard Sauce: Serve Honey-Mustard Dip as a sauce over cooked, chilled asparagus.

AVOCADO YOGURT DIP

Makes: 1¹/₄ cups; serves: 6 to 8

This dip is very well suited to crudités. My personal preference in avocados is the Haas variety, but any avocado will do. The yogurt prevents the avocado from discoloring too quickly.

¾ cup diced or chopped avocado
¼ cup sliced scallions (white and green parts)
1 cup unflavored yogurt

1. Place the avocado and scallions in a food processor container fitted with a steel blade. Cover and process until smooth.

2. Add the yogurt. Cover and process, using an on–off pulse method, until just combined.

Variation: Stir in ⅛ teaspoon ground red pepper for a slight bite.

RED PEPPER AND SUN-DRIED TOMATO DIP

Makes: 1¹/₂ cups; serves: 4 to 6

This dip is slightly sweet and is best suited to a bitter "dipper." I love to use Belgian endive leaves for this. I remove the leaves from the heart and arrange them around the dip bowl, like flower petals.

2 roasted bell peppers (page 276)

1/2 cup water

8 oil-marinated sun-dried tomato halves

1 small clove garlic

1/3 cup mayonnaise

1/4 cup unflavored yogurt

1/8 teaspoon ground red pepper

1. Place the roasted peppers, water, sun-dried tomatoes, and garlic in a blender container. Cover and blend until smooth.

2. Add the mayonnaise, yogurt, and red pepper. Cover and blend until combined.

YOGURT~HORSERADISH DIP

Makes: 1 1/2 cups; serves: 8 to 12

I use prepared white horseradish, available in the refrigerator case in the supermarket. If you choose to grate fresh horseradish, you'll have to check for hotness as you go along because it tends to be much stronger.

1 cup unflavored yogurt

1/2 cup sour cream

2 tablespoons minced onion

2 teaspoons grated horseradish, or more to taste

1 clove garlic, minced

1/2 teaspoon celery seed

1/4 teaspoon anchovy-free Worcestershire sauce

1/4 teaspoon seasoned salt

1. In a medium bowl, stir together all the ingredients.

CARAMELIZED ONION AND SUN~DRIED TOMATO DIP

— [V] —

Makes: 1 cup; serves: 4 to 6

For best results use a good flavorful olive, such as a kalamata.

2 tablespoons olive oil

1 tablespoon butter or margarine

4 cups sliced mild onions

1/4 teaspoon dried rosemary, crumbled

1/8 teaspoon dried thyme

1/3 cup water

2 tablespoons white wine

6 oil-marinated sun-dried tomato halves

1 tablespoon chopped fresh parsley

1/2 teaspoon capers

6 small pitted black olives

1. In a large skillet over medium-high heat, heat the oil and the butter or margarine. Add the onion; cook, stirring until softened, about 2 minutes. Stir in the rosemary and thyme. Lower the heat and cook slowly, uncovered, until onions are golden, stirring occasionally, about 45 minutes.

2. Add the water, wine, sun-dried tomatoes, parsley, and capers. Bring to a boil. Remove from heat and transfer to a food processor container fitted with a steel blade. Add the olives. Cover and process until everything is finely chopped.

Variation: Substitute additional water for the wine.

SOUTHWEST CORN AND BLACK BEAN DIP

Makes: 3 cups; serves: 12 to 20

This recipe makes a large amount of dip, but you can easily halve the recipe. It's best when left to age overnight. Serve with tortilla chips (store-bought, or homemade, page 86), of course! Because this dip is so chunky, it's also a perfect salsa; serve it when you're making tacos or the like.

1 1/2 cups chopped tomatoes
1/2 cup cooked black beans (cooked from dry; or canned, drained)
1/2 cup corn kernels (fresh, cooked; canned, drained; or frozen, thawed)
1/2 cup chopped onions
1/4 cup chopped canned chilies, drained (optional)
1/4 cup mild enchilada sauce
1 clove garlic, minced
1/2 teaspoon chili powder
1/4 teaspoon ground cumin
1/8 teaspoon salt, or to taste

1. In a medium bowl, combine all the ingredients. Refrigerate overnight.

Variation: Add 1/4 cup chopped fresh cilantro.

ARTICHOKE AND PARMESAN DIP

Makes: 3/4 cup; serves: 4 to 6

For a really pretty presentation serve this dip in a hollowed-out cooked artichoke. Guests can then dip the outer leaves as well as other assorted crudités.

1/3 cup oil-marinated artichoke hearts
1/4 cup mayonnaise
2 tablespoons sliced scallions (white and green parts)
1 clove garlic, minced
1/4 cup unflavored yogurt
1/4 cup grated Parmesan cheese
1/4 teaspoon pepper

1. Place the artichoke hearts, mayonnaise, scallions, and garlic in a blender container. Cover and blend until smooth.

2. Transfer to a medium bowl and stir in the yogurt, Parmesan cheese, and pepper.

CHILI CON QUESO

Makes: 1 3/4 cups; serves: 6 to 8

This dip is a little thin when warm, but it thickens as it cools. I think it's best served at room temperature—with lots of tortilla chips.

1 tablespoon vegetable oil
1/3 cup sliced scallions (white and green parts)
1/2 cup finely chopped tomatoes
1 tablespoon all-purpose flour
1/2 cup milk
1 1/2 cups shredded Cheddar cheese
1 cup shredded jalapeño–Monterey Jack cheese

1. In a 1-quart saucepan, heat the oil over medium heat. Add the scallions; cook, stirring, 30 seconds. Add the tomatoes; cook, stirring, 1 minute. Stir in the flour until absorbed.

2. Add the milk; cook, stirring, until mixture comes to a boil.

3. Add the cheese; cook, stirring until melted, about 1 minute.

Variation: Use plain Monterey Jack cheese for a milder version.

SWISS CHEESE FONDUE

— [L] —

Makes: 1 cup fondue; serves: 3 to 4

You don't need a fondue pot to make fondue, just a heavy saucepan. If you have a fondue pot with Sterno, that's great; otherwise you may have to put the saucepan back on the stove periodically to remelt the cheese mixture. Serve the bread cubes with long forks so guests can dip them.

2 cups coarsely shredded Swiss cheese
   (8 ounces)
2 teaspoons all-purpose flour
¼ cup dry white wine
¼ cup vegetable broth (page 93–95)
½ small clove garlic, minced
⅛ teaspoon pepper
1 small French bread, cut into 1-inch cubes

1. In a small bowl, toss together the cheese and flour; set aside.

2. In a heavy-bottomed, 1-quart saucepan, heat the wine, broth, garlic, and pepper over medium heat until scalded (bubbles form around the edges but mixture is not boiling).

3. Gradually stir in the cheese until melted and mixture starts to bubble, about 1 minute.

4. Serve with bread cubes.

Variations: Omit the broth and substitute extra white wine.

German Fondue: Substitute beer for the wine.

FINGER AND TOOTHPICK FOODS

Some of these appetizers, such as nachos or especially the Nachos Grande, can be served as meals, or the various potato pancakes make good side dishes.

NACHOS

— [L] —

Makes: 24 nachos; serves: 4 to 6

I definitely prefer using homemade chips (page 86) for this recipe, since they tend to be sturdier than packaged chips.

24 tortilla chips
2 cups shredded Cheddar cheese
1 to 2 fresh or jarred jalapeño peppers,
   seeded and thinly sliced

1. Preheat broiler.

2. Arrange chips close together on a heat-proof platter. Sprinkle with Cheddar cheese. Sprinkle jalapeño peppers over the cheese.

3. Place under broiler until cheese is melted, about 3 minutes.

NACHOS GRANDE

Makes: 24 nachos; serves: 4 to 6

These are just fancier nachos. You can use homemade or prepared salsa and guacamole.

1 recipe Nachos (page 67)
¼ cup salsa (pages 479–81)
½ cup guacamole (page 56)
¼ cup sour cream

1. Prepare nachos according to the recipe. Drizzle salsa over the top, then dollop with guacamole and sour cream.

Variation: Substitute 1 cup shredded Monterey Jack cheese for 1 cup of the Cheddar in the nachos recipe.

MOZZARELLA BITES

Makes: 3 cups; serves: 8 to 10

These are bite-sized pieces of marinated mozza-rella. You can use packaged mozzarella cheese from the supermarket for this recipe, but it's really best when you use fresh mozzarella or at least the packaged mozzarella that comes floating in water. You can serve these with toothpicks so guests can just pop morsels into their mouths, or serve with bread or crackers.

1 pound mozzarella cheese
3 tablespoons extra virgin olive oil
3 tablespoons chopped fresh basil
3 tablespoons chopped fresh Italian parsley
1 tablespoon minced oil-marinated, sun-dried tomatoes
1 teaspoon garlic, minced
¼ teaspoon red pepper flakes or more, to taste

1. Cut the cheese into ¾-inch cubes.

2. In a medium bowl, stir together the oil, basil, parsley, sun-dried tomatoes, garlic, and pepper flakes. Add the cheese and toss.

3. Refrigerate and let stand overnight.

Variation: Mozzarella Salad: Serve the mozzarella tossed with arugula and radicchio lettuces. The marinade from the cheese should serve as dressing for the salad.

FRIED ZUCCHINI STICKS

Makes: 48 sticks; serves: 6 to 8

These zucchini sticks are just lightly coated with the breading, so that you get a clear taste of the zucchini. Serve this with Honey-Mustard Dip (page 64) or warmed marinara sauce (store bought, or homemade, page 473).

⅔ cup all-purpose flour
1 teaspoon dried oregano
¼ teaspoon salt
¼ teaspoon pepper
2 eggs
2 teaspoons water
48 zucchini sticks (3 × ½ × ½ inches, from 2 large zucchini)
⅔ cup plain bread crumbs
Oil for deep frying

1. On a piece of waxed paper stir together the flour, oregano, salt, and pepper.

2. Beat the eggs with the water.

3. Dip the zucchini in the flour, then in the beaten egg, about 4 to 6 at a time. Coat in bread crumbs. Chill 1 hour.

4. In a 3-quart saucepan, heat the oil over high heat until it bubbles when a few crumbs are tossed in.

5. Add the zucchini sticks a few at a time; cook, turning occasionally, until golden, about 1 to 2 minutes. Drain on paper towels.

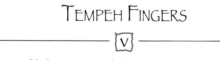 *Variation:* Fried Mozzarella: Cut mozzarella (use packaged, not fresh) into the same-sized sticks as the zucchini; follow recipe.

TEMPEH FINGERS

Makes: 22 tempeh fingers; serves: 6 to 8

Tempeh is a soy vegetable-protein product, and, to be honest, is an acquired taste. (To learn more about tempeh, see page 217.) Serve these with Honey-Mustard Dip (page 64) or Chutney Sauce (page 483).

One 8-ounce package tempeh
Oil for deep frying

1. Slice the tempeh, widthwise, into ¼-inch-thick "fingers."
2. Pour ¼ inch of oil into a large skillet. Heat the oil until it bubbles when a small piece of tempeh is dropped in. Add 4 to 6 fingers at a time. Cook, over medium-high heat, until golden on bottom; turn and cook second side. Drain on paper towels.

Variation: Tempeh Croutons: Cut tempeh into ½-inch cubes and cook as for fingers. Serve over salads.

MOZZARELLA EN CARROZZA

Makes: 12 to 24 pieces; serves: 6 to 12

This is essentially a fried French toast sandwich. Traditionally it's made with anchovies, but I'm using sun-dried tomatoes instead. My dad likes to eat this with powdered sugar (but I think that's weird).

One 8-ounce package mozzarella
12 slices Italian bread (about ¼-inch thick and 4 inches across)
6 tablespoons chopped oil-marinated sun-dried tomatoes
3 eggs
⅔ cup milk
Oil for frying

1. Holding the mozzarella on its side, cut the cheese into six ⅛-inch-thick slices. (You want the slices to be the size of the label, not the smaller slices you would get if you laid the cheese on its face.)
2. Prepare the sandwiches by placing 1 slice mozzarella on each of 6 slices of bread. Sprinkle 1 tablespoon sun-dried tomatoes over each slice mozzarella. Top with remaining slices of bread.
3. In a shallow bowl, beat the eggs lightly. Beat in the milk. Add sandwiches and soak each about 2 minutes per side.
4. In a large skillet, heat the oil over medium heat. Add the sandwiches and cook until browned on the bottom. Turn and cook until second side is browned and cheese is melted. Cut into quarters or halves to serve.

Variation: Add chopped fresh basil to the sandwiches when you sprinkle the sun-dried tomatoes over the mozzarella.

Latkes (Potato Pancakes)

Latkes are a favorite party appetizer. However, they are on the greasy side and may not be for you if you are remotely health-conscious. They can be fully prepared ahead of time; to serve, just place them on a baking sheet and reheat in a 350°F oven for about 8 to 10 minutes, then redrain on paper towels. They will regain their just-fried goodness (or badness, depending on your point of view). Traditionally they are served with either sour cream or applesauce, but I also use unflavored yogurt for dipping. Try applesauce or cinnamon-sugar for the plain and/or Sweet Potato Pancakes; salsa or salsa sauce (page 479) for the plain and/or Corn and Scallion-Potato Pancakes; and Greek Cucumber Salad (page 50) as the dip for the Greek Potato Pancakes.

TRADITIONAL LATKES (POTATO PANCAKES)

Makes: 24 to 28 Latkes; serves: 6 to 8

2 eggs
4 cups coarsely shredded potatoes
1/4 cup matzoh meal, crumbed matzoh, or crumbed water biscuits
2 tablespoons grated onions
1/4 teaspoon salt, or to taste
1/8 teaspoon pepper
Oil for frying

1. In a medium bowl, beat the eggs. Add the potatoes, matzoh meal, onion, salt, and pepper; stir until combined.

2. Pour the oil 1/4 inch deep into a large skillet. Heat the oil over medium-high heat until it bubbles when a little potato is dropped in. Drop the batter by tablespoonsful into the oil and flatten slightly with the back of the spoon. Cook until golden on bottom; turn and cook until golden on second side, about 3 minutes per side. Drain on paper towels.

Variation: Use 1/4 cup chopped scallions (white and green parts) instead of the onions.

GREEK POTATO PANCAKES

Makes: 14 pancakes; serves: 4

1 egg, beaten
2 cups coarsely shredded potatoes
Half 10-ounce package frozen chopped spinach, thawed and well drained
1/2 cup crumbled feta cheese
2 tablespoons bread crumbs
1/8 teaspoon salt, or to taste
Oil for deep frying

1. In a medium bowl, beat the egg. Add the potatoes, spinach, feta cheese, bread crumbs, and salt; stir until combined.

2. Pour the oil 1/4 inch deep into a large skillet. Heat the oil over medium-high heat until it bubbles when a little potato mixture is dropped in. Drop the batter by tablespoonsful into the oil. Cook until golden on bottom; turn and cook until golden on second side, about 3 minutes per side. Drain on paper towels.

Variation: Add 1/2 teaspoon dried oregano when you add the spinach.

CORN AND SCALLION~POTATO PANCAKES

— 〔O〕 —

Makes: 24 pancakes; serves: 6 to 8

2 eggs
2 cups coarsely shredded potatoes
1 cup corn kernels (fresh, cooked; canned, drained; or frozen, thawed)
1/3 cup sliced scallions (white and green parts)
2 tablespoons bread crumbs
1/2 teaspoon salt, or to taste
1/4 teaspoon pepper
Oil for deep frying

1. In a medium bowl, beat the eggs. Add the potatoes, corn, scallions, bread crumbs, salt, and pepper; stir until combined.

2. Pour the oil 1/4 inch deep into a large skillet. Heat the oil over medium-high heat until it bubbles when a little batter is dropped in. Drop the batter by tablespoonful into the oil and flatten slightly with the back of the spoon. Cook until browned and crispy on bottom; turn and cook until browned and crispy on second side, about 3 minutes per side. Drain on paper towels.

Variation: Add 3 tablespoons chopped fresh cilantro when you stir in the bread crumbs.

CORN LATKES

— 〔O〕 —

Makes: 12 3-inch latkes; serves: 4 to 6

Serve these with sour cream or unflavored yogurt or just by themselves.

2 eggs
One 8 1/2-ounce can cream-style corn
1/3 cup cornmeal
1/3 cup all-purpose flour
1 tablespoon sugar
1/2 teaspoon baking powder
1/2 teaspoon salt, or to taste
Oil for frying

1. In a medium bowl, beat the eggs. Add the corn and stir until combined.

2. In a medium bowl or on a piece of waxed paper, stir together the cornmeal, flour, sugar, baking powder, and salt.

3. Stir the cornmeal mixture into the creamed corn, until combined.

4. Pour the oil 1/4 inch deep into a large skillet. Heat the oil over medium-high heat until it bubbles when a little cornmeal is dropped in. Drop the batter 2 tablespoonful at a time into the oil (leave a lot of room between them because they spread). Cook until browned on bottom; turn and cook until browned on second side (turning may be a little tricky since the batter is not completely dried on top). Drain on paper towels.

Variation: Add 1/4 teaspoon ground nutmeg to the batter.

SWEET POTATO PANCAKES

Makes: 12 to 14 pancakes; serves: 4 to 6

1 egg

2 cups coarsely shredded sweet potatoes

2 tablespoons matzoh meal, crumbed matzoh, or crumbed water biscuits

2 tablespoons firmly packed light brown or dark brown sugar

1 teaspoon grated fresh ginger or ½ teaspoon ground ginger

⅛ teaspoon salt, or to taste

Oil for frying

1. In a medium bowl, beat the egg. Add the sweet potatoes, matzoh meal, brown sugar, ginger, and salt; stir until combined.

2. Pour the oil ¼ inch deep into a large skillet. Heat the oil over medium-high heat until it bubbles when a little sweet potato is dropped in. Drop the batter by tablespoonsful into the oil and flatten slightly with the back of the spoon. Cook until golden on bottom; turn and cook until golden on second side. Drain on paper towels.

Variation: Omit the ginger; add ½ teaspoon ground cinnamon.

Dolmas (Stuffed Grape Leaves)

Dolmas are a Greek specialty that can be served warm or at room temperature. You can use grape or vine leaves, but I find that grape are milder and more pleasant. The first recipe with rice filling is closer to a traditional stuffing than the couscous one.

DOLMAS

Makes: 16 to 18 dolmas; serves: 4 to 6

One 16-ounce jar grape leaves

1 teaspoon olive oil

¼ cup chopped onions

¼ cup chopped celery

1 clove garlic, minced

2 cups vegetable broth (pages 93–95), divided

¼ cup white rice

3 tablespoons finely chopped oil-marinated sun-dried tomatoes

¼ cup chopped fresh parsley

2 tablespoons snipped fresh dill

1 cup water

1 tablespoon fresh lemon juice

1. Drain the grape leaves and place in a large bowl. Cover with fresh water and let stand 5 minutes. Drain.

2. In a 1-quart saucepan, heat the oil over medium-high heat. Add the onions, celery, and garlic; cook, stirring, until softened, about 2 minutes. Add ½ cup of the broth; bring to a boil. Add the rice, reduce heat, and simmer, covered, 20 minutes or until liquid is absorbed. Stir in the sun-dried tomatoes, parsley, and dill.

3. Trim the stem from a grape leaf. Lay the leaf flat on a surface. Place a level tablespoon of the filling near the stem end of the leaf. Fold the sides of the leaf over the filling and then roll the leaf away from you, forming a small log. Continue until all the filling has been used.

4. Place half of the remaining leaves in the bottom of a 3-quart saucepan. Place the grape-leaf logs in the bottom of the skillet, seam side down. Top with remaining grape leaves.

5. Pour the remaining 1 1/2 cups of broth and the water and lemon juice into the saucepan, adding extra water, if necessary, to cover the stuffed grape leaves. Place a plate over the leaves to prevent the logs from rising to the surface while cooking. Bring to a boil. Reduce heat and simmer, 45 minutes, uncovered. Remove from saucepan and let cool.

Variation: Place 1/4 cup pine nuts (pignoli) into a dry skillet. Cook over medium-low heat, stirring, until slightly browned, about 2 minutes. Add when you add the herbs.

Couscous-Stuffed Grape Leaves

Makes: 24 stuffed grape leaves; serves: 6 to 8

One 16-ounce jar grape leaves
1 tablespoon olive oil
1/3 cup chopped onions
1 clove garlic, minced
1 1/2 cups vegetable broth (pages 93–95), divided
2 tablespoons port or Madeira wine
1/3 cup couscous
1/2 cup chopped walnuts
1/3 cup chopped dates
3 tablespoons currants
1/4 teaspoon ground cinnamon
1/4 cup chopped fresh mint
1 cup water
1 tablespoon fresh lemon juice

1. Drain the grape leaves and place in a large bowl. Cover with fresh water and let stand 5 minutes. Drain.

2. In a 1-quart saucepan, heat the oil over medium-high heat. Add the onions and garlic; cook, stirring, until softened, about 1 to 2 minutes. Add 1/2 cup of the broth and the wine; bring to a boil. Add the couscous, reduce heat, and simmer, 2 to 4 minutes or until liquid is absorbed. Stir in the walnuts, dates, currants, cinnamon, and mint.

3. Trim the stem from a grape leaf. Lay the leaf flat on a surface. Place a level tablespoon of the filling near the stem end of the leaf. Fold the sides of the leaf over the filling and then roll the leaf away from you, forming a small log. Continue making logs until all the filling has been used.

4. Place half of the remaining leaves in the bottom of a 3-quart skillet. Place the grape-leaf logs in the bottom of the skillet, seam side down. Top with remaining grape leaves.

5. Pour the remaining 1 cup of broth and the water and lemon juice into the saucepan, adding extra water, if necessary, to cover the stuffed grape leaves. Place a plate over the leaves to prevent the logs from rising to the surface while cooking. Bring to a boil. Reduce heat and simmer, 45 minutes, uncovered. Remove from skillet and let cool.

Variation: Couscous with Dates: Double the recipe for the filling and serve as a side dish. Makes 3 1/2 cups.

STRUDEL BITES

Makes: 3 strudels; serves: 8 to 12

These are very flaky—to avoid a mess be sure your guests have napkins or plates to eat these over.

6 phyllo sheets (12 × 17 inches each),
     thawed according to package directions,
     if frozen
2 to 3 tablespoons vegetable oil or melted
     butter or margarine
3 tablespoons unflavored bread crumbs,
     divided
1 recipe of your favorite savory strudel filling
     (pages 177–78)

1. Preheat the oven to 350°F.

2. Remove the thawed phyllo sheets from the package. (Reseal the package tightly so that remaining sheets won't dry out.) Place 1 sheet on a work surface, with the long edge parallel to the edge of the work surface. Lightly brush with oil, butter, or margarine and sprinkle lightly with ¹/₂ tablespoon bread crumbs. Place the next phyllo sheet on top of the first; brush with oil and sprinkle with ¹/₂ tablespoon bread crumbs, as before. Fold in half to form a book 12 × 8¹/₂ inches.

3. Spoon ¹/₃ of the filling onto the phyllo, forming a log 9 inches long, parallel to and 2 inches from the folded border. Fold the short edges over the filling. Starting with the long edge closest to the filling, fold the phyllo up over the filling, encasing it, and then roll up the rest of the phyllo stack. The completed strudel should look like a neat log. Repeat with remaining phyllo leaves, oil, bread crumbs, and filling to make 3 strudels in total.

4. Place the strudels on an ungreased baking sheet and brush the top with any remaining oil. Cut slits into each strudel, 1 inch apart and deep enough to see the filling.

5. Bake 35 to 40 minutes, or until golden. Let cool 7 to 10 minutes. Cut through the slits into 1-inch slices to serve.

SAMOSAS

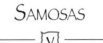

Makes: 16 pastries; serves: 6 to 8

These fried pastries are a real staple at any Indian restaurant. When frying them, be sure the oil is not too hot. You want these to fry slowly enough to cook the pastry all the way through. Serve them with Cilantro Chutney Sauce (page 483).

Dough:
³/₄ cup all-purpose flour
¹/₂ cup whole wheat flour
¹/₂ teaspoon salt
1 tablespoons ghee (page 494) or vegetable oil
¹/₃ cup warm water

Filling:
1 tablespoon ghee (page 494) or vegetable oil
¹/₂ cup chopped onions
3 cloves garlic, minced
1 teaspoon minced fresh ginger
1¹/₂ teaspoons curry powder
¹/₄ teaspoon ground turmeric
¹/₄ teaspoon ground cumin
¹/₈ teaspoon ground red pepper
¹/₂ cup water
1 cup diced potatoes (¹/₄-inch pieces)
¹/₂ cup peas (fresh or frozen)
1¹/₂ tablespoons chopped fresh cilantro
¹/₈ teaspoon salt, or to taste

1. For the dough, place both of the flours and ¹/₂ teaspoon salt in a food processor container fitted with a steel blade. Cover and process until combined.

2. Through the chute, with the motor running, add 1 tablespoon ghee, then as much of the warm water as necessary for the dough to form a ball. Wrap in plastic wrap and chill, 1 to 2 hours.

3. While the dough is chilling, prepare the filling: In a 1-quart saucepan, heat 1 tablespoon ghee or oil over medium-high heat. Add the onions, garlic, and ginger. Cook, stirring, until onions are transparent, about 2 minutes. Stir in the curry powder, turmeric, cumin, and ground red pepper until absorbed. Add $1/2$ cup water and bring to a boil. Add the potatoes and peas. Bring to a boil; reduce heat and simmer, uncovered, 20 minutes or until vegetables are soft and sauce is thick. Stir in cilantro and $1/8$ teaspoon salt.

4. Divide dough into 8 pieces and form each into a ball. Roll out each ball into a 6-inch circle (the dough will be very thin). Cut the circle in half to form 2 half-moons.

5. Moisten the straight edges of the dough and roll to form a cone, using the rounded edge as the top of the cone. Press the flat edge of the dough to seal. Holding the cone in one hand, place about 1 tablespoon of filling in the center. Press the rounded edges of the dough to seal. Be sure all seams are well sealed so the samosa does not come apart in the frying.

6. Pour the oil 2 inches deep into a 3-quart pot and heat over medium-high heat until the oil reaches 350°F or until it bubbles when a small piece of dough is dropped in it.

7. Cook the samosas until nicely browned all over, about 2 to 3 minutes per side. Drain on paper towels.

Variation: Substitute $2/3$ cup cauliflower for $1/2$ cup of the potatoes.

SPINACH~RICE~CHEESE BALLS

Makes: 24 balls; serves: 8 to 12

Pass a platter of these as finger foods for a cocktail party, or serve as an appetizer with Tomato-Leek Coulis (page 99) or other tomato sauce over or under them.

1 cup water
$1/2$ cup white rice
$1/2$ cup shredded mozzarella cheese
$1/2$ cup shredded Fontina cheese
$1/2$ cup grated Parmesan cheese
Half 10-ounce package frozen chopped spinach, thawed and well drained (or $1/2$ cup cooked spinach, chopped)
2 eggs
1 teaspoon water
$2/3$ cup plain dry bread crumbs
Oil for deep frying

1. In a 1-quart saucepan, bring 1 cup water to a boil. Add the rice and simmer, covered, 20 minutes or until water has been absorbed.

2. Stir in the cheeses, then the spinach. Let cool until you are able to handle it. Form into l-inch balls.

3. Beat the eggs with 1 teaspoon water in a medium bowl; set aside.

4. Roll the balls in bread crumbs, dip in the egg, and reroll in the bread crumbs.

5. Pour the oil 2 inches deep into a 3-quart saucepan. Heat the oil over medium-high heat until it bubbles when a few bread crumbs are dropped in. Cook balls a few at a time until golden, about 4 minutes. Drain on paper towels.

Variation: Stir $1/4$ cup chopped marinated sun-dried tomatoes and/or $1/4$ cup chopped fresh basil into the rice mixture when you stir in the cheese.

MINI VEGETABLE DUMPLINGS

V

Makes: 24 to 28 dumplings; serves: 4 to 6

If you cannot find round dumpling skins, buy wonton wrappers and cut them into rounds using a 3- to 3¹/₂-inch cookie or biscuit cutter. Serve these dumplings with Oriental Dipping Sauce (page 482).

1 tablespoon vegetable oil
1¹/₂ teaspoons minced fresh ginger
2 cloves garlic, minced
1¹/₂ cups fresh mung bean sprouts
1 cup lightly packed chopped spinach
¹/₂ cup chopped mushrooms
¹/₂ cup coarsely shredded carrots
¹/₄ cup chopped scallions (white and green parts)
1 teaspoon soy sauce
¹/₂ teaspoon sesame oil
24 to 28 dumpling wrappers or 15 wonton wrappers

1. In a medium skillet, heat the vegetable oil over high heat. Add the ginger and garlic; cook, stirring, 10 seconds. Add the bean sprouts, spinach, mushrooms, carrots, and scallions. Cook, stirring, until vegetables are tender and any liquid has evaporated, about 5 minutes. Stir in the soy sauce and sesame oil.

2. Place one rounded teaspoon of the spinach filling in the center of a dumpling wrapper. Wet the edges with water. Fold in half to form half-moons and pleat the edges in an accordion pleat; press the edges together to seal.

3. Drop the sealed dumplings into salted boiling water and cook until the dumplings rise to the surface and look translucent, about 1 to 2 minutes.

Variation: Add ¹/₄ cup chopped water chestnuts for a crunchier texture.

BAKED BRIE AND SUN-DRIED TOMATOES

Makes: 24 canapés; serves: 6 to 8

How long Brie must bake in order to melt slightly depends upon whether the cheese is at room temperature or is chilled before baking. The degree of ripeness also influences the baking time.

6 slices very thin white or wheat bread
12 oil-marinated sun-dried tomato halves
6 tablespoons ripe Brie, room temperature

1. Preheat oven to 375°F. Butter a baking sheet.

2. Quarter the bread slices and place on the baking sheet. Bake 6 to 8 minutes or until lightly toasted.

3. Halve the tomato pieces and place one piece of tomato on each piece of toast. Top each with 1 teaspoon Brie.

4. Bake about 5 minutes or until the cheese has melted slightly.

Variation: Substitute Camembert for the Brie.

EGG ROLLS

Makes: 10 to 12 egg rolls

Homemade egg rolls have a fresher flavor and crispier texture than those you get in restaurants. The Mini Egg Rolls given in the variation are great at parties. You can prepare and fry them in advance; freeze them until a few minutes before serving, then reheat for 10 to 15 minutes in a 375°F oven.

1 tablespoon mirin (rice wine) or dry sherry
2 teaspoons soy sauce
1 teaspoon cornstarch
½ teaspoon sugar
1 teaspoon sesame oil
2 tablespoons vegetable oil
3 cups shredded cabbage
2 cups mung bean sprouts
½ cup finely diced pressed or baked tofu
⅓ cup chopped scallions (white and green parts)
10 to 12 egg roll skins
1 egg, beaten
Oil for deep frying

1. In a small bowl, stir together the mirin, soy sauce, cornstarch, sugar, and sesame oil; set aside.

2. In a wok or large skillet, heat the vegetable oil over high heat.

3. Add the cabbage and sprouts; cook, stirring until tender-crisp, about 4 minutes. Stir in the tofu and scallions. Add the soy sauce mixture; cook, stirring, until sauce is thickened.

4. Place an egg roll skin so that it forms a diamond on the counter, with the points facing you. Put 3 tablespoons of the filling in a log, 1½ inches beneath the center points.

5. Brush the edges of the wrapper with the beaten egg.

6. Fold the top and bottom points over the filling.

7. Fold the left point over the filling.

8. Roll the entire package toward the right point. Press all exposed edges to seal. Repeat with remaining filling and egg roll skins.

9. Pour the oil 2 inches deep into a wok or large skillet. Heat the oil over medium-high heat until it reaches 375°F or until the oil bubbles when a small piece of egg roll skin is dropped in it.

10. Cook the egg rolls until nicely browned all over, about 3 minutes. Drain on paper towels.

Variation: Mini Egg Rolls: Cut each egg roll skin into 4 smaller squares or use wonton wrappers. Place 1½ teaspoons of filling on each square and prepare as for large egg rolls. Makes 36 egg rolls.

Croustades

These little tart cups are easy to make. Be sure to use very thinly sliced bread (such as that made by Pepperidge Farm or Arnold). You can prepare the cups and the fillings early in the day, but don't combine them too far in advance or they will become soggy instead of delightfully crisp.

You can use any type of filling for these croustades, such as ratatouille or even caponata, but it shouldn't be too liquid because the croustade cups tend to be porous. The yield should be slightly more than 1 cup.

Although I give the yield as 3 to 8, I must confess that I've served a whole recipe of these when I've had only two guests, and although I may eat only two or three, the remainder disappear long before I start to serve the meal. If these are the only appetizers you're serving, this recipe may serve only 3.

CROUSTADE CUPS

Makes: 24 cups; serves: 3 to 8

Butter or margarine
12 slices melba thin white or wheat bread

1. Preheat oven to 400°F. Using butter or margarine, grease 2 miniature muffin pans (24 mini muffin cups).

2. Cut the bread into 24 rounds using a 2-inch biscuit cutter (each slice will make 2 croustade cups). With a rolling pin, flatten the rounds. Fit into prepared muffin cups and press on bottom to flatten into the muffin cup shape. Bake 6 to 8 minutes or until crisp and browned.

Variation: Use very thin rye bread instead of the white or wheat.

MUSHROOM CROUSTADES

Makes: 24 croustades; serves: 4 to 8

2 tablespoons butter or margarine
1/2 cup chopped onions
2 cloves garlic, minced
2 cups finely chopped white mushrooms
1 1/2 tablespoons all-purpose flour
1/2 cup vegetable broth (pages 93–95)
2 tablespoons chopped fresh parsley
1/8 teaspoon dried thyme
1/8 teaspoon salt, or to taste
1/8 teaspoon pepper
1 recipe Croustade Cups (left)

1. Preheat oven to 350°F.

2. In a medium skillet, melt the butter or margarine over medium-high heat. Add the onions and garlic; cook, stirring, until softened, about 1 to 2 minutes. Add the chopped mushrooms; cook, stirring, until softened, about 3 minutes. If mushrooms give off liquid, cook until the liquid is evaporated. Stir in flour until absorbed. Stir in broth, parsley, thyme, salt, and pepper; cook, stirring, until thickened, about 3 minutes.

3. Spoon 1 rounded teaspoon of the filling into each of the croustade cups. Bake 10 minutes or until heated through.

Variation: Use wild mushrooms for some or all of the white mushrooms.

ASPARAGUS CROUSTADES

— L —

Makes: 24 croustades; serves: 4 to 8

1 tablespoon butter or margarine
¼ cup chopped leeks (white and light green parts only)
1 cup finely chopped asparagus
1½ tablespoons all-purpose flour
½ cup vegetable broth (pages 93–95)
⅛ teaspoon pepper
2 tablespoons grated Parmesan cheese
1 recipe Croustade Cups (page 78)

1. Preheat oven to 350°F.

2. In a medium skillet, melt the butter or margarine over medium-high heat. Add the leeks; cook, stirring, until softened, about 2 minutes. Add the chopped asparagus; cook, stirring, until softened, about 3 minutes. Stir in flour until absorbed. Stir in broth and pepper; cook, stirring, until thickened, about 3 minutes. Stir in grated Parmesan.

3. Spoon 1 rounded teaspoon of the filling into each of the croustade cups. Bake 10 minutes or until heated through.

V **Variation:** Omit the Parmesan.

FIRST COURSES

What is the difference between an appetizer and an hors d'oeuvre? Technically, *hors d'oeuvre* is just the French word for appetizer. I like to distinguish the two by using "hors d'oeuvre" to indicate food you serve before people come to the dinner table, and these foods are usually easy to eat with fingers or a toothpick. I think of an "appetizer" as the first course of the meal; it usually requires a plate and a fork or spoon (or even a knife) to eat. Of course, I made up these rules—you can make up your own definition, too. You don't have to limit your selection of appetizers to the recipes in the appetizer chapter. Any entree, side dish, or salad can be served as an appetizer by altering the portion size.

Select an appetizer after you've determined your main course. A "heavy" or large appetizer, such as pasta or another filling dish is better if you're planning a light entree. A light appetizer, such as a vegetable dish or salad, is more suitable to heavier entrees or meals with multiple courses.

LEEKS AND ROASTED RED PEPPERS VINAIGRETTE

[V]

Makes: 3 cups; serves: 4

You want to cook the leeks thoroughly, but not to death. Place them in a skillet of boiling water and cook just until they lose their bright green color. Gently lift them out of the skillet so they hold together. You can also serve this as a salad.

4 medium leeks
1 tablespoon vegetable oil
1 tablespoon extra virgin olive oil
1 tablespoon fresh lemon juice
½ teaspoon Dijon mustard
¼ teaspoon dried tarragon
½ clove garlic, minced
⅛ teaspoon salt, or to taste
½ cup sliced roasted red bell peppers (page 276)
Freshly ground black pepper

1. Cut most of the dark green tops off the leeks (leave 2 to 3 inches of dark green on the leek) and discard the roots. Cut in half lengthwise and rinse very thoroughly. Cook the leeks in a skillet of boiling water until tender, about 6 minutes. Drain and chill.

2. In a small bowl, stir together both oils, the lemon juice, mustard, tarragon, garlic, and salt.

3. Place two halves of leek on each of 4 serving plates. Sprinkle each with 2 tablespoons of the red pepper slices; drizzle each with ¼ of the oil dressing. Grind pepper over the salad.

Variation: Toss the vegetables and dressing in a bowl instead of arranging them on plates (the dressing is distributed more evenly, but the vegetables look less pretty).

SAUTÉED JULIENNED VEGETABLES

[V]

Makes: 3 cups; serves: 6

I use Pepperidge Farm Puff Pastry Sheets. They're easy to use, and since they're made with vegetable shortening they're suitable for the vegan as well as lacto-ovo vegetarians. This dish can be prepared in advance. I serve it at room temperature, although you can serve it hot if you prefer.

½ sheet unbaked puff pastry
1½ tablespoons olive oil
1 cup julienned carrots
1 cup julienned zucchini
1 cup julienned yellow squash
1 cup julienned leeks (white part only)
Hollandaise (page 472) or Tofu Lemon Mayonnaise (page 472)

1. Preheat oven to 350°F.

2. Thaw pastry dough according to package directions. Cut into 2-inch circles or use a cookie cutter to make attractive shapes. Place on ungreased cookie sheets and bake 20 minutes or until puffed and golden. Cool on paper towels.

3. In a large skillet, heat the oil over medium-high heat. Add the carrots; cook, stirring, 1 minute. Add the zucchini, squash, and leeks. Cook, stirring, until just tender, 2 minutes longer.

4. Place the vegetables on four plates; garnish each with 1 or 2 pieces of puff pastry. Drizzle 1 to 2 tablespoons of sauce over the vegetables.

Variation: Omit the sauce and toss chilled vegetables in a vinaigrette to serve as an appetizer salad.

POLENTA WITH GORGONZOLA CHEESE SAUCE

[L]

Makes: 4 molded polenta and 1 cup sauce; serves: 4

This is a very creamy polenta, like a dense pudding. You can prepare the polenta in advance, pour into cups, then chill until you want to serve them. Then reheat in the microwave or in a waterbath in the oven. Then unmold with good result.

Polenta:

2 cups milk

1¾ cups water

2 tablespoons butter or margarine

½ teaspoon salt, or to taste

½ cup yellow cornmeal (polenta)

Sauce:

1 tablespoon butter or margarine

1 tablespoon flour

¼ teaspoon paprika

½ cup vegetable broth (pages 93–95)

¼ cup half-and-half

¼ cup packed soft Gorgonzola or other creamy blue cheese

2 tablespoons grated Parmesan cheese

⅛ teaspoon ground red pepper

1. Grease four 6-ounce custard cups.

2. For the polenta, in a 2-quart saucepan over medium-high heat, bring milk, water, 2 table-spoons butter, and the salt to a boil, stirring frequently.

3. With the liquid still boiling, sprinkle the cornmeal 1 tablespoon at a time over the liquid while stirring, so that no lumps form. Reduce heat to simmer and cook 35 to 45 minutes, stirring very frequently, until the polenta remains mounded when dropped from a spoon. Pour polenta into custard cups; let stand 10 minutes.

4. Meanwhile, make the sauce. In a 1-quart saucepan, melt 1 tablespoon butter or margarine over medium-high heat. Add the flour and paprika; stir until absorbed. Stir in the broth and half-and-half. Cook, stirring, until mixture comes to a boil. Add the cheeses and pepper and stir until cheese is melted.

5. Place 2 tablespoons of sauce on each of 4 small serving plates, unmold the polenta, and top each with some of the remaining sauce.

Variation: Use a different sauce, such as Tomato–Red Pepper Sauce (page 474).

Stuffed Mushrooms

Stuffed mushrooms have been favorites at parties as far back as I can remember. If you're planning to serve them as finger foods, use small or button mushrooms that guests can pop into their mouths in a single bite. Medium or large stuffed mushrooms are more appropriate as appetizers, eaten on a plate with a fork and possibly even a knife. The recipes here call for medium mushrooms, but you can use smaller ones; just go by the given weight, ignore the number called for, and use less filling per mushroom.

Old-Fashioned Stuffed Mushrooms

Makes: 16 mushrooms; serves: 3 to 4

This was the only way to stuff mushrooms when I was a kid. The adventurous cook might use flavored bread crumbs instead of plain.

16 medium white mushrooms (14 ounces)
1 tablespoon butter, margarine, or vegetable oil
1/4 cup minced onion
1 small clove garlic, minced
1/3 cup dry bread crumbs (plain or flavored)
2 tablespoons chopped fresh parsley
1/4 teaspoon salt, or to taste
1/8 teaspoon pepper

1. Preheat oven to 375°F.

2. Wipe the mushrooms clean with a damp cloth and separate the caps from the stems. Chop the stems.

3. In a medium skillet, melt the butter, margarine, or oil over medium-high heat. Add the onion and garlic; cook, stirring, until softened, about 1 to 2 minutes. Add the chopped mushroom stems; cook, stirring, until softened, about 3 minutes. If mushrooms give off liquid, cook until it evaporates. Remove from heat. Stir in bread crumbs, parsley, salt, and pepper.

4. Spoon the filling into each of the mushroom caps. Bake 12 minutes or until heated through.

Variation: Herb-Stuffed Mushrooms: Use seasoned bread crumbs plus 1/2 teaspoon chopped fresh basil and 1/8 teaspoon chopped fresh thyme.

Stilton Stuffed Mushrooms
L

Makes: 16 mushrooms; serves: 3 to 4

16 medium white mushrooms (14 ounces)
2 teaspoons olive oil
2 tablespoons minced shallots
1/2 cup crumbled Stilton
1/3 cup pot cheese or cottage cheese
1/4 cup plain dry bread crumbs, plus additional for top

1. Preheat oven to 375°F.

2. Wipe the mushrooms clean with a damp cloth and separate the caps from the stems. Chop the stems.

3. In a medium skillet, heat the oil over medium-high heat. Add the shallots; cook, stirring, until softened, about 1 minute. Add the chopped mushroom stems; cook, stirring, until softened, about 3 minutes. If mushrooms give off liquid, cook until it evaporates. Remove from heat. Stir in Stilton, pot cheese, and bread crumbs.

4. Spoon the filling into each of the mushroom caps. Sprinkle the top with additional bread crumbs, if desired. Bake 12 minutes or until heated through.

Variation: Cheese-Stuffed Mushrooms: Substitute shredded Gouda for the Stilton.

GARLICKY PARMESAN STUFFED MUSHROOMS

L

Makes: 16 mushrooms; serves: 3 to 4

This is a simple recipe that has held up over all the years. This version is slightly jazzier and less oily than the ones from my youth.

2 slices whole wheat bread
16 medium white mushrooms (about 14 ounces)
1 ½ tablespoons olive oil
2 cloves garlic
¼ cup grated Parmesan cheese
¼ teaspoon salt, or to taste
¼ teaspoon pepper

1. Preheat oven to 375°F.

2. Tear the bread into pieces and place in a blender or food processor container fitted with a steel blade. Cover and process into crumbs (you should have 1 cup of fresh bread crumbs).

3. Wipe the mushrooms clean with a damp cloth and separate the caps from the stems. Chop enough stems to equal ⅓ cup.

4. In a medium skillet, heat the oil over medium-high heat. Add the chopped mushroom stems and garlic; cook, stirring, until softened, about 3 minutes. Remove from heat. Stir in bread crumbs, cheese, salt, and pepper.

5. Spoon the filling into each of the mushroom caps. Bake 12 minutes or until heated through.

Variation: Stir in ½ teaspoon chopped fresh oregano (or ⅛ teaspoon dried) when you add the bread crumbs.

ARTICHOKES WITH CURRIED MAYONNAISE

LO

Makes: 4 artichokes and ½ cup sauce; serves: 4 to 8

Serve this sauce with warm or chilled artichokes. It is thick enough to serve in a hollowed-out artichoke if you like (see page 234 for instructions).

½ cup mayonnaise
2 tablespoons milk
1 tablespoon lemon juice
1 ½ teaspoons curry powder
1 ½ teaspoons distilled white vinegar
¼ teaspoon ground paprika
½ clove garlic, minced
Pinch salt, or to taste
4 cooked artichokes (page 235)

1. In a medium bowl, stir together the mayonnaise, milk, lemon juice, curry, vinegar, paprika, garlic, and salt. Place in 4 small serving bowls.

2. Serve each with an artichoke.

Variation: Add ground red pepper to taste.

STUFFED ARTICHOKES, ITALIAN-STYLE

Makes: 4 artichokes; serves: 4

This is a fairly time-consuming recipe to prepare, but it certainly is impressive to serve.

2 tablespoons olive oil
1/2 cup finely chopped onions
2 cloves garlic, minced
1 juicy lemon
1 1/2 cups dry bread crumbs
1/2 cup finely chopped tomatoes
1/4 cup chopped fresh basil
1/4 cup grated Parmesan cheese (optional)
2 teaspoons chopped capers
1/8 teaspoon pepper
4 artichokes

1. In a large skillet, heat the oil over medium-high heat. Add the onions and garlic; cook, stirring until softened, about 2 minutes. Add 2 tablespoons of juice from the lemon. Remove from heat.

2. Stir in the bread crumbs, tomatoes, basil, Parmesan (if desired), capers, and pepper.

3. Prepare the artichokes by cutting off the bottom stem. Using a sharp knife, cut 1/2 inch off the top of the artichokes (this should remove most of the spiny tips). Snip off any remaining artichoke tips with a pair of scissors. Spread the leaves apart so that you can reach into the center of the artichoke. Grasp the purple-tipped light green leaves; pull out and discard. Using a spoon (the serrated point of a grapefruit spoon works well), scrape out the fine leaves and choke (hairy bottom). Squeeze a little lemon juice into the bottoms to prevent discoloration.

4. Fill the center of the artichokes with the bread crumb mixture.

5. Fill a 6-quart pot with 2 inches of water. Drop the squeezed lemon into the water. Stand the artichokes, stuffing up, in the pot. Cover and bring to a boil over high heat. Reduce heat and simmer, covered, 40 minutes or until artichokes are tender.

ARTICHOKES WITH LEMON-GARLIC MAYONNAISE

Makes: 4 artichokes and 1/2 cup dip; serves: 4 to 8

This dip is very tart, but it complements the artichokes well. Serve it with warm or chilled artichokes.

1/2 cup mayonnaise
2 tablespoons fresh lemon juice
1/4 teaspoon ground paprika
1/2 clove garlic, minced
4 cooked artichokes (page 235)

1. In a medium bowl, stir together the mayonnaise, lemon juice, paprika, and garlic. Place in 4 small bowls.

2. Serve each with an artichoke.

Variation: Add 1/2 teaspoon minced shallot to the sauce.

ARTICHOKES WITH RASPBERRY VINAIGRETTE

Makes: 4 artichokes and 1/2 cup dressing; serves: 4

You can use plain Dijon mustard, but the raspberry mustard, which you can find in some gourmet stores or prepare yourself (page 471), gives this vinaigrette a smoother flavor.

3 tablespoons vegetable oil
3 tablespoons extra virgin olive oil
3 tablespoons fresh lemon juice
1 tablespoon raspberry mustard (see page 471)
1 tablespoon minced shallots
¾ teaspoon salt, or to taste
4 cooked artichokes (page 235)

1. Stir together all the dressing ingredients.

2. Place each artichoke on a serving plate and pour ¼ of the dressing into each cavity.

Variation: Use a plain oil and vinegar vinaigrette for a lighter version.

STUFFED EGGS

Makes: 8 halves; serves: 4

For an attractive presentation, place the egg yolk mixture into a pastry bag fitted with a large star-shaped tip. Pipe the mixture into the egg whites and sprinkle paprika on top. If you're not serving the eggs immediately, be sure to cover them with plastic wrap so the filling doesn't dry out.

4 hard-cooked eggs, peeled (page 448)
1 tablespoon mayonnaise
2 teaspoons milk
½ teaspoon prepared mustard
⅛ teaspoon salt
Dash anchovy-free Worcestershire sauce
   (optional)

1. Cut eggs in half lengthwise. Place yolks in medium bowl.

2. Mash yolks with a fork. Stir in mayonnaise, milk, mustard, salt, and Worcestershire sauce. Whip with fork until fluffy.

3. Place yolk mixture in egg whites.

Variation: Use an additional tablespoon of milk and omit the mayonnaise.

SNACKS

Sometimes you just want to have "a little something" around to nosh on or to have on hand for company. These snacks are better than the store-bought varieties.

CRISPY NOODLES

*Makes: 11 cups (very loosely packed);
serves: 4 to 10*

These are the good, broad noodles that are served in Chinese restaurants to go with soup. Of course, we normally eat them all up, dipping generously in duck sauce and/or mustard long before the soup arrives. Because this snack is so addictive, the yield is more likely to be 4 servings rather than 8 or 10.

6 egg roll skins
Oil for deep frying

1. Slice the egg roll skins into ¾-inch strips.

2. Pour the oil 2 inches deep into a wok or large skillet. Heat over medium-high heat until the oil reaches 375°F or until it bubbles when a small piece of egg roll skin is dropped in.

3. Cook the noodles until nicely browned all over, about 2 minutes.

4. Drain on paper towels.

Variation: Cut the egg roll skins into thicker or thinner strips to your own preference.

Spicy Chickpea Wafers

Makes: 5½ dozen; serves: 10 to 15

These mildly spicy wafers are great served with Chutney Sauce (page 483). Be sure to fry these until browned or they will be soggy. Besan is chickpea flour. You can find it in specialty Middle Eastern stores, or order it by mail (see page 43).

1 cup besan flour
1 cup all-purpose flour
1 teaspoon curry powder
1 teaspoon salt
½ teaspoon ground red pepper, or more to taste
½ teaspoon cumin seeds
¼ teaspoon black pepper
2 tablespoons vegetable oil
½ cup water
Oil for frying

1. Place the two flours, curry powder, salt, red pepper, cumin seeds, and black pepper in a food processor container fitted with a steel blade.

2. With the processor running, pour the oil through the chute. Gradually add water to form the dough into a ball. Turn onto a well-floured surface and knead 10 to 12 times or until dough is not sticky. Let stand 10 minutes, covered with plastic wrap.

3. Pinch off marble-sized pieces of dough and roll into paper-thin wafers (about 3 inches in diameter) on a lightly floured surface.

4. Pour the oil ¼ inch deep in a large skillet. Heat over medium-high heat until the oil bubbles when a small piece of dough is dropped in. Add wafers, in a single layer, and fry until golden brown on each side. Drain on paper towels.

Spicy Garlicky Olives

Makes: 3 cups; serves: 12 to 20, depending on olive size

I make lots and lots of these because they're irresistible, and, if by some miracle they're not eaten immediately, they keep for a few weeks. I use Manzanillo olives, which are small green Israeli olives with a distinctive peppery afterbite. If you can't find them, use another interesting green olive. For very spicy olives, leave the seeds in the jalapeño peppers; for milder olives discard the seeds.

One 12-ounce can small green olives (2 cups), ⅓ cup juice reserved
⅓ cup extra virgin olive oil
2 to 3 tablespoons garlic, sliced paper-thin
1 (or more) jalapeño pepper(s), sliced
1 teaspoon grated lemon rind

1. Combine all the ingredients. Let stand at least overnight, preferably 2 days, for the flavors to meld. Toss occasionally.

Variation: Stir in 1 to 2 tablespoons of chopped fresh rosemary.

Homemade Tortilla Chips

Makes: 24 chips; serves: 3 to 4

If you love the tortilla chips served in most Mexican restaurants, you already know how much better homemade chips are than the ones you buy packaged in the chip department of the supermarket. You don't have to make just 4 tortillas—you can make the whole package. If you use 7-inch tortillas, you can cut them into 8 wedges instead of 6.

Four 5-inch corn tortillas (fresh, or frozen, thawed)
Oil for deep frying
Salt (optional)

1. Place the tortillas in a pile. Cut pile into 6 wedges, creating 24 wedges.

2. Pour the oil ¼ inch deep into a large skillet. Heat over medium-high heat until the oil bubbles when a small piece of tortilla is dropped in. Add a few tortilla wedges to the oil at a time. Cook until tortilla turns a slightly tan color. Turn wedges and cook until second side is tanned as well. Remove from skillet and drain on paper towels. If desired, salt lightly.

3. Repeat in small batches until all wedges are crisped.

Variation: Use wheat tortillas instead of corn.

Sweet Potato Chips

[V]

Makes: 3 to 4 cups; serves: 4 to 6

The thinner you can slice these, the crisper they will fry.

2 cups peeled sweet potato, sliced paper-thin
Oil for deep frying
Salt

1. Pour the oil 2 inches deep into a 2-quart saucepan. Heat the oil until it bubbles when a small piece of sweet potato is dropped in. Place a small handful of potato slices in the oil. Cook until slices lose their dark orange color and have brown blisters on both sides, about 3 minutes. Drain on paper towels.

2. Repeat with remaining potato. Salt chips, if desired.

Variation: Potato Chips: Substitute plain white potatoes for the sweet potatoes; cook until very lightly browned.

Chili Peanuts

Makes: 1½ cups; serves: 4 to 8

The spiciness kind of creeps up on you and then these pack a pretty good punch. You can use more or less ground red pepper to suit your taste.

½ cup confectioners' sugar
2 tablespoons sugar
1 tablespoon chili powder
¼ teaspoon ground red pepper
⅛ teaspoon ground cumin
1 egg white
1 cup salted or unsalted roasted peanuts

1. Preheat oven to 350°F. Grease a 9 × 13-inch baking pan.

2. Place the confectioners' sugar, sugar, chili powder, red pepper, and cumin into a plastic bag. Shake until completely combined.

3. Beat the egg white until foamy. Add the nuts and toss until coated. Pour nuts into a strainer to drain off excess egg white.

4. Add the nuts to the bag with the chili mixture about 1 heaping tablespoon at a time. Shake to coat, then gradually add more nuts until all are in the bag. Spread nuts on the prepared pan.

5. Bake 20 minutes, stirring every 5 minutes. Let cool.

Variation: Use almonds instead of peanuts.

MOLE ALMONDS

Makes: 4 cups; serves: 12

Addictive is a good word to describe these almonds. Everyone who's tasted these has raved—so will your guests. In fact, you'll probably find that this recipe serves fewer than 12 people.

1 egg white
1 tablespoon water
2½ cups almonds
½ cup sugar
1 ounce semisweet chocolate, finely grated
2 tablespoons cocoa powder
1 tablespoon chili powder
1 teaspoon cinnamon

1. Preheat oven to 300°F. Lightly grease a jelly roll pan.

2. In a medium bowl, beat egg with the water until frothy. Stir in almonds. Drain.

3. In a medium bowl, stir together the remaining ingredients. Toss almonds in the chocolate mixture. Spread in prepared pan.

4. Bake 40 minutes or until crispy, stirring every 15 minutes.

Variation: Add 1 teaspoon orange rind.

HOISIN WALNUTS

Makes: 3 cups; serves: 6 to 10

The five-spice powder gives these walnuts a licorice flavor with a spicy afterbite. Also called five-flavor powder or Chinese five spices, five-spice powder is a mixture of anise seed, star anise, clove, cinnamon, and pepper. It can be purchased as a prepared spice mix.

1 egg white
2 tablespoons hoisin sauce
1½ teaspoons cornstarch
2 cups walnut halves
1 cup sugar
1 teaspoon five-spice powder

1. Preheat oven to 300°F. Lightly grease a jelly roll pan.

2. Beat egg white until frothy. Stir in hoisin sauce, then cornstarch. Stir in walnuts. Drain.

3. Stir together sugar and five-spice powder. Toss walnuts until coated. Spread in prepared pan.

4. Bake 40 minutes or until crispy, stirring every 15 minutes.

Variation: Instead of the five-spice powder, use cinnamon and ground cloves for seasonings.

Trail Mix

[v]

Makes: 2 cups; serves: 8 to 12

Pack this healthy snack in lunch boxes or just leave it in a bowl for nibbling. Use raw or roasted, salted or unsalted nuts according to your taste.

¾ cup dark or golden raisins
½ cup peanuts
⅓ cup sunflower seeds
¼ cup soy nuts
¼ cup cashews

1. In a medium bowl, combine all the ingredients.

Variation: Add or omit any dried fruit or nut, as desired.

Roasted Chestnuts

[v]

There's nothing like snacking on chestnuts. Besides being great snacks, they're wonderful in many cooked dishes.

Chestnuts

1. Preheat oven to 350°F.

2. Using a small sharp knife, cut an "X" in the top of each chestnut. Place the chestnuts in a single layer in a baking dish.

3. Bake 30 minutes for small chestnuts, 45 minutes for large.

Seasoned Popcorn

Seasoned popcorn is great at parties, it's easy to make and inexpensive, too. Make a couple of different flavors and place them in bowls around the room. Serving sizes are hard to determine, I know people who can eat one or two quarts at a time.

CHILI POPCORN

Makes: 5 cups; serves: 3 to 6

1 tablespoon corn oil
2 teaspoon chili powder
1/8 teaspoon dried oregano
1/8 teaspoon ground red pepper
1/4 cup popcorn
1/4 teaspoon salt, or to taste

1. Heat the oil in a 2-quart saucepan over medium-high heat. Stir in the chili powder, oregano, and pepper.

2. Add popcorn. Cover, but leave the lid a tiny bit ajar so the popcorn does not become soggy from steam in the pot. Cook until there are 2 to 3 seconds between pops.

3. Toss with salt.

SPICY SEASONED POPCORN

Makes: 6 cups; serves: 3 to 6

1 tablespoon vegetable oil
1/4 teaspoon seasoned salt, or to taste
1/8 teaspoon ground red pepper, or to taste
1/4 cup popcorn

1. Heat the oil in a 2-quart saucepan over medium-high heat. Stir in the salt and pepper.

2. Add popcorn. Cover, but leave the lid a tiny bit ajar so the popcorn does not become soggy from steam in the pot. Cook until there are 2 to 3 seconds between pops.

ITALIAN POPCORN

Makes: 6 cups; serves: 3 to 6

2 teaspoons vegetable oil
1 teaspoon olive oil
1/4 teaspoon dried oregano
1/8 teaspoon garlic powder
1/4 cup popcorn
1/4 cup grated Parmesan cheese

1. Heat both oils in a 2-quart saucepan over medium-high heat. Stir in the oregano and garlic powder.

2. Add popcorn. Cover, but leave the lid a tiny bit ajar so the popcorn does not become soggy from steam in the pot. Cook until there are 2 to 3 seconds between pops.

3. Toss with Parmesan.

SOUPS

Vegetable Soups

Mighty Vegetable Broth   94
Vegetable Juice Broth   95
Mushroom Broth   95
Minestrone   96
Spring Vegetable Soup   96
Randy's Vegetable Soup   96
Fresh Tomato Soup   97
Southwest Salsa Soup   97
Curried Tomato Soup   98
Red Pepper–Tomato
Soup   98
Tomato, Corn, and Spinach
Soup   99
Creamy Tomato and Leek
Soup   99
Tomato–Cheddar Cheese
Soup   100
Tortilla Soup   100
Gumbo Soup   101
Sherried Onion Soup   101
French Onion Soup   102
Bell Pepper–Celery
Soup   102
Spinach Avgolemono
Soup   103
Curried Yellow Pepper
Soup   103
Senegalese Soup   104
Mulligatawny Soup   104
Portuguese Vegetable
Soup   105
Saint Patrick's Day
Soup   105
Lettuce and Pea Soup   106
Zucchini-Leek Soup   106

Crimini Mushroom and
Green Bean Soup   107
Mandarin Soup   107
Chinese Cabbage Soup   108
Hot and Sour Soup   108
Sweet and Sour Cabbage
Soup   109
Manhattan-Style Vegetable
Chowder   109
Corn Chowder   110
Creamy Cauliflower-
Asparagus Soup   110
Carrot-Cauliflower
Soup   111
Basil-Cauliflower Soup   111
Curried Cauliflower
Soup   112
Parsnip-Carrot Soup   112
Caribbean Carrot Soup   113
Cream of Parsley Root
and Parsnip Soup   113
Vichyssoise   114
Peppery Potato-Fennel
Soup   114
Creamy Roasted Garlic
Soup   115
Curried Sweet Potato–
Mango Soup   115
Cream of Corn Soup   116
Cream of Asparagus
Soup   116
Cream of Crudité Soup   117
Cream of Mushroom
Soup   117
Fresh Spinach Cream
Soup   118
Crunchy Broccoli-Cheddar
Soup   118

Buttermilk Broccoli
Soup   119
Peanut Soup   119
Jerusalem Artichoke–Almond
Soup   120
Squash and Apple
Soup   120

Heartier Grain and/or Bean Soups

Kitchen Sink Soup   121
Miso Soup   121
Collard and Black-Eyed Pea
Soup   122
Black Bean Soup   122
Split Pea and Barley
Soup   123
Split Pea Dal   123
Sherried Pea Soup   124
Root Vegetable and Split Pea
Soup   124
Three-Bean Vegetable
Soup   125
Split and Black-Eyed Pea
Soup   125
Mushroom-Barley
Soup   126
Leek and Wild Rice
Soup   126
Escarole-Bean Soup   127
Lentil-Escarole
Soup   127
Lentil-Cauliflower
Soup   128
Creamy French Lentil
Soup   128

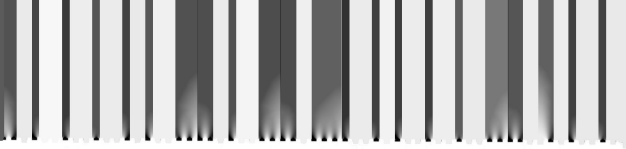

*French Lentil–Vegetable
Soup   129*

*Vegetable Chickpea
Soup   129*

Cold Soups

Gazpacho   130

Green Gazpacho   130

Yellow Gazpacho   130

Borscht   131

Schav   131

*Chilled Cucumber
Soup   132*

*Rich and Creamy
Avocado Soup   133*

*Minted Honeydew
Soup   133*

*Ginger-Cantaloupe
Soup   134*

Yin and Yang Soup   134

*Chilled Strawberry
Soup   135*

Soups are not necessarily just first courses. Teamed up with bread and salad, a hearty soup can make a great entree. Broth makes a good between-meal snack, and fruit soup can be served for dessert. Of course, you can use them as first courses, too.

Vegetable Soups

Vegetable Broth

I don't usually think of broth as my favorite soup, but the broth recipes are probably the most important recipes in this chapter. Aside from being a perfect low-calorie snack, broth is the base of many of the interesting recipes throughout this book. It's broth that makes risotto breathtaking, pilafs exciting, stews fascinating, and other soups scintillating. Although I may be slightly overstating the case for broth, the fact is, broth frequently makes the difference between watery, "thin" dishes and interesting, complex flavors.

It's my practice to make batches of broth whenever I have leftover vegetables. I usually use the Vegetable Juice Broth recipe (page 95), because it's easy and economical. In fact, it's worth the investment in a juice machine just to be able to have homemade broth easily available. I freeze the broth in 1-cup portions, then just defrost as many packages as cups of broth are called for in a recipe.

If you don't have a juicer, Mighty Vegetable Broth (page 94) is very flavorful and a good second best. If you don't have any broth on hand, there are many commercial vegetable broths available, in various forms: canned, frozen or bottled stock, cubes or powder, salted or unsalted. They range in flavor from very acceptable (albeit salty) to totally unpalatable. It's a matter of taste as to which works for you. My personal favorite is Knorr's vegetable cubes; they are quite flavorful, but slightly salty. Unfortunately, they are sometimes hard to find. You can call Best Foods at (1-201-894-2324) if you are having trouble locating them in your area. Mrs. Gooch makes a decent vegetable bouillon, which you can purchase in California, or you can order some by mail from Health Valley Catalog (1-800-423-4846). Otherwise, if you don't like the first bouillon you buy, try, try, again.

Swanson's canned vegetable broth is very easy to use, but I find the flavor a bit heavy on the onion. But try it—if you like it, it certainly makes life easier. Williams Sonoma sells vegetable stock in jars through their mail-order catalog (see mail-order sources). Frozen vegetable broths are also available in gourmet shops, such as Balducci's in New York City. If your local gourmet shop doesn't carry any, perhaps they can special-order it for you.

Unsalted broth has a particular advantage over salted. Beans and certain grains do not soften properly in salted liquids, so unless your broth is unsalted, you'll have to cook them in water, stirring in salted bouillon after the grains and beans are at their desired doneness.

MIGHTY VEGETABLE BROTH

ⓥ ♥

Makes: 4 cups; serves: 4

This is a good all-purpose broth. If you're going to eat or drink it by itself, you may want to add salt to taste. If you're using it for cooking, leave it unsalted, then add salt to taste after you've finished cooking the dish.

8 cups water
3 medium carrots (6 ounces)
2 large ribs celery, with leaves (6 ounces)
2 medium parsnips (6 ounces)
2 leeks (light and dark green parts), thoroughly rinsed
2 small parsley roots, including leaves
1 medium turnip (6 ounces)
1 medium tomato (6 ounces)
½ small celeriac (celery root; knob celery) (3 ounces)
2 cloves garlic

1. Place all the ingredients in a 4-quart pot. Bring to a boil over high heat. Reduce heat and simmer, covered, 1 hour. Uncover and simmer 1 hour longer.

2. Place a large, fine strainer over a large bowl. Pour the broth and vegetables into the strainer. Gently press the vegetables remaining in the strainer, until all the liquid has fallen into the bowl. Discard pressed vegetables.

Variation: Add any vegetables you have on hand: cabbage, spinach, onion, kohlrabi, and so on.

VEGETABLE JUICE BROTH

— v ♥ —

Makes: 6 cups; serves: 6 to 8

This broth requires very few vegetables and is unbelievably flavorful. If you have a juice extractor it is extremely easy to prepare. If you don't have an extractor, you really can't duplicate this broth using any machine, except a Vitamix. As I mentioned on page 93, it's worth purchasing a juicer just to be able to make this broth.

1 small tomato
1 small onion
4 large ribs celery (including leaves), rinsed
2 medium carrots, scrubbed and tops removed
1 medium parsnip, scrubbed and top removed
6 cups water

1. Juice the vegetables, in the order listed, according to your juicer's directions.

2. Place the juice and pulp in a 2-quart saucepan with the water. Bring to a boil over high heat. Simmer, uncovered, 20 minutes.

3. Place a large, fine strainer over a large bowl. Pour the broth through the strainer. Gently press the pulp remaining in the strainer, until all the liquid has fallen into the bowl. Discard the pressed pulp.

Variation: You can use an endless variety of vegetables for this broth. Just follow the proportions of 2 cups vegetable juice, 2 cups pulp, 6 cups water.

MUSHROOM BROTH

— v ♥ —

Makes: 2³/₄ cups; serves: 3 to 4

This really strong, mushroomy broth is suitable for cooking, but you might want to dilute it for eating. Use dried Polish mushrooms, if possible (you can buy the broken pieces, which are less expensive than whole or sliced pieces). Good—and considerably less expensive—mushrooms are imported from Chile; they're usually available in supermarkets in ¹/₂-ounce plastic containers.

One 10-ounce container white mushrooms, chopped
1 cup chopped leeks (white and light green parts only)
One ¹/₂-ounce package dried imported mushrooms
4 cups water

1. Place all the ingredients in a 3-quart saucepan. Bring to a boil over high heat, reduce heat, and simmer, 30 minutes.

2. Pour the broth through a strainer fitted over a large bowl. Press any liquid from the mushrooms and leeks into the bowl before discarding them.

Variation: Add 2 cups vegetable broth (pages 93–95) to the mushroom broth for a less mushroomy flavor.

MINESTRONE

V ♥

Makes: 8 cups; serves: 8 to 12

Any Italian grandmother would be proud of this soup, even without the traditional beef base.

3 cups water
2 cups vegetable broth (pages 93–95)
2 cups chopped tomatoes
1 cup sliced carrots
1 cup sliced celery
³/₄ cup chopped onions
3 tablespoons red wine
¹/₂ teaspoon dried oregano
1 clove garlic, minced
¹/₂ teaspoon salt, or to taste
¹/₄ teaspoon pepper
2 cups sliced zucchini
1 cup diced, peeled potatoes
1¹/₂ cups cooked kidney beans (cooked from dry; or canned, drained)
¹/₄ cup chopped fresh parsley
3 tablespoons small shells or other small pasta, such as orzo

1. Place the water, broth, tomatoes, carrots, celery, onions, wine, oregano, garlic, salt, and pepper in a 4-quart pot. Bring to a boil. Reduce heat and simmer, uncovered, 40 minutes.

2. Add the zucchini, beans, potatoes, parsley, and shells. Cook 20 minutes longer, or until potatoes are tender.

Variation: Use a 14¹/₂-ounce can whole peeled tomatoes (undrained) instead of fresh tomatoes.

SPRING VEGETABLE SOUP

V ♥

Makes: 4 cups; serves: 4 to 6

This very light, broth-based soup is just perfect for a light meal, even brunch.

4 cups vegetable broth (pages 93–95)
¹/₂ cup julienned carrots
¹/₂ cup thinly sliced mushrooms
¹/₄ cup fresh shelled peas
4 to 6 thin asparagus, quartered lengthwise and cut into 2-inch pieces
6 snow peas, julienned
2 tablespoons chopped fresh parsley

1. In a 2-quart saucepan, bring the broth to a boil over medium-high heat. Add the carrots, mushrooms, and peas and simmer, uncovered, 3 minutes or until carrots and peas are tender.

2. Add the asparagus, snow peas, and parsley, and simmer, 2 minutes longer.

Variation: Use almost any julienned seasonal vegetable.

RANDY'S VEGETABLE SOUP

Makes: 11 cups; serves: 10 to 12

Randy says her kids (Dana and Julie) are disappointed if she doesn't make this soup at least once a week—and I can see why. It's great served pureed or unpureed. In fact, I tend to puree only half the recipe; then it seems like two different soups that I cooked in the time it takes to make only one.

8 cups water

4 cups sliced zucchini

2 cups sliced yellow squash

2 cups sliced carrots

2 cups cubed, peeled butternut squash

1½ cups diced, peeled potatoes

1 cup sliced leeks (white and light green parts only)

⅓ cup dry sherry

2 Knorr's Vegetarian Vegetable bouillon cubes

½ teaspoon dried basil

¼ teaspoon salt, or to taste

¼ teaspoon ground white pepper

1. Place all the ingredients in a 6-quart pot. Bring to a boil over medium-high heat. Reduce heat and simmer, uncovered, 1 hour or until vegetables are very tender.

2. For a smooth soup: place the vegetables in a blender or food processor container fitted with a steel blade. Cover and process until smooth. Stir the pureed vegetables into the broth.

Variation: Substitute 4 cups of vegetable broth (pages 93–95) for 4 cups of the water and omit the bouillon cubes.

FRESH TOMATO SOUP

Ⓥ ♥

Makes: 10 cups; serves: 10 to 12

For all you gardeners who end up with buckets of tomatoes, all ripe at the same time, this is one very delightful use for them. If you have the time or patience, you may want to peel the tomatoes before you use them in this soup.

8 medium tomatoes, quartered (3 pounds)

2 cups water

1 cup vegetable broth (pages 94–95)

1 large onion, peeled and halved

1 teaspoon sugar

½ teaspoon salt, or to taste

1. In a 4-quart pot, combine the tomatoes, water, broth, and onion. Bring to a boil. Reduce heat and simmer, uncovered, 1 hour. Stir in sugar and salt.

2. Place the soup in a blender or food processor container fitted with a steel blade. Cover and process until pureed.

Variation: Herbed Tomato Soup: Add fresh herbs to the soup 15 minutes before it has finished cooking. The amount will vary widely depending on the herbs you choose. Use ½ cup chopped fresh basil, mint, parsley, or dill. Use 2 to 3 tablespoons of the stronger-flavored herbs, such as chopped fresh thyme, oregano, rosemary, chervil, or savory.

SOUTHWEST SALSA SOUP

Ⓥ ♥

Makes: 11½ cups; serves: 10 to 12

This recipe takes off where the previous one finishes.

1 recipe Fresh Tomato Soup (left)

¼ cup chopped fresh cilantro

1 tablespoon chili powder

½ teaspoon ground cumin

One 8-ounce can corn kernels, undrained

One 4-ounce can chopped chilies, drained

1. Prepare Fresh Tomato Soup according to recipe, but add cilantro, chili powder, and cumin to the soup before pureeing.

2. After pureeing, stir in corn and chilies; reheat if necessary.

Variation: Omit the chilies for a milder soup.

CURRIED TOMATO SOUP

Makes: 5¹/₂ cups; serves: 6 to 8

This soup is a little on the thick side (which I like); if you prefer, you can add extra water to thin it. Or omit the water and cook this up to be a very interesting sauce. Use it on spaghetti squash, or serve it as a dipping sauce for zucchini sticks or whatever.

1 tablespoon vegetable oil

1 cup chopped onions

1 cup chopped, peeled tart apples

1 tablespoon curry powder

1 teaspoon ground coriander

¹/₂ teaspoon ground ginger

¹/₂ teaspoon ground cardamom

¹/₂ teaspoon ground turmeric

One 28-ounce can crushed tomatoes

2 cups vegetable broth (pages 93–95)

1 cup water

2 tablespoons firmly packed light brown or dark brown sugar

¹/₄ teaspoon salt, or to taste

¹/₄ teaspoon ground red pepper

1. In a 3-quart saucepan, heat the oil over medium-high heat. Stir in the onions and apples; cook until onions are transparent and apples are softened, about 3 minutes. Stir in the curry, coriander, ginger, cardamom, and turmeric until the spices are absorbed.

2. Stir in the crushed tomatoes, broth, and water. Bring to a boil. Reduce heat and simmer, uncovered, 30 minutes. Stir in the brown sugar, salt, and pepper.

3. Place half of the soup in a blender or food processor container fitted with a steel blade. Cover and process until pureed. Repeat with remaining soup.

Variation: Curried Spinach and Tomato Soup: Add a 10-ounce package frozen chopped spinach after you've pureed the soup. Return to heat and cook until spinach is heated through.

RED PEPPER–TOMATO SOUP

Makes: 3¹/₂ cups; serves: 4

The red pepper flavor is subtle, although you definitely get it in the aftertaste. If you want a really strong pepper flavor, use ³/₄ to 1 cup of red peppers instead of the ¹/₂ cup called for in the recipe.

¹/₂ tablespoon olive oil

1 cup chopped onions

2 medium peeled tomatoes, quartered (³/₄ pounds)

1¹/₂ cups vegetable broth (pages 93–95)

1 cup water

¹/₄ teaspoon dried thyme

¹/₂ cup roasted red peppers (page 276)

¹/₄ teaspoon salt, or to taste

¹/₈ teaspoon ground red pepper, or more to taste

1. In a 3-quart saucepan, heat the oil over medium-high heat. Add the onions; cook, stirring, until softened, about 2 minutes. Add the tomatoes; cook, stirring, until softened, about 4 minutes. Add the broth, water, and thyme; bring to a boil.

2. Reduce heat and simmer, uncovered, 40 minutes or until the vegetables are soft.

3. Place the soup, roasted peppers, salt, and ground red pepper in a blender or food processor container fitted with a steel blade. Cover and process until pureed.

TOMATO, CORN, AND SPINACH SOUP

— V ❤ —

Makes: 3³/₄ cups; serves: 3 to 4

Although this soup is based on the previous recipe, the end result is quite different.

1 recipe Red Pepper–Tomato Soup (page 98)
One 16-ounce can of corn kernels, undrained
1 cup chopped fresh spinach
1 tablespoon sugar

1. Cook Red Pepper–Tomato Soup according to directions, omitting the roasted red peppers.

2. After the soup is pureed, return it to saucepan. Stir in the corn (with canning liquid), spinach, and sugar. Cook, over medium heat, until spinach is cooked, about 5 minutes.

Variation: Substitute half of 10-ounce package frozen chopped spinach for the fresh spinach.

CREAMY TOMATO AND LEEK SOUP

— L —

Makes: 4 cups; serves: 4 to 6

Just how creamy you make this soup is up to you. Omit the cream and use just milk (and for an even lower-fat version use skim milk); or use all half-and-half instead of the milk and cream; or use broth instead of any dairy products.

3 tablespoons butter or margarine, divided
1½ cups sliced leeks (white and light green parts only)
4 cups chopped tomatoes
2 tablespoons all-purpose flour
1¼ cups milk
1 cup water
⅓ cup heavy cream
2 teaspoons sugar
¼ teaspoon salt, or to taste
⅛ teaspoon ground red pepper

1. In a 2-quart saucepan, melt 1 tablespoon of the butter or margarine over medium-high heat. Add the leeks; cook, stirring, until softened, about 1 minute. Add the tomatoes. Cook, uncovered, over medium heat 30 minutes, stirring occasionally.

2. Place the tomato mixture in a blender or a food processor container fitted with a steel blade. Cover and process until smooth. Strain, discarding any pieces too large for the strainer.

3. In a 3-quart saucepan, melt the remaining 2 tablespoons butter or margarine. Stir in the flour until absorbed. Add the milk, water, and cream; cook, stirring constantly, until mixture comes to a boil.

4. Gradually stir the strained tomato mixture into the sauce. Stir in the sugar, salt, and pepper.

Variation: Tomato-Leek Coulis: Prepare recipe through step 2, using only the ingredients needed in step 1. Makes 1³/₄ cups.

Tomato-Cheddar Cheese Soup
L

Makes: 8 cups; serves: 10 to 12

For a terrific flavor combination—and an unusual visual presentation, serve this very thick and rich soup with a dollop of Avocado Yogurt (page 64).

3 cups vegetable broth (pages 93–95)
One 28-ounce can whole tomatoes in thick puree
1 cup chopped carrots
1 cup chopped celery
2 tablespoons butter or margarine
³/4 cup chopped onions
2 tablespoons all-purpose flour
2 cups shredded Cheddar cheese
¹/2 teaspoon anchovy-free Worcestershire sauce

1. In a 3-quart saucepan, bring the broth to a boil. Add the tomatoes, carrots, and celery. Cover and simmer 30 minutes or until vegetables are softened.

2. In a 3-quart saucepan, melt the butter or margerine over medium heat. Add the onions; cook until softened, about 3 minutes. Stir in the flour until absorbed. Stir in the vegetables and broth; cook, stirring, until mixture comes to a boil.

3. Place half of broth mixture in a blender or a food processor container fitted with a steel blade. Cover and process until pureed. Repeat with remaining broth.

3. Return to pot and stir in cheese and Worcestershire sauce. Cook, stirring until cheese is melted and soup is heated through.

V **Variation:** Garden Tomato Soup: Omit the Cheddar cheese and Worcestershire sauce.

Tortilla Soup
V

Makes: 4¹/2 cups Serves: 4 to 6

The Rudolph-Weissman-Minsky-Getzoff family gave this soup a four-star rating. You don't have to cut the onions and tomatoes into smaller pieces because they're going to be pureed in the food processor.

3 cups cubed (1¹/2-inch pieces) tomatoes
1 cup cubed (1¹/2-inch pieces) onions
2 tablespoons vegetable oil
1 cup coarsely chopped corn tortillas
4 cloves garlic, minced
1 tablespoon chili powder
³/4 teaspoon ground cumin
3 cups vegetable broth (pages 93–95)
1 cup water
2 tablespoons tomato paste
1 bay leaf
2 corn tortillas, each cut into 8 wedges
1 tablespoon chopped fresh cilantro
1 tablespoon fresh lime juice
¹/2 teaspoon salt, or to taste
Shredded Cheddar (optional)

1. Place the tomato chunks and onion chunks in a blender or food processor container fitted with a steel blade. Cover and process until pureed; set aside.

2. In a 3-quart saucepan, heat the oil over medium-high heat. Add the chopped tortillas and garlic; cook, stirring, until tortillas are softened, about 3 minutes. Stir in the chili powder and cumin until absorbed.

3. Add the broth, water, tomato paste, and bay leaf; bring to a boil. Reduce heat and simmer, 30 minutes. Strain through sieve, pressing the liquid from the chopped tortillas. Discard the bay leaf and chopped tortillas. Return soup to pot. Stir in the tortilla wedges, cilantro, lime juice, and salt. Return to a boil, simmer 3 minutes longer.

4. Serve with Cheddar cheese, if desired.

Variation: Add ¹⁄₄ teaspoon ground red pepper when you stir in the cumin.

GUMBO SOUP

Makes: 5 cups; serves: 4 to 6

As they say in the Campbell's soup ads, this is a soup that eats like a meal. If you're not an okra fan, this soup tastes great even without it.

1 tablespoon vegetable oil
1 cup chopped onions
1 cup chopped celery
³⁄₄ cup chopped green bell peppers
1 teaspoon chili powder
3 cups cubed tomatoes
2 cups vegetable broth (pages 93–95)
1 cup water
2 bay leaves
¹⁄₂ teaspoon dried oregano
¹⁄₂ teaspoon Tabasco sauce, or to taste
¹⁄₄ teaspoon dried basil
¹⁄₄ teaspoon dried thyme
2 tablespoons white rice
1¹⁄₂ cups sliced okra
¹⁄₄ teaspoon salt, or to taste

1. In a 3-quart saucepan, heat the oil over medium-high heat. Add the onions, celery, and bell peppers; cook, stirring, until softened, about 3 minutes. Stir in chili powder until absorbed. Add the tomatoes; cook, stirring, until softened, about 4 minutes. Add the broth, water, bay leaves, oregano, Tabasco, basil, and thyme; bring to a boil.

2. Add rice. Reduce heat and simmer, uncovered, 20 minutes. Stir in okra and salt; return to a boil. Reduce heat and simmer 10 minutes longer or until okra is tender. Discard bay leaves.

SHERRIED ONION SOUP

Makes: 6 cups; serves: 6 to 8

Serve this soup with grated Parmesan cheese, if you like, or use it to make French Onion Soup (see next recipe).

2 tablespoons butter or margarine
4 cups sliced mild onions
6 cups vegetable broth (pages 93–95)
¹⁄₄ cup dry red wine
3 tablespoons dry sherry
¹⁄₂ teaspoon dried thyme
¹⁄₄ teaspoon dried savory
¹⁄₈ teaspoon salt, or to taste
¹⁄₈ teaspoon pepper
1 bay leaf

1. In a 3-quart saucepan melt the butter or margerine over medium-high heat. Add the onions; cook, stirring, until onions are very soft, about 5 minutes.

2. Stir in broth, wine, sherry, thyme, savory, salt, pepper, and bay leaf; bring to a boil. Reduce heat and simmer, uncovered, 50 minutes. Discard the bay leaf.

Variation: Onion Soup: Substitute dry vermouth or additional broth for the sherry.

FRENCH ONION SOUP

Makes: 4 bowls; serves: 4

I used to try to make this soup with shredded cheese and the cheese always ended up on the bottom of the bowl. By hanging the edges of a slice of cheese over the rim of the bowl, the cheese stays afloat. You can use Sherried Onion Soup or any other onion soup for this recipe.

4 cups heated Sherried Onion Soup
    (page 101)
4 slices day-old French bread
¼ cup grated Parmesan, divided
Eight 1-ounce slices Swiss cheese

1. Preheat broiler.

2. Spoon 1 cup of soup into each of 4 ovenproof soup crocks.

3. Float 1 slice of bread over the soup in each crock.

4. Sprinkle 1 tablespoon of the Parmesan over the bread and soup in each crock.

5. Arrange the slices of Swiss cheese over the soup, so that the cheese hangs slightly over the edge of the crock.

6. Broil, 4 inches from the heat source, 4 to 5 minutes, or until the cheese is melted and bubbly.

Variation: Use melba rounds if you don't have any French bread on hand. If the French bread is not stale, toast it until just lightly browned.

BELL PEPPER–CELERY SOUP

Makes: 4½ cups; serves: 4 to 6

Oddly enough, when I first made this soup I was sure it would taste only of the bell and jalapeño peppers. But I found those flavors were quite mild, with the celery being the dominant taste. It could be that I was just using exceptionally mild peppers and a flavorful celery. If you can't find fresh jalapeños, leave them out and just use ground red pepper to taste.

2 tablespoons butter or margarine
1½ cups chopped celery
1½ cups chopped green bell peppers
1 cup chopped onions
2 tablespoons seeded and chopped jalapeño
    peppers (1½ peppers)
2 tablespoons all-purpose flour
3 cups vegetable broth (pages 93–95),
    divided

1. In a 3-quart saucepan melt the butter or margarine over medium-high heat. Add the celery, bell peppers, onions, and jalapeño peppers. Cook, covered, until vegetables are very soft, about 10 minutes. Stir in the flour until absorbed.

2. Place the vegetables and 1 cup of the broth in a blender or food processor container fitted with a steel blade. Cover and process until smooth. Return to saucepan.

3. Stir in remaining broth and bring to a boil, stirring constantly.

Ⓛ ***Variation:*** Cheesy Celery Soup: After the soup has come to a boil, add 1 cup shredded Swiss cheese and 1 cup shredded Monterey Jack cheese, and stir until melted.

SPINACH AVGOLEMONO SOUP

□ ♥

Makes: 4 cups; serves: 4 to 6

The traditional way to serve this soup is without the spinach, but I find the spinach a wonderful addition to a wonderful soup. This recipe calls for bite-sized pieces of fresh spinach, but you can substitute ¹/₂ package frozen chopped spinach (although, personally, I prefer the larger pieces).

3 cups vegetable broth (pages 93–95)
¹/₄ cup white rice
3 cups lightly packed spinach leaves,
    chopped into bite-size pieces
2 eggs
2 tablespoons fresh lemon juice

1. In a 2-quart saucepan, bring the broth to a boil. Add the rice; return to a boil. Reduce heat and simmer, uncovered, 20 minutes. Add the spinach and simmer 5 minutes longer.

2. In a medium bowl, beat the eggs. Beat in the lemon juice. Beating constantly, add 2 cups of the hot broth. Whisk the egg mixture into the remaining soup. Reheat if necessary, but do not boil.

Variation: Avgolemono Soup: Omit the spinach.

CURRIED YELLOW PEPPER SOUP

Ⓥ

Makes: 4 cups; serves: 4

Yum. . . .

1 tablespoon olive oil
³/₄ cup sliced onions
1 tablespoon curry powder
¹/₄ teaspoon ground cumin
2 cups vegetable broth (pages 93–95)
2 cups sliced fennel
¹/₂ cup roasted yellow bell peppers
    (page 276)
¹/₂ cup unsweetened coconut milk (page 497)
¹/₄ teaspoon salt, or to taste

1. In a 2-quart saucepan, heat the oil over medium-high heat. Add the onion; cook, stirring, until softened, about 2 minutes. Add curry powder and cumin and stir until absorbed. Add the broth and bring to a boil. Add the fennel and return to a boil.

2. Reduce heat and simmer, covered, 30 minutes or until the vegetables are soft.

3. Place the soup, peppers, coconut milk, and salt in a blender or food processor container fitted with a steel blade. Cover and process until smooth.

Ⓛ *Variation:* Use buttermilk instead of the coconut milk.

SENEGALESE SOUP

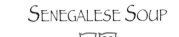

Makes: 4 cups; serves: 4 to 6

This unusual soup combines sweet, tart, and spicy flavors. If you have less adventurous tastes, this one may not be for you.

2 tablespoons butter or margarine
1 cup chopped, peeled tart apples
3/4 cup finely chopped celery
1/3 cup minced shallots
2 teaspoons curry powder
2 tablespoons all-purpose flour
1 1/2 cups vegetable broth (pages 93–95)
3/4 cup milk or unsweetened coconut milk
    (page 497)
3/4 cup apple juice
1/4 cup dry sherry
3 tablespoons chopped fresh cilantro
1/4 teaspoon salt, or to taste
1/8 teaspoon ground red pepper

1. In a 3-quart saucepan, melt the butter or margerine over medium heat. Add the apples, celery, and shallots; cook, stirring, until softened, about 3 to 5 minutes. Add curry powder and stir until absorbed. Add the flour and stir until absorbed. Stir in the broth, milk or unsweetened coconut milk, the juice, sherry, and cilantro. Cook, stirring constantly, until soup comes to a boil. Reduce heat and simmer, uncovered, 15 minutes or until celery is soft.

2. Place the soup, salt, and pepper in a blender or food processor container fitted with a steel blade. Cover and process until smooth. (You may have to do this in two batches.)

Variation: Use diced butternut squash instead of the apples.

MULLIGATAWNY SOUP

Makes: 5 1/2 cups; serves: 4 to 6

This soup is closely related to Senegalese Soup, but is chunkier.

2 tablespoons butter or margarine
1/2 cup finely chopped onions
1/4 cup finely chopped red bell peppers
1 1/2 cups chopped, peeled tart apples
1/2 cup finely chopped carrots
1/2 cup finely chopped celery
2 tablespoons all-purpose flour
1 tablespoon curry powder
2 cups vegetable broth (pages 93–95)
2 cups water
3/4 cup unsweetened coconut milk (page 497)
1/4 cup white rice
1 tablespoon fresh lemon juice
1/4 teaspoon salt, or to taste
1/8 teaspoon ground red pepper
1 tablespoon chopped fresh cilantro or parsley

1. In a 3-quart saucepan, melt the butter or margerine over medium-high heat. Add the onions and bell peppers; cook, stirring, until softened, about 2 minutes. Add the apples, carrots, and celery; cook, stirring, until softened, about 3 minutes.

2. Stir in the flour and curry powder until absorbed.

3. Add the broth, water, coconut milk, and rice. Bring to a boil. Reduce heat and simmer, uncovered, 20 minutes or until rice is tender.

4. Stir in lemon juice, salt, and red pepper; simmer 5 minutes. Stir in cilantro.

Variation: Omit the rice.

PORTUGUESE VEGETABLE SOUP

Makes: 8 cups; serves: 8 to 10

Sausage is usually an element of this soup, but I added wine to substitute for the sausage flavor.

2 tablespoons olive oil

2 cups chopped onions

2 cups chopped cabbage

1 cup thinly sliced leeks (white and light green parts only)

2 cloves garlic, minced

6 cups vegetable broth (pages 93–95)

1 cup sliced, peeled potatoes

1 cup chopped turnips

1 bay leaf

½ teaspoon dried marjoram

½ teaspoon dried thyme

¼ teaspoon dried rosemary, crumbled

⅛ teaspoon grated nutmeg

4 cups lightly packed fresh spinach (thoroughly rinsed, cut into bite-size pieces)

½ cup dry white or red wine

¼ teaspoon salt, or to taste

¼ teaspoon pepper

1. In a 6-quart pot, heat the oil over medium heat. Add the onions, cabbage, leeks, and garlic; cook, stirring occasionally, until the onions are golden, about 20 minutes.

2. Add the broth and bring to a boil. Add the potatoes, turnips, bay leaf, marjoram, thyme, rosemary, and nutmeg. Bring to a boil; reduce heat and simmer, uncovered, 20 minutes. Discard bay leaf.

3. Place 2 cups of the soup in a blender or food processor container fitted with a steel blade. Cover and process until pureed. Stir into soup.

4. Add the spinach, wine, salt, and pepper. Simmer, uncovered, 5 minutes.

Variation: Stir in 1 cup of drained white beans or cannellini (cooked from dry; or canned) when you add the spinach.

SAINT PATRICK'S DAY SOUP

Makes: 8 cups; serves: 8 to 10

I was testing this recipe one March 17th, and I noticed that it only lacked corned beef to make it a "real" Saint Patrick's Day meal. The amount of salt you need may vary with the broth you're using, and I actually added extra pepper to my own serving.

2 tablespoons vegetable oil

6 cups shredded cabbage

1 cup shredded or thinly sliced leeks (white and light green parts only)

6 cups vegetable broth (pages 93–95)

2 cups diced, peeled boiling potatoes

¼ teaspoon salt, or to taste

¼ teaspoon pepper

1. In a 4-quart saucepan, heat the oil over medium-high heat. Add the cabbage and leeks; cook, stirring, until wilted, about 4 minutes.

2. Stir in the broth and bring to a boil. Add the potatoes; reduce heat and simmer, uncovered, 30 minutes or until the potatoes are tender. Stir in salt and pepper.

Variation: Add 1 cup julienned carrots when you add the potatoes.

LETTUCE AND PEA SOUP

Makes: 6¹/₂ cups; serves: 6 to 8

Lovely and elegant are good ways to describe this delicious soup.

1 tablespoon butter or margarine
1 cup sliced leeks (white and light green parts only)
2 cups vegetable broth (pages 93–95)
2 cups water
4 cups shredded iceburg lettuce
One 10-ounce package frozen peas
¼ cup snipped fresh dill
⅛ teaspoon ground red pepper
Yogurt (optional)

1. In a 3-quart saucepan, melt the butter or margarine over medium-high heat. Add the leeks; cook, stirring, until softened, about 1 minute. Add the broth, water, lettuce, peas, dill, and red pepper. Bring to a boil; reduce heat and simmer 10 minutes.

2. Place half of the soup in a blender or food processor container fitted with a steel blade. Cover and process until pureed. Repeat with remaining soup.

3. Serve topped with a dollop of yogurt, if desired.

Variation: Minted Pea and Lettuce Soup: Stir in ¹/₃ cup chopped fresh mint after pureeing the soup.

ZUCCHINI-LEEK SOUP

Makes: 3¹/₄ cups; serves: 3 to 4

Another perfect recipe for all you summer gardeners who are suddenly overwhelmed with zucchini.

1½ teaspoons olive oil
³/₄ cup sliced leeks (white and light green parts only)
2 cups chopped shredded zucchini
2 cups vegetable broth (pages 93–95)
1 cup water
½ teaspoon dried oregano

1. In a 2-quart saucepan, heat the oil over medium-high heat. Add the leeks; cook, stirring, until softened, about 1 minute.

2. Add the zucchini, broth, water, and oregano; bring to a boil. Reduce heat and simmer, uncovered, 10 minutes.

3. Place the soup in a blender or food processor container fitted with a steel blade. Cover and process until smooth. (You may have to do this in more than one batch.) Chill, if desired.

Variation: Add ¹/₄ cup fresh snipped dill instead of the oregano when you add the zucchini.

CRIMINI MUSHROOM AND GREEN BEAN SOUP

Makes: 4 cups; serves: 4

You can use any flavorful mushroom in this soup, such as portobello, shiitake, or porcini.

1 tablespoon butter or margarine
3/4 cup sliced leeks (white and light green part only)
2 cups sliced crimini mushrooms
1 1/2 tablespoons all-purpose flour
2 cups vegetable broth (pages 93–95)
1 cup water
1 1/2 cups cut green beans (fresh or frozen)
1/2 cup chopped fresh parsley
1/4 teaspoon dried thyme

1. In a 2-quart saucepan, melt the butter or margarine over medium-high heat. Add the leeks; cook, stirring, until softened, about 1 minute. Add the mushrooms; cook, stirring, until softened, about 3 minutes.

2. Stir in the flour until absorbed. Add the remaining ingredients; bring to a boil, stirring occasionally.

3. Simmer, uncovered, 10 to 15 minutes or until green beans reach desired consistency.

Variation: For a richer version, substitute 3/4 cup half-and-half for 3/4 cup of the broth.

MANDARIN SOUP

Makes: 4 cups; serves: 4

My tasters all had seconds of this soup—I'd say that's a pretty high recommendation.

1 1/2 cups water
4 dried shiitake mushrooms
1 1/2 cups vegetable broth (pages 93–95)
1 tablespoon cornstarch
1 1/2 teaspoons soy sauce, or to taste
1/4 cup julienned carrots
1 beaten egg (optional)
1 cup diced tofu (6 ounces)
1 cup shredded fresh spinach
1/2 cup sliced, canned bamboo shoots
2 tablespoons thinly sliced scallion (green part only)

1. In a 2-quart saucepan, bring the water to a boil over high heat. Remove from heat, add mushrooms, and let stand 10 minutes or until mushrooms are soft. Remove mushrooms from pot and slice.

2. In a medium bowl, stir together the vegetable broth, cornstarch, and soy sauce. Add the broth mixture, sliced mushrooms, and carrots to the water in the pot. Bring to a boil, stirring constantly. While stirring, gradually add the egg to the soup, if desired. Stir in the tofu, spinach, bamboo shoots, and scallions.

3. Simmer until the spinach is cooked and the tofu is heated through, about 5 minutes.

Variation: Add 1/3 cup cooked fresh or frozen peas when you add the tofu.

CHINESE CABBAGE SOUP

Makes: 7 cups; serves: 6 to 8

With so many vegetables floating in it, this soup is almost a meal. In fact, if you stir in lots of pasta, you could make it a main course (see variation).

1 1/2 tablespoons vegetable oil
2 cups shredded cabbage
1 cup sliced onions
1 clove garlic, minced
5 cups vegetable broth (pages 93–95)
1 tablespoon dry sherry
2 teaspoons soy sauce
3 cups shredded Chinese cabbage or bok choy
1/2 cup julienned carrots
1/2 cup canned straw mushrooms
1/4 cup peas (fresh, cooked; or frozen)
1/4 cup sliced scallions

1. In a 4-quart saucepan, heat the oil over medium-high heat. Add the cabbage, onions, and garlic; cook, stirring, until softened, about 3 minutes.

2. Add the broth, sherry, and soy sauce; bring to a boil. Add the Chinese cabbage, carrots, mushrooms, and peas. Return to a boil, reduce heat, and simmer, uncovered, 7 minutes. Stir in scallions.

Variations: Stir in 1/2 cup water chestnuts, bamboo shoots, and/or snow peas when you add the mushrooms.

Chinese Cabbage and Noodle Soup: Stir in 3 cups cooked noodles when you add the Chinese cabbage. (The best types of noodles to use are the kind you'd use for lo mein or cooked, thin spaghetti.)

HOT AND SOUR SOUP

Makes: 5 cups; serves: 4 to 6

Most of the Asian ingredients called for below are usually available in the ethnic food sections of supermarkets. If you have trouble finding the cloud ears, just use extra shiitake mushrooms; the lily buds can be eliminated altogether. Beaten egg is traditional in this soup, but you can either omit it or use only the white.

3 cups vegetable broth (pages 93–95)
3/4 cup plus 2 tablespoons water, divided
10 dried lily buds
6 dried shiitake mushrooms
2 tablespoons cloud ears (tree fungus)
1 cup diced tofu (6 ounces)
1/3 cup canned, sliced bamboo shoots
1/3 cup canned, sliced water chestnuts
1/4 cup peas (fresh, cooked; or frozen)
1 1/2 tablespoons cornstarch
3 tablespoons red wine vinegar
2 teaspoons dark or black soy sauce
1 teaspoon chili oil
1/4 teaspoon pepper
1 egg or egg white, beaten (optional)
2 tablespoons sliced scallions (green part only)

1. In a 3-quart saucepan, bring the broth and 3/4 cup water to a boil over high heat. Add the lily buds and mushrooms. Simmer them 7 minutes and remove to a cutting board; chop, discarding any tough pieces. Return to the pan. Add the cloud ears, tofu, bamboo shoots, water chestnuts, and peas. Simmer 5 minutes.

2. In a small bowl, blend the cornstarch and the remaining 2 tablespoons water until smooth.

3. Stir the vinegar, soy sauce, chili oil, and pepper into the soup. Stir in the cornstarch mixture and bring to a boil, stirring. Gradually stir in the egg, if desired, then the scallions. Simmer 1 minute longer.

Variation: Use more or less chili oil to increase or reduce the amount of spice.

SWEET AND SOUR CABBAGE SOUP

Makes: 6¹/₂ cups; serves: 6 to 8

If you're a fan of cilantro, sprinkle some into this soup.

2 tablespoons vegetable oil
2 cups shredded cabbage
1¹/₂ cups sliced celery
1 cup sliced onions
2 cloves garlic, minced
6 cups water
One 6-ounce can tomato paste
¹/₄ cup firmly packed light brown or dark brown sugar
2 tablespoons distilled white vinegar
¹/₄ salt, or to taste
¹/₄ teaspoon pepper

1. In a 4-quart saucepan, heat the oil over medium-high heat. Stir in the cabbage, celery, onions, and garlic; cook until onions are transparent and cabbage is softened, about 5 minutes.

2. Stir in the water, tomato paste, brown sugar, vinegar, salt, and pepper. Bring to a boil. Reduce heat and simmer, uncovered, 50 minutes or until vegetables are tender.

Variation: Add 1 cup sauerkraut when you add the water.

MANHATTAN-STYLE VEGETABLE CHOWDER

Makes: 9¹/₂ cups; serves: 8 to 10

The flavor and texture of this soup is very reminiscent of the tomato-based clam chowder served in the Big Apple. This recipe makes quite a lot of soup, but it freezes well.

1 tablespoon vegetable oil
2 cups chopped cabbage
1 cup chopped onions
3 cups water
3 cups vegetable broth (pages 93–95), or fish broth
One 6-ounce can tomato paste
1 cup sliced celery
1 cup sliced zucchini
1 cup sliced carrots
1 cup diced, peeled boiling potatoes
¹/₂ cup frozen lima beans
¹/₂ cup cut green beans (fresh or frozen)
¹/₂ teaspoon dried thyme
¹/₄ teaspoon salt, or to taste
¹/₄ teaspoon pepper

1. In a 4-quart pot, heat the oil over medium-high heat. Add the cabbage and onions; cook, stirring, until softened, about 4 minutes.

2. Stir in the water, vegetable broth, and tomato paste until combined. Add the remaining ingredients. Bring to a boil. Reduce heat and simmer, uncovered, 30 minutes.

Variation: Use corn instead of lima beans.

CORN CHOWDER

Makes: 4³⁄₄ cups; serves: 4 to 6

If you use canned corn, add the canning liquid to the soup for extra corn flavor.

2 tablespoons butter or margarine, divided
1 cup chopped onions
1 cup chopped celery
3 tablespoons all-purpose flour
3 cups vegetable broth (pages 93–95)
1 cup peeled potatoes, diced into ¹⁄₂-inch
    pieces
2 cups corn kernels (fresh, cooked; canned,
    drained; or frozen)
¹⁄₈ teaspoon dried thyme
1 bay leaf
¹⁄₃ cup heavy cream
¹⁄₄ teaspoon pepper
¹⁄₈ teaspoon salt, or to taste

1. In a 3-quart saucepan, melt 1 tablespoon of the butter or margarine. Stir in the onions and celery; cook, stirring, until softened, about 3 minutes. Add the flour and stir until absorbed.

2. Add the broth and bring to a boil. Add the potatoes, corn, thyme, and bay leaf; return to a boil. Reduce heat and simmer 15 minutes or until the potatoes are tender. Discard bay leaf.

3. Stir in the cream, pepper, and salt. Continue to cook, stirring, until heated through.

Ⓥ **Variation:** Omit the cream and substitute extra broth.

CREAMY CAULIFLOWER-ASPARAGUS SOUP

Makes: 8³⁄₄ cups; serves: 8 to 10

My friend Ron Pies was in heaven eating this soup. After proclaiming this one of the best soups ever, he asked what was in it. "It's cauliflower-asparagus soup," I told him. He dropped his spoon and declared, "I hate cauliflower." His wife, Andy Cahill, and I assured him that if he loved it before he knew it was cauliflower soup, he probably would still like it even after he knew the "awful truth." In fact, I think he may even have had seconds.

1 tablespoon vegetable oil
1¹⁄₂ cups sliced leeks, rinsed (white and light
    green parts only)
3 cups vegetable broth (pages 93–95)
3 cups water
4 cups cauliflower florets
1 cup asparagus pieces
2 tablespoons white rice
¹⁄₂ teaspoon salt, or to taste
¹⁄₂ teaspoon lemon rind
¹⁄₄ teaspoon ground sage
¹⁄₈ teaspoon ground nutmeg
¹⁄₈ teaspoon ground red pepper
³⁄₄ cup light cream or half-and-half
Unflavored yogurt (optional)

1. In a 4-quart pot, heat the oil over medium-high heat. Add the leeks; cook, stirring, until wilted, about 2 to 3 minutes. Add the broth and water and bring to a boil.

2. Add the cauliflower, asparagus, and rice and return to a boil. Reduce heat and simmer, covered, 30 minutes or until the vegetables are tender.

3. Stir in the salt, lemon rind, sage, nutmeg, and red pepper.

4. Place a third of the soup in a blender or food processor container fitted with a steel blade. Cover and process until pureed. Repeat with remaining soup.

5. Return soup to pot and stir in the cream or half-and-half. Cook over low heat until heated through.

6. Serve with a dollop of yogurt in each bowl, if desired.

Variations: Chilled Cauliflower-Asparagus Soup: This makes an excellent cold soup. Instead of reheating the soup after pureeing, chill it.

Ⓥ Use additional broth instead of half-and-half. Omit the yogurt dollop.

CARROT~CAULIFLOWER SOUP

Makes: 4¹/₂ cups; serves: 4 to 6

The interesting combination of flavors—carrots, cauliflower, dill, ginger, and honey—works well in this smooth soup.

3 cups sliced carrots
1¹/₂ cups vegetable broth (pages 93–95)
1¹/₂ cups water
1 cup cauliflower florets
3 tablespoons snipped fresh dill
¹/₂ teaspoon ground ginger
¹/₈ teaspoon pepper
1¹/₂ tablespoons honey
¹/₄ teaspoon salt, or to taste

1. In a 3-quart pot, combine the carrots, broth, water, cauliflower, dill, ginger, and pepper. Bring to a boil; reduce heat and simmer, covered, 30 minutes or until the vegetables are tender.

2. Place a third of the soup in a blender or food processor container fitted with a steel blade. Cover and process until smooth. Repeat with remaining soup. Stir in honey and salt.

Ⓛ **Variation:** Stir in ³/₄ cup buttermilk for a creamier soup.

BASIL~CAULIFLOWER SOUP

Makes: 4¹/₂ cups; serves: 4 to 6

The basil in this soup really sings! The soup is smooth and very thick. You can add extra buttermilk if you prefer your soup thinner.

1 tablespoon olive oil
1 cup sliced onions
3 cups vegetable broth (pages 93–95)
3 cups cauliflower florets
¹/₂ cup diced, peeled potatoes
¹/₂ cup packed fresh basil leaves
1 cup buttermilk
¹/₄ teaspoon salt, or to taste
Unflavored yogurt (optional)

1. In a 4-quart pot, heat the oil over medium-high heat. Add the onions; cook, stirring, until softened, about 2 minutes. Add the broth, cauliflower, and potatoes; bring to a boil. Reduce heat and simmer, covered, 30 minutes or until the vegetables are tender. Remove from heat and stir in the basil.

2. Place half of the soup in a blender or food processor container fitted with a steel blade. Cover and process until smooth. Repeat with remaining soup.

3. Return soup to pot and stir in buttermilk and salt. Cook, over low heat, until heated through.

4. Serve with a dollop of yogurt in each bowl, if desired.

Variations: Add ¹/₈ to ¹/₄ teaspoon ground red pepper for a spicy afterbite.

Ⓥ Use additional broth instead of the buttermilk. Omit the yogurt dollop.

CURRIED CAULIFLOWER SOUP

Makes: 3¹/₂ cups; serves: 4

If you use the dairy option, serve this moderately spicy soup with a dollop of yogurt, as suggested in the recipe, or stir in yogurt to taste for a creamier version.

1 tablespoon ghee or vegetable oil
1 cup chopped onions
1 tablespoon minced ginger
3 cloves garlic, minced
½ teaspoon cumin seed
1 tablespoon curry powder
2 cups vegetable broth (pages 93–95)
1 cup water
3 cups cauliflower florets
¼ teaspoon salt, or to taste
Unflavored yogurt (optional)

1. In a 3-quart pot, heat the ghee or oil over medium-high heat. Add the onions, ginger, garlic, and cumin seed; cook, stirring, until softened, about 2 minutes. Add the curry powder and stir until absorbed.

2. Add the broth and water; bring to a boil. Add the cauliflower and salt; bring to a boil. Reduce heat and simmer, covered, 30 minutes or until the vegetables are tender. Remove from heat.

3. Place half of the soup in a blender or food processor container fitted with a steel blade. Cover and process until smooth. Repeat with remaining soup.

4. Serve with a dollop of yogurt in each bowl, if desired.

Variation: Add ¹/₈ to ¹/₄ teaspoon ground red pepper for a spicier version.

PARSNIP-CARROT SOUP

Makes: 3 ¹/₂ cups; serves: 4

There's something especially warming about this soup on a cold day—it's real comfort food.

1 tablespoon olive oil
½ cup sliced leeks (white part only)
2 cups vegetable broth (pages 93–95)
1½ cups sliced parsnips
1¼ cups sliced carrots
½ teaspoon salt, or to taste
½ cup buttermilk
½ cup milk

1. In a 3-quart saucepan, heat the oil over medium-high heat. Add the leeks; cook, stirring, until softened, about 1 minute. Add the broth and bring to a boil. Add the parsnips and carrots and return to a boil.

2. Reduce heat and simmer, covered, 30 minutes or until the vegetables are soft.

3. Place the soup and salt in a blender or food processor container fitted with a steel blade. Cover and process until smooth.

4. Stir in the buttermilk and milk. Reheat until warmed.

Variation: Celeriac-Carrot Soup: Substitute an equal amount of celeriac for the parsnips.

CARIBBEAN CARROT SOUP
[V][♥]

Makes: 6 cups; serves: 4 to 6

Is this a soup you'd really find in the Caribbean? Probably not. But the ginger, jalapeño pepper, and cilantro make me think of islands in the sea. In any case, this is one of my very favorite ways to eat my carrots. If you like, serve it with a dollop of Tomato Raita (page 496) or unflavored yogurt.

2 teaspoons olive oil
1 cup chopped onions
1 tablespoon minced ginger
2 teaspoons minced fresh jalapeño pepper
1 teaspoon ground cumin
3 cups vegetable broth (pages 93–95)
2 cups water
3 cups sliced carrots
2 tablespoons fresh cilantro leaves
1/8 teaspoon salt, or to taste

1. In a 3-quart saucepan, heat the oil over medium-high heat. Add the onions, ginger, and jalapeño pepper. Cook, stirring, until onions are transparent, about 2 minutes. Stir in the cumin until absorbed.

2. Add the broth and water; bring to a boil. Stir in the carrots; return to a boil. Reduce heat and simmer, uncovered, 20 minutes or until carrots are softened.

3. Place the soup, cilantro leaves, and salt in a blender or food processor container fitted with a steel blade. Cover and process until pureed.

Variation: Use 1/8 to 1/4 teaspoon ground red pepper, or to taste, instead of the jalapeños.

CREAM OF PARSLEY ROOT AND PARSNIP SOUP
[V][♥]

Makes: 4 3/4 cups; serves: 4 to 6

It's not often that I find bunches of parsley with large roots, but when I do, I love to make this soup.

2 cups vegetable broth (pages 93–95)
2 cups water
1 1/2 cups peeled parsnip chunks
1 cup peeled parsley root chunks
3/4 cup sliced leeks (white and light green parts only)
1/3 cup lightly packed fresh parsley leaves
1/4 teaspoon salt, or to taste
1/8 teaspoon pepper

1. In a 2-quart saucepan, combine the broth, water, parsnips, parsley roots, leeks, and parsley leaves. Bring to a boil over high heat; reduce heat and simmer, uncovered, 30 minutes or until vegetables are tender.

2. Place the soup in a blender or food processor container fitted with a steel blade. Cover and process until smooth. Stir in salt and pepper. Reheat if necessary.

[L] ***Variation:*** Chilled Parsley Root and Parsnip Soup: Stir in 1/3 cup of half-and-half; chill. Serve with dollops of unflavored yogurt or sour cream.

VICHYSSOISE

Makes: 4¹/₂ cups; serves: 4 to 6

Traditionally served chilled, vichyssoise is also perfectly delicious warm, in which case it's called Potato-Leek Soup (see variation). It's nice to use white pepper in this recipe so you don't have black specks in the otherwise cream-colored soup, but if you don't have any white pepper, the black will taste just fine,.

2 tablespoons butter or margarine
1¹/₂ cups sliced leeks
3 cups vegetable broth (pages 93–95)
2 cups peeled potatoes, cut into 1-inch cubes
¹/₂ cup half-and-half
¹/₈ teaspoon ground white pepper
Snipped fresh chives for garnish

1. In a 2-quart saucepan, melt the butter or margarine over medium-high heat. Add the leeks; cook, stirring, until softened, about 1 minute.

2. Add the broth and bring to a boil. Add the potatoes; reduce heat and simmer, uncovered, 25 minutes or until potatoes are tender.

3. Place the soup in a blender or food processor container fitted with a steel blade. Cover and process until smooth. Add half-and-half, and pepper. Chill.

4. Serve garnished with snipped fresh chives.

Variation: Potato-Leek Soup: Serve warm, reheating if necessary after adding the half-and-half.

PEPPERY POTATO-FENNEL SOUP

Makes: 3³/₄ cups; serves: 4

This soup is rich and creamy, even without any cream. The fennel flavor is mild, not overwhelming.

1 tablespoon butter or margarine
1 cup sliced leeks (white and light green parts only)
1 cup sliced fennel
¹/₂ cup chopped, peeled tart apples
3 cups vegetable broth (pages 93–95)
1 cup diced, peeled potatoes
¹/₄ teaspoon dried tarragon
¹/₄ teaspoon pepper
¹/₄ teaspoon salt, or to taste

1. In a 3-quart saucepan, melt the butter or margarine over medium-high heat. Add the leeks, fennel, and apples; cook until softened, about 3 to 5 minutes. Add the broth and bring to a boil. Add the potatoes, tarragon, and pepper; reduce heat and simmer, uncovered, 25 minutes or until potatoes are tender.

2. Place the soup in a blender or food processor container fitted with a steel blade. Cover and process until smooth. Add salt.

Variation: Creamy Potato Soup: Use celery instead of fennel.

CREAMY ROASTED GARLIC SOUP

[V][♥]

Makes: 3¹/₄ cups; serves: 3 to 4

This soup packs quite a garlic punch. For the less enthusiastic garlic fan, start with fewer garlic cloves and work your way up. One large head of roasted garlic yields about ¹/₄ cup cloves. If you are planning to make a vegan version by omitting the cream, definitely use less garlic, since the cream tones down the bite.

2 cups vegetable broth (pages 93–95)
1 cup water
¹/₂ cup diced carrots
¹/₂ cup diced celery
¹/₂ cup diced, peeled potatoes
¹/₄ cup roasted garlic cloves (page 51), removed from skin
¹/₄ cup heavy cream (optional)
¹/₈ teaspoon pepper, or to taste

1. In a 2-quart saucepan, bring the broth and water to a boil over high heat. Add the carrots, celery, and potatoes; return to a boil. Reduce heat and simmer, uncovered, 25 minutes or until vegetables are very tender.

2. Place the soup and the garlic in a blender or food processor container fitted with a steel blade. Cover and process until smooth. Add the cream and pepper. Reheat if necessary.

Variation: Add 3 tablespoons snipped fresh dill when you add the cream.

CURRIED SWEET POTATO– MANGO SOUP

[V]

Makes: 3¹/₄ cups; serves: 3 to 4

My dad—who really doesn't like curry at all— liked this so much he ate a whole bowlful of this thick, delicious soup.

2 tablespoons butter or margarine
2 tablespoons minced shallots
1 teaspoon curry powder
¹/₂ teaspoon ground ginger
¹/₂ teaspoon ground coriander
¹/₈ teaspoon ground red pepper, or more to taste
3 cups water
1¹/₂ cups cubed, peeled sweet potatoes
1 cup diced mango
¹/₂ teaspoon salt, or to taste

1. In a 3-quart saucepan, melt the butter or margarine over medium-high heat. Stir in the shallots; cook until shallots are softened, about 30 seconds. Stir in the curry powder, ginger, coriander, and red pepper until aborbed.

2. Stir in the water; bring to a boil. Add the potatoes and mango; reduce heat and simmer, uncovered, 30 minutes. Stir in the salt.

3. Place half the soup in a blender or food processor container fitted with a steel blade. Cover and process until pureed. Repeat with remaining soup.

CREAM OF CORN SOUP

Makes: 4¹/₂ cups; serves: 4

If you're using frozen corn kernels, be sure to measure them after they're thawed. If you use canned corn you can substitute the canning liquids for some of the milk, if you like.

2 tablespoons butter or margarine
2 tablespoons all-purpose flour
3 cups milk
3 cups corn kernels (fresh, cooked; canned, drained; or frozen), divided
¹/₈ teaspoon salt, or to taste
¹/₈ teaspoon celery salt, or to taste
¹/₈ teaspoon pepper

1. In a 2-quart saucepan, melt the butter or margarine over medium-high heat. Add the flour; cook, stirring, until absorbed. Add the milk and 2 cups of the corn; bring to a boil, stirring constantly.

2. Place the soup in a blender or food processor container fitted with a steel blade. Cover and process until smooth. (You may have to do this in two batches.) Return to pot and stir in the remaining cup of corn and the salt, celery salt, and pepper. Bring to a simmer and cook until corn is heated through.

[V] **Variation:** Substitute broth for the milk.

CREAM OF ASPARAGUS SOUP

Makes: 3³/₄ cups; serves: 3 to 4

This soup is literally creamier than most of the other creamed soups in this book. If you're watching your fat intake, omit the half-and-half and use additional milk or broth instead.

3 cups vegetable broth (pages 93–95)
3 cups cut asparagus pieces
2 tablespoons butter or margarine
2 tablespoons all-purpose flour
1 cup milk
¹/₂ cup half-and-half
¹/₈ teaspoon salt, or to taste
¹/₈ teaspoon pepper, or to taste

1. In a 1-quart saucepan, bring the broth to a boil over high heat. Add the asparagus pieces and return to a boil. Reduce heat and simmer, uncovered, 15 minutes or until asparagus are very tender.

2. Place the broth and asparagus in a blender or food processor container fitted with a steel blade. Cover and process until pureed.

3. In a 2-quart saucepan, melt the butter or margarine over medium-high heat. Stir in the flour until absorbed. Stir in the milk, half-and-half, and asparagus puree; cook, stirring, until mixture comes to a boil. Add the salt and pepper.

Variation: Cream of Cauliflower Soup: Substitute cauliflower for the asparagus.

CREAM OF CRUDITÉ SOUP

L ♥

Makes: 5 cups; serves 4 to 6

I created this soup the day after a party, when I was looking for a way to use up the many leftover crudités.

2 tablespoons butter or margarine
1 cup finely chopped carrots
1 cup finely chopped celery
1 cup finely chopped red bell peppers
³/₄ cup finely chopped onions
4 cups vegetable broth (pages 93–95)
¹/₄ cup half-and-half

1. In a 3-quart saucepan, melt the butter or margarine over medium-high heat. Add the carrots, celery, bell peppers, and onions; cook, stirring, until vegetables are softened, about 4 minutes. Add the broth; bring to a boil. Reduce heat and simmer 20 minutes.

2. Place half the soup in a blender or food processor container fitted with a steel blade. Cover and process until pureed. Repeat with remaining soup. Stir in half-and-half. Repeat if necessary.

[V] **Variation:** Omit the half-and-half and follow the recipe only through step 1; serve after simmering. Makes 6 cups.

CREAM OF MUSHROOM SOUP

L

Makes: 5 cups; serves: 4 to 6

If your ideal cream of mushroom soup can also double for library paste, you may want to increase the flour by a tablespoon or two. This version is rich and creamy, but not too thick.

3 tablespoons butter or margarine
³/₄ cup chopped leeks (white and light green parts only)
4 cups sliced white mushrooms
3 tablespoons all-purpose flour
3 cups vegetable broth (pages 93–95)
2 tablespoons brandy
¹/₈ teaspoon pepper
Pinch dried thyme
¹/₂ cup half-and-half

1. In a 3-quart saucepan; melt the butter or margarine over medium-high heat. Add the leeks; cook, stirring, until softened, about 1 minute. Add the mushrooms; cook, stirring, until softened, about 3 minutes. Stir in the flour until absorbed.

2. Add the broth, brandy, pepper, and thyme; cook, stirring constantly, until soup comes to a boil. Add the half-and-half. Cook, stirring, until heated through.

Variations: Substitute dry sherry for the brandy.

[V] Omit the half-and-half.

FRESH SPINACH CREAM SOUP

Makes: 4³/₄ cups; serves: 4 to 6

This started out as a cream of celery soup with chopped spinach, but the celery flavor was so mild that I felt it was false advertising to include celery in the title. Nonetheless, it's a delicious soup even if it's not celery soup. Use chopped fresh spinach for the best result.

2 tablespoons butter or margarine
2 cups sliced celery
³/₄ cup chopped onions
2 tablespoons all-purpose flour
3 cups vegetable broth (pages 93–95)
¹/₈ teaspoon pepper
2 cups chopped fresh spinach
¹/₂ cup half-and-half

1. In a 2-quart saucepan; melt the butter or margarine over medium-high heat. Add the celery and onions, cook, stirring, until soft, about 3 minutes. Stir in the flour until absorbed.

2. Add the broth and pepper, stirring constantly, until soup comes to a boil. Add the spinach, reduce heat, and simmer 10 minutes.

3. Stir in the half-and-half. Cook, stirring, until heated through.

Ⓥ *Variation:* For a vegan version, omit the half-and-half.

♥ Use whole milk or even skim milk instead of the half-and-half.

CRUNCHY BROCCOLI-CHEDDAR SOUP

Makes: 5 cups; serves: 4 to 6

The fresh chopped broccoli is cooked for a very short time in this recipe, so the end result is a crunchy soup. If you prefer a softer consistency, use frozen chopped broccoli or precook the fresh broccoli.

1 medium bunch broccoli (1¹/₄ pounds)
3 tablespoons butter or margarine
3 tablespoons all-purpose flour
1¹/₂ cups vegetable broth (pages 93–95)
1 cup milk
1 cup shredded Cheddar cheese
¹/₄ teaspoon salt, or to taste
¹/₄ teaspoon anchovy-free Worcestershire sauce
¹/₈ teaspoon ground red pepper

1. Chop the broccoli florets and stems (this job is perfect for the food processor).

2. In a 2-quart saucepan, melt the butter or margarine over medium-high heat. Add the chopped broccoli; cook, stirring, until bright green, about 3 minutes. Stir in the flour until absorbed.

3. Stir in the broth and milk; cook, stirring, until mixture comes to a boil. Stir in the Cheddar cheese, salt, Worcestershire sauce, and red pepper. Cook, stirring, until cheese is melted.

Variation: Very Rich Broccoli-Cheddar Soup: Substitute half-and-half or light cream for the milk.

BUTTERMILK BROCCOLI SOUP
L ♥

Makes: 5¹/₂ cups; serves: 6 to 8

Based on a recipe my mother's friend Estelle Rinzler gave her, I like this soup served warm or cold.

1½ teaspoon vegetable oil
1 cup sliced leeks (white and light green parts only)
2 cups vegetable broth (pages 93–95)
2 cups water
4 cups broccoli florets
⅓ cup chopped fresh dill
¼ cup white rice
2 cups buttermilk
⅛ teaspoon ground red pepper

1. In a 3-quart saucepan, heat the oil over medium-high heat. Add the leeks; cook, stirring, until softened, about 1 minute.

2. Add the broth and water; bring to a boil. Add the broccoli, dill, and rice; return to a boil. Reduce heat and simmer, uncovered, 30 minutes.

3. Place the soup in a blender or food processor container fitted with a steel blade. Cover and process until smooth. (You may have to do this in more than one batch.)

4. Return to pot and stir in buttermilk and red pepper. Reheat if necessary.

Variation: For a chilled version, don't reheat after stirring in buttermilk; chill instead. Serve with dollops of unflavored yogurt.

PEANUT SOUP
L

Makes: 5 cups; serves: 4 to 6

This soup has an incredibly rich flavor with a slightly unexpected afterbite. Unfortunately, it is fairly high in fat (not to mention calories), so I only serve it occasionally. Be sure to use the unsweetened coconut milk, the type available in Asian markets. To make this soup without coconut milk you can use extra milk, half-and-half, or soy milk.

1 tablespoon vegetable oil
1 cup sliced onions
1 teaspoon curry powder
¼ teaspoon ground red pepper
¼ teaspoon ground ginger
¼ teaspoon salt, or to taste
4 cups vegetable broth (pages 93–95)
2 cups sliced carrots
½ cup smooth peanut butter
½ cup unsweetened coconut milk (page 497)
½ cup milk

1. In a 3-quart saucepan, heat the oil over medium heat. Add onions; cook, stirring, until soft, about 2 minutes. Stir in the curry powder, red pepper, ginger, and salt until absorbed. Add the broth and bring to a boil . Add the carrots; cook uncovered over medium heat, 30 minutes or until carrots are soft.

2. Place the soup and peanut butter in a blender or food processor container fitted with a steel blade. Cover and process until pureed. (You may have to do this in more than one batch.) Return puree to pot.

3. Stir in coconut milk and dairy milk. Cook over low heat, stirring frequently, until heated through.

ⓥ *Variation:* Substitute soy or additional coconut milk for the dairy milk.

JERUSALEM ARTICHOKE~ ALMOND SOUP

Makes: 5 cups; serves: 4 to 6

"Unusual" is a good word to describe this soup, and so is "delicious." It is slightly pink in color and the almonds lend a nice tooth to the texture. It tastes excellent hot or cold, topped with a dollop of unflavored yogurt.

½ cup almonds
3 cups water
1 cup vegetable broth (pages 93–95)
2½ cups cubed Jerusalem artichoke
1 cup chopped tomatoes
3 tablespoons white rice
1 teaspoon fresh lemon juice
½ teaspoon salt, or to taste
⅛ teaspoon ground red pepper
½ cup unflavored yogurt
Additional yogurt for topping

1. Preheat the oven to 350°F. Bake the almonds for 10 minutes or until toasted. Cool.

2. In a 2-quart saucepan, bring the water and broth to a boil. Add the Jerusalem artichoke, tomatoes, and rice. Cover and simmer 30 minutes, or until artichoke cubes are tender. Stir in lemon juice, salt, and red pepper.

3. Place the soup and almonds in a blender or food processor container fitted with a steel blade. Cover and process until smooth. Add ½ cup yogurt and process just enough to blend.

4. Serve warm or cold, topped with dollops of unflavored yogurt.

Variation: For a richer version, substitute sour cream or crème fraîche for the yogurt.

SQUASH AND APPLE SOUP

Makes: 5 cups; serves: 4 to 6

This very smooth soup is good for Thanksgiving if you want a change from pumpkin soup.

2 teaspoons vegetable oil
1½ cups chopped, peeled apples
¾ cup chopped onions
¼ teaspoon ground ginger
⅛ teaspoon ground nutmeg
2 cups vegetable broth (pages 93–95)
1 cup water
2 cups cubed butternut or buttercup squash
⅛ teaspoon salt, or to taste
⅛ teaspoon ground red pepper

1. In a 3-quart saucepan, heat the oil over medium-high heat. Add the apples and onions; cook, stirring, until softened, about 4 minutes. Stir in the ginger and nutmeg until absorbed. Add the broth and water; bring to a boil. Add the squash and return to a boil. Reduce heat and simmer, uncovered, 30 minutes or until vegetables are tender.

2. Place the soup, salt, and red pepper in a blender or food processor container fitted with a steel blade. Cover and process until smooth.

Variation: For a creamier soup, add ½ cup half-and-half.

Heartier Grain and/or Bean Soups

In the winter, thick soups are my favorite lunches. I make large batches and freeze them in individual servings, then at lunchtime I zap a portion in the microwave and I have a perfect meal ready in minutes. Best of all, most of these soups are fat-free.

Kitchen Sink Soup

Makes: 7¹/₂ cups; serves: 6 to 8

This recipe has everything in it except the proverbial kitchen sink.

½ cup baby lima beans
1 tablespoon vegetable oil
1½ cups chopped cabbage
1 cup chopped onions
³/₄ cup chopped celery
6 cups water
³/₄ cup chopped carrots
½ cup chopped parsnips
¼ cup green or yellow split peas
1 bay leaf
2 cloves garlic, minced
³/₄ cup chopped tomatoes
¼ cup barley
1 cup diced, peeled potatoes
³/₄ cup cut green beans (fresh or frozen)
½ cup chopped zucchini
½ cup corn kernels (fresh, cooked; canned, drained; or frozen)
¹/₃ cup chopped fresh parsley
¼ cup snipped fresh dill
½ teaspoon salt, or to taste
¹/₈ teaspoon pepper

1. Soak the lima beans in water overnight, or use the quick-soak method (page 13). Drain.

2. In a 4-quart saucepan, heat the oil over medium-high heat. Add the cabbage, onions, and celery; cook, stirring, until softened, about 4 minutes. Add the water and bring to a boil. Stir in the lima beans, carrots, parsnips, split peas, bay leaf, and garlic. Return to a boil. Reduce heat and simmer, uncovered, 1 hour.

3. Add the tomatoes and barley. Return to a simmer; simmer, uncovered, 25 minutes.

4. Add the remaining ingredients. Return to a simmer; simmer, uncovered, 25 minutes longer. Discard bay leaf.

Variation: Use anything you have in the vegetable bin.

Miso Soup

Makes: 3³/₄ cups; serves: 4

Miso is a fermented soybean product available in health food stores. The soup tends to separate quickly, so be sure to give it a stir before serving, and don't ladle it into bowls too soon before serving either.

1½ cups vegetable broth (pages 93–95)
1½ cups water
3 tablespoons miso
¼ cup finely diced tofu
1 tablespoon thinly sliced scallions (green parts only)

1. Bring broth and water to a boil in a 1¹/₂-quart saucepan. Stir in miso.

2. Spoon into 4 bowls; top with tofu and scallions.

COLLARD AND BLACK-EYED PEA SOUP

Makes: 5½ cups; serves: 6 to 8

This flavorful soup has many elements that I associate with "southern" cooking, so it seemed appropriate to add the baco-bit for a bacon flavor. You can omit them if you prefer. Be sure to use unsalted broth or the beans may not soften correctly.

½ cup dried black-eyed peas
1 tablespoon vegetable oil
2 cups packed, chopped fresh collards
1 cup chopped onions
3 cups unsalted vegetable broth
    (pages 93–95)
2 cups water
1½ cups cubed, peeled potatoes (½-inch
    pieces)
2 teaspoons imitation bacon bits (optional)
½ teaspoon salt, or to taste
¼ teaspoon pepper

1. Soak the beans in water overnight, or use the quick-soak method (page 13). Drain.

2. In a 3-quart saucepan, heat the oil over medium-high heat. Add the collards and onions; cook, stirring, until softened, about 3 minutes.

3. Add the broth and water; bring to a boil. Add the beans; cook 1 hour 15 minutes or until beans are tender.

4. Add the remaining ingredients. Simmer 25 minutes longer.

Variation: You can use chopped Swiss chard or escarole instead of the collards.

BLACK BEAN SOUP

Makes: 6 cups; serves: 6

Serve this soup with salsa (pages 479–81) and tortilla chips (page 86) for a geat lunch or a small dinner.

1 cup dried black beans
1 tablespoon olive oil
2 cups chopped onions
1 cup chopped green or red bell peppers
3 cloves garlic, minced
5 cups water
1 cup diced carrots
1 cup diced celery
¼ cup chopped celery leaves
2 bay leaves
½ teaspoon salt, or to taste
¼ teaspoon pepper

1. Soak the black beans in water to cover, overnight or by the quick soak method (page 13). Drain.

2. In a 3-quart saucepan, heat the oil over medium-high heat. Add the onions, green or red bell peppers, and garlic. Cook, stirring, until softened, about 3 minutes.

3. Add the water and bring to a boil. Add the beans, carrots, celery, celery leaves, and bay leaves. Return to a boil; reduce heat and simmer 2 hours or until the beans are tender. Discard bay leaves. Stir in salt and pepper.

Variation: Stir in 3 tablespoons chopped fresh cilantro 10 minutes before soup is finished cooking.

SPLIT PEA AND BARLEY SOUP

☑️ ❤️

Makes: 10 cups; serves: 8 as lunch, 10 to 12 as appetizer

I like to add pasta to this soup as suggested in the variation.

8 cups water
1 cup chopped onions
1 medium parsnip, peeled
1 parsley root, peeled
1 tablespoon minced garlic
3/4 cup green or yellow split peas, rinsed
1 1/2 cups diced celery
1 1/2 cups sliced mushrooms
1 cup chopped tomatoes
1 cup diced carrots
1/2 cup chopped fresh parsley
1/3 cup pearl barley, rinsed
1/4 cup chopped fresh celery leaves
3/4 teaspoons salt, or to taste
1/4 teaspoon pepper

1. In a 4-quart pot, combine the water, onions, parsnip, parsley root, and garlic. Bring to a boil over high heat. Stir in the split peas and return to a boil. Reduce heat, cover, and simmer 1 hour.

2. Remove the parsnip and parsley root from the pot; set aside.

3. Stir in remaining ingredients. Bring to a boil, reduce heat, and simmer, uncovered, 1 hour longer. Mash the parsnip and parsley root and stir into the soup.

Variation: Add 1/4 cup small dry pasta—such as small bowties, alphabets, or orzo—to the pot 12 minutes before the soup is finished cooking.

SPLIT PEA DAL

☑️ ❤️

Makes: 2 1/4 cups; serves: 2 to 3 as a soup, 4 to 6 as a side dish

Dal is a traditional Indian dish, usually made with red lentils. It's not really a soup, but almost a sauce served with entrees. The consistency, however, is really that of a thick pea soup, and it does make a great untraditional first course.

1 tablespoon vegetable oil
1/2 cup chopped onions
1 teaspoon ground coriander
1/2 teaspoon cumin seed
1/2 teaspoon ground turmeric
5 cups water
3/4 cup yellow split peas
1 bay leaf
1/2 teaspoon salt, or to taste

1. In a 2-quart saucepan, heat the oil over medium-high heat. Add the onions; cook, stirring, until softened, about 2 minutes. Stir in the coriander, cumin, and turmeric until spices are absorbed and the seeds are coated with oil.

2. Add the water and bring to a boil. Stir in the split peas and bay leaf; return to a boil. Reduce heat and simmer, uncovered, 1 hour and 15 minutes or until the split peas have dissolved. Discard the bay leaf. Stir in the salt.

SHERRIED PEA SOUP

Makes: 8 cups; serves: 8 to 12

I served this soup on Thanksgiving and it was a big hit. It's also great served chilled. The cream adds just a bit of richness, but the soup is terrific without the cream for a vegan version.

2 tablespoons butter or margarine
2 cups sliced leeks (white and light green parts)
4 cups vegetable broth (pages 93–95)
3 cups water
1 cup green split peas
2 cups peas (fresh or frozen)
3 tablespoons sherry
1/8 teaspoon salt, or to taste
1/8 teaspoon pepper
1/4 cup heavy cream

1. In a 4-quart saucepan, melt the butter or margarine over medium-high heat. Add the leeks; cook, stirring, until softened, about 1 minute.

2. Add the broth and water; bring to a boil. Add the split peas. Return to a boil; reduce heat and simmer, covered, 1 1/2 hours.

3. Add the peas; return to a boil. Reduce heat and simmer, covered, 30 minutes longer. Stir in the sherry, salt, and pepper; simmer, uncovered, 15 minutes longer.

4. Strain the soup, reserving the broth. Place a third of the solids in a blender container. Cover and blend until smooth. With the motor running, gradually pour a third of the broth into the container and blend until combined. Repeat with remaining soup.

5. Return soup to saucepan. Stir in cream, return to heat, and cook to desired temperature.

Variations: Minted Pea Soup: Stir in 1/4 cup chopped fresh mint instead of the sherry.

[V] Omit the cream.

ROOT VEGETABLE AND SPLIT PEA SOUP

Makes: 5 cups; serves: 5 to 7

This is a kind of thick and chunky pea soup.

4 cups water
1 1/4 cups chopped celeriac (celery root; knob celery)
1 cup chopped onions
1 cup chopped carrots *1 /q*
3/4 cup chopped parsley roots or parsnips
3/4 cup green or yellow split peas
2 cloves garlic, minced
2 cups vegetable broth (pages 93–95)
3/4 cup chopped fresh parsley
1/4 teaspoon salt, or to taste
1/8 teaspoon pepper

1. In a 3-quart saucepan, bring the water to a boil. Add the celeriac, onions, carrots, parsley roots, split peas, and garlic. Return to a boil. Reduce heat and simmer, 1 hour.

2. Add the broth and parsley. Return to a boil. Reduce heat and simmer, uncovered, 30 minutes longer. Stir in the salt and pepper.

Variation: Omit the broth and use additional water instead.

THREE-BEAN VEGETABLE SOUP

— [V][♥] —

Makes: 12 cups; serves: 12 to 16

Don't be intimidated by all the ingredients.

1 cup small dried red (chili) beans
½ cup small dried lima beans
8 cups water
2 cups chopped cabbage
1 cup chopped carrots
1 cup chopped celery
1 cup chopped parsnips
1 cup chopped onions
½ cup chopped turnips
½ cup green or yellow split peas
½ cup chopped fresh parsley
⅓ cup chopped fresh celery leaves
¼ cup chopped fresh dill
⅓ cup small pasta (such as orzo, mini bowties, or small shells)
¾ teaspoon salt, or to taste
¼ teaspoon pepper

1. Soak the red and lima beans overnight in enough water to cover the beans by 2 inches, or use the quick-soak method (page 13). Drain.

2. In a 6-quart pot, combine the water, soaked beans, cabbage, carrots, celery, parsnips, onions, and turnips. Bring to a boil over high heat. Stir in split peas and return to a boil. Reduce heat, cover and simmer 1 hour.

3. Stir in the parsley, celery leaves, and dill. Bring to a boil, reduce heat, and simmer, uncovered, 30 minutes longer. Stir in the pasta, salt, and pepper. Simmer 10 minutes longer or until pasta is cooked.

Variation: Instead of adding salt, stir in 2 to 3 vegetable bouillon cubes.

SPLIT AND BLACK-EYED PEA SOUP

— [V][♥] —

Makes: 8 cups; serves: 8 to 10

Some experts feel you don't have to presoak black-eyed peas; but I prefer to include this step. You can experiment in this recipe, since a little extra cooking time won't hurt the end result.

12 cups water, divided
1 cup dried black-eyed peas
2 cups sliced carrots
2 cups sliced celery
1½ cups chopped onions
1 medium parsnip
½ cup green split peas
½ cup chopped fresh parsley
¼ cup lightly packed chopped fresh dill
½ teaspoon celery salt
½ teaspoon salt, or to taste
¼ teaspoon pepper

1. In a 2-quart saucepan, bring the black-eyed peas and 4 cups of the water to a boil. Let stand 1 hour; drain.

2. In an 8-quart pot, bring the remaining 8 cups of water to a boil. Stir in the black-eyed peas, carrots, celery, onions, parsnips, and split peas. Return to a boil, reduce heat and simmer, uncovered, 40 minutes.

3. Add the parsley and dill; simmer 35 minutes longer or until the beans are softened. Stir in the celery salt, salt, and pepper; discard parsnip.

Variation: Use yellow split peas or red lentils instead of the green split peas.

MUSHROOM-BARLEY SOUP

Makes: 6 cups; serves: 6 to 8

This is a very vegetabley soup—a real favorite in my family. Try to find very dark, imported dried mushrooms. The ones from Poland are the best, but also extremely expensive. The South American dried mushrooms, available in small plastic containers in the supermarket, are also good and not too expensive.

6 cups water, divided
½ ounce dried mushrooms
1 tablespoon vegetable oil
2 cups sliced white mushrooms
1½ cups chopped onions
1 cup diced carrots
1 cup diced celery
1 cup diced parsnip
¼ cup pearled barley
⅓ cup chopped fresh parsley
⅓ cup snipped fresh dill
¼ teaspoon salt, or to taste
¼ teaspoon pepper

1. In a small saucepan, bring ½ cup of the water to a boil. Add the dried mushrooms and let stand 10 minutes or until softened. Chop mushrooms; set aside with the soaking liquid.

2. In a 4-quart saucepan, heat the oil over medium-high heat. Add the white mushrooms and onions; cook, stirring, until softened, about 3 to 5 minutes.

3. Add the remaining water and the carrots, celery, parsnip, barley, and reserved chopped mushrooms and liquid; bring to a boil. Reduce heat and simmer, uncovered, 30 minutes. Add the parsley, dill, salt, and pepper. Simmer 15 minutes longer.

Variation: Add 1 cup diced, peeled potatoes when you add the herbs.

LEEK AND WILD RICE SOUP

L

Makes: 4¾ cups; serves: 4 to 6

This rich, elegant soup is perfect to start any company meal.

2 tablespoons butter, margarine, or olive oil
4 cups thinly sliced leeks (white and light green parts only)
½ cup minced celery
3 cups water
½ cup dry vermouth
1 bay leaf
¼ teaspoon dried thyme
½ cup wild rice
½ cup half-and-half or milk
½ teaspoon salt, or to taste

1. In a 4-quart saucepan, melt the butter or margarine over medium-high heat. Add the leeks and celery; cook, stirring, until softened, about 4 minutes.

2. Add the water, vermouth, bay leaf, and thyme; bring to a boil. Stir in the wild rice; reduce heat and simmer, covered, 1 hour. Discard bay leaf.

3. Stir in half-and-half and salt; cook until heated through.

Variation: Use additional broth instead of the vermouth.

Escarole-Bean Soup

[v][♥]

Makes: 8 cups; serves: 8 to 10

I tasted this divine soup in a local pizzeria. It takes only 20 minutes to prepare.

2 teaspoons vegetable oil

³/₄ cup chopped onions

1 clove garlic, minced

One 14½-ounce can whole peeled tomatoes, undrained

4 cups vegetable broth (pages 93–95)

4 cups lightly packed, bite-sized pieces, escarole

1 cup cooked cannellini beans (cooked from dry; or canned, drained)

¼ cup small bowtie pasta (or other small pasta, such as orzo)

1 teaspoon sugar

½ teaspoon dried oregano

1. In a 3-quart saucepan, heat the oil over medium-high heat. Add the onion and garlic; cook, stirring, until softened, about 2 minutes. Add the tomatoes with liquid and break them up with the back of a spoon.

2. Add the broth and bring to a boil. Add the remaining ingredients; return to a boil. Reduce heat and simmer, uncovered, 10 minutes or until pasta is tender.

Variation: Use kidney beans or chickpeas instead of cannellini.

Lentil-Escarole Soup

[v][♥]

Makes: 8 cups; serves: 8 to 10

Without the bouillon cubes this is a mild-flavored soup. Taste the soup when it's finished cooking. If you find the flavor weak, stir in the bouillon or perhaps add some salt to taste.

1 cup lentils

8 cups water

1 cup chopped carrots

1 cup chopped celery

1 cup chopped onions

¼ cup chopped fresh celery leaves

1 bay leaf

4 cups chopped escarole

½ cup chopped fresh basil

1 teaspoon celery salt

1 clove minced garlic

½ teaspoon poultry seasoning

¼ teaspoon pepper

1 to 2 vegetable bouillon cubes, or 1 to 2 teaspoons vegetable bouillon powder (optional)

1. Rinse the lentils and discard any foreign matter.

2. In a 4-quart pot, bring the water to a boil over high heat. Add the lentils, carrots, celery, onions, celery leaves, and bay leaf; bring to a boil. Reduce heat and simmer, uncovered, 50 minutes, or until lentils are tender; discard the bay leaf.

3. Stir in the escarole, basil, celery salt, garlic, poultry seasoning, and pepper. Let simmer 10 minutes longer. Stir in bouillon, if desired.

Variation: Omit the basil; stir in 1 teaspoon dried oregano instead.

LENTIL-CAULIFLOWER SOUP

Makes: 8¹/₂ cups; serves: 8 to 10

This very simple soup is quite tasty. I like to use small florets so that the cauliflower is pretty well disintegrated by the time the soup is cooked.

4 cups water
4 cups unsalted vegetable broth
  (pages 93–95)
6 cups cauliflower florets
1 cup lentils, rinsed
1 cup sliced leeks (white and light green
  parts only)
2 bay leaves
¹/₄ teaspoon salt, or to taste
¹/₄ teaspoon pepper

1. Place water and broth in a 4-quart pot. Bring to a boil. Add the cauliflower, lentils, leeks, and bay leaves. Return to a boil. Reduce heat and simmer, uncovered, 1 to 1¹/₂ hours or until lentils are cooked to desired doneness.

2. Stir in salt and pepper. Discard bay leaves.

Variation: Add 1 or 2 cloves of garlic (minced) when you add the lentils.

CREAMY FRENCH LENTIL SOUP

— L —

Makes: 6 cups; serves: 6 to 8

French lentils are smaller and slightly more delicately flavored than the ones available in the supermarket. If you use ordinary lentils instead of the French variety, you will have to cook the soup longer until they are tender. This soup is creamy with or without the cream, but it is much richer with it.

1 tablespoon olive oil
2 cups chopped celery
1 cup sliced leeks (white and light green parts
  only)
6 cups water
¹/₄ cup chopped fresh celery leaves
1 cup French lentils
¹/₄ cup medium-sweet Madeira, or other
  fortified wine (optional)
³/₄ teaspoon salt, or to taste
¹/₄ teaspoon dried thyme
¹/₄ teaspoon pepper
3 tablespoons heavy cream

1. In a 3-quart pot, heat the oil over medium-high heat. Add the celery and leeks; cook, stirring, until softened, about 3 minutes.

2. Add the water and bring to a boil. Add the celery leaves and lentils; return to a boil. Reduce heat and simmer, uncovered, 30 minutes.

3. Stir in the Madeira, salt, thyme, and pepper; simmer 10 minutes longer or until lentils are tender.

4. Place the soup in a blender or food processor container fitted with a steel blade. Cover and process until pureed. Stir in the cream.

Ⓥ ***Variation:*** Omit the cream.

FRENCH LENTIL– VEGETABLE SOUP

Ⓛ

Makes: 10 cups; serves: 8 to 10

This is a more peasant-style soup than the previous recipe, on which it is based. It's very thick and makes a great meal.

1 recipe Creamy French Lentil Soup
    (page 128)
2 cups diced potatoes
2 cups sliced carrots
2 cups sliced zucchini
½ cup chopped fresh parsley

1. Follow directions for Creamy French Lentil Soup through step 3, but omit the Madeira.

2. Add the potatoes, carrots, zucchini, and parsley; return to a simmer and cook, uncovered, 20 minutes longer or until potatoes and lentils are tender.

Variation: Use cut green beans instead of zucchini.

VEGETABLE CHICKPEA SOUP

Ⓥ ♥

Makes: 7 cups; serves: 6 to 8

This soup can be served as a light pasta sauce.

1 tablespoon vegetable oil
2 cups chopped cabbage
1 cup chopped escarole or spinach
1 cup sliced leeks (white and light green parts only)
1 clove garlic, minced
4 cups vegetable broth (pages 93–95)
¾ cup chopped tomatoes
½ teaspoon dried basil
⅛ teaspoon dried thyme
1½ cups sliced zucchini
1½ cups cooked chickpeas (cooked from dry; or canned, drained)
¼ cup white wine
⅛ teaspoon salt, or to taste
⅛ teaspoon pepper

1. In a 3-quart saucepan, heat the oil over medium-high heat. Add the cabbage, escarole, leeks, and garlic. Cook, stirring, until vegetables are softened, about 3 minutes.

2. Add the broth and bring to a boil. Stir in the tomatoes, basil, and thyme. Reduce heat and simmer, uncovered, 15 minutes.

3. Add the zucchini, chickpeas, wine, salt, and pepper. Simmer, uncovered, 15 minutes longer.

Variation: Increase the escarole to 2 cups and decrease the cabbage to 1 cup.

Cold Soups

Although these are the soups that are specifically meant to be eaten cold, you'll find additional cold soups as variations of the warm ones (such as Peppery Potato-Fennel Soup, page 114).

Gazpacho

Makes: 3 cups; serves: 3 to 4

This gazpacho is more of a rust color than the red that immediately comes to mind. You may have to make this in two batches.

4 cups tomato wedges
1 cup peeled cucumber chunks
1/2 cup green bell pepper chunks
1 whole medium scallion
2 tablespoons red wine vinegar
2 teaspoons olive oil
1 clove garlic, minced
1/4 teaspoon salt, or to taste

1. Place all the ingredients in a blender or food processor container fitted with a steel blade. Cover and process until smooth. Chill.

Variation: For a spicier version, add 1/2 jalapeño pepper or 1/8 to 1/4 teaspoon ground red pepper.

Green Gazpacho

Makes: 2 3/4 cups; serves: 3

Serve this with a dollop of Salsa Ranchero (page 480) for a little extra zip.

2 1/2 cups peeled cucumber chunks
1 1/2 cups green bell pepper chunks
1/2 cup 1-inch scallion slices (green parts only)
1/2 cup vegetable broth (pages 93–95)
1/4 cup fresh basil leaves
1 teaspoon extra virgin olive oil
1 teaspoon red wine vinegar
1/4 teaspoon salt, or to taste
Pinch ground red pepper

1. Place all the ingredients in a blender or food processor container fitted with a steel blade. Cover and process until smooth. Chill.

Yellow Gazpacho

Makes: 4 cups; serves: 4 to 6

Like all gazpacho, this soup is a real refresher for the summer—and the yellow color is wonderful. Garnish with a sprig of cilantro or snipped chives for a lovely presentation.

3 cups peeled cucumber chunks
1 1/2 cups yellow bell pepper chunks
3/4 cup vegetable broth (pages 93–95)
4 scallions, white part only
1 tablespoon distilled white vinegar
2 teaspoons olive oil
1/2 clove garlic
Dash Tabasco

1. Place all the ingredients in a blender or food processor container fitted with a steel blade. Cover and process until smooth. (You may have to do this in two batches.) Chill.

Variation: Add 5 or 6 sprigs cilantro to the blender.

BORSCHT

V ♥

Makes: 4 1/4 cups; serves: 4 to 6

This traditional Russian soup is eaten warm or cold with a boiled potato or boiled egg. In the old days, before we knew about cholesterol, we ate it cold with sour cream and it was really delicious. Now my family eats it cold with yogurt, cottage cheese, and chopped vegetables (see the variation).

3 cups cubed, peeled beets
2 1/2 cups water
1 1/2 cups vegetable broth (pages 93–95)
1 small onion, quartered
2 tablespoons sugar
1/4 teaspoon salt, or to taste
2 cups shredded beets
Boiled potatoes (optional)
Hard-cooked eggs (optional)
Sour cream (optional)

1. In a 3-quart saucepan over medium-high heat, combine the cubed beets, water, broth, onion, sugar, and salt. Bring to a boil. Reduce heat and simmer 20 minutes. Strain liquid into container, pressing liquid from vegetables into soup; discard vegetables.

2. Return beet broth to pot and add shredded beets. Simmer 5 minutes or until shreds are cooked to desired doneness. Chill.

3. Top with boiled potatoes, boiled egg, or sour cream, if desired.

Variation: Borscht with Spring Salad: For each cup of borscht, stir in 1/2 cup cottage cheese, 1/3 cup chopped cucumber, 1/4 cup unflavored yogurt, 2 tablespoons chopped radish, and 2 tablespoons chopped scallions.

SCHAV

V

Makes: 2 2/3 cups; serves: 3

Schav, also called sorrel or sourgrass, tastes similar to very tender spinach. Serve this soup very chilled. If you're a purist, you may want to use the recipe from my mother's friend Bernice Gurtman: Combine 3 cups water, 1 bunch sourgrass (stems removed), and 1/2 tablespoon salt; simmer until tender—and that's all.

2 cups vegetable broth (pages 93–95)
1 cup water
2 1/2 cups chopped sorrel (stems discarded)
1/8 teaspoon salt
1/8 teaspoon pepper
Thinly sliced scallions (white and green)
Sour cream (optional)

1. In a 2-quart saucepan, bring the broth and water to a boil. Add the sorrel; simmer, uncovered, 20 minutes. Add the salt and pepper.

2. Place the soup in a food processor fitted with a steel blade. Cover and process until sorrel is chopped. (Don't use a blender because it will puree, not chop, the sorrel.) Chill.

3. Spoon into serving bowls and sprinkle with scallions; dollop with sour cream, if desired.

CHILLED CUCUMBER SOUP

Makes: 3½ cups; serves: 4

Summer days and cucumber soup were made for each other. When I'm feeling decadent I make this soup with heavy cream instead of buttermilk. I find the blender better for preparing this soup than the food processor.

2 medium (8-inch-long) peeled, seeded
      cucumbers
3 medium scallions (white and green parts)
1 cup vegetable broth (pages 93–95)
6 sprigs fresh dill, or ½ teaspoon dried dill
      weed
1 cup buttermilk
¼ teaspoon anchovy-free Worcestershire
      sauce
¼ teaspoon salt, or to taste
⅛ teaspoon freshly ground pepper

1. Place the cucumbers, scallions, vegetable broth, and dill in a blender container. Cover and blend until smooth. Add the buttermilk, Worcestershire sauce, salt, and pepper. Cover and blend until combined. Chill.

Variations: Substitute fresh cilantro for the dill.

Ⓥ Use additional broth instead of buttermilk, and ground red pepper instead of black pepper.

RICH AND CREAMY AVOCADO SOUP

Ⓛ

Makes: 4 cups; serves: 6

The texture of this soup is incredibly velvety. For some inexplicable (and happy) reason, it retains its beautiful pale green color, instead of turning brown the way an avocado does when exposed to the air. The vegan variation is just as wonderful as the dairy one.

2 cups vegetable broth (pages 93–95)
1½ cups coarsely chopped ripe avocado
¼ cup white wine (optional)
1 cup buttermilk
¼ teaspoon salt, or to taste

1. In a 2-quart saucepan, bring the broth, avocado, and wine to a boil over medium heat.
2. Place half of the soup in a blender or food processor container fitted with a steel blade. Cover and process until pureed. Repeat with remaining soup.
3. Stir in the buttermilk and salt. Heat to desired temperature or chill.

Variations: Add ¼ cup chopped fresh scallions or cilantro, or both, before pureeing.

Ⓥ Substitute an additional cup of broth for the buttermilk.

MINTED HONEYDEW SOUP

Ⓥ ♥

Makes: 3 cups; serves: 4

If you are looking for a really refreshing start (or end) to a summer meal, this is it! The mint does not overwhelm the delicate flavor of the honeydew, but together they are a delight.

4 cups cut-up honeydew
1 cup apple juice
¼ cup fresh mint leaves

1. In a 2-quart saucepan, bring the honeydew and juice to a boil over medium-high heat. Reduce heat and simmer 5 minutes.
2. Place melon mixture and mint leaves in a blender or food processor container fitted with a steel blade. Cover and process until smooth. (You may have to do this in two batches.) Chill.

Variation: Kiwi-Honeydew Soup: Omit the mint, and add ½ cup cut-up, peeled kiwifruit to the blender container. Makes 3½ cups.

GINGER-CANTALOUPE SOUP

Makes: 3 cups; serves: 4

The ginger adds a slightly spicy sensation. Try serving this soup with a dollop of unflavored yogurt.

4 cups cut-up cantaloupe
1 cup orange juice
1 tablespoon fresh minced ginger, or
    ½ teaspoon ground ginger

1. In a 2-quart saucepan, bring the cantaloupe, orange juice, and ginger to a boil. Reduce heat and simmer, 5 minutes.

2. Place mixture in a blender or food processor container fitted with a steel blade. Cover and process until smooth. Chill.

Variation: Add 1 to 2 tablespoons of rum to the soup.

YIN AND YANG SOUP

Makes: 4 bowls of soup; serves: 4

This is a great combination of flavors, and an incredibly impressive presentation.

½ recipe Kiwi-Honeydew Soup (page 133)
½ recipe Ginger-Cantaloupe Soup (page 133)

1. Pour a quarter of the Kiwi-Honeydew Soup in a circle on one side of each of 4 wide, shallow soup bowls. Using a spoon, drag a little of the soup around the edge of each bowl so that it forms a green comma.

2. Using the Ginger-Cantaloupe Soup, repeat step 1 on the opposite side of the bowls, so that the design resembles a Yin and Yang symbol.

3. For a very dramatic effect, place one drop of green soup in the center of the orange, and one drop of orange soup in the center of the green.

Variation: For a simpler version, just fill half of the bowl with Kiwi-Honeydew Soup and the other half with Ginger-Cantaloupe Soup.

CHILLED STRAWBERRY SOUP

Ⓛ♥

Makes: 3 cups; serves: 4 to 6

Since strawberries vary widely in sweetness, you may want to start by using only 2 tablespoons of sugar, then add more to taste. You can serve the vegan variation as a dessert sauce.

3 cups hulled strawberries
1 cup cranberry juice cocktail
2 to 4 tablespoons sugar
2 tablespoons port wine
⅛ teaspoon ground nutmeg (optional)
½ cup unflavored yogurt

1. Place the strawberries, cranberry juice, sugar, port, and nutmeg in a 1½ quart saucepan. Bring to a boil over medium heat. Simmer, uncovered, 5 minutes.

2. Place in a blender or food processor container fitted with a steel blade. Cover and process until smooth. Chill.

3. Stir in the yogurt.

Ⓥ ***Variation:*** Omit the yogurt.

Grains and Beans

Rattlesnake Stew   139

Cauliflower and Black
Bean Stew   140

Southwestern Stew   140

Rice and Black Beans   141

Cilantro Rice and
Black Beans   141

Creole Red Beans
and Rice   142

Mexicali Stew   142

Zucchini and Yellow Squash
with Chickpeas   143

Broccoli with Black Beans
and Garlic   143

Yellow, Green, and Spaghetti
Squash with Beans   144

Spaghetti Squash with
Curried Carrots
and Beans   144

Moroccan Vegetables
with Couscous   145

Burmese Crispy Vegetables
with Yellow Pea Curry   146

Eggplant with Butter Beans
and Plums   146

Curried Chickpeas
and Kale   147

Lentil Shepherd's Pie   147

Lentil and Mushroom
Stew   148

Vegetables with Kamut
and Beans   148

Moussaka   149

Small White Beans with
Wheat Berries   150

Baby Limas and Barley   150

Stewed Garbanzo Beans
with Zuc-Quinoa   151

Fran's Great Grain Dish   152

Couscous with Vegetable
Sauce and Chickpeas   152

Black Bean Tostadas   153

Brown Rice and Black
Bean Burritos   154

Chili   154

Black Bean Chili   155

Black Bean–Polenta Pie   155

Risotto alla Milanese   156

Risotto with Gorgonzola and
Artichoke Hearts   156

Risotto with Escarole   157

Tomato and Basil
Risotto   158

Rosemary-Mushroom
Risotto   158

Risi e Bisi   159

Zucchini-Leek Melt   159

Wildly Stuffed Peppers   160

Spicy, Cheesy Mushrooms
and Barley   160

Barley-Stuffed Peppers   161

Barley with Vegetables   161

Corn and Millet
Casserole   162

Lentil Burgers   162

Vegetables

Atakilt Acilch'a (Ethiopian
Vegetable Stew)   163

Fajitas   163

Indonesian Vegetable
Stew   164

Spasta   164

Spaghetti Squash
Provençal   165

Spaghetti Squash with
Bulgur Marinara Sauce   165

Butternut Squash with
Curried Millet Filling   166

Sweet and Sour Stuffed
Cabbage   166

Bulgur-Stuffed Eggplant   167

Quinoa-Stuffed
Eggplants   168

Turkish Stuffed
Eggplant   168

Mediterranean Eggplant   169

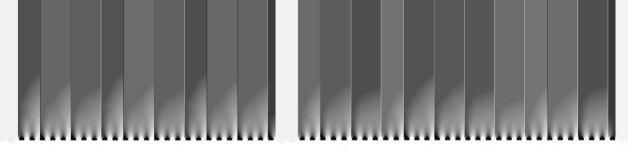

Eggplant with Red Peppers
and Shiitake
Mushrooms   169

Mozzarella Baked Eggplant
and Zucchini   170

Grilled Vegetable
Parmesan   170

Eggplant Parmigiana   171

Eggplant Rollatini   172

Ragout of Wild
Mushrooms   173

Mushrooms Stroganoff   173

Mushroom Paprikash with
Dumplings   174

Tuscan Torta di Funghi
e Patate   175

Spanakopita   176

Entree Strudels

Spinach-Mushroom Strudel
Filling   177

Vegetable-Potato Strudel
Filling   177

Cabbage Kasha Strudel
Filling   178

Wild Rice–Mushroom Strudel
Filling   178

Asian Entrees

Szechuan Broccoli   179

Chinese Cabbage and
Oriental Vegetables   179

Stir-Fried Vegetables with
Mushrooms on a
Bird's Nest   180

Almond Ding
Vegetables   180

Tempura   181

Mixed Vegetable Curry   181

Saag Paneer   182

Cabbage and Mushroom
Curry   182

Okra, Plantain, and Sweet
Potato Curry   183

Pasta, Pizza, Noodles, and Dumplings

Semolina Pasta Dough   185

Tomato Pasta Dough   185

Spinach Pasta Dough   186

Ravioli   186

Goat Cheese Ravioli
Filling   187

Spinach-Pignoli Ravioli
Filling   187

Rosemary-Mushroom Ravioli
Filling   187

Escarole and Cheese Stuffed
Shells   188

Manicotti   188

Pasta with Olive Oil and
Garlic   189

Pasta with Olives, Garlic,
and Pine Nuts   189

Pasta with Tomato and
Eggplant Sauce   190

Pasta Puttanesca   190

Pasta with Yellow
Tomato Sauce   191

Springtime Pasta   191

Randy Kraft's Pasta with
Vegetables and Lentils   192

Ziti with Roasted Red Pepper
and Grilled Eggplant   192

Penne Primavera with
Creamy Tomato Sauce   193

Cavetelli with Cabbage and
Caramelized Onions   193

Pasta with Creamy
Basil Sauce   194

Penne with Vodka
Sauce   194

Tortellini with Wild
Mushroom Sauce   195

Ziti with Broccoli and
Rosemary   195

Vegetable Lasagna   196

Green and White
Lasagna   197

Mushroom Lasagna with Bell
Pepper Cream Sauce   198

Pasta Torte   199

Baked Ziti   199

Whole Wheat Pizza
Crust   201

Semolina Pizza Crust   202

Tomato Sauce for Pizza   202

Pesto Sauce for Pizza   202

White Pizza   203

Gnocchi di Patate   203

Spinach and Ricotta
Gnocchi   204

Gnocchi with Butter
and Cheese   204

Noodles with Broccoli
and Cabbage   204

Noodles with Peanut
Sauce   205

Noodles with Sesame
Sauce   205

Lo Mein   206

Broccoli Rabe with
Rice Noodles   206

Mee Grob   207

Eggs, Cheese, and Dairy

Roquefort Soufflé   208

Broccoli Soufflé   208

Easy Faux Soufflé   209

Savory Mushroom
Bread Pudding   210

Spinach and Dill Savory
Bread Pudding   210

Quiches and Savory Tarts

Vidalia Onion Quiche   211

Dilled Asparagus
Quiche   212

Tomato-Feta Tart   212

Broccoli-Cheddar
Quiche   213

Gorgonzola, Leek, and
Fennel Tart   213

Mushroom-Leek Tart   214

Roasted Eggplant and Red
Pepper Tart   214

Squash and Basil Tart   215

Chili Rellenos   215

Three-Cheese Macaroni
and Cheese   216

Baked Spaghetti   216

Tofu, Tempeh, Seitan, and Textured Vegetable Protein (TVP)

Szechuan Shredded
Vegetables with
Pressed Tofu   217

Sukiyaki   218

Tofu in Brown Sauce   218

Moo Shu Vegetables   219

Sweet and Sour Bean
Curd   220

Eggplant and Tofu with
Plum Sauce   220

Very Quick Barbecue Tofu
and Rice with
Black Beans   221

Bulgur with Tofu and
Cauliflower   221

Spanish-Barbecue Tofu
and Beans   222

Madrid Rice, Beans,
and Tofu   222

Tamale Pie   223

Gado Gado   224

Black Bean Picadillo   225

Chickeny Croquettes   225

Tempeh with Sate
Sauce   226

Noodles with Seitan   226

Seitan with Bean Sprouts
and Mushrooms   227

GRAINS AND BEANS

RATTLESNAKE STEW

[V] [♥]

Makes: 6¹/₂ cups; serves: 4 to 6

Of course there's no rattlesnake meat in this stew—it's rattlesnake beans that are responsible for the name. These slightly exotic beans look like brown vitamin capsules with some black scratches, and they have a smoky flavor. If you can't find rattlesnake beans, you can use adzuki beans, which also have a smoky flavor, or you can use small white beans. If you want help finding the rattlesnake beans, see the mail-order sources (page 43). If you do not have unsalted vegetable broth, use all water; then after the beans are tender, stir in enough bouillon cubes or packets to make 2 cups of broth.

1 cup rattlesnake beans

1 tablespoon vegetable oil

1 ½ cups chopped onions

½ cup chopped green bell peppers

2 cups water

2 cups unsalted vegetable broth
   (pages 93–95)

1 bay leaf

½ teaspoon poultry seasoning

2 cups carrot chunks (1½-inch pieces)

1½ cups celery chunks (1½-inch pieces)

1½ cups boiling potatoes (1-inch pieces)

1 cup corn kernels (fresh, cooked; canned, drained; or frozen)

2 tablespoons tomato paste

¼ teaspoon Tabasco

⅛ teaspoon salt, or to taste

1. Soak the beans in water overnight, or use the quick-soak method (page 13). Drain.

2. In a 6-quart pot, heat the oil over medium-high heat. Add the onions and bell peppers; cook, stirring, until softened, about 3 minutes.

3. Add the water, broth, bay leaf, and poultry seasoning; bring to a boil. Add the soaked beans, carrots, and celery; simmer, uncovered, 1 hour or until beans are tender. Discard the bay leaf.

4. Add the potatoes, corn, tomato paste, Tabasco, and salt. Simmer 30 minutes longer.

Variation: You can use any variety of bean, but be sure to cook it until tender before adding the potatoes.

CAULIFLOWER AND BLACK BEAN STEW

Makes: 4¹/₂ cups; serves: 4

On the day I worked on this recipe I had already tested so many others that I wasn't really hungry. But when I tasted this dish, I suddenly found my appetite.

1½ tablespoons olive oil
1 cup chopped onions
1 cup chopped green bell peppers
3 cloves garlic, minced
¼ teaspoon cumin seed
4 cups cauliflower florets
1½ cups cooked black beans (cooked from dry; or canned, drained)
1 cup chopped tomatoes
½ cup water
½ teaspoon salt, or to taste
¼ teaspoon Tabasco (optional)

1. In a 4-quart pot, heat the oil over medium-high heat. Add the onions, bell peppers, and garlic. Cook, stirring, until the vegetables are softened, about 2 minutes.

2. Add the cumin seed and stir for 30 seconds. Add the remaining ingredients. Cook, stirring occasionally, for 25 minutes or until vegetables are tender and stew is slightly thickened.

Variation: Use chickpeas or other beans instead of the black beans.

SOUTHWESTERN STEW

Makes: 3³/₄ cups; serves: 4

I add the carrots toward the end of cooking time so they retain some of their crunchiness. If you prefer soft carrots, add them when you add the beans.

1 tablespoon vegetable oil
1 cup chopped green bell peppers
3 cloves garlic, minced
1 tablespoon chili powder
¼ teaspoon ground cumin
¼ teaspoon ground cinnamon
One 14¼-ounce can whole peeled tomatoes, undrained
1½ cups cooked black beans (cooked from dry or canned), drained
1 cup corn kernels (fresh, frozen, or canned), drained
¼ cup water
1 teaspoon sugar
¼ teaspoon ground sage
¼ teaspoon salt, or to taste
¼ teaspoon Tabasco (optional)
1 cup diced carrots
⅓ cup chopped fresh cilantro

1. In a 3-quart pot, heat the oil over medium-high heat. Add bell peppers and garlic. Cook, stirring, until the vegetables are softened, about 2 minutes. Stir in the chili powder, cumin, and cinnamon until absorbed.

2. Add the tomatoes, breaking them up with the back of a spoon. Add the black beans, corn, water, sugar, sage, salt, and Tabasco. Cook, uncovered, stirring occasionally, for 15 minutes. Stir in the carrots and cilantro. Cook, uncovered, 10 minutes longer or until vegetables are tender and stew is slightly thickened.

Variation: Substitute 1 cup diced zucchini for the carrots or add it with the carrots.

RICE AND BLACK BEANS

Makes: 2¹/₂ cups; serves: 4

This is my favorite dish to order at any Cuban restaurant—it's especially good when topped with Cilantro–Two Onion Relish (page 484) and served with Fried Sweet Bananas (page 279). The finished dish should not be so watery as to be souplike, nor so thick as to be gloppy.

1 cup black beans
3¹/₂ to 4 cups water, divided
1 tablespoon vegetable oil
1 cup chopped onions
¹/₃ cup chopped green bell peppers
4 cloves garlic, minced
¹/₂ teaspoon ground cumin
¹/₄ teaspoon dried oregano
1 bay leaf
¹/₄ teaspoon salt, or to taste
¹/₄ teaspoon pepper
3 cups cooked white or brown rice

1. Place the beans in a large bowl, add water to cover by 2 inches, and let stand overnight (or use the quick-soak method: page 13). Drain.

2. In a 2-quart saucepan, heat the oil over medium-high heat. Add the onions, bell peppers, and garlic; cook, stirring, until softened, about 3 minutes. Stir in the cumin until absorbed.

3. Add 3¹/₂ cups of the water; bring to a boil. Add the drained beans, oregano, and bay leaf. Return to a boil. Reduce heat and simmer, uncovered, 2 to 2¹/₂ hours or until beans are very soft and mixture is thick; if necessary add the final ¹/₂ cup water during cooking time. Stir in salt and pepper. Discard the bay leaf.

4. Serve over rice.

Variation: Mooros y Christianos: Stir 2 cups of cooked white rice into the cooked black beans. Bake 25 minutes.

CILANTRO RICE AND BLACK BEANS

[V]

Makes: 4 cups; serves: 4

This recipe was tested using leftover rice (from a Chinese take-out dinner) and canned beans; if you are using freshly cooked, still-warm rice and beans, just stir the ingredients together and serve. If either is not hot, it's easiest to use a microwave, as called for below. If you don't own a microwave, reheat on the stove top, adding a tablespoon or two of water to prevent the rice from sticking to the pot.

2 cups cooked white or brown rice
    (I use white)
2 cups cooked black beans (cooked from dry
    or canned), drained
6 tablespoons (¹/₂ recipe) Cilantro Pesto
    (see page 476)
¹/₄ teaspoon salt, or to taste

1. In a 1¹/₂-quart microwave-safe bowl, stir together the rice, beans, pesto, and salt. Cover the bowl loosely and microwave on high power (100%) 2 minutes. Stir; microwave on high power 1 minute longer or until heated through.

Variation: Parsley Rice and Black Beans: Substitute Parsley Pesto (page 476) for the Cilantro Pesto.

CREOLE RED BEANS AND RICE

[V][♥]

Makes: 5 1/2 cups; serves: 4 to 6

The type of bean you use is really not going to affect the outcome of the dish, except that some types may take longer than others to cook. Just keep tasting until the beans are soft.

1 cup dry red, pinto, black, or kidney beans
1 tablespoon vegetable oil
1 cup chopped onions
1 cup chopped celery
1 cup chopped green bell peppers, divided
3 cloves garlic, minced, divided
1 teaspoon chili powder
2 cups water
One 14 1/2-ounce can whole peeled tomatoes, undrained
1/2 teaspoon salt, or to taste
4 cups cooked white or brown rice

1. Place the beans in a 1 1/2-quart saucepan; cover with water. Bring to a boil over medium heat. Let boil 2 minutes. Remove from heat and let stand 1 hour. Drain.

2. In a 3-quart saucepan, heat the oil over medium-high heat. Add the onions, celery, green peppers, and garlic. Cook, stirring, until softened, about 3 minutes. Stir in chili powder until absorbed. Add water and beans; bring to a boil. Reduce heat and simmer, covered, 1 1/2 hours or until beans are tender.

3. Add the tomatoes and salt; break up the tomatoes with the back of a spoon. Simmer, covered, 25 minutes longer.

4. Serve over cooked rice.

Variation: Add ground red pepper to taste.

MEXICALI STEW

[V][♥]

Makes: 4 3/4 cups; serves: 4 to 6

This is a first cousin to chili; in fact, it's so closely related it may be a step-sister. This stew, however, has a distinct sweetness and a mild spiciness. Mexicorn is a Green Giant product that has some red peppers and chili peppers mixed in with the corn. If you can't find it, any canned corn kernels will do.

1 tablespoon olive oil
1 cup chopped onions
1/2 cup chopped green bell peppers
2 cloves garlic
1 tablespoon chili powder
1 teaspoon cocoa powder
2 cups ripe tomato wedges
3/4 cup water
1 1/2 teaspoons sugar
1 teaspoon dried oregano
1 1/2 cups cooked kidney beans (cooked from dry; or canned, drained)
1 1/2 cups peeled, cubed potatoes
One 7-ounce can Mexicorn kernels, undrained
1/4 teaspoon salt, or to taste

1. In a 3-quart saucepan, heat the oil over medium-high heat. Add the onions, green peppers, and garlic; cook, stirring, until vegetables are softened, about 3 minutes. Stir in the chili powder and cocoa powder until absorbed.

2. Stir in the tomatoes, water, sugar, and oregano. Cook 5 minutes, stirring constantly. Stir in the beans, potatoes, and corn. Bring to a boil; reduce heat and simmer, 40 minutes, stirring occasionally, or until potatoes are tender and almost ready to disintegrate. Stir in salt.

Variation: For a spicier version, substitute Mexican-style stewed tomatoes for the tomato wedges, or add ground red pepper.

ZUCCHINI AND YELLOW SQUASH WITH CHICKPEAS

[V] [♥]

Makes: 6 cups; serves: 4 to 6

Serve this as a sauce over pasta or polenta, or just as a stew with a chunk of crusty bread.

2 teaspoons olive oil
3 cloves garlic, minced
One 14½-ounce can whole peeled tomatoes, undrained
3 cups cubed zucchini (1-inch pieces)
3 cups cubed yellow squash (1-inch pieces)
1½ cups cooked chickpeas (cooked from dry; or canned, drained)
¼ cup chopped fresh basil
¼ cup chopped fresh parsley
½ teaspoon dried oregano
¼ teaspoon sugar
⅛ teaspoon salt, or to taste
⅛ teaspoon pepper

1. In a 3-quart saucepan, heat the oil over medium-high heat. Add the garlic; cook, stirring, 10 seconds. Stir in the tomatoes with the canning liquid; break them up with the back of a spoon. Add the remaining ingredients.

2. Bring to a boil; reduce heat and simmer, uncovered, 30 minutes.

Variation: Add ¾ cup chopped green bell peppers when you add the garlic; cook until softened, and continue with the recipe.

BROCCOLI WITH BLACK BEANS AND GARLIC

[V] [♥]

Makes: 5½ cups; serves: 3 to 4

Served over polenta or brown rice, this dish makes a very satisfying meal.

1½ tablespoons olive oil
4 cloves garlic, minced
6 cups broccoli florets
1 cup vegetable broth (pages 93–95)
1½ cups cooked black beans (cooked from dry; or canned, drained)

1. In a large skillet, heat the oil over high heat. Add the garlic; cook, stirring, 10 seconds. Add the broccoli; cook, stirring, until tender crisp, about 4 minutes.

2. Add the broth and bring to a boil. Add the beans. Return to a boil and cook, stirring, until heated through, about 3 minutes.

Variation: Add 1 cup sliced red bell peppers when you add the broccoli.

Yellow, Green, and Spaghetti Squash with Beans

— ⓥ —

Makes: 2 cups squash and 4 cups sauce;
serves: 3 to 4

I used freshly juiced carrots (it took about 1
pound of carrots to make the ³/₄ cup juice). If you
are not one of the 2 million or so people who have
a juice extractor, you can just substitute vegetable
broth for the carrot juice.

1 small spaghetti squash (1¼ pounds)
2 tablespoons olive oil
2 cups sliced yellow squash
2 cups sliced zucchini
1 cup sliced leeks (white and light green
    parts only)
2 cloves garlic, minced
¾ cup fresh carrot juice
1½ cups cooked butter beans (cooked
    from dry; or canned, drained)
¼ teaspoon salt, or to taste
¼ teaspoon ground nutmeg
¼ teaspoon pepper

1. Preheat the oven to 350°F. Cut the spaghetti
squash in half widthwise; place in a baking pan,
cut side down, and bake for 1 hour or until tender. Discard the seeds. Pull out the squash
threads and place in large bowl.

2. While the squash is baking, heat the oil
in a large skillet over medium-high heat. Add
the yellow squash, zucchini, leeks, and garlic.
Cook, stirring, until softened, about 4 minutes.
Add the juice and bring to a boil. Add the
beans; cook, 5 minutes, until heated through
and sauce has thickened slightly. Stir in the salt,
nutmeg, and pepper.

3. Pour the sauce over the spaghetti squash
and toss to combine.

Variation: Curried Squash with Beans: Stir
in 2 teaspoons curry powder until absorbed
(add it after the vegetables are softened,
before adding juice). If desired, add ⅛ to ¼
teaspoon ground red pepper for a spicier
curry.

Spaghetti Squash with Curried Carrots and Beans

— ⓥ ♥ —

Makes: 4 cups squash and 4 cups sauce;
serves: 4 to 6

I guess I find butter beans a great match for
spaghetti squash, since I used this combination in
the last recipe, too. You can substitute chickpeas if
you like.

1 large spaghetti squash (3 pounds)
2 tablespoons vegetable oil
2 cups chopped onions
1 tablespoon minced fresh ginger
1 tablespoon curry powder
½ teaspoon ground coriander
⅛ teaspoon ground red pepper
1 cup vegetable broth (pages 93–95)
3 cups carrots, sliced 1-inch thick
1½ cups cooked butter beans (cooked from
    dry; or canned, drained)
¼ teaspoon salt, or to taste

1. Preheat the oven to 350°F. Cut the spaghetti
squash in half widthwise; place in a baking pan,
cut side down, and bake for 1 hour or until
tender. Discard the seeds. Pull out the squash
threads and place in large bowl.

2. While the squash is baking, heat the oil in a
large skillet over medium-high heat. Add the
onions and ginger; cook, stirring, until softened,
about 2 minutes. Stir in the curry powder,
coriander, and red pepper, until absorbed. Add
the broth and bring to a boil. Add the carrots;

return to a boil. Reduce heat and simmer, uncovered, 45 minutes.

3. Add the beans; cook, 10 minutes, until heated through and sauce has thickened slightly. Stir in the salt.

4. Pour the sauce over the spaghetti squash and toss to combine.

Moroccan Vegetables with Couscous

Makes: 6³/₄ cups; serves: 4 to 6

Although fava beans are very nice in this dish, butter beans or chickpeas make good substitutes. If you don't have saffron, you can substitute ¹/₂ teaspoon extra turmeric to give this dish the nice deep yellow color it gets from the saffron.

2 tablespoons butter or margarine
2 cups coarsely chopped cabbage
2 cups chopped onions
1 ¹/₂ cups cubed eggplant (1-inch pieces)
1 teaspoon ground turmeric
¹/₂ teaspoon ground cinnamon
¹/₂ teaspoon ground ginger
¹/₈ teaspoon ground allspice
¹/₈ teaspoon saffron threads
2 cups vegetable broth (pages 93–95) or water
1 ¹/₂ cups carrot chunks (1-inch pieces)
1 ¹/₂ cups cubed rutabaga (1-inch pieces)
1 cup chopped tomatoes
1 bay leaf
2 cups cooked fava beans (cooked from dry; or canned, drained)
¹/₂ cup golden or dark raisins

1. In a 6-quart pot, melt the butter or margarine over medium-high heat. Add the cabbage and onions; cook, stirring, until the vegetables are softened, about 4 minutes. Add the eggplant; cook, stirring until softened, about 3 minutes.

2. Stir in the turmeric, cinnamon, ginger, allspice, and saffron until absorbed. Add the broth and bring to a boil. Add the carrots, rutabaga, tomatoes, and bay leaf; cook, covered, stirring occasionally, for 40 minutes or until vegetables are tender.

3. Add the fava beans and raisins; cook, covered, 20 minutes longer or until stew is slightly thickened. Discard the bay leaf.

Variation: Use chickpeas or other beans instead of the fava beans.

BURMESE CRISPY VEGETABLES WITH YELLOW PEA CURRY

— V —

Makes: 5 cups; serves: 4 to 6

I ordered this yellow pea curry at a local Burmese restaurant and was pleasantly surprised to find that unlike most curries, these vegetables were still tender-crisp. The sauce should be thicker than most curries, more like a thick pea soup. If yours is too thick, add a little extra water.

3 tablespoons vegetable oil, divided
1/2 cup chopped onions
4 cloves garlic, minced
1 1/2 tablespoons curry powder
1 teaspoon ground ginger
1/2 teaspoon ground cumin
1/2 teaspoon ground turmeric
1/8 teaspoon ground red pepper
3/4 cup yellow split peas
4 3/4 cups water
1 cup sliced carrots
3 cups broccoli florets
1 cup thickly sliced onions
1/2 cup cut green beans
1/2 teaspoon salt, or to taste

1. In a 3-quart saucepan, heat 1 tablespoon of the oil over medium-high heat. Add the chopped onions and garlic; cook, stirring, until softened, about 2 minutes. Stir in the curry powder, ginger, cumin, turmeric, and red pepper until absorbed.

2. Add the peas and stir until coated with spices. Add the water and bring to a boil. Reduce heat and simmer, uncovered, 45 minutes, stirring occasionally. Cook 20 to 30 minutes longer, stirring frequently, until most split peas have dissolved.

3. When the sauce has just about finished cooking, heat the remaining oil in a wok or large skillet. Add the carrots; cook, stirring, until almost tender, about 3 minutes. Add the broccoli, sliced onions, and green beans. Cook, stirring, until tender-crisp, about 3 minutes.

4. Stir the vegetables into the split pea mixture and add the salt.

Variation: Add other vegetables to the stir-fry, such as snow peas, bell peppers, or tomatoes.

EGGPLANT WITH BUTTER BEANS AND PLUMS

— V —

Makes: 4 cups; serves: 4

I serve this stew with couscous, but it would be equally good with rice (especially brown), or with wild rice for a more elegant presentation. I use my eggplant unpeeled, but you can peel it if you prefer.

3 tablespoons vegetable oil
6 cups cubed eggplant (3/4-inch pieces)
1 cup chopped onions
1 1/2 cups coarsely chopped fresh plums
1 cup chopped tomatoes
1 tablespoon soy sauce
1 1/2 cups cooked butter beans (cooked from dry; or canned, drained)
1 teaspoon balsamic vinegar
3 tablespoons chopped fresh cilantro or parsley
1/8 teaspoon salt, or to taste

1. In a 4-quart saucepan, heat the oil over medium-high heat. Add the eggplant and onions; cook, stirring, until softened, about 4 minutes. Add the plums, tomatoes, and soy sauce. Bring to a boil. Cook over medium heat, uncovered, 15 minutes.

2. Add the butter beans and vinegar; simmer 10 minutes longer. Add the cilantro and salt and simmer 3 minutes longer.

CURRIED CHICKPEAS AND KALE

[v]

Makes: 4¹/₂ cups; serves: 4

This is a mild curry. If you like yours spicy, stir in ground red pepper when you add the curry powder.

2 tablespoons ghee (page 494) or vegetable oil
1½ cups chopped onions
4 cloves garlic, minced
½ teaspoon cumin seeds
3 cups chopped kale
1½ tablespoons curry powder
1 teaspoon ground ginger
1 teaspoon ground coriander
1½ cups vegetable broth (pages 93–95)
3 cups cooked chickpeas (cooked from dry; or canned, drained)
1 cup chopped tomatoes
¼ teaspoon salt, or to taste

1. In a 2-quart saucepan, heat the ghee or oil over medium-high heat. Add the onions, garlic, and cumin; cook, stirring, until softened, about 2 minutes. Add the kale; cook, stirring, until softened, about 2 minutes.

2. Stir in the curry, ginger, and coriander until absorbed. Stir in the broth and bring to a boil. Add the chickpeas, tomatoes, and salt; bring to a boil. Reduce heat and simmer, uncovered, 25 minutes.

Variation: Substitute Swiss chard or a 10-ounce package frozen chopped spinach for the kale.

LENTIL SHEPHERD'S PIE

[v]

Makes: 6 cups; serves: 4

The 2 cups of mashed potatoes—which can be homemade or reconstituted from a package—is not too generous a portion. If you love potatoes you may want to increase the amount to 3 cups; just be sure not to cover the entire top but leave a little air space in the middle to vent.

2 tablespoons vegetable oil
¾ cup chopped onions
1 clove garlic, minced
2 tablespoons all-purpose flour
1⅓ cups vegetable broth (pages 93–95)
¼ teaspoon dried thyme
⅛ teaspoon salt, or to taste
⅛ teaspoon pepper
2 cups cooked lentils
One 10-ounce package frozen mixed vegetables
2 cups mashed potatoes (page 281)

1. Preheat the oven to 350°F. Grease a 9 × 5 × 3-inch loaf pan.

2. In a 1½-quart saucepan, heat the oil over medium-high heat. Add the onions and garlic; cook, stirring, until softened, about 2 minutes. Stir in the flour until absorbed. Add the broth, thyme, salt, and pepper. Cook, stirring, until mixture comes to a boil. Stir in the lentils and mixed vegetables. Spoon into pan.

3. Place the potatoes into a pastry bag fitted with a large star tip. Pipe the potatoes around the edge of the pan.

4. Bake 40 minutes or until potatoes brown on top.

Variation: Use any cooked vegetables you like, such as zucchini, mushrooms, or celery.

LENTIL AND MUSHROOM STEW

— [V][♥] —

Makes: 4¹/₂ cups; serves: 4 to 5

I used mushroom ketchup (which is available in gourmet shops and is not like tomato ketchup) to give a slight flavor boost. If you don't have any, just leave it out or use a little anchovy-free Worcestershire sauce, or a tablespoon of steak sauce.

1 ½ tablespoons olive oil
1 cup sliced leeks (white and light green parts only)
2 cloves garlic, minced
2 cups chopped portobello or shiitake mushrooms
2 cups sliced white mushrooms
2 cups water
¾ cup lentils
1 bay leaf
1 cup sliced carrots
1 cup fresh cut green beans
1 cup diced, peeled potatoes (¾-inch pieces)
⅓ cup chopped fresh parsley
1 tablespoon mushroom ketchup
¼ teaspoon dried thyme
¼ teaspoon salt, or to taste
⅛ teaspoon pepper

1. In a 2-quart saucepan, heat the oil over medium-high heat. Add the leeks and garlic; cook until softened, about 30 seconds.

2. Add both mushrooms; cook, until softened, about 3 minutes. Add the water and bring to a boil. Add the lentils and bay leaf; return to a boil. Reduce heat and simmer, covered, 25 minutes.

3. Stir in the remaining ingredients. Simmer, covered, 15 minutes or until vegetables and lentils are tender. Discard the bay leaf.

Variation: Use peas instead of the green beans or the potatoes.

VEGETABLES WITH KAMUT AND BEANS

— [V][♥] —

Makes: 4 cups; serves: 4

Kamut is a whole grain available in natural food stores or by mail (see page 43). If you have trouble finding it, substitute cooked whole grain wheat, spelt, or barley. The "gravy" in this stew is somewhat starchy, but very appealing. My tasters declared it delicious.

1 tablespoons vegetable oil
1 cup chopped onions
2 cloves garlic, minced
1 ½ cups vegetable broth (pages 93–95)
1 cup sliced carrots
1 cup sliced celery
1 bay leaf
1 ½ cups cooked small white beans (cooked from dry; or canned, drained)
1 cup sliced zucchini
1 cup cooked kamut
¼ cup chopped fresh parsley

1. In a 3-quart saucepan, heat the oil over medium-high heat. Add the onions and garlic; cook, stirring, until softened, about 2 minutes.

2. Add the broth; bring to a boil. Add the carrots, celery, and bay leaf. Return to a boil; reduce heat and simmer, uncovered, 20 minutes. Discard the bay leaf.

3. Add the beans, zucchini, kamut, and parsley. Simmer, uncovered, 10 minutes or until vegetables are tender and beans are heated through.

Variation: Add ¹/₃ cup snipped fresh dill when you add the parsley.

MOUSSAKA

Makes: one 9-inch-square pan; serves: 4 to 6

Traditionally a lamb dish, this translates very successfully to a vegetarian meal.

3 tablespoons olive oil, divided
2 cloves garlic
1 medium eggplant (1¼ pounds), thinly sliced
1 cup chopped onions
2 cups chopped tomatoes
1 tablespoon tomato paste
⅓ cup chopped fresh parsley
½ teaspoon salt, or to taste
½ teaspoon ground cinnamon
¼ teaspoon ground cloves
¼ teaspoon ground allspice
¼ teaspoon pepper
2 cups cooked lentils
¾ cup cooked diced potatoes
2 tablespoons butter or margarine
3 tablespoons all-purpose flour
1½ cups milk
⅓ cup grated Parmesan cheese, divided
Pinch ground nutmeg
1 egg

1. Preheat the grill or broiler.

2. Stir 1½ tablespoons of the oil and the garlic together and let stand 10 minutes. Brush each side of the sliced eggplant lightly with some oil. Broil 4 to 6 inches from heat for 5 minutes per side or until browned or lightly charred.

3. In a large skillet, heat the remaining 1½ tablespoons of oil. Add the onions; cook, stirring, until softened, about 2 minutes. Add the tomatoes, tomato paste, parsley, salt, cinnamon, cloves, allspice, and pepper. Cook, stirring occasionally, 10 minutes. Stir in the lentils and potatoes; set aside.

4. In a 1-quart saucepan, melt the butter or margarine over medium heat. Stir in the flour until absorbed. Stir in the milk; cook, stirring, until mixture comes to a boil. Stir in 3 tablespoons of the Parmesan cheese and nutmeg. In a medium bowl, beat the egg. Beat ½ cup of the white sauce into the egg. Stir egg mixture into remaining white sauce.

5. Preheat the oven to 375°F. Grease a 9-inch-square pan. Make a layer of overlapping slices of eggplant. Top with the lentil mixture. Place another layer of eggplant over the mixture. Pour the cream sauce over the eggplant. Sprinkle with the remaining Parmesan cheese.

6. Bake 25 minutes or until heated through and the top has browned. Let stand 10 minutes before serving

Variation: Use 3 cups of lentils instead of lentils and potatoes.

SMALL WHITE BEANS WITH WHEAT BERRIES

v ♥

Makes: 3¹/₂ cups; serves: 4

This recipe is very adaptable to being a "melt." After cooking, place in oven-proof casserole, sprinkle generously with shredded cheese (such as Gouda, Jarlsberg, Fontina, or Swiss), then place under broiler until bubbly.

1 tablespoon olive oil
¹/₂ cup chopped onions
¹/₂ cup chopped zucchini
¹/₂ cup chopped yellow squash
1 cup lightly packed chopped escarole
1¹/₂ cups cooked small white beans (cooked from dry; or canned, drained)
1 cup cooked wheat berries (whole grain wheat)
¹/₄ teaspoon salt, or to taste
¹/₈ teaspoon pepper

1. In a large skillet, heat the oil over medium-high heat. Add the onions, zucchini, and yellow squash; cook, stirring, until vegetables are softened, about 4 minutes. Add the escarole; cook, stirring, until wilted, about 3 minutes longer.

2. Add the beans, wheat berries, salt, and pepper; cook, stirring until heated through, about 2 minutes.

Variation: Stir in ¹/₂ cup grated Parmesan cheese just before serving.

BABY LIMAS AND BARLEY

v ♥

Makes: 5 cups; serves: 4 to 6

Dried limas are one type of bean that does not come canned (canned limas are fresh, not dried). If you want to skip step 1 and use canned beans, use drained, rinsed butter beans.

³/₄ cup dried baby lima beans
2¹/₂ cups vegetable broth (pages 93–95), divided
¹/₂ ounce imported dried mushrooms
2 teaspoons vegetable oil
1 cup chopped onions
1 cup barley, rinsed
¹/₃ cup chopped fresh parsley
3 tablespoons snipped fresh dill
¹/₄ teaspoon pepper

1. Soak the beans overnight or use the quick-soak method (page 13). Simmer in 4 cups water for 40 minutes or until tender. Drain. (You will have 2 cups of beans.)

2. Heat ¹/₂ cup of the vegetable broth to boiling. Add the mushrooms and let soak 10 minutes. Remove the mushrooms and chop, reserving the soaking water.

3. In a 3-quart saucepan, heat the oil over medium-high heat. Add the onions; cook, stirring, until softened, about 2 minutes. Add the remaining 2 cups vegetable broth and bring to a boil. Add the barley, mushrooms, and reserved mushroom soaking water and return to a boil. Reduce heat and simmer, 30 minutes.

4. Add the beans, parsley, dill, and pepper. Simmer 10 minutes longer or until the barley is tender and the beans are heated through.

Variation: Stir in ¹/₂ cup chopped green bell peppers when sautéing onions.

STEWED GARBANZO BEANS WITH ZUC~QUINOA

V ♥

*Makes: 3 cups beans and 3 cups zuc-quinoa;
serves: 4 to 6*

*If you prefer, you can serve these recipes separately
as side dishes. The chickpea stew goes well with
cooked spaghetti squash.*

For the beans:

2 teaspoons olive oil

¾ cup chopped onions

¾ cup chopped green bell peppers

One 14½-ounce can whole peeled tomatoes,
  undrained

2 tablespoons tomato paste (Italian-style or
  plain)

1½ cups cooked chickpeas (cooked from dry;
  or canned, drained)

For the zuc-quinoa:

¾ cup quinoa

2 teaspoons vegetable oil

½ cup chopped red onions

1½ cups vegetable broth (pages 93–95) or
  water

½ teaspoon dried oregano

2 cups sliced zucchini

½ teaspoon salt, or to taste

1. For the beans, in a 1½-quart saucepan, heat
the olive oil over medium-high heat. Add
¾ cup onions and the bell peppers; cook, stirring, until softened, about 3 minutes.

2. Stir in the tomatoes with juice; break them
up with the back of a spoon. Stir in the tomato
paste. Add the chickpeas. Return to a boil. Reduce heat and simmer, uncovered, 20 minutes.

3. While the beans are cooking, place the
quinoa in a large bowl; fill the bowl with cool
water and then drain into strainer. Repeat
4 more times or until the water no longer
looks soapy.

4. In a 2-quart saucepan, heat the vegetable oil
over medium-high heat. Add ½ cup onions;
cook, stirring, until softened, about 2 minutes.
Add the broth and oregano; bring to a boil. Stir
in the quinoa. Return to a boil. Reduce heat
and simmer, covered, 10 minutes. Add the
zucchini and salt; cook, covered, 10 minutes
longer.

Variation: Use kidney beans instead of
chickpeas; use yellow squash instead of
zucchini.

FRAN'S GREAT GRAIN DISH

— ◻♥ —

Makes: 9 cups; serves: 8 to 10

My cousin Fran Slote developed this recipe for the book. She cooks the grains in salted broth because she likes the extra chewiness that salted water imparts to whole grains. She serves this over cooked basmati rice. If you don't want to use bouillon cubes, you can substitute 4 cups of vegetable broth for the water and bouillon.

4 cups water
2 cups firmly packed sliced leeks (light and
    green parts only)
1 cup chopped celery
1 cup sliced carrots
1 cup chopped fresh parsley
2 Knorr's vegetarian vegetable bouillon cubes
2 teaspoons garlic, minced
2 teaspoons dried dill weed
1 egg
1 cup hulled barley
½ cup wheat berries (whole grain wheat)
½ cup whole grain oats
2 tablespoons vegetable oil
1 cup minced onions
½ cup diced shiitake mushrooms
One 16-ounce can kidney beans, undrained

1. In a 6-quart pot, combine the water, leeks, celery, carrots, parsley, bouillon cubes, garlic, and dill weed. Bring to a boil; reduce heat and simmer, covered, while you continue with the recipe.

2. In a medium bowl, beat the egg. Add the hulled barley, wheat berries, and oats; set aside.

3. In a large skillet, heat the oil over medium-high heat. Add the onions and mushrooms; cook, stirring, until softened, about 3 minutes. Add the grain mixture; cook until grains separate and onions are browned. Add the grain

mixture and the beans to the pot with the broth.

4. Bring to a boil. Reduce heat and simmer, covered, 2 hours or until liquid is absorbed.

Variation: Substitute pearled barley for some of the hulled barley.

COUSCOUS WITH VEGETABLE SAUCE AND CHICKPEAS

— ⓥ♥ —

Makes: 2¼ cups couscous and 5 cups sauce; serves: 4 to 6

Although I use this sauce with couscous, it's also excellent served with polenta.

1½ tablespoons olive oil
1 cup chopped onions
¾ cup chopped celery
3 cloves garlic, minced
3 cups diced eggplant (peeled or unpeeled)
3 cups chopped tomatoes
¾ cup chopped carrots
⅓ cup red wine
1½ teaspoons sugar
½ teaspoon salt, or to taste, divided
1½ cups cooked chickpeas (cooked from
    dry; or canned, drained)
1¼ cups water
1 cup couscous

1. In a 3-quart saucepan, heat the oil over medium heat. Add the onions, celery, and garlic; cook, stirring, until the vegetables are tender, about 3 minutes. Add the eggplant; cook, stirring, until softened. Add the tomatoes, carrots, wine, sugar, and ¼ teaspoon of the salt. Bring to a boil. Reduce heat and simmer, uncovered, 15 minutes.

2. Stir in the chickpeas; return to a boil. Reduce heat and simmer, uncovered, 15 minutes, stirring occasionally.

3. Meanwhile, bring the water to a boil in a 1-quart saucepan. Stir in the couscous; return to a boil. Remove from heat and let stand 5 minutes or until water is absorbed; stir in remaining ¼ teaspoon salt. Serve with sauce.

Variation: Substitute any bean for the chickpeas.

BLACK BEAN TOSTADAS
[V]

Makes: 4 tostadas; serves: 2 to 4

For an even quicker version, you can make these tostadas using canned refried beans instead of the black bean puree given here. If you have any leftover bean puree, use it for the dip suggested in the variation.

1 tablespoon vegetable oil
¾ cup chopped onions, divided
¼ cup chopped green bell peppers
3 cloves garlic, minced
½ teaspoon ground cumin
1½ cups cooked black beans (cooked from dry; or canned, drained)
¼ cup water
2 tablespoons chopped fresh cilantro
¼ teaspoon salt, or to taste
⅛ teaspoon ground red pepper
4 tostada shells
¼ cup salsa (homemade, pages 479–481, or jarred), divided
1 cup shredded lettuce, divided
½ cup chopped tomatoes, divided
½ cup shredded Cheddar cheese, divided (optional)

1. In a 1½-quart saucepan, heat the oil over medium-high heat. Add ½ cup of the onions, the bell peppers, and garlic; cook, stirring, until vegetables are tender, about 3 minutes. Add the cumin and stir until absorbed. Add the

black beans, water, cilantro, salt, and red pepper. Bring to a boil, stirring frequently. Simmer, uncovered, 15 minutes or until mixture is thick.

2. Place the bean mixture in a food processor container fitted with a steel blade. Cover and process until smooth.

3. Spread ¼ of the bean mixture on each tostada shell. Top each with 1 tablespoon salsa, then ¼ cup lettuce, 2 tablespoons tomatoes, and 1 tablespoon of the remaining chopped onions. If desired, sprinkle 2 tablespoons Cheddar over each tostada.

Variations: Serve with guacamole (page 56) over the bean mixture.

Black Bean Dip: Stir ½ cup sour cream into ½ cup of the black bean filling. If desired, add extra ground cumin and/or ground red pepper. Makes ⅔ cup.

Brown Rice and Black Bean Burritos

Makes: 4 burritos; serves: 4 to 6

You can prepare these burritos using store-bought or homemade salsa (pages 479–81) and/or guacamole (page 56). I usually cut these burritos in half because they yield slightly too much food for some people. Or, instead of making giant burritos, you can use smaller tortillas and make 6 smaller ones.

4 large (10-inch) flour tortillas
1/3 cup finely chopped, seeded tomatoes
3 tablespoons minced onion
2 tablespoons minced green bell peppers
2 cups cooked brown rice
1 cup cooked black beans (cooked from dry; or canned, drained)
1/2 cup mild or medium salsa
1/2 cup shredded Monterey Jack cheese
1 cup guacamole

1. Preheat the oven to 350°F. Wrap the tortillas in foil and place in oven; heat about 5 to 10 minutes or until tortillas are warm and pliable.

2. While the tortillas are heating, combine the tomatoes, onion, and green pepper in a small bowl; set aside.

3. In a 1-quart saucepan, stir together the brown rice, beans, and salsa. Cook over low heat until heated through, about 4 minutes.

4. Remove the tortillas from the oven. Place one on a serving plate. Place 1/4 of the bean mixture (a generous 1/2 cup) in the center of the tortilla. Top with 2 tablespoons shredded cheese, then 1/4 cup guacamole and 1/4 of the tomato mixture.

5. Fold two opposite sides of the tortilla over the filling. Lift the edge of one of the remaining sides; fold it over filling and roll to form a very wide log. Repeat with remaining tortillas.

Variations: Substitute Cheddar for the Monterey Jack.

[v] Omit the cheese completely.

Chili

Makes: 4 2/3 cups; serves: 4 to 6

I think this is one of the best vegetarian chili recipes I've ever tasted. Serve this, or any chili, topped with sour cream or yogurt, and/or chopped onion or scallions, and/or shredded Cheddar.

2 tablespoons vegetable oil
2 cups chopped onions
6 cloves garlic, minced
1/4 cup chili powder
1 tablespoon paprika
1 teaspoon ground cumin
1 teaspoon dried oregano
4 cups chopped tomatoes
1 bay leaf
1/2 teaspoon sugar
1/2 teaspoon salt, or to taste
1/8 teaspoon ground red pepper (optional)
3 cups cooked kidney beans (cooked from dry; or canned, drained)

1. In a 4-quart saucepan, heat the oil over medium-high heat. Add the onions and garlic; cook, stirring, until softened, about 2 minutes. Stir in the chili powder, paprika, cumin, and oregano until absorbed.

2. Stir in the tomatoes, bay leaf, sugar, salt, and red pepper; bring to a boil. Reduce heat and simmer, covered, 20 minutes, stirring occasionally.

3. Add the beans; simmer, covered, 15 to 20 minutes longer or until chili is slightly thick, stirring occasionally. Discard the bay leaf.

Variation: Add 1 cup chopped green bell peppers when you add the onions.

BLACK BEAN CHILI

— [V][♥] —

Makes: 6¹/₂ cups; serves: 4 to 6

This is a fairly spicy chili. For a much milder one, omit the canned chilies; for a moderately brave palate, use only ¹/₂ can of chilies. I like the variation with the TVP (textured vegetable protein); my father preferred the regular recipe.

1 tablespoon vegetable oil
1 cup chopped onions
³/₄ cup chopped green bell peppers
3 cloves garlic, minced
3 tablespoons chili powder
1 teaspoon ground cumin
¹/₂ teaspoon dried oregano
¹/₂ teaspoon ground cinnamon
One 28-ounce can crushed tomatoes
1 cup water
One 4-ounce can chopped green chilies
3 cups black beans (cooked from dry; or canned, drained)
¹/₂ teaspoon sugar
¹/₄ teaspoon salt, or to taste

1. In a 4-quart saucepan, heat the oil over medium-high heat. Add the onions, bell peppers, and garlic; cook, stirring, until softened, about 2 minutes. Stir in the chili powder, cumin, oregano, and cinnamon; cook, stirring, until absorbed.

2. Stir in the tomatoes, water, and chilies (undrained); bring to a boil. Add the black beans, sugar, and salt; return to a boil. Reduce heat and simmer, covered, 30 minutes, stirring occasionally. Uncover and simmer 15 minutes longer, stirring occasionally.

Variation: For a meaty texture, stir in ³/₄ cup reconstituted TVP or cooked bulgur 10 minutes before chili is finished cooking.

BLACK BEAN–POLENTA PIE

— [LO] —

Makes: one 9-inch pie; serves: 6

In order to form a smooth crust, the polenta has to be freshly cooked and spread into the pie plate as soon as it has finished cooking. Try to make the crust a little higher than the sides of the dish.

2¹/₂ cups cooked polenta (1 basic recipe, page 307)
1 tablespoon vegetable oil
1 cup chopped onions
1 cup chopped green bell peppers
1 cup chopped tomatoes, or one 8-ounce can whole peeled tomatoes, undrained
1¹/₂ cups cooked black beans (cooked from dry; or canned, drained)
1 cup cooked corn kernels (fresh, cooked; canned, drained; or frozen)
One 4-ounce can chopped chilies, drained
1¹/₂ cups shredded Cheddar cheese, divided
1 egg
¹/₃ cup sour cream

1. Preheat the oven to 375°F.

2. Spread the polenta into a greased 9-inch pie plate to form a thick crust, making sure to make a high crust over the edge of the dish.

3. In a large skillet, heat the oil over medium-high heat. Add the onions and bell peppers; cook, stirring, until tender, about 3 minutes. Add the tomatoes; cook, stirring, until most of the liquid has evaporated. Stir in the beans, corn, and chilies. Stir in 1 cup of the Cheddar cheese.

4. In a small bowl, beat the egg; beat in the sour cream. Add to the bean mixture and stir until combined. Spoon into the polenta shell. Top with the remaining cheese. Bake 35 minutes or until bean mixture has heated through and cheese has melted.

Variation: Substitute unflavored yogurt for the sour cream.

Risotto

Risotto, a very popular, creamy Italian rice dish, is made with a special medium-short-grain rice called Arborio. Risotto gets its creamy texture from the starchiness of the rice, which is developed by the constant stirring. Look for Arborio rice in your local gourmet or Italian specialty stores. Unfortunately, you can't substitute regular long-grain rice.

I have ordered risotto at restaurants that serve it quite *al dente;* my preference is for softer risotto. If you prefer the toothier style, use ¹/₄ to ¹/₂ cups less broth or water, and taste it as you get close to the end of the cooking time. Although risotto can be served as a side dish, it is more common to serve it as an entree. A crusty bread and crispy salad make this a meal to remember.

RISOTTO ALLA MILANESE

Makes: 2²/₃ cups; serves: 3 to 4

This is the classic way of preparing risotto. The Marsala adds a slight sweetness. You need only a pinch of saffron to flavor and color the rice.

2¹/₂ cups vegetable broth (pages 93–95)
1 cup water
¹/₃ cup Marsala
Pinch saffron
2 tablespoons butter or margarine
¹/₃ cup finely chopped onions
1 cup Arborio rice
¹/₂ cup grated Parmesan cheese (optional)

1. In a 2-quart saucepan, heat the broth, water, Marsala, and saffron until simmering. Keep on low heat so that the liquids stay warm throughout the cooking time.

2. While the broth is heating, melt the butter or margarine in a 3-quart saucepan, over medium heat. Add the onions; cook, stirring, until golden, about 10 minutes. Add the rice; cook, stirring, until rice is coated with butter or margarine.

3. Add the broth to the rice mixture, ¹/₄ cup at a time, stirring constantly, until the rice has absorbed the liquid. (You should make the next addition of liquid when you can draw a clear path on the bottom of the pot as you scrape through the rice with a wooden spoon. This will happen rather quickly at first and will take longer as you near the end of the cooking time.)

4. Stir in the cheese, if desired.

Variation: Omit the cheese and stir in ¹/₂ cup chopped oil-marinated sun-dried tomatoes when you add the last ¹/₄ cup broth.

RISOTTO WITH GORGONZOLA AND ARTICHOKE HEARTS

———— [L] ————

Makes: 3³/₄ cups; serves: 4 to 6

If you're using fresh artichoke hearts, follow the recipe as written. If you're using canned or frozen artichoke hearts, stir them in three-quarters of the way through the cooking.

2 cups vegetable broth (pages 93–95)
1³/₄ cups water
2 tablespoons butter or margarine
1 cup chopped fresh or frozen artichoke hearts
2 cloves garlic, minced
1 cup Arborio rice
¹/₂ cup crumbled Gorgonzola
¹/₄ cup grated Parmesan cheese (optional)

1. In a 2-quart saucepan, heat the broth and water until simmering. Keep on low heat so that the liquids stay warm throughout the cooking time.

2. While the broth is heating, heat the butter or margarine in a 3-quart saucepan over medium heat. Add the artichokes and garlic; cook, stirring, 10 seconds. Add the rice; cook, stirring, until rice is coated with butter or margarine.

3. Add the broth to the rice mixture, $^{1}/_{4}$ cup at a time, stirring constantly, until the rice has absorbed the liquid. (You should make the next addition of liquid when you can draw a clear path on the bottom of the pot as you scrape through the rice with a wooden spoon. This will happen rather quickly at first and will take longer as you near the end of the cooking time.)

4. Stir in the cheeses until melted.

Variation: Substitute chopped, peeled Jerusalem artichokes for the artichoke hearts.

RISOTTO WITH ESCAROLE

Makes: 3$^{1}/_{2}$ cups; serves: 4 to 6

Two of my favorite foods, together with garlic . . . Heaven!

2 cups vegetable broth (pages 93–95)
1¾ cups water
2 tablespoons olive oil
3 cloves garlic, minced
1 cup Arborio rice
4 cups lightly packed chopped escarole
½ cup grated Parmesan cheese (optional)

1. In a 2-quart saucepan, heat the broth and water until simmering. Keep on low heat so that the liquids stay warm throughout the cooking time.

2. While the broth is heating, heat the oil in a 3-quart saucepan, over medium heat. Add the garlic; cook, stirring, 10 seconds. Add the rice; cook, stirring, until rice is coated with oil. Add the escarole; cook, stirring, until wilted, about 1 minute.

3. Add the broth to the rice mixture, $^{1}/_{4}$ cup at a time, stirring constantly, until the rice has absorbed the liquid. (You should make the next addition of liquid when you can draw a clear path on the bottom of the pot as you scrape through the rice with a wooden spoon. This will happen rather quickly at first and will take longer as you near the end of the cooking time.)

4. Stir in the cheese, if desired.

Variation: Spinach Risotto: Substitute chopped spinach for the escarole.

TOMATO AND BASIL RISOTTO

Makes: 3³/₄ cups; serves: 4 to 6

This is one of the few recipes where I overcome my laziness and actually seed and peel the tomatoes. You don't have to—the recipe will taste the same, but the texture will be a little crunchier.

2 cups vegetable broth (pages 93–95)
1¹/₂ cups water
1¹/₂ tablespoons butter or margarine
¹/₃ cup finely chopped onions
1 clove garlic, minced
1 cup Arborio rice
2 cups chopped tomatoes (seeded and peeled, if desired)
¹/₃ cup grated Parmesan cheese (optional)
¹/₃ cup chopped fresh basil, or 1¹/₂ teaspoons dried basil
¹/₄ teaspoon salt, or to taste
¹/₈ teaspoon pepper

1. In a 2-quart saucepan, heat the broth and water until simmering. Keep on low heat so that the liquids stay warm throughout the cooking time.

2. While the broth is heating, melt the butter or margarine in a 3-quart saucepan over medium heat. Add the onions and garlic; cook, stirring, until softened, about 30 seconds. Add the rice; cook, stirring, until rice is coated with butter or margarine. Stir in the tomatoes; cook, stirring, until the tomatoes are softened, about 2 minutes.

3. Add the broth to the rice mixture, ¹/₄ cup at a time, stirring constantly, until the rice has absorbed the liquid. (You should make the next addition of liquid when you can draw a clear path on the bottom of the pot as you scrape through the rice with a wooden spoon. This will happen rather quickly at first and will take longer as you near the end of the cooking time.)

4. Stir in the cheese, if desired, the basil, salt, and pepper.

Variation: Add ¹/₃ cup chopped fresh parsley when you add the basil.

ROSEMARY-MUSHROOM RISOTTO

Makes: 3¹/₂ cups; serves: 4 to 6

Although I use white mushrooms in this recipe, shiitake mushrooms would be a wonderful substitution. If you don't want to go through the bother of making mushroom broth, you can just use additional vegetable broth instead, but, of course, the mushroom flavor will not be nearly as intense.

1 cup mushroom broth (page 95)
1 cup vegetable broth (pages 93–95)
1³/₄ cups water
¹/₂ teaspoon dried rosemary, crumbled
¹/₄ teaspoon dried thyme
2 tablespoons olive oil
1¹/₂ cups chopped white mushrooms
2 tablespoons minced shallots
1 cup Arborio rice
¹/₄ cup chopped fresh parsley
¹/₂ teaspoon salt, or to taste
¹/₈ teaspoon pepper

1. In a 2-quart saucepan, heat both of the broths, the water, rosemary, and thyme until simmering. Keep on low heat so that the liquids stay warm throughout the cooking time.

2. While broth is heating, heat the oil in a 3-quart saucepan over medium heat. Add the mushrooms and shallots; cook, stirring, until mushrooms are softened. Add the rice; cook, stirring, until rice is coated with oil.

3. Add the broth to the rice mixture, $^1/_4$ cup at a time, stirring constantly, until the rice has absorbed the liquid. (You should make the next addition of liquid when you can draw a clear path on the bottom of the pot as you scrape through the rice with a wooden spoon. This will happen rather quickly at first and will take longer as you near the end of the cooking time.)

4. Add the parsley, salt, and pepper when you add the last portion of broth.

Variation: Stir in $^1/_3$ cup grated Parmesan cheese when the parsley is stirred in.

Risi e Bisi

Makes: 3$^3/_4$ cups; serves: 4 to 6

When my Aunt Emma made Risi e Bisi, she just stirred peas into white rice. This one, which is really risotto with peas, is more authentic.

2 cups vegetable broth (pages 93–95)
1 $^1/_4$ cups water
$^1/_3$ cup white wine
2 tablespoons olive oil
$^1/_4$ cup finely chopped onions
1 cup Arborio rice
1 cup peas (fresh, cooked; or frozen)
$^1/_3$ cup grated Parmesan cheese (optional)

1. In a 2-quart saucepan, heat the broth, water, and wine until simmering. Keep on low heat so that the liquids stay warm throughout the cooking time.

2. While the broth is heating, in a 3-quart saucepan, over medium heat, heat the oil. Add onions; cook, stirring, until transparent, about 1 minute. Add the rice; cook, stirring, until rice is coated with oil.

3. Add the broth to the rice mixture, $^1/_4$ cup at a time, stirring constantly, until the rice has absorbed the liquid. (You should make the next addition of liquid when you can draw a clear path on the bottom of the pot as you scrape through the rice with a wooden spoon. This will happen rather quickly at first and will take longer as you near the end of the cooking time.)

4. Stir in the peas and cheese, if desired; cook, stirring, until heated through.

Zucchini-Leek Melt

Makes: 6$^1/_2$ cups; serves: 4

This is an especially good dish to prepare in advance, then just pop into the oven for heating when guests arrive or the family gets home.

1 $^1/_2$ tablespoons butter or margarine
4 cups sliced zucchini
1 cup sliced leeks (white and light green parts only)
3 $^1/_2$ cups cooked brown rice
$^1/_3$ cup grated Parmesan cheese
1 $^1/_2$ cups shredded Swiss cheese

1. Preheat the oven to 375°F.

2. In a large skillet, melt the butter or margarine over medium-high heat. Add the zucchini and leeks; cook, stirring, until tender crisp, about 2 to 3 minutes.

3. In a buttered 9-inch-square pan, stir together the brown rice and Parmesan cheese. Top with zucchini mixture, then sprinkle with Swiss cheese.

4. Bake 25 minutes or until cheese is melted and casserole is heated through.

Variation: Use shredded Gouda instead of Swiss.

WILDLY STUFFED PEPPERS

Makes: 4 halves; serves: 4

Stuffed with wild rice and wild mushrooms, these can be served with the marinara sauce (homemade or prepared), as suggested in the recipe, or just plain. There is quite a lot of filling, enough to fill two halved large peppers or four small peppers. You can use cultivated white mushrooms instead of the wild ones, but the filling will be less wildly flavorful. In that case, opt for the broth instead of the water.

2 large or 4 small red or green bell peppers
2 tablespoons vegetable oil
1 cup chopped onions
2 cloves garlic, minced
1 1/2 cups chopped wild mushrooms
    (portobello, shiitake, or porcini)
1 tablespoon all-purpose flour
3/4 cup water or broth
1 1/2 cups cooked wild rice
1 cup cooked small pasta (such as orzo
    or ancini)
1/4 cup chopped fresh parsley
1/4 teaspoon dried thyme
1/4 teaspoon salt, or to taste
1/8 teaspoon pepper
2 cups marinara sauce (page 473) or store
    bought

1. Preheat the oven to 375°F.

2. If using large bell peppers, cut them in half through the stem, discard seeds and pith; or, if using small peppers, cut off the top with the stem, then remove seeds and pith. Blanch in boiling water 4 minutes; drain.

3. In a medium skillet, heat the oil over medium-high heat. Add the onions and garlic; cook, stirring, until softened, about 2 minutes. Add the mushrooms; cook, stirring, until

softened, about 3 minutes. Stir in the flour, then the water (or broth); cook, stirring until thickened. Add the wild rice, pasta, parsley, thyme, salt, and pepper. Spoon 1/4 of the mixture into each of the prepared pepper shells.

4. Pour the sauce into a 9-inch square pan. Place the stuffed peppers over the sauce. Bake 25 minutes or until filling is heated through.

Variation: Add 1/4 teaspoon crumbled dried rosemary when you add the other herbs.

SPICY, CHEESY MUSHROOMS AND BARLEY

Makes: 4 cups; serves: 4

The barley in this dish is slightly al dente. For softer barley you may want to use slightly more water and cook until absorbed. The cheese makes a wonderful velvety sauce.

1 tablespoon vegetable oil
1 1/2 cups sliced white mushrooms
1/2 cup chopped onions
2 1/2 cups water
1 cup pearled barley, rinsed
1 1/2 cups shredded jalapeño Monterey Jack
    cheese
3/4 teaspoon salt, or to taste

1. In a 2-quart saucepan, heat the oil over medium-high heat. Add the mushrooms and onions; cook, stirring, until softened, about 3 minutes.

2. Add the water and bring to a boil. Stir in the barley. Reduce heat and simmer, covered, 40 minutes, or until liquid is absorbed.

3. Stir in the cheese until melted, and salt, if desired.

Variation: Use plain Monterey Jack cheese for a nonspicy version.

BARLEY-STUFFED PEPPERS

Makes: 4 peppers; serves: 4

I like these peppers with Parmesan cheese, as suggested in the variation.

2 large or 4 small green or red bell peppers
1 tablespoon vegetable oil
1/2 cup chopped onions
2 cloves garlic, minced
1 1/2 cups chopped tomatoes
1/4 cup snipped fresh dill
1/4 cup chopped fresh parsley
3 cups cooked barley (pages 301, 302)
1/2 teaspoon salt, or to taste
1/4 teaspoon pepper

1. Preheat the oven to 375°F.

2. If using large peppers, cut them in half through the stem, discard seeds and pith; or, if using small peppers, cut off the top with the stem, then remove seeds and pith. Blanch in boiling water 4 minutes; drain.

3. In a medium skillet, heat the oil over medium-high heat. Add the onions and garlic; cook, stirring, until softened, about 2 minutes. Add the tomatoes, dill, and parsley. Cook, stirring until tomatoes are softened, about 3 minutes. Stir in the barley, salt, and pepper. Spoon 1/4 of the barley mixture into each of the prepared pepper shells.

4. Bake 20 minutes or until filling is heated through.

Variation: Add 1/4 cup grated Parmesan cheese when you add the barley.

BARLEY WITH VEGETABLES

Makes: 5 cups; serves: 4 to 6

You can use a 10-ounce package of frozen chopped spinach instead of the fresh.

1 tablespoon vegetable oil
1 cup chopped onions
1 cup chopped celery
2 1/2 cups vegetable broth (pages 93–95)
1 cup barley, rinsed
1 cup chopped carrots
4 cups spinach, in bite-size pieces
1/3 cup grated Parmesan cheese (optional)
1/4 teaspoon pepper

1. In a 2-quart saucepan, heat the oil over medium-high heat. Add the onions, and celery; cook, stirring, until softened, about 3 minutes. Add the broth and bring to a boil.

2. Add the barley; return to a boil. Reduce heat and simmer, covered, 30 minutes. Add the carrots and spinach; simmer, covered, 15 minutes longer.

3. Stir in cheese, if desired, and pepper.

Variation: Stir in one cup fresh or frozen peas when you add the spinach.

CORN AND MILLET CASSEROLE

[V] [♥]

Makes: 2³/₄ cups; serves: 4 to 6

This is a kind of brunchy, lunchy entree; it also makes a good side dish.

³/₄ cup water
2 tablespoons sugar
¹/₂ teaspoon salt, or to taste
¹/₄ cup cornmeal
1¹/₂ teaspoons vegetable oil
¹/₂ cup finely chopped onions
¹/₂ cup finely chopped green bell peppers
1 tablespoon minced jalapeño pepper
1¹/₂ cups cooked millet (page 301)
1 cup corn kernels (fresh, cooked; canned, drained; or frozen)
3 tablespoons chopped fresh cilantro

1. Preheat the oven to 350°F. Heavily grease a 1-quart casserole dish.

2. In a 1-quart saucepan, stir together the water, sugar, and salt. Stir in the cornmeal. Cook over medium-high heat, stirring, until mixture comes to a boil. Set aside.

3. In a small skillet, heat the oil over medium-high heat. Add the onions and both types of peppers. Cook, stirring, until softened about 2 to 3 minutes.

4. Stir the onion-pepper mixture, millet, corn, and cilantro into the cornmeal mixture. Spoon into prepared pan.

5. Bake 1 hour, or until browned around the edges.

Variation: Substitute ¹/₈ teaspoon ground red pepper for the jalapeño.

LENTIL BURGERS

[V]

Makes: 4 patties; Serves: 4

Serve these on a bun, like a regular burger, or on a plate with a sauce, such as Tomato–Red Pepper Sauce (page 474).

1 tablespoon vegetable oil
1 cup chopped mushrooms
¹/₂ cup chopped onions
1 cup cooked lentils (pages 13–14)
1 tablespoon soy sauce
¹/₂ cup cooked barley (pages 301, 302)
¹/₃ cup finely chopped walnuts
2 tablespoons bread crumbs
¹/₄ teaspoon pepper
Additional vegetable oil

1. In a medium skillet, heat 1 tablespoon oil over medium-high heat. Add the mushrooms and onions; cook, stirring, until softened, about 3 minutes. Reduce heat to low; add the lentils and soy sauce. Mash with fork; continue cooking until a film forms on the pan.

2. Remove from heat. Stir in the barley, walnuts, bread crumbs, and pepper. Let cool.

3. Form into 4 patties. Chill at least 1 hour.

4. Pour ¹/₄ inch oil into a large skillet. Heat over medium-high heat until the oil bubbles when a few bread crumbs are dropped in. Cook patties until browned and crusty on bottom; turn and cook on second side.

Variation: Use chopped pecans instead of walnuts.

VEGETABLES

ATAKILT ACILCH'A (ETHIOPIAN VEGETABLE STEW)

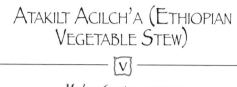

Makes: 6 cups; serves: 4

I usually like my vegetables tender-crisp; however, the long cooking time gives this vegetable dish a very sweet flavor. Ethiopian dishes are usually served on a large spongy crepe called injera, and the crepe is also used for picking up the food. Feel free to use spoons and/or forks and plates and serve the stew with warm pita bread instead.

3 tablespoons vegetable oil
4 cups coarsely chopped cabbage
3 cups chopped onion
3 cloves garlic, minced
1 teaspoon turmeric
2 cups water
2 tablespoons tomato paste
3 cups carrot chunks (1½- to 2-inch pieces)
3 cups green beans (whole or halved; ¾ pound)
1½ cups potato chunks (I use red bliss or other boiling potatoes)
½ teaspoon salt, or to taste
¼ teaspoon pepper

1. In a 6-quart pot, heat the oil over medium-high heat. Add the cabbage, onion, and garlic. Cook, stirring, until wilted, about 4 minutes. Stir in the turmeric until absorbed.

2. Add the water and tomato paste; stir until combined. Add the carrots and green beans. Bring to a boil. Reduce heat and simmer, covered, 1¼ hours. Add the potatoes, salt, and pepper; simmer, covered, 25 to 30 minutes longer. If necessary add ¼ cup additional water.

Variation: You can vary the vegetables to your taste. Use green peas, turnips, squash (but add squash when you add the potatoes), or any other you like.

FAJITAS

Makes: 8 fajitas; serves: 4

You can serve these vegetables over rice instead of rolled in tortillas.

1 tablespoon vegetable oil
1 tablespoon fresh lime juice
1 teaspoon chili powder
1 teaspoon dried oregano
¼ teaspoon ground cumin
2 large cloves garlic, minced
⅛ teaspoon salt, or to taste
6 cups cut vegetables (such as zucchini, yellow squash, or eggplant)
Eight 7-inch flour tortillas
½ cup salsa

1. In a large bowl, stir together the oil, lime juice, chili powder, oregano, cumin, garlic, and salt. Add the vegetables and toss to coat; let marinate at least 1 hour.

2. Preheat the broiler. Line a pan with foil; cook vegetables until desired doneness, turning once.

3. Warm the tortillas on the grill or in the oven. Place ½ cup of the vegetables in the center of each tortilla, top each with 1 tablespoon salsa. Fold one side over the vegetables, then roll to form a tube.

Variation: Top vegetables with 2 tablespoons guacamole (you'll need 1 cup total for the recipe) before adding salsa.

Indonesian Vegetable Stew

Makes: 5 cups; serves: 3 to 4

I like to serve this vegetable dish on jasmine rice, and to include the tofu suggested in the variation. It makes the meal seem more complete.

3 tablespoons distilled white vinegar
3 shallots, quartered
1 tablespoon minced fresh ginger
4 cloves garlic
2 teaspoons paprika
2 teaspoons sugar
1½ teaspoons ground turmeric
½ teaspoon salt, or to taste
3 tablespoons vegetable oil
2 cups julienned carrots
1½ cups julienned celery
1 cup julienned green bell peppers
1 seeded, slivered jalapeño pepper
3 cups whole green beans, trimmed (about ¾ pound)
¾ cup canned or homemade unsweetened coconut milk (page 497)
2 tablespoons peanut butter

1. Place the vinegar, shallots, ginger, garlic, paprika, sugar, turmeric, and salt into a blender container. Cover and blend until smooth.

2. In a wok or large skillet, heat the oil over high heat. Add the spice paste; cook, stirring, 30 seconds. Add the carrots, celery, both kinds of peppers, and the beans. Cook, stirring, until vegetables are tender-crisp, about 3 minutes.

3. Add the coconut milk and peanut butter to the blender container (with any spices that remain). Cover and blend until combined. Add the blender mixture to the skillet and deglaze the bottom of the pan. Cook, covered, 3 to 5 minutes or until the vegetables reach desired consistency.

4. Remove the cover and cook, stirring, until vegetables are tender and sauce is thickened.

Variation: Stir julienned baked tofu (page 217) into the vegetables just after you uncover the skillet.

Spasta

Makes: 6 cups; serves: 4

The Boulevard, a restaurant in my neighborhood, serves this extremely delicious dish. This is my version. You can make everything from scratch, or you can use prepared sauces—both marinara and pesto—on vegetables you've sautéed.

1 large spaghetti squash (2 pounds)
2 tablespoons pine nuts (pignoli)
1 recipe Pesto Vegetables (page 291)
2 to 3 cups marinara sauce (page 473)

1. Bake the spaghetti squash at 350°F, 1 hour and 15 minutes or until tender.

2. While squash is baking, toast the pine nuts in a dry skillet over medium heat until lightly browned, about 1 minute.

3. Prepare Sautéed Pesto Vegetables.

4. Prepare marinara sauce, or heat purchased sauce.

5. When the squash is tender, cut in half widthwise; discard seeds. Using a fork, scrape the flesh into a bowl, pulling into "spaghetti" strands.

6. Spread ¼ of the marinara sauce around the edge of each of 4 dinner plates. Place ¼ of the squash in the center of each plate. Top with ¼ of Sautéed Pesto Vegetables. Top each with ¼ of the toasted pine nuts.

Variation: Spaghettti Squash with Tomato Sauce: Omit the Sautéed Pesto Vegetables and pine nuts; serve with 3 cups marinara sauce.

Spaghetti Squash Provençal

V ♥

Makes: 7 cups squash and 4 cups sauce;
serves: 4 to 6

The zucchini and yellow squash are basically
interchangeable in this recipe, so if you have lots of
one or the other, just use it. Similarly, you can use
either red or green bell pepper instead of both.

2 spaghetti squash (1 1/4 pounds each)
1 tablespoon olive oil
1 cup chopped onions
2 cloves garlic, minced
1/2 cup green bell pepper strips
1/2 cup red bell pepper strips
One 28-ounce can whole tomatoes in thick
    puree, undrained
1 1/2 cups sliced zucchini
1 1/2 cups sliced yellow squash
2 tablespoons Galiano, anisette, or orange
    liqueur (optional)
1/2 teaspoon dried basil
1/2 teaspoon dried rosemary, crumbled
1/2 teaspoon grated orange rind
1/4 teaspoon dried savory
1/4 teaspoon dried thyme
1/4 teaspoon salt, or to taste
1/4 teaspoon pepper

1. Preheat the oven to 350°F. Bake the
spaghetti squash 1 hour 15 minutes or until
tender. Cut in half; discard seeds. Using a fork,
scrape the flesh into a bowl, pulling into
"spaghetti" strands.

2. While the squash is baking, in a 3-quart
saucepan, heat the oil over medium-high heat.
Add the onions and garlic; cook, stirring, until
onions are transparent, about 2 minutes. Stir in
the bell peppers; cook, stirring, until softened,
about 3 minutes.

3. Add the undrained tomatoes and break
them up with the back of a spoon. Stir in the
remaining ingredients.

4. Bring to a boil. Reduce heat and simmer,
uncovered, 35 minutes or until sauce is thickened. Serve over spaghetti squash.

Variation: Add 1 cup sliced carrots to the
sauce when you add the zucchini.

Spaghetti Squash with Bulgur Marinara Sauce

V

Makes: 5 1/2 cups; serves: 4

This is one recipe where I usually use prepared
marinara sauce. Of course, if you prefer home-
made marinara, I think the Garlic Marinara
(page xxx) would work well with this recipe.

1 medium spaghetti squash (1 1/2 pounds)
2 cups marinara sauce
1/2 recipe Bulgur with Summer Squash
    (page 165)

1. Preheat the oven to 350°F. Bake the
spaghetti squash 1 hour 15 minutes or until
tender. Cut in half; discard seeds. Using a fork,
scrape the flesh into a bowl, pulling into
"spaghetti" strands.

2. In a 3-quart pot, heat the marinara sauce to
boiling. Add the bulgur with vegetables and
spaghetti squash. Cook, tossing, until heated
through.

Variation: Use 1 cup plain cooked bulgur
(page 302) instead of the Bulgur with
Summer Squash.

BUTTERNUT SQUASH WITH CURRIED MILLET FILLING

L ♥

Makes: 4 stuffed squash halves; serves: 4

You can use any of the chutneys in the relish chapter (pages 468–97), or you can use a commercially available chutney such as Major Grey's mango chutney. This stuffing works well with acorn squash, buttercup squash, and dumpling squash (although dumpling squash are so small that you should allow 2 halves per person).

Two 2-pound butternut squash, halved and seeded
1 tablespoon vegetable oil
½ cup chopped onions
2 teaspoons curry powder
½ teaspoon ground cinnamon
⅛ teaspoon ground red pepper
3 cups cooked millet (page 301)
⅓ cup golden or dark raisins
⅓ cup chopped cashews
⅓ cup unflavored yogurt
¼ cup cooked peas (fresh or frozen)
¼ cup chopped chutney

1. Preheat the oven to 350°F. Place squash on a baking sheet and bake 30 minutes.

2. While the squash is baking, heat the oil in a large skillet over medium-high heat. Add the onions; cook, stirring, until softened, about 2 minutes. Stir in the curry powder, cinnamon, and red pepper until absorbed.

3. Remove skillet from heat and stir in the millet, raisins, cashews, yogurt, peas, and chutney.

4. Place ¼ of the millet mixture into the hollows of the 4 squash halves. Return to oven and bake 30 minutes more or until stuffing is heated through and squash halves are tender.

Variation: For a quicker filling, use cooked couscous instead of millet.

SWEET AND SOUR STUFFED CABBAGE

O

Makes: 8 cabbage rolls; serves: 4

I think the sweet and sour flavors complement the kasha, but if you don't like the flavor of buckwheat, you can substitute cooked bulgur for the kasha.

Filling:
1 egg
1½ cups cooked kasha (page 303)
½ cup finely chopped walnuts
½ cup finely chopped dried apricots
⅛ teaspoon salt, or to taste
1 large head cabbage

Sauce:
1 tablespoon vegetable oil
1 cup chopped onions
2 cloves garlic, minced
½ teaspoon ground cinnamon
¼ teaspoon ground ginger
One 28-ounce can crushed tomatoes
2 cups water
One 2-pound package sauerkraut, drained
½ cup golden or dark raisins
½ cup firmly packed light brown or dark brown sugar

1. For the filling, in a medium bowl, beat the egg. Stir in the kasha, walnuts, apricots, and salt.

2. Cook the cabbage in boiling water until the outer leaves are pliable. Place in cool water; drain. Carefully peel 8 of the outer leaves off the head of the cabbage.

3. Place a cabbage leaf on a flat surface. Place ¼ cup filling on the leaf near the stem end. Fold the stem over the top of the filling, then fold the two sides over the filling. Roll up. Repeat with remaining leaves.

4. For the sauce, in a large pot (at least 6 quarts), heat the oil over medium-high heat. Add the onion and garlic; cook, stirring, until onions are transparent, about 2 minutes. Stir in the cinnamon and ginger. Add the tomatoes, water, sauerkraut, raisins, and brown sugar; stir until combined.

5. Place the cabbage rolls in the sauce. Bring to a boil. Reduce heat and simmer, uncovered, 1 hour.

Variation: Use an additional ¹/₂ cup raisins in the filling instead of the dried apricots.

Bulgur-Stuffed Eggplant

Makes: 4 eggplant halves; serves: 4

Substitute cooked brown rice for the bulgur and the result is equally good, but then it's no longer called Bulgur-stuffed Eggplant.

2 medium eggplants (1 pound each)
1 tablespoon vegetable oil
1 cup chopped onions
³/₄ cup chopped green bell peppers
1 cup chopped zucchini
¹/₄ cup chopped fresh parsley
³/₄ teaspoon dried rosemary, crushed
¹/₂ teaspoon dried basil
¹/₄ teaspoon dried thyme
¹/₄ teaspoon salt, or to taste
¹/₄ teaspoon pepper
¹/₄ cup white wine
2 cups cooked bulgur (page 302)

1. Preheat the oven to 350°F.

2. Cut the eggplants in half lengthwise. Scoop out and chop the flesh, leaving about ¹/₄ inch of flesh in the eggplant shells.

3. Place the eggplant shells in the oven and bake 20 minutes.

4. Heat the oil in a large skillet. Add the chopped eggplant, onions, and bell peppers. Cook, stirring, until softened, about 3 minutes. Add the zucchini; cook, stirring, until softened, about 2 minutes. Stir in the parsley, rosemary, basil, thyme, salt, and pepper. Stir in the wine, then the bulgur.

5. Place ¹/₄ of the filling into each eggplant shell. Bake 20 minutes or until heated through.

Ⓛ **Variation**: Add 2 cups shredded Monterey Jack or Swiss cheese to the filling before stuffing the shells.

QUINOA-STUFFED EGGPLANTS

— V —

Makes: 2 eggplant halves; serves: 2

The fluffy quinoa is well suited to the fruit-and-herb combination.

1 medium eggplant (1 1/4 pound)
2 tablespoons vegetable oil
1 cup chopped, peeled apples
3/4 cup chopped onions
1/2 cup chopped celery
1/4 cup chopped fresh parsley
1/4 teaspoon dried rosemary, crushed
1/4 teaspoon dried sage, crushed
1/4 teaspoon salt, or to taste
1/4 teaspoon pepper
1 cup cooked quinoa (page 301)

1. Preheat the oven to 350°F.

2. Cut the eggplant in half lengthwise. Scoop out and chop the flesh, leaving about 1/4 inch of flesh in the eggplant shells.

3. Place the eggplant shells in the oven and bake 20 minutes.

4. Heat the oil in a large skillet. Add the chopped eggplant, apples, onions, and celery. Cook, stirring, until softened, about 4 minutes. Stir in the parsley, rosemary, sage, salt, and pepper. Stir in the quinoa.

5. Place 1/4 of the filling into each eggplant shell. Bake 20 minutes or until heated through.

Variation: Add 1 cup chopped walnuts when you add the quinoa.

TURKISH STUFFED EGGPLANT

— V ♥ —

Makes: 4 eggplant halves; serves: 2 to 4

I don't know if this is a Turkish dish or not, but I used Turkish apricots in it, hence the name. If you don't want to use brown rice, you can substitute couscous or bulgur.

2 small eggplants (about 3/4 pound each)
1 1/2 tablespoons vegetable oil
1 cup chopped onions
2 cups cooked brown rice (page 303)
1/2 cup chopped dried apricots
1/3 cup dried currants
1/4 teaspoon salt, or to taste
1/8 teaspoon pepper

1. Preheat the oven to 350°F.

2. Cut eggplants in half lengthwise. Scoop out the flesh, leaving about 1/4 inch of flesh in the eggplant shells. Dice the scooped eggplant into 1/2-inch pieces. (You should have 3 cups of diced eggplant).

3. Place the eggplant shells onto a baking dish and bake 20 minutes.

4. While the shells are baking, heat the oil in a large skillet over medium-high heat. Add the onions; cook, stirring until softened, about 2 minutes. Add diced eggplant; cook, stirring, until tender, about 3 minutes. Stir in the rice, apricots, currants, salt, and pepper.

5. Place 1/4 of the rice mixture into each of the eggplant halves.

6. Place on baking sheet and cover with aluminum foil. Bake 20 minutes or until heated through.

Variation: Add 1/2 cup chopped walnuts when you add the rice.

MEDITERRANEAN EGGPLANT

— L —

Makes: 3 cups; serves: 3 to 4

Fresh herbs really contribute to the subtle flavors of this dish; they're worth the effort, if you can find them. Serve this with polenta or couscous.

2 tablespoons olive oil
4 cups cubed eggplant (¾-inch pieces)
4 cloves garlic, minced (almost a tablespoon)
3 tablespoons white wine
2 tablespoons dry vermouth
4 cups chopped, peeled, seeded tomatoes
¼ cup chopped fresh parsley
2 teaspoons chopped fresh oregano, or
    ½ teaspoon dried oregano
½ teaspoon chopped fresh rosemary, or
    ⅛ teaspoon dried rosemary
½ cup crumbled feta cheese
⅛ teaspoon salt, or to taste
⅛ teaspoon ground red pepper

1. In a large skillet, heat the oil over medium-high heat. Add the eggplant and garlic; cook, stirring, until oil is absorbed, about 1 minute.

2. Add the wine and vermouth; cook, stirring, until eggplant is softened, about 3 minutes. Add the tomatoes, parsley, oregano, and rosemary. Cook over medium heat, uncovered, 10 minutes or until all the vegetables are cooked through. Add the feta cheese, salt, and red pepper.

V **Variation:** Omit the cheese and add 1 to 1½ cups cooked chickpeas when you add the tomatoes.

EGGPLANT WITH RED PEPPERS AND SHIITAKE MUSHROOMS

— V —

Makes: 5 cups; serves: 4

I usually serve this over couscous, but it also makes a great pasta sauce. I like to use it with penne, rigatoni, or similar medium-sized pasta.

2 tablespoons vegetable oil
1 cup chopped onions
2 cups sliced red bell peppers
1 clove garlic, minced
6 cups cubed, unpeeled eggplant (1-inch pieces; ¾ pound)
2 cups coarsely chopped shiitake mushrooms
1 tablespoon all-purpose flour
½ cup vegetable broth (pages 93–95)
¼ cup port wine or Madeira
1½ tablespoons dry sherry
1 tablespoon red wine vinegar
2 tablespoons chopped fresh parsley
⅛ teaspoon pepper

1. In a large skillet, heat the oil over medium-high heat. Add the onions, bell peppers, and garlic; cook, stirring, until softened, about 3 minutes.

2. Add the eggplant and mushrooms; cook, stirring, until softened, about 3 minutes. Stir in the flour until absorbed.

3. Stir in the broth, wine, sherry, and vinegar. Stir in the parsley and pepper. Cook, stirring, until mixture comes to a boil and sauce is thickened.

Variation: Use green bell peppers instead of the red and/or sliced cultivated mushrooms instead of the shiitake.

Mozzarella Baked Eggplant and Zucchini

Makes: one 9-inch-square; serves: 4 to 6

Even when you let this dish stand after cooking, there tends to be a fair amount of liquid in the bottom of the baking dish; just spoon some of the sauce over each serving as you dish it out. I like to use the Garlic Tomato Sauce (page 473) for this recipe, but store-bought is okay, too. Serve this with garlic bread (page 428).

1 medium eggplant (1½ pounds)
2¼ cups marinara sauce, divided
¼ cup chopped fresh basil, divided
1½ cups shredded mozzarella cheese
½ cup grated Parmesan cheese
1½ cups sliced zucchini

1. Preheat the oven to 375°F. Grease a 9-inch-square baking dish.

2. Cut the eggplant into ½-inch-thick slices. Layer ½ of the slices on the bottom of the dish. Top with ½ cup of the sauce and 1 tablespoon of the basil.

3. Toss together the mozzarella and Parmesan. Sprinkle ⅔ cup of the cheese mixture over the sauce.

4. Layer the zucchini over the cheese. Top with ¾ cup of the sauce, 2 tablespoons of the basil, and ⅔ cup of the cheese mixture.

5. Top with remaining eggplant slices and the remaining sauce, basil, and cheese mixture.

6. Cover with aluminum foil and bake 15 minutes. Uncover and bake 25 minutes longer. Let stand 10 minutes to set before serving.

Grilled Vegetable Parmesan

Makes: 8 cups; serves: 4 to 6

This recipe is slightly lower in fat than usual, because you grill the vegetables instead of frying them. You can further lower the fat content by using part-skim mozzarella.

3 cups tomato sauce (homemade, page xxx, or prepared)
6 cups grilled sliced eggplant and/or zucchini
2 cups shredded mozzarella cheese (about 8 ounces)
2 tablespoons grated Parmesan cheese

1. Preheat the oven to 350°F.

2. Spread 1 cup sauce into the bottom of an 8-inch-square pan. Layer 3 cups of the grilled vegetables in the pan. Top with 1 cup more sauce. Sprinkle with 1 cup of the mozzarella. Layer the remaining vegetables, then the sauce, then the mozzarella. Sprinkle with Parmesan.

3. Bake 40 minutes or until heated through.

EGGPLANT PARMIGIANA

Makes: about 7 cups; serves: 4 to 6

This is a really delicious Eggplant Parmigiana. However, the fat content is pretty high because you fry the eggplant before putting it into the baking dish. For a slightly lower-fat version, make the Grilled Vegetable Parmesan (page 170) and substitute it for the fried eggplant in this recipe.

1 large eggplant (1 1/2 pounds)
3 eggs
3 tablespoons water
1/3 cup all-purpose flour
1/8 teaspoon salt, or to taste
Oil for deep frying
2 cups marinara sauce, divided
2 cups shredded mozzarella cheese
   (about 8 ounces)
1/3 cup grated Parmesan cheese, divided

1. Preheat the oven to 375°F.

2. Cut the eggplant into 1/4-inch-thick slices.

3. In a large, shallow bowl, beat the eggs with the water. Using a whisk, stir in the flour and salt until smooth.

4. In a large skillet, heat the oil over medium heat until it bubbles when a drop of batter is tossed in.

5. Dip 3 or 4 of the eggplant slices into the batter, then fry in a single layer until browned on the bottom. Turn and cook until browned on second side. Remove from skillet and drain on paper towels. Repeat with remaining eggplant slices until all are fried.

6. Spread 1/2 cup of the sauce in the bottom of a 9 × 13 × 2-inch baking pan. Layer 1/2 of the slices on the bottom of the pan. Top with 1 cup of the sauce, spreading to cover the eggplant slices. Sprinkle 1 cup of the mozzarella over the sauce and top with 2 tablespoons of the Parmesan.

7. Place the remaining eggplant slices over the cheese and spread the remaining 1/2 cup of the sauce over the eggplant. Sprinkle the remaining 1 cup of mozzarella over the sauce. Sprinkle with the remaining Parmesan.

8. Cover with aluminum foil and bake 20 to 25 minutes or until heated through and the cheese has melted.

EGGPLANT ROLLATINI

Makes: 12 rollatini; serves: 4 to 6

This is similar to manicotti, but instead of pasta tubes you use cooked sliced eggplant to hold the cheese filling.

2 to 3 medium eggplants, unpeeled
    (each about 7 inches long)
Salt

Sauce:
1 tablespoon olive oil
³/₄ cup chopped onions
2 cloves garlic, minced
One 14¹/₂-ounce can whole peeled tomatoes,
    undrained
3 tablespoons tomato paste
¹/₄ teaspoon salt, or to taste
²/₃ cup heavy cream

Filling:
One 15-ounce container ricotta cheese
1 cup shredded mozzarella cheese
¹/₄ cup chopped fresh parsley
3 tablespoons grated Parmesan cheese
1 clove garlic, minced
¹/₈ teaspoon pepper
Oil for frying (optional method)

1. Cut the eggplants lengthwise into 12 slices (¹/₈- to ¹/₄-inch thick). Discard the end slices that are mostly skin. Salt each slice lightly and place in a colander to drain while you cook the sauce.

2. To prepare the sauce: In a 2-quart saucepan, heat the 1 tablespoon oil over medium-high heat. Add the onions and 2 cloves minced garlic; cook, stirring, until softened, about 2 minutes. Add the tomatoes, with liquid, and break them up with the back of a spoon. Stir in the tomato paste and ¹/₄ teaspoon salt. Bring

to a boil. Reduce heat and simmer, uncovered, 20 minutes, stirring occasionally. Place sauce in a blender. (A blender is better than a food processor for this recipe, but if you only have a processor, that will do—just get the sauce as smooth as possible.) Cover and blend until smooth. Return to pot and stir in cream; set aside.

3. While the sauce is simmering, preheat the oven to 375°F and prepare the filling. In a medium bowl, stir together the ricotta, mozzarella, parsley, Parmesan, 1 clove minced garlic, and the pepper; set aside.

4. Rinse the salt off each slice of eggplant; pat dry. Cook the eggplant slices by frying them in oil (which they soak up like a sponge) or broiling them (see page 255). The cooking method doesn't matter; it's just important that the eggplant be completely cooked, because it doesn't soften more in the baking.

5. Place 3 tablespoons of the filling on the thick end of each of the eggplant slices; roll to completely encase the filling.

6. Pour 1 cup of the sauce into the bottom of a 10³/₄ × 7 × 1¹/₂-inch baking dish (if you don't have this size dish, a 9-inch-square baking dish should do). Place the rolls, seam down, into the dish. Top with the remaining sauce. Bake, uncovered, 15 minutes at 375°F, or until cheese is heated through and slightly runny.

♥ *Variation:* Broil the eggplant, omit the cream from the sauce (it tastes good even without the cream), and use part-skim ricotta and mozzarella.

Ragout of Wild Mushrooms
V ♥

Makes: 5 cups; serves: 4 to 6

*I like this very much served with Basic Polenta
(page 307). Although I found that this particular
combination of mushrooms worked extremely well,
you can substitute portobello, crimini, or the like.*

1 tablespoon butter or margarine
1 tablespoon vegetable oil
12 small white onions (peeled)
2 cups oyster mushrooms
2 cups white mushrooms
2 cups shiitake mushrooms
2 tablespoons all-purpose flour
2 cups vegetable broth (pages 93–95)
3 cups carrot chunks (1-inch pieces)
1/2 cup chopped fresh parsley
2 tablespoons brandy (optional)
1 tablespoon dry sherry (optional)
1 tablespoon Madeira (optional)
1/2 teaspoon sugar
1/4 teaspoon dried rosemary, crumbled
1/4 teaspoon dried thyme
1/8 teaspoon salt, or to taste
1/8 teaspoon pepper

1. In a 3-quart saucepan melt the butter or
margarine with the oil over medium-high heat.
Add the onions; cook, stirring occasionally, until
browned in spots, about 4 minutes.

2. While the onions are browning, toss all the
mushrooms in the flour until lightly coated.
Add to the saucepan; cook, stirring, until mushrooms are softened, about 3 minutes. Add the
broth, carrots, parsley, brandy, sherry, Madeira,
sugar, rosemary, and thyme. Bring to a boil.
Reduce heat and simmer, uncovered, 1 hour 15
minutes. Stir in salt and pepper.

Variation: Add 1 1/2 cups cubed potatoes to
the pot 25 minutes before the stew has
finished cooking.

Mushrooms Stroganoff
L

Makes: 2 1/2 cups; serves: 4

*I use portobello mushrooms for this dish
because they are large and meaty. I slice them
into strips similar to the pieces of meat used in
traditional Beef Stroganoff. I like to serve this
with broad noodles, although rice is probably
more traditional.*

1/4 cup sour cream
1/4 cup unflavored yogurt
1 teaspoon Dijon mustard
2 tablespoons snipped fresh dill
1/8 teaspoon salt, or to taste
1/8 teaspoon pepper
6 medium portobello mushrooms (5 to 6
    inches in diameter; 1 1/4 pounds total)
2 tablespoons butter or margarine
2 tablespoons minced onion
2 tablespoons all-purpose flour
1/2 cup vegetable broth (pages 93–95)

1. In a small bowl, stir together the sour cream,
yogurt, mustard, dill, salt, and pepper.

2. Slice the mushrooms into 1/4-inch-thick
strips.

3. In a large skillet, melt the butter or margarine over medium-high heat. Add the mushrooms and onion; cook, stirring, until soft, about
6 minutes.

4. Stir in the flour until absorbed. Stir in the
broth to deglaze the pan. Cook, stirring, until
broth boils. Stir in the sour cream mixture.
Cook, stirring, until heated through, about
1 minute longer.

Variation: Omit the dill and substitute
1/4 cup chopped fresh parsley.

Mushroom Paprikash with Dumplings

Makes: 5 cups stew (3 cups dumplings); serves: 4

Hungarian food is "home cooking" to me, but all the paprikashes and goulashes Mom prepared were made with beef and/or poultry. This paprikash is just as good as any prepared with meat.

Stew:

1/2 cup sour cream
2 teaspoons all-purpose flour
1/4 teaspoon pepper
1/8 teaspoon salt, or to taste
2 tablespoons vegetable oil
1 1/2 cups chopped onions
3 cloves garlic, minced
1 1/2 tablespoons paprika
7 cups quartered white mushrooms
    (two 10-ounce containers)
1 cup vegetable broth (pages 93–95)

Dumplings:

3 eggs
3/4 cup all-purpose flour
1/3 cup whole wheat flour
2 tablespoons vegetable oil
1 teaspoon salt

1. For the stew, in a small bowl, stir together the sour cream, 2 teaspoons flour, the pepper and 1/8 teaspoon salt. Set aside.

2. In a 4-quart saucepan, heat 2 tablespoons oil over medium-high heat. Add the onions and garlic; cook, stirring, until softened, about 2 minutes. Add the paprika; cook, stirring, until absorbed.

3. Add the mushrooms and stir until coated with the paprika mixture. Add the broth and bring to a boil. Reduce heat and simmer, uncovered, 20 minutes.

4. While the mushrooms are cooking, prepare the dumplings. In a medium bowl, beat the eggs. Add both flours, 2 tablespoons oil, and 1 teaspoon salt. Stir until completely combined. Drop the dumplings by rounded teaspoonsful into a large pot of boiling water. Let boil over high heat until the dumplings rise to the top of the water. Remove from pot with slotted spoon. (Makes 24 to 30 dumplings.)

5. Add the dumplings to the cooked mushrooms. Stir in the sour cream mixture. Cook until heated through.

♥ **Variation:** Substitute unflavored yogurt for the sour cream.

Tuscan Torta Di Funghi e Patate

— V —

Makes: one 8-inch pie; serves: 6

This very impressive entree will bring oohs and aahs from your guests, but be sure to observe the standing time after baking. Cutting into the torte early will leave you with a runny mess.

Olive oil pastry dough for two-crust pie
 (page 517)
4 cups peeled, thinly sliced baking potatoes
2 tablespoons olive oil
2 cups sliced onions
3 cloves garlic, minced
3 cups sliced wild mushrooms (such as
 shiitake, portobello, porcini, or crimini)
2 cups sliced white mushrooms
1/3 cup chopped fresh parsley
1/2 teaspoon dried sage leaves, crumbled
1 tablespoon butter or margarine
1 1/2 tablespoons all-purpose flour
1 cup vegetable broth (pages xxx–xxx)
1 teaspoon salt, or to taste
1/4 teaspoon pepper

1. Preheat the oven to 350°F.

2. Divide dough into 2 pieces, one about 2/3 and the other 1/3 of the dough. Roll the larger piece into a 14-inch circle. Fit dough into the bottom and up the side of an 8-inch springform pan. Roll out the second piece of dough into a 9- to 10-inch circle; set aside.

3. Cook the potato slices in boiling water for 5 minutes; drain. Set aside.

4. In a large skillet, heat the oil over medium-high heat. Add the onions and garlic; cook, stirring until softened, about 2 minutes. Add both kinds of mushrooms; cook, stirring, until softened, about 4 minutes. If mushrooms release liquid, cook until liquid has evaporated. Stir in parsley and sage.

5. In a 1-quart saucepan, melt the butter or margarine over medium-high heat. Stir in the flour until absorbed. Stir in the broth, salt, and pepper. Cook, stirring constantly, until mixture comes to a boil; set aside.

6. Layer 1/3 of the mushroom mixture in the bottom of the pastry. Top with 1/2 of the potatoes, making an overlapping layer. Top with half of the remaining mushrooms, then with remaining potatoes, and finally top with remaining mushrooms. Pour sauce over the mushrooms.

7. Place second crust over mushrooms and make slits to vent. Seal edges by crimping the dough attractively.

8. Bake 1 hour 15 minutes or until crust is lightly browned. Let stand 20 minutes before serving.

Variation: You can use oregano or basil or any other herb of choice in place of the sage.

SPANAKOPITA

Makes: 24 pieces; serves: 8 to 14

This also makes a wonderful appetizer—just cut it into smaller pieces. Also, you can reheat this for 10 to 15 minutes at 350°F and the layers will recrisp nicely.

1 tablespoon olive oil
1½ cups chopped onions
2 cloves garlic, minced
2 eggs
1½ cups (12 ounces) ricotta cheese
One 8-ounce package feta cheese, crumbled
Two 10-ounce packages frozen chopped spinach, thawed and squeezed dry
²/₃ to ¾ cup plain bread crumbs, divided
3 tablespoons snipped fresh dill
⅛ teaspoon salt, or to taste
⅛ teaspoon pepper
16 sheets phyllo dough (12 × 17 inches)
½ cup melted butter or margarine

1. Preheat the oven to 350°F.

2. In a large skillet, heat the oil over medium-high heat. Add the onions and garlic; cook, stirring, until softened, about 2 minutes.

3. In a medium bowl, beat the eggs. Beat in the ricotta and feta. Stir in the onion mixture, spinach, 2 tablespoons of the bread crumbs, the dill, salt, and pepper; set aside.

4. Remove the thawed phyllo sheets from the package. (Reseal the package tightly so that remaining sheets won't dry out.) Place 1 sheet on a flat surface. Brush with butter or margarine and sprinkle with about 2 teaspoons of the bread crumbs.

5. Place the next phyllo sheet on top of the first, brush with more butter or margarine, and sprinkle with bread crumbs, as before. Repeat with the third through seventh sheets. Place the eighth sheet of phyllo on top of the stack, but don't brush with butter or margarine or sprinkle with crumbs.

6. Fit the stack of phyllo into a greased 9 × 13 × 2-inch pan. Spoon the spinach-cheese filling onto the phyllo and spread to the edges. On a flat surface, layer the remaining sheets of phyllo, brushing butter or margarine and sprinkling with bread crumbs between each layer, as in step 5. Place on top of the spinach filling, and tuck edges into the pan. Using a sharp knife, score the top layers of phyllo dough into 2-inch diamonds or squares.

7. Bake 1 hour 15 minutes or until leaves are flaky and browned.

ENTREE STRUDELS

Best known as dessert items, strudels also make wonderful entrees. Prepare the fillings as suggested below, then turn to page 528 for strudel-making techniques. When preparing savory strudels, use bread crumbs instead of cornflake crumbs. The entree fillings yield about 2 cups.

To make mini strudels for appetizers, see page 74.

SPINACH-MUSHROOM STRUDEL FILLING

—————— [V] ——————

Makes: enough filling for 1 strudel; serves: 3 to 4

See page 528 for the strudel-making technique.

1 tablespoon vegetable oil
1½ cups chopped mushrooms
½ cup chopped onions
1 clove garlic, minced
One 10-ounce package frozen chopped
    spinach, thawed and squeezed dry
½ teaspoon salt, or to taste
¼ teaspoon dried thyme
⅛ teaspoon dried savory
⅛ teaspoon dried marjoram
⅛ teaspoon pepper
1 cup cannellini (cooked from dry; or canned,
    drained and rinsed)

1. In a medium skillet, heat the oil over medium-high heat. Add the mushrooms, onions, and garlic; cook, stirring, until soft, about 4 minutes. Remove from heat and stir in the spinach, salt, thyme, savory, marjoram, and pepper.

2. Add the cannellini and mash slightly with the back of a spoon.

VEGETABLE-POTATO STRUDEL FILLING

—————— [V] ——————

Makes: enough filling for 1 strudel; serves: 3 to 4

See page 528 for the strudel-making technique.

2 cups cubed, peeled potatoes
3 tablespoons vegetable broth (pages
    93–95) or milk
¼ teaspoon salt, or to taste
⅛ teaspoon pepper
1 tablespoon vegetable oil
1 cup chopped cabbage
½ cup chopped onions
⅓ cup coarsely shredded carrots
⅓ cup coarsely shredded rutabaga
    (yellow turnip)
1 clove garlic, minced

1. In a 1-quart saucepan, cook the potatoes in enough water to cover it by 1 inch. Bring to a boil over high heat. Reduce heat to medium-high and cook 15 to 20 minutes or until potatoes are fork-tender. Drain immediately. Return potatoes to pot; add the broth, salt, and pepper. Mash with fork until smooth.

2. In a medium skillet, heat the oil over medium-high heat. Add the cabbage, onions, carrots, rutabaga, and garlic; cook, stirring, until soft, about 4 minutes. Stir into the potatoes.

CABBAGE KASHA STRUDEL FILLING

Makes: 4 cups, enough to fill 2 strudels; serves: 4

See page 528 for the strudel-making technique.

1 cup vegetable broth (pages 93–95)
2 tablespoons vegetable oil
2 cups chopped cabbage
¾ cup chopped onions
¾ cup coarsely shredded carrots
½ cup kasha
1 cup shredded Swiss, Monterey Jack, or
   Gouda cheese
¼ cup chopped fresh parsley
3 tablespoons snipped fresh dill
⅛ teaspoon salt, or to taste
¼ teaspoon pepper

1. In a 1-quart saucepan bring the broth to a boil; set aside.

2. In a 1½-quart saucepan, heat the oil over medium-high heat. Add the cabbage, onions, and carrots; cook, stirring, until cabbage is softened, about 3 minutes. Add the kasha and stir until coated with oil.

3. Stir in the broth. Cook, covered, over low heat 12 to 15 minutes or until liquid is almost but not completely absorbed. Remove from heat and stir in the cheese, parsley, dill, salt, and pepper.

Variation: Use jalapeño Monterey Jack for more of a bite.

WILD RICE–MUSHROOM STRUDEL FILLING

Makes: 2 cups, enough to fill 1 strudel; serves: 3 to 4

See page 528 for the strudel-making technique.

2 tablespoons butter or margarine
⅓ cup sliced leeks (white and light green
   parts only)
⅓ cup coarsely shredded carrots
1½ cups chopped wild or white mushrooms
2 tablespoons all-purpose flour
½ cup vegetable broth (pages 93–95)
1 cup cooked wild rice (page 301)
¼ cup chopped fresh parsley
¼ cup snipped fresh dill
3 tablespoons grated Parmesan cheese
⅛ teaspoon salt, or to taste
⅛ teaspoon pepper

1. In a large skillet, melt the butter over medium-high heat. Add the leeks and carrots; cook, stirring, until softened, about 3 minutes. Add the mushrooms, cook, stirring, until softened, about 3 minutes.

2. Stir in the flour until absorbed. Add the broth; cook, stirring, until mixture comes to a boil. Stir in the remaining ingredients.

Ⓥ **Variation:** Omit the cheese.

ASIAN ENTREES

SZECHUAN BROCCOLI

──────── [V] ────────

Makes: 9 cups; serves: 3 to 4

This recipe will serve only 3 if it is the sole entree. If other dishes are served this can feed 4 or more. Serve with brown or white rice.

3 tablespoons water
2 tablespoons mirin (rice wine) or dry sherry
2 teaspoons soy sauce
1 tablespoon hoisin sauce
1 teaspoon cornstarch
2 large bunches broccoli
3 tablespoons vegetable oil
1 tablespoon minced fresh ginger
3 cloves garlic, minced
¼ teaspoon red pepper flakes (optional)
1 teaspoon sesame oil

1. In a medium bowl, stir together the water, mirin, soy sauce, hoisin, and cornstarch; set aside.

2. Cut the broccoli heads into florets; peel the stems and slice thin. Set aside (about 14 cups cut up broccoli).

3. In a wok or large skillet, heat the vegetable oil over high heat. Add the ginger, garlic, and red pepper flakes; cook, stirring, 30 seconds. Add the broccoli; cook, stirring, until tender-crisp, about 5 minutes.

4. Add the sauce; cook, stirring, until broccoli is coated, about 1 minute. Add the sesame oil.

Variation: Add 1 cup sliced red or green bell peppers when you add the ginger and garlic.

CHINESE CABBAGE AND ORIENTAL VEGETABLES

──────── [V] ────────

Makes: 5 cups; serves: 3 to 4

Chinese cabbage comes in a head like celery, with flat stalks and light green leaves. If you can't find it, use bok choy, which also comes in a head like celery but has plumper stalks and dark green leaves. I like to add 2 cakes diced, pressed, baked tofu for extra protein, texture, and flavor. I add the tofu when I add the water chestnuts.

¼ cup vegetable broth (pages 93–95)
2 tablespoons mirin (rice wine) or sherry
1 tablespoon cornstarch
1 tablespoon soy sauce
1 teaspoon sugar
2 tablespoons vegetable oil
1 cup sliced onions
2 cloves garlic, minced
8 cups shredded Chinese cabbage
   (1 small head)
1 cup baby corn (canned)
1 cup sliced water chestnuts (canned)
¾ cup straw mushrooms (canned)

1. In a medium bowl, stir together the broth, mirin, cornstarch, soy sauce, and sugar; set aside.

2. In a wok or large skillet, heat the oil over high heat. Add the onion and garlic; cook, stirring, until onions are transparent, about 1 minute. Add the cabbage; cook, stirring, until wilted, about 2 minutes.

3. Add the corn, water chestnuts, and mushrooms; cook, stirring, until heated, about 1 minute. Add the sauce; cook, stirring until thickened, about 2 minutes longer.

Variations: Add 1 cup julienned snow peas when you add the cabbage.

Add 1 cup sliced pressed, baked tofu.

STIR-FRIED VEGETABLES WITH MUSHROOMS ON A BIRD'S NEST

[V]

Makes: 5¹/₂ cups; serves: 4

If you don't have any rice sticks with which to make the bird's nests, brown or white rice works fine, too.

2 ounces rice sticks
oil for deep frying
1 cup boiling water
12 dried shiitake mushrooms
1 tablespoon mirin (rice wine) or dry sherry
1 tablespoon cornstarch
1¹/₂ teaspoons soy sauce
1 teaspoon sugar
3 tablespoons vegetable oil
2 cups snow peas
1 cup sliced onions
1 cup julienned carrots
¹/₂ cup sliced scallions (1¹/₂-inch pieces; white and green parts)
3 cloves garlic, minced
4 cups Chinese cabbage or bok choy, cut into bite-size pieces
¹/₂ cup sliced bamboo shoots (canned)

1. Fry the noodles until they puff.

2. In a medium bowl, combine the water and mushrooms. Let stand 10 minutes, stirring once or twice until mushrooms are softened. Drain off the liquid, reserving ¹/₃ cup; let cool. Slice the mushrooms, discarding the tough stems; set aside.

3. In a small bowl combine the reserved mushroom liquid, the mirin, cornstarch, soy sauce, and sugar; set aside.

4. In a wok or large skillet, heat the oil over high heat. Add the snow peas, onions, carrots, scallions, and garlic. Cook, stirring, until tender-crisp, about 2 minutes. Add the Chinese cabbage and bamboo shoots; cook, stirring,

until tender-crisp, about 1 minute. Add the mushrooms and the cornstarch mixture; cook, stirring, until mixture is thickened and heated through, about 2 minutes.

5. Serve over bird's nests.

Variation: Use snap peas instead of snow peas.

ALMOND DING VEGETABLES

[V]

Makes: 5 cups; serves: 4

When I was a kid we'd go to Ding Ho Palace for Chinese food and we frequently ordered Chicken Almond Ding. This is a lovely nonmeat version of that dish.

¹/₂ cup coarsely chopped almonds
¹/₄ cup water
3 tablespoons mirin (rice wine) or sherry
1 tablespoon soy sauce
1 tablespoon cornstarch
¹/₂ teaspoon sugar
2 tablespoons vegetable oil
4 cups diced celery (¹/₂-inch pieces)
1 cup coarsely chopped onions
3 cloves garlic, minced
One 8-ounce can whole water chestnuts, drained and quartered
One 8-ounce can bamboo shoots, drained and diced

1. Toast almonds in a 350°F oven for 10 minutes; set aside.

2. In a small bowl, stir together the water, mirin, soy sauce, cornstarch, and sugar; set aside.

3. In a wok or large skillet, heat the oil over high heat. Add the celery, onions, and garlic; cook, stirring, until tender-crisp, about 3 minutes. Add the water chestnuts and bamboo shoots; cook, stirring, until heated through.

4. Add the cornstarch mixture; cook, stirring, until thickened, about 1 to 2 minutes. Stir in the toasted almonds.

Variation: Add 1 cup chopped snow peas when you add the celery.

TEMPURA

Makes: 7 to 8 cups; serves: 4 to 6

The theory behind crispy tempura is to have cold batter and hot oil. The batter is supposed to be thin and slightly lumpy. Good vegetable choices for tempura are thinly sliced winter squash, sweet potatoes, and carrots; and summer squash, green beans, bell peppers, eggplant, and broccoli.

¾ cup all-purpose flour and additional flour for dusting
2 tablespoons cornstarch
1 egg yolk
1 cup ice water
Oil for deep frying
4 cups cut-up vegetables
1 recipe Oriental Dipping Sauce (page 482)

1. Stir together the ¾ cups flour and cornstarch; set aside.

2. In a medium bowl, beat the egg yolk lightly. Stir in the water until just combined. Add the flour mixture and, using a pastry cutter in an up-and-down motion, combine the flour with the egg mixture (there should still be lumps).

3. Dust the vegetables with flour.

4. Pour oil 3 inches deep into a 3-quart pot and heat until a small piece of tempura rises to the surface after about 10 seconds. Dip the vegetables in the batter; deep fry until lightly crispy and the vegetables are cooked, turning once if necessary. Drain on paper towels.

5. Serve with dipping sauce.

MIXED VEGETABLE CURRY

Makes: 8 cups; serves: 4

For a spicy version, add ground red pepper when you add the curry. Serve with Dal (page 123) and Yellow Indian rice (page 316).

1½ tablespoons ghee (page 494) or vegetable oil
2 cups chopped onions
3 cloves garlic, minced
1 tablespoon curry powder
1 teaspoon ground cinnamon
1 teaspoon ground ginger
1 teaspoon ground turmeric
½ teaspoon ground cumin
¾ cup water
3 cups carrot chunks (1-inch pieces)
3 cups green beans (2-inch pieces)
2 cups cubed potatoes (1-inch pieces)
2 cups tomato wedges
1 cup peas, fresh or frozen
½ teaspoon salt, or to taste

1. In a 4-quart saucepan, heat the ghee or oil over medium heat. Add the onions and garlic; cook, stirring, until onions are transparent, about 2 minutes. Stir in the curry powder, cinnamon, ginger, turmeric, and cumin until absorbed. Add the water; bring to a boil.

2. Add the carrots, green beans, potatoes, tomato wedges, and peas. Bring to a boil; reduce heat and simmer, uncovered, 30 minutes or until vegetables are soft. Stir in salt.

Variation: Stir in 1 to 2 cups of cubed tofu when the vegetables have finished cooking and cook until heated through.

SAAG PANEER

Makes: 2 cups; serves: 2 to 3

This is spinach with homemade cheese (paneer, page 495). It's a great dish that's quite quick to cook once you have the paneer ready.

2 tablespoons water
2 teaspoons minced fresh ginger
2 cloves garlic
1 dried hot pepper, or 1/2 teaspoon crushed red pepper, or to taste
1 teaspoon ground coriander
1 teaspoon cumin seed
1 teaspoon paprika
1/2 teaspoon ground turmeric
1/2 teaspoon salt, or to taste
1 recipe paneer (page 495)
2 tablespoons ghee (page 494) or vegetable oil
Two 10-ounce packages frozen chopped spinach, thawed but undrained
1/4 cup unsweetened coconut milk (page 497)

1. Place the water, ginger, garlic, pepper, coriander, cumin seed, paprika, turmeric, and salt into a blender container. Cover and blend until pureed.

2. Cut the paneer into bite-size pieces.

3. In a 3-quart saucepan, heat the ghee over medium-high heat. Fry the paneer until golden, about 5 minutes; remove from pan and set aside.

4. Add the spice puree to the pan. Cook until heated. Stir in the spinach, then the paneer and coconut milk. Cook 5 minutes or until heated through.

Variation: Substitute cream for the coconut milk; omit pepper if desired.

CABBAGE AND MUSHROOM CURRY

Makes: 5 1/2 cups; serves: 4 to 6

3 tablespoons ghee (page 494) or vegetable oil
1 1/2 cups onions
1 tablespoon minced ginger
3 cloves garlic, minced
6 cups coarsely chopped cabbage
3 cups small whole mushrooms or larger mushrooms halved
2 tablespoons curry powder
1 teaspoon ground coriander
1/2 teaspoon ground cumin
1/2 teaspoon salt, or to taste
1/4 teaspoon ground red pepper
1 cup vegetable broth (pages 93–95)
2 cups tomato wedges
1 cup peas (fresh or frozen)
1/4 cup chopped fresh cilantro

1. In a 6-quart pot, heat the ghee or oil over medium-high heat. Add the onions, ginger, and garlic; cook, stirring, until softened, about 2 minutes. Add the cabbage and mushrooms; cook, stirring until cabbage is wilted, about 3 minutes. If mushrooms give off liquid, continue cooking until liquid has evaporated.

2. Stir in the curry powder, coriander, cumin, salt, and red pepper until absorbed. Add the broth and tomatoes. Bring to a boil. Reduce heat and simmer, covered, 15 minutes.

3. Stir in the peas; simmer, uncovered, 15 minutes. Stir in the cilantro; simmer, uncovered, 10 minutes longer.

Variation: Add 1 cup cubed potatoes when you add the tomatoes.

OKRA, PLANTAIN, AND SWEET POTATO CURRY

—————— [V] ——————

Makes: 5 cups; serves: 5 to 6

If the okra are small, use them whole; otherwise, cut them in half or slice them. The lemon grass is tough to chew (kind of like fingernail trimmings), but adds great flavor. If you can't find lemon grass, add 1 teaspoon grated lemon rind instead. To peel the plantain, cut into slices before peeling.

1 large onion
2 tablespoons vegetable oil
1 clove garlic, minced
1 1/2 tablespoons curry powder
1 teaspoon paprika
1/2 teaspoon ground cardamom
1/4 teaspoon ground cinnamon
2 cups water
3/4 cup unsweetened coconut milk (page xxx)
2 cups cubed sweet potatoes (1-inch pieces)
2 cups sliced green plantains (1/2-inch slices)
2 teaspoons dried lemon grass
1/2 teaspoon dried basil
2 cups whole okra, tops trimmed
2 tablespoons chopped fresh cilantro
1/4 teaspoon salt, or to taste

1. Peel and cut onion in half through the blossom. Cut into 1/4-inch-thick slices.

2. In a 3-quart saucepan, heat the oil over medium-high heat. Add the onions and garlic; cook, stirring, until softened, about 2 minutes. Stir in the curry powder, paprika, cardamom, and cinnamon until absorbed.

3. Add the water and coconut milk; bring to a boil. Add the sweet potatoes, plantains, lemon grass, and basil; return to a boil. Reduce heat and simmer, uncovered, 40 minutes. Add the okra, cilantro, and salt; return to a boil. Simmer, uncovered, 10 minutes or until okra are tender.

Variation: Add 1 cup peas when you add the okra.

Pasta, Pizza, Noodles, and Dumplings

Homemade Pasta Techniques

Mixing and Kneading by Hand

1. Stir together the flour or flours, and salt (if using). Form into a large mound. Make a well in the mound (like a volcano crater).

2. Beat the wet ingredients (this may include egg, water, vegetable or vegetable paste, and/ or oil). Pour into the well.

3. Working in a stirring motion with your hands, start mixing the flour into the liquid ingredients. (You will be using the flour from the inside of the well to mix with the liquid in-gredients; as you add more flour the walls of the "volcano" become thinner until all the flour is stirred in.) Continue working in the flour until all the runny liquid has been incorporated into a thick paste. Start to squeeze the dough and any loose flour through your fingers until the mixture is a fairly stiff dough.

4. Gather the dough into a ball and knead for 10 minutes, until the dough is smooth and elastic. (This will require more elbow grease than bread dough because this dough is intended to be stiffer.) If the dough is sticky (because your eggs were a little too large or it was a humid day), you may have to knead in extra flour.

5. Let dough rest, under a damp towel or greased plastic wrap, at least 30 minutes. (The longer you let the dough rest, the easier it will be to roll out—2 hours is really excellent.)

Mixing and Kneading by Pasta Machine or Bread Machine

Both of these appliances will mix and knead the dough for you. The pasta machine will also roll or shape and cut the dough. The bread machine only mixes and kneads.

Place all the ingredients into the machine and start it. With a bread maker, you may have to stop the machine occasionally to push the dough toward the paddle. Remove the dough after the knead cycle and let it rest at least 30 minutes, covered with a damp towel or greased plastic wrap. Then roll as desired.

Rolling by Hand

1. Cut the dough into 4 pieces. On a floured surface, using a floured rolling pin, roll out the dough as thinly as possible. Start rolling from the center of the dough and work toward the edges to keep the dough from being thicker in the center than on the edges. Lift the dough frequently and move to make sure dough has not started to stick to the board. If so, add more flour to the rolling surface. You should be able to see the counter through the dough when it is fully rolled out.

2. Cut to shape as required for the type of pasta you are making.

Rolling by Hand-Crank Machine

1. Cut dough in half, keeping unused portion covered with plastic wrap. Dust the dough with flour. Set the rolling slot to the widest setting (#1). Flour the rollers. Roll the dough out 2 to 3 times. If you find the dough is not coming out in a smooth sheet, it probably is too moist and needs extra flour. Dust the dough on both sides with flour before reinserting it into the rollers. Roll through the machine, dust with flour again, fold dough in half, and reroll. Continue rolling and flouring until you get a nice, smooth sheet of pasta coming out of the machine.

2. Set the rolling slot to one setting thinner (#2). Roll the dough out. Fold dough in half; return setting to widest position (#1). Roll out folded dough.

3. Set the rolling slot one setting thinner (#3). Roll out dough, once. Fold dough in half, return setting to one wider (#2), and roll out folded dough.

4. Set rolling slot one setting thinner (#3); roll once.

5. Roll once through each thinner setting until you get to desired thinness of dough (I like #4 or #5 for ravioli, linguini, fettuccini, and spaghetti, and #6, the thinnest setting, for angel hair pasta).

6. Switch the crank handle to the cutting side and put the pasta sheet through the cutting blades (if you are making ravioli, skip the cutting step). Hang the pasta to dry for at least $\frac{1}{2}$ hour before cooking.

Cutting the Pasta by Hand

For Long, Thin Pasta

1. Flour the dough to prevent it from sticking when folded.

2. Fold dough in half, then quarters, then eighths widthwise. Slice into desired thickness.

3. Cook immediately or hang and let dry for future use.

For Ravioli, Tortellini, or Other Stuffed Pasta

1. Use a sharp knife, pastry or pizza wheel, or biscuit or cookie cutters to cut into desired shapes.

2. Fill, shape, and seal according to directions in recipe.

3. Dry for 30 minutes; then cook immediately or refrigerate or freeze for future use.

Semolina Pasta Dough

Makes: 14$\frac{1}{2}$ ounces (enough for 48 ravioli)
Serves: 4

This is a very traditional Italian dough. It is hard to knead, but it rolls out like a dream. It requires a longer cooking time than other homemade fresh pasta doughs—at least 15 minutes.

1 to 1$\frac{1}{4}$ cups all-purpose flour
$\frac{3}{4}$ cups semolina (pasta flour)
3 eggs
$\frac{1}{2}$ teaspoon salt, or to taste

1. Prepare dough according to Homemade Pasta Techniques (pages 184–85).

Tomato Pasta Dough

Makes: 15 ounces (enough for 48 ravioli);
Serves: 4

This dough can be a little sticky and hard to roll. Be sure to coat the dough with flour before rolling, and have the board and rolling pin well floured to avoid difficulties. It cooks up extremely quickly (about 2 to 3 minutes) and makes a very tender pasta.

1$\frac{3}{4}$ cups all-purpose flour
2 eggs
2 tablespoons olive oil
2 tablespoons tomato paste
$\frac{1}{2}$ teaspoon salt, or to taste

1. Prepare dough according to Homemade Pasta Techniques (pages 184–85).

Variation: Use Italian tomato paste (flavored with oregano and other spices) instead of plain.

Spinach Pasta Dough

⟦V⟧⟦♥⟧

Makes: 14 ounces (enough for 48 ravioli);
serves: 4

1 cup semolina flour
¾ cup all-purpose flour
½ teaspoon salt, or to taste
⅓ cup warm water
¼ cup cooked chopped spinach, well
    drained
1 tablespoon olive oil

1. Prepare dough according to Homemade
Pasta Techniques (pages 184–85).

Ravioli

Makes: 48 ravioli; serves: 4 to 6

Ravioli are squares of pasta with any filling of
choice. If you are preparing the ravioli well in
advance of cooking them, store them carefully. Use
plastic wrap or aluminum foil between layers,
and be sure to dust well the tops and bottoms of
the ravioli with flour to prevent them from
sticking to the foil or wrap. Refrigerate or freeze
until needed.

1 pound (14 or 15 ounces are okay, if thinly
    rolled) pasta dough of choice
    (pages 184–85)
1 cup filling (1 teaspoon per ravioli)

By Hand
1. Divide the dough into two pieces, one
slightly larger than the other. Roll out the
smaller piece into a rectangle.

2. Place the filling on the rectangle (one teaspoon per ravioli), spaced 1 inch apart. Brush
the dough between the filling mounds with
water.

3. Roll out the larger piece of dough into a
larger rectangle. Carefully lay it over the piece
with the filling. Gently press around each of the
filling mounds to seal the dough. Cut into
squares (one per filling mound) with a pizza or
pastry wheel or a sharp knife.

By Machine
Both electric and hand-crank machines have
ravioli attachments. Follow manufacturer's
directions.

Ravioli Form
This relatively inexpensive gadget provides a
small rolling pin, plus 2 trays that help shape
the ravioli. Ravioli making is very easy to do
this way. Follow manufacturer's directions.

To Cook
1. Bring salted water to a boil. Add the ravioli.
Cook 3 to 15 minutes until *al dente* (cooking
times vary widely depending on the pasta
dough used).

2. Serve with sauce.

Fillings for Pasta

GOAT CHEESE RAVIOLI FILLING

Makes: 1 scant cup, enough for: 48 ravioli

1/2 cup soft goat cheese (such as Montrachet)
1/2 cup shredded mozzarella cheese
1 1/2 tablespoons grated Parmesan cheese
1/4 teaspoon pepper (preferably white)

1. In a medium bowl, stir together the goat cheese, mozzarella, Parmesan, and pepper.

2. Fill ravioli according to directions on page 186.

SPINACH~PIGNOLI RAVIOLI FILLING

Makes: 1 1/4 cups, enough for: 60 ravioli

1/3 cup pine nuts (pignoli)
1/2 cup diced tofu
3 tablespoons olive oil
2 cloves garlic, minced
1/4 teaspoon dried thyme
1/4 teaspoon salt, or to taste
One 10-ounce package frozen chopped spinach, thawed and squeezed dry

1. In a dry skillet over medium heat, cook the pine nuts, stirring constantly, until most of the nuts are at least partially browned. Cool, chop coarsely, and set aside.

2. Place the tofu in a food processor container fitted with a steel blade. Cover and process until smooth. While the processor is running, pour the oil into the processor through the chute. Add the garlic, thyme, and salt; continue to process until combined.

3. Place the spinach and pine nuts in a large bowl. Add the tofu mixture and stir until completely combined.

4. Fill ravioli according to directions on page 186.

L *Variation*: Substitute 1/2 cup ricotta cheese for the tofu.

ROSEMARY~MUSHROOM RAVIOLI FILLING

Makes: 1 cup, enough for: 48 ravioli

1 tablespoon olive oil
2 tablespoons minced shallots
2 cups chopped white or wild mushrooms
1 tablespoon white wine
1/4 teaspoon dried rosemary, crumbled
Pinch salt, or to taste
Pinch freshly ground black pepper
1/2 cup shredded Swiss cheese
1 tablespoon grated Parmesan cheese

1. In a medium skillet, heat the oil over medium-high heat. Add the shallots; cook, stirring, until softened, about 30 seconds. Add the mushrooms; cook, stirring, until softened, about 3 minutes. Add the wine, rosemary, salt, and pepper. Cook, stirring, until any liquid evaporates. Stir in the cheeses.

2. Fill ravioli according to directions on page 186.

ESCAROLE AND CHEESE STUFFED SHELLS

———— L ————

Makes: 20 jumbo shells; serves: 4 to 5

I find Garlic Tomato Sauce (page 473) to be especially wonderful with these shells, but you can use any marinara or similar sauce.

1 tablespoon olive oil
¼ cup finely chopped onions
1 clove garlic, minced
2 cups chopped escarole
1½ cups ricotta cheese
½ cup shredded mozzarella cheese
¼ cup grated Parmesan cheese
¼ teaspoon salt, or to taste
⅛ teaspoon pepper
20 jumbo shells
3½ to 4 cups sauce

1. Preheat the oven to 350°F.

2. In a medium skillet, heat the oil. Add the onions and garlic; cook, stirring, until onions are softened, about 1 to 2 minutes. Add the escarole; cook, stirring, until wilted, about 2 minutes. Cool.

3. In a medium bowl, stir together the ricotta, mozzarella, and Parmesan cheeses. Add the escarole mixture, the salt, and pepper.

4. Cook the shells according to package directions until just *al dente*. Drain and rinse in cool water, then drain again.

5. Stuff a heaping tablespoon of the cheese mixture into each of the shells.

6. Spread 2 to 3 cups of sauce over the bottom of a 9 × 13-inch baking pan. Arrange the shells on the sauce. Pour the remaining sauce over the shells.

7. Bake 30 minutes or until the cheese is melted and the shells are heated through.

Variations: Stuffed Shells: Omit step 2 of the recipe, leaving out the olive oil, onions, garlic, and escarole.

Stuffed Shells Parmigiana: Combine 1 cup of additional shredded mozzarella plus 2 tablespoons additional grated Parmesan cheese. Sprinkle over the shells after you've added all the sauce.

MANICOTTI

———— ————

Makes: 10 manicotti; serves: 4 to 5

No matter what you do, manicotti are quite a bother to make, but the result is always satisfying. If you can't find manicotti shells, you can make a batch of crepes (page 553) and roll the filling in the crepes, then proceed as if you'd used the shells. (You may need more than 10 crepes, however.)

1 egg
One 15-ounce container ricotta cheese
One 8-ounce package mozzarella, shredded, divided
⅓ cup grated Parmesan cheese
¼ teaspoon salt, or to taste
¼ teaspoon pepper
10 manicotti shells
3 cups marinara sauce

1. Preheat the oven to 350°F.

2. In a medium bowl, beat the egg; stir in the ricotta, 1 cup of the mozzarella, the Parmesan cheese, salt, and pepper.

3. Cook the shells according to package directions until just *al dente*. Drain and rinse in cool water, then drain again.

4. Stuff a heaping tablespoon of the cheese mixture into each of the shells, or place on crepe and roll.

5. Spread 1 cup of sauce over the bottom of a 9 × 13-inch baking pan. Arrange the shells on the sauce. Pour the remaining sauce over the shells. Sprinkle with the remaining mozzarella.

6. Bake 40 minutes or until the cheese is melted and the shells are heated through.

Variation: Add ¹/₂ cup chopped cooked spinach to the filling.

PASTA WITH OLIVE OIL AND GARLIC

[V] [♥]

Makes: 6 cups; serves: 4 to 6

This simple dish is a favorite among most real pasta lovers.

12 ounces long dry pasta (such as spaghetti, linguini, fusilli, or angel hair)
2 tablespoons extra virgin olive oil
2 cloves garlic, put through a garlic press
¹/₈ teaspoon salt, or to taste
Freshly ground black pepper, to taste
Shaved or grated Parmesan cheese (optional)

1. Cook the pasta according to package directions. Drain.

2. Heat the oil over medium-high heat. Add the garlic; cook, stirring, 30 seconds. Add drained pasta and toss. Add salt and pepper to taste.

3. Serve with Parmesan cheese, if desired.

Variation: Pasta with Broccoli and Garlic: Add 2 cups cooked broccoli pieces to the garlic and oil. Saute until broccoli is heated through. Toss with pasta.

PASTA WITH OLIVES, GARLIC, AND PINE NUTS

[V]

Makes: 6¹/₂ cups; serves: 4 to 6

I used regular canned black olives for this recipe—no need for fancier ones. Linguini was my pasta of choice, but ziti or any pasta will do.

12 ounces pasta
2 tablespoons pine nuts (pignoli)
1¹/₂ tablespoons extra virgin olive oil
2 cloves garlic, minced
2 cups chopped tomatoes
¹/₄ cup chopped fresh parsley
3 tablespoons chopped fresh basil
¹/₂ cup small pitted black olives, halved
¹/₄ teaspoon salt, or to taste
Freshly ground black pepper, to taste
Shaved or grated Parmesan cheese (optional)

1. Cook the pasta according to package directions.

2. While pasta is cooking, toast the pine nuts in a dry medium-sized skillet over medium heat until partially browned, about 2 minutes. Remove from skillet; set aside.

3. Heat the oil in the skillet used to cook the pine nuts. Add the garlic; cook, stirring, 20 seconds. Add the tomatoes, parsley, and basil. Cook, stirring, 5 minutes or until tomatoes are softened. Add the olives, salt, and drained pasta; cook until heated through. Grind pepper over pasta, and sprinkle with Parmesan, if desired. Add toasted pine nuts and toss to combine.

PASTA WITH TOMATO AND EGGPLANT SAUCE

[V][♥]

Makes: 3¹/₂ cups sauce; serves: 4 to 6

This recipe is also very well suited to Baked Ziti (page 199).

2 tablespoons olive oil

1¹/₂ cups chopped onions

3 cloves garlic, minced

4 cups diced eggplant (¹/₂-inch pieces)

One 14¹/₂-ounce can whole peeled tomatoes, undrained

²/₃ cup red wine

2 tablespoons tomato paste

1¹/₂ teaspoons sugar

1 teaspoon dried oregano

¹/₂ teaspoon dried thyme

¹/₄ teaspoon dried rosemary, crumbled

¹/₄ teaspoon salt, or to taste

¹/₈ teaspoon pepper

12 ounces dry pasta (such as rigatoni, penne, or the like)

1. In a 3-quart saucepan, heat the oil over medium-high heat. Add the onions and garlic; cook, stirring, until softened, about 2 minutes. Add the eggplant; cook, stirring, until softened, about 3 minutes.

2. Add the tomatoes, with liquid, and break them up with the back of a spoon. Stir in the wine, tomato paste, sugar, oregano, thyme, rosemary, salt, and pepper. Bring to a boil. Reduce heat and simmer, uncovered, 30 minutes or until thickened, stirring occasionally.

3. Cook the pasta according to package directions; drain. Either toss with sauce or serve topped with sauce.

Variation: Use dry white wine or broth instead of the red wine.

PASTA PUTTANESCA

[V]

Makes: 3¹/₂ cups sauce; serves: 3 to 4

I tested this recipe using 12 ounces of thin spaghetti, and although the flavor was very good, I really like my pasta dishes saucier, so I reduced the amount of pasta to 8 ounces. If you like your pasta less saucy, you can serve this sauce on 12 ounces of pasta.

1¹/₂ tablespoons olive oil

1 cup chopped onions

3 cloves garlic, minced

One 14¹/₂-ounce can whole peeled tomatoes, undrained

¹/₂ cup water

¹/₄ cup tomato paste

¹/₃ cup chopped oil-marinated sun-dried tomatoes

1¹/₂ teaspoons sugar

¹/₈ teaspoon red pepper flakes

One 5.75-ounce jar pitted black olives, drained and chopped

¹/₂ cup chopped fresh parsley

1 tablespoon chopped capers

8 to 12 ounces pasta (spaghetti, thin spaghetti, or linguine)

1. In a 2-quart saucepan, heat the oil over medium-high heat. Add the onions and garlic; cook, stirring, until softened, about 2 minutes.

2. Add the whole tomatoes, with liquid, and break them up with the back of a spoon. Stir in the water, tomato paste, sun-dried tomatoes, sugar, and red pepper flakes. Bring to a boil. Reduce heat and simmer, uncovered, 30 minutes or until thickened, stirring occasionally. Stir in the olives, parsley, and capers; cook until heated through, 2 minutes longer.

3. Cook the pasta according to package directions; drain. Either toss with sauce or serve topped with sauce.

Variation: Add ⅓ cup chopped fresh basil when you add the tomatoes.

PASTA WITH YELLOW TOMATO SAUCE

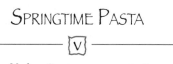

Makes: 3 cups sauce; serves: about 6 (volume of pasta varies with shape chosen)

One morning while I was walking my dog, Poppy, in the park, my friend Aaron Stoner (and his dog, Archie) came over to us and asked if I knew of a recipe for tomato sauce that was low in acid. I suggested making tomato sauce with yellow tomatoes since they are low in acid and yet taste just like red tomatoes—they only look weird.

1½ tablespoons olive oil
1½ cups chopped onions
3 cloves garlic, minced
5 cups coarsely chopped yellow tomatoes
1½ teaspoons dried oregano
½ teaspoon salt, or to taste
½ teaspoon dried basil
¼ teaspoon dried thyme
⅛ teaspoon pepper
1 pound pasta (any long or medium pasta works well—try ziti, linguini, angel hair, or the like)

1. In a 3-quart saucepan, heat the oil over medium-high heat. Add the onions and garlic; cook, stirring, until softened, about 2 minutes.

2. Stir in the tomatoes, oregano, salt, basil, thyme, and pepper. Bring to a boil; cook until tomatoes have given up enough juice to almost cover the pieces. Reduce heat and simmer, uncovered, 1 hour.

3. Ten minutes before sauce is finished, cook the pasta according to package directions; drain.

4. Toss pasta with sauce.

Variation: Easy Fresh Marinara Sauce: Use regular red tomatoes instead of yellow.

SPRINGTIME PASTA

Makes: 8 cups; serves: 4 to 6

Though there is really hardly any demarcation between seasons now (since both asparagus and sugar-snap peas are available pretty much year-round), I like to think of these elements as harbingers of summer anyway.

12 ounces rigatoni or other medium-size pasta
2 tablespoons olive oil
2 cups chopped asparagus (1½-inch pieces)
1 cup sugar-snap peas
2 cloves garlic, minced
½ cup chopped oil-marinated sun-dried tomatoes
¼ cup dry white wine
2 tablespoons chopped capers
½ cup grated Parmesan cheese (optional)

1. Cook the pasta according to package directions; drain.

2. In a large skillet, heat the olive oil over medium-high heat. Add the asparagus, peas, and garlic; cook, stirring, until vegetables are tender-crisp, about 4 minutes. Add the tomatoes, wine, and capers. Cook, stirring, 30 seconds.

3. Add the drained pasta; cook, tossing until pasta is heated through. Remove from heat; add Parmesan, if desired, and toss.

Variation: Use snow peas if you can't find sugar-snap peas.

RANDY KRAFT'S PASTA WITH VEGETABLES AND LENTILS

[V][♥]

Makes: 3 cups sauce plus pasta; serves: 4

While I was on the phone with Randy (an almost daily event), she raved about a pasta sauce she had just invented. She insisted I get a pencil and write it down immediately for my book so I wouldn't forget it. The sauce also makes a good side dish, or, with extra broth, a great soup.

3 cups vegetable broth (pages 93–95; Randy used water plus Knorr's vegetable cubes)
²/₃ cup julienned carrots
½ cup sliced onions
1 clove garlic, minced
1 cup sliced zucchini
1 cup sliced yellow squash
½ cup sliced red bell peppers
⅓ cup lentils
¼ teaspoon pepper
12 ounces penne (or similar, such as ziti or rigatoni)
Grated Parmesan cheese (optional)

1. In a 3-quart saucepan, bring the broth to a boil over high heat. Add the carrots, onions, and garlic; reduce heat and simmer, uncovered, 5 minutes. Add the zucchini, squash, bell peppers, lentils, and pepper. Return to a boil; reduce heat and simmer 30 minutes or until lentils are tender.

2. Cook the pasta according to package directions; drain. Add pasta to sauce and toss to combine.

3. Serve with grated Parmesan, if desired.

Variation: Add 1 cup broccoli florets with the vegetables.

ZITI WITH ROASTED RED PEPPER AND GRILLED EGGPLANT

[V]

Makes: 8 cups; serves: 4 to 6

I apologize for all the cross-references here. If you don't feel like checking out those recipes, just broil some sliced eggplant brushed with oil, and use jarred roasted red peppers and prepared pesto.

12 ounces ziti
2 cups grilled eggplant (page 232), cut into strips
1 cup sliced roasted red bell peppers (page 276)
¾ cup Spinach-Parsley Pesto (page 477)
⅛ teaspoon salt, or to taste

1. In a 3-quart saucepan, cook the ziti according to package directions; drain. Return to saucepan; add eggplant, bell peppers, pesto, and salt. Cook over medium heat, tossing, until heated through.

Variation: Add ¹/₃ cup chopped oil-marinated sun-dried tomatoes.

PENNE PRIMAVERA WITH CREAMY TOMATO SAUCE

L

Makes: 8 cups; serves: 4

This is really more of a cream sauce with tomato flavor than a tomato sauce with cream (you'll find that on page 194—Penne with Vodka Sauce).

⅓ cup pine nuts (pignoli)
12 ounces penne
2 tablespoons olive oil, divided
1 cup julienned carrots
1 cup julienned zucchini
1 cup julienned yellow squash
1 tablespoon all-purpose flour
1 cup half-and-half
1 tablespoon tomato paste
⅓ cup grated Parmesan cheese (optional)
⅛ teaspoon pepper

1. Toast the pine nuts in a dry skillet over medium heat until all the nuts are slightly browned, about 2 minutes; set aside.

2. Cook the pasta according to package directions; drain.

3. While pasta is cooking, heat 1 tablespoon of the oil in a large skillet over medium-high heat. Add the carrots; cook, stirring 30 seconds. Add the zucchini and squash; cook, stirring, until tender, about 3 minutes. Remove vegetables from skillet.

4. Add the remaining tablespoon of oil to the skillet; stir in flour until absorbed. Stir in the half-and-half and tomato paste. Cook, stirring, until mixture comes to a boil and thickens. Stir in pasta and vegetables. Cook, tossing, until heated through. Remove from heat; stir in Parmesan cheese, pine nuts, and pepper.

Ⓥ ***Variation:*** Use vegetable broth (pages 93–95) instead of the half-and-half.

CAVETELLI WITH CABBAGE AND CARAMELIZED ONIONS

L

Makes: 7½ cups; serves: 4 to 6

If you prefer to have color in your dishes, add some red or green bell peppers when you cook the onions for this otherwise off-white dish.

12 ounces cavetelli (or other medium-size pasta)
2 tablespoons butter or margarine
2 cups sliced onions
4 cups thinly sliced cabbage
⅓ cup heavy cream
¼ teaspoon salt, or to taste
⅛ teaspoon pepper

1. Cook pasta according to package directions; drain.

2. In a large skillet, melt the butter or margarine over medium heat. Add the onions; cook, stirring occasionally, until caramelized, about 20 minutes. Add the cabbage; cook, stirring until wilted, about 4 minutes.

3. Add the cream; cook until bubbling all over the surface of the skillet, about 3 minutes. Add the pasta, salt, and pepper; cook, tossing, until heated through.

Ⓥ♥ ***Variation:*** Use broth (page 93–95) instead of heavy cream.

PASTA WITH CREAMY BASIL SAUCE

Makes: 7 cups; serves: 4 to 6

Just how creamy this sauce is depends on the liquid you use. If you use milk or broth instead of the half-and-half, the result will be less creamy tasting. Also, if you omit the basil, you'll have a nice Parmesan cream sauce.

¼ cup pine nuts (pignoli)
12 ounces ziti, penne, or tortellini pasta
1 tablespoon butter or margarine
1 clove garlic, minced
1½ tablespoons all-purpose flour
1 cup half-and-half or light cream
⅛ teaspoon salt, or to taste
½ cup chopped fresh basil, or 1 tablespoon dried basil
¼ cup grated Parmesan cheese
Fresh black pepper, to taste

1. In a dry skillet, cook the pine nuts over medium heat until lightly browned, shaking the skillet occasionally. Remove from the skillet and set aside.

2. Cook the pasta in salted boiling water according to package directions; drain.

3. While the pasta is cooking, melt the butter or margarine in a 1-quart saucepan over medium-high heat. Add the garlic and cook 10 seconds. Add the flour; cook, stirring, until absorbed. Add the half-and-half and salt; cook, stirring, until the mixture comes to a boil and has thickened.

4. Remove from heat and stir in the basil and grated Parmesan.

5. Put the pasta and sauce in a large bowl; toss until combined. Grind pepper on top and toss.

Variation: Use heavy cream for an even creamier version.

PENNE WITH VODKA SAUCE

Makes: 7 cups; serves: 4 to 6

If you don't have vodka on hand you can use gin or even white wine. If you prefer not to use alcohol you can substitute broth, but it's not quite the same without the vodka.

1 tablespoon olive oil
1 cup chopped onions
2 cloves garlic, minced
One 14½-ounce can whole peeled tomatoes, undrained
¼ cup vodka
3 tablespoons tomato paste
1½ teaspoons sugar
¼ teaspoon salt, or to taste
⅛ teaspoon crushed red pepper
12 ounces penne pasta
¼ cup heavy cream

1. In a 1½ quart saucepan, heat the oil over medium-high heat. Add the onions and garlic; cook, stirring, until softened, about 2 minutes.

2. Add the tomatoes and break them up with the back of a spoon. Stir in the vodka, tomato paste, sugar, salt, and red pepper. Cook, uncovered, over medium heat 20 minutes, stirring occasionally.

3. While the sauce is cooking, cook the pasta according to package directions; drain.

4. Stir the cream into the sauce; cook, stirring, until heated through. Do not allow to boil. Pour sauce over pasta and toss.

Variation: Stir in ¼ to ⅓ cup grated Parmesan cheese when you add the cream.

TORTELLINI WITH WILD MUSHROOM SAUCE

Makes: 2 cups sauce; serves: 4 to 6

I use a combination of mushrooms for this dish. The sauce calls for cream and Parmesan cheese; these ingredients certainly enhance the flavor and consistency of the dish, but the vegan variation is extremely tasty too (and considerably lower in fat).

1½ tablespoons olive oil
2 tablespoons minced shallots
3 cups coarsley chopped wild mushrooms (portobello, crimini, and/or shiitake)
1½ cups vegetable broth (pages 93–95)
½ cup water
2 tablespoons medium sweet Madeira or Marsala wine
¼ teaspoon dried thyme
⅛ teaspoon salt, or to taste
⅛ teaspoon pepper
2 tablespoons butter or margarine
3 tablespoons all-purpose flour
3 tablespoons heavy cream
2 tablespoons grated Parmesan cheese
¼ cup chopped fresh parsley
Two 12-ounce packages fresh cheese tortellini

1. In a 2-quart saucepan, heat the oil over medium-high heat. Add the shallots; cook, stirring, until tender, about 30 seconds. Add the mushrooms; cook, stirring, until softened, about 4 minutes. Add the broth, water, Madeira, thyme, salt, and pepper. Bring to a boil. Reduce heat and simmer uncovered, 10 minutes.

2. In a 1½-quart saucepan, melt the butter or margarine over medium-high heat. Stir in the flour until absorbed. Stir in the mushrooms and broth; cook, stirring, until mixture comes to a boil, about 2 minutes. Add the cream and Parmesan cheese. Add the parsley.

3. Cook the pasta according to package directions; drain. Place the pasta in a serving bowl or individual serving bowls. Add the mushroom sauce.

Variations: Gnocchi with Wild Mushroom Sauce: Use gnocchi (pages 203–204) instead of pasta.

[V] Omit the heavy cream and cheese.

ZITI WITH BROCCOLI AND ROSEMARY

[V]

Makes: 10 cups; serves: 4 to 6

This is one of my "lazy days" recipes. I cook the broccoli in the same pot as the pasta—that way I have one less pot to clean.

12 ounces ziti (or other medium-size pasta, such as rotelli or rigatoni)
4 cups broccoli florets
3 tablespoons butter or margarine
1 tablespoon fresh rosemary, or 1 teaspoon dried rosemary, crumbled
Grated Parmesan cheese (optional)

1. Cook pasta according to package directions. Two minutes before the pasta has finished cooking, add the broccoli to the pot. Continue cooking the pasta until done. Drain pasta and broccoli.

2. Return pasta and broccoli to the pot and add butter or margarine and the rosemary. Cook, stirring, until butter or margarine is melted. Serve with grated Parmesan, if desired.

Lasagna

Lasagna is an ideal dish to prepare for company or parties: It serves a lot of people; it's easy to make ahead and then just heat before serving; it stays warm a relatively long time; it's easy to serve; most people enjoy it (even nonvegetarians find vegetarian lasagna a satisfying meal); and it's a fairly complete meal (you need only prepare a salad to go with it and have some bread on the side).

VEGETABLE LASAGNA

Makes: one 9 × 13-inch lasagna; serves: 8 to 12

Vegetable Filling:
1 tablespoon vegetable oil
4 cups thinly sliced zucchini
3 cups diced eggplant (1/2-inch pieces)
2 cups chopped wild mushrooms (such as shiitake, crimini, or portobello)
1 cup shredded carrots
1 cup chopped onions
1 1/2 cups marinara sauce
1/2 cup cooked chopped spinach (from fresh or frozen, squeezed dry)
1/2 cup grated Parmesan cheese
1/2 cup chopped fresh parsley
1/8 teaspoon salt, or to taste

Ricotta Filling:
1 egg, beaten
3 cups ricotta cheese
1 1/2 cups shredded mozzarella cheese
1/4 teaspoon pepper

Topping:
1/2 cup shredded mozzarella cheese
1/4 cup grated Parmesan cheese

To finish the dish:
12 lasagna noodles
1 1/2 cups marinara sauce, divided

1. For the vegetable filling, heat the oil in a large skillet. Add the zucchini, eggplant, mushrooms, carrots, and onions; cook, stirring, until softened, about 4 minutes. Stir in the 1 1/2 cups marinara sauce, the spinach, 1/2 cup Parmesan, the parsley, and salt.

2. For the ricotta filling, in a large bowl, beat the egg; add the ricotta, 1 1/2 cups mozzarella, and the pepper.

3. In a small bowl, toss together 1/2 cup mozzarella and 1/4 cup Parmesan for the topping.

4. Cook the noodles according to package directions; drain.

5. Preheat the oven to 400°F.

6. Thinly spread 3/4 cup marinara sauce in the bottom of a 9 × 13-inch baking dish. Use 4 of the noodles to line the bottom of the dish.

7. Spread 1/2 of the ricotta filling over the noodles. Cover with 1/2 of the vegetable filling.

8. Top with 4 more noodles. Spread with remaining ricotta filling and top with remaining vegetable filling.

9. Top with remaining noodles. Spread remaining 3/4 cup marinara sauce over noodles.

10. Bake, covered, 30 minutes. Sprinkle with cheese topping; continue baking 20 minutes longer. Remove from oven and let stand 15 minutes before cutting into squares.

Variation: You can vary the vegetables however you like—use more of some and less of others.

GREEN AND WHITE LASAGNA

Makes: one 9 × 13-inch lasagna; serves: 8 to 12

This is not a huge lasagna, but it's so rich it easily serves 8 hearty eaters or 12 smaller eaters.

Basil-Cream Sauce:
3 tablespoons butter or margarine
3 tablespoons all-purpose flour
3 cups milk
½ cup chopped fresh basil
½ cup grated Parmesan cheese
1 clove garlic, minced
¼ teaspoon salt, or to taste

Filling:
⅓ cup pine nuts (pignoli)
Two 10-ounce packages frozen chopped
    spinach, thawed and squeezed dry
One 15-ounce container ricotta cheese
2 cups shredded mozzarella, divided
1½ cups shredded Fontina cheese
¾ cup grated Parmesan cheese
1 egg, beaten
¼ teaspoon freshly ground pepper

To finish the dish:
12 lasagna noodles

1. For the basil-cream sauce, in a 2-quart saucepan, melt the butter or margarine over medium heat. Stir in the flour until absorbed. Add the milk; cook, stirring constantly, until mixture comes to a boil and has thickened. Remove from heat; stir in the basil, ½ cup Parmesan, the garlic, and salt. Place plastic wrap on surface of sauce and set aside.

2. To begin the filling, over low heat, cook the pine nuts in a dry, small skillet until all the nuts are at least partially browned. Chop.

3. Place pine nuts in large bowl. Add the spinach, ricotta, ½ cup of the mozzarella, the Fontina, ¾ cup Parmesan, the egg, and pepper. Stir to combine; set aside.

4. Cook the noodles according to package directions; drain.

5. Preheat the oven to 375°F.

6. Thinly spread 1 cup of the basil-cream sauce in the bottom of a 9 × 13-inch baking dish. Use 4 of the noodles to line the bottom of the dish.

7. Spread ½ of the ricotta filling over the noodles. Spread ½ of the remaining basil-cream sauce over the cheese.

8. Top with 4 more noodles. Spread with remaining ricotta filling.

9. Top with remaining noodles. Spread remaining sauce over noodles.

10. Bake 30 minutes. Sprinkle with remaining 1 cup mozzarella; continue baking 20 minutes longer. Remove from oven and let stand 15 minutes before cutting into squares.

Variation: Instead of making the basil-cream sauce, use 2½ to 3 cups of marinara sauce or some other tomato sauce.

MUSHROOM LASAGNA WITH BELL PEPPER CREAM SAUCE

———— LO ————

Makes: one 9 × 13-inch lasagne; serves: 8 to 12

If using jarred roasted peppers, add ¹/₂ teaspoon sugar to the bell pepper sauce when you add the broth.

Bell Pepper Cream Sauce:

3 tablespoons butter or margarine
2 cloves garlic, minced
¼ cup all-purpose flour
2 cups vegetable broth (pages 93–95)
⅛ teaspoon salt, or to taste
⅛ teaspoon ground red pepper
1 cup roasted red bell peppers (page 276)
¼ cup heavy cream

Mushroom Filling:

2 tablespoons butter or margarine
¼ cup chopped shallots
6 cups sliced white mushrooms
4 cups sliced wild mushrooms

Ricotta Filling:

1 egg, beaten
Two 15-ounce containers ricotta cheese
2 cups shredded mozzarella cheese
½ cup grated Parmesan cheese
⅓ cup chopped fresh parsley
1 clove garlic, minced
¼ teaspoon pepper

Topping:

1 cup shredded mozzarella cheese
¼ cup grated Parmesan cheese

To finish the dish:

12 lasagna noodles

1. For the bell pepper cream sauce, in a 2-quart saucepan, melt 3 tablespoons butter or margarine over medium heat. Add 2 cloves garlic; cook, stirring, 15 seconds. Stir in the flour until absorbed. Add the broth; cook, stirring constantly, until mixture comes to a boil and has thickened, about 4 minutes. Remove from heat, stir in the salt and ground red pepper. Put the roasted bell peppers into a blender along with ¹/₂ cup of the sauce. Cover and blend until smooth. Stir the bell pepper puree into the remaining sauce; stir in the cream. Place plastic wrap on surface of sauce and set aside.

2. For the mushroom filling, melt 2 tablespoons butter or margarine in a large skillet. Add the shallots; cook, stirring, 30 seconds. Add both types of mushrooms; cook, stirring, until softened, about 5 minutes. If mushrooms give off liquid, cook until liquid evaporates. Stir 1¹/₂ cups of the bell pepper cream sauce into the mushrooms; set aside.

3. For the ricotta filling, in large bowl, beat the egg; add the ricotta, 2 cups mozzarella, ¹/₂ cup Parmesan, the parsley, 1 clove garlic, and the pepper.

4. In a small bowl, toss together 1 cup mozzarella and ¹/₄ cup Parmesan for the topping.

5. Cook the noodles according to package directions; drain.

6. Preheat the oven to 375°F.

7. Thinly spread ³/₄ cup of the cream sauce in the bottom of a 9 × 13-inch baking dish. Use 4 of the noodles to line the bottom of the dish.

8. Spread ¹/₂ of the ricotta filling over the noodles. Cover with ¹/₂ of the mushroom filling.

9. Top with 4 more noodles. Spread with remaining ricotta filling and mushroom filling.

10. Top with remaining noodles. Spread remaining cream sauce over noodles.

11. Bake, covered, 30 minutes. Sprinkle with cheese topping; continue baking 20 minutes longer. Remove from oven and let stand 15 minutes before cutting into squares.

PASTA TORTE

Makes: one 8-inch torte; serves: 6

This dish makes a great presentation. Serve it with a salad and maybe some garlic bread.

12 ounces spaghetti
1 tablespoon olive oil
1 cup chopped fresh spinach
2 cloves garlic, minced
3 cups chopped tomatoes
1/2 cup chopped fresh basil
2 eggs
1/8 teaspoon salt, or to taste
1 cup ricotta or cottage cheese
1 cup shredded mozzarella cheese
1 cup shredded Fontina cheese
1/2 cup grated Parmesan cheese
1/8 teaspoon pepper

1. Preheat the oven to 375°F. Grease an 8-inch springform pan.

2. Cook spaghetti according to package directions; drain.

3. While the spaghetti is cooking, heat the oil in a medium skillet. Add the spinach and garlic; cook, stirring, until wilted, about 2 minutes. Add the tomatoes and basil; cook, stirring, until tomatoes are softened, about 3 minutes. Stir into drained spaghetti.

4. In a medium bowl, beat the eggs with the salt. Stir in the ricotta. Stir into spaghetti. Stir in the remaining ingredients. Turn into prepared pan and press with the back of a spoon to compress.

5. Bake 45 minutes or until browned on top. Run a knife around the edge before releasing ring. Cut into wedges.

Variation: Add 1/4 cup pesto sauce (page 476–77) to the beaten egg and omit the fresh basil.

BAKED ZITI

Makes: 10 cups; serves: 6 to 8

My first memory of baked ziti is when I was in college in Florida. My pals and I would go to a restaurant called Rocky's, where they made great baked ziti—I had to order it every time. Now I make it at home and love it just as much.

2 tablespoons olive oil
1/2 cup chopped onions
2 cups water
One 14 1/2-ounce can whole peeled tomatoes, undrained
One 6-ounce can tomato paste
1/3 cup chopped fresh parsley
1 teaspoon dried oregano
1/2 teaspoon dried basil
1 pound ziti
3 medium roasted red bell peppers (page 276), sliced
2 cups shredded mozzarella, divided
1/2 cup grated Parmesan cheese
1/3 cup chopped sun-dried tomatoes (optional)

1. In a 2-quart saucepan, heat the oil over medium-high heat. Add the onions; cook, stirring, until softened, about 2 minutes. Add the water, tomatoes (with liquid), tomato paste, parsley, oregano, and basil. Break up the tomatoes with the back of a spoon. Bring to a boil. Reduce heat and simmer 20 minutes, stirring occasionally.

2. Preheat the oven to 350°F.

3. Cook pasta according to package directions; drain. Return to pot, but do not heat; stir in the tomato sauce, the roasted bell peppers, 1 1/2 cups of the mozzarella, the Parmesan, and sun-dried tomatoes.

4. Spoon into 9-inch square baking dish. Sprinkle remaining mozzarella over top. Bake 20 minutes or until heated through and the cheese has melted.

Pizza

Making pizza at home is fun to do and the results are so far superior to any pizza in the freezer case—or even in a pizzeria—you won't believe it. However, it's extremely hard to make a "large" pie. I like to make 4 manageable smaller pies. Since I don't have 4 ovens, I bake one at a time, cut it into quarters or sixths (depending on how many you're serving), and eat it while the next one is baking. Then you can vary the toppings too.

Preparing Pizza Crust

Pizza dough is not especially quick-rising. Allow at least an hour or even $1^1/_2$ hours for the dough to rise. The more the dough rises, the easier it is to shape into a pizza crust. If you haven't left enough rising time, you may find your dough acting more like a rubber band than a well-behaved crust.

I usually make my crusts by hand, but you can make them in a food processor or bread maker. The food processor may require a little extra flour. The bread maker does a great job of mixing and kneading, and you can even let the dough rise in the machine. Either machine makes much less work for the pizza maker.

Shaping the crust takes some practice, I frequently find myself serving amoeba-shaped pizzas, but so far, no one has ever complained. Here's how you do it:

Divide the dough into quarters. On a well-floured surface, pat one piece of the dough into as flat a circle as possible. Lift the dough and rest it on top of your two fists. Gently pull your fists apart, stretching the dough. Stretch the middle and then the edges of the dough. When the dough is close to the desired thickness, if the center of the crust is much thinner than the edges, hold the dough with both hands, suspending the dough in the air. Squeeze the edges as you rotate the dough, until the crust is of a fairly even thickness.

Pizza Sauces

You can use any sauce you like on pizza, but ideally it should be slightly thicker than a sauce you would use on pasta. I also prefer a less complicated flavor for pizza sauces, so the toppings can shine. I also don't add garlic to the sauces, since I add fresh garlic to the pizza before spreading the sauce (page 201).

Pizza Toppings

You can use anything as a topping for pizza. Here are just a few suggestions:

minced fresh garlic

sauce of choice

olive oil

sliced mushrooms (cultivated or wild; raw or sautéed)

sliced onions (raw or caramelized)

sliced bell peppers (red, green, yellow, orange, or purple)

roasted bell peppers

roasted red peppers

blanched broccoli florets

grilled eggplant

zucchini or yellow squash (raw or sautéed)

sliced tomatoes

marinated artichoke hearts

oil-marinated sun-dried tomatoes

capers

fennel (raw, grilled, sautéed, or roasted)

spinach (whole leaves or chopped)

fresh or dried herbs

Assembling and Baking Pizza

Have ready:

Cornmeal (yellow or white)

1 recipe pizza crust of choice (pages 201–202)

4 teaspoons fresh garlic, minced

1 recipe pizza sauce of choice (pages 202–203)

3 cups coarsely shredded mozzarella cheese (2 cups fresh and 1 cup packaged)

Toppings of choice

Olive oil (optional)

1. For a gas oven: Remove the racks from the oven; place a large baking sheet on the floor of the oven, with the lip toward the back and the flat edge toward the front. For an electric oven: Set the rack to the lowest shelf setting; place a large baking sheet on that shelf, with the lip toward the back and the flat edge toward the front. Preheat the oven to 450°F.

2. Generously dust a pizza peel (a large wooden cutting board shaped like a paddle) or a second baking sheet with cornmeal. Lay the rolled-out crust on top.

3. Sprinkle the crust with 1 teaspoon of the garlic. Spread 1/4 of pizza sauce over the garlic, to within 1/2 inch of the edge of the crust. Sprinkle 3/4 cup of the mozzarella over the crust. Use additional toppings, if desired. Sprinkle lightly with olive oil, if desired. Don't be too generous with your sauce and cheese or they will run off the pie onto the baking sheet and start to smoke like crazy.

4. Slide the pizza off the pizza peel or baking sheet onto the preheated sheet in the oven (this may require a jerking motion, especially if you weren't generous enough with the cornmeal).

5. Bake 7 to 12 minutes or until crust is browned and cheese is melted.

6. To remove from oven, slide the peel or extra baking sheet under the pizza and lift, leaving the preheated baking sheet in the oven for the next pizza. Repeat with remaining crusts.

WHOLE WHEAT PIZZA CRUST

[V] [♥]

Makes: 4 pies (each 6 to 10 inches, depending on desired thickness); serves: 4 to 6

1/2 cup very warm water (105°–115°F)

1/2 teaspoon sugar

1 package active dry yeast

1 1/2 cups whole wheat flour

1 1/2 cups all-purpose flour, divided

1 tablespoon salt

3/4 cup water

1 tablespoon olive oil

1. In a glass measuring cup, stir together 1/2 cup warm water and the sugar. Stir in yeast and let proof (page 413).

2. In a large bowl combine the whole wheat flour, 1/2 cup of the all-purpose flour, and salt. Stir the yeast mixture, 3/4 cup water, and the oil into the flour. Stir in 1/2 cup more all-purpose flour or as much more as necessary to make a dough that is firm enough to handle.

3. Turn the dough onto a well-floured surface and knead in enough of the remaining all-purpose flour to make a dough that is manageable and no longer sticky.

4. Place the dough in a large, greased bowl and cover with greased plastic wrap. Set in a warm, draft-free spot until doubled in bulk. Punch down the dough; divide into 4 pieces.

5. Shape into pizza crust (see page 200). Use desired toppings to finish the pie.

SEMOLINA PIZZA CRUST

Makes: 4 pies (each 6 to 10 inches, depending on desired thickness); serves: 4 to 6

If you can't find semolina just substitute additional all-purpose flour, or make the whole wheat crust (page 201).

½ cup very warm water (105°–115°F)
½ teaspoon sugar
1 package active dry yeast
2 to 3 cups all-purpose flour, divided
¾ cup semolina
1 tablespoon salt
¾ cup water
1 tablespoon olive oil

1. In a glass measuring cup, stir together ½ cup warm water and the sugar. Stir in the yeast and let proof (see page 413).

2. In a large bowl combine 1½ cups of the flour and the semolina and salt. Stir the yeast mixture, ¾ cup water, and the oil into the flour mixture. Stir in ½ cup more flour or as much of the flour as necessary to make a dough that is firm enough to handle.

3. Turn the dough onto a well-floured surface and knead in enough of the remaining flour to make a dough that is manageable and no longer sticky.

4. Place the dough in a large, greased bowl and cover with greased plastic wrap. Set in a warm, draft-free spot until doubled in bulk. Punch down the dough; divide into 4 pieces.

5. Shape into pizza crust (page 200).

6. Use desired toppings to finish the pie.

TOMATO SAUCE FOR PIZZA

Makes: 3 cups (enough for four 8-inch pizzas)

2 tablespoons olive oil
1½ cups chopped onions
One 28-ounce can whole peeled Italian tomatoes in puree, undrained
2 tablespoons tomato paste
⅛ teaspoon salt, or to taste

1. In a 2-quart saucepan, heat the oil over medium-high heat. Add the onions; cook, stirring, until onions are softened, about 2 minutes.

2. Stir in the tomatoes, breaking them up with the back of a spoon. Stir in the tomato paste and salt.

3. Bring to a boil. Reduce heat and simmer, uncovered, 30 to 40 minutes or until thickened.

Variation: Stir in ½ cup chopped fresh basil or 2 teaspoons dried with the tomato paste.

PESTO SAUCE FOR PIZZA

Makes: 1 cup (enough for four 8-inch pizzas)

This recipe is less oily and is thicker than regular pesto (page 476). It also has no garlic, pine nuts, or cheese, and is pureed in the processor instead of just chopped.

2 cups packed fresh basil leaves
½ cup extra virgin olive oil
¼ teaspoon salt, or to taste

1. Place the basil in a food processor container fitted with a steel blade (a blender will not work for this purpose). Cover and process until finely chopped.

2. With the motor running, gradually pour the oil into the processor and process until pureed.

3. Stir in salt.

Variation: Substitute 1 cup parsley for 1 cup of the basil.

WHITE PIZZA

Makes: 4 pizzas; serves: 4

1 1/2 cups (12 ounces) ricotta cheese
1 cup shredded provolone cheese
1/4 cup grated Parmesan cheese
1/2 teaspoon dried basil
1 recipe pizza dough (page 201–2)
1 tablespoon garlic, minced
1 1/3 cups shredded mozzarella cheese

1. In a medium bowl, stir together the ricotta, provolone, Parmesan, and basil.

2. Prepare pizza dough according to directions (pages 201, 202).

3. Sprinkle 1/4 of the garlic on each pizza dough, spread 1/4 of the cheese mixture over each dough, and top with 1/4 of the mozzarella.

4. Bake at 425°F for 10 to 12 minutes.

Gnocchi

My method for making gnocchi is slightly unorthodox. Authentic gnocchi are shaped by rolling the dough around the handle of a wooden spoon and making fork marks on the outside. My method is easier, and tastes great.

Serve gnocchi with the sauces suggested below, or any type of sauce: cream, pesto, tomato, or the like. They're very versatile.

GNOCCHI DI PATATE

Makes: 80 gnocchi; serves: 4 to 6

2 cups mashed potatoes
1 cup all-purpose flour
1/3 cup whole wheat flour
1 tablespoon olive oil
1 teaspoon salt, or to taste

1. In a large bowl, stir together all the ingredients until mixture is a soft dough.

2. Turn onto floured board and knead 20 times.

3. Divide the dough into fourths. Roll each quarter into a rope 12 inches long. Slice each log into 20 pieces; set pieces onto a surface dusted with flour. Flatten each piece using the tines of a fork. Fold the gnocchi in half with the tine marks on the outside.

4. Bring a large pot of salted water to a boil. Add the gnocchi and cook until they float to the top. (You may have to do this 1/3 at a time, if you don't have at least an 8-quart pot.) Drain.

Variation: Spinach Gnocchi: Add to the dough 1/2 of a 10-ounce package of frozen chopped spinach, thawed and squeezed dry. Add up to 1/2 cup extra all-purpose flour if the dough is sticky.

SPINACH AND RICOTTA GNOCCHI

Makes: 60 gnocchi; serves: 4 to 6

One 10-ounce package frozen chopped
  spinach, thawed and squeezed dry
1 cup ricotta cheese
¼ cup grated Parmesan cheese
¼ teaspoon salt, or to taste
2 egg yolks
¾ to 1 cup all-purpose flour

1. In a large bowl, stir together the spinach,
ricotta, Parmesan, and salt. Stir in the yolks. Stir
in flour until mixture is a soft dough.

2. Divide dough into fourths. On a floured
board with floured hands, roll each quarter into
a rope 12 inches long. Slice each log into
15 pieces. Flatten each piece using the tines of
a fork. Fold the gnocchi in half with the tine
marks outside.

3. Bring a large pot of salted water to a boil.
Add the gnocchi and cook until they float to the
top. (You may have to do this ⅓ at a time, if you
don't have at least an 8-quart pot.) Drain.

GNOCCHI WITH BUTTER AND CHEESE

Makes: 60 to 80 gnocchi; serves: 4 to 6

1 recipe gnocchi (potato, page 203, or
  spinach, page 204)
⅓ cup melted butter or margarine
¾ cup grated Parmesan cheese

1. Preheat broiler.

2. Place the gnocchi in a 9 × 13-inch baking
pan. Pour the butter or margarine over the
gnocchi and stir to coat completely. Sprinkle
with cheese.

3. Place under broiler, 4 inches from the heat
source. Broil 2 to 3 minutes or until the cheese
is browned.

Variation: Substitute hard Asiago cheese for
the Parmesan.

NOODLES WITH BROCCOLI AND CABBAGE

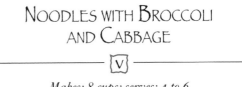

Makes: 8 cups; serves: 4 to 6

*I used Mrs. Dash or a similar (unsalted) sea-
soning mix and dried lo mein noodles. If you can't
find lo mein noodles, use thin spaghetti.*

¾ cup vegetable broth (pages 93–95)
1 tablespoon soy sauce
2 tablespoons mirin (rice wine) or sherry
2 teaspoons all-purpose seasoning
1 teaspoon cornstarch
8 ounces dried noodles
2 tablespoons vegetable oil
3 cups cubed cabbage
1 cup sliced scallions (1-inch pieces; white
  and green parts)
2 cloves garlic, minced
4 cups broccoli florets
1½ teaspoons sesame oil

1. In a small bowl, stir together the broth, soy
sauce, mirin, seasoning, and cornstarch; set
aside.

2. Cook the noodles according to package
directions; drain.

3. While the noodles are cooking, heat the oil
in a wok or large skillet. Add the cabbage, scallions, and garlic; cook, stirring, until slightly
softened, about 2 minutes. Add the broccoli;
cook, stirring, until tender-crisp, about 3
minutes.

4. Add the noodles and soy sauce and mixture. Cook, stirring, until heated through. Add the sesame oil; toss until combined.

Variation: Substitute chili oil for ¼ teaspoon sesame oil, or to taste.

Noodles with Peanut Sauce

Makes: 4 ¹⁄₂ cups; serves: 4 to 6

I get my noodles for this dish in Chinatown, where the lo mein noodles are sold fresh, not dried. These noodles are square egg noodles, similar in diameter to spaghetti. If you don't have access to fresh lo mein noodles, you can use 8 ounces of thin spaghetti.

12 ounces lo mein noodles
¼ cup smooth peanut butter
3 tablespoons soy sauce
1 tablespoon mirin (rice wine) or dry sherry
2 teaspoons cider vinegar
2 teaspoons sugar
1 teaspoon chili oil
½ small clove garlic
⅓ cup sliced scallions (white and light green parts)

1. Cook the noodles according to package directions. Drain and rinse under cold water until cool.

2. While the noodles are cooking, place the peanut butter, soy sauce, mirin, vinegar, sugar, chili oil, and garlic in a blender or food processor container fitted with a steel blade. Cover and process until thoroughly combined.

3. Toss noodles with peanut sauce and scallions.

Variation: Toss 1 cup blanched bean sprouts or julienned cucumber with the noodles.

Noodles with Sesame Sauce

Makes: 5 cups; serves: 3 to 4

This light, delicate dish can be made slightly spicy with the chili oil or left mild without it. Tomoshiraga somen is available at Asian groceries. If you can't find it, use angel hair pasta instead.

8 ounces Tomoshiraga somen (very thin noodles)
½ cup tahini (sesame paste)
3 tablespoons mirin (rice wine) or dry sherry
1½ tablespoons dark soy sauce
3 tablespoons water
1½ tablespoons sugar
2 teaspoons sesame oil
½ teaspoon ground ginger
½ teaspoon chili oil (optional)
3 cloves garlic
1 cup chopped snow peas or sugar-snap peas
¾ cup coarsely shredded cucumber
⅓ cup sliced scallions (white and green parts)

1. Cook the noodles in boiling salted water 2 to 3 minutes or until tender. Drain into strainer and run under cold water until chilled. Place in a large bowl.

2. Place the tahini, mirin, soy sauce, water, sugar, sesame oil, ginger, and chili oil into a blender container. Cover and process until smooth. While blender is running, remove cap and drop in the garlic. Continue blending until garlic is completely minced.

3. Add the snow peas, cucumber, and scallions to the bowl with the noodles. Pour sesame sauce over the noodle salad; toss until completely combined.

Variation: Add 1 cup mung bean sprouts to the salad.

LO MEIN

Makes: 8 cups; serves: 4 to 6

My dad's favorite Chinese dish is pork lo mein, but since he's a good guy, he orders vegetable lo mein so I can share with him. He likes this homemade version.

1½ tablespoons soy sauce
1 tablespoon mirin (rice wine) or sherry
1 teaspoon cornstarch
12 ounces dry lo mein noodles or very thin spaghetti
2 tablespoons vegetable oil
1 cup julienned carrots
1 cup julienned celery
2 cups shredded bok choy or Chinese cabbage
1 cup sliced mushrooms
½ cup sliced scallions (1½-inch pieces; white and green parts)
2 cloves garlic, minced

1. In a small bowl, stir together the soy sauce, mirin, and cornstarch.

2. Cook the noodles according to package directions; drain.

3. In a wok or large skillet, heat the oil over high heat. Add the carrots, celery, bok choy, mushrooms, scallions, and garlic. Cook, stirring, until tender-crisp, about 5 minutes. Add the noodles and toss. Add the sauce and cook, stirring, until noodles are coated and heated through.

Variation: Add 1 cup baby corn when you add the noodles.

BROCCOLI RABE WITH RICE NOODLES

Makes: 6½ cups; serves: 4 to 6

I go to Chinatown to get fresh rice noodles, but you can use the dried kind available in Asian markets. Just cook them according to package direction, then use as fresh. I like to use the wider noodles (about ¾ inch) for this recipe, although thinner noodles also work. The black bean sauce is also available in Asian markets.

3 tablespoons vegetable oil
4 cloves garlic, minced
4 cups chopped broccoli rabe
1 cup sliced scallions (1-inch pieces; white and green parts)
1 cup mung bean sprouts
1 tablespoon black bean sauce
3 tablespoons soy sauce
1½ pounds fresh rice noodles

1. In wok or large skillet, heat the oil over high heat. Add the garlic; stir-fry 10 seconds.

2. Add the broccoli rabe, scallions, and bean sprouts. Stir-fry until tender-crisp, about 4 minutes. Stir in the bean and soy sauces.

3. Add the noodles; cook, stirring, until heated through, 2 minutes longer.

Variation: Substitute regular broccoli for the broccoli rabe and/or soy bean sprouts for the mung bean sprouts.

MEE GROB

Makes: 5 cups; serves: 4

*The basic principal of Thai cooking is to combine
all four of the basic tastes in each dish, so look for
the elements of sweet, sour, hot, and salty in these
next two dishes. Mee Grob uses rice noodles, which
you can find dried in many Asian markets.*

¼ cup fresh lemon juice
¼ cup *nam pla* (page 482)
¼ cup sugar
2 tablespoons tomato paste
1 tablespoon rice vinegar
Vegetable oil for deep frying
6 ounces rice sticks
3 tablespoons vegetable oil, divided
2 eggs, beaten
1 tablespoon minced shallot
1 tablespoon minced garlic
¼ teaspoon red pepper flakes
3 cups mung bean sprouts
¾ cup finely chopped pressed bean curd
⅓ cup sliced scallions (white and green parts)
2 tablespoons chopped fresh cilantro
2 tablespoons chopped peanuts

1. In a 1-quart saucepan, stir together the
lemon juice, nam pla, sugar, tomato paste, and
rice vinegar. Cook over high heat 3 minutes or
until liquid is reduced by half.

2. Pour vegetable oil 1½ inches deep into a
3-quart saucepan; heat until a small piece of
rice stick puffs up and turns white when
dropped in. Break the rice sticks into small
bundles. Fry quickly on each side until puffed.
Remove from oil; drain. Repeat until all rice
sticks are cooked.

3. In a small skillet, heat 1 tablespoon of the
vegetable oil over high heat. Add the eggs; cook
until dry. Chop and set aside.

4. In a wok or large skillet, heat the remaining
2 tablespoons of oil over high heat. Add the
shallot, garlic, and red pepper flakes; cook, stirring, 30 seconds. Add the bean sprouts; cook,
stirring, until softened, about 2 minutes. Add
the rice sticks, sauce, bean curd, scallions,
cilantro, and peanuts. Cook, stirring, until
heated through, 2 minutes longer.

Eggs, Cheese, and Dairy

Look for more egg recipes in the Breakfast, Brunch, Lunch chapter (pages 432–67).

Roquefort Soufflé

Serves: 4 as a main dish, 6 as an appetizer

Since the saltiness of cheeses varies, judge the amount of salt needed for this recipe accordingly. If your cheese is salty, decrease added salt by half.

Melted butter or margarine
1 tablespoon Parmesan cheese
1½ cups milk
4 ounces Roquefort cheese
2 teaspoons dry mustard
½ teaspoon anchovy-free Worcestershire sauce
¼ teaspoon salt, or to taste
⅛ teaspoon ground red pepper
¼ cups (½ stick) butter or margarine
¼ cup all-purpose flour
4 egg yolks
5 egg whites
¼ teaspoon cream of tartar

1. Preheat the oven to 375°F. Grease a 7-inch soufflé dish with melted butter or margarine. Dust with Parmesan; set aside.

2. Place the milk, Roquefort, mustard, Worcestershire sauce, salt, and red pepper in a blender or food processor container fitted with a steel blade. Cover and process until smooth.

3. In a medium saucepan, melt ¼ cup butter or margarine over medium heat. Stir in the flour until smooth. Stir in cheese mixture. Cook, stirring constantly, until mixture comes to boil, about 5 minutes. Remove from heat; cool 20 minutes.

4. In a medium bowl, lightly beat the egg yolks. Stir 1 cup of the cooled cheese mixture into yolks, then stir the yolk mixture into the pot with the cheese mixture.

5. In a large bowl with clean beaters, beat the egg whites with the cream of tartar until stiff but not dry. Fold the egg whites into the cheese mixture. Pour into prepared dish. Bake 30 minutes, Serve immediately.

Variation: Use Stilton or other blue cheese instead of Roquefort.

Broccoli Soufflé

Serves: 4 as a main dish, 6 as an appetizer

My guests couldn't believe how light and airy this soufflé is; they also couldn't stop eating it.

Melted butter or margarine
1 to 2 tablespoons grated Parmesan cheese
¼ cup butter or margarine
¼ cup all-purpose flour
1½ cups milk
1 cup shredded Cheddar cheese
½ teaspoon anchovy-free Worcestershire sauce
¼ teaspoon salt, or to taste
⅛ teaspoon ground red pepper
2 egg yolks
1½ cups chopped cooked broccoli (fresh, cooked until tender, or frozen, thawed)
6 egg whites
¼ teaspoon cream of tartar

1. Preheat the oven to 375°F. Grease an 8-cup soufflé dish with melted butter or margarine. Dust with Parmesan cheese; set aside.

2. In a 2-quart saucepan, melt ¼ cup butter or margarine over medium heat. Stir in the flour until smooth. Using a whisk, stir in the milk. Cook, stirring constantly, until mixture comes

to boil, about 5 minutes. Remove from heat. Stir in the Cheddar, Worcestershire sauce, salt, and red pepper until cheese is melted. Cool 20 minutes.

3. In a medium bowl, lightly beat the egg yolks. Stir 1 cup of cooled cheese mixture into yolks. Stir in broccoli.

4. In a large bowl with clean beaters, beat the egg whites with cream of tartar until stiff but not dry. Fold the egg whites into the broccoli-cheese mixture. Pour into prepared pan. Bake 30 minutes. Serve immediately.

Savory Bread Puddings

Savory bread pudding is a first cousin to spoon bread, a second cousin to poultry stuffing, and a third cousin, once removed, to a soufflé. It's perfect as a brunch or lunch entree or as a side dish. I like to use squishy whole wheat bread (Wonder) to absorb the custard as evenly as possible.

EASY FAUX SOUFFLÉ

Makes: 3 ¹/₂ cups; serves: 4

7 slices whole wheat bread, cubed
½ cup grated Cheddar cheese
3 tablespoons melted butter or margarine
3 eggs
¼ cup grated Parmesan cheese
½ teaspoon anchovy-free Worcestershire sauce
¼ teaspoon salt, or to taste
⅛ teaspoon pepper
2 cups scalded milk

1. Preheat the oven to 350°F. Grease a 2-quart soufflé dish.

2. In a large bowl, toss the bread, Cheddar, and melted butter or margarine together. Put into prepared soufflé dish.

3. Beat together the eggs, Parmesan, Worcestershire sauce, salt, and pepper. Gradually beat in milk. Pour over bread cubes.

4. Bake 45 minutes. Serve immediately.

Variation: Use shredded Swiss or Gouda instead of the Cheddar.

SAVORY MUSHROOM BREAD PUDDING

Makes: 3¹/₂ cups; serves: 3 to 6

I used shiitake mushrooms, but regular cultivated mushrooms would be just fine too.

¼ cup (½ stick) butter or margarine, divided
½ cup finely chopped celery
¼ cup finely chopped onions
1 cup chopped mushrooms
¼ cup chopped fresh parsley
½ teaspoon poultry seasoning
¼ teaspoon dried thyme
6 slices whole wheat bread, cubed (about 4½ cups)
3 eggs
1⅓ cups milk
¼ teaspoon salt, or to taste
⅛ teaspoon pepper

1. Preheat the oven to 350°F. Grease a 1½-quart casserole.

2. In a medium skillet, melt 1 tablespoon of the butter or margarine over medium-high heat. Add the celery and onions; cook, stirring, until onions are softened, about 3 minutes. Add the mushrooms; cook, stirring, until mushrooms are softened, about 3 minutes. Stir in the parsley, poultry seasoning, and thyme.

3. Place the remaining 3 tablespoons butter or margarine in the casserole and put in the oven to melt (about 7 minutes). Add the bread and toss until coated with the butter or margarine. Add the mushroom mixture; toss.

4. In a medium bowl, beat the eggs. Beat in the milk, salt, and pepper.

5. Pour the egg mixture over the bread and toss. Let stand 10 minutes, tossing once or twice.

6. Bake 50 to 60 minutes or until a knife inserted in center comes out fairly clean (there is no liquid clinging to the knife) and the top is browned and pudding is puffed.

Variation: Add ⅓ cup finely chopped green bell peppers when you add the celery.

SPINACH AND DILL SAVORY BREAD PUDDING

Makes: 3³/₄ cups; serves: 3 to 6

3 tablespoons butter or margarine
6 slices whole wheat bread, cubed (about 4½ cups cubes)
1 cup chopped spinach
¼ cup chopped scallions (white and green parts)
3 tablespoons snipped fresh dill
3 eggs
1¾ cups scalded milk
¼ teaspoon salt, or to taste
⅛ teaspoon pepper

1. Preheat the oven to 350°F. Grease a 1½-quart casserole.

2. Place the butter or margarine in the casserole and put in the oven to melt (about 7 minutes). Add the bread and toss until coated with the butter or margarine. Add the spinach, scallions, and dill; toss.

3. In a medium bowl, beat the eggs. Beat in the milk, salt, and pepper.

4. Pour the egg mixture over the bread and toss. Let stand 10 minutes, tossing once or twice.

5. Bake 50 to 60 minutes or until a knife inserted in the center comes out fairly clean (there is no liquid clinging to the knife) and the top is browned and pudding is puffed.

Variation: Add 1 cup shredded Gouda when you add the spinach.

QUICHES AND SAVORY TARTS

I usually serve quiches or savory tarts to company. They're easy to prepare and only require a green salad to make a complete meal (they're also great for brunch and lunch). It's the kind of meal I feel comfortable inviting both vegetarians and nonvegetarians to because no one ever feels left out or deprived (unless, of course, my guests are vegans—in which case I'd make a different menu entirely).

Quiches and savory tarts are also excellent for large crowds because they are easy to serve and are fine just slightly warm. For a buffet, I'd generally serve two or three different types of quiche or tart—and the best part is that you can bake them in advance and freeze until needed. Just reheat about 20 minutes at 350°F (although, honestly, I do prefer them fresh from the oven). A large salad and some bread complete the meal.

When baking a quiche or tart it's essential that the crust be intact with no little cracks or holes; otherwise the custard will seep through the cracks and into the crust, making it extremely soggy.

VIDALIA ONION QUICHE

Makes: one 9-inch quiche; serves: 6

Pastry for one 9-inch pie (page 518), or one 9-inch frozen deep-dish crust
2 tablespoons butter or margarine
3 cups sliced Vidalia, Maui, or other sweet onions
1 cup grated Swiss cheese
2 eggs
1 cup half-and-half or milk
½ teaspoon salt, or to taste
¼ teaspoon dried thyme
¼ teaspoon dried tarragon
⅛ teaspoon pepper

1. Preheat the oven to 425°F.

2. Roll the pastry into an 11-inch circle. Line a 9-inch pie dish with the rolled dough; crimp the edges. Weigh down the pastry using pie weights or dried beans to prevent the crust from rising. Bake 20 minutes, or until lightly browned. Remove weights and cool.

3. In a large skillet, melt the butter or margarine over medium-high heat. Add the onions and stir until coated. Reduce heat to low; cover and cook 20 minutes or until very soft but not browned.

4. Sprinkle the cheese into pie shell; add the onions and toss gently.

5. In a large bowl, beat the eggs; stir in remaining ingredients. Pour into pie shell.

6. Reduce oven temperature to 350°F. Bake 50 minutes or until knife inserted in center comes out clean. Cool on rack 5 minutes before slicing.

Variation: Use Gouda or another cheese with a similar consistency.

DILLED ASPARAGUS QUICHE

Makes: one 9-inch quiche; serves: 6

Pastry for one 9-inch pie (page 518), or one
    9-inch frozen deep-dish crust
1 tablespoon butter or margarine
1 1/4 cups chopped fresh asparagus (1/4-inch
    pieces)
1/2 cup chopped onions
1 cup shredded Gouda cheese
3 eggs
1 1/2 cups milk
1/4 cup snipped fresh dill, or 1 1/2 teaspoons
    dried dill weed
1/4 teaspoon salt, or to taste
1/8 teaspoon pepper

1. Preheat the oven to 425°F.

2. Roll the pastry into an 11-inch circle. Line
a 9-inch pie dish with the rolled dough; crimp
the edges. Weigh down the pastry using pie
weights or dried beans to prevent the crust
from rising. Bake l0 minutes. Remove weights
and cool.

3. In a medium skillet, melt the butter or margarine over medium-high heat. Add the asparagus and onions; cook, stirring, until onions are
transparent, about 3 minutes. Sprinkle the
cheese into pie shell; add the asparagus and
onions and toss gently to combine.

4. In a large bowl, beat eggs; stir in remaining
ingredients. Pour into pie shell.

5. Reduce oven temperature to 350°F. Bake
50 minutes or until knife inserted in center
comes out clean. Cool on rack 5 minutes before
slicing.

Variation: Use Swiss or another cheese with
a similar consistency.

TOMATO-FETA TART

Makes: one 10-inch tart; serves: 6

*The sliced tomatoes on top make this tart as
attractive as it is tasty. However, the skin on the
tomato can make it a little hard to slice into neat
pieces. If you are feeling ambitious, you can skin
the tomatoes before slicing. Dip into boiling water
for 2 minutes, then plunge into ice water and peel
off the skin.*

Pastry for one 9-inch pie (page 518), or one
    9-inch frozen deep-dish crust
3 eggs
1 1/3 cups milk
1 clove garlic, minced
1/4 teaspoon salt, or to taste
1/4 teaspoon dried oregano
Dash Tabasco
1 1/2 cups crumbled feta cheese (about
    8 ounces)
15 thin slices tomato

1. Preheat the oven to 375°F.

2. Roll the pastry into an 11-inch circle. Line
a 10-inch tart pan with the rolled dough. Weigh
down the pastry using pie weights or dried
beans to prevent the crust from rising. Bake
20 minutes or until just lightly browned.
Remove from oven and remove weights.

3. Decrease oven temperature to 350°F.

4. In a large bowl, beat the eggs lightly. Add
the milk, garlic, salt, oregano, and Tabasco; beat
until combined.

5. Sprinkle the feta cheese into the bottom of
the tart shell. Pour in the egg mixture. Arrange
the tomato slices on top.

6. Bake 1 hour or until puffy and slightly
browned on top.

Variation: Sprinkle 1/4 cup sliced black
olives over the tomatoes.

Broccoli-Cheddar Quiche

Makes: one 9-inch quiche; serves: 6

Pastry for one 9-inch pie (page 518), or one
   9-inch frozen deep-dish crust

3 eggs

1 ½ cups milk

1 teaspoon anchovy-free Worcestershire sauce

½ teaspoon salt, or to taste

¼ teaspoon pepper

1 ½ cups shredded Cheddar cheese
   (6 ounces)

2 cups chopped broccoli (fresh, cooked; or
   frozen, thawed)

½ cup thinly sliced scallions (white and green
   parts)

1. Preheat the oven to 425°F.

2. Roll the pastry into an 11-inch circle. Line
a 9-inch pie dish with the rolled dough. Weigh
down the pastry using pie weights or dried
beans to prevent the crust from rising. Bake
10 minutes. Remove from oven and remove
weights.

3. Decrease oven temperature to 350°F.

4. In a large bowl, beat the eggs lightly. Add
the milk, Worcestershire sauce, salt, and pepper; beat until combined.

5. Sprinkle the cheese into the bottom of the
tart shell. Add the broccoli and scallions,
and toss gently to combine. Pour in the egg
mixture.

6. Bake 50 to 60 minutes or until puffy and
slightly browned on top. Let stand 10 minutes
before slicing.

Variation: Use Gouda or another hard
cheese instead of the Cheddar.

Gorgonzola, Leek, and Fennel Tart

Makes: one 10-inch tart; serves: 6 to 8

Pastry for one 10-inch pie (page 518)

1 ½ tablespoons olive oil

2 cups sliced fennel

¾ cup sliced leeks (white and light green
   parts only)

¾ cup crumbled Gorgonzola cheese

3 eggs

1 ½ cups milk

½ teaspoon dried tarragon

¼ teaspoon salt, or to taste

¼ teaspoon pepper

1. Preheat the oven to 425°F.

2. Roll the pastry into an 11-inch circle. Line
a 10-inch tart pan with the rolled dough. Weigh
down the pastry using pie weights or dried
beans to prevent the crust from rising. Bake
10 minutes. Remove from oven and remove
weights.

3. Decrease oven temperature to 325°F.

4. In a medium skillet, heat the oil over
medium-high heat. Add the fennel and leeks;
cook, stirring, until softened, about 3 minutes.

5. Sprinkle the cheese into baked tart shell.
Spoon the fennel mixture over the cheese. Toss
gently to combine.

6. In a large bowl, beat the eggs lightly. Add
the remaining ingredients; beat until combined. Pour the egg mixture into the tart.

7. Bake 50 minutes or until puffy and slightly
browned on top. Let stand 10 minutes before
slicing.

MUSHROOM-LEEK TART

Makes: one 10-inch tart; serves: 6 to 8

1½ tablespoons butter or margarine
¾ cup sliced leeks (white and light green parts only)
3½ cups sliced mushrooms
1½ cups shredded Jarlsberg cheese
One 10-inch fully baked tart shell
2 eggs
1 cup vegetable broth (pages 93–95)
½ cup sour cream
1 tablespoon Dijon mustard
¼ teaspoon dried thyme
¼ teaspoon dried tarragon
¼ teaspoon salt, or to taste
¼ teaspoon pepper

1. Preheat the oven to 325°F.

2. In a medium skillet, melt the butter or margarine over medium-high heat. Add the leeks; cook, stirring, 30 seconds. Add the mushrooms; cook, stirring, until softened, about 4 minutes.

3. Sprinkle the cheese into the baked tart shell. Spoon the mushrooms over the cheese. Toss gently to combine.

4. In a large bowl, beat the eggs lightly. Add the remaining ingredients; beat until combined. Pour the egg mixture into the tart.

5. Bake 45 minutes or until puffy and slightly browned on top. Let stand 10 minutes before slicing.

Variation: Wild Mushroom and Leek Tart: Instead of the cultivated mushrooms, use a mixture of wild mushrooms, such as shiitake, portobello, crimini, and chanterelles. For a less expensive version, use half wild mushrooms and half cultivated.

ROASTED EGGPLANT AND RED PEPPER TART

Makes: one 9-inch tart; serves: 6

As with the tomatoes in the Tomato-Feta Tart, the eggplant skin is tough, and slicing the tart is easier if you peel the eggplant. However, the peel does make the tart look more interesting. It's your call.

Pastry for one 9-inch pie (page 518)
2 eggs
1¼ cups milk
½ cup grated Parmesan cheese
½ teaspoon dried basil
¼ teaspoon salt, or to taste
⅛ teaspoon pepper
½ cup sliced roasted red peppers (homemade, page 276, or jarred)
12 slices grilled eggplant (½ inch thick), peeled or unpeeled (page 233)

1. Preheat the oven to 400°F.

2. Roll the pastry into an 11-inch circle. Line a 9-inch tart pan with the rolled dough. Weigh down the pastry using pie weights or dried beans to prevent the crust from rising. Bake 12 minutes or until just lightly browned. Remove from oven and remove weights.

3. Decrease oven temperature to 375°F.

4. In a large bowl, beat the eggs lightly. Add the milk, Parmesan cheese, basil, salt, and pepper; beat until combined.

5. Sprinkle the roasted peppers into the bottom of the tart shell. Arrange the eggplant slices on top. Pour in the egg mixture.

6. Bake 25 to 35 minutes or until puffy and slightly browned on top.

SQUASH AND BASIL TART

Makes: one 9-inch tart; serves: 4 to 6

If you're entertaining and want to make this tart look spectacular, arrange the squash slices in concentric circles instead of just tossing them in the tart shell.

1½ cups shredded Fontina cheese
1 fully baked 9-inch tart shell (pages 517–18)
⅓ cup chopped scallions (white and green parts)
⅓ cup chopped fresh basil
¾ cup sliced zucchini
¾ cup sliced yellow squash
3 eggs
¾ vegetable broth (pages 93–95)
¾ cup milk
½ teaspoon dried oregano
¼ teaspoon dried thyme
¼ teaspoon salt, or to taste
⅛ teaspoon pepper

1. Preheat the oven to 350°F.

2. Sprinkle the Fontina into the baked tart shell. Top with the scallions and basil. Add the zucchini and squash and toss gently to combine.

3. In a large bowl, beat the eggs lightly. Add the broth, milk, oregano, thyme, salt, and pepper; beat until combined. Pour the egg mixture into the tart.

4. Bake 1 hour to 1 hour 10 minutes or until puffy and slightly browned on top. Let stand 10 minutes before slicing.

CHILI RELLENOS

Makes: 8 chili rellenos; serves: 4

If you are fortunate enough to be able to find fresh Anaheim chilies, roast them, skin them, and seed them. If you can't find fresh, use canned whole chilies. Be sure to pat them dry before stuffing them.

8 ounces Monterey Jack cheese, cut lengthwise into eighths (6 × ½ × ½-inch sticks)
8 whole green chilies, seeded (see note above)
½ cup cornmeal
⅓ cup all-purpose flour
¼ cup whole wheat flour
¼ teaspoon baking powder
¼ teaspoon salt, or to taste
1 egg
1 egg white
⅔ cup milk
Vegetable oil for deep frying

1. Place 1 piece of cheese into the cavity of each chili; set aside.

2. In a medium bowl or on a piece of waxed paper, stir together the cornmeal, both flours, the baking powder, and salt.

3. In a large bowl, beat the egg and egg white. Beat in the milk. Add the dry ingredients and stir until combined.

4. Pour the oil about 2 inches deep into a large pot. Heat the oil to 375°F.

5. Dip the stuffed chilies into the batter. Drop into the oil and cook until golden all over, about 5 minutes. Drain on paper towels.

Variation: You can also stuff these with Cheddar or mozzarella, or any combination of these and Monterey Jack.

THREE-CHEESE MACARONI AND CHEESE

Makes: 7 cups; serves: 4 to 6

This is definitely an American classic. Unfortunately, I think many kids who have grown up with the packaged versions may be disappointed with the real thing—it won't taste "right" to them. Old-timers, however, will love this very creamy comfort food.

12 ounces elbow macaroni
¼ cup butter or margarine
¼ cup all-purpose flour
3 cups milk
1½ cups shredded Cheddar cheese
1 cup shredded Gouda cheese
½ cup shredded mozzarella cheese
¼ teaspoon anchovy-free Worcestershire sauce
¼ teaspoon salt, or to taste
Bread crumbs (optional)

1. Preheat the oven to 350°F.

2. Cook the macaroni according to package directions, for the minimum suggested time; drain.

3. In a 3-quart saucepan, over medium-high heat, melt the butter or margarine. Stir in the flour until absorbed.

4. Using a whisk, stir in the milk. Cook over medium heat, stirring constantly, until mixture comes to a boil (make sure you get all the edges of the pot so that there are no clumps in the bottom). Stir in all cheeses, the Worcestershire sauce, and salt. Remove from heat and continue stirring until cheeses are melted. Stir in the cooked macaroni. Pour into a greased 9-inch-square baking pan. Sprinkle with bread crumbs, if desired.

5. Bake 30 to 45 minutes or until bread crumbs are browned and mixture is heated through and bubbly.

Variation: Good Old Macaroni and Cheese: Use an additional 1½ cups of shredded Cheddar instead of the Gouda and mozzarella.

BAKED SPAGHETTI

Makes: one 9 × 9-inch panful; serves: 4

The only way my mother could get us to eat fish was to serve it with baked spaghetti. We all loved the side dish so much that we would force down some of the fish. Now that I don't have to eat the fish, I can just enjoy the baked spaghetti. I have no idea where my mother found this recipe (although I suspect it may have been in an ad for Campbell's soup), but we especially loved the crispy top of this baked dish.

8 ounces spaghetti
3 tablespoons butter or margarine
One 10¾-ounce can Campbell's tomato soup
1½ cups shredded Cheddar cheese

1. Preheat the oven to 375°F. Grease a 9-inch-square baking pan.

2. Cook the spaghetti according to package directions; drain.

3. Return the spaghetti to the empty pot and stir in the butter until melted. Stir in the soup and Cheddar cheese. Spoon into pan.

4. Bake 45 minutes or until top is nicely browned.

Variation: Bake in a 9 ×13-inch pan for more browned top.

TOFU, TEMPEH, SEITAN, AND TEXTURED VEGETABLE PROTEIN (TVP)

Tofu is made from soymilk, which is coagulated and then pressed into cakes. Tofu comes in different consistencies: firm or soft, as well as silken, which is custardlike. It can be purchased fresh (usually found floating in a tub of water) or packaged in plastic tubs. Silken tofu is usually sold in aseptic packages. Look for expiration dates on the packages. It is fairly bland and can be added to most dishes when you want to give a dish a protein boost.

In addition to the "fresh" tofu, many health food stores sell "pressed" and/or baked tofu. Pressed tofu is usually flavored and is firmer and chewier than "fresh" tofu.

Tempeh is made of cooked soybeans, fermented with a mold culture. As the beans ferment, they are bound into blocks or cakes by the mold. Tempeh can be purchased in packages in the refrigerator case of health food stores. Be sure to check expiration dates.

The flavor of tempeh is not everyone's cup of tea, although many people feel that frying improves the flavor greatly. The texture of fried tempeh is somewhat like french fries.

Seitan, also called "wheat gluten," is just that, cooked gluten from wheat. A dough is formed and then rinsed and kneaded until all that remains is the gluten, which is then cooked. It is rather chewy and meatlike in texture. It's frequently sold packed in a diluted soy sauce, which makes the seitan easily suitable to dishes with Oriental flavors.

Textured Vegetable Protein (TVP) is made from soy flour which is pressed into granules. When re-hydrated, these granules have a consistency very similar to chopped meat. TVP is quite flavorless and will assume the flavor of the dish it is cooked in.

SZECHUAN SHREDDED VEGETABLES WITH PRESSED TOFU

─── V ───

Makes: 5½ cups; serves: 4 to 6

I think this dish is spiced just right; however, the definition of "right" varies greatly. Use more or less of the red pepper flakes to suit your own tastes.

⅓ cup vegetable broth (pages 93–95) or water
1 tablespoon soy sauce
1 tablespoon mirin (rice wine) or sherry
1 tablespoon cornstarch
2 tablespoons vegetable oil
1 tablespoon minced fresh ginger
3 cloves garlic, minced
¼ teaspoon red pepper flakes
3 cups julienned carrots
2 cups julienned celery
1 cup julienned snow peas
½ cup julienned scallions (white and green parts)
2 cups julienned, pressed tofu
1 teaspoon sesame oil

1. In a small bowl, stir together the broth, soy sauce, mirin, and cornstarch; set aside.

2. In a wok or large skillet, heat the oil over high heat. Add the ginger, garlic, and red pepper flakes; cook, stirring, 10 seconds.

3. Add the carrots, celery, snow peas, and scallions; cook, stirring until softened, about 4 minutes. Add the tofu; cook, stirring, until heated through, about 2 minutes.

4. Add the soy mixture to the wok; cook, stirring, until sauce is thickened, about 1 minute longer. Stir in the sesame oil.

Variation: Use julienned red or green bell peppers instead of—or in addition to—the snow peas.

SUKIYAKI

— V̄ —

Makes: 6 cups; serves: 2 to 3

If you can't find cellophane noodles—also called bean threads—just leave them out.

2 ounces cellophane noodles
Boiling water for soaking noodles and mushrooms
6 dried shiitake mushrooms
¼ cup vegetable broth (pages 93–95)
3 tablespoons saki, mirin (rice wine), or sherry
3 tablespoons dark soy sauce
1½ tablespoons sugar
1 tablespoon vegetable oil
1 cup thinly sliced Spanish onions
2 sliced scallions (2-inch pieces; white and green parts)
1 bunch fresh watercress (6 to 8 ounces), thoroughly rinsed
1 cup mung bean sprouts
½ cup thinly sliced carrots
2 cakes silken tofu, cubed (8 ounces)

1. In a medium bowl, soak noodles in boiling water to cover for 15 minutes or until softened; drain and set aside.

2. In a small bowl, soak the mushrooms in ½ cup boiling water for 5 minutes. Discard the tough stems, halve the mushrooms, and set aside; reserve soaking liquid.

3. In a small bowl, stir together the broth, saki, soy sauce, sugar, and reserved mushroom liquid; set aside.

4. In a large skillet, heat the oil over high heat. Add the onions and scallions; cook, stirring, 30 seconds. Push to one side of the skillet. Add the remaining vegetables, tofu, mushrooms, and noodles, placing each in a separate section of the skillet. Pour the soy mixture into the skillet. Cover and cook on high 5 minutes or until vegetables are tender-crisp.

Variation: Vary your vegetable choices—perhaps use bok choy, spinach, or some bamboo shoots instead of, or in addition to, the watercress.

TOFU IN BROWN SAUCE

Makes: 6 cups; serves: 4 to 6

This dish has to be served as soon as it's cooked because the sauce gets thinner as it cools, rather than thicker, which is usually the case with cornstarch-based sauce. Serve this with brown rice.

½ cup vegetable broth (pages 93–95)
2 tablespoons hoisin sauce
2 tablespoons mirin (rice wine) or dry sherry
1 tablespoon black beans in garlic sauce (available in Asian markets)
1 tablespoon cornstarch
1½ teaspoons sugar
2 teaspoons vegetable oil
½ cup sliced scallions (1-inch pieces; white and green parts)
1 tablespoon minced fresh ginger
3 cloves garlic, minced
¼ teaspoon red pepper flakes, or to taste
6 cups cubed tofu
1 cup cooked peas (fresh or frozen)

1. In a small bowl, stir together the broth, hoisin sauce, mirin, black beans, cornstarch, and sugar.

2. In a wok or large skillet, heat the oil over high heat. Add the scallions, ginger, garlic, and red pepper flakes. Cook, stirring, until softened, about 30 seconds.

3. Add the tofu, peas, and brown sauce. Cook, stirring, until sauce is thickened and tofu is heated through, about 2 minutes longer.

MOO SHU VEGETABLES

[V]

Makes: 6 cups; serves: 4 to 6

Moo shu vegetables are usually served with a dollop of hoisin sauce and a pancake, which gets rolled up like an eggroll, but I just serve this over rice. You can use wonton skins or flour tortillas to roll these vegetables in instead of the pancakes.

¾ cup vegetable broth (pages 93–95)

6 dried Chinese mushrooms (available in Asian markets)

¼ cup cloud ears (available in Asian markets)

12 lily buds (available in Asian markets)

2 tablespoons mirin (rice wine) or sherry

1 tablespoon soy sauce

2 teaspoons hoisin sauce

½ teaspoon sugar

1½ teaspoons cornstarch

3 tablespoons vegetable oil, divided

1 egg, beaten (optional)

½ cup sliced scallions (1½-inch pieces; white and green parts)

2 teaspoons minced fresh ginger

3 cloves garlic, minced

3 cups shredded Chinese cabbage or bok choy

2 cups shredded green cabbage

1 cup julienned carrots

1 cup julienned bamboo shoots

1½ cups diced pressed tofu

Hoisin sauce for serving

1. Over high heat, bring the broth to a boil in a 1-quart saucepan. Add the mushrooms, cloud ears, and lily buds. Let stand 5 minutes; drain, reserving the broth. On a cutting board; chop the drained vegetables, discarding any tough pieces.

2. In a small bowl, blend the reserved broth, the mirin, soy sauce, hoisin sauce, and sugar. Add cornstarch and stir until smooth.

3. If using egg: In a wok or large skillet, heat 1½ tablespoons of the oil over high heat. Stir in the beaten egg; cook until scrambled. Remove from the wok and chop.

4. Add the remaining 1½ tablespoons oil to the wok (or skillet) and heat over high heat. Add the scallions, ginger, and garlic. Cook, stirring, until softened, about 30 seconds.

5. Add the Chinese cabbage, green cabbage, and carrots. Cook, stirring, until tender crisp, about 5 minutes. Add the bamboo shoots, tofu, mushroom mixture, and egg; stir. Add the sauce. Cook, stirring, until sauce is thickened and tofu is heated through, about 2 minutes.

SWEET AND SOUR BEAN CURD

[v]

Makes: 5 cups; serves: 4

If you prepare this recipe without the tofu, it makes a lovely side dish.

One 8-ounce can juice-packed pineapple
    chunks, undrained
3 tablespoons ketchup
3 tablespoons firmly packed light brown or
    dark brown sugar
2 tablespoons distilled white vinegar
1 tablespoon dark or black soy sauce
1 tablespoon cornstarch
2 tablespoons vegetable oil
1 cup sliced celery
1 cup sliced onions
1 cup cubed red bell peppers
1 cup cubed green bell peppers
2 cloves garlic, minced
3 cups cubed tofu

1. Drain the pineapple juice into a measuring cup. If necessary, add enough water to equal $^1/_3$ cup. Stir in the ketchup, brown sugar, vinegar, soy sauce, and cornstarch; set aside.

2. In a wok or large skillet, heat the oil over high heat. Add the celery, onions, both bell peppers, and garlic; cook until tender-crisp, about 4 minutes.

3. Add the sauce mixture; cook, stirring, until thickened, about 1 minute. Stir in the tofu and pineapple chunks. Cook, stirring, until heated through, about 2 minutes longer.

Variations: Add 1 cup baby corn when you add the tofu.

Add 1 cup snow peas when you add the celery.

EGGPLANT AND TOFU WITH PLUM SAUCE

[v]

Makes: 10 cups; serves: 4

This is a sweet and rich dish. I like to serve it over short-grain brown rice with Szechuan Broccoli (page 179) as a side dish.

$^1/_2$ cup water, divided
$^1/_3$ cup plum sauce
3 tablespoons mirin (rice wine) or dry sherry
3 tablespoons honey
2 tablespoons soy sauce
$^1/_4$ teaspoon five-spice powder (available in
    Asian markets)
6 firm tofu cakes
$^1/_3$ cup cornstarch
Oil for deep frying
3 tablespoons vegetable oil
1 tablespoon minced fresh ginger
3 cloves garlic, minced
$^1/_4$ teaspoon red pepper flakes
4 cups cubed eggplant
2 cups cubed red bell peppers
$^1/_2$ cup sliced scallions (1-inch pieces; white
    and green parts)
$^1/_2$ cup cashew halves (or chopped)

1. In a small bowl, stir together $^1/_4$ cup of the water, plum sauce, mirin, honey, soy sauce, and five-spice powder; set aside.

2. Cut each of the tofu cakes into 4 pieces. Dredge each in cornstarch to coat lightly.

3. Pour 2 inches of oil into a 3-quart pot and heat until 375°F, or until the oil bubbles when a few sprinkles of cornstarch are tossed in the pot. Add the tofu, a few pieces at a time, and fry until crispy (they will not brown); drain and set aside.

4. In a wok or very large skillet, heat 3 tablespoons oil over high heat. Add the ginger,

garlic, and pepper flakes; cook for 30 seconds. Add the eggplant, bell peppers, and scallions; cook, stirring, until oil is absorbed, about 2 minutes. Add the remaining ¼ cup water and continue stir-frying until the vegetables are tender-crisp, about 3 minutes.

5. Add the tofu, sauce, and cashews; stir-fry until tofu is heated through and sauce is thickened, about 2 minutes longer.

Variation: Instead of frying the tofu, stir 2 teaspoons of cornstarch into the sauce mixture and just stir in the uncooked tofu when you would add the fried.

VERY QUICK BARBECUE TOFU AND RICE WITH BLACK BEANS

Makes: 5 ½ cups; serves: 4

This is one of my leftover-rice-from-the-Chinese-restaurant recipes. Canned beans, prepared barbecue sauce, and tofu combine for a very quick, very nutritious entree. Of course, if you prefer, you can prepare your beans and barbecue sauce from scratch.

1½ cups cooked rice (I use white rice, page 304)
One 10½-ounce can black beans, drained and rinsed
⅓ cup barbecue sauce
¼ cup water
4 cakes tofu, diced into ½-inch pieces (4 cups)

1. In a 2-quart saucepan, stir together the rice and beans. Add the barbecue sauce and water; stir until combined. Cook over medium heat, stirring occasionally, 10 minutes or until heated through.

2. Stir in the tofu and cook until heated through, about 2 minutes longer.

Variation: Use kidney or any other bean. You can also use brown rice instead of white.

BULGUR WITH TOFU AND CAULIFLOWER

Makes: 5 cups; serves: 4 to 6

This dish is slightly moister than most bulgur dishes.

1 tablespoon vegetable oil
1 cup chopped onions
2 cups vegetable broth (pages 93–95)
One 8-ounce can stewed tomatoes
½ teaspoon dried basil
¼ teaspoon dried oregano
2 cups cauliflower florets
1 cup bulgur
1½ cups diced tofu

1. In a 3-quart saucepan, heat the oil over medium-high heat. Add the onions; cook, stirring, until softened, about 2 minutes. Add the broth, tomatoes, basil, and oregano; bring to a boil.

2. Add the cauliflower and bulgur. Simmer 5 minutes. Add the tofu and simmer 10 to 15 minutes longer or until bulgur is soft.

Variation: Kasha with Tofu and Cauliflower: Beat 1 egg and toss with 1 cup of kasha until coated. Cook in ungreased skillet until the egg is dried; set aside. Follow the recipe directions, using the kasha instead of the bulgur. Increase final cooking time to 15 minutes.

SPANISH-BARBECUE TOFU AND BEANS

— V ♥ —

Makes: 4 1/2 cups; serves: 4 to 6

This sauce is a cross between barbecue sauce and the filling for a Spanish omelet. Serve over rice to sop up the sauce. Provide chopped onions, shredded Cheddar, and unflavored yogurt as condiments, if desired.

1 tablespoon vegetable oil
1 cup chopped onions
1/2 cup chopped green bell peppers
2 cloves garlic, minced
One 8-ounce can tomato sauce
3 tablespoons vegetable broth (pages 93–95) or water
2 tablespoons firmly packed light brown or dark brown sugar
1 tablespoon molasses
2 teaspoons distilled white vinegar
1 teaspoon anchovy-free Worcestershire sauce
1/8 teaspoon Tabasco sauce
1 1/2 cups cooked kidney beans (cooked from dry; or canned, drained)
2 to 3 cakes cubed tofu (1/2-inch pieces; 3 cups)

1. In a 3-quart saucepan, heat the oil over medium-high heat. Add the onions, bell peppers, and garlic; cook, stirring, until softened, about 2 minutes. Stir in the tomato sauce, broth, brown sugar, molasses, vinegar, Worcestershire sauce, and Tabasco.

2. Stir in the beans and bring to a boil. Reduce heat and simmer, uncovered, 20 minutes, stirring occasionally.

3. Stir in the tofu; cook, stirring once or twice, until heated through, about 2 minutes.

Variation: Use red bell peppers instead of green and any type of bean.

MADRID RICE, BEANS, AND TOFU

— V ♥ —

Makes: 7 cups; serves: 6 to 8

Although I used pressed tofu in this recipe, you can substitute fresh tofu, but choose the firm tofu instead of soft.

2 teaspoons vegetable oil
1 cup chopped onions
2 cloves garlic, minced
1 cup vegetable broth (pages 93–95)
3/4 cup water
One 14 1/2-ounce can whole peeled tomatoes, undrained
1 cup white rice
1/4 teaspoon dried thyme
1/4 teaspoon ground cumin
1/8 teaspoon ground red pepper
1 1/2 cups cooked kidney beans (cooked from dry; or canned, drained)
1 1/4 cups pressed tofu, diced into 1/4-inch pieces (6 ounces)
1/2 cup fresh or frozen peas
1/3 cup chopped pimiento
1 tablespoon chopped capers

1. In a 3-quart saucepan, heat the oil over medium-high heat. Add the onions and garlic; cook, stirring, until softened, about 2 minutes.

2. Add the broth and water; bring to a boil. Add the tomatoes; break them up using the back of a spoon. Return to a boil.

3. Add the rice, thyme, cumin, and red pepper. Return to a boil. Reduce heat and simmer, covered, 15 minutes. Add the remaining ingredients. Simmer, covered, 10 minutes longer or until liquid is absorbed and beans, tofu, and peas are heated through.

Variation: Add 1/3 cup chopped fresh cilantro before serving.

Tamale Pie

Makes: one 9-inch-square pie; serves: 4 to 6

This is not really a pie, since the filling is on the bottom and the crust is on the top.

Stew:

1 tablespoon vegetable oil
¾ cup chopped onions
¾ cup chopped green bell peppers
3 cloves garlic, minced
2 tablespoons chili powder
½ teaspoon ground cumin
One 28-ounce can crushed tomatoes
1½ cups diced firm tofu (¼-inch pieces)
1½ cups cooked kidney beans (cooked from dry; or canned, drained)
1 cup corn kernels (fresh, cooked; canned, drained; or frozen)

Topping:

½ cup cornmeal
½ cup all-purpose flour
2 teaspoons baking powder
2 teaspoons sugar
½ teaspoon salt
1 egg
1 egg white
⅔ cup milk
3 tablespoons melted butter or margarine

1. For the stew, in a 2-quart saucepan, heat the oil over medium-high heat. Add the onions, bell peppers, and garlic; cook, stirring, until softened, about 2 minutes. Stir in the chili powder and cumin until absorbed.

2. Add the tomatoes and bring to a boil. Stir in the tofu, kidney beans, and corn. Spoon into a greased 9 × 9-inch-square baking pan.

3. Preheat the oven to 400°F.

4. For the topping, in a large bowl, stir together the cornmeal, flour, baking powder, sugar, and ½ teaspoon salt.

5. In a medium bowl, beat the egg and egg white. Add the milk and melted butter or margarine; beat until completely combined.

6. Stir the liquid ingredients into the dry until the dry ingredients are moistened. Spread over the stew.

7. Bake 30 to 35 minutes or until top is browned and a wooden pick inserted in center comes out clean.

Variations: Add one 4-ounce can chopped chilies, drained, when you add the beans.

Ⓥ Just serve the stew and skip the cornbread topping.

GADO GADO

Makes: 9 cups; serves: 4

A versatile Indonesian dish that can be eaten as a salad or a main course, this is traditionally served with shrimp chips, dried wafers that puff up when deep-fried. You can use potato chips to provide the desired crunchiness. Another traditional accompaniment is hard-cooked eggs, which you can add, quartered, if you like.

Dressing:

½ cup water, divided

½ small onion, cut into chunks

1½ tablespoons firmly packed light brown or dark brown sugar

1½ teaspoons distilled white vinegar

1½ teaspoons paprika

1½ teaspoons fresh lime juice

2 cloves garlic

½ jalapeño pepper, seeded

2 teaspoons vegetable oil

¼ cup peanut butter, preferably smooth

¼ teaspoon salt, or to taste

Salad:

1 cup diced tofu (½-inch pieces)

2 tablespoons water

1 tablespoon dark soy sauce

1½ teaspoons fresh lime juice

¼ teaspoon salt

2 tablespoons vegetable oil

3 cups coarsely shredded cabbage

2 cups fresh green beans, cut into bite-size pieces

1 cup thinly sliced carrots

1 cup mung bean sprouts

4 small red potatoes, cooked and sliced

1 small cucumber, sliced

2 hard-cooked eggs (optional)

1 cup potato chips (optional)

1. For the dressing, place ¼ cup of the water, the onion, brown sugar, vinegar, paprika, 1½ teaspoons lime juice, the garlic, and jalapeño pepper in a blender container. Cover and process until smooth.

2. In a 1-quart saucepan, heat 2 teaspoons oil over medium-high heat. Add the spice paste from the blender; stir-fry 1 minute. Stir in the peanut butter, the remaining ¼ cup water, and ¼ teaspoon salt. Bring to a boil; reduce heat and simmer, stirring often, 10 minutes, or until the oils rise to the surface. Cool.

3. For the salad, marinate the tofu in 2 tablespoons water, the soy sauce, 1½ teaspoons lime juice, and ¼ teaspoon salt for 20 minutes. Drain on paper towels.

4. Heat 2 tablespoons oil in a large skillet; add the tofu. Sauté until the tofu is golden, about 3 minutes. Set aside.

5. Blanch the cabbage, green beans, carrots, and sprouts by cooking in 8 or 9 cups of salted water for 2 or 3 minutes, or until the vegetables turn a bright color. Drain the vegetables and plunge under cold water to stop the cooking. Drain and chill.

6. On a large plate, arrange the blanched vegetables and the potatoes and cucumber. Top with the tofu and, if desired, hard-cooked eggs and potato chips. Serve the dressing on the side.

BLACK BEAN PICADILLO

[V]

Makes: 4 1/2 cups; serves: 4

If you are using powder or cubes to make the broth, make the broth double strength. If you're using homemade broth, boil 1 cup broth until reduced to 1/2 cup.

1/2 cup double-strength vegetable broth (pages 93–95)
1/2 cup granular TVP (see mail-order list or purchase in health food store)
1 tablespoon vegetable oil
1 1/2 cups chopped onions
3/4 cup chopped green bell peppers
3/4 cup chopped red bell peppers
One 14-ounce can whole peeled tomatoes
One 8-ounce can tomato sauce
1 cup black beans (cooked from dry; or canned, drained)
1/2 cup sliced stuffed green olives
1/2 cup dark or golden raisins
1/2 teaspoon ground cinnamon
1/2 teaspoon salt, or to taste
1/8 teaspoon ground red pepper

1. Bring the vegetable broth to a boil. Remove from heat and add TVP. Let stand 10 minutes. Set aside.

2. In a large skillet, heat the oil to medium-high. Add the onions and both bell peppers; cook, stirring, until softened, about 2 minutes. Stir in the tomatoes, breaking them up with the back of a spoon. Stir in the TVP and remaining ingredients.

3. Bring to a boil. Reduce heat and simmer, uncovered, 20 minutes or until the sauce is thick.

Variation: Use pinto, white, or pink beans instead of the black beans.

CHICKENY CROQUETTES

[V]

Makes: 8 patties; serves: 4

These are quite tasty as is, but you can also serve them with marinara or tomato sauce.

2 1/3 cups vegetable broth (pages 93–95), divided
1 1/2 cups granular TVP
2 slices whole wheat bread
2 tablespoons butter or margarine
1/4 cup all-purpose flour
1/3 cup finely chopped celery
1/4 cup chopped scallions (white and green parts)
3 tablespoons chopped fresh parsley
2 tablespoons whole wheat flour
1 teaspoon distilled white vinegar
1/2 teaspoon poultry seasoning
1/2 teaspoon dry mustard
1/2 teaspoon salt, or to taste
1/4 teaspoon pepper
1/2 cup unflavored dry bread crumbs
Oil for frying

1. In a 1-quart saucepan, bring 1 1/3 cups of the vegetable broth to a boil over high heat. Remove from heat and stir in the TVP; let stand until absorbed.

2. Tear the bread into pieces and place in a blender or food processor container fitted with a steel blade. Cover and process until bread becomes crumbed (makes about 3/4 cup).

3. In a 2-quart saucepan, melt the butter or margarine over medium heat. Stir in the all-purpose flour until absorbed. Using a whisk, gradually stir in the remaining 1 cup vegetable broth. Cook, stirring constantly, until mixture comes to a boil and thickens, about 4 minutes.

4. Stir in the celery, scallions, parsley, whole wheat flour, vinegar, poultry seasoning, mustard, salt, and pepper. Stir in the rehydrated

TVP and the fresh whole wheat bread crumbs; cover and chill 2 hours.

5. Shape into 8 patties; roll each croquette in the dry bread crumbs to coat.

6. Fill a large skillet with ¹/₂ inch oil. Heat the oil over medium-high heat to 375 F, or until it bubbles when a few crumbs are dropped in.

7. Fry patties 2 to 3 minutes per side or until golden brown. Drain on paper towels.

Variation: Use chopped green bell peppers instead of the chopped celery.

TEMPEH WITH SATE SAUCE

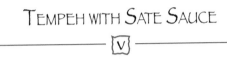

Makes: 20 squares with 1 cup sauce; serves: 4

I use any leftover sauce (and there probably will be some) as a salad dressing or dip for grilled vegetables.

2 teaspoons vegetable oil
2 cloves garlic, minced
2 teaspoons curry powder
1 cup unsweetened coconut milk (page 497)
¹/₄ cup peanut butter
2 tablespoons firmly packed light brown or dark brown sugar
1 tablespoon soy sauce
Two 8-ounce packages tempeh (page 217)
Oil for deep frying

1. In a 1-quart saucepan, heat 2 teaspoons of oil over medium-high heat. Add the garlic; cook 10 seconds, stirring, or until softened. Add the curry powder; cook, stirring, until absorbed. Stir in the coconut milk, peanut butter, brown sugar, and soy sauce. Cook, uncovered, stirring occasionally, until thickened, about 10 minutes.

2. Cut the tempeh into 2-inch squares and deep-fry until browned. Serve with peanut sauce.

Variation: Add ¹/₈ teaspoon ground red pepper (or more) to the sauce when you add the curry powder.

NOODLES WITH SEITAN

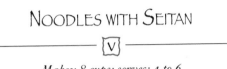

Makes: 8 cups; serves: 4 to 6

¹/₂ cup vegetable broth (pages 93–95)
2 tablespoons mirin (rice wine) or dry sherry
1 tablespoon black bean sauce (available in Asian markets)
2 teaspoons sugar
1 teaspoon soy sauce
1 teaspoon cornstarch
1 pound fresh lo mein noodles or thin spaghetti
2 tablespoons vegetable oil
3 cups lightly packed shredded Chinese cabbage or bok choy
1 cup sliced onions
2 cloves garlic, minced
1 cup mung bean sprouts
One 8-ounce container seitan in soy sauce, drained and sliced (page 217)
1 teaspoon sesame oil

1. In a small bowl, stir together the broth, mirin, black bean sauce, sugar, soy sauce, and cornstarch; set aside.

2. Cook the noodles according to package directions; drain.

3. While the noodles are cooking, heat the vegetable oil in a wok or large skillet. Add the Chinese cabbage, onions, and garlic. Cook, stirring, until tender-crisp, about 4 minutes. Add bean sprouts and seitan; cook, stirring, until wilted, about 2 minutes. Stir in the sesame oil.

4. Add the noodles and reserved sauce. Cook, stirring, until heated through, about 2 minutes.

Variation: Add 1 cup julienned carrots when you add the Chinese cabbage.

SEITAN WITH BEANS SPROUTS AND MUSHROOMS

—————— [V] ——————

Makes: 4 1/2 cups; serves: 4

1/4 cup dried cloud ears or tree fungus
(available in Asian markets)
1/2 cup boiling water
3 tablespoons hoisin sauce
1 tablespoon mirin (rice wine) or dry sherry
2 teaspoons soy sauce
2 teaspoons cornstarch
2 tablespoons vegetable oil
2 cups sliced white or shiitake mushrooms
1 cup snow peas
1 cup sliced scallions (1-inch pieces; white
and green parts)
3 cloves garlic, minced
4 cups bean sprouts
1 1/4 cups julienned seitan (8 ounces)
(page 217)

1. In a small bowl, combine the cloud ears and water; let stand 10 minutes or until softened. Pour the liquid into a small bowl; stir in the hoisin sauce, mirin, soy sauce, and cornstarch. Chop the cloud ears.

2. In a wok or very large skillet, heat the oil over high heat. Add the mushrooms, snow peas, scallions, and garlic; stir-fry until snow peas are tender-crisp, about 5 minutes. Add the bean sprouts; cook, stirring, until tender-crisp, about 1 minute. Add the seitan, cloud ears, and reserved sauce, continue stir-frying until heated, about 2 minutes longer.

Variation: Add 1/2 cup baby corn when you add the bean sprouts.

Vegetables

Vegetable Kebabs   233

Basic Grilled or Broiled
Vegetables   233

Teriyaki Grilled
Vegetables   234

Steamed Artichokes   235

Asparagus with Walnuts
and Browned Butter   236

Asparagus with Lemon
Butter   236

Sautéed Asparagus,
Tomatoes, and
Red Onion   236

Sesame Asparagus   237

Szechuan Asparagus with
Water Chestnuts   238

Stir-Fried Mung Bean
Sprouts   238

Hoisin Sprouts with
Cloud Ears   239

Soybean Sprouts in Black
Bean Sauce   239

Beets in Red Wine
and Honey   240

Beets with Cranberries   240

Sweet and Sour Beets   240

Stir-Fried Bok Choy   241

Puree of Broccoflower   241

Broccoli with Oyster
Mushrooms   242

Sautéed Broccoli
with Garlic   242

Sautéed Broccoli and
Zucchini   242

Broccoli with Orange
and Almonds   243

Broccoli Rabe with Yellow
Peppers and Carrots   243

Sautéed Broccoli Rabe
with Chestnuts   244

Braised Brussels
Sprouts   244

Autumn Brussels
Sprouts   245

Winter Vegetables for
a Crowd   245

Spiced Boiled Cabbage   246

Sautéed Cabbage with
Snow Peas   246

Sauerkraut with Apples and
Caraway Seeds   246

Sautéed Red Cabbage with
Balsamic Vinegar   247

Braised Red Cabbage
with Apples   247

Parslied Carrots   248

Sesame Carrots   248

Jalapeño Carrots   248

Gingered Carrot Puree   249

Bali Vegetables   249

Cauliflower with Parsley
and Lemon   250

Cauliflower Polonaise   250

Cauliflower in Cheese
Sauce   250

Batter-Fried Cauliflower   251

Julienned Celeriac and
Celery Sauté   251

Braised Celery with
Wild Mushrooms   252

Boiled Corn on the Cob   252

Microwaved Corn on
the Cob   252

Corn Pudding   253

Tex-Mex Corn Pudding   253

Corn Fritters   254

Creamed Corn   254

Sautéed Cucumbers
with Tarragon   255

Baked Eggplant   255

Broiled Eggplant   255

Microwaved Eggplant   255

Sautéed Eggplant with
Tomatoes, Capers,
and Garlic   256

Barbecued Eggplant   256

Stuffed Young Eggplants   256

Ratatouille   257

Braised Fennel   258

Sautéed Fennel and Celery
with Water Chestnuts and
Toasted Almonds   258

Fennel au Gratin   258

Garlic Green Beans   259

Italian-Style Green Beans
and Fennel   260

Spicy Green Beans with
Shallots   260

Creamy Parmesan
Green Beans   260

Szechuan Green Beans   261

Green Beans with Chickpeas
in Groundnut Sauce   262

Collards, Zucchini,
and Tomatoes   262

Collards   263

Creamy Swiss Chard with
Cranberry Beans   263

Sautéed Escarole   263

Escarole and Sliced
Cucumber   264

Escarole with
Mushrooms   264

Jerusalem Artichokes with
Black Beans   265

Lime-Sautéed Jícama
with Grapes   265

Parmesan Baked
Kohlrabi   266

Leeks Provençal   266

Sautéed Mushrooms with
Water Chestnuts   267

Button Mushrooms
Persiller   268

Sautéed Wild Mushrooms
and Peas   268

Chili-Fried Okra   269

Creole Okra with Corn   269

Curried Okra with
Green Beans   270

Onion Timbales   270

Fried Onion Rings   271

Sweet and Sour Pearl
Onions   271

Baked Stuffed Onions   272

Orange-Glazed Parsnip   272

Sugar Snap Sauté   273

Sautéed Snow Peas, Peas,
and Wild Mushrooms   273

Snow Peas with Scallions
and Ginger   274

Snow Peas, Cauliflower,
and Red Bell Peppers   274

Creamed Peas   275

Minted Peas   275

Pureed Peas   276

Roasted Red Bell
Peppers   276

A Trio of Sautéed
Peppers   277

Sautéed Peppers, Onions,
and Cauliflower   277

Baked Plantains   278

Plantain and Sweet
Potato Loaf   278

Tostones (Fried Green
Plantains)   279

Honey-Lemon Glazed
Plantains   279

Baked Potatoes   280

Microwaved Baked
Potatoes   280

Parslied Boiling
Potatoes   281

Perfect Mashed
Potatoes   281

Ruthie's Thanksgiving Chive
Mashed Potatoes   282

Colcannon   282

Oven Fries   283

Stuffed Baked Potatoes   283

Potatoes au Gratin   284

Stilton Potatoes au
Gratin   284

Yellow Potatoes with Red
Swiss Chard, Rosemary, and
Garlic   285

Mashed Sweets with
Hazelnut Praline   285

Brandied Candied Sweet
Potatoes   286

Pecan Mashed Sweet
Potatoes   286

Tzimmes   287

Creamed Spinach   288

Creamy Spinach   288

Spinach-Herb Timbales   288

Sautéed Young
Zucchini   289

Zucchini Italian-Style   290

Curried Zucchini
and Fennel   290

Zucchini with Shiitake
Mushrooms   290

Stuffed Yellow Squash   291

Pesto Vegetables   291

Baked Whole Squash   292

Microwaved Squash   292

Apple-Stuffed Acorn
Squash   292

Pureed Winter Squash
with Pear   293

Sweet Potato–Stuffed
Chayote   293

Basil-Garlic Spaghetti
Squash   294

Spaghetti Squash with
Fennel   294

Spaghetti Squash
with Bok Choy   295

Cheesy Broiled
Tomatoes   295

Stewed Tomatoes   296

Sautéed Tomatoes   296

Basil-Stuffed
Baked Tomatoes   296

Broccoli-Stuffed
Tomatoes   297

Scalloped Tomatoes   297

Orzo-Stuffed Tomatoes   298

Turnips and Apples   298

Mashed Rutabaga   299

Ginger-Baked Root
Vegetables   299

Orange-Sautéed Rutabaga
and Carrots   300

Grains

Millet   301

Kasha   303

Basic Short-Grain White
Rice (Glutinous)   304

Barley with
Mushrooms   304

Zucchini Barley   304

Barley with Rutabaga
and Carrots   305

Barley with Spinach   305

Kasha Varniskas   306

Kasha with Jícama
and Apples   306

Basic Polenta   307

Fried Polenta   307

Hush Puppies   308

Grits with Cheese   308

Thanksgiving Kamut   309

Kamut with Sautéed
Escarole and Yellow
Squash   309

Spelt and Peas   310

Curried Millet   310

Chili Millet with
Peppers   311

Mexican Millet   311

Orange-Almond Millet   312

Millet with Dried Fruits   312

Quinoa with Shredded
Vegetables   313

Quinoa with Mixed
Vegetables   313

Quinoa with Jerusalem
Artichokes and Fennel   314

Quinoa Italiano   314

Parslied Rice   315

Saffron Rice   315

Coconut Rice   315

Yellow Indian Rice   316

Paprikash Rice   316

Spanish Rice   317

Chili Rice with
Tomatillos   317

Curried Fried Rice   318

Fried Rice   318

Continental Fried Rice   318

Barbecue Rice with
Beans and Corn   319

Spinach Brown Rice   319

Brown Rice with Onion
and Red Bell Pepper   320

Autumn Brown Rice   320

Apricot-Pineapple
Brown Rice   320

Fiddlehead Ferns
with Wild Rice   321

Lemon Wild and
White Rice   321

Wild Rice and Corn   322

Wild Rice with Orzo and
Three-Color Peppers   322

Wild Rice with Apples
and Almonds   323

Rizcous, Corn,
and Beans   323

Bulgur with Summer
Squash   324

Tomato Bulgur with
Eggplant   324

Bulgur with Squash,
Carrots, and Collards   325

Bulgur with Celery   325

Couscous with Golden
Fruits and Vegetables   326

Couscous-Stuffed
Papaya   326

Couscous with Eggplant   326

Spiced Couscous with
Diced Vegetables   327

Wheat Berries Provençal   327

Wheat Berries with
Gingered Eggplant   328

Wheat Berries with
Cashews   328

Wheat Berries with Calabaza
and Cabbage   328

Wheat Berries with
Cardoon   329

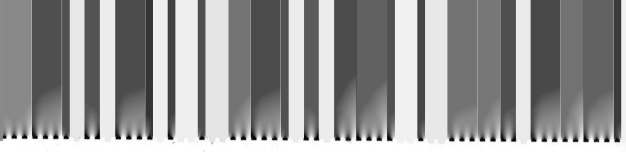

*Dilled Wheat Berries with
Brown Rice   329*

Noodle Pudding   330

Savory Noodle Pudding   330

*Noodles with Sour Cream
and Apple Sauce   331*

Beans

Frijoles   331

Refried Beans   332

Barbecue Beans   332

Baked Beans   332

*Black Beans with
Celery   333*

*Garbanzo Beans with
Escarole   333*

Succotash   334

*Lentils in Tomato
Sauce   334*

*Pureed Lima Beans
with Dill   334*

*White Beans with Tomatoes
and Basil   335*

Side Dishes

What makes a side dish a side dish and not an entree? If this sounds like a riddle to you, let me assure you that it was definitely a hard one for me. In truth, any side dish *can* be a main dish, and vice versa; it just depends on what you choose to eat at a meal. But, unless I were just to make one giant chapter called "Entrees and Side Dishes," there had to be some cut-off to differentiate the two. I chose to resolve this question by the following criteria:

- Recipes containing primarily one vegetable became side dishes.
- Recipes that yield small portions became side dishes.
- Dishes traditionally served as side dishes (such as refried beans) became side dishes.
- Dishes that need "support" dishes to become an entree (such as polenta, which really needs a sauce or vegetable to support it) became side dishes.

Considering the reasons that side dishes are not main dishes, here are some suggestions to help make side dishes into main entrees:

- Couple a starch with a vegetable or two.
- Couple a vegetable or starch with an appetizer.
- Combine a grain dish with a bean dish.
- Double the recipe.

This chapter is divided into three sections: vegetable dishes, grain dishes, and bean dishes. The general cooking instructions for vegetables are given on page 232; cooking instructions for grains are given on pages 300–4; and cooking instructions for beans are given on pages 13–14. Each section is grouped alphabetically, with a brief description about the type of vegetable, grain, or bean, and sometimes with shopping or cooking tips.

VEGETABLES

Steaming Vegetables

Steaming (cooking vegetables in a covered pot, on a rack, over—not *in*—boiling water) is the ideal way to cook vegetables because they retain most of their vitamin content. Although some vitamins are destroyed by heat even during steaming, other vitamins (those that are water-soluble) are retained after steaming.

Steamers are available in many different styles. Some are perforated metal disks with collapsible sides; others fit into the top of pots, similar to a double boiler but with holes. Asian steamers are stackable bamboo or metal cylinders that fit into a wok, which holds the boiling water. You can also improvise a steamer by placing a round rack into a pot (with a lid) and adding enough water to boil in the bottom, but not to immerse the vegetables.

The cooking times for steaming can only be approximated, since the size of the pieces as well as the quantity you place in the steamer will affect the cooking time. Furthermore, doneness is strictly a matter of taste. You will need considerably less cooking time for tender-crisp vegetables than for the same vegetables to be cooked until soft. The best test for doneness is to take a bite and see if you like the consistency.

If you don't have a steamer, you can toss the vegetables into a pot with a little boiling water and cook, covered, until done, then drain. Boiling vegetables gives about the same result as steamed vegetables, but you lose the water-soluble vitamins that steaming retains.

Microwaving Vegetables

If you are cooking only one or two portions of vegetables in the microwave, my favorite method is to wet a microwave-safe paper towel, wrap the vegetables in the towel, then microwave on high for a minute or two or until the vegetables reach the desired doneness. Be careful when you remove them from the oven because the towel will be quite hot.

A more conventional method of microwaving vegetables is to use a microwave steamer (two nesting bowls, the inner one with holes or slots, plus a top) and cook until the vegetables are al dente or to desired doneness.

Grilling Vegetables

Although many recipes in this book call for grilled vegetables, in fact, I usually cook them in the broiler until slightly charred. Vegetables "grilled" in the broiler have several advantages: They are easier to turn; they can be "grilled" year round; and of course the broiler is easier to start than a charcoal grill (though a gas-grill is just as easy to start as a broiler). Other options for indoor "grilling" are electric and stove-top smoke-free grills. Electric grills have heating units under the grill, whereas the "minute" grills have heating units on both top and bottom, which speeds up the cooking time. Top-of-the-stove grills are made of two round pieces of metal. The bottom part fits over the burner and gets filled with water. To cook, food is placed on the nonstick top, which has slots cut into it.

If you don't have any type of grill, you can grill vegetables by slicing them and placing them on a greased baking sheet (or for easier cleanup, lining the baking sheet with aluminum foil before greasing), then broiling as described on page 233. A more flavorful method is to brush the vegetables with olive or vegetable oil, or melted butter or margarine. You can also flavor the oil with pressed garlic cloves, or chili powder, or curry powder, or various herbs. Be as creative as you like.

Almost any vegetable can be "grilled." Zucchini, yellow squash, eggplant, and bell peppers grill extremely well. But you can also grill root vegetables (onions, carrots, beets, jícama, and so on) and potatoes (the potatoes tend to come out like tender-crisp carrots rather than as soft as baked potatoes).

For actual grilling on a barbecue, cutting the vegetables into chunks and then stringing them on skewers makes them easier to turn. You can brush kebabs with any of the same items as you would for plain "grilled" vegetables.

VEGETABLE KEBABS

—————— $\boxed{V}\boxed{\heartsuit}$ ——————

Makes and serves: depends on quantities used

You can string vegetables onto wooden or metal skewers. If you use wooden ones, soak the skewers in water for an hour or two beforehand so they don't burn too badly. Choose metal skewers if you are planning on cooking hard vegetables, such as jícama, potatoes, carrots, or beets.

Bell peppers, cherry tomatoes, mushrooms, onion wedges, yellow squash, and zucchini all make nice kebabs. You can make single-vegetable kebabs or you can use an assortment of vegetables on the same skewer. If you make single-vegetable kebabs, you don't have to worry that one vegetable will take too long to cook while another is cooking too quickly.

As with grilled vegetables, kebabs are enhanced by being brushed with barbecue sauce or marinades. Use any of the ones in this book (pages 477–78, 482), or store-bought products.

Cubed vegetables of choice (1- to 1½-inch pieces)
Olive or vegetable oil, or marinade or sauce of choice

1. Preheat the grill or broiler.

2. Lightly brush each side of the vegetable slices with oil.

3. Broil 4 to 6 inches from heat, 5 minutes per side or until browned or lightly charred on the outside and tender or tender-crisp on the inside.

BASIC GRILLED OR BROILED VEGETABLES

—————— $\boxed{V}$ ——————

Makes and serves: depends on vegetable chosen and quantity used

Vegetable of choice, sliced ½ inch thick
Olive or vegetable oil

1. Preheat the grill or broiler.

2. Lightly brush each side of the vegetable slices with oil.

3. Broil 4 to 6 inches from heat, 5 minutes per side or until browned or lightly charred on the outside and tender or tender-crisp on the inside.

Variation: Barbecued Vegetables: Instead of brushing the vegetables with oil, brush them with barbecue sauce.

TERIYAKI GRILLED VEGETABLES

[V][♥]

Makes: 4 to 8 cups, depending on vegetables chosen; serves: 4 to 8

Good vegetables to use for this recipe are bell peppers, eggplant, onions, zucchini, yellow squash, carrots, tomatoes, and/or mushrooms. The yield for teriyaki vegetables depends on the vegetables chosen; for example, mushrooms shrink quite a lot, whereas carrots retain their full volume.

⅓ cup soy sauce
2 tablespoons mirin (rice wine) or dry sherry
1 tablespoon sugar
1 tablespoon minced fresh ginger
2 cloves garlic, minced
8 cups vegetable slices

1. Combine the marinade ingredients and toss with the vegetables. Let stand 30 minutes.

2. Heat the grill or broiler.

3. Broil 4 to 6 inches from heat, 5 minutes per side or until browned or lightly charred on the outside and tender or tender-crisp on the inside.

Artichokes

These thistles have a delicate flavor prized by many. Very small (baby) artichokes are totally edible. Larger ones generally require a fair amount of work to prepare, and quite a bit of the plants are inedible, but the parts that are edible are certainly worth the effort. The "choke" is actually the inedible hairy fibers found in the middle of the plant. Remove the choke by scraping it with a spoon (I find a grapefruit spoon with a serrated tip works quite well). The heart—the most prized part—is also available canned in water or frozen. Shop for artichokes that are tightly closed and preferably with a good bright color.

Artichokes are most often served as appetizers, so look for more recipes in the appetizer chapter (pages 44–91).

To eat a cooked artichoke, pluck an outer leaf from the bottom of the plant. You will see a slightly grayish fleshy mound at the bottom of the leaf; dip it in melted butter or other dip of choice. Place the bottom of the leaf between your teeth and scrape the fleshy part off the leaf; discard the remainder of the leaf (the host or hostess should provide a bowl for the discarded leaves). Continue plucking and eating the leaves until you get to the little, very light leaves with the purple thorns on the top; these are fairly inedible. Pull them off and discard to reveal the choke attached to the fleshy heart. Scrape the choke off the heart and discard the choke. Cut the heart with a knife and/or fork and dip the chunks in any sauce you've been using for the leaves.

STEAMED ARTICHOKES

[V] [♥]

*Makes: depends on quantities used; serves:
1 artichoke per person*

*Cooking the artichokes is not really difficult; the
more work-intensive part is preparing them for
cooking. Unless you're microwaving the artichokes, it doesn't matter how many you cook at
once, since cooking times will vary according to the
size of the artichoke, not the number. I like these
best when served traditionally, with melted butter.*

3 to 4 quarts water
1 tablespoon lemon juice
Fresh artichokes
½ lemon

1. In a 6-quart pot, bring the water and lemon
juice to a boil.

2. While the water is coming to a boil, prepare the artichokes. Using a sharp knife, cut
the stems off flush with the bottom of the
artichoke. Pull off any small leaves from the
bottom. Rub the cut lemon over the cut part
of the bottom of the artichoke to prevent it
from browning.

3. Lay the artichoke on its side on a cutting
board. Slice off 1 inch from the top of the artichoke (don't be too concerned about wasting
too much of the artichoke since you eat only
the bottom portions of the leaves). This should
remove most of the pointy tips. Rub the cut
lemon over the exposed inner artichoke. Using
a scissor, snip off any of the remaining artichoke
points.

4. Cook the artichokes in a covered pot, in the
boiling water until tender, or until an outer leaf
comes off easily when pulled and the bottom
is tender when pierced with a fork (about 30
to 40 minutes for small artichokes and 45 to 55
minutes for large ones). Drain, upside down, in
a colander before serving.

5. If you want to serve the artichokes hollowed
out to hold dip, spread the leaves apart so that
you can reach into the center. Grasp the purple-
tipped light green leaves; pull out and discard.
Using a spoon (I like to use a grapefruit spoon
with a serrated point), scrape out the fine leaves
and choke (hairy bottom). Fill with dipping
sauce; serve warm or cold.

Variation: Microwaved Artichokes: Wrap
each in plastic wrap, tucking ends under
artichoke. Cook as follows:

1 artichoke:	4 minutes
2 artichokes:	7 minutes
3 artichokes:	10 minutes
4 artichokes:	12 minutes

Rotate and let stand, wrapped, 5 minutes.

Asparagus

There are different schools of thought on the ideal asparagus, and there is no right or wrong. While I prefer pencil-thin asparagus, my mother's taste is for very thick stalks. In either case, look for a bright green stem with tips that are tightly closed. Prepare asparagus by holding the middle of the stalk in one hand and the bottom in the other. Bend the stalk; it will snap where the tender part starts. Asparagus that are shriveled, or that bend but do not snap, are beyond their prime.

ASPARAGUS WITH WALNUTS AND BROWNED BUTTER

Makes: 2¹/₂ cups; serves: 4 to 6

Be sure to stir the butter as it cooks; remove it from the heat as soon as it's lightly browned to prevent burning.

¹/₂ cup chopped walnuts
1 pound asparagus, bottoms snapped (above)
2 tablespoons butter or margarine
¹/₂ teaspoon grated lemon rind

1. Preheat the oven to 350°F. On a baking sheet, bake the walnuts 15 minutes; set aside.

2. Steam the asparagus to desired doneness (page 232); place on serving platter.

3. In a small skillet, melt the butter or margarine over medium heat; cook, stirring, until butter browns and smells nutty. Stir in the toasted walnuts and lemon rind. Pour over asparagus.

Variation: Substitute orange rind for the lemon.

ASPARAGUS WITH LEMON BUTTER

Makes: 18 asparagus; serves: 3 to 4

¹/₂ cup water
18 medium asparagus, bottoms snapped (left)
1 tablespoon butter or margarine
1 tablespoon fresh lemon juice
Pinch salt, or to taste

1. In a large skillet, bring the water to a boil. Add the asparagus; cook, covered, about 4 minutes or to desired doneness; drain.

2. Return the asparagus to the skillet and add the butter or margarine; cook over medium heat, tossing until butter or margarine melts. Add the lemon juice and salt; toss.

Variation: Green Beans with Lemon Butter: Substitute ¹/₂ pound (3 cups) whole green beans for the asparagus.

SAUTÉED ASPARAGUS, TOMATOES, AND RED ONION

Makes: 5 cups; serves: 4 to 8

These vegetables are perfect summer fare. They're sautéed very quickly so that the vegetables retain their texture and taste, accented by just a hint of lemon juice.

1 tablespoon olive oil
¹/₂ cup sliced red onion wedges
3 cups fresh asparagus (cut into 2-inch pieces)
2 cups tomato wedges
1¹/₂ teaspoons fresh lemon juice
¹/₈ teaspoon salt, or to taste
¹/₈ teaspoon pepper

1. In a large skillet, heat the oil over medium-high heat. Add the onions; cook, stirring, until just transparent, about 2 minutes.

2. Add the asparagus; cook, stirring, until almost tender-crisp, about 3 minutes. Add the tomatoes; cook, stirring, until softened and the asparagus are tender-crisp, about 2 minutes. Stir in the lemon juice, salt, and pepper.

Variation: Sautéed Summer Vegetable Salad: Chill the cooked vegetables and toss with 1 tablespoon white wine vinegar. This salad is also great to toss with Mozzarella Bites (page 68).

SESAME ASPARAGUS

Makes: 4 cups; serves: 4 to 6

You can make this into an entree by doubling the sauce and stirring in diced tofu.

3 tablespoons water
1 ½ tablespoons soy sauce
1 ½ tablespoons mirin (rice wine) or dry sherry
1 tablespoon plum sauce
1 tablespoon sugar
1 teaspoon cornstarch
1 teaspoon distilled white vinegar
1 ½ tablespoons vegetable oil
3 cloves garlic, minced
6 cups asparagus, cut into 2-inch pieces
    (1 pound)
¾ cup sliced scallions (½-inch pieces; white
    and green parts)
1 ½ tablespoons sesame seeds
1 teaspoon sesame oil

1. In a small bowl, stir together the water, soy sauce, mirin, plum sauce, sugar, cornstarch, and vinegar; set aside.

2. In a wok or large skillet, heat the oil over high heat. Add the garlic; cook, stirring, 10 seconds. Add the asparagus and scallions; cook, stirring, until about half the asparagus have turned bright green, about 3 minutes.

3. Add the soy sauce mixture; cook, stirring, until thickened, about 2 minutes. Add the sesame seeds and sesame oil; toss until combined.

Variations: Spicy Sesame Asparagus: Add ¼ teaspoon hot chili oil when you add the sesame oil.

Sesame Green Beans: Use green beans instead of asparagus.

SZECHUAN ASPARAGUS WITH WATER CHESTNUTS

— [V] —

Makes: 2¹/₂ cups; serves: 4

This is not a very spicy dish, but you can add extra chili oil to taste.

¹/₃ cup water

2 tablespoons mirin (rice wine) or sherry

1 tablespoon soy sauce

2 teaspoons cornstarch

¹/₂ teaspoon sugar

1¹/₂ tablespoons vegetable oil

¹/₂ cup sliced scallions (2-inch pieces; white and green parts)

¹/₂ cup julienned red bell peppers

1 tablespoon minced fresh ginger

2 cloves garlic, minced

2 cups cut-up asparagus stems and tips (2-inch pieces)

One 8-ounce can sliced water chestnuts, drained

1 teaspoon sesame oil

¹/₄ teaspoon chili oil

1. In a small bowl, stir together the water, mirin, soy sauce, cornstarch, and sugar; set aside.

2. In a wok or large skillet, heat the vegetable oil over high heat. Add the scallions, bell peppers, ginger, and garlic; cook, stirring, 30 seconds. Add the asparagus; cook, stirring, until tender-crisp, about 4 minutes. Add the sauce mixture and water chestnuts; cook, stirring, until sauce thickens and water chestnuts are heated through, about 2 minutes. Stir in the sesame and chili oils.

Variation: Double recipe and serve as an entree.

Bean Sprouts

Sprouts are beans or peas that have been soaked in water and drained until they sprout shoots. You can buy many types of sprouts in gourmet shops, Asian markets, or supermarkets. Look for sprouts that are crisp and bright white on the sprout part. Grayish or brownish sprouts or sprouts that look transparent and limp are old. Soybean sprouts have to be cooked through and are not suitable for eating raw.

STIR-FRIED MUNG BEAN SPROUTS

— [V][♥] —

Makes: 2¹/₂ cups; serves: 4 to 6

1 tablespoon water

1 tablespoon soy sauce, or to taste

1 tablespoon mirin (rice wine) or sherry

¹/₂ teaspoon sugar

1 teaspoon cornstarch

1 tablespoon vegetable oil

6 cups fresh mung bean sprouts

1 cup sliced scallions (1¹/₂-inch pieces; white and green parts)

3 cloves garlic, minced

¹/₂ teaspoon sesame oil (optional)

1. In a small bowl, stir together the water, soy sauce, mirin, sugar, and cornstarch; set aside.

2. In a large skillet or wok, heat the oil over high heat. Add the sprouts, scallions, and garlic; cook, stirring, until tender, about 2 minutes. Stir in the sauce; cook until thickened, about 2 minutes. Stir in the sesame oil.

Variation: Use soybean sprouts instead of mung.

HOISIN SPROUTS WITH CLOUD EARS

— V —

Makes: 3 cups; serves: 4 to 6

Cloud ears are dried mushrooms available at Asian markets. You can substitute tree fungus for them, or, if you must, use 1 cup sliced white mushrooms and add them with the carrots.

½ cup hot water
¼ cup cloud ears
2 tablespoons hoisin sauce
2 tablespoons mirin (rice wine) or dry sherry
1½ teaspoons cornstarch
1 teaspoon soy sauce
2 tablespoons vegetable oil
1 cup julienned carrots
2 cloves garlic, minced
4 cups fresh soybean sprouts
¼ teaspoon chili oil

1. In a medium bowl, combine the hot water and cloud ears; let stand 10 minutes; drain, reserving 3 tablespoons of the liquid.

2. In a small bowl, stir together the reserved liquid, the hoisin sauce, mirin, cornstarch, and soy sauce; set aside.

3. In a large skillet or wok, heat the oil over high heat. Add the carrots and garlic; cook, stirring, until tender-crisp, about 3 minutes. Add the sprouts; cook, stirring, until tender, about 3 minutes. Stir in the sauce; cook until thickened. Stir in the chili oil.

Variation: Use mung bean sprouts instead of soybean.

SOYBEAN SPROUTS IN BLACK BEAN SAUCE

— V ♥ —

Makes: 3 cups; serves: 4 to 6

2 tablespoons mirin (rice wine) or dry sherry
2 tablespoons water
2 tablespoons black bean–garlic sauce (available at Asian grocery stores)
2 teaspoons cornstarch
1 tablespoon vegetable oil
1 pound fresh soybean sprouts (6 cups)
½ cup thinly sliced scallions (white and green parts)

1. In a small bowl, stir together the mirin, water, black bean–garlic sauce, and cornstarch; set aside.

2. In a large skillet or wok, heat the oil over high heat. Add the sprouts and scallions; cook, stirring, until tender, about 4 minutes. Stir in the sauce; cook until thickened, about 2 minutes.

Variation: Use mung bean sprouts instead of soybean.

Beets

These naturally sweet roots can be purchased with or without their leaves. If you buy them with the leaves, you can be assured of their freshness by the perkiness of the leaves, and you can also cook up the leaves in any recipe calling for greens (such as collards). Smaller beets are more tender (less woody) than larger ones. Peel beets as you would potatoes, using a vegetable peeler or paring knife, or if you are going to boil or steam them, they will easily slip out of their skins when they are tender.

BEETS IN RED WINE AND HONEY

Makes: 2¹/₂ cups; serves: 4

The honey and wine go so well with the beets you don't even notice them, except that the beets taste delicious. I thought these were a tiny bit too sweet, but all my tasters loved them.

4 cups peeled, sliced beets (¼ inch thick)
¾ cup dry red wine
½ cup water
¼ cup honey

1. In a 2-quart saucepan, combine all the ingredients. Bring to a boil over high heat. Reduce heat to medium; cook, uncovered, 30 minutes, stirring occasionally, or until beets are tender.

Variation: Add 8 whole cloves to the pan with the other ingredients.

BEETS WITH CRANBERRIES

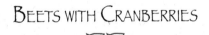

Makes: 2 cups; serves: 4

There are not very many cranberries in this recipe; they just add zip to the flavor of the juice.

2½ cups diced, peeled beets (½-inch pieces)
½ cup water
½ cup orange juice
3 tablespoons sugar
⅓ cup chopped fresh cranberries
⅛ teaspoon salt, or to taste

1. Combine the beets, water, orange juice, and sugar in a 2-quart saucepan. Bring to a boil over medium-high heat, stirring until sugar dissolves. Reduce heat and simmer, uncovered, 20 minutes or until beets reach desired doneness.

2. Add the cranberries and salt; simmer, uncovered, 5 minutes longer.

Variation: Use apple juice instead of orange.

SWEET AND SOUR BEETS

Makes: 2¹/₂ cups; serves: 4

I'm not sure whether these are actually sweet and sour or whether they'd be considered pickled beets; either way, they're good.

3 cups sliced, peeled fresh beets
½ cup sliced mild onions
½ cup water
½ cup apple juice concentrate
1 tablespoon cider vinegar
6 whole cloves
1 bay leaf
⅛ teaspoon salt, or to taste

1. Place all the ingredients in a 2-quart saucepan. Bring to a boil over high heat. Reduce heat and simmer, uncovered, 20 minutes, stirring occasionally, or until beets are tender. Discard the bay leaf.

Variation: Add 1 tablespoon minced fresh ginger with the other ingredients.

Bok Choy

This Chinese vegetable is often mistaken for Chinese cabbage. They do have many similarities, and the two can be used interchangeably. Both grow in heads, like celery with green leaves, but bok choy has white stems and dark oval leaves (similar to collards), whereas Chinese cabbage has pale leaves and broad, pale green stems. Look for heads that are crisp, not wilted.

STIR-FRIED BOK CHOY

Makes: 3¹/₂ cups; serves: 4 to 6

¾ cup vegetable broth (pages 93–95)
2 tablespoons mirin (rice wine) or dry sherry
1 tablespoon cornstarch
1 teaspoon soy sauce
1 teaspoon sugar
2 tablespoons vegetable oil
½ cup scallions (1-inch pieces; white and green parts)
2 cloves garlic, minced
6 cups packed bok choy
1 cup fresh mung bean sprouts

1. In a medium bowl, stir together the broth, mirin, cornstarch, soy sauce, and sugar; set aside.

2. In a wok or large skillet, heat the oil over high heat. Add the scallions and garlic; cook, stirring, 10 seconds. Add the bok choy and sprouts; cook, stirring, until softened, about 3 minutes.

3. Add the sauce; cook, stirring, until thickened, about 1 minute.

Variation: Add 1 cup baby corn when you add the bok choy.

Broccoflower

A hybrid between broccoli and cauliflower, broccoflower looks like a green cauliflower and tastes more like cauliflower. Look for tight, slightly cone-shaped florets without any dark patches.

PUREE OF BROCCOFLOWER

Makes: 2 cups; serves: 3 to 4

2 tablespoons butter or margarine, divided
¾ cup sliced leeks (white and light green parts only)
4 cups broccoflower florets
¾ cup vegetable broth (pages 93–95) or water
⅛ teaspoon salt
⅛ teaspoon pepper

1. In a 2-quart saucepan, melt 1 tablespoon of the butter or margarine over medium-high heat. Add the leeks; cook, stirring until softened, about 30 seconds.

2. Add the broccoflower and broth. Bring to a boil over medium-high heat. Cover and simmer 15 minutes or until the vegetables are quite soft.

3. Place the broccoflower with any remaining cooking liquid, the remaining 1 tablespoon of butter or margarine, and the salt and pepper in a food processor container fitted with a steel blade. Cover and process until smooth.

Variation: Substitute broccoli or cauliflower for the broccoflower.

Broccoli

A good source of calcium, broccoli has its devoted fans as well as those who can't stand it. Like other members of the cabbage family, it can be "gassy." Don't throw away the stalks; they make very tasty crudités when peeled. Look for firm stalks and no yellowing of the florets.

BROCCOLI WITH OYSTER MUSHROOMS

Makes: 2 1/2 cups; serves: 3 to 4

The delicate flavor of the oyster mushrooms does not clash with the strong flavor of the broccoli. If you can't find oyster mushrooms, you may be better off substituting cultured white mushrooms instead of a different wild mushroom.

1 tablespoon butter or margarine
2 tablespoons minced shallots
3 cups broccoli florets
1 cup oyster mushrooms, cut in bite-size pieces if necessary
2 tablespoons water
2 tablespoons chopped fresh parsley
1/8 teaspoon salt, or to taste
1/8 teaspoon pepper

1. In a large skillet, melt the butter or margarine over medium-high heat. Add the shallots; cook, stirring, until softened, about 30 seconds. Add the broccoli and mushrooms; cook, stirring, until softened, about 4 minutes.

2. Stir in the water, parsley, salt, and pepper. Cook, stirring, to desired doneness, about 3 minutes longer.

Variation: Substitute zucchini or yellow squash for the broccoli.

SAUTÉED BROCCOLI WITH GARLIC

Makes: 3 cups; serves: 4 to 6

These cook up tender-crisp when cooked according to the recipe. If you like your broccoli on the soft side, cover the skillet after adding the water and let the broccoli steam for a minute or two.

1 tablespoon olive oil
4 cups broccoli florets
1 tablespoon slivered garlic
1/4 teaspoon red pepper flakes
3 tablespoons water
Pinch salt

1. In a large skillet, heat the oil over medium-high heat. Add the broccoli, garlic, and red pepper flakes; cook, stirring, until tender-crisp, about 4 minutes. Add the water and salt; cook, stirring, until the liquid has evaporated and the vegetables reach the desired doneness, about 3 minutes longer.

Variation: Add 2 teaspoons lemon juice plus 1/2 teaspoon grated lemon rind to the skillet when you add the water.

SAUTÉED BROCCOLI AND ZUCCHINI

Makes: 3 3/4 cups; serves: 4 to 6

If you prefer crunchy vegetables, use the broccoli raw. If you prefer softer vegetables, blanch and drain the broccoli before sautéing.

1 1/2 tablespoons olive oil
1/2 cup sliced leeks (white and light green only)
2 cups broccoli florets
2 cups sliced zucchini
1/8 teaspoon salt, or to taste

1. In a large skillet, heat the oil over medium-high heat. Add the leeks; cook, stirring, until softened, about 1 minute. Add the broccoli and zucchini; cook, stirring, until tender-crisp, about 4 minutes. Stir in the salt.

Variation: Use butter or margarine instead of oil.

BROCCOLI WITH ORANGE AND ALMONDS

Makes: 2²/₃ cups; serves: 4

This unusual combination is surprisingly nice.

1 orange
¼ cup slivered almonds
1½ tablespoons butter or margarine
3 cups broccoli florets
1 tablespoon water
¼ teaspoon salt, or to taste

1. Grate the orange to yield ½ teaspoon orange rind. Using a sharp knife, cut away all the white pith. Remove the orange segments from the membrane by slicing between segment and membrane. (Reserve 1 tablespoon of the juice that falls during this process.) Set aside the segments, juice, and rind.

2. In a dry skillet over medium heat, stir the almonds until most are lightly browned, about 2 minutes; remove from skillet and set aside.

3. In a large skillet, melt the butter or margarine over medium-high heat. Add the broccoli; cook, stirring, just until it turns bright green, about 3 minutes. Add the water, orange juice, and rind; cook, stirring, until combined. Add the orange segments, almonds, and salt. Cook, stirring, until heated through.

Variation: Use Brussels sprouts instead of broccoli.

Broccoli Rabe

This vegetable looks somewhat like its namesake, broccoli, but with more (pointy) leaves and much smaller florets. The flavor is slightly bitter. Look for bunches with fresh-looking leaves; avoid florets that are turning yellow.

BROCCOLI RABE WITH YELLOW PEPPERS AND CARROTS

Makes: 5 cups; serves: 4 to 6

This is excellent when served with polenta (page 307) and can be served as an entree for four.

1 cup vegetable broth (page 93–95)
2 teaspoons cornstarch
2 tablespoons vegetable oil
2 teaspoons slivered garlic
1 bunch broccoli rabe (1¼ pounds)
2 cups sliced yellow bell peppers
1 cup julienned carrots

1. In a small bowl, stir together the broth and cornstarch; set aside.

2. In a large skillet, heat the vegetable oil over high heat. Add the garlic; cook, stirring, 10 seconds. Add the broccoli rabe, bell peppers, and carrots; cook, stirring, until tender-crisp, about 5 minutes.

3. Add the sauce; cook, stirring, until thickened, about 1 minute.

Variation: Add 1 cup tomato wedges when you add the vegetables. Also, substitute red, orange, or green bell peppers for the yellow.

SAUTÉED BROCCOLI RABE WITH CHESTNUTS

Makes 4½ cups; serves: 6

The bitterness of the rabe blends perfectly with the sweetness of the chestnuts. You can use freshly cooked or canned chestnuts equally well in this recipe.

2 tablespoons butter or margarine
4 cups chopped broccoli rabe
1½ tablespoons fresh lemon juice
¾ cup chopped cooked, peeled chestnuts (page 89)
¼ teaspoon salt, or to taste

1. In a large skillet, melt the butter or margarine over medium-high heat. Add the broccoli rabe; cook, stirring, until tender-crisp, about 4 minutes. Deglaze the pan with the lemon juice.

2. Add the chestnuts and salt; cook, stirring, until heated through.

Variation: Use chopped Swiss chard instead of the broccoli rabe.

Brussels Sprouts

Available fresh mainly in the winter, these tend to be a love-or-hate-them vegetable. They are a member of the cabbage-broccoli-cauliflower family and, like their cousins, have a strong flavor and can leave one with a certain gassiness. Traditionally these are cooked to death, but in fact, they taste quite delicious when left al dente. Look for Brussels sprouts that are quite firm and avoid those that have started to turn yellow.

BRAISED BRUSSELS SPROUTS

Makes: 2½ cups; serves: 4 to 6

Cook these whole if small, halved if large.

1 tablespoon vegetable oil
⅓ cup chopped onions
3 cups Brussels sprouts
1 cup vegetable broth (pages 93–95)

1. In a 3-quart saucepan, heat the oil over medium-high heat. Add the onions; cook, stirring, until softened, about 2 minutes. Add the Brussels sprouts; cook, stirring, until softened, about 4 minutes.

2. Add the broth and bring to a boil. Reduce heat and simmer, covered, 20 minutes or until sprouts reach desired doneness.

AUTUMN BRUSSELS SPROUTS

V ♥

Makes: 3³/₄ cups; serves: 4 to 6

Apples, chestnuts, and Brussels sprouts are all at their best in the autumn, and also in this dish. You can use fresh chestnuts that you've roasted or boiled and peeled, or you can use canned chestnuts.

3 cups halved Brussels sprouts
1 tablespoon butter or margarine
1 cup chopped, peeled apples
½ cup chopped onion
½ cup chopped, cooked chestnuts
½ cup vegetable broth (pages 93–95)
⅛ teaspoon salt, or to taste
⅛ teaspoon pepper

1. Cook the Brussels sprouts in boiling water to desired doneness; drain.

2. In a large skillet, melt the butter or margarine over medium-high heat. Add the apples and onions; cook, stirring until softened, about 4 minutes. Add the Brussels sprouts, chestnuts, broth, salt, and pepper; cook, stirring, until most of the broth has evaporated, about 3 minutes.

Variation: Use apple juice instead of the broth.

WINTER VEGETABLES FOR A CROWD

L

Makes: 9 cups; serves: 12 to 14

This was a great hit at my Thanksgiving dinner.

3 cups halved Brussels sprouts
3 cups cauliflower florets
2 cups sliced carrots
2 cups small white onions
4½ tablespoons butter or margarine, divided
3 tablespoons all-purpose flour
1 cup milk
1 cup vegetable broth (pages 93–95)
1½ cups shredded Gouda
½ cup unflavored bread crumbs

1. Preheat the oven to 350°F.

2. Cook the Brussels sprouts, cauliflower, carrots, and onions in boiling water until tender, about 10 minutes; drain.

3. In a 3-quart saucepan, melt 3 tablespoons of the butter or margarine over medium-high heat. Stir in the flour until absorbed. Stir in the milk and broth; bring to a boil, stirring constantly. Stir in the Gouda.

4. Add the vegetables and toss. Spoon into a buttered 3-quart casserole.

5. In a small saucepan, melt the remaining 1½ tablespoons of butter or margarine over medium heat. Remove from heat; add the bread crumbs and stir until butter or margarine is absorbed. Sprinkle the bread crumbs over the creamed vegetables.

6. Bake 30 minutes or until topping is browned.

Variation: Substitute Cheddar or Swiss cheese for the Gouda.

Cabbage

This very versatile vegetable is good cooked as well as raw. Cabbage is available in a variety of types, the best known of which are green cabbage, red cabbage, and savoy (which has wrinkled leaves). Chinese cabbage is really closer to bok choy in flavor and consistency than to green cabbage. When buying cabbage, look for heads that are heavy for their size, with no yellow or brown on the leaves (although Chinese cabbage may have pale yellow inner leaves). Outer leaves, which are frequently removed before sale, should be dark green and firm.

SPICED BOILED CABBAGE

Makes: 4 quarters; serves 4 to 8

This is not a spicy dish; in fact, the spices are quite subtle. I like my cabbage cooked until really soggy. You may want to cook yours less.

1 small head green cabbage
1/2 teaspoon salt, or to taste
1 clove garlic
2 bay leaves
4 peppercorns
4 whole cloves
4 whole allspice
4 whole juniper berries

1. Quarter the cabbage through the stem, so that the wedges are held together by the heart of the cabbage.

2. In a 6-quart pot of boiling water, add the cabbage and remaining ingredients. Simmer, covered, 45 minutes or until the cabbage is very tender. Drain and cut into serving portions.

Variation: Boiled Cabbage: Omit the spices.

SAUTÉED CABBAGE WITH SNOW PEAS

Makes: 2 cups; serves: 3 to 4

The sesame oil flavor is subtle but definitely there.

1 1/2 tablespoons vegetable oil
3 cups shredded cabbage
1 cup julienned snow peas
1 cup sliced leeks (white and light green parts only)
1 teaspoon sesame oil
1/8 teaspoon salt, or to taste
1/8 teaspoon pepper

1. In a large skillet, heat the vegetable oil over medium-high heat. Add the cabbage, snow peas, and leeks; cook, stirring, until softened, about 4 minutes.

2. Add the sesame oil, salt, and pepper; cook, stirring, until combined.

Variation: Omit the snow peas and add 1 more cup shredded cabbage.

SAUERKRAUT WITH APPLES AND CARAWAY SEEDS

Makes: 2 1/2 cups; serves: 3 to 4

2 teaspoons vegetable oil
1/3 cup sliced onions
1 cup sliced apples
One 1-pound package sauerkraut, drained (2 cups)
1 cup apple juice
1/3 cup chopped prunes
2 teaspoons caraway seeds

1. In a 1½-quart saucepan, heat the oil over medium-high heat. Add the onions; cook, stirring, until softened, about 2 minutes. Add the apples; cook, stirring, until softened, about 2 minutes.

2. Add the sauerkraut, apple juice, prunes, and caraway seeds. Cook, stirring occasionally, 15 minutes.

SAUTÉED RED CABBAGE WITH BALSAMIC VINEGAR

──────── V ♥ ────────

Makes: 3¼ cups; serves: 4 to 6

Unlike many cabbage dishes, which I prefer cooked to death, this one I sauté until just tender-crisp. If the balsamic vinegar you're using is not properly aged and the dish tastes too acidic, just stir in ½ teaspoon sugar to mellow the flavor.

1½ tablespoons butter or margarine
4 cups shredded red cabbage
1½ cups sliced onions
1½ tablespoons balsamic vinegar
¼ teaspoon salt, or to taste
¼ teaspoon pepper

1. In a large, nonreactive skillet, melt the butter or margarine over medium-high heat. Add the cabbage and onion; cook, stirring, until softened, about 3 minutes.

2. Add the vinegar, salt, and pepper; cook, stirring, until vinegar evaporates and cabbage is tender, about 4 minutes longer.

Variation: Use green cabbage instead of red.

BRAISED RED CABBAGE WITH APPLES

──────── V ♥ ────────

Makes: 4 cups; serves: 4 to 6

This is an old Germanic-style recipe I developed on a crisp autumn day.

2 tablespoons butter or margarine
4 cups shredded red cabbage
½ cup sliced onions
2 cups chopped, peeled tart apples
¼ cup water
3 tablespoons light brown or dark brown sugar
1 tablespoon cider vinegar
⅛ teaspoon ground cloves
⅛ teaspoon salt, or to taste
⅛ teaspoon pepper

1. In a 3-quart saucepan, melt the butter or margarine over medium-high heat. Add the cabbage and onions; cook, stirring, until wilted, about 3 minutes. Add the apples; cook, stirring, until softened, about 3 minutes.

2. Add the water, brown sugar, vinegar, cloves, salt, and pepper. Cook, stirring, until the liquid is absorbed, about 4 minutes.

Variation: Use pears instead of apples.

Carrots

An incredible source of beta carotene, the common carrot adds character to many dishes but is frequently overlooked as a vegetable on its own. Look for carrots that are firm. If they still have their tops, the leaves should be fresh-looking. Carrots that have sprouted roots or are limp are over the hill.

PARSLIED CARROTS

Makes: 3 cups; serves: 4 to 6

For a slightly more elegant version, use whole baby carrots; you can use fresh or frozen.

3 cups sliced carrots (¼ inch thick)
1 tablespoon butter or margarine
½ cup chopped fresh parsley

1. Cook the carrots in boiling water 10 minutes or until tender; drain.

2. Return to pot and stir in butter or margarine and parsley; cook, stirring, until butter melts.

♥ *Variation:* For a lower-fat version, use only one teaspoon butter or margarine.

SESAME CARROTS

[V]

Makes: 4 cups; serves: 6 to 8

These carrots are not overly sweet; if you'd like them sweeter, add extra honey.

2 tablespoons sesame seeds
4 cups sliced carrots (¼ inch thick)
2 teaspoons butter or margarine
1 tablespoon honey
¼ teaspoon ground cardamom
¼ teaspoon salt, or to taste

1. Cook the sesame seeds in a dry skillet over medium heat, until lightly browned, about 2 minutes.

2. Cook the carrots in boiling water until tender, about 5 to 7 minutes. Drain.

3. In a medium skillet, melt the butter or margarine over medium heat. Add the carrots, honey, cardamom, and salt. Cook, stirring, until carrots are coated. Add the sesame seeds and toss.

Variation: Use nutmeg instead of cardamom.

JALAPEÑO CARROTS

Makes: 2¼ cups; serves: 3 to 4

These are really not as spicy as you would imagine.

1½ tablespoons butter or margarine
3 cups julienned carrots
3 tablespoons slivered, seeded jalapeño
    peppers
1½ tablespoons sugar
1 tablespoon water
1 teaspoon fresh lime juice
⅛ teaspoon salt, or to taste

1. In a large skillet, melt the butter or margarine over medium-high heat. Add the carrots and peppers; cook, stirring, until tender-crisp, about 3 minutes.

2. Add the sugar, water, lime juice, and salt. Cook, stirring, until carrots are glazed and liquid has evaporated, about 5 minutes.

Variation: Jalapeño Jícama: Substitute jícama for the carrots.

GINGERED CARROT PUREE

[V][♥]

Makes: 2 cups; serves: 4

For a thicker puree, you can substitute sweet potatoes for part of the carrots.

3 cups sliced carrots (¼ inch thick)
½ cup orange juice
2 teaspoons minced fresh ginger
3 tablespoons apricot preserves
1 tablespoon butter or margarine
⅛ teaspoon salt, or to taste

1. Place the carrots, orange juice, and ginger into a 1-quart saucepan. Bring to a boil over high heat. Reduce heat and simmer, covered, 30 minutes or until the carrots are very soft.

2. Place the carrots with any remaining juice, the preserves, butter or margarine, and salt in a blender or food processor container fitted with a steel blade. Cover and process until smooth.

Variation: Substitute orange marmalade for the apricot preserves; sweeten to taste, if necessary.

BALI VEGETABLES

[V]

Makes: 2½ cups; serves: 4

This recipe starts by preparing a spice paste, a common technique in Indonesian cooking. The vegetables are slightly sweet from the coconut milk; serve them warm or at room temperature. If the sauce is too thick for your taste, stir in a tablespoon or two of water.

2 tablespoons water
½ small onion
1 tablespoon distilled white vinegar
3 cloves garlic
2 shallots
½-inch-thick slice fresh ginger
1 whole dried red pepper, or ¼ teaspoon red pepper flakes
1 teaspoon paprika
1 teaspoon ground turmeric
¼ teaspoon ground cardamom
¼ teaspoon salt, or to taste
2 tablespoons vegetable oil
1½ cups julienned carrots
1 cup julienned celeriac (knob celery)
1 cup julienned celery
½ cup julienned green bell peppers
½ cup unsweetened coconut milk

1. Place the water, onion, vinegar, garlic, shallots, ginger, red pepper, paprika, turmeric, cardamon, and salt in a blender container. Cover and process until pureed.

2. In a large skillet, heat the oil over medium-high heat. Add the spice puree; cook, stirring, 30 seconds. Add the vegetables; cook, stirring, until coated with the spices. Add the coconut milk. Cook, stirring, until vegetables are tender, about 5 minutes.

Variation: Substitute julienned cucumber or green beans for the celeriac.

Cauliflower

Like broccoli, cauliflower is a member of the cabbage family. Look for a creamy white color, with the florets tightly closed and no black splotches (although you can just cut the black away).

CAULIFLOWER WITH PARSLEY AND LEMON

Makes: 3 cups; serves: 4 to 6

You can use thawed frozen cauliflower if you can't find fresh or if fresh is too expensive.

1 tablespoon butter or margarine
½ cup chopped fresh parsley
2 tablespoons chopped lemon segments
2 teaspoons chopped capers
⅛ teaspoon salt, or to taste
⅛ teaspoon pepper
3 cups cooked cauliflower florets

1. In a large skillet, melt the butter or margarine over medium-high heat. Add the parsley, lemon, and capers; cook, stirring, until parsley is wilted, about 2 minutes. Add the salt and pepper. Add the cauliflower; cook, stirring, until coated and heated through.

Variation: Add 1 clove garlic, minced, before adding the parsley; cook, stirring, 10 seconds.

CAULIFLOWER POLONAISE

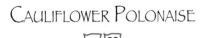

Makes: 4 cups; serves: 4 to 6

Traditionally, polonaise contains chopped egg (as in the variation), but I find it even more delicious without it.

4 cups cauliflower florets
2 tablespoons butter or margarine
⅓ cup unflavored bread crumbs
⅛ teaspoon salt, or to taste
⅛ teaspoon pepper

1. Cook the cauliflower in boiling water until just tender, or to desired doneness, about 5 minutes; drain.

2. In a large skillet, melt the butter or margarine over medium-high heat. Stir in the bread crumbs; cook, stirring, until lightly browned. Stir in the salt and pepper.

3. Add the drained cauliflower; cook, stirring, until heated through.

Variation: Add a hard-cooked egg, finely chopped, when you add the cauliflower.

CAULIFLOWER IN CHEESE SAUCE

Makes: 3 cups; serves: 4 to 6

The cheese sauce is moderately thin and, if you want, can accommodate 2 cups more cauliflower.

4 cups cauliflower florets
2 tablespoons butter or margarine
2 tablespoons all-purpose flour
¾ cup milk
1 cup shredded Cheddar cheese
3 tablespoons grated Parmesan cheese
⅛ teaspoon pepper

1. Cook the cauliflower in boiling water until just tender or to desired doneness, about 5 minutes; drain.

2. In a 1½-quart saucepan, melt the butter or margarine over medium-high heat. Stir in the flour until absorbed. Stir in the milk; cook, stirring, until mixture comes to a boil. Stir in both cheeses. Stir in the pepper.

3. Add the drained cauliflower; cook, stirring, until heated through.

Variation: Broccoli in Cheese Sauce: Substitute broccoli for the cauliflower.

BATTER-FRIED CAULIFLOWER

Makes: 4¹/₂ cups; serves: 4 to 6

You can serve these as hors d'oeuvres as well as a side dish.

3 cups cauliflower florets
¼ cup whole wheat flour
¼ cup all-purpose flour
¼ teaspoon salt, or to taste
¼ teaspoon baking powder
¼ teaspoon pepper
1 egg
¼ cup water
¼ cup chopped fresh parsley
Oil for deep frying

1. Blanch the cauliflower in boiling water until tender-crisp, about 4 minutes; drain.

2. In a medium bowl or on a piece of waxed paper, stir together both flours, the salt, baking powder, and pepper.

3. In a medium bowl, beat the egg with the water. Stir in the dry ingredients and the parsley.

4. In a large pot, pour the oil 2 inches deep and heat until it bubbles when a small drop of batter is dropped in. Drop the drained florets in the batter and toss to coat. Fry a few at a time until golden. Remove from oil and drain on paper towels.

Variation: Use chopped cilantro instead of the parsley.

Celeriac

Also known as celery root or knob celery, this vegetable is not the root of a celery, but obtains its name from its celerylike flavor. Larger roots can be woody, so look for small or medium roots. The tough, hairy brown skin is best removed with a paring knife. Celeriac can be substituted for parsnip in most recipes, and it's especially nice in soups.

JULIENNED CELERIAC AND CELERY SAUTÉ

Makes: 3¹/₄ cups; serves: 6

1 tablespoon butter or margarine
2 cups julienned celeriac
2 cups julienned celery
2 tablespoons white wine
2 tablespoons chopped celery leaf
⅛ teaspoon salt, or to taste

1. In a large skillet, melt the butter or margarine over medium-high heat. Add the celeriac and celery; cook, stirring, until tender-crisp, about 3 minutes.

2. Add the wine, celery leaf, and salt. Cook, stirring, until wine evaporates, about 3 minutes.

Variation: Substitute parsnip or carrots for the celeriac.

Celery

I find that the celery with very deep green color is more pungent than the lighter heads. Some people covet the very small light green, almost yellow, inner stalks known as the heart. Celery leaves are perfectly edible and excellent in soups or as substitutes for parsley.

BRAISED CELERY WITH WILD MUSHROOMS

Makes: 3 cups; serves: 4 to 6

The mushrooms add depth to the flavor of the broth.

1 tablespoon olive oil
¾ cup sliced leeks (white and light green parts only)
3 cups sliced celery (¼ inch thick)
1 cup sliced shiitake mushrooms
⅓ cup vegetable broth (pages 93–95)
2 tablespoons chopped fresh parsley
¼ teaspoon dried thyme
⅛ teaspoon pepper

1. In a large skillet, heat the oil over medium-high heat. Add the leeks; cook, stirring, until softened, about 30 seconds.

2. Add the celery and mushrooms; cook, stirring, until just barely tender-crisp, about 3 minutes.

3. Add the broth, parsley, thyme, and pepper. Cook, stirring, until vegetables are tender-crisp, about 2 minutes.

Variation: Use cultivated mushrooms instead of wild, and substitute tarragon for the thyme.

Corn

Maize, as it was called by the Indians, was the greatest gift to early American settlers. Though technically a grain, it is generally thought of as a vegetable and is still one of the most popular vegetables today. Fresh corn is sweetest when just picked, so buy corn the same day you are planning to eat it. Look for corn still in the husk. The husk should be bright in color, not dull. Both the husk and the tassels (corn silk) should be moist, not dried out. Corn is also available canned and frozen, both interchangeable with fresh kernels.

Dried corn (a variety different from the sweet corn we eat fresh) is ground into cornmeal (yellow, white, or blue), and even more finely ground into masa harina (from which tortillas are made). Corn treated with lye becomes hominy (posole), from which grits are made.

Cooking Corn on the Cob

Corn can be cooked in many different fashions.

Boiled Corn on the Cob: Shuck corn and remove the silk, then put into a large pot of boiling water (you can add 1 tablespoon sugar and/or ½ cup milk to the water to sweeten the corn, if desired). Return to a boil and cook 4 to 6 minutes or until corn is tender.

Microwaved Corn on the Cob: Version I: Peel back the husk but don't remove it. Remove the cornsilk. Close the husk and microwave for the appropriate time (see below). Version II: Remove the husk and the silk. Wrap the corn in waxed paper or plastic wrap. Microwave for the appropriate time (see below). (You may want to brush the corn with softened butter or margarine before wrapping.) To cook either version, place corn in a circle around the outer edge of the microwave and cook for half the specified time. Turn corn over and cook for the remaining time.

MICROWAVE TIMING FOR CORN

The cooking times given here are based on a 650-watt oven. Times may vary depending on the microwave wattage:

1 ear:	2 to 4 minutes
2 ears:	5 to 7 minutes
4 ears:	10 to 15 minutes

CORN PUDDING

Makes: 4¹/₂ cups; serves 6

This is not a sweet corn pudding, but it is "sweetish." It's a good dish to serve for brunch or as a side dish with something like Lentil Burgers (page 162). Make fresh bread crumbs by placing 5 torn slices of bread (I use whole wheat) in a blender or food processor container fitted with a steel blade. Cover and process until crumbed.

1 tablespoon butter or vegetable oil
1 cup chopped onions
3 eggs
1¹/₂ cups milk
¹/₂ teaspoon salt, or to taste
¹/₄ teaspoon ground nutmeg
2 cups corn kernels (fresh, cooked; canned, drained; or frozen)
1¹/₂ cups fresh whole wheat bread crumbs (see note above)

1. Preheat the oven to 350°F. Grease a 2-quart casserole.

2. In a medium skillet, melt the butter over medium-high heat. Add the onions; cook, stirring, until softened, about 2 minutes; set aside.

3. In a large bowl, beat the eggs. Beat in the milk, salt, and nutmeg. Stir in the corn, bread crumbs, and sautéed onions. Pour into the prepared casserole.

4. Bake 50 minutes to 1 hour or until a knife inserted in the center comes out clean.

Variation: Add ¹/₂ cup chopped red bell peppers when you sauté the onions.

TEX~MEX CORN PUDDING

Makes: 4¹/₂ cups; serves 6

Serve this as a side dish or as a main entree for brunch.

1 tablespoon butter or margarine or vegetable oil
1 cup chopped onions
1 cup chopped green bell peppers
1 teaspoon minced, seeded jalapeño peppers
2 teaspoons chili powder
3 eggs
1¹/₂ cups milk
¹/₂ teaspoon salt, or to taste
2 cups corn kernels (fresh, cooked; canned, drained; or frozen)
1¹/₂ cups fresh whole wheat bread crumbs (about 5 slices bread, crumbed in blender or food processor)

1. Preheat the oven to 350°F. Grease a 2-quart casserole.

2. In a medium skillet, melt the butter or margarine over medium-high heat. Add the onions, and both types of peppers; cook, stirring, until softened, about 3 minutes. Stir in the chili powder until absorbed; set aside.

3. In a large bowl, beat the eggs. Beat in the milk and salt. Stir in the corn, bread crumbs, and sautéed onion-pepper mixture. Pour into the prepared casserole.

4. Bake 50 minutes to 1 hour or until a knife inserted in the center comes out clean.

Variation: Omit the jalapeño for a milder version, or add more for a spicier one.

CORN FRITTERS

Makes: 3¹/₂ dozen; serves: 6 to 8

I was introduced to corn fritters at summer camp and, frankly, they're the only good food I can remember camp ever serving! These are so delicious that they'll disappear before you can blink your eyes.

1 cup yellow cornmeal
¾ cup all-purpose flour
3 tablespoons sugar
1 teaspoon baking powder
Pinch nutmeg (optional)
1 egg
½ cup milk
One 6-ounce can corn (reserve ¼ cup liquid and discard remainder)
Oil for deep frying

1. In a medium bowl or on a piece of waxed paper, stir together the cornmeal, flour, sugar, baking powder, and nutmeg.

2. In a large bowl, beat the egg. Stir in the milk and reserved corn liquid. Stir in the dry ingredients until combined. Stir in the corn.

3. In a large pot, pour the oil 2 inches deep and heat until it bubbles when a small drop of batter is dropped in. Drop the batter by rounded tablespoons into the oil. Cook until golden on one side. Turn and cook until golden on second side. Remove from the oil and drain on paper towels.

Variations: Omit the sugar and add 1 tablespoon chopped onion with the corn.

Stir in ¼ teaspoon ground red pepper for a non-traditional, spicier version.

CREAMED CORN

Ⓛ

Makes: 2²/₃ cups; serves: 4 to 6

¾ vegetable broth (pages 93–95)
3 cups corn kernels (fresh, cooked; canned, drained; or frozen)
1½ tablespoons butter or margarine
2 tablespoons all-purpose flour
3 tablespoons heavy cream
⅛ teaspoon pepper

1. In a 1-quart saucepan, bring the broth to a boil over medium-high heat. Add the corn and simmer, covered, 7 minutes.

2. In a 1½-quart saucepan, melt the butter or margarine over medium-high heat. Stir in the flour until absorbed. Add the corn-broth mixture, the cream, and pepper; stir with a whisk until smooth. Cook, stirring, until mixture comes to a boil and sauce is thickened, about 1 minute.

Variations: Add 1 tablespoon snipped fresh dill to the broth when you add the corn.

Ⓥ Use additional broth instead of cream.

Cucumbers

Cucumbers (except kirbys—pickling cucumbers) are usually waxed before they are brought to market, and should be peeled before use. Look for ones that are thin; fatter cucumbers tend to be more "seedy." Tough seeds indicate old cucumbers. Cucumbers should not be wrinkled at the ends. English cucumbers, the very long ones usually wrapped in plastic, are considered "burpless" (easier to digest).

SAUTÉED CUCUMBERS WITH TARRAGON

Makes: 2¼ cups; serves: 3 to 4

If you are not fond of tarragon, you can substitute chopped cilantro.

1½ tablespoons butter or margarine
2 cloves garlic, minced
3 cups julienned cucumber
1 cup julienned green bell peppers
2 tablespoons chopped fresh parsley
1 tablespoon white wine
½ teaspoon dried tarragon, or 1 teaspoon chopped fresh tarragon
⅛ teaspoon salt, or to taste
⅛ teaspoon pepper

1. In a large skillet, melt the butter or margarine over medium-high heat. Add the garlic; cook, stirring, 10 seconds. Add the cucumber and bell peppers; cook, stirring, until just barely tender-crisp, about 2 minutes.

2. Add the parsley, wine, tarragon, salt, and pepper; cook, stirring, until vegetables are tender-crisp, about 3 minutes longer.

Eggplant

The texture and mild flavor of the eggplant make it a very important vegetable in meatless cooking. Look for eggplants with unblemished skin that are firm, but not rock hard. Sometimes eggplant has a bitter flavor, which you can eliminate by sprinkling salt on the cut or sliced eggplant, letting it stand for 30 minutes, then rinsing. I think the cooking process eliminates much of the bitterness, and in truth, I usually skip the salting step and just use the eggplant as is. I've rarely found the finished dish bitter.

Eggplant Basics

For the purposes of this book, eggplants are sized as follows:

1 small eggplant	=	¾ pound
1 medium eggplant	=	1 pound
1 large eggplant	=	1½ pounds

Baked Eggplant: Eggplant is not usually eaten this way, but rather this method of cooking eggplant is a first step in many dips and spreads. Place any size whole eggplant directly on rack of a preheated 375°F oven. Bake 45 minutes or until skin is charred and eggplant has collapsed and is extremely soft. Cut in half lengthwise and scrape out flesh; discard skin. Serves: 2 to 4, depending on use.

Broiled Eggplant: Preheat broiler. Slice eggplant ¼-inch thick. Brush lightly with olive oil. Place on greased baking pan. Broil 5 minutes per side.

Microwaved Eggplant: Adjust cooking time according to size (see page 256). Pierce an eggplant in several places with a fork. Place in microwave oven and microwave on high, turning over once, halfway through cooking time.

MICROWAVE TIMING FOR EGGPLANT

The cooking times given here are based on a 650-watt oven. Times may vary, depending on the microwave wattage.

Small:	5 minutes
Medium:	7 minutes
Large:	8 minutes

SAUTÉED EGGPLANT WITH TOMATOES, CAPERS, AND GARLIC

Makes: 3¹/₂ cups; serves: 4 to 6

This is quite tangy and can even be used as a pasta sauce.

2 tablespoons olive oil
4 cups cubed eggplant
3 cloves garlic, minced
2 cups tomato wedges
¼ cup chopped fresh parsley
1 tablespoon fresh lemon juice
1 tablespoon chopped capers
⅛ teaspoon salt, or to taste
⅛ teaspoon ground red pepper

1. In a large skillet, heat the oil over medium-high heat. Add the eggplant and garlic; cook, stirring, until slightly softened, about 3 minutes.

2. Add the tomatoes, parsley, lemon juice, capers, salt, and red pepper. Cook, stirring, until the tomatoes have softened, about 3 minutes.

Variation: Substitute dry vermouth for the lemon juice.

BARBECUED EGGPLANT

Makes: 12 to 16 slices; serves: 3 to 4

I used the Orange-Flavored Barbecue Sauce (page 478) for this recipe, but if you prefer, you can use any homemade or even bottled barbecue sauce. Serve these slices over rice.

2 medium eggplants (about 1 pound each)
1 cup barbecue sauce

1. Preheat the broiler. Line broiling pan with aluminum foil; grease the foil with butter or margarine.

2. Cut the eggplant into 1-inch-thick slices. Place on the broiling pan so that the slices do not overlap. Generously brush the eggplant with sauce.

3. Broil about 4 inches from the heat source for 5 minutes or until the eggplant with sauce is browned and bubbly. Turn the slices and brush the second side generously with the remaining sauce. Broil 5 minutes longer.

STUFFED YOUNG EGGPLANTS

Makes: 6 eggplant halves; serves: 6 (3 as entree)

If you cannot find small eggplants, you can use one large or two medium ones, as long as the total weight is 1¹/₂ pounds. Many stuffing mixes use animal products. I used Arnold's Premium Seasoned Stuffing, which has no animal products. If you can't find it, you can use plain, unflavored stuffing and add herbs to your taste, or you can use boxed croutons.

3 small eggplants (about 6-inch diameter each, 1½ pounds total)

Salt

2 tablespoons olive oil

⅓ cup chopped onions

1 clove garlic, minced

1 cup chopped tomatoes

½ cup vegetable broth (pages 93–95)

2 cups dry stuffing mix

¼ cup chopped fresh parsley

1. Cut the eggplants in half lengthwise. Scoop out the flesh, leaving about ¼ inch in the shell. Chop the scooped eggplant and place 1½ cups (save any extra for another use or discard) in a strainer or colander and sprinkle lightly with salt, tossing to disperse the salt evenly. Lightly sprinkle the shells with salt. Let stand 20 minutes. Rinse salt from chopped eggplant and shells.

2. Preheat the oven to 350°F. Bake the empty shells for 20 minutes.

3. While the shells are baking, in a large skillet, heat the oil over medium-high heat. Add the onions and garlic; cook, stirring, until softened, about 2 minutes. Add the chopped eggplant and tomatoes to the skillet; cook, stirring, until softened, about 4 minutes. Add the broth and bring to a boil. Stir in the stuffing and parsley until liquid is absorbed.

4. Fill the eggplant shells with the stuffing mixture. Place in a 9 × 13-inch baking pan. Bake 20 minutes or until stuffing is crisped on top.

⌐ *Variation:* Add ⅓ cup grated Parmesan after you've added the stuffing and parsley.

RATATOUILLE

Ⓥ ♥

Makes: 6½ cups; serves: 8 to 12

This is one of my very favorite vegetable dishes. Serve it warm or at room temperature as a vegetable and as an hors d'oeuvre, or over starch (such as pasta or polenta) as a main dish, or top with shredded cheese and melt to serve au gratin.

2 tablespoons olive oil

2 cups chopped onions

3 cloves garlic, minced

4 cups diced eggplants

1 cup red bell pepper chunks

½ cup green bell pepper chunks

3 cups tomato wedges

2 cups sliced zucchini

1 cup sliced yellow squash

⅓ cup chopped fresh parsley

¼ cup red wine

2 tablespoons tomato paste

1 teaspoon sugar

1 teaspoon dried basil

½ teaspoon dried rosemary, crumbled

¼ teaspoon dried thyme

¼ teaspoon dried sage

2 teaspoons red wine vinegar

½ teaspoon salt, or to taste

⅛ teaspoon pepper

1. In a 6-quart pot, heat the oil over medium-high heat. Add the onions and garlic; cook, stirring, until softened, about 2 minutes. Add the eggplant and both bell peppers; cook, stirring, until softened, about 4 minutes.

2. Add the tomatoes, zucchini, yellow squash, parsley, wine, tomato paste, sugar, basil, rosemary, thyme, and sage. Bring to a boil. Reduce heat and simmer, uncovered, 25 minutes, stirring occasionally. Add the vinegar, salt, and pepper, simmer 5 minutes longer.

Fennel

Fennel looks like short, rounded celery with fluffy dill on top. It has a mild licorice flavor. You can use the bulbs as a vegetable and the "leaves" as an herb, if you like. Fennel with stalks that look dryish are past their prime.

BRAISED FENNEL

Makes: 12 wedges; serves: 3 to 4

2 medium heads fennel
1 tablespoon olive oil
1 teaspoon slivered garlic
2 cups vegetable broth (pages 93–95)

1. Trim the stalks and feathery leaves from the fennel bulbs. Cut each bulb, through the root, into 6 wedges.

2. In a 2-quart saucepan, heat the oil over medium-high heat. Add the garlic; cook, stirring, 10 seconds. Add the fennel; cook, stirring, until tender-crisp, about 3 minutes.

3. Add the broth; bring to a boil. Reduce heat and simmer, 20 minutes or until fennel is very tender.

Variation: Braised Celery: Substitute 1½-inch slices of celery for the fennel and omit the garlic.

SAUTÉED FENNEL AND CELERY WITH WATER CHESTNUTS AND TOASTED ALMONDS

$$\boxed{V}$$

Makes: 3 cups; serves: 4 to 6

The small changes made in the variation make an enormous difference in the final result. They're both terrific, but one is slightly sweet.

½ cup whole almonds
1 tablespoon vegetable oil
1½ cups diced fennel
1 cup diced celery
½ cup canned, diced water chestnuts
¼ teaspoon salt, or to taste

1. Toast the almonds in a baking pan in a 350°F oven for 10 minutes.

2. In a large skillet, heat the oil over medium-high heat. Add the fennel and celery; cook, stirring, until softened, about 4 minutes. Add the almonds, water chestnuts and salt; cook, stirring, until heated through.

Variation: Omit the water chestnuts and stir in ½ cup dark or golden raisins instead.

FENNEL AU GRATIN

Makes: 2 cups; serves: 3 to 4

I'm usually not overjoyed with fennel, but I loved this dish so much that I almost licked out the casserole. Aged Asiago cheese is similar to Parmesan and is used for grating; "fresh" Asiago can be used for eating or shredding and is the one I've chosen here. If Asiago is not available where you live, Swiss or Jarlsberg will be good in this recipe, too.

2½ tablespoons butter or margarine, divided
3 tablespoons dry, unflavored bread crumbs
3 cups sliced fennel (about ½ pound)
2 tablespoons all-purpose flour
¾ cup milk
½ cup shredded Asiago cheese
1 tablespoon grated Parmesan cheese
¼ cup chopped fresh parsley
⅛ teaspoon pepper

1. Preheat the oven to 350°F.

2. In a 2-quart saucepan, melt ¹/₂ tablespoon of the butter or margarine. Add the bread crumbs and stir until they absorb the butter or margarine; remove from pan and set aside.

3. Melt the remaining butter or margarine over medium-high heat in the now-empty saucepan. Add the fennel; cook, stirring, until softened, about 4 minutes.

4. Stir in the flour until absorbed. Stir in the milk; cook, stirring, until mixture comes to a boil. Stir in both cheeses. Stir in the parsley and pepper. Pour mixture into a 1-quart casserole. Sprinkle with the reserved bread crumbs.

5. Bake 20 minutes or until bread crumbs are browned and mixture is bubbly.

Variation: Celery au Gratin: Substitute sliced celery for the fennel.

Green Beans

Call them green beans or string beans, they're the pods of immature beans. Green beans can be yellow (wax beans) or purple, rounded or flat (Italian), or long (Chinese long beans). Wax beans have a milder flavor than green beans, and the very small green beans (haricots verts) are probably the most flavorful. Look for thin, crisp beans with smooth skin (the bumpier the skin, the tougher the bean). Frozen whole green beans can stand in fairly well for cooked fresh ones.

Garlic Green Beans

Makes: 2¹/₂ cups; serves: 3 to 4

I found these surprisingly mild, considering how much garlic I'd added.

1 tablespoon olive oil
4 cups whole green beans, ends trimmed (³/₄ pound)
1 tablespoon slivered garlic
2 teaspoons fresh lemon juice
1 tablespoon water
¹/₈ teaspoon salt, or to taste

1. In a large skillet, heat the oil over high heat. Add the beans and garlic; cook, stirring, 1 minute. Add the lemon juice, water, and salt. Cook, stirring, until liquid evaporates and beans reach desired doneness, about 4 minutes.

Variation: Orange-glazed Garlic Green Beans: Add 2 teaspoons orange juice concentrate when you add the lemon juice.

ITALIAN-STYLE GREEN BEANS AND FENNEL

Makes: 3½ cups; serves: 4 to 6

These are equally good served warm or at room temperature. They're a good buffet or party dish.

1½ tablespoons olive oil
3 cups whole green beans, ends trimmed
     (½ pound)
2 cups sliced fennel
2 cloves garlic, minced
One 8-ounce can tomato sauce
1 cup vegetable broth (pages 93–95)
⅓ cup chopped fresh parsley
2 tablespoons red wine
1 teaspoon sugar
½ teaspoon dried oregano
⅛ teaspoon pepper

1. In a 3-quart saucepan, heat the oil over medium-high heat. Add the green beans, fennel, and garlic; cook, stirring, until softened, about 4 minutes.

2. Add the tomato sauce, broth, parsley, wine, sugar, oregano, and pepper. Bring to a boil; reduce heat and simmer, uncovered, 20 minutes. Serve warm or let cool to room temperature.

Variation: For a stronger fennel flavor, add ½ to 1 teaspoon fennel seeds when you add the tomato sauce.

SPICY GREEN BEANS WITH SHALLOTS

Makes: 7 cups; serves 6 to 8

Slightly sweet from the hoisin sauce, these beans rate moderate on the hotness scale.

2 tablespoons mirin (rice wine) or dry sherry
2 tablespoons soy sauce
1 tablespoon hoisin sauce
3 tablespoons vegetable oil
1 cup halved shallots
1 tablespoon garlic, minced
1 tablespoon minced fresh ginger
3 whole dried chilies
9 cups whole green beans, ends trimmed
     (1½ pounds)

1. In a small bowl, stir together the mirin, soy sauce, and hoisin sauce; set aside.

2. In a wok or large skillet, heat the oil over high heat. Add the shallots, garlic, ginger, and chilies. Cook, stirring, 30 seconds.

3. Add the green beans; cook, stirring, until the beans turn bright green, about 3 minutes. Add the sauce; cook, stirring, until the beans are coated with the sauce.

Variation: For a less spicy version, omit the chilies.

CREAMY PARMESAN GREEN BEANS

Ⓛ

Makes: 4 cups; serves: 4 to 6

As written, this recipe produces beans that are quite al dente (tender-crisp), which is the way I like them. My father just considered them undercooked. If you like your beans less than crispy, add 2 or 3 tablespoons of broth or water to the heavy cream before adding the beans; then cook, covered, for a few minutes—this way the beans will be softer before the liquid evaporates.

⅓ cup heavy cream

6 cups whole green beans, ends trimmed (1 pound)

¼ cup grated Parmesan cheese

⅛ teaspoon salt, or to taste

⅛ teaspoon pepper

1. In a large skillet, heat the heavy cream to boiling. Add the green beans; cook, stirring, until the liquid evaporates and the beans are tender-crisp and bright green, about 3 minutes. Stir in the Parmesan, salt, and pepper. Cook, stirring, until beans are coated with slightly melted cheese mixture.

Variation: Creamy Parmesan Broccoli: Use 5 cups broccoli florets instead of the green beans.

SZECHUAN GREEN BEANS

[V]

Makes: 5 cups; serves: 4 to 6

Just slightly hotter than Spicy Green Beans with Shallots (page 260).

3 tablespoons mirin (rice wine) or dry sherry

2 tablespoons soy sauce

½ teaspoon sugar

1 teaspoon cornstarch

2 tablespoons vegetable oil

1 tablespoon slivered garlic

1 tablespoon julienned fresh ginger

4 whole dried chili peppers, or ¼ teaspoon red pepper flakes

6 cups whole green beans, ends trimmed (1 pound)

1 cup sliced red bell peppers

1 teaspoon sesame oil

1. In a small bowl, stir together the mirin, soy sauce, sugar, and cornstarch; set aside.

2. In a wok or large skillet, heat the vegetable oil over high heat. Add the garlic, ginger, and dried peppers. Cook, stirring, 30 seconds. Add the green beans and bell peppers; cook, stirring, until tender-crisp, about 4 minutes.

3. Add the sauce mixture; cook, stirring, until mixture comes to a boil and is thickened, about 1 minute.

4. Stir in the sesame oil.

Variation: Cold Marinated Szechuan Green Beans: Omit the cornstarch; chill overnight.

GREEN BEANS WITH CHICKPEAS IN GROUNDNUT SAUCE

— Ⓥ —

Makes: 5 1/2 cups; serves: 6 to 8

Peanuts are called groundnuts in many African nations. This curry is unusual in that it doesn't complement rice nearly as well as it does bread— especially paratha, roti, or naan.

6 tablespoons, divided
2 shallots
2 cloves garlic
One 1-inch piece fresh ginger
2 teaspoons curry powder
1 teaspoon ground coriander
1/2 teaspoon salt, or to taste
1/4 teaspoon ground red pepper
1 tablespoon vegetable oil
4 cups whole green beans, ends trimmed
   (about 3/4 pound)
1/2 cup unsweetened coconut milk
1/4 cup peanut butter
2 cups chopped tomatoes
1 1/2 cups chickpeas (cooked from dry; or
   canned, drained)
1/2 teaspoon dried basil or 2 tablespoons
   chopped fresh basil

1. In a blender container, combine the 2 tablespoons water, the shallots, garlic, ginger, curry powder, coriander, salt, and red pepper. Cover and blend until smooth.

2. In a 3-quart saucepan, heat the oil over medium-high heat. Add the spice mixture; cook, stirring, until heated. Add the green beans; cook, stirring, until coated with spices. Stir in the remaining 1/4 cup water, the coconut milk, and peanut butter until smooth. Bring to a boil.

3. Add the tomatoes, chickpeas, and basil. Return to a boil. Reduce heat and simmer, uncovered, 20 minutes.

Greens

Any dark edible leaf can be considered a "green," however, the more tender leaves that are eaten raw are categorized as lettuce. Most greens are at least partially bitter and need to be cooked rather than eaten raw. Collard greens, beet greens, kale, turnip greens, mustard greens, Swiss chard, and vine leaves are all considered "greens." You can use greens interchangeably in recipes. Look for firm leaves which are not brown at the edges and are not at all slimy.

COLLARDS, ZUCCHINI, AND TOMATOES

Makes: 3 cups; serves: 4 to 6

Substitute kale or escarole for the collards, if you prefer.

1 1/2 tablespoons olive oil
4 cups chopped collards
1 cup sliced leeks (white and light green parts
   only)
2 cups tomato wedges
1 cup sliced zucchini
1/8 teaspoon salt, or to taste
1/8 teaspoon pepper

1. In a large skillet, heat the oil over medium-high heat. Add the collards and leeks; cook, stirring, until softened, about 3 minutes.

2. Add the tomato wedges. Cook over low heat, covered, 10 minutes. Add the zucchini, salt, and pepper; cook, covered, 5 minutes longer.

Variation: Substitute corn for the zucchini.

COLLARDS

Makes: 2³/₄ cups; serves: 3 to 4

This is a very basic way to prepare collards; it's so good and simple, I couldn't think of a variation.

1 tablespoon olive oil
1 cup chopped onions
6 cups chopped collards
½ cup vegetable broth (pages 93–95)

1. In a large skillet, heat the oil over high heat. Add the onions; cook, stirring, until transparent, about 2 minutes. Add the collards; cook, stirring, until the collards are wilted, about 2 minutes. Add the broth; simmer, covered, 15 minutes.

CREAMY SWISS CHARD WITH CRANBERRY BEANS

Makes: 3 cups; serves: 4 to 6

I developed this recipe one day after I'd found fresh cranberry beans in the farmer's market. I thought cooked fresh beans would be ever so different from dried or canned. Unfortunately, they were remarkably similar to dried. That means that you don't have to wait until fresh cranberry beans are available on the market to try this recipe—just cook up dried, or use canned, drained.

1½ tablespoons vegetable oil
½ cup finely chopped onions
4 cups bite-size pieces Swiss chard
1½ cups cooked cranberry beans (cooked from dry; or canned, drained)
½ cup sour cream
¼ teaspoon salt, or to taste
⅛ teaspoon pepper

1. In a large skillet, heat the oil over medium-high heat. Add the onions; cook, stirring, until onions are softened, about 2 minutes. Add the Swiss chard; cook, stirring until wilted, about 3 minutes. Add the beans; cook, stirring, until heated through.

2. Remove from heat. Stir in the sour cream, salt, and pepper.

Variation: Substitute kidney or cannellini beans for the cranberry beans.

SAUTÉED ESCAROLE

Makes: 3 cups; serves: 4

One of my favorite dinners is Sautéed Escarole with Creamy Polenta (page 307) and a salad.

2 tablespoons olive oil
1 tablespoon slivered garlic
1 large head escarole (1 pound; 12 cups bite-size pieces), rinsed well

1. In a large skillet, heat the oil over medium-high heat. Add the garlic; cook, stirring, 30 seconds. Add the escarole; cook, stirring occasionally, until most of the liquid evaporates.

Variations: Sautéed Spinach: Use 1 pound of spinach instead of the escarole.

Escarole and Beans: Stir in 1 cup white beans or cannellini (cooked from dry; or canned, drained), and cook until heated through.

ESCAROLE AND SLICED CUCUMBER

Makes: 2 cups; serves: 3 to 4

I prepared this recipe early one day. When supper came, I had too many other dishes in the microwave to reheat this one—so I served it at room temperature. It was just fine, almost like a salad (I guess that's because most people don't think of eating cucumbers cooked).

1 tablespoon olive oil
4 cups lightly packed coarsely chopped escarole (bite-size pieces)
1 cup peeled, sliced cucumber
½ cup sliced scallions (1-inch pieces; white and green parts)
⅛ teaspoon salt, or to taste
⅛ teaspoon pepper

1. In a large skillet, heat the oil over high heat. Add the escarole, cucumber, and scallions. Cook, stirring, until the vegetables are wilted, about 3 minutes. Stir in the salt and pepper.

Variation: Use Swiss chard instead of the escarole; add 1 teaspoon garlic, minced, when you add the vegetables.

ESCAROLE WITH MUSHROOMS

[V]

Makes: 2 cups; serves: 3 to 4

You can also add tomato wedges when you add the escarole for a nice variation.

1½ tablespoons olive oil
½ cup sliced leeks (white and light green parts only)
1½ cups sliced mushrooms
4 cups coarsely chopped escarole (bite-size pieces)
2 teaspoons fresh lemon juice
⅛ teaspoon salt, or to taste
⅛ teaspoon pepper

1. In a large skillet, heat the oil over high heat. Add the leeks; cook, stirring, until softened, about 30 seconds. Add the mushrooms; cook, stirring, until softened, about 3 minutes. Add the escarole, lemon juice, salt, and pepper; cook, stirring, until wilted, about 3 minutes.

Variation: Add 1 tablespoon white wine when you add the escarole.

Jerusalem Artichokes

Neither from Jerusalem nor an artichoke, these roots—which resemble fresh ginger in appearance—are densely crisp, similar to water chestnuts, and slightly sweet, similar to jícama. When cooked, they do taste somewhat like artichoke hearts. They're also good raw in salads.

JERUSALEM ARTICHOKES WITH BLACK BEANS

Makes: 2²/₃ cups; serves: 4

1 tablespoon olive oil
½ cup sliced leeks (white and light green parts only)
2 cups diced Jerusalem artichokes
¼ cup vegetable broth (pages 93–95)
1 tablespoon fresh lemon juice
1 cup cooked black beans (cooked from dry; or canned, drained)

1. In a 2-quart saucepan, heat the oil over medium-high heat. Add the leeks; cook, stirring, until softened, about 1 minute. Add the Jerusalem artichokes, vegetable broth, and lemon juice. Cook, stirring, 5 minutes or until the vegetables are tender.

2. Stir in the black beans. Cook, stirring, until heated through.

Jícama

This newcomer to the marketplace is a root vegetable with a thick, light-brown skin. The flesh is white and crispy, with texture somewhere between an unripe pear and a radish. The flavor is on the sweet side and is well suited to salads and crudités. Cooked, the texture is similar to a water chestnut. When choosing jícama, be sure the vegetable is quite firm and the skin has a sheen.

LIME-SAUTÉED JÍCAMA WITH GRAPES

Makes: 3¹/₄ cups; serves: 4 to 6

I used red seedless grapes because visually they contrast nicely with the white jícama and green cilantro, but you can use green grapes, if you prefer.

1 tablespoon butter or margarine
3 cups diced jícama (½-inch pieces)
½ cup water
1 tablespoon fresh lime juice
¾ cup seedless or pitted grapes, halved
2 tablespoons chopped fresh cilantro
½ teaspoon grated lime rind
⅛ teaspoon salt, or to taste

1. In a large skillet, melt the butter or margarine over medium-high heat. Add the jícama; cook, stirring, until tender-crisp, about 4 minutes. Add the water and lime juice; cook, stirring, until liquid evaporates. Add the grapes, cilantro, lime rind, and salt; cook, stirring, until grapes are heated through.

Variation: Substitute lemon juice and rind for the lime.

Kohlrabi

Kohlrabi can be "woody" if they are too large, so look for medium or small ones. If possible, buy them in bunches with the leaves on, so you can check that the leaves are still fresh and not wilted. Kohlrabi leaves can be eaten as "greens."

PARMESAN BAKED KOHLRABI

Makes: 3 cups; serves: 4 to 6

The baking time is kind of long, but it's well worth the wait.

Bread crumbs, for dusting
3 cups sliced kohlrabi (¼-inch-thick pieces)
1 tablespoon butter or margarine, melted
2 tablespoons grated Parmesan cheese
1 tablespoon unflavored bread crumbs
⅛ teaspoon pepper

1. Preheat the oven to 350°F. Grease an 8-inch-round cake pan and dust with bread crumbs.

2. Cook the kohlrabi in boiling water until just tender, about 7 to 10 minutes; drain. Toss with the melted butter or margarine.

3. Place the kohlrabi in the prepared pan, then sprinkle with Parmesan cheese, 1 tablespoon bread crumbs, and the pepper. Bake 1 hour or until topping is browned.

Variation: Parmesan Baked Celeriac: Substitute celeriac (or rutabaga) for the kohlrabi.

Leeks

Leeks are part of the onion family, and as such, are usually an ingredient in recipes rather than the primary vegetable. Look for leeks that have a long white bottom (since that's the best part of the leek). Sometimes leeks have a thick core in the center, so check that there are a lot of "leaves" in the center of the leek you're about to buy, not a stem. You can use the tough, dark-green parts of the leek when you prepare broth, but don't use them in recipes calling for leek.

As with spinach, cleaning is an essential part of cooking leeks. Halve the leeks lengthwise and be sure to rinse between each "leaf"; or slice leeks in rounds and rinse thoroughly in a strainer.

LEEKS PROVENÇAL

Makes: 2 cups; serves: 3 to 4

This dish is just cooked vegetables; it's not saucy. If you'd like it more tomato saucy, add ⅓ cup water when you add the vermouth.

1 tablespoon olive oil
2 cups sliced leeks (1-inch pieces; white parts only)
1 cup coarsely chopped tomatoes
½ cup small black olive halves
¼ cup chopped fresh parsley
2 tablespoons dry vermouth
2 tablespoons water
½ teaspoon grated lemon rind
¼ teaspoon dried thyme
⅛ teaspoon salt, or to taste
⅛ teaspoon pepper

1. In a large skillet, heat the oil over high heat. Add the leeks; cook, stirring, until almost tender-crisp, about 30 minutes.

2. Add the tomatoes, olives, parsley, vermouth, water, lemon rind, thyme, salt, and pepper. Cook, covered, 3 minutes or until vegetables are tender.

Variation: Add 2 tablespoons chopped fresh basil when you add the parsley.

Mushrooms

The most commonly available mushroom is the white or cultivated mushroom; however, there are many other mushrooms available to those interested. Most varieties can be described as earthy, with a consistency that is "meaty" or chewy. For the vegetarian this makes mushrooms an excellent entree ingredient. There is a world of "wild" mushrooms (most of which are now also cultivated or farmed), such as the delicate chanterelle, morel, enoki, and oyster mushrooms, and the heartier portobello, crimini, and shiitake mushrooms. Mushrooms are available canned and dried as well as fresh. Dried mushrooms tend to have even more intense flavor when rehydrated than their fresh counterparts. Look for cultivated mushrooms that have tightly closed caps. Wild mushrooms should be moist without being wet.

SAUTÉED MUSHROOMS WITH WATER CHESTNUTS

V ♥

Makes: 1³/₄ cups; serves: 4

A lovely combination of chewy (mushrooms) and crunchy (water chestnuts).

1 tablespoon vegetable oil
½ cup sliced onions
3 cups sliced white mushrooms
½ cup canned water chestnuts, chopped
2 teaspoons soy sauce

1. In a large skillet, heat the oil over medium-high heat. Add the onions; cook, stirring until softened, about 2 minutes. Add the mushrooms; cook, stirring, until softened, about 3 minutes.

2. Add the water chestnuts and soy sauce; cook, stirring, until any liquid has evaporated.

Variation: Substitute 1 cup of shiitake mushrooms for 1 cup of the white.

BUTTON MUSHROOMS PERSILLER

⟦V⟧

Makes: 2 cups; serves: 4

Button mushrooms are very small, cultivated mushrooms (they're cute as a . . .). If you can't find button mushrooms, use medium mushrooms and quarter them.

1½ tablespoons butter or margarine
3 cups button mushrooms
1 clove garlic, minced
¼ cup chopped fresh parsley
⅛ teaspoon salt, or to taste
Pinch black pepper

1. In a medium skillet, melt the butter or margarine over medium-high heat. Add the mushrooms and garlic; cook, stirring, until softened, about 3 minutes. Stir in the parsley, salt, and pepper; cook, stirring, until any liquid in the pan has evaporated.

Variation: Add 1 tablespoon brandy, sherry, or Marsala when you add the parsley.

SAUTÉED WILD MUSHROOMS AND PEAS

⟦V⟧

Makes: 2 cups; serves: 4

I've always loved sautéed mushrooms and onions; in fact, my mother would serve them over toast points as a real treat for lunch. One evening when I had dinner at the home of my friends Danusia and Elliot Cohen, Elliot (who was the cook that night) took my old favorite one giant step forward. He used portobello mushrooms instead of regular cultivated ones—and it was heaven on earth.

3 tablespoons olive oil
1½ cups chopped onions
4 cups diced wild mushroom caps and stems (¾-inch pieces; choose portobello, shiitake, crimini, porcini, or the like)
1½ cups cooked peas (fresh or frozen)
⅛ teaspoon salt, or to taste
⅛ teaspoon pepper

1. In a medium skillet, heat the oil over medium heat. Add the onions; cook, stirring, until onions start to brown, about 4 minutes. Add the mushrooms and peas; cook, stirring, until softened, about 4 minutes. Sprinkle with the salt and pepper.

Variation: Add such chopped fresh herbs as parsley, rosemary, oregano, or thyme when you add the onions.

Okra

Many people are turned off to okra because of its sliminess when cooked; others value it for the thickening it affords to sauces. You can avoid a slimy consistency and still enjoy okra by breading and frying it or keeping the pod enclosed. It only gets slimy when you cut the okra and the juices mix in with the cooking liquids, so just slice the top stem off the okra, but don't cut deep enough to see the seeds.

When shopping for okra look for a good green color and not too many black scratches. It should snap when you try to bend the tip. I personally prefer small okra to the larger ones.

CHILI-FRIED OKRA

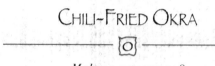

Makes: 3 cup; serves: 8

These are not really as spicy as the title may suggest. For more heat, stir in some ground red pepper when you add the chili powder.

1 egg
1 tablespoon water
3 tablespoons cornmeal
2 tablespoons all-purpose flour
1 tablespoon chili powder
1/2 teaspoon salt, or to taste
1/4 teaspoon pepper
2 cups sliced okra (1/2-inch-thick pieces; about 1/2 pound)
Oil for deep frying

1. In a medium bowl, beat the egg and water until combined.

2. In a medium bowl or on a piece of waxed paper, stir together the cornmeal, flour, chili powder, salt, and pepper until combined.

3. Add the okra slices to the egg mixture. Stir until coated. Lift out with a slotted spoon and roll in cornmeal mixture until coated (do this in small batches).

4. Pour the oil 2 inches deep and heat the oil to 375°F, or until it bubbles when a few specks of cornmeal are dropped in. Add the okra, in small batches, and fry until lightly browned, about 2 minutes. Remove from pot with slotted spoon and drain on paper towels. Continue with remaining okra, until all is cooked.

Variation: Fried Okra: Use 1 tablespoon extra flour instead of the chili powder, and reduce the pepper to 1/8 teaspoon.

CREOLE OKRA WITH CORN

Makes: 3 1/2 cups; serves: 4 to 6

1 tablespoon vegetable oil
1/2 cup chopped onions
1/2 cup chopped green bell peppers
1/2 cup chopped celery
1 1/2 cups whole okra, top stems sliced off
One 11-ounce can corn kernels, undrained
One 8-ounce can tomato sauce
1/4 teaspoon salt
1/8 teaspoon ground red pepper or more, to taste

1. In a 1 1/2 cup saucepan, heat the oil over medium-high heat. Add the onions, green peppers, and celery; cook, stirring, until tender-crisp, about 3 minutes. Add the okra; cook, stirring, until okra turns brighter green, about 2 minutes.

2. Add the corn, tomato sauce, salt, and red pepper. Bring to a boil; reduce heat and simmer, covered, 10 to 15 minutes or until the okra is tender.

Variation: Add 1 teaspoon chili powder before adding the tomato sauce.

CURRIED OKRA WITH GREEN BEANS

— L —

Makes: 3 cups; serves: 4 to 6

Double this recipe for a great entree.

1 tablespoon ghee (page 494) or
   vegetable oil
1 cup chopped onions
3 cloves garlic, minced
1 tablespoon curry powder
1 teaspoon paprika
1 teaspoon ground coriander
¼ teaspoon ground red pepper
1½ cups whole okra, trimmed
   (see page 269)
1 cup whole green beans, trimmed
¾ cup vegetable broth (pages 93–95)
½ teaspoon sugar
⅛ teaspoon salt, or to taste
1 tablespoon half-and-half

1. In a 1½ quart saucepan, heat the ghee or oil over medium-high heat. Add the onions and garlic; cook, stirring, until transparent, about 2 minutes. Stir in the curry powder, paprika, coriander, and red pepper until absorbed. Add the okra and green beans, stirring until vegetables are coated with the curry.

2. Add the broth, sugar, and salt. Bring to a boil; reduce heat and simmer, covered, 10 to 15 minutes or until the okra is tender. Stir in the half-and-half.

[v] *Variation:* Substitute unsweetened coconut milk for the half-and-half.

Onions

What would we do without the lowly onion? It adds flavor to almost any savory recipe. When cooked a long time onions turn positively sweet. Larger onions tend to be milder than smaller ones, and certain varieties, such as Vidalia and Maui, are extremely mild. Red onions add color as well as flavor to salads. Look for onions that are quite hard and have a nice sheen to the skin (avoid ones that are sprouting green out the top).

ONION TIMBALES

— LO —

Makes: 6 timbales; serves: 6

Use such mild onions as Spanish, Maui, or Vidalia for the timbales, which are like mini crustless quiches. Serve this as a side dish, or as an appetizer using the sauce in the variation.

1 tablespoon butter or margarine
1½ cups coarsely chopped onions
3 eggs
3 egg whites
1½ cups milk
¼ cup bread crumbs
¼ teaspoon dried thyme
¼ teaspoon salt, or to taste
¼ teaspoon pepper
¾ cup shredded Swiss cheese

1. Preheat the oven to 375°F. Heavily grease six 6-ounce custard cups.

2. In a medium skillet, melt the butter or margarine over medium-high heat. Add the onions; cook over low heat, stirring occasionally, until onions are golden, about 40 minutes.

3. In a medium bowl, beat the eggs and egg whites. Beat in the milk, bread crumbs, thyme, salt, and pepper.

4. Spoon ⅙ onion mixture into each cup; top with 2 tablespoons Swiss cheese. Pour the egg mixture evenly into the 6 cups.

5. Cut 6 rounds of waxed paper to fit the custard cups; grease. Place the rounds, greased sides down, on the surface of the custard.

6. Place the cups into a 9 × 13 × 2-inch pan, filled with 1 inch of very hot water. Bake 25 to 30 minutes or until a knife inserted in the center comes out clean. Discard waxed paper and unmold timbales to serve.

Variation: Serve these timbales as an appetizer with Tomato–Red Pepper Sauce (page 474). Spoon some of the sauce onto each plate before unmolding the timbales. For Curried Tomato–Red Pepper Sauce, stir 1 tablespoon curry powder into the skillet after the onions have softened when preparing the sauce.

FRIED ONION RINGS

Makes: 6 cups; serves: 4

You have to prepare these just before serving or they will get soggy. You can use Spanish, Bermuda, Vidalia, Maui, or any other mild-flavored onion for this recipe.

1 large mild onion (8-ounces), cut into ½-inch-thick rings
½ cup all-purpose flour
⅓ cup whole wheat flour
½ teaspoon salt
1 egg
⅔ cup buttermilk
½ cup beer
Oil for deep frying

1. Soak the onion rings in cold water for 15 minutes; drain.

2. On a piece of waxed paper, stir together both flours and the salt.

3. In a shallow bowl, beat the egg with the buttermilk and beer. Stir in the flour.

4. Dip the onion rings into the egg-flour mixture.

5. In a 3-quart saucepan, heat the oil over medium-high heat, until the oil bubbles when a little flour is sprinkled in. Add the onions, a few at a time; cook, turning once, until golden brown all over, about 1 to 2 minutes. Drain on paper towels.

SWEET AND SOUR PEARL ONIONS

Makes: 2 cups; serves: 4 to 6

The sauce cooks down to a glaze when the onions are ready.

1 tablespoon butter or margarine, melted
3 cups peeled pearl onions
½ cup orange juice
3 tablespoons sugar
2 tablespoons distilled white vinegar
1 tablespoon ketchup

1. In a large skillet, melt the butter or margarine over medium-high heat. Add the onions; cook, stirring, until transparent, about 3 minutes.

2. Add the orange juice, sugar, vinegar, and ketchup. Simmer, covered, for 10 minutes. Uncover and cook until liquid evaporates and onions are glazed, about 3 minutes longer.

Variation: Add ½ cup dark raisins when you add the juice.

Baked Stuffed Onions

Makes: 4 onions; serves: 4

These can be made ahead, then baked before serving time.

4 Spanish onions (12 ounces each)
1 ½ tablespoons butter or margarine
1 ½ cups chopped apple
½ cup cooked wild rice
⅓ cup chopped dried apricots
2 tablespoons chopped fresh parsley
⅛ teaspoon salt, or to taste
⅛ teaspoon pepper

1. Peel the onions; cut off the hairy root, but leave the root bottom intact. Cut off about ½ inch of the tops (deeply enough to see all layers). Cook in boiling water 15 minutes. Drain and cool.

2. Preheat the oven to 350°F.

3. Carefully cut the center layers out of the onions, leaving the root and two outer layers on each onion. Chop the onion from the middle layers equal to 1 cup total.

4. In a large skillet, melt the butter or margarine over medium-high heat. Add the chopped onion and apple. Cook, stirring, until both are starting to brown and are tender, about 6 minutes. Stir in the wild rice, apricots, parsley, salt, and pepper.

5. Place the stuffing into the hollowed-out onions. Wrap each in aluminum foil. Bake 20 minutes or until onions are heated through.

Variation: Substitute dried currants for the apricot.

Parsnip

Primarily used for soups in this country, parsnips are very flavorful roots. Look for ones that are crisp, not limp or wrinkled.

Orange-Glazed Parsnip

Makes: 2 ½ cups; serves: 4

These are only lightly glazed; for a stronger glaze add extra honey. You can julienne the parsnips instead of slicing them.

⅔ cup orange juice
1 tablespoon honey
1 tablespoon mirin (rice wine) or sherry
½ teaspoon soy sauce
¼ teaspoon ground ginger
1 tablespoon butter or margarine
3 cups thinly sliced parsnips

1. In a small bowl, stir together the orange juice, honey, mirin, soy sauce, and ginger; set aside.

2. In a medium skillet, melt the butter or margarine over medium-high heat. Add the parsnips; cook, stirring, about 5 minutes. Add the orange juice mixture; cook, uncovered, stirring frequently, until parsnips are tender and glazed, about 5 minutes longer.

Variation: Substitute carrots for some of the parsnips.

Pea Pods

Snow peas and sugar snaps (also called snap peas or sugar-snap peas) have small (totally edible) peas inside. If you have regular peas that you are shelling, you can also use those pods in these recipes. Just remove the top and bottom strings, then peel out the thin membrane on the inside of the pod. It's especially important to remove the string from the top and bottom of snap peas and the top string from snow peas. Look for pods that are crisp, not wilted, with good color and no black spots.

SUGAR SNAP SAUTÉ

Makes: 3¹/₂ cups; serves: 4 to 6

If sugar snaps are not available or are too expensive, use snow peas instead (assuming they're available and less expensive).

1¹/₂ tablespoons vegetable oil
3 cups sugar snaps, tough strings removed
¹/₂ cup julienned red bell peppers
3 cloves garlic, minced
¹/₄ cup vegetable broth (pages 93–95)
¹/₄ cup dry white wine
¹/₄ cup chopped fresh parsley
¹/₄ teaspoon salt, or to taste
¹/₈ teaspoon pepper

1. In a large skillet, heat the oil over high heat. Add the sugar snaps, bell peppers, and garlic. Cook, stirring, until almost tender-crisp, about 4 minutes.

2. Add the broth, wine, parsley, salt, and pepper. Cook, stirring, until tender, about 3 minutes, or to taste.

Variation: Broccoli with Sautéed Vegetables: Substitute broccoli for the sugar snaps.

SAUTÉED SNOW PEAS, PEAS, AND WILD MUSHROOMS

Makes: 3 cups; serves: 4 to 6

I usually associate snow peas with Chinese recipes—with good reason. However, this sort-of-French vegetable dish is just divine and doesn't even hint of Asia. If you don't have fresh peas, use frozen, but add them at the end, cooking just long enough to heat them through.

1¹/₂ tablespoons olive oil
3 tablespoons minced shallots
1¹/₂ cups sliced wild mushrooms (preferably shiitake, portobello, or similar meaty mushrooms)
1 cup fresh shelled peas
2 tablespoons white wine, or broth, or water
3 cups snow peas, trimmed
¹/₄ teaspoon salt, or to taste
¹/₈ teaspoon pepper

1. In a large skillet, heat the oil over medium-high heat. Add the shallots; cook, stirring, until softened, about 1 minute. Add the mushrooms and peas; cook, stirring, until softened, about 4 minutes. Add the wine; cook, stirring, until evaporated.

2. Add the snow peas; cook, stirring, until tender-crisp, about 3 minutes.

3. Add the salt and pepper and toss.

Variation: Add ¹/₂ cup julienned red peppers when you sauté the shallots.

SNOW PEAS WITH SCALLIONS AND GINGER

Makes: 2¼ cups; serves: 3 to 4

To make this dish spicy, substitute chili oil for part or all of the sesame oil.

1 tablespoon vegetable oil
½ cup sliced scallions (1-inch pieces)
1 tablespoon minced fresh ginger
3 cups snow peas
2 teaspoons mirin (rice wine) or sherry
1 teaspoon soy sauce
½ teaspoon sesame oil

1. In a large skillet, heat the vegetable oil over high heat. Add the scallions and ginger; cook until scallions are wilted, about 1 minute.

2. Add the snow peas; cook, stirring, until snow peas are tender-crisp, about 3 minutes. Add the mirin, soy sauce, and sesame oil; toss until combined.

Variation: Add ½ cup julienned red bell peppers when you add the snow peas.

SNOW PEAS, CAULIFLOWER, AND RED BELL PEPPERS

Makes: 4 cups; serves: 6 to 8

If, by any chance, you have leftovers, chill them and toss them with vinaigrette for a yummy salad.

1½ tablespoons vegetable oil
1 cup sliced red bell peppers
2 cloves garlic, minced
1½ cups cauliflower florets
2 tablespoons water
3 cups snow peas

1. In a large skillet, heat the oil over medium-high heat. Add the garlic and bell peppers; cook, stirring, until softened, about 2 minutes.

2. Add the cauliflower and water; cook, stirring, until almost tender-crisp, about 3 minutes. Add the snow peas; stir-fry until tender-crisp, about 2 minutes.

Variations: You can use broccoli instead of cauliflower or sugar-snap peas instead of snow peas.

Oriental Snow Peas, Cauliflower, and Red Bell Peppers: Stir 1 tablespoon soy sauce and 1 teaspoon sesame oil into the vegetables when they are just finished cooking.

Peas

Technically peas are legumes, not vegetables. Fresh peas are a different variety from the ones used dried. Younger peas tend to be sweeter and more tender than older. If buying in the pods, look for bright-colored pods that are firm, not limp, and avoid any with mildew spots. Peas that have tiny shoots are too old to be tasty (although they will not harm you).

CREAMED PEAS

Makes: 2 scant cups; serves: 3 to 4

The peas made with milk are creamier than those made with vegetable broth; however, both are delicious.

1 tablespoon butter or margarine
1 1/2 tablespoons minced onion
1 1/2 tablespoons flour
3/4 cup milk or vegetable broth (pages 93–95)
2 cups cooked peas (fresh or frozen)
1/4 teaspoon salt, or to taste
1/8 teaspoon poultry seasoning
1/8 teaspoon pepper

1. In a 1 1/2-quart saucepan, melt the butter or margarine over medium-high heat. Add the onion; cook, stirring, until softened, about 2 minutes.

2. Stir in the flour until absorbed. Gradually stir in the milk or broth. Cook, stirring constantly, until mixture comes to a boil.

3. Stir in the remaining ingredients. Cook, stirring occasionally, 5 minutes or until heated through.

Variations: Richer Creamed Peas: Use half-and-half instead of milk.

♥ Lower-Fat Creamed Peas: Use only one tablespoon of butter or margarine instead of two. Use skim milk instead of whole milk.

MINTED PEAS

Makes: 2 cups; serves: 4

You can used dried mint (about 1 teaspoon), but try to find fresh because it's really better.

1 tablespoon butter or margarine
1/4 cup sliced leeks (white and light green parts only)
2 cups shelled peas
3 tablespoons water
3 tablespoons chopped fresh mint
1/8 teaspoon salt, or to taste

1. In a 1 1/2-quart saucepan, melt the butter or margarine over medium-high heat. Add the leeks; cook, stirring, until softened, about 30 seconds.

2. Add the peas and water. Cover and cook, 10 minutes or until peas are tender. Add the mint and salt; cook, stirring, until any liquid has evaporated.

Variation: Dilled Peas: Substitute dill for the mint.

PUREED PEAS

Makes 2 cups; serves 3 to 4

If you're serving this with a "fancy" meal, you can place the puree into a pastry bag fitted with a large star tip and pipe the puree onto the plate.

One 1-pound package frozen peas
¾ cup vegetable broth (pages 93–95)
2 tablespoons sliced scallions (green part only)
1 tablespoon butter or margarine
⅛ teaspoon salt
⅛ teaspoon pepper

1. In a 1½-quart saucepan, combine the peas and broth. Bring to a boil. Cook, covered, 10 minutes or until peas are thoroughly cooked.
2. Place the peas and any remaining broth with the remaining ingredients in a blender or food processor container fitted with a steel blade. Cover and process until smooth.

Variation: Add 3 tablespoons chopped fresh dill when you add the scallions.

Peppers

Whether sweet or hot, red or green, peppers always lend a distinctive flavor to any dish. Bell peppers are most commonly available in green and red but can also be found in yellow, orange, and purple. Red bell peppers are the sweetest, followed by orange. Green bell peppers are more pungent, with yellow and purple milder but similar to the green.

Hot peppers are also available in a variety of colors and range from mildly hot, such as the Anaheim (also called New Mexico), to the spicier, such as the jalapeño. When adding "hot" peppers to recipes, you can lessen the spiciness by seeding them, since most of the heat is in the seeds. It's best to handle "hot" peppers with rubber gloves to avoid the burning they can cause to the skin. Hot peppers are also available dried.

All fresh peppers should be firm, with a good sheen to the skin.

ROASTED RED BELL PEPPERS

Makes: 8 halves; serves: depends on use

Roasted peppers are a very versatile ingredient. Chop them up and toss them in any salad or cooked rice dish, add them to pasta, or just munch on them for a flavorful snack. Homemade roasted red peppers are much sweeter than the ones you buy in a jar, but you can use the jarred ones in recipes when you're in a pinch. Although this recipe calls for four peppers, the method works with only one or as many as can comfortably fit on a pan that goes under your broiler.

4 red bell peppers

1. Preheat the broiler.

2. Cut the peppers in half lengthwise. Discard the seeds and pith. Place peppers in one layer in a large pan. Broil, 4 inches from the heat, 5 minutes or until quite charred. Turn and cook until second side is charred.

3. Place in paper bag and cool.

4. Peel and discard skin.

Variation: Roasted Yellow or Orange Bell Peppers: Use orange or yellow peppers instead of the red.

A TRIO OF SAUTÉED PEPPERS

Makes: 2¹/₂ cups; serves: 4

In addition to being a good side dish, you can use this recipe as a filling for omelets.

1 tablespoon olive oil
1 cup sliced onions
1 cup sliced green bell peppers
¹/₂ cup sliced red bell peppers
¹/₂ cup sliced orange or yellow peppers
¹/₄ teaspoon dried thyme
¹/₈ teaspoon salt, or to taste
¹/₈ teaspoon pepper

1. In a large skillet, heat the oil over high heat. Add the onions and all three bell peppers; cook, stirring, until slightly tender, about 3 minutes.

2. Add the thyme, salt, and pepper; cook, stirring, until the peppers are tender-crisp, about 2 minutes longer.

Variations: Use only one or two types of bell peppers instead of three.

Rice with Three Peppers: Stir in 1¹/₂ cups cooked white rice.

SAUTÉED PEPPERS, ONIONS, AND CAULIFLOWER

Makes: 4 cups; serves: 4 to 6

Serve with polenta or couscous as a main dish.

2 teaspoons vegetable oil
2 teaspoons olive oil
1 ¹/₂ cups sliced onions
1 cup sliced green bell peppers
4 cups cauliflower florets
¹/₂ cup vegetable broth (pages 93–95)
¹/₂ teaspoon oregano
¹/₄ teaspoon salt, or to taste
2 tablespoons grated Parmesan cheese
    (optional)

1. In a large skillet, heat both oils over medium-high heat. Add the onions and peppers; cook, stirring, until onions are browned, about 3 minutes.

2. Add the cauliflower, broth, oregano, and salt. Cook, stirring, until vegetables are softened and liquid has evaporated, about 5 minutes. Remove to serving bowl and add the Parmesan, if desired; toss to combine.

Variation: Use red bell peppers instead of green and/or broccoli instead of cauliflower.

Plantains

Usually found in Hispanic markets, these bananalike vegetables are sweet when ripe (but are not eaten raw, even when ripe) and very starchy when green. For ripe plantains, look for yellow skin with lots of black on it; they're even good when the skin is completely black. Green plantains should be bright green. Plantains are quite difficult to peel when green; the best method is to slice the plantain first, then make two or three slits in the skin and peel off small portions at a time.

BAKED PLANTAINS

Makes: 4 plantains; serves: 4 to 8, depending on size

You need to use fully ripe plantains for this really easy dish. You can tell when they are ripe because the skin should be mostly or almost completely black. Baked plantains have a slightly sweet taste, with a texture similar to, but slightly drier than, baked sweet potatoes. I serve them right in the skin and dig the plantain out with a fork. Try serving them to your family for a really nice change of pace.

4 plantains (skin black)

1. Preheat the oven to 350°F.

2. Make a lengthwise slit in the skin of the plantain, to prevent bursting.

3. Bake 40 minutes or until fork tender.

Variation: Serve with lemon wedges and sprinkle the plantain with the juice.

PLANTAIN AND SWEET POTATO LOAF

Makes: 1 loaf; serves: 4 to 6

This loaf holds together well enough to make a nice presentation, but not really to serve in slices. If you like you can just scoop them into a serving bowl and forget the loaf effect.

3 cups thinly sliced sweet potatoes, peeled (1 pound)
2 tablespoons butter or margarine
¼ cup firmly packed light brown or dark brown sugar
1 tablespoon orange juice concentrate
1½ cups peeled, thinly sliced ripe plantain (1 large plantain; yellow with lots of black on the skin), divided

1. Preheat the oven to 350°F. Grease an 8 × 5 × 2¾-inch loaf pan.

2. Boil the sweet potato slices 5 minutes; drain.

3. While the potatoes are cooking, melt the butter or margarine. Stir in the brown sugar and orange juice concentrate; keep warm enough to remain liquid.

4. Arrange ⅓ of the potato slices in a layer in the bottom of the pan. Drizzle about 1 tablespoon of the sugar mixture over the potatoes. Top with ½ of the plantains.

5. Top with ⅓ more potato slices. Drizzle about 1 tablespoon of the sugar mixture over the potatoes. Top with remaining plantains. Arrange remaining ⅓ sweet potato slices on top. Drizzle the remaining sugar mixture over the potatoes.

6. Bake, uncovered, 45 minutes or until potatoes are tender. Invert onto serving platter, if desired.

Variation: Stir ¼ teaspoon nutmeg into the brown sugar.

TOSTONES (FRIED GREEN PLANTAINS)

— ⟦V⟧ —

Makes: 36 slices; serves: 5 to 8

I confess that I prefer the Sweet Fried Bananas variation to the plantains. One of my favorite dinners is Rice and Black Beans (page 141) and fried bananas.

3 green (unripe) plantains
¼ cup vegetable oil
Salt

1. Slice the plantains diagonally into ½-inch-thick oval pieces. Cut one or two slits in the skin (from top of the slice through the bottom), then remove the peel.

2. In a large skillet, heat the oil until it bubbles when a small piece of plantain is thrown in. Add the plantain pieces a few at a time so they are in a single layer; fry until very lightly browned on the bottom, about 3 minutes. Turn and lightly brown second side. Remove from oil; drain on paper towels.

3. Using a meat pounder (the flat-bottom type) or the bottom of a heavy skillet, pound the fried plantain until it is only ¼ inch thick.

4. Return smashed plantains to oil and fry until well browned on each side, about 2 minutes per side longer. Remove from oil; drain on paper towels. Season with salt.

Variation: Fried Sweet Bananas: Substitute ripe plantains for the green ones and skip the smashing step; just fry until browned and omit the salt.

HONEY-LEMON GLAZED PLANTAINS

— ⟦V⟧⟦♥⟧ —

Makes: 3 cups; serves: 4 to 6

These are a nice twist on the more common candied sweet potatoes.

3 tablespoons honey
2 tablespoons lemon juice
2 tablespoons firmly packed light brown or
    dark brown sugar
1 tablespoon water
1 tablespoon melted butter or margarine
4 cups sliced ripe plantains (1 inch thick)

1. Preheat the oven to 350°F.

2. In a medium bowl, stir together the honey, lemon juice, brown sugar, water, and butter or margarine. Add the plantain slices and toss. Spoon into an 8-inch-square baking dish.

3. Bake, uncovered, 40 minutes. Turn the plantains over and bake 20 minutes longer, or until the liquid is syrupy and plantains are soft and glazed.

Variation: Add ½ teaspoon grated lemon rind to the glaze when you add the plantains.

Potatoes

There's hardly a home or restaurant that doesn't have potatoes on hand. Although technically there are many different varieties, for cooking purposes only three categories are important: boiling potatoes, baking potatoes, and sweet potatoes. Boiling potatoes are firmer and don't disintegrate as quickly as baking potatoes. They can be found in a variety of colors (white, gold, or purple fleshed, and brown, red, or purple skinned), but still they have that familiar firm, creamy texture. Baking potatoes are drier and mealier than boiling potatoes and tend to disintegrate much more quickly when boiled; this is not necessarily a disadvantage, since it makes them ideal for thickening soups or stews.

Sweet potatoes are an entirely different creature from boiling or baking potatoes. Usually orange in color (although they can be found in white), as the name would imply, they have a flavor that ranges from mildly to very sweet.

When peeled, raw potatoes tend to oxidize (turn brown or black), so if you are going to peel in advance of cooking the potatoes, store the peeled potatoes in water to prevent oxidation.

When shopping for boiling or baking potatoes, look for ones that feel firm and have no eyes (small white sprouts), greening (a slight green tinge of the flesh), black patches, cuts, or bruises. For sweet potatoes, look for firmness and darker skins, which can indicate sweeter flesh.

Potato Basics

I love the texture of baked potatoes that you get in a restaurant—they're dense and super-moist. My home-baked potatoes always seemed too dry. I finally figured out that for restaurant-type texture, you have to bake the potatoes in advance and let them sit for a while to allow the potatoes to condense. If you prefer the "fluffier" style of baked potato, serve them as soon as they are baked. Microwaved potatoes are never as good as baked, but they certainly are ready much faster. There are many nutrients in the potato peel, so scrub the outside well (I have a special brush that I use just for this purpose) and then you can eat the peels.

Baked Potatoes: Four medium baking potatoes (8 ounces each), or as many as you want—the number doesn't affect the baking time. Bake 1 hour in a 350°F oven or until potatoes are tender when lightly squeezed. Turn off oven and leave potatoes in it for 40 minutes.

Microwaved Baked Potatoes: It's very important to pierce the potatoes before placing them in the microwave oven; otherwise steam builds up as they cook and they will explode when there is no place for the steam to vent. Lightly sprinkle salt over an 8-ounce potato. Wrap in microwave-safe paper towel (if you are cooking more than one at a time, wrap each potato in a separate paper towel). Microwave on high power, turning potato upside down halfway through the cooking time (see below). Bake until potato is tender when lightly squeezed. Let stand.

MICROWAVE TIMING FOR POTATOES

The cooking times given here are based on a 650-watt oven. Times may vary depending on the microwave wattage.

1 potato:	3 minutes
2 potatoes:	6 minutes
3 potatoes:	8 minutes
4 potatoes:	11 minutes

PARSLIED BOILING POTATOES

[V]

Makes: about 3 cups; serves: 4

I usually use small red bliss potatoes for this type of dish, and I leave them unpeeled. However, any boiling potato can be used. They can be cut into 1½-inch pieces or left whole; if whole, they can be peeled or tuxedoed (a thin strip of peel removed from around the center of the potato, rather like a belt or cummerbund). These can also be prepared in the microwave: Pierce potatoes if using whole, and place in a microwave-safe bowl. Microwave, lightly covered, on high for 6 minutes; add butter or margarine, parsley, and salt (if desired), then toss. Recover and cook 2 to 4 minutes longer or until potatoes are tender. Let stand 2 minutes.

12 small boiling potatoes (or 6 medium, halved; or 4 large, quartered; total weight, 1 pound)
1 tablespoon butter or margarine (optional)
¼ cup chopped fresh parsley
Salt to taste

1. In a 2-quart saucepan of boiling salted water, cook the potatoes 15 to 20 minutes or until tender. Drain.

2. Return potatoes to pot and toss with butter or margarine until melted. Add parsley and salt; toss until evenly distributed.

Variations: Boiled Potatoes: Omit the butter or margarine and parsley.

Dilled Potatoes: Substitute chopped fresh dill for the parsley.

PERFECT MASHED POTATOES

[L][♥]

Makes: 2½ cups; serves: 4

There is nothing as wonderful as mashed potatoes when you're feeling in need of a soothing food. Add as much of the milk as needed to make mashed potatoes that are your idea of perfect.

3 cups peeled, cubed all-purpose potatoes (¾ pound)
¼ cup warm milk
1 tablespoons butter or margarine
¼ teaspoon salt, or to taste

1. In a 2-quart saucepan, cook the potatoes in enough water to cover the potatoes by 1 inch. Bring to a boil over high heat. Reduce heat to medium-high and cook 15 to 20 minutes or until potatoes are fork-tender. Drain immediately.

2. Return potatoes to the pot and add the remaining ingredients. For smooth mashed potatoes, mash with an electric beater until smooth (but don't overbeat or the potatoes will become gooey). For lumpy potatoes, mash with a fork to desired consistency.

Variation: Stir in chopped fresh dill, chives, or scallions.

RUTHIE'S THANKSGIVING CHIVE MASHED POTATOES

—————— Ⅼ ——————

Makes 5 cups; serves: 4 to 8

I spend Thanksgivings with my second family—the Rudolphs (my friend Paula's family). Ruthie Getzoff (Paula's sister) always brings these fabulous mashed potatoes as one of her specialties. Throw your calorie counter away when you dig in here! Not only are they loaded with delicious cream cheese, but you're also sure to go back for seconds (and if there are any potatoes left, thirds). You can use fresh snipped chives, but Ruthie uses the freeze-dried kind and I don't tamper with perfection. If you're serving more than four people you may want to double this recipe, because although it theoretically serves up to eight, I've never known anyone to eat only one serving!

6 cups peeled, cubed all-purpose potatoes
     (1½ pounds)
½ cup milk
Two 3-ounce packages cream cheese
⅓ cup freeze-dried chives
1 teaspoon salt, or to taste
⅛ teaspoon pepper

1. In a 4-quart saucepan, cook the potatoes in enough water to cover them by 1 inch. Bring to a boil over high heat. Reduce heat to medium-high and cook 15 to 20 minutes or until potatoes are fork-tender. Drain immediately.

2. Return potatoes to pot and add the remaining ingredients.

3. For smooth mashed potatoes, mash with an electric beater until smooth (but don't overbeat or the potatoes will become sticky). For lumpy potatoes, mash with a fork to desired consistency.

COLCANNON

——————  ——————

Makes 3¼ cups; serves: 4 to 6

This traditional Irish dish also makes a great filling for strudels and knishes.

3 cups peeled, cubed all-purpose potatoes
     (¾ pound)
1½ tablespoons butter or margarine
2 cups chopped cabbage
⅓ cup finely chopped onions
¼ cup milk or vegetable broth (pages 93–95)
¼ teaspoon salt, or to taste
¼ teaspoon pepper

1. In a 3-quart saucepan, cook the potatoes in enough water to cover them by 1 inch. Bring to a boil over high heat. Reduce heat to medium-high and cook 15 to 20 minutes or until potatoes are fork-tender.

2. While the potatoes are cooking, in a medium skillet, melt the butter or margarine over medium-high heat. Add the cabbage and onions. Cook, stirring, until cabbage has wilted, about 4 minutes.

3. Drain the potatoes as soon as tender. Return potatoes to pot and add the milk, salt, and pepper.

4. For smooth mashed potatoes, mash with an electric beater until smooth (but don't overbeat or the potatoes will become sticky). For lumpy potatoes, mash with a fork to desired consistency.

5. Add cabbage-onion mixture; stir until combined.

Variation: Add 1 cup shredded carrots when you sauté the cabbage.

Oven Fries
⟦v⟧⟦♥⟧

Makes: 2 cups; serves: 6

You use less oil when you prepare baked French fries than when you fry them.

2 medium baking potatoes, unpeeled and
    scrubbed (1 pound)
2½ teaspoons vegetable or olive oil
Salt (optional)

1. Preheat the oven to 425°F. Line a jelly roll pan (10×15×1 inches) with aluminum foil.

2. Cut the potatoes into ¼-inch-thick rounds. In a medium bowl, toss the potatoes with the oil until completely coated.

3. Place the potato slices in a single layer on the baking sheet.

4. Bake 20 minutes or until golden on top. Turn and bake 7 to 10 minutes longer until golden on both sides. Sprinkle with salt, if desired.

Variation: Barbecue Oven Fries: Generously brush the tops of the baked fries with barbecue sauce. Broil 1 to 2 minutes until bubbly. Turn and repeat on other side.

Stuffed Baked Potatoes
⟦L⟧⟦♥⟧

Makes: 8 potato boats; serves: 4 or 8

This recipe is very flexible. If you don't have buttermilk, just use regular milk (although you may need a little less). If you prefer a less tangy flavor use only milk and no yogurt or buttermilk. If you don't have fresh dill, use 1 teaspoon dried dill weed. For a slightly smoother flavor, you may want to stir in 1 tablespoon butter (but, of course, you'll be adding lots of fat).

4 medium baking potatoes (2 pounds)
½ cup unflavored yogurt
½ cup buttermilk
3 tablespoons finely chopped scallions
3 tablespoons finely chopped fresh parsley
2 tablespoons snipped fresh dill
¾ teaspoon salt, or to taste
⅛ teaspoon pepper

1. Preheat the oven to 350°F.

2. Scrub potatoes. Bake for 1 hour or until tender.

3. Cut baked potatoes in half lengthwise. Leaving ⅛ inch in the shell, scoop the potato into a medium bowl.

4. Mash with a fork, then stir in the remaining ingredients.

5. Spoon the mashed-potato mixture back into the potato skins. Return to oven and bake 10 to 15 minutes longer or until heated through.

Variation: Decadent Baked Stuffed Potatoes: Use sour cream instead of yogurt and whole milk instead of buttermilk.

POTATOES AU GRATIN

L

Makes one 8-inch square; serves: 8 to 12

This is a real comfort food, especially on a cold winter's eve.

6 cups peeled, sliced baking potatoes
　　(1/4-inch-thick pieces)
2 tablespoons butter or margarine
2 tablespoons all-purpose flour
1 3/4 cups milk
1 1/4 cups shredded Swiss cheese, divided
3 tablespoons grated Parmesan cheese,
　　divided
1/2 teaspoon salt, or to taste
1/8 teaspoon pepper
1 clove garlic, minced
Paprika

1. Preheat the oven to 350°F. Grease an 8-inch-square baking dish.

2. Cook the potatoes in boiling water 5 to 7 minutes or until tender; drain.

3. In a 1-quart saucepan, melt the butter or margarine over medium-high heat. Stir in the flour until absorbed. Using a whisk, stir in the milk. Cook, stirring, until mixture comes to a boil. Remove from heat; stir in 3/4 cup of the Swiss cheese, 2 tablespoons of the grated Parmesan, the salt, pepper and garlic.

4. Arrange half of the potatoes in layers in the baking pan. Pour 1/2 of the sauce over the potatoes. Repeat with remaining potatoes and sauce. Sprinkle top with remaining 1/2 cup Swiss and 1 tablespoon Parmesan cheese; sprinkle lightly with paprika.

5. Bake 30 to 40 minutes or until browned on top. Let stand 10 minutes before serving.

Variation: Use Cheddar cheese instead of Swiss.

STILTON POTATOES AU GRATIN

L

Makes 4 cups; serves: 6 to 8

Although similar in consistency to plain Potatoes au Gratin (left), the flavor here is much tangier.

6 cups peeled, sliced boiling potatoes
　　(1/8-inch-thick pieces)
2 tablespoons butter or margarine
1/2 cup sliced leeks
3 tablespoons all-purpose flour
1/2 cup vegetable broth (pages 93–95)
1/2 cup milk
1/2 teaspoon salt, or to taste
1/4 teaspoon pepper
1 cup crumbled Stilton cheese

1. Preheat the oven to 350°F. Grease an 8-inch-square baking dish.

2. Cook the potatoes in boiling water 5 to 7 minutes or until tender; drain.

3. In a 1-quart saucepan, melt the butter or margarine over medium-high heat. Add the leeks; cook, stirring, until softened, about 30 seconds. Stir in the flour until absorbed. Using a whisk, stir in the broth, milk, salt, and pepper. Cook, stirring, until mixture comes to a boil; remove from heat.

4. Arrange half of the potatoes in layers in the baking pan. Pour half of the sauce over the potatoes. Sprinkle on the crumbled Stilton. Repeat with remaining potatoes and sauce.

5. Bake 30 to 40 minutes or until browned on top. Let stand 10 minutes before serving.

Variation: Use Gorgonzola cheese instead of Stilton.

YELLOW POTATOES WITH RED SWISS CHARD, ROSEMARY, AND GARLIC

— [V] —

Makes: 2¹⁄₄ cups; serves: 3 to 4

Yellow potatoes are what is known as "boiling" or "waxy" potatoes. They don't fall apart or dissolve the way baking potatoes do. Red bliss or new potatoes will be a good substitute if yellow potatoes are not available. For an exotic touch, you can even use purple potatoes. Both the salt and the pepper in this recipe are coarse, making them milder in flavor than ordinary spices. If you use table salt and pepper, you may want to decrease the amounts. You can also stir in 2 cups cooked beans to make this an entree.

3 tablespoons olive oil
2 cups peeled, cubed yellow potatoes
    (¹⁄₂-inch pieces; about ³⁄₄ pound)
6 cloves garlic, whole, unpeeled
2 tablespoons chopped fresh rosemary, or
    2 teaspoons dried rosemary, crumbled
2 cups chopped red or green Swiss chard
¹⁄₂ teaspoon coarse salt, or to taste
¹⁄₄ teaspoon café grind pepper

1. In a large skillet, heat the oil over medium-high heat. Add the potatoes and garlic; cook, stirring, until browned, about 9 minutes. Add the rosemary; cook, stirring, 1 minute.

2. Add the Swiss chard, salt, and pepper. Cook, stirring, until the chard is tender, about 2 minutes.

Variation: Bok choy or collards can be substituted for the Swiss chard. Substitute 1 tablespoon chopped fresh thyme or oregano for the rosemary.

MASHED SWEETS WITH HAZELNUT PRALINE

— [L] —

Makes: 7 cups; serves: 10 to 14

You can make the sweet potatoes by mashing canned or by baking fresh potatoes until tender and then mashing them.

1 cup hazelnuts
³⁄₄ cup sugar
¹⁄₄ cup water
6 cups mashed sweet potatoes
¹⁄₂ cup sour cream
¹⁄₂ cup firmly packed light brown or dark
    brown sugar
¹⁄₄ cup honey
2 teaspoons ground cinnamon

1. Preheat the oven to 350°F. In a baking pan, bake the hazelnuts 15 minutes; chop coarsely, set aside. Keep the oven on.

2. Line a baking sheet with foil; grease the foil.

3. To make the praline, in a 1¹⁄₂-quart sauce-pan, stir together the sugar and water. Bring to a boil over high heat, stirring until the sugar dissolves. Continue to boil, without stirring, until any sugar on the sides of the pan turns brown. Stir until sugar syrup turns amber. Stir in the hazelnuts. Pour onto foil-lined pan. Let cool completely; chop.

4. In a large bowl, stir together the sweet potatoes, sour cream, brown sugar, honey, and cinnamon. Spoon into an ovenproof casserole. Bake 20 minutes or until heated through. Sprinkle praline on top before serving.

Variation: Substitute pecans for the hazelnuts.

BRANDIED CANDIED SWEET POTATOES

Makes: 3 cups; serves: 4

These incredibly delicious potatoes are easy to make, but do keep a close eye on them during the last 5 minutes, stirring fairly frequently, since there is a fine line between glazed and incinerated.

½ cup water
½ cup firmly packed light brown or dark brown sugar
¼ cup brandy
2 tablespoons butter or margarine
¼ teaspoon salt, or to taste
4 cups cubed sweet potatoes (1-inch pieces; about 1½ pounds)

1. In a 2-quart saucepan, combine the water, brown sugar, brandy, butter or margarine, and salt. Bring to a boil. Add the sweet potatoes; return to a boil. Reduce heat to medium; cook, stirring occasionally, 20 minutes or until all liquid has evaporated and potatoes are soft and glazed.

Variations: For a nonalcoholic version, use orange juice or apple juice instead of the brandy.

Butter Rum Sweet Potatoes: Substitute rum for the brandy.

PECAN MASHED SWEET POTATOES

L

Makes: 1¾ cups; serves: 4

To be honest, I "bake" my potatoes for this in the microwave, 8 minutes (4 minutes per side) on high power.

2 large baked sweet potatoes (about 1 pound)
1 tablespoon firmly packed light brown or dark brown sugar
2 tablespoons half-and-half
⅛ teaspoon salt, or to taste
⅓ cup chopped pecans

1. Cut the potatoes in half lengthwise. Scoop out the flesh into a medium-sized bowl; add the brown sugar, half-and-half, and salt. Mash with a fork, or beat with an electric mixer, until light and fluffy. Stir in the pecans.

2. Heat in a microwave, if necessary.

V **Variation:** Orange Mashed Sweet Potatoes: Substitute orange juice for the half-and-half, and add 1 teaspoon grated orange rind.

Tzimmes

V ♥

Makes: 8 cups; serves: 12 to 16

In Yiddish tzimmes means a fuss or big deal, as in "Why are you making such a tzimmes about this?" It also means mishmash, and since this really isn't a great deal of fuss to make, I guess the second definition applies. Tzimmes is a staple on any holiday meal table.

4 cups sliced carrots
One 6-ounce can frozen apple juice
    concentrate, thawed
1 cup water
3 cups cubed sweet potatoes (1-inch pieces)
One 12-ounce package prunes with or
    without pits
¾ cup dried apricots
½ cup diced dried papaya (optional)
2 to 3 tablespoons firmly packed light brown
    or dark brown sugar, or to taste
¼ teaspoon salt, or to taste

1. In a 4-quart saucepan, bring the carrots, juice concentrate, and water to a boil over medium-high heat. Reduce heat and simmer, covered, 40 minutes or until the carrots are soft. Add the sweet potatoes; simmer, covered, 15 minutes longer.

2. Stir in the prunes, apricots, papaya, brown sugar, and salt. Return to a boil. Reduce heat and simmer, covered, 10 minutes longer. Uncover and simmer 5 to 10 minutes longer or until syrup is thick.

Variation: For a more traditional tzimmes, omit the apricots and papaya and use additional prunes instead.

Spinach

It's impossible to praise the delights and benefits of spinach too highly (unless, of course, you're one of the people who hate it). Technically, spinach fits into the "greens" category, but I list it separately because of its fragile leaf and its mildness of flavor, as compared to most other vegetables in that grouping, which tend to be tougher and/or more bitter. Like other "greens," spinach is an excellent source of beta carotene, folacin, and pantothenic acid, and a good source of calcium, vitamin E, iron, riboflavin, potassium, and pyridoxine. If you don't know what all those things are, trust me, they're really good for you.

There are two types of spinach commonly available. One has a relatively flat, lighter green leaf; the other has a very dark green, crinkled leaf. Both should be fresh-looking, not wilted. Both are most unpleasant if not properly rinsed to remove sand, but the grit tends to get caught particularly in the crinkled type, which can ruin an entire dish. To clean, plunge the spinach in a large bowl of cold water, gently swishing the leaves around. Empty the bowl; refill and reswish until there is no sand in the bottom of the bowl when you empty out the water. (This is easiest to do in a salad spinner; fill the bowl with water, leaving the basket in the bowl, then lift out the basket with the leaves and pour out the water from the outer bowl.) For good measure, then rinse each leaf under running water.

CREAMED SPINACH

Makes: 1³/4 cups; serves 3 to 4

I must confess that I'm a great fan of Seabrook Farms frozen creamed spinach, but this one is even better. The fresh-chopped spinach adds a real spinach flavor.

2 tablespoons butter or margarine
1 small clove garlic, minced
2 tablespoons all-purpose flour
²/3 cup vegetable broth (pages 93–95)
2 tablespoons half-and-half
2 cups packed chopped spinach (about 10 ounces before trimming)
¹/8 teaspoon salt, or to taste

1. In a 1¹/2-quart saucepan, melt the butter or margarine over medium-high heat. Add the garlic; cook, stirring 10 seconds. Stir in the flour until absorbed.

2. Add the broth and half-and-half; cook, stirring with a whisk, until no lumps remain. Add the spinach and salt. Cook, stirring frequently, until spinach is cooked through, about 3 to 5 minutes.

v **Variation:** Substitute additional broth for the half-and-half.

CREAMY SPINACH

Makes: generous 1 cup; serves: 2 to 3

Not creamed spinach, which contains a white sauce and uses chopped spinach, this recipe uses leaf spinach with cream cheese for a finisher.

1 pound spinach
1 teaspoon olive oil
1 tablespoon minced shallots
2 tablespoons cream cheese
¹/8 teaspoon salt, or to taste
Pinch ground nutmeg

1. Rinse the spinach thoroughly (page 287) and discard the tough stems.

2. In a large skillet, heat the oil over medium-high heat. Add the shallots; cook, stirring, until softened, about 30 seconds.

3. Add the spinach; cook, stirring, until wilted, about 2 minutes. If there is liquid in the bottom of the skillet, drain off as much as possible.

4. Add the cream cheese, salt, and nutmeg. Cook, stirring, until the cheese melts and any liquid evaporates.

Variation: Use chive cream cheese.

SPINACH-HERB TIMBALES

Makes: 6 timbales; serves: 6

Timbales are like mini crustless quiches. Instead of serving these as a side dish, you could use them as brunch entrees.

4 eggs
2 egg whites
1 1/2 cups milk
1/4 cup bread crumbs
1/4 teaspoon salt, or to taste
1/4 teaspoon anchovy-free Worcestershire sauce
1 10-ounce package frozen chopped spinach, thawed and drained
1 tablespoon chopped fresh parsley
1/4 teaspoon dried tarragon
1/4 teaspoon dried marjoram
1/8 teaspoon dried thyme
Pinch ground nutmeg
3/4 cup grated Cheddar cheese

1. Preheat the oven to 375°F. Heavily grease six 6-ounce custard cups.

2. In a medium bowl, beat the eggs and egg whites. Beat in the milk, bread crumbs, salt, and Worcestershire sauce.

3. In a separate bowl, combine the spinach, parsley, tarragon, marjoram, thyme, and nutmeg.

4. Spoon 1/6 of the spinach mixture into each cup; add 2 tablespoons Cheddar to each cup. Pour the egg mixture evenly into the six cups.

5. Cut 6 rounds of waxed paper to fit the custard cups; grease. Place the rounds, greased sides down, on the surface of the custard.

6. Place the cups into a 9 × 13 × 2-inch pan, filled with 1 inch of very hot water. Bake 25 to 30 minutes or until a knife inserted in the center comes out clean.

7. Turn out of the cups and serve immediately.

Variation: Broccoli Herb Timbales: Use chopped broccoli instead of spinach.

Squash, Summer

As the name implies, summer squash (zucchini, yellow, crookneck, and pattypan) used to be available only in the summer, but now they are pretty much available year-round. They are harvested while the skin and seeds are tender and edible. Squash grow quite quickly and it's not unusual for the weekend gardener to leave home Sunday with only squash blossoms and come back the following Friday to find zucchini baseball bats. The smaller squash are more flavorful than the giants, but even the large ones are quite usable. You can also use baby squash, which are about 3 inches long, and squash blossoms, which can be sautéed.

SAUTÉED YOUNG ZUCCHINI

Makes: 3 cups; serves: 4 to 6

Young zucchini should be about 5 inches long. Of course, you can use larger squash; just cut them into 5-inch-long wedges.

1 1/2 tablespoons olive oil
2 cloves garlic, minced
6 young zucchini, ends trimmed, quartered lengthwise
1/2 teaspoon dried rosemary, crumbled

1. In a large skillet, heat the oil over medium-high heat. Add the garlic; cook, stirring, 30 seconds. Add the zucchini and rosemary; cook, stirring, until tender, about 4 minutes.

Variation: Use dried oregano, thyme, or basil instead of the rosemary.

ZUCCHINI ITALIAN-STYLE

[V][♥]

Makes: 2³/₄ cups; serves: 4 to 6

This recipe makes a fine topping for pasta, as well as a side dish.

1 tablespoon olive oil
½ cup chopped onions
2 cloves garlic, minced
One 14½-ounce can whole peeled
    tomatoes, undrained
1 bay leaf
½ teaspoon dried oregano
½ teaspoon dried basil
¼ teaspoon sugar
¼ teaspoon salt, or to taste
⅛ teaspoon pepper
3 cups sliced zucchini

1. In a 2-quart saucepan, heat the oil over medium-high heat. Add the onions and garlic; cook, stirring, until onions are softened, about 2 minutes. Add the tomatoes with canning liquid, breaking up the tomatoes with the back of a spoon.

2. Add the bay leaf, oregano, basil, sugar, salt, and pepper. Bring to a boil. Reduce heat and simmer, uncovered, 15 minutes. Add the zucchini; simmer, uncovered, 5 to 8 minutes longer or until zucchini reaches desired doneness. Discard the bay leaf.

Variation: Add 1 to 2 tablespoons tomato paste for a thicker sauce.

CURRIED ZUCCHINI AND FENNEL

[V][♥]

Makes: 2¹/₂ cups; serves: 4

I prepared this recipe along with the one for Okra, Plantain, and Sweet Potato Curry (page 183), so I had some unused coconut milk to toss into this dish. If you don't have coconut milk on hand, and don't want to prepare fresh or open a can for just 1 tablespoonful, substitute 3 tablespoons broth for the coconut milk and omit the water.

1 tablespoon butter or margarine
2 cups sliced zucchini
1½ cups thinly sliced fennel
1 clove garlic, minced
1 teaspoon curry powder
2 tablespoons water
1 tablespoon unsweetened coconut milk
⅛ teaspoon salt, or to taste

1. In a large skillet, melt the butter or margarine over medium-high heat. Add the zucchini, fennel, and garlic; cook, stirring, until vegetables are tender-crisp, about 3 minutes.

2. Stir in the curry powder until absorbed. Add the water, coconut milk, and salt; cook, stirring, until vegetables are tender, about 5 minutes.

Variation: Substitute celery for the fennel.

ZUCCHINI WITH SHIITAKE MUSHROOMS

[V]

Makes: 2 cups; serves: 3 to 4

Use any fresh wild mushroom, such as portobello, crimini, or chanterelle; plain white mushrooms are fine, too.

1 1/2 tablespoons olive oil

2 tablespoons minced shallots

2 1/2 cups sliced zucchini

1 1/2 cups sliced shiitake mushrooms

1/2 teaspoon finely chopped fresh rosemary,
    or 1/8 teaspoon dried rosemary

1/2 teaspoon finely chopped fresh thyme,
    or 1/8 teaspoon dried thyme

1/8 teaspoon salt, or to taste

1/8 teaspoon pepper

3 tablespoons white wine or water

1. In a large skillet, heat the oil over medium-high heat. Add the shallots; cook, stirring, until softened, about 30 seconds. Add the zucchini, mushrooms, rosemary, thyme, salt, and pepper. Cook until oil is absorbed, abour 1 minute. Add the wine; cook, stirring, until vegetables are tender, about 4 minutes longer.

Variation: Substitute yellow squash for the zucchini. Add 1 cup halved cherry tomatoes when you add the vegetables.

STUFFED YELLOW SQUASH

Makes: 4 halves; serves: 4

2 large yellow squash (12 ounces each)

2 teaspoons vegetable oil

1/2 cup chopped red bell peppers

1/4 cup chopped onions

1 clove garlic, minced

1/3 cup corn kernels (fresh, cooked; canned, drained; or frozen)

1/4 cup unflavored bread crumbs

2 tablespoons fresh parsley

2 tablespoons snipped fresh dill

1/8 teaspoon salt, or to taste

1/8 teaspoon pepper

1. Preheat the oven to 350°F.

2. Cut the squash in half lengthwise. Scoop out the centers, leaving shells 1/2-inch thick. Chop the scooped-out flesh.

3. In a medium skillet, heat the oil over medium-high heat. Add the chopped squash, bell peppers, onions, and garlic; cook, stirring, until softened, about 3 minutes. Stir in the corn, breadcrumbs, parsley, dill, salt, and pepper.

4. Spoon 1/4 of the filling into each half squash. Wrap each half in aluminum foil. Place on baking sheet and bake 20 minutes or until squash shells are tender.

Variation: Use cooked bulgur instead of the corn.

PESTO VEGETABLES

Makes: 3 1/2 cups; serves: 6

I always keep some homemade pesto in my freezer to snazz up simple recipes. If you didn't make pesto this summer, you can buy pesto in the supermarket.

1 tablespoon olive oil

1 cup julienned carrots

2 cups diced zucchini (1/4-inch pieces)

1 cup diced yellow squash (1/4-inch pieces)

3 tablespoons pesto (page 476)

2 tablespoons grated Parmesan cheese (optional)

1. In a large skillet, heat the olive oil. Add the carrots and sauté 1 minute. Add the zucchini and yellow squash; cook, stirring until softened, about 3 minutes. Add the pesto, and the cheese, if desired.

Squash, Winter

Winter squash comes in many varieties, colors, and sizes, which can be used interchangeably in many recipes. (Winter squash and summer squash, however, are not interchangeable.) I use butternut squash most frequently because of all the winter squash they are easiest to peel and have a pleasing, sweet flavor. Most of the other squash have ridged skins that make them difficult to peel before cooking, but once cooked, the different squash can be used interchangeably for things like pureeing or filling with stuffing, or whatever you like. In general, winter squash are starchy vegetables and tend to range from slightly sweet to fairly sweet; the flesh ranges in color from yellow to deep orange. Shop for winter squash that are very firm.

Cooking Winter Squash

Baked whole squash: Preheat the oven to 350°F.

> Acorn squash: 40 to 50 minutes or until tender
>
> Butternut squash (1 medium; 2 pounds): 40 to 50 minutes
>
> Spaghetti squash (8 inches long; 3½ pounds): 1 hour 15 minutes or until tender. Cut in half; discard seeds. Using a fork, scrape the flesh into a bowl, pulling into strands. Makes 3½ cups.

Microwaved squash: Cut squash in half; discard seeds. Place in microwave oven, cut side up. Cover lightly with waxed paper. Cook on high, turning once halfway through cooking time, according to the specified times (see right) or until tender.

MICROWAVE TIMING FOR SQUASH

The cooking times given here are based on a 650-watt oven. Times may vary, depending on the microwave wattage:

> Acorn Squash (1½ pounds): 8 to 10 minutes
>
> Butternut (3 pounds): 10 to 14 minutes
>
> Spaghetti squash (7 inches long; 3 pounds): 10 to 14 minutes

APPLE-STUFFED ACORN SQUASH

Makes: 4 halves; serves: 4

This sweet side dish is especially nice served in combination with anything lentil.

2 acorn squash, halved and seeded
3 cups cubed, peeled apples
½ cup chopped walnuts
¼ cup firmly packed light brown or dark brown sugar
2 tablespoons golden or dark raisins
2 tablespoons melted butter or margarine
½ teaspoon ground cinnamon

1. Preheat the oven to 350°F. Place the squash, cut side down, in a baking pan filled with ¼ inch hot water. Bake 30 minutes.

2. While the squash is baking, in a large bowl, toss together the apples, walnuts, brown sugar, raisins, melted butter or margarine, and cinnamon.

3. Remove the pan from the oven; discard the water. Place the squash, cut side up, in pan and fill each half with ¼ of the apple mixture. Bake 30 minutes longer.

Variation: Omit the raisins and add ¼ cup chopped dried apricots or prunes instead.

PUREED WINTER SQUASH WITH PEAR

— V ♥ —

Makes: 1²/₃ cups; serves: 3 to 4

It's very important to use ripe and juicy pears, since the squash cooks in the liquid formed from the cooking pears. This dish is slightly but not overly sweet; you may choose to add a bit more brown sugar to your own taste.

2 cups peeled, diced calabaza or butternut squash
2 cups peeled, diced ripe pears
2 tablespoons white wine or water
1 tablespoon firmly packed light brown or dark brown sugar
½ teaspoon ground cinnamon
1 teaspoon fresh lemon juice

1. Place the squash, pears, wine, brown sugar, and cinnamon in a 1½-quart saucepan. Bring to a boil over medium heat. Reduce heat and simmer, 30 minutes, uncovered, until the squash is soft.

2. Place the squash, pears, and any liquid, along with the lemon juice, in a blender or food processor container fitted with a steel blade. Cover and process until smooth.

Variation: Add ⅛ to ¼ teaspoon ground nutmeg when you add the cinnamon.

SWEET POTATO– STUFFED CHAYOTE

— V —

Makes: 4 halves; serves: 4

This interesting squash has to cook for a long time because it is quite hard, but the cooked flesh is not starchy like other winter squash, rather somewhat like a cooked melon, but firmer. The soft seed is edible, but you don't have to use it in this recipe.

2 whole chayote
1 cup diced cooked sweet potatoes
½ cup chopped dried apricots
2 tablespoons firmly packed light brown or dark brown sugar
¼ teaspoon ground cinnamon

1. Cook the chayote in simmering water 45 minutes or until tender. Scoop out the flesh, leaving about ¼ inch in the shell. Chop the scooped chayote to equal ¾ cup (save any extra for another use or discard).

2. Preheat the oven to 350°F.

3. In a medium bowl, combine the chopped chayote, sweet potatoes, apricots, brown sugar, and cinnamon. Place ¼ of the mixture into each of the chayote shells.

4. Bake 20 minutes, or until heated through.

Variation: Add ½ cup chopped pecans to the filling.

BASIL~GARLIC SPAGHETTI SQUASH

Makes: 3 cups; serves: 4 to 6

If you have any Basil-Garlic Butter (page 489) prepared, just stir a tablespoon of it into cooked spaghetti squash. The basil is quite subtle and you can use extra if you like.

1 medium spaghetti squash (8 inches long)
2 tablespoons chopped fresh basil,
   or ½ teaspoon dried basil
1 tablespoon butter or margarine
1 clove garlic, minced
⅛ teaspoon salt, or to taste

1. Preheat the oven to 350°F. Bake the spaghetti squash 1 hour 15 minutes or until tender. Cut in half; discard the seeds. Using a fork, scrape the flesh into a bowl, pulling into strands.

2. In a small bowl, stir together the basil, butter or margarine, garlic, and salt. Stir the basil-butter into the squash until melted.

Variation: Use any of the savory butters (pages 489, 491–93) instead of the Basil-Garlic Butter.

SPAGHETTI SQUASH WITH FENNEL

Makes: 4 cups; serves: 6 to 8

You can easily serve this as an entree.

1 tablespoon olive oil
1½ cups sliced fennel
2 cloves garlic, minced
1 cup halved cherry tomatoes
¼ cup chopped fresh basil
¼ cup chopped fresh parsley
3 cups cooked spaghetti squash strands
⅛ teaspoon salt, or to taste
⅛ teaspoon pepper

1. In a large skillet, heat the oil over medium-high heat. Add the fennel and garlic; cook, stirring, until softened, about 3 minutes. Add the tomatoes, basil, and parsley; cook, stirring, until tomatoes are slightly softened, about 3 minutes.

2. Add the spaghetti squash, salt, and pepper. Cook, stirring, until heated through.

SPAGHETTI SQUASH WITH BOK CHOY

Makes: 5 cups; serves: 6 to 8

Although I don't usually think of spaghetti squash as an Asian ingredient, it acts like bean threads in this recipe. (Even my nonvegetable-eating mother had seconds.)

1½ tablespoons vegetable oil
¾ cup sliced onions
½ cup julienned carrots
2 cloves garlic, minced
4 cups coarsely chopped bok choy
3 tablespoons mirin (rice wine) or dry sherry
1 tablespoon soy sauce
3 cups cooked spaghetti squash (one 3-pound squash, cooked)

1. In a wok or large skillet, heat the oil over high heat. Add the onions, carrots, and garlic; cook, stirring, until onions are transparent, about 2 minutes. Add the bok choy; cook, stirring, until wilted, about 2 minutes. Add the mirin and soy sauce.

2. Add the squash; cook, stirring, until heated through.

Variation: Add red bell pepper strips or snow peas when you add the bok choy.

Tomatoes

Like onions and bell peppers, tomatoes are among the most versatile of vegetables. Raw or cooked, they add zip to most dishes. Tomatoes come in a wide variety of sizes and shapes, from large Jersey beefsteaks to small bell-shaped cherry tomatoes. The best tomatoes are vine-ripened, and many home gardeners have access to excellent tomatoes that the average shopper never gets to see, let alone taste. Most tomatoes brought to market are picked green, but it's best to buy them at least partially ripened. The good news is that tomatoes ripen quite well at home; just let them sit a few days at room temperature until deep red and slightly softened.

CHEESY BROILED TOMATOES

Makes: 4 halves; serves: 2 to 4

These simple-to-make broiled tomatoes are extremely tasty. I'm never sure whether to consider a half or a whole tomato as a serving.

2 ripe tomatoes
2 tablespoons grated Parmesan cheese

1. Preheat the broiler.

2. Cut tomatoes in half widthwise. Place in a broiler pan, cut side up. Broil, 4 inches from heat source, for 5 minutes, or until cooked through.

3. Remove from the broiler. Sprinkle the top of each tomato with 1½ teaspoons Parmesan. Return to broiler; cook about 1 minute or until cheese is bubbly and browned.

⊽ *Variation:* Broiled Tomatoes: Lightly salt and pepper the tomato halves before broiling; omit the cheese.

STEWED TOMATOES

Makes: 2 cups; serves: 4

I used plum tomatoes for this recipe and sliced them ¹/₂ inch thick. These are much more delicious than the canned ones you can buy. If your tomatoes are not very juicy, add 1 tablespoon of water to the pot when you add the other ingredients.

4 cups peeled, thickly sliced tomatoes
2 basil leaves
1 clove garlic, minced
¹/₈ teaspoon salt

1. Place all the ingredients in a 1¹/₂-quart saucepan. Cook, uncovered, over medium heat until tomatoes have given up enough liquid to almost completely cover the tomato pieces and the liquid starts to boil. Reduce heat and simmer, covered, 5 minutes.

SAUTÉED TOMATOES

Makes: 3 cups; serves: 4 to 6

I came to love these when I was staying in a youth hostel in London. They served tomatoes every morning with breakfast. Of course, they're equally delicious served for lunch or dinner.

1 tablespoon butter or margarine
3 cups tomato wedges
¹/₄ teaspoon salt, or to taste
¹/₈ teaspoon pepper

1. In a large skillet, melt the butter or margarine over medium-high heat.

2. Add the tomatoes; cook, stirring, until softened, about 3 minutes. Stir in the salt and pepper.

Variation: Use halved cherry tomatoes instead of the larger tomato wedges.

BASIL-STUFFED BAKED TOMATOES

Makes: 4 halves; serves: 4

Stuffed tomatoes are great side dishes for any meal.

2 ripe medium tomatoes
1 tablespoon olive oil
¹/₄ cup finely chopped onions
1 clove garlic, minced
¹/₂ cup dry unflavored bread crumbs
3 tablespoons fresh basil, or ¹/₂ teaspoon dried basil
¹/₈ teaspoon salt, or to taste
¹/₈ teaspoon pepper

1. Preheat the oven to 350°F.

2. Cut the tomatoes in half. Scoop out the center tomato pulp and chop; set aside.

3. In a medium skillet, heat the oil over medium-high heat. Add the onions and garlic; cook, stirring, until onions are softened, about 2 minutes. Add the chopped tomato pulp; cook, stirring, until softened, about 2 minutes. Stir in the bread crumbs, basil, salt, and pepper.

4. Fill each tomato half with ¹/₄ of the bread crumb mixture.

5. Bake 15 minutes or until heated through.

Variation: Use flavored bread crumbs instead of unflavored. Add 2 tablespoons grated Parmesan cheese, if desired.

BROCCOLI-STUFFED TOMATOES

L

Makes: 4 tomatoes; serves: 4

This is a great use for those tomatoes that looked good when you bought them but turned out to have an unpleasant mealy texture.

4 ripe medium tomatoes
Salt and pepper
1 ½ cups chopped broccoli (fresh, cooked; or frozen, thawed)
½ cup lightly packed shredded Monterey Jack cheese

1. Preheat the oven to 350°F.

2. Slice off the blossom ends of the tomatoes. Scoop out the tomato pulp and discard. Lightly season the shells with salt and pepper.

3. In a small bowl, combine the broccoli and cheese.

4. Fill each tomato with ¼ of the broccoli mixture.

5. Bake 15 minutes or until vegetables are heated through and cheese is melted.

Variation: Use Cheddar, Gouda, or Jarlsberg instead of Monterey Jack.

SCALLOPED TOMATOES

L

Makes: 5½ cups; serves: 6 to 8

I made large (1-inch) croutons for this dish.

1 tablespoon olive oil
½ cup chopped onions
2 cloves garlic, minced
4 cups diced tomatoes (¾-inch pieces)
3 cups cubed flavored croutons (page 427)
1 cup shredded Jarlsberg or Swiss cheese
¼ cup grated Parmesan cheese
¼ teaspoon pepper

1. Preheat the oven to 350°F. Grease a 1½-quart casserole.

2. In a large skillet, heat the oil over medium-high heat. Add the onions and garlic; cook, stirring, until softened, about 2 minutes; remove from heat. Add the tomatoes, croutons, both cheeses, and pepper. Toss until combined. Spoon into the prepared casserole.

3. Bake 40 minutes or until casserole is heated through and cheese has melted.

Variation: Add ¼ cup chopped fresh basil.

ORZO~STUFFED TOMATOES

Makes: 4 tomatoes; serves: 4

You can omit the cheese for a vegan variation. If you don't have orzo on hand, you can use cooked rice.

4 ripe medium tomatoes
1 cup cooked orzo
²/₃ cup shredded Monterey Jack cheese
¹/₃ cup peas (fresh, cooked; or frozen, thawed)
¹/₄ cup chopped fresh parsley
2 tablespoons chopped fresh dill,
    or 1 teaspoon dried dill weed
2 teaspoons melted butter or margarine
¹/₈ teaspoon salt, or to taste
¹/₈ teaspoon pepper

1. Preheat the oven to 350°F.

2. Slice off the blossom ends of the tomatoes. Scoop out the tomato pulp and discard.

3. In a small bowl, combine the remaining ingredients.

4. Fill each tomato with ¹/₄ of the orzo mixture.

5. Bake 15 to 20 minutes or until vegetables are heated through.

Variation: Italian Stuffed Tomatoes: Use ¹/₄ cup chopped fresh basil or 2 teaspoons dried basil instead of the dill; use shredded Fontina instead of the Monterey Jack.

Turnips and Rutabaga

Turnips were much more popular at the turn of the century, when they were one of the few winter vegetables available in the market. Turnips are white with a light purple bottom; when yellow they are called rutabagas (see below). White turnips have a slightly sharp bite when eaten raw, but sweeten somewhat when cooked. Always buy turnips that are very firm and not too large.

I had a friend who used to give up rutabaga for Lent every year, but I think that's because he'd never tasted one in his life. If he had, he might not have been so eager to give them up. They have a kind of natural sweetness, like carrots. They're great just peeled and cut into sticks to serve with dips or to snack on. Rutabagas, also called yellow turnips, come dipped in a thick wax coating; therefore, they must always be peeled. Avoid ones that are growing green tops—they must have been around quite a while.

TURNIPS AND APPLES

Makes: 2³/₄ cups; serves: 4

The nutmeg flavor is very subtle, so you can easily double the nutmeg quantity.

2 tablespoons butter or margarine, divided
1 cup peeled, thinly sliced apples
3 cups coarsely shredded turnips
¹/₈ teaspoon ground nutmeg
¹/₈ teaspoon salt, or to taste
¹/₂ cup apple juice

1. In a large skillet, melt one tablespoon of the butter or margarine over medium-high heat. Add the apples; cook, stirring, until slightly browned, about 5 minutes. Remove from skillet and set aside.

2. Add the remaining butter or margarine and melt; add the turnips, nutmeg, and salt; cook, stirring, until butter or margarine has been absorbed. Add the juice; cook, stirring, until turnips are soft, about 7 minutes. Return the apples to the skillet; cook, stirring, until heated through.

Variation: Add ½ cup chopped walnuts when you return the apples to the skillet.

MASHED RUTABAGA

Ⓥ | ♥

Makes: 2 cups; serves: 3 to 4

There's just a hint of sweetness in these rutabaga. If you'd like more, increase the brown sugar to taste.

4 cups cubed rutabaga (1-inch pieces)
1 tablespoon firmly packed light brown or
    dark brown sugar
2 teaspoons butter or margarine
½ teaspoon salt, or to taste
⅛ teaspoon ground nutmeg

1. Cook the rutabaga in boiling water for 20 minutes or until tender; drain.

2. Place in a large bowl. Add the remaining ingredients. Mash with a fork, electric mixer, or food processor.

Variation: Omit the brown sugar and nutmeg.

GINGER-BAKED ROOT VEGETABLES

Ⓥ | ♥

Makes: 2¼ cups; serves: 4

You don't have to make this a mixture of vegetables—any of these vegetables alone taste great prepared this way.

1 cup julienned rutabaga
1 cup julienned beets
1 cup julienned carrots
¼ cup water
2 tablespoons honey
1 tablespoon minced fresh ginger

1. Preheat the oven to 350°F.

2. In a 1-quart casserole, toss together the rutabaga, beets, and carrots.

3. In a small bowl, stir together the remaining ingredients. Pour over the vegetables and bake 1 hour, uncovered, stirring occasionally, until vegetables are tender.

Variation: Substitute orange or apple juice for the water.

ORANGE~SAUTÉED RUTABAGA AND CARROTS

—— Ⓥ ♥ ——

Makes: 2³⁄₄ cups; serves: 4

I usually julienne vegetables thin as match sticks; in this recipe, however, the pieces are about ¹⁄₄ inch thick. When cooked, the rutabaga and carrots are still tender-crisp. If you like vegetables softer, cut the pieces thinner or add water (or additional orange juice) and continue cooking until they reach the desired doneness.

1 tablespoon butter or margarine
2 cups julienned rutabaga
2 cups julienned carrots
¹⁄₂ cup orange juice
2 tablespoons light brown or dark
    brown sugar

1. In a large skillet, melt the butter or margarine over medium-high heat. Add the rutabaga and carrots; cook, stirring until slightly tender, about 3 minutes. Add the orange juice and brown sugar. Cook, stirring occasionally, until liquid evaporates and vegetables are glazed, about 3 minutes longer.

Variation: Add ground nutmeg when you add the orange juice.

GRAINS

Until the late 1980s, most Americans' idea of grains was rice, wheat, corn, and barley. The wheat was usually eaten in flour form, although an occasional bulgur or couscous dish was a possibility.

As the medical community began acknowledging that less meat leads to healthier outcomes, food writers started venturing further afield to find dishes that would fill in the meat gap.

When it came to healthy eating, vegetarians had quite a jump on the population at large. Brown rice, oats, and millet were already known commodities and "newer" such grains as quinoa and kamut were not unheard of.

Cooking Basics: Whole Grains with Hulls

You will see that whole grains are sometimes referred to as "berries." Both terms refer to grains that are intact, with only the outer husks removed; the bran, germ, and endosperm remain.

Because of the hulls, completely unprocessed grains require long cooking times. These grains absorb the water best when there is no salt in the cooking liquid (and that includes any broths). Since the long cooking time also turns most vegetables into mush, I prefer to cook grains separately.

The flavor and consistencies of these grains are fairly similar, and you can use them interchangeably. The advantage of interchanging grains can be important for people who are allergic to a certain grain (usually wheat); by substituting another grain they can still use the recipes. Practically speaking, since the cooking times are long, it makes sense to cook up a batch large enough for more than one recipe, then use the remainder in any recipe calling for cooked whole grain products, regardless of whether the grain called for is exactly the one you've cooked.

COOKING WHOLE GRAINS

1. Bring water to a boil in a 1½- or 2-quart saucepan.
2. Add the grain.
3. Reduce heat; simmer, covered, for specified time (see below) or until water is absorbed.
4. Stir lightly to fluff (adding salt to taste, if desired).
5. Let stand for specified time.

MILLET

Makes: 4¼ cups; serves: depending on use

Although millet can be simmered the same way as most whole grains, the result is dense and soggy. For a fluffier outcome, try this cooking method.

1 tablespoon oil
1 cup millet
2 cups boiling water

1. Heat the oil in a 1½-quart saucepan. Add the millet; cook, stirring, until some grains have browned.

2. Add the boiling water. Cover and simmer 30 minutes or until liquid is absorbed. Let stand 5 minutes.

WHOLE GRAIN COOKING TABLE

Grain 1 cup	Water (cups)	Cooking Time	Standing Time	Yield (cups)
Barley,				
Hulless	2½	1 hr. 20 min.	10 min.	4¼
Barley, or Pot Barley,				
Unhulled	2½	1 hr. 20 min.	10 min.	3¼
Kamut	1½	1 hr.	3 min.	2½
Millet	2	30 min.	5 min.	3
Oats	2	1 hr.	7 min.	2½
Quinoa*	3	20 min.	2 min.	3
Rice (Brown)	2¼	45 min.	2 min.	3½
Rye	2½	2 hrs. 15 min.	10 min.	3½
Spelt	2	1½ hrs.	5 min.	3
Wheat	2¼	1½–2 hrs.	5 min.	3½
Wild Rice	2	50 min.	5 min.	3

*In order to remove a natural but bitter-tasting coating, quinoa must be thoroughly rinsed, until there are no frothy bubbles in the bowl. Place the quinoa in a large bowl, fill with cool water, then drain into a strainer. Repeat 4 more times or until the water no longer looks soapy.

Cooking Basics: Processed Grains

Processed grains are those that have been pre-treated in some manner before packaging, such as having the hulls removed or being cracked. Following are explanations of how various grains are processed.

Barley

Hulless barley: Specifically grown without hull. Treat like whole unprocessed grains (see chart, page 301).

Pearl barley: Barley with hull polished, re-moved by grounding.

Buckwheat

Kasha: Toasted buckwheat; can be whole or cracked into coarse, medium, or fine grains.

Wheat

Bulgur wheat: Wheat that has been hulled, then steamed and dried.

Cereal, farina: Very finely cracked endosperm of wheat.

Cereal, wheatena: Very finely cracked wheat.

Couscous: Endosperm of durum wheat, bro-ken up, then cooked and pressed together

Cracked wheat: Whole wheat that has been broken into pieces.

Flour

All-purpose flour: Ground endosperm. May be bleached or unbleached.

Bread flour: Ground endosperm from high-gluten wheat.

Cake flour: Ground endosperm from bleached low-gluten wheat.

Graham flour: Finely ground wheat, includ-ing bran and germ.

Pastry flour: Ground endosperm from low-gluten wheat.

Self-rising flour: All-purpose or cake flour, plus baking powder and salt.

Whole wheat flour: Finely ground wheat, in-cluding the bran but not the germ. (Because the germ has a high oil content, omitting it gives the whole wheat flour a longer shelf life.)

COOKING PROCESSED GRAINS

1. Bring water to a boil in a 1½-quart saucepan.
2. Add the grain.
3. Reduce heat; simmer, covered, for specified time or until water is absorbed.
4. Stir lightly to fluff (adding salt to taste, if desired).
5. Let stand for specified time.

PROCESSED GRAIN COOKING TABLE

Grain 1 cup	Water (cups)	Cooking Time	Standing Time	Yield (cups)
Barley (pearl)	2½	40 min.	4 min.	3½
Bulgur and				
cracked wheat	2	20 min.	3 min.	3
Couscous	1¾	2 min.	3 min.	2¾
Grits (quick)	4	5 min.	1 min.	4
Kasha (whole*)	2	10–15 min.	5 min.	3

*Medium and fine kasha will require the shorter cooking times.

KASHA

Makes: 3 ¹/₂ cups; serves: depending on use

Although kasha can be simmered the same way as most grains, the result is dense and soggy. For a fluffier outcome, try this cooking method.

1 egg
1 cup kasha
2 cups boiling water

1. Beat the egg and stir in the kasha. Cook in a dry 1½-quart saucepan until the beaten egg has dried onto the kasha.
2. Add the boiling water. Cover and simmer 10 to 12 minutes or until liquid is absorbed. Let stand 5 minutes.

Cooking Basics: Rice

In addition to long-grain white rice there are medium- and short-grain white rices. Shorter grains yield stickier cooked rice. *Arborio* rice, which is medium grain, is prized for the creamy result it produces in risottos (see pages 156–59 for recipes). Short-grain rice is most frequently used in Asian cooking, notably for sashimi and other dishes in which the rice is molded.

Imported rices such as jasmine (my favorite) and basmati have a very fragrant aroma and delicate flavor (some describe it as a popcorn flavor). In fact, they are called aromatic rice. American growers are also producing aromatic rices called basmati, jasmati, texmati, and calmati.

Brown rice, previously designated for "health food nuts," is gaining respectability among the masses. It has a nuttier flavor and chewier consistency than white. It comes in long and short grains. It also has a higher fiber and vitamin profile. Brown rice takes longer to cook than white, but it's worth the effort.

Instant rice is widely available in supermarkets. It is precooked rice that has been dehydrated. Instant rice is available in both white and brown varieties. It is "cooked" by simply adding to boiling water for a few minutes. My personal view is that the flavor and consistency of instant rices are not very desirable; I'd rather wait the 20 minutes for regular rice to cook.

COOKING RICE

1. Bring water to a boil in a 1½-quart saucepan.
2. Add the rice.
3. Reduce heat; simmer, covered, for specified time (see below) or until water is absorbed.
5. Stir lightly to fluff (adding salt to taste, if desired).
6. Let stand for specified time.

RICE COOKING TABLE

Type of Rice 1 cup	Water (cups)	Cooking Time	Standing Time	Yield (cups)
Basmati	2	20 min.	5 min.	3²/₃
Brown	2¼	45 min.	2 min.	3½
Converted	2½	25 min.	5 min.	3½
Jasmine	2	20 min.	5 min.	3
Texmati	2	20 min.	5 min.	4
White, long-grain	2	20 min.	5 min.	3

BASIC SHORT-GRAIN WHITE RICE (GLUTINOUS)

Makes 3 cups; serves: depending on use

1 cup rice
1 ½ cups water

1. Thoroughly rinse the rice until water is no longer cloudy. Place in bowl, cover with some water, and let soak 30 minutes; drain.

2. Place rice in 1½-quart heatproof dish. Add the 1½ cups water. Place on rack in steamer over boiling water. Steam in covered steamer (the dish should not be covered, only the pot), 30 minutes or until water is absorbed. Fluff with a fork.

Barley

Barley is most often sold (and eaten) pearled (the outer husk is polished off). It's great in stews, soups, sautéed with vegetables, or just by itself.

BARLEY WITH MUSHROOMS

Makes: 3¼ cups; serves: 4 to 6

Dress up this everyday favorite by substituting wild mushrooms for the white, or adding chopped dill and/or parsley to the dish.

1 ½ tablespoons vegetable oil
½ cup chopped onions
½ cup chopped green bell peppers
1 ½ cups sliced white mushrooms
1 ⅔ cups water
½ teaspoon salt, or to taste
¼ teaspoon pepper
¾ cup pearl barley

1. In a 2-quart saucepan, heat the oil over medium-high heat. Add the onions and bell peppers; cook, stirring, until softened, about 3 minutes. Add the mushrooms; cook, stirring, until softened, about 3 minutes.

2. Add the water, salt, and pepper; bring to a boil. Stir in the barley; return to a boil. Reduce heat and simmer, covered, 40 minutes or until liquid is absorbed.

Variation: Substitute broth for the water and adjust salt accordingly.

ZUCCHINI BARLEY

Makes: 4 cups; serves: 6 to 8

So much flavor in such a simple dish.

2 teaspoons olive oil
½ cup chopped onions
1½ cups vegetable broth (pages 93–95)
1 cup water
1 cup pearl barley
1 cup chopped zucchini
¼ cup chopped fresh parsley
¼ teaspoon salt, or to taste
⅛ teaspoon pepper

1. In a 1½-quart saucepan, heat the oil over medium-high heat. Add the onions; cook, stirring, until softened, about 2 minutes.

2. Add the broth and water; bring to a boil. Stir in the barley and return to a boil. Reduce heat and simmer, covered, 35 minutes. Stir in the remaining ingredients. Simmer, covered, 5 to 10 minutes longer or until liquid is absorbed and vegetables are tender.

Variation: Toast ⅓ cup pine nuts and stir into the cooked barley. Substitute broccoli or yellow squash for the zucchini.

BARLEY WITH RUTABAGA AND CARROTS

Makes: 3¼ cups; serves: 4 to 6

The important consideration for this recipe is that you have to really like rutabaga (also known as yellow or waxy turnip), since that is definitely the dominant flavor.

2 teaspoons vegetable oil
½ cup chopped onions
1¼ cups water
½ cup pearl barley
1 cup diced rutabaga
¾ cup diced carrots
¼ teaspoon salt, or to taste
¼ teaspoon pepper

1. In a 2-quart saucepan, heat the oil over medium-high heat. Add the onions; cook, stirring, until softened, about 2 minutes. Add the water and bring to a boil.

2. Add the barley, rutabaga, and carrots; return to a boil. Reduce heat and simmer, covered, 40 minutes. Remove from heat; stir in the salt and pepper; let stand 4 minutes.

Variation: Use broth instead of water; use all carrots instead of rutabaga.

BARLEY WITH SPINACH

Makes: 3½ cups; serves: 4 to 6

You can use a package of frozen chopped spinach, but the pieces will be smaller than if using fresh spinach.

2 teaspoons vegetable oil
¾ cup chopped onions
¾ cup chopped celery
1⅔ cups vegetable broth (pages 93–95)
¾ cup pearl barley, rinsed
3 cups bite-size pieces fresh rinsed spinach
¾ cup chopped carrots
¼ teaspoon pepper

1. In a 2-quart saucepan, heat the oil over medium-high heat. Add the onions and celery; cook, stirring, until softened, about 3 minutes. Add the broth and bring to a boil.

2. Add the barley; return to a boil. Reduce heat and simmer, covered, 30 minutes. Add the spinach, carrots, and pepper. Simmer, covered, 15 minutes longer.

Buckwheat

It's uncommon to find buckwheat in its raw form. Most often people confuse kasha, which is roasted buckwheat, for raw. Kasha has a very distinctive flavor and most people either love it or hate it, but few feel indifferent.

KASHA VARNISKAS

Makes: 3 cups; serves: 4 to 6

This is an old Russian–Eastern European favorite. Use whole, coarse, or medium-coarse kasha (not fine), and for extra flavor cook the kasha with broth instead of water.

2 tablespoons vegetable oil
1 cup chopped onions
1 1/2 cups cooked kasha (page 302)
1 1/2 cups cooked bowtie pasta
1/4 teaspoon salt, or to taste
1/4 teaspoon pepper

1. In a large skillet, heat the oil over medium-high heat. Add the onions; cook, stirring, until onions are transparent, about 2 minutes.

2. Stir in the kasha, pasta, salt, and pepper. Cook, stirring, until heated through.

Variation: Although not traditional for this dish, add 1/2 cup chopped green bell peppers when you add the onions.

KASHA WITH JÍCAMA AND APPLES

Makes: 3 cups; serves: 4 to 6

If your kasha was not just freshly cooked for this recipe, you may want to stir in 1 tablespoon apple juice or water with the kasha to moisten it.

1 1/2 tablespoon butter or margarine, divided
1/2 cup sliced leeks (white or light green parts only)
1 cup diced jícama
1 cup peeled, sliced apples
1 1/2 cups cooked kasha (page 302)
1/3 cup golden or dark raisins
1/8 teaspoon salt, or to taste
1/8 teaspoon pepper

1. In a large skillet, melt 1 tablespoon of the butter or margarine over medium-high heat. Add the leeks; cook, stirring, until softened, about 30 seconds. Add the jícama; cook, stirring, until tender-crisp, about 4 minutes. Add the remaining butter or margarine and melt. Add the apples; cook until they start to brown, about 3 minutes longer.

2. Stir in the kasha, raisins, salt, and pepper. Cook, stirring, until heated through.

Variation: Add 1/2 cup chopped walnuts when you add the raisins.

Cornmeal

Except as polenta, cornmeal is generally used as an ingredient in baking, rather than as a dish on its own. It brings a pleasant grittiness to most prepared dishes.

BASIC POLENTA

Makes: 2¹/₂ cups; serves: 4

This Italian specialty makes a very filling side dish to accompany vegetables and stews. It's very versatile and can be served with just about any sauce you'd serve on pasta. My personal favorite dinner is polenta (basic or creamy) with a side of Sautéed Escarole (page 263). Many people prefer the taste of Creamy Polenta (the variation), but I think the basic recipe really allows the sauces to shine. If you're planning to slice the polenta, use the basic recipe, since the creamy one will be a little too loose.

2¹/₂ cups water
³/₄ cup polenta (yellow cornmeal)
¹/₂ teaspoon salt, or to taste
1 tablespoon butter or margarine (optional)

1. In a 2-quart saucepan, stir together the water, cornmeal, and salt until there are no lumps.

2. Bring to a boil over medium-high heat, stirring frequently. Reduce heat to simmer; cook, stirring constantly, until the polenta leaves a clean path when you scrape the bottom of the pan (and your arms feel like they are falling off), about 20 to 30 minutes.

3. Add the butter or margarine, if desired, and stir until melted.

4. Serve immediately or place in loaf pan to cool for slicing.

⌊ *Variation:* Creamy Polenta: Stir in ¹/₂ cup half-and-half or milk when you add the butter or margarine. For a second version of creamy polenta, see page 81.

FRIED POLENTA

Makes: 12 to 14 slices; serves: 6 to 8

You can serve these yummy slices of polenta with any vegetable, sauce, or stew that you would serve with basic polenta.

1 recipe basic polenta (left)
Oil for frying

1. Place the polenta into a greased 7-inch loaf pan. Chill.

2. Turn onto cutting board and slice into ¹/₂-inch-thick pieces.

3. Pour ¹/₄ inch of oil into a large skillet. Heat over medium-high heat until oil bubbles when a small piece of polenta is dropped in. Place slices of polenta into pan in a single layer. Cook until golden on bottom; turn and cook until golden on second side, about 3 minutes in all. Drain on paper towels. Repeat with remaining slices.

Hush Puppies

Makes: 20; serves: 4 to 5

You can find Hush Puppies without corn kernels, and many Southerners will declare that that's the right way to do them. But what does a girl from New York (actually New Jersey) know? I like the kernels. You can leave them out if you're feeling Southern.

1 cup yellow cornmeal
2 tablespoons all-purpose flour
1 teaspoon baking powder
1 teaspoon salt, or to taste
1/4 teaspoon baking soda
1 egg
2/3 cup buttermilk
1 cup corn kernels (fresh, cooked; canned, drained; or frozen)
1/4 cup minced onions
Oil for deep frying

1. In a medium bowl or on a piece of waxed paper, stir together the cornmeal, flour, baking powder, salt, and baking soda.

2. In a medium bowl, beat the egg. Stir in the buttermilk, then the corn and onions. Stir in the dry ingredients until thoroughly combined.

3. In a 3-quart saucepan, pour the oil 2 inches deep and heat until it bubbles when a small amount of batter is dropped in. Drop the batter by rounded tablespoons into the oil. Cook until golden on one side. Turn and cook until golden on second side, about 2 minutes in all. Remove from oil and drain on paper towels.

Grits

Grits is similar in texture to hot cereal and is most commonly served as a breakfast side dish in many Southern states.

Grits with Cheese

Makes: 3 1/2 cups; serves: 4 to 6

Cooked grits has a consistency similar to polenta, which shouldn't be surprising since both are corn products. For a firmer consistency, let this dish stand about 10 minutes before serving.

1 tablespoon vegetable oil
1/2 cup chopped onions
1/2 cup chopped green bell peppers
1 1/2 cups water
One 8-ounce can tomato sauce
1/2 cup old-fashioned grits
1/2 cup corn kernels (fresh, cooked; canned, drained; or frozen)
1/8 teaspoon salt, or to taste
Dash Tabasco (optional)
1 cup coarsely shredded Cheddar cheese

1. In a 2-quart saucepan, heat the oil over medium-high heat. Add the onions and bell peppers; cook, stirring, until vegetables are softened, about 3 minutes.

2. Add the water and tomato sauce; bring to a boil. Stir in the grits. Reduce heat and simmer 5 minutes. Stir in the corn, salt, and Tabasco. Cook, stirring constantly, until thickened, about 5 minutes longer. Stir in the cheese until melted. Let stand 5 to 10 minutes before serving.

Variation: Add 1 1/2 teaspoons chili powder before you add the water.

Kamut and Spelt

Kamut and spelt (along with quinoa and amaranth) are what are known as "ancient" grains. Spelt is believed to be the predecessor of wheat. Neither grain was commonly available until recently. Now they can be found in health food stores as whole grains as well as flour. Both have mild flavors and a nice chewy texture. I use them interchangeably.

THANKSGIVING KAMUT

⸺ [V][♥] ⸺

Makes: 7¹/₂ cups; serves: 10 to 15

This dish has been highly complimented by all the guests when I've brought it to Thanksgiving dinner, which is why the recipe serves so many. For a more festive presentation, place the mixture into a greased mold and press slightly with a spoon, then turn onto a serving platter.

3¾ cups water
1 cup kamut
1 cup brown rice
¹/₂ cup sliced almonds
3 cups diced butternut squash (¹/₂-inch pieces)
1 cup chopped dried apricots
¹/₂ cup chopped fresh cranberries
2 tablespoons honey
1 teaspoon salt, or to taste

1. In a 3-quart saucepan, bring the water to a boil. Add the kamut and return to a boil. Reduce heat and simmer 1 hour. Add the rice and simmer 30 minutes longer.

2. While the rice is cooking, bake the almonds in a baking pan for 10 minutes in a 350°F oven; set aside.

3. Stir the squash into the saucepan; simmer 10 minutes. Stir in the remaining ingredients. Simmer 5 minutes longer.

Variation: If kamut is not available, use wheat berries and simmer 1 hour 15 minutes before adding brown rice.

KAMUT WITH SAUTÉED ESCAROLE AND YELLOW SQUASH

⸺ [L] ⸺

Makes: 3¹/₄ cups; serves: 4 to 6

Besides being an excellent side dish, this can be made into an entree by placing it in a baking dish, topping with shredded Swiss cheese, and baking or broiling until cheese is melted.

2 tablespoons pine nuts (pignoli)
1 tablespoon vegetable oil
2 cups lightly packed, coarsely chopped escarole
1 cup sliced yellow squash
¹/₂ cup sliced leeks (white and light green only)
1¹/₂ cups cooked kamut (page 301)
2 tablespoons grated Parmesan cheese
¹/₄ teaspoon salt, or to taste
¹/₈ teaspoon pepper

1. In a large skillet, cook the pine nuts over medium heat until somewhat browned; remove from skillet and set aside.

2. Add the oil to the skillet; heat over medium-high heat. Add the escarole, squash, and leeks; cook, stirring, until tender-crisp, about 3 minutes. Add the kamut; cook, stirring, until heated through. Stir in the pine nuts, Parmesan, salt, and pepper.

[V] *Variation:* Omit the Parmesan cheese.

Spelt and Peas

Makes: 3 cups; serves: 4 to 6

Although very basic, this dish is a wonderful accompaniment to almost everything.

1 tablespoon vegetable oil
⅔ cup chopped onions
2 cups cooked spelt (page 301)
1 cup peas (fresh or frozen), cooked
⅓ cup chopped fresh parsley
¼ teaspoon salt, or to taste
¼ teaspoon pepper

1. In a large skillet, heat the oil over medium-high heat. Add the onions; cook, stirring, until softened, about 2 minutes. Add the remaining ingredients. Cook, stirring, until heated through.

Variation: Add ¼ cup snipped fresh dill when you add the parsley.

Millet

Millet is usually associated with "health food nuts." It's a grain that may take some getting used to—it has a slightly bitter flavor and can also have a chalky texture if simmered without sautéing first. The dishes to serve with millet are ones that appeal to the basic taste sensors: sweet, sour, hot, or salty.

Curried Millet

Makes: 3⅓ cups; serves: 4 to 6

This curry has a pretty good kick to it. If you prefer a milder curry, use only ¼ teaspoon of the ground red pepper.

1½ tablespoons vegetable oil
¾ cup millet, rinsed
¾ cup chopped onions
2 cloves garlic, minced
1 tablespoon curry powder
½ teaspoon ground cumin
½ teaspoon ground turmeric
¼ teaspoon ground red pepper
1½ cups water
½ teaspoon salt, or to taste

1. In a 1½-quart saucepan, heat the oil over medium-high heat. Add the millet; cook, stirring, until the millet crackles, about 2 minutes.

2. Add the onions and garlic; cook, stirring, until vegetables are softened, about 2 minutes. Stir in the curry powder, cumin, turmeric, and red pepper until absorbed.

3. Add the water and salt. Reduce heat and simmer, covered, 20 to 25 minutes or until liquid is absorbed. Remove from heat and fluff with a fork. Let stand 5 minutes.

Variation: Add ½ cup frozen peas 5 minutes before the millet has finished cooking.

CHILI MILLET WITH PEPPERS

▢

Makes: 3 cups; serves: 4 to 6

For a main course, stir in 1½ cups cooked kidney beans during the last five minutes of cooking (especially good with the cheese variation). Serve topped with sliced scallions.

2 tablespoons vegetable oil
½ cup millet, rinsed
¾ cup chopped onions
½ cup chopped red bell peppers
½ cup chopped green bell peppers
½ to 1 tablespoon minced (seeded) jalapeño pepper
1 clove garlic, minced
2 teaspoons chili powder
1 cup boiling water
½ teaspoon salt, or to taste

1. In a 2-quart saucepan, heat the oil over medium-high heat. Add the millet; cook, stirring, until the millet crackles, about 2 minutes.

2. Add the onions, all the peppers, and garlic. Cook, stirring, until vegetables are softened, about 3 minutes. Stir in the chili powder until absorbed.

3. Add the boiling water. Reduce heat and simmer, covered, 30 minutes. Remove from heat, stir in the salt, and fluff with a fork. Let stand 5 minutes.

Variation: Chili Millet with Cheese: Stir in 1 cup shredded Cheddar when you add the salt.

MEXICAN MILLET

▢ ♥

Makes: 5 cups; serves: 6 to 8

I used a medium-spicy green salsa and the result was fairly spicy; use mild or very spicy salsa according to your taste. If you don't have green salsa, red will be fine. If you haven't prepared the Cilantro–Two Onion Relish, you can just add chopped scallions and/or onion, plus chopped cilantro and/or parsley to taste.

2 tablespoons vegetable oil
1 cup millet, rinsed
1 cup chopped onions
1 clove garlic, minced
1½ cups water
¾ cup salsa (pages 479–81)
⅔ cup chopped black olives
½ cup chopped Cilantro–Two Onion Relish (page 484)
2 teaspoons olive oil
¼ teaspoon salt, or to taste

1. In a 2-quart saucepan, heat the vegetable oil over medium-high heat. Add the millet; cook, stirring, until the millet crackles, about 2 minutes.

2. Add the onions and garlic; cook, stirring, until onions are softened, about 2 minutes.

3. Add the water and salsa; bring to a boil. Reduce heat and simmer, covered, 20 to 30 minutes, or until liquid has been absorbed. Remove from heat; stir in the olives, relish, olive oil, and salt; fluff with a fork. Let stand 5 minutes.

Variation: Add ¾ cup finely chopped, seeded tomatoes when you add the olives.

ORANGE-ALMOND MILLET

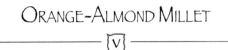

Makes: 3½ cups; serves: 4 to 6

Just the right balance of sweet and tart. Spoon this millet into a baked, halved acorn or butternut squash for a great side dish.

2 tablespoons vegetable oil
1 cup millet, rinsed
1 cup water
1 cup orange juice
¼ cup honey
½ cup chopped toasted slivered almonds (page 371)
2 teaspoons grated orange rind
¼ teaspoon salt, or to taste

1. In a 2-quart saucepan, heat the oil over medium-high heat. Add the millet; cook, stirring, until the millet crackles, about 2 minutes.

2. Add the water, juice, and honey. Bring to a boil; reduce heat and simmer, covered, 20 to 30 minutes, or until the liquid is absorbed. Remove from heat, stir in the almonds, orange rind, and salt; fluff with a fork. Let stand 5 minutes.

Variation: Stir in drained mandarin oranges when you add the almonds.

MILLET WITH DRIED FRUITS

Makes: 4¾ cups; serves: 6 to 8

You can also use this as a stuffing for baked butternut or acorn squash.

2 tablespoons vegetable oil
1 cup millet, rinsed
1¼ cups apple juice
1 cup water
3 tablespoons firmly packed light brown or dark brown sugar
1 teaspoon ground cinnamon
1 cup chopped dried apricots
¾ cup chopped dates
½ teaspoon salt, or to taste

1. In a 2-quart saucepan, heat the oil over medium-high heat. Add the millet; cook, stirring, until the millet crackles, about 2 minutes.

2. Add the juice, water, brown sugar, and cinnamon. Bring to a boil; reduce heat and simmer, covered, 15 minutes. Remove from heat; stir in the apricots, dates, and salt. Simmer 10 minutes longer. Remove from heat; let stand 5 minutes, then fluff with a fork.

Variation: Add ½ cup chopped walnuts when you add the dates.

Quinoa

Quinoa has a light, fluffy consistency and a melt-in-the-mouth quality, as opposed to the chewiness one usually associates with grain. Don't forget to rinse the quinoa well before cooking or it will have a bitter taste.

QUINOA WITH SHREDDED VEGETABLES

Makes: 3 cups; serves: 4 to 6

Shredded vegetables are particularly compatible with the light fluffy texture of cooked quinoa.

1/2 cup quinoa
1 tablespoon butter or margarine
1/2 cup chopped onions
1 cup vegetable broth (page 93–95) or water
3/4 cup coarsely shredded carrots
3/4 cup coarsely shredded rutabaga
3/4 cup coarsely shredded zucchini
1/4 teaspoon salt, or to taste

1. Place the quinoa in a large bowl; fill bowl with cool water and then drain into a strainer. Repeat 4 more times or until the water no longer looks soapy.

2. In a 1 1/2-quart saucepan, melt the butter or margarine over medium-high heat. Add the onions; cook, stirring, until softened, about 2 minutes. Add the quinoa; cook, stirring until quinoa makes popping sounds, about 1 to 2 minutes. Add the broth and bring to a boil.

3. Add the carrots, rutabaga, zucchini, and salt. Reduce heat and simmer, covered, 15 minutes or until the liquid is absorbed.

Variation: Quinoa Pilaf: Omit the shredded vegetables.

QUINOA WITH MIXED VEGETABLES

Makes: 3 cups; serves: 4 to 6

I wrote this recipe to be cooked with barley, but when I went to the pantry I was out of barley so I used quinoa instead—another happy accident.

1/2 cup quinoa
1 tablespoon vegetable oil
1 cup chopped white mushrooms
3/4 cup chopped carrots
1/2 cup chopped onions
1/2 cup chopped green bell peppers
1/2 cup chopped celery
3/4 cup vegetable broth (pages 93–95)
1/2 cup corn kernels (fresh, cooked; canned, drained; or frozen)
1/8 teaspoon pepper

1. Place the quinoa in a large bowl; fill bowl with cool water and then drain into a strainer. Repeat 4 more times or until the water no longer looks soapy.

2. In a 2-quart saucepan, heat the oil over medium-high heat. Add the mushrooms, carrots, onions, bell peppers, and celery. Cook, stirring, until vegetables are softened, and any liquid has evaporated, about 4 minutes.

3. Add the broth; bring to a boil. Stir in the quinoa; return to a boil. Reduce heat and simmer, covered, 15 minutes.

4. Stir in the corn; return to a simmer. Simmer, covered, 5 minutes longer or until liquids are absorbed. Remove from heat; stir in pepper. Let stand 3 minutes.

Variation: Substitute chopped zucchini for the corn.

QUINOA WITH JERUSALEM ARTICHOKES AND FENNEL

V ♥

Makes: 3 cups; serves: 4 to 6

For a strong licorice flavor, use the anise seeds; otherwise omit them.

½ cup quinoa
1 tablespoon butter or margarine
¾ cup diced fennel
¾ cup chopped red bell peppers
½ cup chopped onions
1 cup vegetable broth (pages 93–95)
     or water
¼ teaspoon anise seed
¾ cup chopped Jerusalem artichokes
¼ teaspoon salt, or to taste
¼ cup chopped fresh parsley

1. Place the quinoa in a large bowl; fill bowl with cool water and then drain into strainer. Repeat 4 more times or until the water no longer looks soapy.

2. In a 1½-quart saucepan melt the butter or margarine over medium-high heat. Add the fennel, bell peppers, and onions; cook, stirring, until softened, about 4 minutes. Add the quinoa; cook, stirring until quinoa makes popping sounds, about 1 to 2 minutes. Add the broth and anise seed; bring to a boil.

3. Add the Jerusalem artichokes and salt. Reduce heat and simmer, covered, 15 minutes or until the liquid is absorbed. Stir in the parsley; let stand 3 minutes.

Variation: Add ⅓ cup chopped carrots when you add the Jerusalem artichokes.

QUINOA ITALIANO

V ♥

Makes: 3¼ cups; serves: 4 to 6

Stirring in extra sauce at the end of the cooking time really boosts the tomato flavor.

1 cup quinoa
2 teaspoons olive oil
½ cup chopped onions
1 cup marinara sauce, divided
1 cup water
½ teaspoon dried oregano
⅛ teaspoon salt, or to taste
⅛ teaspoon pepper

1. Place the quinoa in a large bowl; fill bowl with cool water and then drain into strainer. Repeat 4 more times or until the water no longer looks soapy.

2. In a 2-quart saucepan, heat the oil over medium-high heat. Add the onions; cook, stirring, until onions are softened, about 1 to 2 minutes.

3. Add ¾ cup sauce and the water; bring to a boil. Stir in the quinoa and oregano; return to a boil. Reduce heat and simmer, covered, 20 minutes.

4. Remove from heat; stir in the remaining ¼ cup sauce, the salt, and pepper. Let stand 3 minutes.

Variation: Add 3 tablespoons chopped fresh basil when you stir in the salt.

Rice

There are so many different kinds of rice available nowadays that it's sad to think that many people are still just using run-of-the-mill long-grain white rice and letting all the other dishes in the meal be the stars, relegating the rice to the chorus line. For rice cooking basics, see pages 303–4.

PARSLIED RICE

Makes: 3 cups; serves: 4 to 6

This is really just buttered rice with parsley. I find that adding the butter after cooking enhances the buttery flavor.

2 cups water (2½ cups if you're using
    converted rice)
1 cup long-grain white rice
¼ cup chopped fresh parsley
1 tablespoon butter or margarine
½ teaspoon salt, or to taste

1. In a 1-quart saucepan, bring the water to a boil. Add the rice. Return to a boil. Reduce heat and simmer, covered, 20 to 25 minutes or until the water is absorbed.

2. Stir in the parsley, butter, and salt.

SAFFRON RICE

Makes: 3¾ cups; serves: 5 to 7

I used converted white rice for this recipe. If you use regular or aromatic rice (basmati, jasmine, or texmati), you may need only 2 cups of broth and may also need to decrease cooking time by 5 minutes. The saffron is measured very loosely packed.

1 tablespoon butter or margarine
1 cup chopped onions
1 clove garlic, minced
2¼ cups vegetable broth (pages 93–95)
¼ teaspoon saffron threads
1 cup converted white rice
¼ teaspoon salt, or to taste

1. In a 1½-quart saucepan, melt the butter or margarine over medium-high heat.

2. Add the onions and garlic; cook, stirring, until softened, about 2 minutes. Add the broth and saffron and bring to a boil.

3. Add the rice; return to a boil. Reduce heat and simmer, covered, 25 minutes or until the liquid is absorbed. Remove from heat, stir in the salt, and let stand 3 to 5 minutes.

Variation: Add chopped fresh cilantro or parsley when you add the salt.

COCONUT RICE

Makes: 2⅔ cups; serves: 4 to 6

I make this whenever I open a can of unsweetened coconut milk and don't use the whole can. This rice is very creamy and a perfect flavor for any curry.

1¼ cup water
¾ cup unsweetened coconut milk
1 cup long-grain white rice
½ teaspoon salt, or to taste

1. In a 1-quart saucepan, bring the water and coconut milk to a boil. Add the rice and return to a boil. Reduce heat and simmer, covered, 25 minutes or until the liquid is absorbed. Stir in the salt.

Variation: Sweetened Coconut Rice: Stir in 2 tablespoons firmly packed brown sugar.

YELLOW INDIAN RICE

[V][♥]

Makes: 4 cups; serves: 6 to 8

This flavorful rice dish is made even more so by the jasmine rice, sometimes called Thai rice, which is a very aromatic variety. If you cannot find jasmine rice, Indian basmati is second choice, followed by texmati and lastly by ordinary white rice.

1 tablespoon ghee (page 494), butter, or
   vegetable oil
1 teaspoon cumin seeds
1/2 teaspoon black mustard seeds
1/2 teaspoon ground turmeric
1 3/4 cups water
1 cup jasmine rice, rinsed
2 tablespoons chopped fresh cilantro
1/2 teaspoon salt, or to taste

1. In a 2-quart saucepan, heat the ghee, butter, or oil over medium-high heat. Add the cumin and mustard seeds; cook, stirring, 30 seconds. Add the turmeric; cook, stirring, until absorbed. Add the water and bring to a boil.

2. Stir in the rice; return to a boil. Reduce heat and simmer, covered, 20 minutes or until the liquid has been absorbed.

3. Stir in the cilantro and salt.

PAPRIKASH RICE

[V][♥]

Makes: 4 cups; serves: 6 to 8

When Mom prepares chicken paprikash, she serves it with either nockerly (dumplings), as I did in Mushrooms Paprikash (page 316), or she cooks rice in the sauce. I love that rice, and this is very very close.

2 teaspoons vegetable oil
1 cup chopped onions
2 cloves garlic
2 teaspoons Hungarian sweet paprika
1 cup converted white rice
1 1/4 cups vegetable broth (pages 93–95)
1 cup water
1/4 teaspoon salt, or to taste
1/8 teaspoon pepper

1. In a 1 1/2-quart saucepan, heat the oil over medium-high heat. Add the onions and garlic; cook, stirring, until onions are very soft, about 4 minutes. Stir in the paprika until absorbed.

2. Stir in the rice; cook, stirring, until coated with paprika. Add the broth and water; bring to a boil. Reduce heat and simmer, covered, 25 minutes or until liquid is absorbed. Stir in the salt and pepper. Fluff with a fork; let stand 3 minutes.

Variation: Add 1/4 cup finely chopped red or green bell peppers when you add the onions and garlic.

SPANISH RICE

— V —

Makes: 4 cups; serves: 6 to 8

You can use homemade sofrito (page 484) or purchase it in the Spanish food section of your supermarket.

1 tablespoon olive oil
¾ cup chopped onions
3 tablespoons sofrito
One 14½-ounce can whole peeled tomatoes, undrained
One 8-ounce can tomato sauce
½ cup water
¼ teaspoon ground cumin
1 cup long-grain white rice
¾ cup peas (fresh or frozen)
¼ teaspoon salt, or to taste
⅛ teaspoon pepper

1. In a 1½-quart saucepan, heat the oil over medium-high heat. Add the onions and sofrito; cook, stirring, until softened, about 2 minutes. Add the tomatoes, break up with the back of a wooden spoon. Add the tomato sauce, water, and cumin; bring to a boil.

2. Add the rice and return to a boil. Reduce heat and simmer, covered, 20 minutes or until liquid is absorbed. Add the peas; cook, covered, 5 minutes longer. Remove from heat; stir in the salt and pepper with a fork; let stand, covered, 5 minutes.

Variation: To make this into an entree, add 2 cups cooked black beans.

CHILI RICE WITH TOMATILLOS

— V ♥ —

Makes: 3⅓ cups; serves: 4 to 6

Two cups of water yield a very moist rice; 1¾ cups water is on the dry side. Adjust to your own tastes. I like chili rice very much, but you lose some of the character of the tomatillos to the chili flavor.

2 teaspoons vegetable oil
¾ cup chopped onions
¼ cup finely chopped green bell peppers
1 teaspoon chili powder
1½ cups chopped tomatillos
1¾ cups water
1½ teaspoons fresh lemon juice
1 cup long-grain white rice
½ teaspoon salt, or to taste
⅛ teaspoon pepper

1. In a 1½-quart saucepan, heat the oil over medium-high heat. Add the onions and bell peppers; cook, stirring, until softened, about 3 minutes. Stir in chili powder until absorbed. Add the tomatillos; cook, stirring, until softened, about 3 minutes.

2. Add the water and lemon juice; bring to a boil. Stir in the rice and return to a boil. Reduce heat and simmer, covered, 25 minutes or until liquid is absorbed. Remove from heat; stir in the salt and pepper with a fork; let stand, covered, 5 minutes.

Variation: For a spicy rice, stir in ground red pepper to taste when you add the chili.

CURRIED FRIED RICE

Makes: 3¹/₂ cups; serves: 4 to 6

Neither of my parents is a fan of curry—my father has even been quoted as saying, "You know I don't eat anything with that Green stuff in it." But they both really enjoyed this dish. My father concluded that it didn't taste like curry . . . so it was okay.

2 tablespoons vegetable oil
1 cup chopped onions
½ cup chopped snow peas
½ cup chopped celery
2 teaspoons curry powder
2 cups cooked rice (white or brown, pages 303–4)
¼ teaspoon salt, or to taste
⅛ teaspoon pepper
½ cup chopped peanuts
¼ cup chopped fresh cilantro or Italian parsley

1. In a large skillet, heat the oil over medium-high heat. Add the onions, snow peas, and celery; cook, stirring, until softened, about 4 minutes.

2. Stir in the curry powder until absorbed. Add the rice, salt, and pepper; cook, stirring, until heated through. Stir in the peanuts and cilantro.

Variation: Stir in ⅓ cup golden or dark raisins when you add the peanuts.

FRIED RICE

Makes: 4 cups; serves: 6 to 8

This is a little greasy, which is the way I like my fried rice. However, you can reduce the oil by 1¹/₂ teaspoons and still have a very tasty dish. You can

use frozen peas, frozen peas and carrots, or frozen mixed vegetables—just use a total of 1¹/₂ cups.

1½ tablespoons soy sauce
1 tablespoon water
2 teaspoons mirin (rice wine) or sherry
2 tablespoons vegetable oil
1 cup chopped onions
¾ cup chopped snow peas
⅓ cup sliced scallions (white and green parts)
2 cups cooked rice (white or brown)
¾ cup diced, blanched carrots
¾ cup cooked fresh or frozen peas

1. In a small bowl, stir together the soy sauce, water, and mirin; set aside.

2. In a wok or large skillet, heat the oil over high heat. Add the onions; cook, stirring, until transparent, about 2 minutes. Add the snow peas and scallions; cook, stirring, until softened, about 2 minutes.

2. Add the rice, carrots, peas, and soy sauce mixture. Cook, stirring, until heated through.

Variation: Add chopped scrambled egg when you add the carrots and peas.

CONTINENTAL FRIED RICE

Makes: 3¹/₄ cups; serves: 4 to 6

This recipe is based on the same concept as any Asian fried rice: Start with leftover cooked rice (which I usually have after I've had Chinese food delivered to my apartment) and sauté it with vegetables and seasonings. This is a very loose recipe and you can vary the vegetables to your taste; for example, use carrots, celery, and zucchini instead of the bell peppers, mushrooms, and peas.

1½ tablespoons vegetable oil

½ cup chopped onions

½ cup chopped green bell peppers

½ cup chopped mushrooms

¼ teaspoon dried thyme

2 cups cooked white or brown rice
  (pages 303–4)

½ cup cooked peas (fresh or frozen)

2 tablespoons white wine, broth, or water

1. In a medium skillet, heat the oil over medium-high heat. Add the onions and bell peppers; cook, stirring, until softened, about 3 minutes. Add the mushrooms and thyme; cook, stirring, until softened, about 2 minutes.

2. Add the rice, peas, and wine; cook stirring, until heated through.

Variation: Stir in ½ cup toasted chopped almonds.

BARBECUE RICE WITH BEANS AND CORN

Makes: 3½ cups; serves: 4 to 6

I used the barbecue sauce on page 478 and the result was superb. The sauce makes this dish a little moister than standard rice dishes.

1 tablespoon vegetable oil

½ cup chopped onions

½ cup chopped green bell peppers

1¼ cups water

½ cup converted white rice

1 cup corn kernels (fresh; canned, drained; or frozen)

1 cup kidney beans (cooked from dry; or canned, drained)

⅓ cup barbecue sauce

1. In a 2-quart saucepan, heat the oil over medium-high heat. Add the onions and bell peppers; cook, stirring, until softened, about 3 minutes.

2. Stir in the water; bring to a boil. Stir in the rice; return to a boil. Reduce heat and simmer, covered, 20 minutes.

3. Stir in the corn, beans, and barbecue sauce. Simmer, covered, 10 minutes longer.

Variation: Use spicy barbecue sauce or smoky barbecue sauce to add different flavors.

SPINACH BROWN RICE

Makes: 4 cups; serves: 6 to 8

The spinach flavor is quite strong in this dish.

¼ cup pine nuts (pignoli)

2 teaspoons vegetable oil

¾ cup chopped onions

2 cups vegetable broth (pages 93–95)

1 cup brown rice

One 10-ounce package frozen chopped spinach, thawed and drained

1. In a 1½-quart saucepan, toast the pine nuts over medium heat until browned; remove from pan and set aside.

2. Add the oil to the saucepan and heat. Add the onions; cook, stirring, until softened, about 2 minutes. Add the broth; bring to a boil. Add the brown rice; return to a boil. Reduce heat and simmer, covered, 30 minutes.

2. Stir in the spinach. Simmer 10 to 15 minutes longer or until all the liquid has been absorbed. Stir in the pine nuts.

Variation: Add ½ cup chopped red bell peppers when you add the onions.

BROWN RICE WITH ONION AND RED BELL PEPPER

Makes: 3¹/₂ cups; serves: 4 to 6

The pine nuts are hard to see among the brown rice kernels, so it's a nice surprise when you bite into one.

3 tablespoons pine nuts (pignoli)
1 tablespoon olive oil
1 cup chopped onions
1 cup chopped red bell peppers
2 cups cooked brown rice (page 303)
2 tablespoons vegetable broth (pages 93–95)
    or water
¼ cup chopped fresh parsley
¼ teaspoon salt, or to taste
⅛ teaspoon pepper

1. In a large skillet, toast the pine nuts over medium heat until lightly browned; remove from skillet and set aside.

2. Add the oil to the skillet and increase heat to medium-high. Add the onions and bell peppers; cook, stirring, until onions are transparent and peppers are softened, about 3 minutes.

2. Add the rice; cook, stirring, until rice starts to stick to the skillet, about 2 minutes. Add the broth; cook, stirring, until heated through. Add parsley, salt, and pepper.

Variation: Substitute ¹/₂ cup green bell peppers for ¹/₂ cup of the red.

AUTUMN BROWN RICE

Makes: 3 cups; serves: 4 to 6

Squash and cranberries are a natural contrast between sweet and tart.

1¹/₂ cups water
²/₃ cup brown rice
³/₄ cup peeled, diced butternut squash
³/₄ cup chopped walnuts or pecans
¹/₂ cup chopped cranberries
2 tablespoons honey
¹/₄ teaspoon salt, or to taste

1. In a 1¹/₂-quart saucepan, bring the water to a boil over high heat. Add the rice; return to a boil. Reduce heat and simmer; covered, 35 minutes.

2. Add the squash; cover and simmer 10 minutes longer or until the water is absorbed and the squash and rice are tender.

3. Stir in the nuts, cranberries, honey, and salt. Cook until heated through.

Variation: Use apples instead of cranberries.

APRICOT–PINEAPPLE BROWN RICE

Makes: 3¹/₂ cups; serves: 4 to 6

I use short-grain brown rice because I find the slightly stickier texture to be very compatible with the slightly sticky dried fruits.

1¹/₂ cups water
²/₃ cup brown rice
¹/₂ cup chopped dried apricots
¹/₂ cup chopped dried pineapple
¹/₂ cup chopped pecans
2 tablespoons currants
¹/₂ teaspoon salt, or to taste

1. In a 2-quart saucepan, bring the water to a boil. Add the rice and return to a boil. Reduce heat and simmer, covered, 45 minutes or until the water is absorbed.

2. Stir in the apricots, pineapple, pecans, currants, and salt.

Variation: Use ¹/₄ cup golden or dark raisins instead of the currants.

FIDDLEHEAD FERNS WITH WILD RICE

— [v] —

Makes: 3 cups; serves: 4

Fiddlehead ferns are available in the spring; some writers suggest they taste similar to asparagus. They look like coiled stems around a leafy center. Choose small ones to assure tenderness.

2 tablespoons pine nuts (pignoli)
2 tablespoons butter or margarine
¹/₂ teaspoon slivered garlic
2 cups fiddlehead ferns, well rinsed
1 cup cooked wild rice
¹/₈ teaspoon salt, or to taste

1. In a large skillet, cook the pine nuts over medium heat until partly browned; remove from skillet and set aside.

2. Melt the butter or margarine over medium-high heat. Add the garlic; cook, stirring, 10 seconds. Add the ferns; cook, stirring until tender-crisp, about 3 to 4 minutes. Stir in the rice and salt; cook, stirring, until heated through.

Variation: Omit the wild rice and serve the fiddleheads as a sautéed vegetable.

LEMON WILD AND WHITE RICE

— [v][♥] —

Makes: 4 cups; serves: 6 to 8

Despite the fact that there is so little lemon juice in this recipe, the flavor comes through loud and clear.

1¹/₂ tablespoons butter or margarine
¹/₂ cup chopped onions
1 cup broccoli florets
1 cup sliced yellow squash or zucchini
¹/₂ cup julienned carrots
2 teaspoons lemon juice
1 cup cooked wild rice
1 cup cooked white (or brown) rice
¹/₄ teaspoon salt, or to taste

1. In a large skillet, melt the butter or margarine over medium-high heat. Add the onions; cook, stirring, until transparent, about 2 minutes. Add the broccoli, squash, and carrots; cook, stirring, until tender-crisp, about 4 minutes. Remove from the skillet and set aside.

2. Add the lemon juice to the skillet to deglaze the pan. Return the vegetables; add both rices and salt. Cook, stirring, until heated through.

Variation: Use cauliflower instead of the squash.

WILD RICE AND CORN

Makes: 3 cups; serves: 4 to 6

This dish started out as a filling for stuffed tomatoes, but since it's very flavorful and the tomato overwhelmed the subtle flavors, it's now a recipe all by itself!

1 tablespoon vegetable oil
⅔ cup chopped onions
½ cup chopped red or green bell peppers
1½ cups corn kernels (fresh, cooked; canned, drained; or frozen)
1 cup cooked wild rice
2 tablespoons chopped fresh parsley
½ teaspoon poultry seasoning
½ teaspoon salt, or to taste

1. In a large skillet, heat the oil over medium-high heat. Add the onions and bell peppers; cook, stirring, until softened, about 3 minutes. Stir in the remaining ingredients. Cook, stirring, until heated through.

Variation: Wild Rice and Corn Salad: Instead of heating the wild rice and corn, place in a large bowl with the sautéed vegetables and remaining ingredients. Add 2 tablespoons of Italian dressing or vinaigrette of choice and toss.

WILD RICE WITH ORZO AND THREE-COLOR PEPPERS

Makes: 3¼ cups; serves: 4 to 6

This started out as a rice dish, but I was concerned that cooking the peppers with the rice might result in overcooked vegetables. Fortune stepped in—I had cooked orzo to use in another dish, so that's how this one got developed.

1 tablespoon olive oil
¾ cup chopped onions
½ cup chopped green bell peppers
½ cup chopped red bell peppers
½ cup chopped yellow bell peppers
1 cup cooked orzo
¾ cup cooked wild rice
¼ teaspoon salt, or to taste

1. In a medium skillet, heat the oil over medium-high heat. Add the onions and all three bell peppers; cook, stirring, until softened, about 4 minutes.

2. Stir in the orzo, wild rice, and salt. Cook until heated through.

Variation: Wild and White Rice with Three-Color Peppers: Use cooked white or brown rice instead of the orzo.

WILD RICE WITH APPLES AND ALMONDS

[V]

Makes: 3¹/₂ cups; serves: 4 to 6

This elegant dish is suitable for any company dinner.

2 teaspoons vegetable oil
¹/₂ cup chopped onions
¹/₃ cup chopped celery
1 ¹/₄ cups water
²/₃ cup wild rice
¹/₂ cup sliced almonds
1 tablespoon butter or margarine
2 cups chopped, peeled tart apples
¹/₄ teaspoon salt, or to taste

1. In a 1¹/₂-quart saucepan, heat the oil over medium-high heat. Add the onions and celery; cook, stirring, until softened, about 3 minutes. Add the water; bring to a boil. Add the rice; return to a boil. Reduce heat and simmer, covered, 50 minutes.

2. While the rice is cooking, toast the almonds in a baking pan in a 350°F oven for 10 minutes; set aside. In a medium skillet, melt the butter or margarine over medium-high heat. Add the apples; cook, stirring, until apples start to brown, about 5 minutes; set aside.

3. When the rice has cooked, stir in the almonds, apples, and salt.

Variation: Add ¹/₄ teaspoon crumbled dried rosemary when you add the wild rice.

Rizcous

A hybrid grain, rizcous is a cross between instant brown rice and couscous. Its flavor is closer to couscous, and the quick cooking time is quite an asset. You can find it in gourmet shops.

RIZCOUS, CORN, AND BEANS

Makes: 5 cups; serves: 8 to 10

I threw together this recipe as a last-minute emergency dish to fill in a slightly skimpy meal at the homeless shelter for which I occasionally cook. I thought it was quite tasty—not to mention filling!

1 tablespoon vegetable oil
³/₄ cup chopped onions
2 ¹/₄ cups vegetable broth (pages 93–95)
1 cup rizcous
1 cup corn kernels (fresh, cooked; canned, drained; or frozen)
1 cup kidney beans (cooked from dry; or canned, drained)
1 cup frozen peas
¹/₂ teaspoon salt, or to taste
¹/₂ teaspoon poultry seasoning

1. In a 2-quart saucepan, heat the oil over medium-high heat. Add the onions; cook, stirring, until transparent, about 2 minutes.

2. Add the broth; bring to a boil. Add the remaining ingredients. Return to a boil. Reduce heat and simmer, covered, 5 minutes.

Variation: Use chickpeas instead of kidney beans.

Wheat

Although the popularity of cooked whole grain wheat has increased only recently in the U.S., wheat products—be they bread or noodles, bulgur or couscous—have always been central in diets the world over.

Whole grain wheat, also called wheat berries, like most whole grains, takes a long time to cook (close to 2 hours). It is versatile and can be combined with almost any vegetable to produce a yummy entree or side dish.

Bulgur

Bulgur has been widely used throughout the Middle East. Besides bulgur being really delicious, its short cooking time is a good selling point.

BULGUR WITH SUMMER SQUASH

Makes: 3³/₄ cups; serves: 6

Use just zucchini or just yellow squash, if you prefer.

1 tablespoon olive oil
½ cup chopped onions
¾ cup chopped zucchini
¾ cup chopped yellow squash
½ cup chopped green bell peppers
¾ cup vegetable broth (pages 93–95)
²/₃ cup water
¾ cup bulgur
½ teaspoon dried oregano
¼ teaspoon salt, or to taste

1. In a 1¹/₂-quart saucepan, heat the oil over medium-high heat. Add the onions; cook, stirring, until softened, about 2 minutes. Add the zucchini, squash, and bell peppers; cook, stirring, until just softened, about 3 minutes. Add the broth and water; bring to a boil.

2. Stir in the bulgur and oregano. Return to a boil; reduce heat and simmer, covered, 20 to 25 minutes. Remove from heat. Using a fork, stir in the salt; let stand, covered, 3 minutes.

Variation: For crunchier vegetables, cook the bulgur in the water-broth with the oregano. Sauté the vegetables separately, then toss together and stir in the salt.

TOMATO BULGUR WITH EGGPLANT

Makes: 3³/₄ cups; serves: 6

Tomato bulgur is a popular item on many upscale salad tables in Manhattan. I added the eggplant for a moist texture.

1 tablespoon olive oil
1½ cups diced eggplant
3 cloves garlic, minced
1½ cups water
¼ cup tomato paste
¾ cup bulgur
¼ teaspoon salt, or to taste

1. In a 1¹/₂-quart saucepan, heat the oil over medium-high heat. Add the eggplant and garlic; cook, stirring, until softened, about 4 minutes. Add the water and tomato paste; bring to a boil.

2. Stir in the bulgur; return to a boil. Reduce heat and simmer, covered, 20 minutes. Remove from heat. Using a fork, stir in the salt; let stand, covered, 3 minutes.

BULGUR WITH SQUASH, CARROTS, AND COLLARDS

[V] [♥]

Makes: 4 cups; serves: 6 to 8

This could alternatively be called Vitamin A Delight.

1 tablespoon vegetable oil
1 ½ cups chopped collard greens or kale
⅔ cup chopped onions
1 ¾ cups water
1 cup sliced carrots
1 cup diced butternut or buttercup squash
¾ cup bulgur
¼ teaspoon salt, or to taste

1. In a 2-quart saucepan, heat the oil over medium-high heat. Add the collard greens and onions; cook, stirring, until vegetables are softened, about 3 minutes.

2. Add the water, carrots, and squash; bring to a boil. Add the bulgur. Return to a boil; reduce heat and simmer, covered, 20 minutes or until liquid is absorbed. Stir in the salt.

Variation: Substitute chopped spinach for the collards.

BULGUR WITH CELERY

[V] [♥]

Makes: 3²⁄₃ cups; serves: 6

This is a bulgur pilaf.

1 tablespoon vegetable oil
1 ½ cups chopped celery
1 cup chopped onions
1 ½ cups vegetable broth (pages 93–95)
3 tablespoons chopped fresh parsley
¾ cup bulgur
¼ teaspoon salt, or to taste
¼ teaspoon pepper

1. In a 1½-quart saucepan, heat the oil over medium-high heat. Add the celery and onions; cook, stirring, until softened, about 3 minutes. Add the broth and parsley; bring to a boil.

2. Stir in the bulgur; return to a boil. Reduce heat and simmer, covered, 20 minutes. Remove from heat. Using a fork, stir in the salt and pepper; let stand, covered, 3 minutes.

Variation: Add ½ cup chopped green bell peppers when you add the celery.

Couscous

Couscous is a staple in the Moroccan diet. To cook couscous the authentic way, you would steam it in a "couscousinere," letting the grains cook, then dry several times. Cooking couscous the "instant" way tastes just fine, too.

COUSCOUS WITH GOLDEN FRUITS AND VEGETABLES

Makes: 4 cups; serves: 6 to 8

This is a wonderful accompaniment to all curries, especially Curried Chickpeas and Kale (page 147).

2 teaspoons vegetable oil
1/3 cup chopped onions
1 teaspoon curry powder
1/2 teaspoon ground cinnamon
1 1/3 cups water
1/2 cup chopped carrots
3/4 cup chopped butternut squash
    (or buttercup or calabaza)
3/4 cup couscous
1/2 cup chopped dried apricots
1/4 cup golden raisins
1/3 cup chopped pecans
1/2 teaspoon salt, or to taste

1. In a 2-quart saucepan, heat the oil over medium-high heat. Add the onions; cook, stirring, until transparent, about 2 minutes.

2. Stir in the curry powder and cinnamon until absorbed. Add the water and bring to a boil. Add the carrots and squash; simmer, covered, 7 minutes or until vegetables are tender.

3. Add the couscous, apricots, and raisins. Cover and simmer 2 minutes. Remove from heat and let stand, covered, 3 minutes longer. Add the pecans and salt; toss to combine.

Variation: Use chopped rutabaga (yellow turnip) instead of the squash.

COUSCOUS-STUFFED PAPAYA

Makes: 4 halves; serves: 4

You can just serve the couscous stuffing as a side dish without the papaya halves (this recipe makes about 2 1/3 cups of stuffing).

2 ripe papayas
2 cups cooked couscous
2/3 cup chopped pecans
1 tablespoon honey
1/8 teaspoon salt

1. Preheat the oven to 350°F.

2. Peel the papayas; cut in half lengthwise. Scoop out the seeds and discard. Place each papaya half on a 12-inch-square piece of aluminum foil.

3. In a medium bowl, stir together the couscous, pecans, honey, and salt. Spoon 1/4 of the couscous mixture into the well of each papaya half. Pull up the corners of the foil and fold to seal in the papaya. Place on a baking sheet.

4. Bake 20 minutes or until papaya is heated through.

Variation: Add 1/4 teaspoon ground nutmeg when you add the honey.

COUSCOUS WITH EGGPLANT

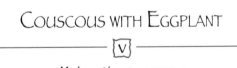

Makes: 2 2/3 cups; serves: 4

This is not a sweet dish, although smelling the cinnamon while cooking may lead to that expectation. If you would like it sweet, you can stir in some brown sugar.

1½ tablespoons vegetable oil
½ cup chopped onions
½ teaspoon ground cinnamon
1 cup chopped eggplant
1 cup water
⅔ cup couscous
⅓ cup chopped prunes
½ teaspoon salt, or to taste

1. In a 1½-quart saucepan, heat the oil over medium-high heat. Add the onions; cook, stirring, until softened, about 2 minutes. Stir in the cinnamon until absorbed. Add the eggplant; cook, stirring, until tender, about 3 minutes.

2. Add the water and bring to a boil. Add the couscous, prunes, and salt. Return to a boil; reduce heat and simmer, covered, 5 minutes or until the liquid has been absorbed.

Variation: Stir in ⅓ cup chopped mint before serving.

SPICED COUSCOUS WITH DICED VEGETABLES

Makes: 4¾ cups; serves: 6 to 8

Add diced tofu for an excellent entree.

1 tablespoon vegetable oil
½ cup chopped onions
1½ teaspoons ground turmeric
½ teaspoon ground coriander
¼ teaspoon ground cardamom
⅛ teaspoon ground allspice
1⅓ cups water
1 cup diced carrots, blanched
1 cup small cauliflower florets, blanched
½ cup diced zucchini, blanched
½ cup chopped fresh parsley
1 cup couscous
⅛ teaspoon salt, or to taste

1. In a 2-quart saucepan, heat the oil over medium-high heat. Add onions; cook, stirring, until softened, about 2 minutes. Stir in the turmeric, coriander, cardamom, and allspice until absorbed.

2. Add the water, carrots, cauliflower, zucchini, and parsley; bring to a boil. Add the couscous and salt. Return to a boil; reduce heat and simmer, covered, 5 minutes or until the liquid has been absorbed.

Variation: Add ½ cup chopped red bell pepper when you add the onions.

WHEAT BERRIES PROVENÇAL

Makes: 2½ cups; serves: 3 to 4

I think the vermouth suggested in the variation adds a nice touch to the dish, but if you don't have any on hand, the recipe is still very flavorful.

2 tablespoons olive oil
1 cup chopped onions
2 cloves garlic, mincesd
1½ cups cubed eggplant (¾-inch pieces)
1 cup diced tomatoes (¾-inch pieces)
½ cup chopped fresh parsley
1 cup cooked wheat berries (whole grain wheat, page 301)
¼ teaspoon salt
¼ teaspoon pepper

1. In a large skillet, heat the oil over medium-high heat. Add the onions and garlic; cook, stirring, until softened, about 2 minutes. Add the eggplant; cook, stirring, until slightly softened, about 2 minutes. Add the tomatos and parsley; cook, stirring, until the vegetables are cooked through, about 4 minutes.

2. Add the wheat berries, salt, and pepper. Cook, stirring, until heated through.

Variation: Add 1 tablespoon dry vermouth or white wine when you add the tomatoes.

WHEAT BERRIES WITH GINGERED EGGPLANT

Makes: 1³/₄ cups; serves: 3 to 4

This recipe started out as a tasty eggplant spread but was even better with the addition of the wheat berries.

1½ tablespoons vegetable oil
1 tablespoon minced fresh ginger
2 cloves garlic, minced
2 cups finely diced eggplant
2 tablespoons mirin (rice wine) or dry sherry
1 teaspoon soy sauce
1½ cups cooked wheat berries (page 301)
1½ teaspoons rice vinegar
¼ teaspoon chili oil

1. In a large skillet, heat the vegetable oil over medium-high heat. Add the ginger and garlic; cook, stirring, until softened, 30 seconds.

2. Add the eggplant; cook, stirring, until oil is absorbed, about 2 minutes. Add the mirin and soy sauce; cook 5 minutes or until eggplant is cooked through. Add the wheat berries; cook until heated through. Stir in the vinegar and chili oil.

Variation: For a milder version, use sesame oil instead of chili oil.

WHEAT BERRIES WITH CASHEWS

Makes: 2²/₃ cups; serves: 4 to 5

Serve these warm or at room temperature.

1 tablespoon vegetable oil
½ cup chopped onions
1½ cups cooked wheat berries (page 301)
¾ cup golden or dark raisins
½ cup coarsely chopped cashews
1 tablespoon fresh lemon juice
¼ teaspoon salt

1. In a large skillet, heat the oil over medium-high heat. Add the onions; cook, stirring, until softened, about 2 minutes. Add the remaining ingredients; cook, stirring, until heated through.

Variation: Add ½ cup chopped celery when you add the onions.

WHEAT BERRIES WITH CALABAZA AND CABBAGE

Makes: 3¹/₂ cups; serves: 4 to 6

This dish is quite peppery, but that's what gives it personality. If spicy is not your favorite flavor, just cut the pepper to ¹/₄ teaspoon—but be warned, the dish may seem bland. Calabaza is a sweet, large winter squash. If you can't find it, substitute buttercup or butternut squash.

1½ tablespoons vegetable oil
2 cups chopped cabbage
1 cup chopped onions
2 teaspoons minced fresh ginger
⅓ cup water
3 cups cubed calabaza (¾-inch pieces)
1 cup cooked wheat berries (page 301)
½ teaspoon pepper
¼ teaspoon salt, or to taste

1. In a large skillet, heat the oil over medium-high heat. Add the cabbage, onions, and ginger; cook, stirring, until softened, about 3 minutes. Add the water. Add the calabaza; cook, covered, over low heat, 15 minutes or until tender.

2. Stir in the wheat berries, pepper, and salt. Cook, stirring occasionally, until heated through.

Variation: Omit the wheat berries and just serve this as a vegetable dish.

WHEAT BERRIES WITH CARDOON

Ⓥ ♥

Makes: 3²/₃ cups; serves: 4 to 6

If you can't find cardoon (a vegetable that looks like celery with a serious thyroid problem and tastes similar to artichoke), you can use steamed diced celery, Jerusalem artichoke, or jícama—just cook them until tender, not as long as the cardoon.

1¾ cups diced cardoon (¾-inch pieces)
1 tablespoon olive oil
1 cup chopped onions
1 cup halved cherry tomatoes
1½ cups cooked wheat berries (page 301)
¼ teaspoon salt, or to taste
⅛ teaspoon pepper

1. Cook the cardoon in simmering water for 45 minutes or until tender; drain.

2. In a large skillet, heat the oil over medium-high heat. Add the onions; cook, stirring, until softened, about 2 minutes. Add the cardoon and tomatoes; cook, stirring, until tomatoes are slightly softened, about 3 minutes.

3. Add the wheat berries, salt, and pepper. Cook, stirring, until heated through.

Variation: Add ⅓ cup chopped fresh basil when you add the tomatoes.

DILLED WHEAT BERRIES WITH BROWN RICE

Ⓥ ♥

Makes: 3 cups; serves: 4 to 6

I think brown rice and wheat berries are particularly well suited to be served together.

1 tablespoon vegetable oil
1 cup sliced celery
½ cup chopped onions
1 cup cooked wheat berries (page 301)
1 cup cooked brown rice (page 301)
2 tablespoons vegetable broth (pages 93–95) or water
¼ cup snipped fresh dill
¼ teaspoon salt, or to taste
⅛ teaspoon pepper

1. In a large skillet, heat the oil over medium-high heat. Add the celery and onions; cook, stirring, until vegetables are tender, about 3 minutes.

2. Add the wheat berries and rice; cook, stirring, until rice starts to stick to the pan. Stir in the remaining ingredients. Cook, stirring, until heated through.

Variation: Add ½ cup chopped green bell peppers when you add the onions.

Noodles

Noodles show up in almost every culture. In Chinese cuisine you can find them made of rice and even soybeans, as well as the more common wheat.

NOODLE PUDDING

Makes: 12 squares; serves: 12

Although technically a side dish, noodle pudding also makes a delicious dessert. Serve it warm or cold.

One 12-ounce package wide noodles, cooked according to package directions and drained
One 8-ounce can crushed pineapple, undrained
1 cup golden raisins
3 eggs
1½ cups cottage cheese
1 cup milk
One 8-ounce container sour cream (¾ cup)
⅔ cup sugar
1½ teaspoons ground cinnamon
1 teaspoon vanilla
¼ teaspoon salt, or to taste

1. Preheat the oven to 350°F. Grease a 9-inch-square baking pan.

2. In a large bowl, toss together the noodles, pineapple, and raisins.

3. In a medium bowl, beat the eggs. Beat in the remaining ingredients. Pour over noodles and toss.

4. Spoon into prepared pan and bake 1 hour. Let cool to warm, or chill. Cut into 12 squares.

Variation: Substitute unflavored yogurt for the sour cream.

SAVORY NOODLE PUDDING

Makes: 12 squares; serves: 12

This dish is almost hearty enough for a main course, and it certainly makes a good luncheon entree.

2 tablespoons vegetable oil
2 cups shredded zucchini
2 cups shredded carrots
2 cups chopped mushroom
2 cups cooked broccoli florets
One 12-ounce package wide noodles, cooked according to package directions and drained
1 tablespoon dried dill weed
½ teaspoon anchovy-free Worcestershire sauce
3 eggs
One 1-pound container small curd cottage cheese
1 cup unflavored yogurt
¾ teaspoon salt, or to taste
¼ teaspoon pepper
⅛ teaspoon seasoned salt, or to taste
2 cups shredded Cheddar cheese

1. Preheat the oven to 350°F. Grease a 9 × 13-inch baking pan.

2. In a large skillet, heat the oil over medium-high heat. Add the zucchini, carrots, mushrooms, and broccoli. Cook, stirring, until softened, about 4 minutes. Stir in the noodles, dill weed, and Worcestershire sauce.

3. In a medium bowl, beat the eggs. Beat in the cottage cheese, yogurt, salt, pepper, and seasoned salt. Pour over noodle-vegetable mixture and toss. Add the Cheddar and toss again.

4. Spoon into prepared pan and bake 1 hour. Cut into 12 squares

Variation: Substitute Swiss cheese for the Cheddar.

Noodles with Sour Cream and Apple Sauce

Makes: 4¹/₂ cups; serves: 6 to 8

Although this is a side dish, it's a real comfort food for me, and I occasionally have a bowl for dinner.

8 ounces broad noodles (egg or no-yolk)
One 8-ounce container sour cream (³/₄ cup)
³/₄ cup chunky applesauce
¹/₂ cup golden or dark raisins
2 tablespoons sugar
¹/₂ teaspoon salt, or to taste

1. Cook noodles according to package directions, drain.

2. Return noodles to pot and stir in the sour cream, applesauce, raisins, sugar, and salt. Cook, stirring, until heated through.

Variation: Stir in ¹/₂ teaspoon ground cinnamon.

Beans

Since I usually use beans as an entree, I have not included many bean side dishes.

Frijoles

Makes: 2¹/₂ cups; serves: 3 to 4

The Mexican method is to cook beans without presoaking them. These beans are unbelievably delicious. Use them on tostadas, in burritos, or as a filling in other Mexican entrees.

3 cups water
1 cup dry pinto, black, or kidney beans
¹/₂ cup chopped onions
1 tablespoon minced, seeded jalapeño peppers, or more to taste
3 cloves garlic, minced, divided
1 bay leaf
¹/₄ teaspoon salt, or to taste
1 tablespoon vegetable oil
¹/₂ cup peeled, seeded, and chopped tomatoes

1. Place the water, beans, onions, peppers, 2 cloves of the minced garlic, and the bay leaf in a 2-quart saucepan. Bring to a boil over medium heat. Reduce heat and simmer, covered, 1¹/₂ hours or until beans are tender. Stir in the salt and discard the bay leaf; simmer 30 minutes longer.

2. In a small skillet, heat the oil over medium-high heat. Add the tomatoes and remaining clove of the garlic. Cook, stirring, until tomatoes soften, about 3 minutes.

3. Place the tomatoes and ¹/₄ cup of the beans in a food processor container fitted with a steel blade. Cover and process until smooth. Stir into the bean pot and cook 10 minutes longer.

REFRIED BEANS

Makes: 1¹/₃ cups; serves: 2 to 4

You can use frijoles left over from a previous meal, or buy Mexican beans (elRio makes some), which are pinto beans with chili sauce.

2 tablespoons vegetable oil
3 tablespoons minced onion
1 clove garlic, minced
¼ teaspoon ground cumin
1½ cups Frijoles (page 331) or Mexican beans

1. In a medium skillet, heat the oil over medium-high heat. Add the onion and garlic; cook, stirring, until onion is tender, about 2 minutes. Stir in the cumin until absorbed.

2. Add the beans and mash with a fork. Cook until dry.

Variation: For a spicier version, add ⅛ teaspoon ground red pepper when you add the cumin.

BARBECUE BEANS

Makes: 2¹/₂ cups; serves: 4

When I call for pepper sauce in this recipe I'm not referring to Tabasco or any other hot sauce, but rather a thick, brown sauce with a fruit base that usually includes tamarind (one brand is Pick-a-Pepper Sauce). If you don't have pepper sauce, you can substitute steak sauce.

1 cup chopped tomatoes
½ cup water
2 tablespoons tomato paste
1½ tablespoons firmly packed light brown or dark brown sugar
1½ tablespoons distilled white vinegar
1 tablespoon molasses
2 teaspoons pepper sauce (see note above)
½ teaspoon anchovy-free Worcestershire sauce
2 cloves garlic, minced
⅛ teaspoon salt, or to taste
4 drops Tabasco, or to taste
2 teaspoons vegetable oil
½ cup chopped onions
½ cup finely chopped green bell peppers
2 cups red kidney beans (cooked from dry; or canned, drained)

1. In a medium bowl, stir together the tomatoes, water, tomato paste, brown sugar, vinegar, molasses, pepper sauce, Worcestershire sauce, garlic, salt, and Tabasco; set aside

2. In a 2-quart saucepan, heat the oil over medium-high heat. Add the onions, and bell peppers; cook, stirring, until softened, about 3 minutes. Stir in the sauce mixture; bring to a boil. Reduce heat and simmer 15 minutes.

3. Stir in the beans. Simmer 10 minutes longer or until heated through.

Variation: Barbecue Sauce: Omit the beans and use the sauce as desired. Makes 1¹/₂ cups sauce.

BAKED BEANS

Makes: 2³/₄ cups; serves: 4

These sweet beans are not too hard to make, especially if you start with canned beans.

3 cups cooked, small white, navy, or great northern beans (cooked from dry; or canned, drained)

⅓ cup molasses

2 tablespoons firmly packed light brown or dark brown sugar

¼ cup minced onions

1 tablespoon distilled white vinegar

1 teaspoon dry mustard

½ teaspoon salt, or to taste

1¼ cups boiling water

1. Preheat the oven to 325°F.

2. In a 1½-quart casserole, combine the beans, molasses, brown sugar, onions, vinegar, mustard, and salt. Pour the water over the mixture. Bake, tightly covered, 3 to 4 hours or until sauce is thickened.

Variation: Add ¼ teaspoon Tabasco for a zippier bean.

BLACK BEANS WITH CELERY

Makes: 2 cups; serves: 4

Cooked according to this recipe, the beans get very soft and the dish looks like a mush, but tastes de-lish. For a better-looking (but equally tasty) dish, use the variation.

1 tablespoon olive oil

2 cups sliced celery

½ cup chopped onions

¼ cup chopped red bell peppers

2 cloves garlic

1 cup black beans (cooked from dry; or canned, drained)

¼ cup vegetable broth (pages 93–95)

1 tablespoon chopped fresh cilantro

⅛ teaspoon ground red pepper

1. In a 2-quart saucepan, heat the oil over medium-high heat. Add the celery, onions, bell peppers, and garlic; cook, stirring, until softened, about 3 minutes. Add the beans and broth; simmer, uncovered, 5 minutes. Stir in the cilantro and red pepper.

Variation: Sautéed Black Beans and Celery: Omit the broth and simmering step. Just add the beans, cilantro, and pepper; cook, stirring, until heated through.

GARBANZO BEANS WITH ESCAROLE

Makes: 2 cups; serves: 4

Garbanzo beans are just another name for chickpeas.

1 tablespoons olive oil

2 cloves garlic, minced

4 cups lightly packed chopped escarole

1½ cups garbanzo beans (cooked from dry; or canned, drained)

½ cup vegetable broth (pages 93–95)

1. In a 1½-quart saucepan, heat the oil over medium-high heat. Add the garlic; cook 10 seconds. Add the escarole; cook, stirring, until softened, about 2 minutes. Add the beans and broth. Simmer, uncovered, 10 minutes.

Variation: Use small white beans or cannellini instead of the garbanzo beans.

SUCCOTASH

Makes: 2¹⁄₃ cups; serves: 4

As written, this is a very rich side dish, which I serve only occasionally. The variation offers a lower-fat, vegan version.

1 tablespoon butter or margarine
1 tablespoon minced onion
One 10-ounce package frozen lima beans
One 8-ounce can corn kernels, undrained
3 tablespoons heavy cream
3 tablespoons water or vegetable broth
    (pages 93–95)
1⁄8 teaspoon salt, or to taste
1⁄8 teaspoon pepper

1. In a large skillet, melt the butter or margarine over medium-high heat. Add the onion; cook, stirring, until softened, about 1 minute. Add the remaining ingredients. Cook, uncovered, stirring occasionally, until the liquid has almost completely evaporated and vegetables are glazed, about 5 minutes.

Variation: For a vegan version, substitute broth for the heavy cream.

LENTILS IN TOMATO SAUCE

Makes: 3 cups; serves: 3 to 4

This highly seasoned dish tastes equally good served warm or at room temperature. If you puree the lentils, as suggested in the variation, you get a puree similar to an Ethiopian dish—just add extra ground red pepper.

1 tablespoon olive oil
1⁄2 cup chopped onions
2 cloves garlic, minced
1⁄2 cup water
2 tablespoons tomato paste
1⁄8 teaspoon salt, or to taste
1⁄4 teaspoon ground red pepper
1 1⁄2 cups cooked lentils (pages 13–14)

1. In a 1¹⁄₂-quart saucepan, heat the oil over medium-high heat. Add the onions and garlic; cook, stirring, until softened, about 2 minutes.

2. Add the water, tomato paste, salt, and red pepper; stir until combined. Add the lentils; cook, uncovered, 5 minutes or until heated through.

Variation: Place the lentils in a food processor container fitted with a steel blade. Cover and process until pureed.

PUREED LIMA BEANS WITH DILL

Makes: 1¹⁄₂ cups; serves: 3 to 4

These are the consistency of mashed potatoes, but I think they taste even better and look prettier.

One 10-ounce package frozen baby
    lima beans
1⁄4 cup vegetable broth (pages 93–95)
1⁄4 cup water
2 tablespoons fresh chopped dill
1 tablespoon butter or margarine
1⁄8 teaspoon salt, or to taste
1⁄8 teaspoon pepper

1. Place the beans, broth, and water in a 1-quart saucepan. Bring to a boil over medium-high heat. Cover and simmer 15 minutes or until the beans are quite soft.

2. Place the beans, along with any remaining cooking liquid, and the dill, butter or margarine, salt, and pepper in a food processor container fitted with a steel blade. Cover and process until smooth. If necessary, add 1 to 2 tablespoons extra water or broth to help puree the beans.

Ⓛ *Variation:* Buttered Lima Beans with Dill: Cook the beans according to directions, then instead of pureeing, drain them and toss with the butter, dill, salt, and pepper.

WHITE BEANS WITH TOMATOES AND BASIL

Makes: 2 cups; serves: 4

Black beans or chickpeas work just as well as white beans here.

1 tablespoon olive oil
1½ cups chopped tomatoes
2 cloves garlic, minced
1 cup white beans (cooked from dry; or canned, drained)
¼ cup chopped fresh basil
¼ cup chopped fresh parsley
¼ teaspoon salt, or to taste
⅛ teaspoon pepper

1. In a large skillet, heat the oil over medium-high heat. Add the tomatoes and garlic; cook, stirring, until heated through, about 3 minutes.

2. Add the beans, basil, parsley, salt, and pepper; cook, stirring, until heated through.

Variation: Add 2 tablespoons vinaigrette and serve as a warm or chilled salad.

SALADS

Vegetable Salads

The Gelles Family
Salad   339

Spanish Restaurant
Salad   340

Caesar Salad   340

Greek Salad   341

Antipasto Salad   341

Farmer's Market Salad   342

Mixed Greens with Vegetable
Threads   342

Mixed Greens with Grilled
Mushrooms   343

Romaine, Avocado, and
Cucumber Salad   343

Parsley Salad   344

Spinach Salad with Goat
Cheese Dressing   344

Spinach and Mushroom
Salad I   344

Spinach and Mushroom
Salad II   345

Baby Spinach Salad   345

Julienned Endive Salad with
Graeta Olive Dressing   346

Salad Greens with Baked
Goat Cheese   346

Endive Salad with Roasted
Red Pepper and Boursin
Dressing   347

Watercress, Cucumber, and
Onion Salad with Creamy
Pepper Dressing   347

Watercress and Romaine
with Roquefort
Dressing   348

Red, White, and Green Salad
with Balsamic Vinegar   348

South of the Border
Salad   348

Garden Vegetable
Salad   349

Chunky Salad   349

Tomato-Scallion Salad   350

Tomato-Mozzarella
Salad   350

Warm Tomato Salad   350

Tomato, Endive, and Hearts
of Palm Salad   351

Tomato and Feta Cheese
Salad   351

Tomato-Avocado Salad   351

Grilled Vegetable and Bread
Salad   352

Snap Pea–Tomato
Salad   352

Zucchini Salad   352

Asparagus and Hearts of
Palm Salad   353

Red Radish Salad   353

Wilted Cucumber
Salad   354

Cucumber Fennel
Salad   354

Cilantro Cucumber
Salad   354

Greek Cucumber
Salad   355

Cucumber, Endive, and
Radish Salad with Creamy
Mustard Dressing   355

Dilled Cucumber Salad   356

Basil-Mint Cucumber and
Pea Salad   356

Israeli Salad   356

Green Bean Salad with
Creamy Mustard
Dressing   357

Bell Pepper Salad   357

Broccoli Salad   357

Cardoon Salad with Roasted
Red Peppers   358

Health Salad   358

Pesto Cauliflower
Salad   358

Shredded Carrot and Jícama
Salad   359

Shredded Turnip with
Chopped Vegetables   359

Shredded Carrot and
Yellow Turnip Salad with
Cardamom Dressing   360

Moroccan Carrot
Salad   360

Coleslaw   360

Tricolor Coleslaw   361

Zucchini Coleslaw   361

Cabbage and Cashew
Salad   362

Red Cabbage Salad with
Ketchup Dressing   362

Wilted Sprout and
Watercress Salad   362

Potato Salad   363

Green Potato Salad   363

Broccoli-Potato Salad   364

Vegetable and Potato
Salad   364

Roasted Red Pepper and
Potato Salad   365

Fruit and Vegetable Salads

Waldorf Salad   365

Carrot-Apple Slaw   366

Shredded Red Cabbage and
Asian Pear Salad   366

Red Cabbage and Apple
Salad   366

Arugula Salad with Fruit
and Lime-Ginger
Dressing   367

Arugula, Honeydew, and
Raspberries with Honey-
Mustard Dressing   367

Arugula with Fresh Figs and
Feta Cheese   367

Strawberry–Belgian Endive
Salad   368

Endive and Radicchio Salad
with Fresh Raspberries   368

Blackberry-Endive
Salad   368

Bitter Greens with Pears and
Stilton Dressing   369

Spinach, Strawberry, and
Nectarine Salad   369

Pineapple, Red Pepper, and
Celery Salad   370

Fennel-Apple-Gouda
Salad   370

Beet and Pear Salad with
Honey-Yogurt Dressing   370

Grilled Fennel and Orange
Salad   371

Boston Lettuce with Jícama,
Oranges, and Almonds   371

Grain and Bean Salads

Wheat Berry Salad with
Tomatoes and Goat
Cheese   372

Wheat Berry–Vegetable
Salad   372

Wheat Berry–Corn
Salad   372

Tropical Wheat Berry
Salad   373

Tabouli   373

Apple-Bulgur Salad   374

Bulgur S-D-T Salad   374

Bulgur Salad with Sofrito
Dressing   374

Fruited Couscous
Salad   375

Creamy Couscous
Salad   375

Couscous Salad with
Oranges   376

Dilled Rice and Pea Salad   376

Spanish Rice Salad   376

Curried Coconut Rice Salad   377

Brown Rice and Lentil Salad   377

Brown Rice, Cantaloupe, and Apple Salad   378

Wild Rice Salad with Apples and Walnuts   378

Wild and White Rice Salad   379

Wild Rice and Rice Bean Salad   379

Kasha, Jícama, and Mandarin Orange Salad   380

Asian Millet Salad   380

Curried Millet Salad   380

Mandarin Quinoa Salad   381

Pasta Salad   381

Macaroni and Bean Salad   382

Stuffed Olive, Rice, and Roman Bean Salad   382

Sautéed Portobello Mushroom and Pinto Bean Salad   382

Lentil and Mushroom Salad   383

Warm Lentil Salad with Balsamic Dressing   383

French Lentil Salad with Hearts of Palm   384

Corn and Black Bean Salad   384

Black Bean and Olive Salad   384

Black Bean and Tomato Salad   385

Three-Bean Salad   385

Pigeon Bean and Corn Salad   386

Marinated Chickpea Salad   386

Chickpea and Grilled Vegetable Salad   386

Chickpea and Sprouted-Pea Salad   387

Fruit Salads

Jamaican Kiwi-Strawberry Salad   387

Grapefruit-Kiwi Salad   388

Winter Salad   388

Blueberry-Nectarine Salad   388

Peach and Strawberry Salad   388

Berry Berry Berry Good Fruit Salad   389

Papaya-Banana-Orange Salad   389

Calypso-Berry Salad   389

Mango-Strawberry Salad   389

Cantaloupe-Blueberry Salad   390

Summer Brunch Fruit Salad   390

Cottage Cheese and Fruit Salad   390

Dressings

Italian Dressing   391

French Vinaigrette   391

Russian Dressing   391

Herbed Buttermilk Dressing   392

Tahini Dressing   392

Feta Dressing   392

Fresh Herb Balsamic Vinaigrette   393

I think many people consider lettuce to be synonymous with the word *salad*. Although in the past lettuce and tomatoes were the most commonly available salads, nowadays anything goes. Pasta salad, rice salad, potato salad, bean salad, and even bread salad add interest and zing to meals. Furthermore, lettuce is not just iceberg anymore. Look for exciting lettuces and greens, such as mache, oak leaf (red or green), arugula, and endive, not to mention spinach, leaf (red or green), chicory, romaine, and Boston. There are no hard and fast rules to salad except that the end result should taste delicious. I suspect that salads, more than any other part of the meal, tend to be spontaneous creations rather than carefully followed recipes and I hope that some of these recipes will be jumping-off points for your artistic endeavors.

VEGETABLE SALADS

THE GELLES FAMILY SALAD

———————— V ♥ ————————

Makes: 7 cups; serves: 4

My mother's idea of a perfect salad is a wedge of iceburg lettuce with lots of Russian dressing (page 391), but Dad always preferred romaine, so romaine was the primary salad in our family. Dad's the dressing maker; his formula is once around the bowl with oil and twice with vinegar. So here's our salad. I usually prepare it with raw onion (as suggested in the variation), and I sometimes add a hit of garlic powder to the dressing.

8 cups bite-size pieces romaine lettuce
2 tablespoons red wine vinegar
1 tablespoon vegetable oil
Pinch salt
Pinch freshly ground black pepper

1. Place the lettuce in a large salad bowl. Add the vinegar, oil, salt, and pepper. Toss until combined.

Variation: Add sliced onion and/or tomato wedges to the salad.

SPANISH RESTAURANT SALAD

V ♥

Makes: 5 cups; serves: 4 to 6

The name speaks for itself. Be sure the onion is sliced paper-thin.

4 cups shredded iceberg lettuce
1½ cups halved and thinly sliced tomatoes
⅓ cup thinly sliced onions
1 tablespoon vegetable oil
1 tablespoon distilled white vinegar
⅛ teaspoon salt, or to taste
Freshly ground black pepper, to taste

1. In a large bowl toss together the lettuce, tomatoes, and onions. Sprinkle the oil, vinegar, salt, and pepper over the salad. Toss to combine.

Variation: Add pimientos and ¼ teaspoon dried oregano.

CAESAR SALAD

lo

Makes: 7 cups; serves: 4 to 6

Who needs anchovies for an outstanding Caesar salad? Not me! For a creamier dressing, prepare the dressing in a blender or food processor.

1 egg
1 tablespoon extra virgin olive oil
1 tablespoon minced oil-marinated sun-dried tomatoes
1 clove garlic, pressed
1½ tablespoons fresh lemon juice
1 teaspoon red wine vinegar
1 teaspoon Dijon mustard
¼ teaspoon anchovy-free Worcestershire sauce
¼ teaspoon salt, or to taste
8 cups bite-size pieces romaine lettuce
Freshly ground black pepper, to taste
3 tablespoons grated Parmesan cheese
Croutons (homemade, page 427, or store-bought)

1. Place the egg in boiling water for 1 minute. Crack the egg and discard the white. Place the yolk in a large salad bowl. Add the oil, sun-dried tomatoes, and garlic. Using a whisk, stir until combined. Add the lemon juice, vinegar, mustard, Worcestershire sauce, and salt. Whisk until completely combined.

2. Add the lettuce to the bowl. Toss until the dressing coats the lettuce. Grind some pepper over the salad and sprinkle with cheese and croutons. Toss again.

Variation: Add tomatoes, cucumbers, or other vegetables to the salad.

GREEK SALAD

— L —

Makes: 11 cups; serves: 6 to 8

This salad is large and satisfying enough to serve as a main dish. It is also a large side dish for 6. Try to use a really fine-quality feta cheese since it will set the character of the salad.

8 cups lightly packed bite-size pieces romaine lettuce
1½ cups tomato wedges
½ cup sliced scallions (1-inch pieces; white and green parts)
½ cup sliced radishes
3 tablespoons red wine vinegar
1 tablespoon vegetable oil
1 tablespoon extra virgin olive oil
1 teaspoon fresh lemon juice
¼ teaspoon dried oregano, crumbled
1 cup cucumber slices
12 green bell pepper rings
½ cup black olives
2 cups crumbled feta cheese

1. In a large bowl, toss together the lettuce, tomato wedges, scallions, and radishes.

2. In a small bowl, stir together the vinegar, both oils, the lemon juice, and oregano. Pour the dressing over the salad and toss to combine.

3. Arrange the salad on 6 or 8 serving plates. Top each with some the cucumber slices, green pepper rings, and olives. Sprinkle some feta cheese over the top.

Variations: For an even heartier salad, garnish each plate with 3 or 4 Stuffed Grape Leaves (homemade, page 72, or store-bought).

V Omit the feta cheese.

ANTIPASTO SALAD

— V —

Makes: 8 cups; serves: 6 to 8

This is an ideal salad to use as an entree, especially if you add the provolone cheese as suggested in the variation.

3 cups iceberg lettuce
1 cup cooked chickpeas (cooked from dry; or canned, drained)
1 cup celery chunks (1-inch pieces)
1 cup tomato wedges
½ cup sliced green bell peppers
½ cup marinated artichoke hearts (optional)
12 olives (black or green)
⅓ cup sliced red onions
¼ cup sliced roasted red peppers
6 pepperonici (pickled Italian peppers; optional)
2½ tablespoons red wine vinegar
1 tablespoon vegetable oil
1½ teaspoons extra virgin olive oil
½ clove garlic, minced
¼ teaspoon dried oregano, crumbled

1. In a large bowl, toss together the lettuce, chickpeas, celery, tomato wedges, bell peppers, artichoke hearts, olives, red onions, roasted peppers, and pepperonici.

2. In a small bowl, stir together the vinegar, both oils, and the garlic and oregano. Pour the dressing over the salad and toss to combine.

L **Variation:** Add 4 ounces provolone cheese, cut into strips.

FARMER'S MARKET SALAD

Makes: 3 cups; serves: 3 to 4

Some of the items in this salad I can only find at the large farmer's market that carries unusual produce. Gourmet produce markets carry these ingredients seasonally (in the spring); or you can grow them in your own garden. (Pea shoots are not sprouts, but about 2- to 4-inch-long vines with green leaves on top.)

1½ cups halved cherry tomatoes
1½ cups sliced Belgian endive
½ cup lightly packed pea shoots
½ cup lightly packed purslane
2 tablespoons chopped fresh basil
1 tablespoon extra virgin olive oil
1½ teaspoons white wine vinegar
¼ teaspoon dry mustard
⅛ teaspoon sugar
Pinch salt, or to taste
Pinch freshly ground black pepper, or to taste

1. In a large bowl, toss together the tomatoes, endive, pea shoots, and purslane.

2. In a small bowl, stir together the basil, oil, vinegar, mustard, sugar, salt, and pepper. Combine with the vegetables and serve.

Variations: Use seasoned vinegar, such as tarragon or garlic, instead of white wine vinegar.

Use halved tomato wedges instead of the cherry tomatoes.

MIXED GREENS WITH VEGETABLE THREADS

Makes: 5 cups; serves: 4

To make vegetable threads, you need a special gadget—a 4- or 5-holed zester. It looks like teeny weeny brass knuckles on a handle. If you don't have that, you can use a mandolin (the grater, not the musical instrument) set very fine. If all else fails, you can make long, thin strips with a vegetable peeler and then slice the strips into microthin julienne using a sharp knife.

1 peeled carrot
1 peeled beet
2 cups bite-size pieces red or green leaf lettuce
2 cups arugula (leave small leaves intact but very large leaves should be halved or quartered)
1 cup frisee or the inner leaves of chicory
2 tablespoons vegetable oil
2 teaspoons balsamic vinegar
2 teaspoons fresh lemon juice
2 teaspoons minced shallots
1 teaspoon Dijon mustard

1. At least 30 minutes before serving time, prepare the vegetable threads by running the length of the vegetable (carrot and beet) with a zester. Make enough threads to have 1 cup of each vegetable. Place in ice water to crisp until serving time. (You can prepare the threads well in advance and let them crisp in the refrigerator until you need them.)

2. In a large bowl, toss together the lettuce, arugula, and frisee.

3. In a small bowl, whisk together the oil, vinegar, lemon juice, shallots, and mustard. Pour over lettuce and toss to combine.

4. Place salad on 4 plates and top each with tangles of carrot and beet threads.

Variation: Use any mixture of salad greens.

MIXED GREENS WITH GRILLED MUSHROOMS

—————— V ——————

Makes: 4¹/₂ cups; serves: 4

Although I suggest cooling the mushrooms before adding to the salad, you can use them warm, too. You can use other wild mushrooms (like shiitake or porcini) and if they are small, you may only want to half them instead of slicing.

2½ tablespoons olive oil, divided
1 clove garlic, minced
¼ teaspoon dried thyme
3 medium portobello mushrooms (4- to 5-inch diameter; ½ pound)
6 cups bite-size pieces mixed lettuce (romaine, endive, radicchio, chicory, and leaf lettuce make a nice mixture)
1½ tablespoons red wine vinegar

1. Preheat the grill or broiler.

2. In a small bowl, stir together 1¹/₂ tablespoons of the olive oil and the garlic and thyme. Brush over the top of the mushroom(s). Place 4 inches from heat and cook, brushed side up, 4 minutes, until mushroom is cooked through. Cool and slice; set aside.

3. In a large bowl, toss together the lettuces with the remaining 1 tablespoon olive oil and the vinegar. Place ¹/₄ of the salad on each of 4 serving plates. Top each salad with ¹/₄ of the mushroom slices.

Variation: Use cultivated mushrooms instead of portobellos.

ROMAINE, AVOCADO, AND CUCUMBER SALAD

—————— L ——————

Makes: 4 cups; serves: 3 to 4

Use any blue cheese if you don't have Roquefort.

4 cups bite-size pieces romaine lettuce
1 cup avocado slices
1 cup sliced cucumber
¹/₃ cup sliced red onions
¹/₄ cup unflavored yogurt
2 tablespoons mayonnaise
3 tablespoons firmly packed Roquefort cheese
Freshly ground black pepper to taste

1. In a large bowl, toss together the lettuce, avocado, cucumber, and onions.

2. In a small bowl, stir together the yogurt and mayonnaise. Add the Roquefort and pepper and stir until combined. Pour the dressing over the salad, grind pepper over the top, and toss to combine.

Variation: Add tomato wedges or cherry tomatoes.

PARSLEY SALAD

Makes: 2¹/₂ cups; serves: 4

Serve this salad with spicy-garlicky dishes (the parsley should neutralize the garlic breath).

2 cups coarsely chopped fresh parsley
½ cup diced tomatoes (¼-inch pieces)
⅓ cup finely chopped mild onions
2 tablespoons fresh lime juice
1 tablespoon vegetable oil
⅛ teaspoon salt, or to taste
Freshly ground black pepper to taste

1. In a medium bowl, toss together the parsley, tomatoes, and onions. Add the lime juice, oil, salt, and pepper; toss to combine.

Variation: Add ⅓ cup finely chopped celery.

SPINACH SALAD WITH GOAT CHEESE DRESSING

Makes: 5 cups; ¹/₂ cup dressing; serves: 4 to 6

You have to use a soft goat cheese so it will blend into the dressing. You may even want to make the dressing in the blender.

6 cups lightly packed bite-size pieces fresh
     spinach
½ cup julienned red bell peppers
¼ cup sliced red onions
¼ cup buttermilk
3 tablespoons soft goat cheese
1 tablespoon mayonnaise
½ clove garlic, minced
⅛ teaspoon dried thyme
Freshly ground black pepper to taste

1. In a large bowl, toss together the spinach, bell peppers, and onions.

2. In a small bowl, stir together the buttermilk, goat cheese, mayonnaise, garlic, and thyme. Pour the dressing over the salad, grind pepper on top, and toss to combine.

Variation: Use a combination of lettuces instead of just spinach.

SPINACH AND MUSHROOM SALAD I

Makes: 6¹/₂ cups; serves: 4 to 6

If you serve this as a main dish salad, you may want to garnish it with sliced or chopped hard-cooked eggs for a heartier dish.

6 cups lightly packed bite-size pieces fresh
     spinach
1½ cups sliced mushrooms
⅓ cup thinly sliced red onions
3 tablespoons extra virgin olive oil
1½ tablespoons fresh lemon juice
1 teaspoon Dijon mustard
¼ teaspoon dried tarragon
½ clove garlic, minced
Pinch salt
Pinch freshly ground black pepper

1. In a large bowl, toss together the spinach, mushrooms, and onions.

2. In a small bowl, stir together the oil, lemon juice, mustard, tarragon, garlic, salt, and pepper. Pour the dressing over the salad and toss to combine.

Variation: Add hard-cooked egg slices or wedges.

SPINACH AND MUSHROOM SALAD II

[V] [♥]

Makes: 6 cups; serves: 4 to 6

I know many people are turned off by imitation bacon bits, but if you're fond of them, this is a good place to sprinkle them.

6 cups lightly packed bite-size pieces fresh spinach

2 cups sliced mushrooms

1/3 cup sliced Vidalia onions (or other mild onions, such as Bermuda)

2 tablespoons imitation bacon bits (optional)

2 tablespoons balsamic vinegar

1 tablespoon vegetable oil

1 teaspoon raspberry mustard (page 471) or Dijon mustard

1. In a large bowl, toss together the spinach, mushrooms, onions, and bacon bits.

2. In a small bowl, stir together the vinegar, oil, and mustard. Pour the dressing over the salad and toss to combine.

▣ *Variation:* Use Caesar dressing (page 340) instead of the balsamic.

BABY SPINACH SALAD

[V]

Makes: 8¹/₂ cups; serves: 6 to 8

Baby spinach is just that, but it has very tender leaves and a delicious flavor. If you can't find baby spinach, grown-up spinach will be fine too— just tear the leaves into bite-size pieces.

8 cups loosely packed baby spinach leaves, thoroughly rinsed

1 large Belgian endive, cut into bite-size pieces

1/2 cup sliced red onions

1/2 cup sliced red bell peppers

2 tablespoons pumpkin seeds

3 tablespoons balsamic vinegar

1¹/₂ tablespoons vegetable oil

2 teaspoons country-style Dijon mustard

1/2 teaspoon grated orange rind

1. In a large bowl, toss together the spinach, endive, onions, bell peppers, and pumpkin seeds.

2. In a small bowl, stir together the vinegar, oil, mustard, and orange rind.

3. Pour the dressing over the salad and toss to combine.

Variation: Lemon-Scented Balsamic Dressing: Use 1 teaspoon regular Dijon mustard (instead of country-style) and lemon rind instead of orange rind.

JULIENNED ENDIVE SALAD WITH GRAETA OLIVE DRESSING

Makes: 4 cups; serves: 3 to 4

Graeta olives are very flavorful small black olives. If you can't find them, Kalamata olives would be a suitable substitution.

2 large Belgian endives
3 tablespoons finely chopped Graeta olives
1½ tablespoons extra virgin olive oil
1 tablespoon fresh lemon juice
½ teaspoon grated lemon rind
½ teaspoon Dijon mustard
½ clove garlic, minced
Pinch salt

1. Cut endives in half lengthwise; remove core from root end. Julienne the halves and place in a large bowl.

2. In a medium bowl, stir together the olives, oil, lemon juice, lemon rind, mustard, garlic, and salt until combined. Pour the dressing over the endives and toss to combine.

Variation: Substitute 2 cups arugula for one of the endives.

SALAD GREENS WITH BAKED GOAT CHEESE

[L]

Makes: 4½ cups; serves: 4 to 6

It's nice to serve this salad with slices of French bread on each plate so the cheese can be eaten on the bread.

¼ cup extra virgin olive oil, divided
2 tablespoons chopped fresh basil
2 tablespoons chopped fresh parsley
1 teaspoon minced shallots
¼ teaspoon dried rosemary, crumbled
⅛ teaspoon dried thyme
One 6-ounce log soft goat cheese (such as Montrachet)
¼ cup unflavored dry bread crumbs
6 cups bite-size pieces assorted greens (lettuce, Belgian endive, radicchio, arugula, watercress, and the like)
1 tablespoon red wine vinegar
1 teaspoon Dijon mustard

1. Pour 3 tablespoons of the oil into an 8-inch-square baking pan. Stir in the basil, parsley, shallots, rosemary, and thyme.

2. Slice the cheese into 8 rounds. Place in the pan with the herbs; turn once to coat. Let stand 1 hour.

3. Remove the cheese from the pan. Dredge the cheese in the bread crumbs.

4. Drain the oil into a small bowl (scrape any herbs in the pan into the bowl with the oil); set aside.

5. Return breaded cheese rounds to the pan (which is now fairly empty but oiled) and bake at 375°F for 7 minutes or until warm and soft.

6. While the cheese is baking, in a large bowl, combine the various lettuces.

7. Add the remaining tablespoon of oil and the vinegar and mustard to the bowl with the herbs; stir until combined. Pour the dressing over the salad and toss to combine. Divide salad onto 4 or 6 serving plates and place 1 or 2 cheese rounds on each.

ENDIVE SALAD WITH ROASTED RED PEPPER AND BOURSIN DRESSING

— L —

Makes: 5¹/₂ cups; serves: 4 to 6

Boursin is a garlic-herb cheese widely available in supermarkets. If yours doesn't carry it, Allouette is a similar product, or you can use Garlic-Herb Cheese Spread (page 46).

3 cups Belgian endive slices (cut crosswise into 1-inch pieces)
2 cups lightly packed arugula
½ cup julienned red bell peppers
⅓ cup sliced red onions
⅓ cup buttermilk
¼ cup softened Boursin
Pinch salt, or to taste
Freshly ground black pepper, to taste

1. In a large bowl, toss together the endive, arugula, bell peppers, and onions.

2. In a small bowl, stir together the buttermilk, Boursin, and salt until combined. Pour the dressing over the salad, grind pepper on top, and toss to combine.

Variation: Add tomato wedges or halved cherry tomatoes.

WATERCRESS, CUCUMBER, AND ONION SALAD WITH CREAMY PEPPER DRESSING

— L ♥ —

Makes: 4 cups; serves: 4 to 6

Watercress is a fairly bitter, peppery green. If you prefer sweeter lettuce such as green or red leaf, substitute it for half or most of the watercress.

3 cups lightly packed watercress (1 bunch)
1 cup sliced, peeled cucumber
⅓ cups sliced red onions
¼ cup sour cream
¼ cup buttermilk
1 small clove garlic, minced
¼ teaspoon coarsely ground pepper, or more to taste
⅛ teaspoon dried oregano

1. In a large bowl, toss together the watercress, cucumber, and onions.

2. In a small bowl, stir together the remaining ingredients. Pour the dressing over the salad and toss to combine.

Variations: Crumble Stilton, Roquefort, or other blue cheese over the dressed salad.

♥ For a lower-fat version, use unflavored yogurt instead of the sour cream.

WATERCRESS AND ROMAINE WITH ROQUEFORT DRESSING

L

Makes: 6 cups; serves: 4 to 6

Although I used Roquefort, Danish blue or Stilton would work as well.

4 cups bite-size pieces romaine lettuce
2 cups watercress
1/3 cup sliced red onions
3 tablespoons buttermilk
3 tablespoons Roquefort cheese
1 tablespoon mayonnaise
Freshly ground black pepper, to taste

1. In a large bowl, toss together the lettuce, watercress, and onions.

2. In a small bowl combine the buttermilk, cheese, and mayonnaise, using a fork to mash the cheese. Pour the dressing over the salad, top with ground pepper, and toss to combine.

Variation: Add halved cherry tomatoes.

RED, WHITE, AND GREEN SALAD WITH BALSAMIC VINEGAR

V

Makes: 7 cups; serves: 5 to 7

Arugula, called rocket on the West Coast, has a bitter, peppery flavor that some people are crazy about and others are not too fond of. I prefer to use homemade roasted red peppers (page 276), but you can use jarred ones without losing too much flavor. You can add other vegetables, such as cucumber or fresh fennel slices, to this salad.

6 cups arugula
1 1/2 cups bite-size pieces Belgian endive
3/4 cup roasted red pepper strips
1/4 cup chopped walnuts
2 tablespoons balsamic vinegar
2 tablespoons minced red onion
1 tablespoon extra virgin olive oil
1 teaspoon fresh lemon juice
1 teaspoon orange liqueur (optional)

1. In a large bowl, toss together the arugula, endive, pepper strips, and walnuts.

2. In a small bowl, stir together the remaining ingredients. Pour the dressing over the salad and toss to combine.

Variation: Use spinach or romaine lettuce instead of some or all of the arugula.

SOUTH OF THE BORDER SALAD

Makes: 4 cups; serves: 4 to 6

Although all the ingredients are available most places in the country, the lime and cilantro dressing gives this a Mexican feeling.

1 1/2 cups peeled, cubed cucumbers
1 cup cubed tomatoes
1 cup celery chunks (3/4-inch pieces)
12 pitted ripe olives, halved
1/4 cup chopped red onions
3 tablespoons fresh lime juice
1 1/2 tablespoons extra virgin olive oil
1/4 cup chopped fresh cilantro
1/8 teaspoon salt, or to taste

1. In a large bowl, toss together the cucumbers, tomatoes, celery, olives, and onions.

2. In a small bowl, stir together the remaining ingredients. Pour the dressing over the salad and toss to combine.

Variation: Add 1 cup green bell pepper chunks.

GARDEN VEGETABLE SALAD

Makes: 4¹/₂ cups; serves: 4 to 6

This salad is made with vegetables commonly grown by the summer gardener, who is usually looking for new ways to use the season's crop.

1 cup sliced green beans (1¹/₂-inch pieces)
2 cups chopped tomatoes
1 cup peeled, sliced cucumber
1 cup green bell pepper chunks
2 tablespoons chopped fresh basil
2 tablespoons sliced scallions (white and
    green parts)
1 tablespoon vegetable oil
1 tablespoon red wine vinegar
1 teaspoon extra virgin olive oil
¹/₄ teaspoon salt, or to taste
Freshly ground black pepper, to taste

1. Blanch the green beans in boiling water 1 minute, or until bright green. Drain and chill.

2. In a large bowl, combine the tomatoes, cucumber, pepper chunks, basil, scallions, and chilled green beans.

3. In a small bowl, combine the vegetable oil, vinegar, olive oil, and salt. Add to the salad, grind pepper on top, and toss to combine.

Variation: Add (or substitute) zucchini, red peppers, cherry tomatoes, or any vegetable that you like to eat raw.

CHUNKY SALAD

Makes: 5 cups; serves: 4 to 6

Don't prepare this too far in advance of serving or the avocado will turn brown.

1¹/₂ cups celery chunks (1-inch pieces)
1¹/₂ cups diced tomatoes
1 cup peeled, cubed cucumber (1-inch pieces)
³/₄ cup diced avocado
¹/₂ cup sliced green bell peppers
12 ripe olives, halved
2 tablespoons chopped fresh cilantro
2 tablespoons red wine vinegar
1 tablespoon vegetable oil
2 teaspoons extra virgin olive oil
¹/₂ clove garlic, minced

1. In a large bowl, toss together the celery, tomatoes, cucumber, avocado, peppers, olives, and cilantro.

2. In a small bowl, stir together the remaining ingredients. Pour the dressing over the salad and toss to combine.

Variation: Add 4 ounces sliced provolone cheese, cut into strips.

TOMATO-SCALLION SALAD

Makes: 4 cups; serves: 4 to 6

This so-simple salad is really tasty, especially if you let it stand for even longer than the recommended minimum time.

4 cups chopped tomatoes
½ cup sliced scallions (¼-inch pieces; white and green parts)
1 tablespoon red wine vinegar
¼ teaspoon salt, or to taste
Freshly ground black pepper, to taste

1. Combine all the ingredients in a large bowl. Let stand at least 10 minutes to let the flavors meld.

Variations: Stir in ¼ cup chopped fresh basil or 2 teaspoons dried basil.

Tomato-Bean Salad: Add 1 to 2 cups cooked white beans to the salad (with or without herbs).

TOMATO-MOZZARELLA SALAD

L

Makes: 4½ cups; serves: 4 to 6

I like to use fresh mozzarella in this recipe. If you live near an Italian grocery you may be able to find it. Otherwise, Polly-O makes a fresh mozzarella cheese that comes packed in water.

3 cups chopped tomatoes
1½ cups diced mozzarella (½-inch pieces)
½ cup chopped fresh basil
2 teaspoons extra virgin olive oil
¼ teaspoon salt, or to taste
¼ teaspoon pepper

1. In a large bowl toss together all the ingredients.

Variation: Arranged Tomato-Mozzarella Salad: Use 12 slices of tomato and 12 slices mozzarella and arrange in concentric circles on a platter. Sprinkle with the basil, oil, salt and pepper.

WARM TOMATO SALAD

V

Makes: 2¾ cups; serves: 4

Sort of a cross between a vegetable and a salad, this delicious dish can be served as an appetizer as well as a salad.

1½ tablespoons extra virgin olive oil
4 cups tomato wedges
¼ cup sliced scallions (white and green parts)
2 teaspoons red wine vinegar
⅛ teaspoon salt, or to taste
Freshly ground black pepper, to taste

1. In a large skillet, heat the oil over medium-high heat. Add the tomatoes; cook, stirring, until warmed and slightly softened, about 2 minutes.

2. Remove from heat and stir in the remaining ingredients. Serve warm.

Variation: Add ¼ cup chopped fresh basil when you add the scallions.

TOMATO, ENDIVE, AND HEARTS OF PALM SALAD

Makes: 2¹/₂ cups; serves: 3 to 4

I've never seen fresh hearts of palm, so I always use the canned ones.

1¹/₂ cups chopped tomatoes
1 cup sliced Belgian endive
1 cup chopped hearts of palm
¹/₃ cup diced green bell peppers
¹/₃ cup sliced scallions (white and green parts)
1 tablespoon red wine vinegar
2 teaspoons extra virgin olive oil
Freshly ground black pepper, to taste

1. In a large bowl, toss together the tomatoes, endive, hearts of palm, peppers, and scallions. Add the remaining ingredients. Toss to combine.

Variation: Add ¹/₂ cup chopped walnuts.

TOMATO AND FETA CHEESE SALAD

L

Makes: 3¹/₂ cups; serves: 4 to 6

Kalamata olives are really excellent in this salad, but you'll have to pit them.

3 cups diced tomatoes
¹/₂ cup halved ripe black olives
¹/₃ cup sliced red onions
1 tablespoon extra virgin olive oil
1 tablespoon red wine vinegar
¹/₂ cup crumbled feta cheese
Freshly ground black pepper, to taste

1. In a large bowl, toss together the tomatoes, olives, and onions. Add the oil and vinegar. Toss to combine. Add the feta cheese, grind the pepper on top, and toss again.

Variation: Add ¹/₂ teaspoon dried oregano.

TOMATO~AVOCADO SALAD

V

Makes: 4 cups; serves: 4 to 6

The vinegar prevents the avocado from turning brown too quickly.

3 cups coarsely chopped tomatoes
1 cup chopped avocado
¹/₄ cup sliced scallions (¹/₄-inch pieces; white and green parts)
1 tablespoon red wine vinegar
2 teaspoons vegetable oil
¹/₈ teaspoon salt, or to taste
Freshly ground black pepper, to taste

1. In a large bowl, toss together the tomatoes, avocado, and scallions. Add the remaining ingredients; toss to combine.

Variation: Use red onion instead of scallions.

GRILLED VEGETABLE AND BREAD SALAD

——— V ———

Makes: 5 cups; serves: 4 to 6

The best bread for this salad would be a foccacia or other coarse-grained bread; semolina bread would also be very good.

2 cups diced tomatoes
2 cups diced assorted grilled vegetables
    (page 233)
1½ tablespoons red wine vinegar
1 tablespoon extra virgin olive oil
⅛ teaspoon salt, or to taste
1½ cups cubed (¾-inch) day-old bread
Freshly ground black pepper, to taste

1. In a large bowl, toss together the tomatoes, vegetables, vinegar, oil, and salt. Let stand ½ hour.

2. Just before serving, toss in bread cubes. Grind pepper on top and toss again.

Variation: Add ⅓ cup chopped ripe olives.

SNAP PEA–TOMATO SALAD

——— V ———

Makes: 3 cups; serves: 4

Snap peas, also called sugar snaps, are available in late spring and early summer. If you can't find them, substitute snow peas. Prepare this salad just before serving so the snap peas retain their nice bright color; if you dress it too far in advance they turn a sort of khaki color.

2 cups cubed tomatoes
1½ cups blanched snap peas
¼ cup sliced scallions (green and white parts)
¼ cup chopped fresh parsley
1 tablespoon red wine vinegar
2 teaspoons extra virgin olive oil
⅛ teaspoon dried thyme
⅛ teaspoon salt, or to taste
Freshly ground black pepper, to taste

1. In a large bowl, toss together the tomatoes, snap peas, scallions, and parsley. Pour the oil and vinegar over the salad and toss to combine. Add the thyme, salt, and pepper and toss again.

Variation: Add ½ cup chopped red bell peppers.

ZUCCHINI SALAD

——— V ♥ ———

Makes: 4½ cups; serves: 6 to 8

Substitute yellow squash for all or part of the zucchini if you like.

3 cups diced zucchini (½-inch pieces)
¾ cup diced green bell peppers
¾ cup chopped celery
⅓ cup chopped red onions
1½ tablespoons vegetable oil
1½ tablespoons cider vinegar
1 teaspoon sugar
⅛ teaspoon salt, or to taste
Freshly ground black pepper, to taste

1. In a large bowl, toss together the zucchini, green peppers, celery, and onions.

2. In a small bowl, stir together the oil, vinegar, sugar, and salt until sugar dissolves. Pour the dressing over the salad, grind pepper on top, and toss to combine.

Variations: Add 1 cup corn (fresh, cooked; canned, drained; or frozen, thawed).

Add 1 cup chopped tomatoes.

ASPARAGUS AND HEARTS OF PALM SALAD

— [V] —

Makes: 4 cups; serves: 4 to 6

This elegant and delicious salad can be served as described, or you can cut the asparagus into bite-size pieces instead of leaving them whole. If your asparagus are thick, you may want to quarter them lengthwise.

36 blanched thin asparagus (about ¾ pound)
One 14-ounce can hearts of palm, drained and quartered lengthwise
⅓ cup sliced pitted black olives
1 tablespoon extra virgin olive oil
2 teaspoons vegetable oil
2 teaspoons white wine vinegar
1 teaspoon Dijon mustard
¼ teaspoon dried tarragon

1. On a large plate, combine the asparagus and hearts of palm; sprinkle the olives over them.

2. In a small bowl, stir together the remaining ingredients. Pour the dressing over the salad and toss to combine.

Variation: Add roasted red pepper strips.

RED RADISH SALAD

— [O] —

Makes: 2 cups; serves: 4

Salting the radishes (and onion) before adding the dressing decreases the sharpness of the ingredients.

3 cups thinly sliced red radishes
¼ cup sliced red onions
Salt
2 tablespoons sour cream
2 tablespoons mayonnaise
2 tablespoons chopped fresh dill or 1 teaspoon dried dill weed
Freshly ground black pepper, to taste

1. In a large bowl, liberally sprinkle the radishes and onions with salt. Let stand 20 minutes. Rinse thoroughly to remove salt; drain.

2. In a small bowl, stir together the sour cream, mayonnaise, and dill. Pour the dressing over the radishes and onions, grind pepper on top, and toss to combine.

Variation: Use chopped fresh parsley instead of dill.

WILTED CUCUMBER SALAD

Makes: 2½ cups; serves: 4 to 6

We eat this salad on all holidays. It's great-tasting and light because it doesn't have any oil.

6 cups peeled, very thinly sliced cucumbers
    (3 large cucumbers)
¾ cup very thinly sliced onions
1½ teaspoons salt
1 cup water
2 tablespoons distilled white vinegar
1 tablespoon sugar
Freshly ground black pepper, to taste

1. In a large bowl, place 2 cups of the cucumbers and ¼ cup of the onions, then sprinkle liberally with ½ teaspoon of the salt. Repeat with 2 cups more cucumbers, ¼ cup onions, ½ teaspoon salt, then the last 2 cups of cucumbers, ¼ cup onions, and remaining ½ teaspoon salt. Place a small plate over the cucumbers and weight them down (I usually use a quart jar filled with water). Let stand at room temperature at least 1 hour.

2. Drain off any water that has accumulated around the cucumbers. Pick up a large handful of the wilted vegetables and squeeze them until all the water runs out. Place the squeezed vegetables into a clean bowl. Continue squeezing until all the salt water is out of the cucumbers and onions.

3. In a medium bowl, combine 1 cup water, the vinegar, sugar, and pepper. Stir until sugar has dissolved. Pour over vegetables and chill.

Variation: Add ½ clove garlic, minced, to the dressing.

CUCUMBER FENNEL SALAD

Makes: 3 cups; serves: 4

The flavors of the fennel and basil are somewhat similar and complement each other.

2 cups sliced cucumbers
1 cup sliced fennel
2 tablespoons chopped fresh basil
1 tablespoon extra virgin olive oil
1 tablespoon white wine vinegar

1. In a large bowl, combine the cucumbers, fennel, and basil. Add the oil and vinegar and toss to combine.

Variation: Use chopped fresh parsley instead of basil.

CILANTRO CUCUMBER SALAD

Makes: 3 cups; serves: 4 to 6

I find that most people either love or hate the flavor of cilantro. In most recipes, you can substitute chopped fresh parsley for the cilantro and not lose too much flavor. In this recipe, however, the cilantro is a very important element—and if you're not fond of it, try a different cucumber salad.

3 cups chopped peeled cucumbers (seeded, if
    desired)
2 tablespoons chopped cilantro
2 tablespoons chopped scallions (white and
    green parts)
2 tablespoons minced red bell peppers
2 tablespoons fresh lime juice
2 teaspoons vegetable oil
¼ teaspoon salt, or to taste
Freshly ground black pepper, to taste

1. In a large bowl, stir together the cucumbers, cilantro, scallions, and red peppers.

2. In a small bowl, stir together the lime juice, oil, and salt. Pour the dressing over the salad, grind pepper on top, and toss to combine.

Variation: Use green bell peppers instead of red.

GREEK CUCUMBER SALAD

— ⬜ —

Makes: 3³/₄ cups; serves: 4 to 6

If your feta cheese is very salty, soak it in cool water for 10 minutes before crumbling.

3 cups diced, peeled cucumbers (³/₄-inch pieces)
¹/₃ cup sliced scallions (¹/₄-inch pieces; green parts only)
¹/₄ cup snipped fresh dill
1¹/₂ tablespoons fresh lemon juice
1¹/₂ tablespoons extra virgin olive oil
¹/₈ teaspoon salt
¹/₂ cup crumbled feta cheese
Freshly ground black pepper, to taste

1. In a medium bowl, toss together the cucumbers, scallions, and dill. Add the lemon juice, oil, and salt. Toss to combine. Add the feta cheese, grind the pepper on top, and toss again.

Variation: Add ¹/₂ teaspoon oregano when you add the dill.

CUCUMBER, ENDIVE, AND RADISH SALAD WITH CREAMY MUSTARD DRESSING

— 🔲❤️ —

Makes: 4¹/₂ cups; Serves: 4 to 6

Although sliced red radishes add a lovely color to the salad, they tend to be quite sharp. For a milder salad, you may want to use sliced daikon radish (large white Japanese radish) instead of the red.

2 cups peeled, thinly sliced cucumbers
2 cups julienned endive
1 cup thinly sliced radishes
¹/₄ cup paper-thin sliced red onions
2 tablespoons mayonnaise
1 tablespoon unflavored yogurt
1¹/₂ teaspoons Dijon mustard
1 teaspoon white wine vinegar
¹/₄ teaspoon dried tarragon

1. In a medium bowl, toss together the cucumbers, endive, radishes, and onions.

2. In a small bowl, stir together the remaining ingredients. Pour the dressing over the salad and toss to combine.

Variation: Omit the tarragon from the dressing.

DILLED CUCUMBER SALAD

Makes: 3 cups; serves: 4 to 6

The combination of dill, cucumbers, and yogurt makes this an especially refreshing salad—a perfect accompaniment to spicy foods.

3 cups sliced cucumbers
⅓ cup sliced scallions (white and green parts)
½ cup unflavored yogurt
¼ cup chopped fresh dill
1 clove garlic, minced
⅛ teaspoon salt, or to taste
Freshly ground black pepper, to taste

1. In a medium bowl combine the cucumbers and scallions.

2. In a small bowl, stir together the yogurt, dill, garlic, and salt. Pour over cucumbers, grind pepper on top, and toss to combine.

Variation: Use chopped fresh cilantro instead of dill (of course, then it's not dilled anymore).

BASIL~MINT CUCUMBER AND PEA SALAD

Makes: 2½ cups; serves: 3 to 4

The herbs complement each other and the result is a super salad.

2 cups seeded, chopped, peeled cucumbers
½ cup peas (fresh, cooked and cooled; or frozen, thawed)
2 tablespoons chopped fresh basil
1 tablespoon chopped fresh mint
3 tablespoons unflavored yogurt
1 tablespoon mayonnaise

⅛ teaspoon salt, or to taste
Freshly ground black pepper, to taste

1. In a medium bowl, toss together the cucumbers, peas, basil, and mint.

2. In a small bowl, stir together the yogurt, mayonnaise, and salt. Pour the dressing over the salad, grind pepper on top, and toss to combine.

Variation: Add ¼ cup chopped red bell peppers.

ISRAELI SALAD

Makes: 3 cups; serves: 4 to 6

It's common practice in Israel to have salad for breakfast. You dice up anything that appeals to you (pieces should be about ¼ inch) and set the bowl of vegetables on the table. The vegetables I've suggested here are just a few of the multitude of possibilities (radishes and even pickles are also popular ingredients in these salads).

1½ cups diced tomatoes
1 cup diced cucumbers
½ cup diced green bell peppers
2 tablespoons chopped onion
2 teaspoons extra virgin olive oil
¼ teaspoon salt, or to taste
Freshly ground black pepper, to taste

1. In a medium bowl, combine all the ingredients.

Variations: If you're used to tart salads, you can add red wine vinegar or distilled white vinegar to taste.

Bean, Olive, and Vegetable Salad: Stir together one recipe of Israeli Salad with a recipe of Black Bean and Olive Salad (page 384) for a delicious new dish entirely.

GREEN BEAN SALAD WITH CREAMY MUSTARD DRESSING

— 🔲 —

Makes: 7 cups; Serves: 6 to 8

This divine, rich salad is great for party buffets. The green beans look great whole but are a little hard to eat gracefully, so feel free to cut them in half for more bite-size pieces.

6 cups whole green beans, ends trimmed (about 1 pound)
1 cup sliced white mushrooms
½ cup walnut halves
3 tablespoons mayonnaise
2 tablespoons unflavored yogurt
2 teaspoons Dijon mustard
⅛ teaspoon salt, or to taste
Freshly ground black pepper, to taste

1. Cook the green beans in boiling water to desired doneness. Drain and rinse under cold water until cooled; drain.

2. Place green beans in large bowl with mushrooms and walnuts.

3. In a small bowl, stir together the mayonnaise, yogurt, mustard, and salt. Pour the dressing over the salad, grind pepper on top, and toss to combine.

Variation: For an even richer dressing, substitute sour cream for the yogurt.

BELL PEPPER SALAD

— 🔲🔲 —

Makes: 3 cups; serves: 4 to 6

Naked, this salad is nice for topping pita sandwiches or stirring into cottage cheese. I diced all my vegetables into ¹⁄₂-inch pieces.

1½ cups diced red bell peppers
1 cup diced cucumber
½ cup diced green bell peppers
⅓ cup diced onions
2 tablespoons chopped fresh cilantro or parsley
1 tablespoon distilled white vinegar
1 teaspoon extra virgin olive oil
¼ teaspoon salt, or to taste
Freshly ground black pepper, to taste

1. In a large bowl, toss together all the ingredients.

Variation: Black Bean–Bell Pepper Salad: Add 1 cup cooked black beans and ¹⁄₂ cup sliced black olives; add 2 teaspoons vegetable oil and 1 more teaspoon white vinegar.

BROCCOLI SALAD

— 🔲🔲 —

Makes: 4 cups; serves: 4 to 6

My mom always made this simple salad with leftover cooked broccoli. Frankly, I always preferred broccoli this way to warm. I've even been known to just defrost frozen broccoli spears and use them in this salad.

5 cups bite-size pieces broccoli (stems and florets)
3 tablespoons red wine vinegar
1½ tablespoons vegetable oil
Salt and pepper, to taste

1. Cook the broccoli in salted boiling water until tender. Chill.

2. Toss broccoli with the remaining ingredients.

Variation: You can make this salad with any leftover cooked vegetable: cauliflower, green beans, and others.

CARDOON SALAD WITH ROASTED RED PEPPERS

Makes: 4 cups; serves: 6 to 8

Cardoon looks like a mean celery with a thyroid problem, but the flavor is quite mild. Although you can use jarred roasted red peppers in this recipe, I think homemade (page 276) are much better in dishes where their flavor is such an important factor.

3 cups cooked, diced cardoon (¾-inch pieces; page 329)
¾ cup diced roasted red bell peppers
⅓ cup sliced scallions (white and green parts)
2 tablespoons chopped fresh parsley
1 tablespoon extra virgin olive oil
2 teaspoons fresh lemon juice
2 teaspoons red wine vinegar
1 small clove garlic, pressed

1. In a large bowl, toss together the cardoon, red peppers, scallions, and parsley.

2. In a small bowl, combine the oil, lemon juice, vinegar, and garlic. Pour the dressing over the salad and toss to combine.

Variation: Add 3 tablespoons chopped fresh basil when you add the parsley.

HEALTH SALAD

Makes: 4 cups; serves: 4 to 6

I'm not sure why delicatessens call this "health salad" since it uses more oil than almost any other salad in this chapter. It's one of the few recipes for which I choose to use the food processor for slicing and shredding. This recipe stays fresh up to 10 days.

3 cups shredded cabbage
1 cup peeled, thinly sliced cucumber
1 cup thinly sliced carrots
¾ cup thinly sliced onions
½ cup thinly sliced red or green bell peppers
⅓ cup vegetable oil
¼ cup distilled white vinegar
1½ teaspoons sugar
2 cloves garlic, pressed
½ teaspoon salt, or to taste
Freshly ground black pepper, to taste

1. In a large bowl, toss together the cabbage, cucumber, carrots, onions, and peppers. In a medium bowl, stir together the remaining ingredients. Add to salad and toss to combine. Let stand at least 4 hours, or preferably overnight, for the flavors to meld.

Variation: You can use thinly sliced celery instead of the cucumber, and add ½ teaspoon celery seed.

PESTO CAULIFLOWER SALAD

Makes: 4 cups; serves: 4 to 6

Use homemade or store-bought pesto for this dressing.

½ medium head cauliflower
1 tablespoon extra virgin olive oil
1 tablespoon vegetable oil
1 tablespoon red wine vinegar
1 tablespoon pesto (homemade, page 476, or store-bought)
1 teaspoon Dijon mustard
½ cup chopped red bell peppers

1. Break the cauliflower into florets (you should have 4 cups); blanch in boiling water. Drain and cool.

2. In a large bowl, stir together both oils and the vinegar, pesto, and mustard. Add the cauliflower and peppers; toss to combine.

SHREDDED CARROT AND JÍCAMA SALAD

Makes: 3 cups; serves: 4 to 6

This is a very lightly dressed salad. If you're comfortable with a more conventional dressing, just add extra oil. The coriander flavor is very subtle here—add more to taste.

2 cups coarsely shredded carrots
1 1/2 cups coarsely shredded jícama
1 tablespoon cider vinegar
2 teaspoons vegetable oil
1/8 teaspoon ground coriander
1/8 teaspoon salt, or to taste

1. In a medium bowl, toss together the carrots and jícama. Add the remaining ingredients and toss to combine.

Variation: Stir in 1/2 cup finely diced fresh pineapple or crushed canned pineapple, drained.

SHREDDED TURNIP WITH CHOPPED VEGETABLES

Makes: 3 cups; serves: 4 to 6

I used shredded white turnip, but you can use yellow (rutabaga) or even celeriac (knob celery) instead.

2 cups coarsely shredded turnips
1/2 cup finely diced red bell peppers
1/2 cup finely chopped celery
1/4 cup sliced scallions (green and white parts)
1/4 cup snipped fresh dill
1 1/2 tablespoons vegetable oil
1 tablespoon cider vinegar
1 teaspoon honey mustard
1/8 teaspoon salt, or to taste
Freshly ground black pepper, to taste

1. In a large bowl, toss together the turnips, peppers, celery, scallions, and dill.
2. In a small bowl, stir together the oil, vinegar, mustard, and salt. Pour the dressing over the salad, grind pepper on top, and toss to combine.

Variation: Add 1/3 cup chopped fresh parsley when you add the dill.

SHREDDED CARROT AND YELLOW TURNIP SALAD WITH CARDAMOM DRESSING

— [V] —

Makes: 3¹/₂ cups; serves: 4 to 6

Yellow turnip, also know as rutabaga, is much sweeter and less sharp than its cousin, the white turnip.

¹/₂ cup slivered almonds
1¹/₂ cups coarsely shredded yellow turnips
1¹/₂ cups coarsely shredded carrots
1 cup coarsely shredded apples
1 tablespoon vegetable oil
1 tablespoon fresh lemon juice
1 tablespoon apple juice
1¹/₂ teaspoons honey
1 teaspoon soy sauce
¹/₂ teaspoon ground cardamom

1. Bake the almonds on a piece of aluminum foil in a 350°F oven for 10 minutes; set aside.

2. In a large bowl, combine the turnips, carrots, and apples.

3. In a small bowl, stir together the remaining ingredients, except the almonds. Pour the dressing over the salad and toss to combine. Add the almonds and toss again.

[L] **Variation:** Shredded Carrot and Yellow Turnip Salad with Cheese: Add 1 cup of coarsely shredded Monterey Jack cheese and ¹/₂ cup golden raisins to the salad when you add the almonds.

MOROCCAN CARROT SALAD

— [V] —

Makes: 2 cups; serves: 4

This features a really unusual combination of flavors. If you're not fond of mint, use chopped fresh cilantro or parsley instead.

2 cups coarsely shredded carrots
¹/₂ cup golden raisins
2 tablespoons chopped fresh mint
2 tablespoons extra virgin olive oil
1¹/₂ tablespoons fresh lemon juice
1 clove garlic, minced
¹/₂ teaspoon sugar
¹/₄ teaspoon ground cinnamon
¹/₈ teaspoon ground cumin
¹/₈ teaspoon salt, or to taste
¹/₈ teaspoon ground red pepper

1. In a large bowl toss together the carrots, raisins, and mint.

2. In a small bowl, stir together the remaining ingredients. Pour the dressing over the salad and toss to combine.

Variation: Omit the red pepper. Add ¹/₂ cup drained, crushed pineapple.

COLESLAW

— [LO] —

Makes: 4¹/₂ cups; serves: 6 to 8

You can serve this right away, but it's really better if you let it stand at least one hour, to let the cabbage wilt.

5 cups shredded cabbage
1 cup shredded carrots
1/2 cup mayonnaise
2 tablespoons unflavored yogurt
2 teaspoons distilled white vinegar
1/2 teaspoon salt, or to taste
Freshly ground black pepper, to taste

1. In a large bowl, toss together the cabbage and carrots.

2. In a small bowl, stir together the remaining ingredients. Pour the dressing over the salad and let stand.

Variations: Stir in 1/4 to 1/2 teaspoon celery seed.

Use all mayonnaise instead of yogurt.

TRICOLOR COLESLAW

Makes: 4 cups; serves: 6 to 8

Lorraine Klein thought this salad was wonderful, but she would have liked some caraway seeds in it—I was thinking celery seed. You can add either, or even poppy seed if you like.

2 cups shredded red cabbage
2 cups shredded green cabbage
1 cup shredded carrots
1/4 cup chopped fresh parsley, or 1 1/2
    tablespoons dried parsley
3 tablespoons vegetable oil
2 tablespoons cider vinegar
1 teaspoon dried mustard
1 teaspoon sugar
1/2 teaspoon salt, or to taste
Freshly ground black pepper, to taste

1. In a large bowl, toss together both cabbages, the carrots, and parsley.

2. In a small bowl, stir together the oil, vinegar, mustard, sugar, and salt. Pour the dressing over the salad, grind pepper on top, and toss to combine. Let stand at least one hour to wilt.

Variation: Add 1/2 cup finely chopped green bell peppers to the salad.

ZUCCHINI COLESLAW

Makes: 2 1/2 cups; serves: 4

If you don't like the idea of a slightly sweet coleslaw, just leave out the pineapple.

1 1/2 cups chopped cabbage
1 cup coarsely shredded zucchini
3/4 cup finely chopped fresh pineapple
1/3 cup finely chopped green bell peppers
1/4 cup mayonnaise
1 tablespoon thinly sliced scallions (green
    part only)
1/8 teaspoon salt, or to taste
Freshly ground black pepper, to taste

1. In a large bowl, toss together the cabbage, zucchini, pineapple, and peppers. Add the remaining ingredients; toss to combine.

Variation: Substitute coarsely shredded carrots for the zucchini.

CABBAGE AND CASHEW SALAD

— V —

Makes: 6 cups; serves: 4 to 6

I came up with this particular combination of ingredients by happy accident. I was snacking on some cashews while preparing the ingredients for Ethiopian Vegetable Stew (page 163). I had some extra cabbage and tried the two together—et voilà.

4 cups shredded cabbage
1 cup coarsely chopped roasted cashews
1/3 cup thinly sliced red onions
1/4 cup chopped fresh parsley
2 tablespoons vegetable oil
1 tablespoon white wine vinegar
1 tablespoon fresh lemon juice
1/2 teaspoon salt, or to taste

1. In a large bowl, toss together the cabbage, cashews, onions, and parsley. Add the remaining ingredients and toss to combine.

Variation: Add 1/2 cup raisins.

RED CABBAGE SALAD WITH KETCHUP DRESSING

— V —

Makes: 4 1/2 cups; serves 6 to 8

I know it may sound weird, but this is one of my mother's great recipes. She would make this salad whenever we were running low on ketchup. She'd just add oil and vinegar to the mostly empty ketchup bottle and shake and pour over the salad. This tangy salad is perfect to pep up a dish like vegetarian burgers.

6 cups shredded red cabbage
1 1/2 cups shredded carrots
6 tablespoons ketchup
1/4 cup vegetable oil
2 tablespoons red wine vinegar
1/4 teaspoons salt, or to taste
Freshly ground black pepper, to taste

1. In a large bowl, toss together the cabbage and carrots.

2. In a small bowl stir together the ketchup, oil, vinegar, and salt. Pour the dressing over the salad, grind pepper on top, and toss to combine.

3. Let stand an hour or two, stirring occasionally, before serving.

WILTED SPROUT AND WATERCRESS SALAD

— V —

Makes: 2 1/2 cups; serves: 4

Serve this salad warm or at room temperature.

1 tablespoon vegetable oil
2 cups fresh mung bean sprouts
4 cups lightly packed watercress (1 bunch)
1/2 cup sliced scallions (1-inch pieces; green and white parts)
2 teaspoons mirin (rice wine) or dry sherry
2 teaspoons rice vinegar
1 1/2 teaspoons sesame oil
1/4 teaspoon soy sauce, or to taste
1/2 clove garlic, minced

1. In a large skillet, heat the oil over medium-high heat. Add the sprouts, watercress, and scallions; cook, stirring, until wilted, about 2 minutes.

2. Add the mirin, vinegar, oil, soy sauce, and garlic. Let cool.

Variation: Add 1 tablespoon toasted sesame seeds.

POTATO SALAD

Makes: 3 cups; serves: 4 to 6

I like to use boiling potatoes for potato salad because I think the texture is better than baking potatoes.

3 cups sliced cooked potatoes (peeled or unpeeled)
1/4 cup mayonnaise
2 tablespoons unflavored yogurt
1 teaspoon cider vinegar
1 teaspoon grated onion or onion juice
1/2 teaspoon spicy brown mustard
1/4 teaspoon salt, or to taste
Freshly ground black pepper, to taste

1. Place the potatoes in a large bowl. In a small bowl, stir together the mayonnaise, yogurt, vinegar, onion, mustard, and salt. Pour the dressing over the potatoes, grind pepper on top, and toss to combine.

Variation: Add 1/2 cup finely chopped green peppers and/or celery.

GREEN POTATO SALAD

Makes: 4 cups; serves: 6 to 8

I'm not a great lover of commercial potato salad, but I do love this homemade one.

3 cups cubed red bliss or boiling potatoes (1-inch pieces; 1 pound)
1/2 cup lightly packed fresh parsley leaves
2 tablespoons extra virgin olive oil
1 tablespoon red wine vinegar
1 cup diced celery
1/2 cup sliced scallions (green part only)
1/4 cup finely chopped green bell peppers
1/2 teaspoon salt, or to taste
Freshly ground black pepper, to taste

1. Cook the cubed potatoes in boiling, salted water, 15 to 20 minutes or until tender; drain and cool to room temperature.

2. Place the parsley, oil, and vinegar into a blender or food processor container fitted with a steel blade. Cover and process until finely chopped.

3. In a large bowl, combine the potatoes, celery, scallions, bell peppers, salt, and parsley mixture. Grind pepper on top and toss until combined. Chill until serving time.

Variations: Greek Potato Salad: Add 1/2 cup chopped Kalamata olives when you add the celery. For a lacto version, you can also stir in crumbled feta cheese. Taste before salting since the olives and cheese are both very salty ingredients.

Broccoli-Potato Salad

Makes: 4 cups; serves: 6 to 8

If you're fond of caraway seeds, you can add them to this salad.

3 cups cubed red bliss or boiling potatoes
(¾-inch pieces; 1 pound)
2 cups broccoli florets
½ cup shredded carrots
¼ cup chopped scallions (green and
white parts)
3 tablespoons unflavored yogurt
2 tablespoons vegetable oil
1 tablespoon mayonnaise
1 tablespoon cider vinegar
2 teaspoons balsamic vinegar
2 teaspoons spicy brown mustard
1 teaspoon sugar
½ teaspoon salt, or to taste
Freshly ground black pepper, to taste

1. Cook the cubed potatoes in boiling water 10 to 15 minutes, until tender. Drain and chill.

2. Cook the broccoli in boiling water until tender-crisp, about 4 minutes; drain and chill.

3. In a large bowl, toss together the potatoes, broccoli, carrots, and scallions.

4. In a small bowl, stir together the yogurt, oil, mayonnaise, both vinegars, the mustard, sugar, and salt. Pour the dressing over the salad, grind pepper on top, and toss to combine.

Variations: Use green beans instead of broccoli.

♥ Lower-fat version: Use ¼ cup nonfat yogurt instead of the yogurt plus mayonnaise; decrease the oil to 1 tablespoon and the cider vinegar to 1 teaspoon.

Vegetable and Potato Salad

Makes: 4½ cups; serves: 4 to 6

The vegetables add a nice crunchy texture to the potato salad. Add chopped hard-cooked eggs for a creamier salad.

3 cups cooked, cubed potatoes (¾-inch
pieces; 1 pound; peeled or unpeeled)
¾ cup chopped celery
¾ cup shredded carrots
½ cup finely chopped green bell peppers
½ cup cooked peas (fresh or frozen)
¼ cup chopped fresh parsley
½ cup mayonnaise
2 teaspoons spicy brown mustard
1 teaspoon distilled white vinegar
½ teaspoon caraway seeds
½ teaspoon salt, or to taste
Freshly ground black pepper, to taste

1. In a large bowl, toss together the potatoes, celery, carrots, bell peppers, peas, and parsley.

2. In a small bowl, stir together the mayonnaise, mustard, vinegar, caraway seeds, and salt. Pour the dressing over the salad, grind pepper on top, and toss to combine.

Variation: Substitute ¼ teaspoon celery seed for the caraway seeds.

ROASTED RED PEPPER AND POTATO SALAD

Makes: 3 cups; serves: 4 to 6

The red pepper is an important flavor here, so I like to use homemade roasted peppers instead of the jarred ones.

3 cups cooked, cubed potatoes (¾-inch pieces; 1 pound; peeled or unpeeled)
½ cup diced roasted red bell peppers (page 276)
¼ cup chopped fresh parsley
1½ tablespoons mayonnaise
1 tablespoon vegetable oil
2 teaspoons cider vinegar
1½ teaspoons spicy brown mustard
½ teaspoon salt, or to taste
Freshly ground black pepper, to taste

1. In a large bowl, toss together the potatoes, roasted peppers, and parsley.

2. In a small bowl, stir together the mayonnaise, oil, vinegar, mustard, and salt. Pour the dressing over the salad, grind pepper on top, and toss to combine.

Variation: Add ½ cup finely chopped celery.

FRUIT AND VEGETABLE SALADS

Fruits add a particularly delicious contrast to vegetable salads.

WALDORF SALAD

Makes: 3½ cups; serves: 4

This is an update of an old standard, but lower-fat yogurt is substituted for some of the mayonnaise. For a pretty presentation, serve on a bed of red or green leaf lettuce or Boston lettuce.

2 cups chopped apples
2 teaspoons fresh lemon juice
1 cup chopped celery
½ cup chopped walnuts
2 tablespoons golden or dark raisins or currants
½ cup vanilla yogurt
2 tablespoons mayonnaise

1. In a medium bowl, toss the apples with the lemon juice. Add the celery, walnuts, and raisins and toss to combine.

2. In a small bowl, stir together the yogurt and mayonnaise. Pour the dressing over the salad and toss to combine.

Variation: Substitute lemon yogurt for the vanilla.

CARROT-APPLE SLAW

Makes: 3 cups; serves: 4 to 6

Crunchy like coleslaw, but sweeter.

3 cups coarsely shredded carrots
1 cup coarsely shredded tart apples
½ cup thinly sliced celery
¼ cup mayonnaise
¼ teaspoon celery seeds
¼ teaspoon salt, or to taste

1. In a large bowl, toss together the carrots, apples, and celery. Add the remaining ingredients. Toss until combined.

Variation: Use ½ teaspoon caraway seeds instead of the celery seeds.

SHREDDED RED CABBAGE AND ASIAN PEAR SALAD

Makes: 2⅔ cups; serves: 3 to 5

Asian pears, sometimes called apple-pears, taste similar to pears, with the consistency of crisp apples. Like apples and pears, you can use them peeled or unpeeled (although I prefer peeling them for this recipe). If you can't find them in your market, you'd be better off substituting shredded jícama than apple or pear.

2 cups shredded red cabbage
1 cup coarsely shredded Asian pears
⅓ cup golden raisins
1 tablespoon fresh lemon juice
1 tablespoon extra virgin olive oil
⅛ teaspoon salt, or to taste

1. Place all the ingredients in a large bowl and toss to combine. Let stand at least 15 minutes for the flavors to meld.

Variation: Add 1 cup chopped walnuts.

RED CABBAGE AND APPLE SALAD

Makes: 6 cups; serves: 4 to 6

This "slaw" is a very nice alternative to more conventional coleslaws. It's lighter and prettier, too, and perfect for picnics or barbecues.

3 cups shredded red cabbage
1½ cups chopped McIntosh apples (peeled or unpeeled)
1 cup thinly sliced celery
3 tablespoons vegetable oil
1½ tablespoons cider vinegar
1 tablespoon fresh lemon juice
1½ teaspoons sugar
1 teaspoon dry mustard
½ teaspoon salt, or to taste

1. In a large bowl, toss the cabbage, apples, and celery until combined.

2. In a small bowl, stir together the oil, vinegar, lemon juice, sugar, mustard, and salt. Pour the dressing over the salad and toss to combine.

Variation: Stir in ½ cup golden raisins.

Arugula, Radicchio, and Belgian Endive

The bitterness of arugula, radicchio, and Belgian endive contrasts nicely with fruit. If you can't find arugula or radicchio (or don't like them), you can use romaine lettuce or watercress instead.

ARUGULA SALAD WITH FRUIT AND LIME~GINGER DRESSING

Makes: 6¹/₂ cups; serves: 4 to 6

2 cups packed arugula leaves (1 bunch)
2 cups radicchio leaves (1 small head)
1 cup chopped McIntosh apples
½ cup fresh orange segments
½ cup sliced red onions
⅓ cup chopped kiwifruit
2 tablespoons fresh lime juice
1½ tablespoons extra virgin olive oil
1 teaspoon dried mustard
1 teaspoon grated fresh ginger, or
    ¼ teaspoon ground ginger
1 teaspoon sugar

1. In a large bowl, toss together the arugula, radicchio, apples, orange, onions, and kiwifruit.

2. In a small bowl, stir together the remaining ingredients. Pour the dressing over the salad and toss to combine.

Variation: Use endive instead of the radicchio and/or watercress instead of the arugula.

ARUGULA, HONEYDEW, AND RASPBERRIES WITH HONEY~ MUSTARD DRESSING

Makes: 4¹/₂ cups; serves: 4

2 cups loosely packed arugula leaves (cut into bite-size pieces, if large)
1 cup julienned endive
1 cup chopped honeydew (¾-inch pieces)
½ cup raspberries
1 tablespoon balsamic vinegar
2 teaspoons extra virgin olive oil
1 teaspoon honey mustard

1. In a large bowl, toss together the arugula, endive, honeydew, and raspberries.

2. In a small bowl, stir together the remaining ingredients. Pour the dressing over the salad and toss to combine.

Variation: Use cantaloupe instead of honeydew and blackberries instead of raspberries.

ARUGULA WITH FRESH FIGS AND FETA CHEESE

Makes: 5 cups; serves: 3 to 4

4 cups loosely packed arugula leaves
2 cups quartered fresh figs
½ cup crumbled feta cheese
2 tablespoons sunflower seeds
4 teaspoons raspberry vinegar
1 tablespoon extra virgin olive oil

1. Place all the ingredients in a large bowl and toss to combine.

Variation: Substitute coarsely chopped walnuts for the sunflower seeds.

STRAWBERRY–BELGIAN ENDIVE SALAD

Makes: 6 cups; serves: 4 to 6

Use a light hand with the nutmeg so it doesn't overwhelm the other flavors in the salad. If your strawberries are very tart, you may want to use extra honey in the dressing.

2 large Belgian endives (about 7 ounces each)
2 cups sliced strawberries
¼ cup paper-thin slices red onions
2 tablespoons fresh lemon juice
1 tablespoon extra virgin olive oil
1½ teaspoons honey
⅛ teaspoon salt
Pinch ground nutmeg

1. Slice the endives, widthwise, into ¼-inch-thick semicircles. Toss in a large bowl with the strawberries and red onion.

2. In a small bowl, stir together the lemon juice, oil, honey, salt, and nutmeg. Pour the dressing over the salad and toss to combine.

Variation: Add ½ cup sliced kiwifruit.

ENDIVE AND RADICCHIO SALAD WITH FRESH RASPBERRIES

Makes: 4 cups; serves: 4

This is one of my "company" dishes. When I make this for a casual meal, I treat it as a regular tossed salad, but when I serve it to guests I arrange the ingredients carefully: first a bed of radicchio leaves, then the julienned endive, topped with the raspberries and walnuts.

1 large head endive, julienned
1 small head radicchio
1 tablespoon chopped fresh cilantro or Italian parsley
2 tablespoons balsamic vinegar
1 tablespoon extra virgin olive oil
1 teaspoon Dijon mustard
½ cup fresh raspberries
¼ cup chopped walnuts

1. Place the endive, radicchio, and cilantro in a large bowl.

2. In a small bowl, stir together the vinegar, oil, and mustard. Pour over greens and toss to combine.

3. Place on 4 serving plates and top each with 2 tablespoons of the raspberries and 1 tablespoon of the walnuts.

Variation: Substitute orange segments for the raspberries.

BLACKBERRY–ENDIVE SALAD

Makes: 5 cups; serves: 4

4 cups bite-size pieces red leaf lettuce
2 cups julienned endive
1 cup blackberries
1 tablespoon Raspberry Vinegar (page 470–71)
1 tablespoon extra virgin olive oil
1 teaspoon Raspberry Mustard (page 471)

1. In a large bowl, toss together the lettuce, endive, and blackberries.

2. In a small bowl, stir together the remaining ingredients until combined. Pour the dressing over the salad and toss to combine.

BITTER GREENS WITH PEARS AND STILTON DRESSING

——————— 🔲 ———————

Makes: 8 cups; serves: 6 to 8

Stilton is called the "queen of cheeses" for good reason—it's divine. But it must be ripe; underripe Stilton tends to taste more like the queen of soap. Ask the salesperson to let you taste the cheese before purchasing it. If you can't find ripe Stilton, Roquefort is a good substitute.

1 large head endive, cut into 1-inch pieces
1 bunch watercress
1 large ripe pear, cut into thin slices
½ cup crumbled ripe Stilton
⅓ cup buttermilk
2 tablespoons sour cream
2 tablespoons mayonnaise
Additional Stilton

1. Toss together the endive and watercress. Place on 6 or 8 serving plates. Place some of the pear slices on top.

2. In a medium bowl, stir together ¹/₂ cup Stilton, the buttermilk, sour cream, and mayonnaise. Spoon over each salad. Top each with additional Stilton.

Variations: Substitute a tart apple for the pear. Sprinkle with chopped walnuts.

Stilton Dip: Prepare dressing as described in this recipe (or you may want to double it), and serve as a dip with crudités.

SPINACH, STRAWBERRY, AND NECTARINE SALAD

——————— 🔲 ———————

Makes: 6 cups; serves: 4 to 6

My friend Irwin Srob loved this salad so much he insisted on having the recipe right away—he didn't want to wait the two years for the book to come out. (P.S. He entered the recipe in a cooking contest and won first prize!)

6 cups lightly packed bite-size pieces fresh spinach
1 cup sliced nectarines
1 cup sliced strawberries
1 tablespoon vegetable oil
1 tablespoon fresh lemon juice
1 tablespoon balsamic vinegar
1 teaspoon sugar
1 teaspoon dry mustard
1 tablespoon sunflower seeds (optional)

1. In a large bowl, toss together the spinach, nectarines, and strawberries.

2. In a small bowl, stir together the remaining ingredients. Pour the dressing over the salad and toss to combine. Sprinkle with seeds.

Variation: Substitute peaches for the nectarines and raspberries for the strawberries.

PINEAPPLE, RED PEPPER, AND CELERY SALAD

V ♥

Makes: 4 cups; serves: 4 to 6

This is another of those lightly dressed salads. You can add more oil if you prefer that style of salad.

2 cups fresh pineapple chunks (¾-inch pieces)
1 cup celery chunks (1-inch pieces)
¾ cup cubed red bell peppers (1-inch pieces)
1 teaspoon dried mint
1 tablespoon fresh lime juice
1 teaspoon extra virgin olive oil
½ teaspoon minced crystallized or fresh ginger
½ teaspoon sugar
⅛ teaspoon salt, or to taste

1. In a large bowl, toss together the pineapple, celery, and bell peppers.

2. In a small bowl, stir together the remaining ingredients. Pour the dressing over the salad and toss to combine.

Variation: Omit the mint and use chopped fresh coriander instead.

FENNEL-APPLE-GOUDA SALAD

L

Makes: 4½ cups; serves: 4 to 6

My student intern, Martha Lee, felt this would be a perfect salad to take on a picnic. I agreed and suggested that with the caraway seeds, you wouldn't even notice any ants that might wander into the salad. She didn't think I was funny! Vegans can omit the cheese for a delightful salad.

2 cups sliced fennel
1½ cups chopped tart apple
1 cup diced Gouda cheese
1 tablespoon vegetable oil
1 tablespoon fresh lemon juice
2 teaspoons cider vinegar
1 teaspoon caraway seeds
½ teaspoon dried mustard
¼ teaspoon sugar

1. In a large bowl, toss together the fennel, apple, and Gouda.

2. In a small bowl, stir together the remaining ingredients. Pour the dressing over the salad and toss to combine.

Variation: Use celery instead of fennel.

BEET AND PEAR SALAD WITH HONEY-YOGURT DRESSING

L ♥

Makes: 2½ cups; serves: 4

The beets turn the yogurt magenta, but hopefully that won't put you off.

2 cups shredded, peeled fresh beets
1 cup peeled, thinly sliced pear
2 tablespoons chopped fresh cilantro
1 tablespoon chopped scallions (green and white parts)
¼ cup unflavored yogurt
2 teaspoons honey
½ teaspoon grated orange rind
¼ teaspoon salt, or to taste

1. In a medium bowl, stir together the beets, pear, cilantro, and scallions.

2. In a small bowl, stir together the remaining ingredients. Pour the dressing over the salad and toss to combine.

Variation: Use sliced apple instead of pear.

GRILLED FENNEL AND ORANGE SALAD

[V]

Makes: 4 cups; serves: 6

It always amazes me how much flavor tiny pignoli add to any recipe—this recipe is a great example.

2 tablespoons pine nuts (pignoli)
2 large fennel bulbs, or several smaller fennel bulbs (2 pounds total)
2 oranges
1/3 cup red onion wedges
1 tablespoon extra virgin olive oil
1 1/2 tablespoon white wine vinegar
1 teaspoon fresh rosemary, or 1/4 teaspoon dried rosemary

1. Cook the pine nuts in a dry skillet over medium heat until toasted; set aside.

2. Cut the fennel into wedges 1/4 to 1/2 inch thick.

3. Preheat the grill or broiler (if using a broiler, place the fennel on a lightly greased pan). Grill or broil 7 to 10 minutes per side (6 inches from the heat) or until blackened. Cool.

4. Remove the skin and pith from the oranges. Slice and cut the slices into quarters.

5. In a medium bowl, combine the fennel, oranges, and onion.

6. In a small bowl, stir together the remaining ingredients. Pour the dressing over the fennel mixture and toss to combine.

Variation: For a very unusual salad, try grapefruit segments instead of oranges.

BOSTON LETTUCE WITH JÍCAMA, ORANGES, AND ALMONDS

[V]

Makes: 6 cups; serves: 4 to 6

This salad can also make a very pretty composition. Instead of tossing all the ingredients together, dress the lettuce and onions, then arrange the orange slices on top and sprinkle with the almonds.

1/3 cup slivered almonds
6 cups bite-size pieces Boston lettuce
3/4 cup fresh orange segments
3/4 cup julienned jícama
1/2 cup sliced red onions
1 1/2 tablespoons vegetable oil
1 tablespoon orange juice
2 teaspoons balsamic vinegar
2 teaspoons red wine vinegar
1/2 teaspoon dry mustard
1/2 teaspoon sugar
Freshly ground black pepper, to taste

1. Toast the almonds in a 350°F oven for 10 minutes; set aside.

2. In a large bowl, toss together the lettuce, oranges, jícama, onions, and almonds.

3. In a small bowl, stir together the oil, orange juice, both vinegars, the mustard, and sugar. Pour the dressing over the salad, grind pepper on top, and toss to combine.

Variation: For a bittersweet salad, replace half the orange segments with grapefruit sections.

Grain and Bean Salads

These salads can easily be used as main dishes by altering the portion size.

Wheat Berry Salad with Tomatoes and Goat Cheese

Makes: 3¹/4 cups; serves: 6

If you use a fairly hard goat cheese such as feta, it will hold together better than a softer one, such as Montrachet, which will almost become part of the dressing (although it tastes great this way, too).

1½ cups cooked and cooled wheat berries (whole grain wheat, page 301)
1 cup chopped tomatoes
³/4 cup chopped cucumber
¼ cup chopped scallions (green and white parts)
¼ cup chopped fresh parsley
1½ tablespoons vegetable oil
1 tablespoon wine vinegar
½ teaspoon Dijon mustard
¼ teaspoon salt, or to taste
½ cup crumbled goat cheese

1. In a large bowl, toss together the wheat berries, tomatoes, cucumber, scallions, and parsley.

2. In a small bowl, stir together the oil, vinegar, mustard, and salt. Pour the dressing over the salad and toss to combine.

3. Sprinkle the cheese over the salad and toss again.

Ⓥ *Variation:* Omit the goat cheese.

Wheat Berry–Vegetable Salad

Makes: 3¹/4 cups; serves: 4 to 6

If your balsamic vinegar is sharp, you may want to use 2 teaspoons instead of the 1 tablespoon of mellow balsamic. If Kalamata olives are too strong-tasting for you, or are hard to find, small black olives will do fine.

1½ cups cooked and cooled wheat berries (whole grain wheat, page 301)
1 cup diced cucumber
½ cup diced red bell peppers
½ cup halved Kalamata olives
¼ cup chopped scallions (green and white parts)
1 tablespoon vegetable oil
1 tablespoon balsamic vinegar
¼ teaspoon salt, or to taste
Freshly ground black pepper, to taste

1. In a large bowl, combine the wheat berries, cucumber, bell peppers, olives, and scallions. Add the remaining ingredients and toss to combine.

Variation: Use celery instead of cucumber.

Wheat Berry–Corn Salad

Makes: 3 cups; serves: 4 to 6

This salad is dressed more heavily than most. You can start with 1 tablespoon oil and 2 teaspoons cider vinegar and see what you think. I felt it needed the extra.

1 ½ cups cooked and cooled wheat berries
  (whole grain wheat, page 301)
1 cup corn kernels (fresh, cooked; canned,
  drained; or frozen, thawed and cooked)
½ cup chopped green bell peppers
⅓ cup chopped roasted red peppers
¼ cup sliced scallions (green and white parts)
1 ½ tablespoons vegetable oil
1 tablespoon cider vinegar
¼ teaspoon salt, or to taste
Freshly ground black pepper, to taste

1. In a large bowl, combine the wheat berries, corn, bell peppers, roasted peppers, and scallions. Add the remaining ingredients and toss to combine.

Variation: Add ½ cup chopped celery.

TROPICAL WHEAT BERRY SALAD

— Ⅴ —

Makes: 3 cups; serves: 4 to 6

I don't know if strawberries are really tropical, but papaya certainly is.

1 ½ cups cooked and cooled wheat berries
  (whole grain wheat, page 301)
1 cup sliced strawberries
½ cup chopped papaya
½ cup chopped jícama
¼ cup sliced scallions (green and white parts)
3 tablespoons shredded coconut (fresh
  or sweetened)
2 tablespoons fresh lime juice
1 ½ tablespoons extra virgin olive oil
2 teaspoons sugar
¼ teaspoon salt, or to taste
⅛ teaspoon ground red pepper

1. In a large bowl, toss together the wheat berries, strawberries, papaya, jícama, scallions, and coconut.

2. In a small bowl, stir together the lime juice, oil, sugar, salt, and red pepper. Pour the dressing over the salad and toss to combine.

Variation: Add 1 cup sliced banana.

TABOULI

Makes: 3⅓ cups; serves: 4 to 6

The key elements in this Middle Eastern salad are bulgur, chopped vegetables, and mint. The dressing is quite light and the mint adds to the refreshing feeling. If you are using bulgur that is already cooked, use 1½ cups and omit step 1.

1 cup water
½ cup bulgur
¾ cup chopped tomatoes
¾ cup chopped cucumber
⅓ cup chopped fresh parsley
¼ cup chopped fresh mint
¼ cup chopped scallions (green and white
  parts)
1 ½ tablespoons olive oil
1 tablespoon fresh lemon juice
1 teaspoon red wine vinegar
¼ teaspoon salt, or to taste
⅛ teaspoon pepper

1. In a one-quart saucepan, bring the water to a boil. Add the bulgur and return to a boil. Reduce heat and simmer, covered, 20 minutes or until the liquid is absorbed. Let cool.

2. In a large bowl, toss the bulgur, tomatoes, cucumber, parsley, mint, and scallions until combined.

3. In a small bowl, stir together the oil, lemon juice, vinegar, salt, and pepper. Pour over the salad and toss to combine.

Variation: Use all parsley if you are not fond of mint.

APPLE-BULGUR SALAD

Makes: 4¹/₂ cups; serves: 6 to 8

This salad is sweet from the apple juice cooked with the bulgur and the raisins, and tart from the chopped apples and vinegar.

1 cup apple juice
¹/₄ cup water
¹/₂ cup bulgur
1¹/₂ cups chopped tart apple
³/₄ cup chopped celery
¹/₂ cup golden raisins
¹/₄ cup chopped scallions (green and white parts)
1¹/₂ tablespoons extra virgin olive oil
2 teaspoons cider vinegar
¹/₈ teaspoon salt, or to taste
Freshly ground black pepper, to taste

1. In a one-quart saucepan, bring the juice and water to a boil. Add the bulgur and return to a boil. Reduce heat and simmer, covered, 20 minutes or until the liquid is absorbed. Let cool.

2. In a large bowl, combine the bulgar, apple, celery, raisins, and scallions.

3. In a small bowl, stir together the remaining. Pour the dressing over the salad and toss to combine.

Variation: Add ³/₄ cup chopped walnuts or pecans.

BULGUR S-D-T SALAD

Makes: 3¹/₄ cups; serves: 4 to 6

I was at an Italian restaurant where many of the daily specials featured "S-D-T." Neither my sister nor I could figure out what S-D-T stood for—the waiter finally revealed it to be sun-dried tomatoes!

1¹/₂ cups cooked and cooled bulgur (page 302)
¹/₂ cup chopped yellow or red bell peppers
¹/₂ cup sliced hearts of palm
¹/₃ cup chopped oil-marinated sun-dried tomatoes
¹/₃ cup chopped fresh parsley
¹/₄ cup sliced scallions (white and green parts)
1 tablespoon extra virgin olive oil
2 teaspoons white wine vinegar
¹/₄ teaspoon salt, or to taste
Freshly ground black pepper, to taste

1. Place all the ingredients in a large bowl and toss to combine.

Variation: Add 1 cup chopped fresh apricot or apple.

BULGUR SALAD WITH SOFRITO DRESSING

Makes: 3 cups; serves: 4 to 6

I used homemade sofrito (page 484), but you can buy it prepared in the supermarket. Look for it with Goya products in the freezer case or on the shelves.

1½ cups cooked and cooled bulgur
   (page 302)
¾ cup chopped tomatoes
¾ cup chopped avocado
½ cup chopped cucumber
2 tablespoons sofrito
1 tablespoon extra virgin olive oil
1 tablespoon fresh lime juice
¼ teaspoon salt, or to taste

1. In a large bowl, stir together the bulgur, tomatoes, avocado, and cucumber.

2. In a small bowl, stir together the remaining ingredients. Pour the dressing over the salad and toss to combine.

Variation: Use 1 extra tablespoon sofrito for a slightly spicier dressing.

FRUITED COUSCOUS SALAD

Makes: 5 cups; serves: 6 to 8

If you've prepared the Couscous with Golden Fruits and Vegetables in advance and chilled it, be sure to bring it back to room temperature so that the grains soften somewhat.

1 recipe Couscous with Golden Fruits and
   Vegetables (page 326), room temperature
1 cup chopped fresh pineapple (or canned,
   crushed pineapple, drained)
¼ cup unflavored yogurt
2 tablespoons mayonnaise

1. In a large bowl, combine the prepared couscous recipe with the pineapple.

2. In a small bowl, stir together the yogurt and mayonnaise. Pour the dressing over the salad and toss to combine.

Variation: Use chopped apple instead of the pineapple.

CREAMY COUSCOUS SALAD

Makes: 3 cups; serves: 4 to 6

This makes a nice change from macaroni or potato salad.

1½ cups cooked couscous (page 302)
¾ cup chopped celery
½ cup chopped red bell peppers
½ cup peas (fresh, cooked; or frozen,
   thawed)
¼ cup chopped fresh parsley
¼ cup mayonnaise
2 teaspoons distilled white vinegar
¼ teaspoon salt, or to taste
Freshly ground black pepper, to taste

1. In a large bowl, combine the couscous, celery, bell peppers, peas, and parsley.

2. In a small bowl, stir together the mayonnaise, vinegar, and salt. Pour the dressing over the salad, grind pepper on top, and toss to combine.

Variation: Substitute fresh dill for the parsley.

COUSCOUS SALAD WITH ORANGES

Makes: 3¹/₂ cups; serves: 4 to 6

You can buy prepared orange segments in the dairy case of the supermarket, but I prefer to make my own from fresh oranges.

2 cups cooked couscous (page 302)
1 cup orange segments
³/₄ cup chopped celery
¹/₄ cup sliced scallions (green and white parts)
1 tablespoon extra virgin olive oil
1 tablespoon orange juice
2 teaspoons fresh lemon juice
¹/₂ teaspoon grated orange rind
¹/₄ teaspoon sugar
¹/₈ teaspoon salt, or to taste
Freshly ground black pepper, to taste

1. In a large bowl, combine the couscous, orange segments, celery, and scallions.

2. In a small bowl, stir together the olive oil, both juices, orange rind, sugar, and salt. Pour the dressing over the salad, grind pepper on top, and toss to combine.

Variation: Substitute chopped green bell peppers for the celery.

DILLED RICE AND PEA SALAD

Makes: 3 cups; serves: 4 to 6

This is one of the dishes I make with rice left over from Chinese takeout. Remember to bring the rice to room temperature or it will be hard and dry (I cook it in the microwave for about 1 minute with a teaspoon or two of water added to soften the grains).

2 cups cooked white rice
1 cup peas (fresh, cooked; or frozen, thawed)
¹/₄ cup snipped fresh dill
¹/₄ cup chopped scallions (white and green parts)
¹/₄ cup unflavored yogurt
3 tablespoons mayonnaise

1. Place all the ingredients in a large bowl and toss to combine.

Variations: Use brown rice instead of white.

Add ¹/₄ cup toasted pine nuts (pignoli).

SPANISH RICE SALAD

Makes: 3 cups; serves: 4 to 6

I had dinner at a Spanish restaurant with my family, and there was so much good food to eat that we completely ignored the yellow rice. When it was time to leave, the waiter asked if we wanted him to wrap it up. Our first inclination was to say no, but then I figured surely I could use it in a recipe for the book, and here it is. If you don't happen to have leftover yellow rice on hand, you can substitute any other cooked rice.

1¹/₂ cups cooked yellow rice, at room temperature
³/₄ cup peas (fresh, cooked; or frozen, thawed)
³/₄ cup chopped pimiento-stuffed olives
¹/₂ cup chopped Spanish or other mild onions
¹/₂ cup chopped celery
1 tablespoon extra virgin olive oil
1 tablespoon red wine vinegar
1¹/₂ teaspoons vegetable oil
¹/₈ teaspoon salt, or to taste
¹/₈ teaspoon pepper

1. Place all the ingredients in a large bowl and toss to combine.

Variation: Picadillo Rice Salad: Stir in ¹/₂ cup dark or golden raisins, ¹/₂ cup chopped almonds, and ¹/₄ cup chopped fresh parsley.

CURRIED COCONUT RICE SALAD

Makes: 2³/₄ cups; serves: 4 to 6

A little sweet, a little spicy. If you don't want to make the Coconut Rice, you can use any cooked rice instead, but the salad won't be quite as interesting.

1¹/₂ cups cooked Coconut Rice (page 315)
³/₄ cup peas (fresh, cooked; or frozen, thawed)
¹/₃ cup chopped cashews
2 tablespoons mayonnaise
2 tablespoons unflavored yogurt
2 teaspoons curry powder
1 teaspoon distilled white vinegar
¹/₄ teaspoon ground turmeric
¹/₈ teaspoon ground red pepper

1. In a large bowl, stir together the rice, peas, and cashews.

2. In a small bowl, stir together the mayonnaise, yogurt, curry powder, vinegar, turmeric, and pepper. Pour the dressing over the rice mixture and toss to combine.

Variation: Add one 8-ounce can unsweetened crushed pineapple, drained.

BROWN RICE AND LENTIL SALAD

─────── $\boxed{\text{V}}$ ───────

Makes: 4¹/₂ cups; serves: 4

The sun-dried tomatoes give this a slight picante bite.

2¹/₃ cups water
¹/₂ cup long-grain brown rice
¹/₂ cup lentils, rinsed
1 cup chopped red bell peppers
¹/₄ cup chopped oil-marinated sun-dried tomatoes
¹/₄ cup chopped scallions
2 tablespoons chopped fresh parsley
2 tablespoons olive oil
1 tablespoon red wine vinegar
1 tablespoon lemon juice
¹/₂ teaspoon salt, or to taste
¹/₄ teaspoon pepper

1. In a medium saucepan, bring the water to a boil. Add the rice and return to a boil; reduce heat and simmer 10 minutes. Add the lentils; return to a boil. Reduce heat, cover, and simmer 35 minutes or until water has been absorbed and grains are tender. Chill.

2. In a large bowl, combine the rice, lentils, and remaining ingredients; toss to combine.

Variation: Use ¹/₂ cup chopped roasted red peppers instead of the sun-dried tomatoes, and use green bell peppers instead of the red.

BROWN RICE, CANTALOUPE, AND APPLE SALAD

[V][♥]

Makes: 3 cups; serves: 4 to 6

You can dress up this salad by adding cashews, peas, nectarines, and/or mangoes—anything goes.

1½ cups cooked brown rice
1 cup diced cantaloupe
1 cup chopped apples
¼ cup sliced scallions (green and white parts)
2 tablespoons currants
1½ tablespoons cider vinegar
1 tablespoon vegetable oil
¾ teaspoon curry powder
¼ teaspoon salt, or to taste

1. In a large bowl, toss together the rice, cantaloupe, apples, scallions, and currants.

2. In a small bowl, stir together the vinegar, oil, curry powder, and salt. Pour the dressing over the salad and toss to combine.

[L] *Variation:* Creamy Brown Rice, Cantaloupe, and Apple Salad: Stir in ¼ to ⅓ cup unflavored yogurt. For an even creamier dressing, use sour cream instead of yogurt.

WILD RICE SALAD WITH APPLES AND WALNUTS

[V]

Makes: 3⅓ cups; serves: 4 to 6

You can prepare this salad using cooked brown or white rice instead of part or all of the wild rice.

1½ cups wild rice
1 cup diced tart apples
¾ cup diced celery
½ cup chopped walnuts
1½ tablespoons balsamic vinegar
1 tablespoon vegetable oil
1 tablespoon extra virgin olive oil
2 teaspoons honey mustard
1 teaspoon grated orange rind
½ clove garlic, minced
⅛ teaspoon salt, or to taste

1. In a large bowl, toss together the wild rice, apples, celery, and walnuts.

2. In a small bowl, stir together the remaining ingredients. Pour the dressing over the salad and toss to combine.

Variation: Add ½ cup raisins when you add the apples.

WILD AND WHITE RICE SALAD

— [V] —

Makes: 3¹/₂ cups; serves: 4 to 6

One great thing about living in New York City is the wonderful (not to mention free) events featured in Central Park. Unfortunately, if you want to be able to see or hear the concerts, you have to get to the park quite early in the day to get a good spot for your blanket. To fill the time between arriving at the park and the start of the concerts, most people have picnics. Dinners vary from wine and cheese to truly elaborate banquets. I developed this salad as one of the dishes for a 4th of July concert (with fireworks).

¼ cup pine nuts (pignoli)
¾ cup cooked wild rice
¾ cup cooked white rice
1 cup chopped tomatoes
½ cup chopped cucumber
⅓ cup sliced scallions (green and white parts)
¼ cup chopped fresh basil
1 tablespoon vegetable oil
1 tablespoon red wine vinegar
1 teaspoon balsamic vinegar
¼ teaspoon salt, or to taste
Freshly ground black pepper, to taste

1. In a small skillet, cook the pine nuts over medium heat until all the nuts are at least partially browned, about 1 to 2 minutes; set aside.

2. In a large bowl, toss together the pine nuts and remaining ingredients.

Variation: Use either all wild rice or all white rice. Substitute brown rice for either the wild or white rice.

WILD RICE AND RICE BEAN SALAD

— [V] —

Makes: 4 cups; serves: 4 to 6

Rice beans are very small and white, almost as small as grains of rice, hence the name. Thinking they would cook up quickly, I was eager to use them in a recipe. Unfortunately, they took 50 minutes to cook after soaking, so they're not really that different from any other bean. If you don't have rice beans you can substitute any cooked bean, or orzo, or white or brown rice instead.

1½ cups cooked wild rice
1 cup cooked rice beans
1 cup chopped tomatoes
½ cup sliced hearts of palm
¼ cup sliced scallions (green and white parts)
2 tablespoons extra virgin olive oil
1 tablespoon wine vinegar
½ clove garlic, minced
¼ teaspoon salt, or to taste
Freshly ground black pepper, to taste

1. Place all the ingredients in a large bowl and toss to combine.

Variation: Add ¹/₂ cup chopped red or green bell peppers.

KASHA, JÍCAMA, AND MANDARIN ORANGE SALAD

Makes: 4 cups; serves: 6 to 8

The kasha really requires a lot of dressing to make this salad work. If you are watching your fat intake, substitute rice for the kasha and use $^1/_3$ to $^1/_2$ less dressing.

1½ cups cooked kasha
One 11-ounce can mandarin orange
    segments, drained
1 cup sliced strawberries
¾ cup chopped jícama
½ cup chopped yellow or red bell peppers
¼ cup chopped scallions (green and white
    parts)
3 tablespoons vegetable oil
1½ tablespoons cider vinegar
1 teaspoon sugar
1 teaspoon grated orange rind
¼ teaspoon salt
Freshly ground black pepper, to taste

1. In a large bowl, combine the kasha, orange segments, strawberries, jícama, bell peppers, and scallions.

2. In a small bowl, stir together the oil, vinegar, sugar, orange rind, and salt. Pour the dressing over the salad, grind pepper on top, and toss to combine.

Variation: Use 1 cup fresh orange segments instead of the canned mandarin oranges.

ASIAN MILLET SALAD

Makes: 4$^1/_4$ cups; serves: 4 to 6

Millet gets quite hard when chilled. If you've refrigerated the millet between cooking it and preparing this salad, add a teaspoon of water and reheat it slightly in the microwave.

2 cups cooked millet, at room temperature
1 cup mung bean sprouts
½ cup chopped cucumber
½ cup chopped snow peas
½ cup chopped red bell peppers
⅓ cup sliced scallions (green and white parts)
1 tablespoon soy sauce
1 tablespoon mirin or dry sherry
1 tablespoon rice vinegar
2 teaspoons vegetable oil
1 teaspoon sesame oil

1. In a large bowl, toss together the millet, sprouts, cucumber, snow peas, bell peppers, and scallions.

2. In a small bowl, stir together the remaining ingredients. Pour the dressing over the salad and toss to combine.

Variation: Use couscous instead of millet.

CURRIED MILLET SALAD

Makes: 4 cups; serves: 4 to 6

If you only have unflavored cooked millet, just use the following mixture instead of the unflavored dressing. Stir together the vinegar and oil, add 1$^1/_2$ teaspoons curry powder, $^1/_4$ teaspoon ground cumin, $^1/_2$ clove minced garlic, and $^1/_8$ teaspoon ground red pepper.

2 cups Curried Millet (page 310)

1 cup chopped tomatoes

¾ cup chopped cucumber

½ cup peas (fresh, cooked; or frozen, thawed)

¼ cup sliced scallions (white and green parts)

2 tablespoons cider vinegar

1½ tablespoons vegetable oil

1. Place all the ingredients in a large bowl and toss to combine.

Variation: Add ¹/₃ cup toasted sliced almonds.

MANDARIN QUINOA SALAD

Makes: 3 cups; serves: 4 to 6

Slightly exotic but delicious, this recipe includes salted cocktail peanuts.

2 cups cooked quinoa

One 11-ounce can mandarin orange segments in light syrup, drained, 1 tablespoon syrup reserved

½ cup chopped salted peanuts

¼ cup sliced scallions (white and green parts)

1 tablespoon vegetable oil

1 tablespoon rice wine vinegar

1 teaspoon sesame oil

⅛ teaspoon ground ginger

⅛ teaspoon salt, or to taste

⅛ teaspoon ground red pepper

1. In a large bowl, toss together the quinoa, orange segments, peanuts, and scallions.

2. In a small bowl, stir together the remaining ingredients. Pour the dressing over the salad and toss to combine.

Variation: Curried Quinoa Salad: Add 2 teaspoons curry powder to the salad dressing.

PASTA SALAD

[V]

Makes: 5¹/₂ cups; serves: 6

For an even heartier salad, use a filled pasta such as tortellini. This is the type of salad I like to make when I'm invited to potluck dinners—this way I feel I know there'll be something substantial for vegetarians, and the carnivores will enjoy it too.

2 cups cooked and cooled medium-sized pasta (such as ziti, rotini, cavatelli, or radiatori)

1 cup celery chunks

1 cup green bell pepper chunks

1 cup sliced zucchini

½ cup sliced chopped pimiento-stuffed olives

½ cup chopped drained marinated artichoke hearts

¹/₃ cup chopped pimientos or roasted red peppers

1½ tablespoons extra virgin olive oil

1 tablespoon fresh lemon juice

1 tablespoon red wine vinegar

1 clove garlic, minced

1. Place all the ingredients in a large bowl and toss to combine.

Variation: Add 1 cup cooked, drained chickpeas (cooked from dry; or canned, drained) and perhaps ¹/₃ cup grated Parmesan and serve this as a main dish salad for 3 to 4 people.

MACARONI AND BEAN SALAD

Makes: 2¼ cups; serves: 4

Beans add a great texture—not to mention protein and fiber profile—to this traditional salad.

1½ cups cooked macaroni
¾ cup cooked red kidney beans
⅓ cup chopped celery
2 tablespoons chopped fresh parsley
3 tablespoons mayonnaise
½ teaspoon distilled white vinegar
¼ teaspoon salt, or to taste
⅛ teaspoon pepper

1. In a large bowl, toss together the macaroni, beans, celery, and parsley.

2. In a small bowl, stir together the remaining ingredients. Pour the dressing over the salad and toss to combine.

Variation: Add ½ cup chopped red or green bell peppers.

STUFFED OLIVE, RICE, AND ROMAN BEAN SALAD

Makes: 4½ cups; serves: 6 to 8

I used a Goya product (Spicy Stuffed Olives) for this recipe, but regular stuffed olives will be fine, too. The spicy olives are not too noticeable when you first eat the salad, but they leave an afterburn. Roman beans are also called cranberry beans; if you can't find them, pinto or kidney beans will be suitable substitutes.

1½ cups cooked white or brown rice
1½ cups Roman beans (cooked from dry; or canned, drained)
1 cup chopped celery
⅓ cup chopped red-hot pepper-stuffed olives
¼ cup finely chopped green bell peppers
2 tablespoons chopped fresh parsley
2 tablespoons olive oil
1 tablespoon fresh lemon juice
1 tablespoon red wine vinegar
¼ teaspoon dried rosemary, crumbled

1. Place all the ingredients in a large bowl and toss to combine.

Variation: Add ¼ cup chopped fresh cilantro and omit the rosemary.

SAUTÉED PORTOBELLO MUSH-ROOM AND PINTO BEAN SALAD

Makes: 4 cups; serves: 6 to 8

The beans and mushrooms both contribute an "earthiness" to the salad. You can use white mushrooms if you can't find portobellos.

1½ tablespoons vegetable oil
4 cups diced portobello mushrooms (¾-inch pieces)
2 tablespoons water
1½ cups cooked pinto beans
¾ cup chopped green bell peppers
⅓ cup chopped mild onions
⅓ cup chopped fresh parsley
2 tablespoons balsamic vinegar
1 tablespoon extra virgin olive oil
⅛ teaspoon salt, or to taste
Freshly ground black pepper, to taste

1. In a large skillet, heat the vegetable oil over medium-high heat. Add the mushrooms; cook, stirring, until oil is absorbed, about 1 minute. Add the water; cook, stirring, until softened, about 3 minutes (if liquid accumulates, continue cooking until evaporated); cool.

2. Place the cooled mushrooms and the remaining ingredients in a medium bowl and toss to combine.

Variation: Add ³/₄ cup chopped cucumber.

LENTIL AND MUSHROOM SALAD

Makes: 3 cups; serves: 4

Cultivated white mushrooms are fine if you can't find wild mushrooms.

2 tablespoons vegetable oil
½ cup sliced leeks (white and light green parts only)
2 cups sliced crimini, shiitake, or portobello mushrooms
1½ cups cooked lentils
1 cup chopped tomatoes
1 tablespoon red wine vinegar
1 teaspoon extra virgin olive oil
1 teaspoon Dijon mustard

1. In a small skillet, heat the vegetable oil over medium-high heat. Add the leeks; cook, stirring, until softened, about 2 minutes. Add the mushrooms; cook, stirring, until softened, about 3 minutes. Cool.

2. In a medium bowl, toss together the lentils, tomatoes, and mushroom mixture.

3. In a small bowl, stir together the remaining ingredients. Pour the dressing over the salad and toss to combine.

☐ *Variation:* Add ½ cup crumbled feta cheese.

WARM LENTIL SALAD WITH BALSAMIC DRESSING

Ⓥ ♥

Makes: 6 cups; serves: 8 to 12

The lentils tend to make the salad look a little mushy, but it's really not. This makes an excellent main dish salad; serve on a bed of lettuce and top with crumbled feta cheese, if desired (it will serve 4 to 6 as a main course). You can also serve it at room temperature instead of warm.

3 cups water
1 cup lentils
1 bay leaf
1 cup chopped celery
1 cup chopped apples
³/₄ cup chopped red or green bell peppers
½ cup chopped onions
½ cup chopped dried apricots
3 tablespoons balsamic vinegar
1½ tablespoons extra virgin olive oil
1½ teaspoons honey mustard
¼ teaspoon salt, or to taste
Freshly ground black pepper, to taste

1. In a 1½-quart saucepan, bring the water to a boil. Add the lentils and bay leaf. Return to a boil. Reduce heat and simmer, uncovered, 30 to 45 minutes or until lentils are tender. Drain. Discard the bay leaf and place lentils in large bowl.

2. Add the celery, apples, bell peppers, onions, and apricots.

3. In a small bowl, stir together the vinegar, oil, mustard, and salt. Pour the dressing over the salad, grind pepper on top, and toss to combine.

Variation: Substitute chopped fennel for the celery.

FRENCH LENTIL SALAD WITH HEARTS OF PALM

⟦V⟧⟦♥⟧

Makes: 3 cups; serves: 4 to 6

French lentils are darker and smaller than regular lentils, and they cook in 30 minutes or less. If you can't find French lentils, use regular lentils and cook until tender.

1½ cups cooked French lentils
¾ cup sliced hearts of palm
¾ cup chopped dried apricots
¼ cup thinly sliced red onions
3 tablespoons chopped fresh cilantro leaves
3 tablespoons chopped fresh parsley leaves
1 tablespoon extra virgin olive oil
1 tablespoon fresh lemon juice
⅛ teaspoon salt, or to taste
Freshly ground black pepper, to taste

1. Place all the ingredients in a large bowl and toss to combine.

Variation: Use chopped tart apples instead of the dried apricots.

CORN AND BLACK BEAN SALAD

⟦V⟧⟦♥⟧

Makes: 3¼ cups; serves: 4 to 6

The sweet, crunchy corn contrasts nicely with the soft black beans. This easy-to-prepare salad is a real favorite at any gathering.

1½ cups corn (fresh, cooked; canned, drained; or frozen, thawed, cooked)
1 cup cooked black beans (cooked from dry; or canned, drained)
⅔ cup chopped red bell peppers
⅓ cup chopped onions
¼ cup chopped fresh parsley
1½ tablespoons red wine vinegar
1 tablespoon vegetable oil
½ teaspoon sugar
⅛ teaspoon salt, or to taste
Freshly ground black pepper, to taste

1. In a large bowl, toss together the corn, beans, peppers, onions, and parsley.
2. In a small bowl, stir together the remaining ingredients. Pour the dressing over the salad and toss to combine.

Variation: Add ½ cup canned, drained, chopped chilies.

BLACK BEAN AND OLIVE SALAD

⟦V⟧

Makes: 2½ cups; serves: 4 to 5

Because I make this salad with black beans, you don't see the black olives, and they come as a taste surprise. It might be prettier to use a lighter-color bean, but then the olives are no longer a mysterious ingredient.

1½ cups black beans (cooked from dry; or canned, drained)

½ cup chopped celery

⅓ cup sliced or chopped black olives

¼ cup chopped onions

¼ cup sliced or chopped pimiento-stuffed green olives

¼ cup chopped fresh cilantro or parsley

2 tablespoons minced green bell peppers

1½ tablespoons extra virgin olive oil

1 tablespoon white wine vinegar

¼ teaspoon salt, or to taste

Freshly ground black pepper, to taste

1. Place all the ingredients in a medium bowl and toss to combine.

Ⓛ *Variation:* Add chopped jalapeño peppers or cayenne pepper to taste, or diced avocado. Serve with a dollop of unflavored yogurt, sour cream, or diced or shredded Cheddar cheese.

BLACK BEAN AND TOMATO SALAD

Makes: 3 cups; serves: 4 to 6

If you have cilantro pesto on hand, you can add it instead of the fresh cilantro.

1½ cups black beans (cooked from dry; or canned, drained)

1 cup chopped tomatoes

¾ cup chopped avocado

¼ cup sliced scallions (green and white parts)

1 tablespoon chopped fresh cilantro

1 tablespoon vegetable oil

1 tablespoon fresh lime juice

2 teaspoons red wine vinegar

⅛ teaspoon ground cumin

½ clove garlic

1. In a large bowl, stir together the beans, tomatoes, avocado, scallions, and cilantro. Add the remaining ingredients and toss to combine.

Variation: Add 1 tablespoon sofrito (page 484) instead of the cilantro.

THREE-BEAN SALAD

Makes: 2½ cups; serves: 3 to 4

I make this the cheater's way by using frozen green beans and canned chickpeas and kidney beans.

1 cup cooked, cut green beans (fresh, cooked; or frozen)

¾ cup cooked chickpeas (cooked from dry; or canned, drained)

¾ cup cooked kidney beans (cooked from dry; or canned, drained)

¼ cup finely chopped red onions

1½ tablespoons vegetable oil

1 tablespoon cider vinegar

½ clove garlic, minced

¼ teaspoon salt, or to taste

Freshly ground black pepper, to taste

1. In a large bowl, toss together the green beans, chickpeas, kidney beans, and onions.

2. In a small bowl, combine the remaining ingredients. Pour the dressing over the salad and toss to combine.

Variation: Add ½ cup chopped green bell peppers or celery.

PIGEON BEAN AND CORN SALAD

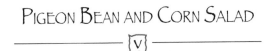

Makes: 3³/₄ cups; serves: 4 to 6

If pigeon beans are not available, use small white beans instead.

1½ cups cooked pigeon beans (cooked from dry; or canned, drained)
1 cup corn kernels (fresh, cooked; canned, drained; or frozen, thawed)
1 cup sliced raw zucchini (large slices halved or quartered)
½ cup sliced red onions
¼ cup chopped fresh cilantro
2 tablespoons vegetable oil
1½ tablespoons cider vinegar
1 teaspoon sugar
½ teaspoon dried mustard

1. In a large bowl, combine the beans, corn, zucchini, onions, and cilantro.

2. In a small bowl, stir together the remaining ingredients. Pour the dressing over the salad and toss to combine.

Variation: Add ¹/₃ cup chopped roasted red peppers or pimientos.

MARINATED CHICKPEA SALAD

Makes: 2¹/₂ cups; serves: 4

My parents frequent a diner that usually has interesting marinated salads on the table for patrons to munch on while waiting for their orders. This is similar to one that I enjoyed a lot.

1½ cups cooked chickpeas (cooked from dry; or canned, drained)
½ cup finely chopped celery
½ cup chopped black olives

¼ cup finely chopped onions
3 tablespoons distilled white vinegar
2 tablespoons extra virgin olive oil
1 teaspoon dried oregano
1 clove garlic, minced
⅛ teaspoon salt, or to taste.
Freshly ground black pepper, to taste

1. Place all the ingredients in a large bowl and toss to combine. Let stand at least 30 minutes before serving.

Variation: Add ¹/₃ cup finely chopped green bell peppers.

CHICKPEA AND GRILLED VEGETABLE SALAD

Makes: 3¹/₂ cups; serves: 4 to 6

You can substitute grilled yellow squash or eggplant for the zucchini.

1½ cups cooked chickpeas (cooked from dry; or canned, drained)
½ cup grilled, sliced zucchini (1-inch pieces)
½ cup coarsely chopped roasted red peppers (see page 276)
½ cup chopped celery
½ cup chopped marinated artichoke hearts
¹/₃ cup chopped red onions
2 tablespoons chopped fresh parsley
2 tablespoons red wine vinegar
1 tablespoon extra virgin olive oil
1 tablespoon fresh lemon juice
1 clove garlic, minced
⅛ teaspoon salt, or to taste
Freshly ground black pepper, to taste

1. Place all the ingredients in a large bowl and toss to combine.

Variation: Add ½ cup chopped green bell peppers.

CHICKPEA AND SPROUTED-PEA SALAD

[V][♥]

Makes: 4¼ cups; serves: 6 to 8

Sprouted beans are frequently available in supermarket produce departments. Sometimes you can find just sprouted peas, or peas in combination with bean sprouts. Either is good in this salad.

1½ cups chickpeas (cooked from dry; or canned, drained)
1 cup crunchy sprouted peas
¾ cup chopped celery
¾ cup chopped jícama
½ cup chopped red bell peppers
2 tablespoon vegetable oil
1 tablespoon cider vinegar
½ teaspoon dry mustard
½ teaspoon grated orange rind
Freshly ground black pepper, to taste

1. In a large bowl, toss together the chickpeas, sprouted peas, celery, jícama, and bell peppers.

2. In a small bowl, stir together the remaining ingredients. Pour the dressing over the salad and toss to combine.

Variation: Use pears instead of jícama and add ½ cup raisins.

FRUIT SALADS

I tend to make large batches of fruit salad because it lasts a few days (as long as it doesn't include bananas), and makes an ideal something-nutritious-to-grab when you're feeling a little hungry between meals. I also love to have fruit salad on hand for a quick lunch with cottage cheese.

You'll notice that many of my fruit salads have a little liqueur in them, because I find that liqueur helps to meld the various fruit flavors. Feel free to substitute fruit juice or just a little sweetener for the liqueur.

Fruit salad is an excellent choice for dessert after a heavy meal. Guests don't need creamy desserts when you've already served them a creamy main dish. If you think fruit salad by itself feels skimpy, serve crisp cookies or sorbet or sherbet along with it. On the other hand, I must admit that using fruit salad as a topping for vanilla ice cream is pretty delicious, too.

JAMAICAN KIWI-STRAWBERRY SALAD

[V][♥]

Makes: 3½ cups; serves: 4 to 6

Serve this salad with lemon sorbet.

2 cups peeled, cubed kiwifruit
1½ cups strawberry halves
3 tablespoons Jamaican rum
2 tablespoons sugar

1. In a medium bowl, toss together the kiwifruit and strawberries.

2. In a small bowl, stir together the rum and sugar until the sugar dissolves. Pour the dressing over the salad and toss to combine. Let stand at least 15 minutes before serving.

Variation: For a nonalcoholic version, use orange juice instead of rum.

GRAPEFRUIT~KIWI SALAD

Makes: 5¹/₂ cups; serves: 6 to 8

You can buy prepared grapefruit segments in the dairy case of the supermarket, or even canned, but I prefer to prepare my own from fresh grapefruits.

3 cups grapefruit segments
2 cups chopped, peeled pears
1½ cups sliced kiwifruit
2 tablespoons orange liqueur
2 tablespoons grenadine

1. Place all the ingredients in a medium bowl and toss to combine.

Variations: Substitute pineapple for the grapefruit.

For a nonalcoholic version, use orange juice instead of orange liqueur.

WINTER SALAD

Makes: 4 cups; serves: 4 to 6

All these fruits are readily available year-round, not just in the winter.

1 cup fresh pineapple chunks
1 cup apple chunks
1 cup red grapes (halve large ones)
1 cup orange segments
2 tablespoons orange liqueur or juice
1 tablespoon sugar

1. Place all the ingredients in a large bowl and toss to combine.

2. Let stand 20 minutes for the flavors to meld.

Variation: Vary the fruits to your liking—use pears instead of apples, canned pineapple if fresh is not available or too expensive, or even nonwinter fruits if available. Anything will taste fine.

BLUEBERRY~NECTARINE SALAD

Makes: 4 cups; serves: 4 to 6

1½ cups blueberries
1½ cups sliced nectarines
1 cup sliced banana
2 tablespoons orange juice
Sweetener to taste (optional)

1. In a medium bowl, toss the fruits and juice together. Sweeten if necessary. Let stand at least 30 minutes for the flavors meld.

Variation: Use pineapple instead of banana.

PEACH AND STRAWBERRY SALAD

Makes: 3³/₄ cups; serves: 4 to 6

2 cups sliced peaches
2 cups sliced strawberries
1 tablespoon peach schnapps or orange liqueur
Sweetener to taste (optional)

1. In a medium bowl, toss both fruits and the schnapps together. Sweeten if necessary. Let stand at least 30 minutes for the flavors to meld.

Variation: Use nectarines instead of peaches.

BERRY BERRY BERRY GOOD FRUIT SALAD

Makes: 3¹/₂ cups; serves: 4 to 6

1½ cups blueberries
1½ cups sliced strawberries
1 cup raspberries
2 tablespoons raspberry liqueur (framboise) or cherry liqueur (kirsch)
Sugar to taste

1. In a large bowl, toss all the berries and liqueur together. Sweeten if necessary. Let stand at least 30 minutes for the flavors to meld.

Variation: July 4th Salad: Add 1¹/₂ cups chopped peeled pears and use pear liqueur instead of raspberry liqueur.

PAPAYA~BANANA~ORANGE SALAD

Makes: 4 cups; serves: 4 to 6

I don't know why, but this salad just screams out for maraschino cherries. Maybe it's the grenadine, which I add for the color.

2 cups papaya chunks
1 cup banana slices
1 cup orange segments
2 tablespoons orange juice
2 teaspoons grenadine, or to taste

1. In a large bowl, combine all the fruits, the juice (as well as any juice that accumulates from cutting the orange into segments), and the grenadine. Let stand at least 30 minutes for the flavors to meld.

Variation: Be wild—throw in some maraschino cherry halves.

CALYPSO~BERRY SALAD

Makes: 6 cups; serves: 6 to 8

Berries are not exactly calypso, but the combination is great. The sloe gin is optional, or you can substitute a little grenadine.

2 cups sliced strawberries
1 cup blueberries
1 cup chopped papaya
1 cup chopped mango
1 cup sliced banana
1½ tablespoons sloe gin
1 tablespoon lime juice

1. Place all the ingredients in a medium bowl and toss to combine.

Variation: Substitute nectarines for the mangoes and/or extra banana for the papaya.

MANGO~STRAWBERRY SALAD

Makes: 4 cups; serves: 4 to 6

If your strawberries or mangoes are tart instead of sweet, you may want to add sweetener to taste.

2 cups sliced strawberries
2 cups diced mango
½ cup chopped walnuts
1 tablespoon apricot brandy or orange juice
1 tablespoon fresh lemon juice

1. Place all the ingredients in a medium bowl and toss to combine.

Variation: Substitute nectarines for the mangoes.

CANTALOUPE-BLUEBERRY SALAD

Makes: 4 cups; serves: 4 to 6

You can just use lemon-flavored yogurt instead of making the lemon dressing; but it won't taste as fresh.

2 cups cubed cantaloupe
2 cups blueberries
¼ cup unflavored yogurt
2 teaspoons sugar
2 teaspoons fresh lemon juice
¼ teaspoon grated lemon rind

1. Toss the cantaloupe and blueberries together in a large bowl.

2. In a small bowl, stir together the yogurt, sugar, lemon juice, and lemon rind. Pour the dressing over the fruit and toss to combine.

Variation: Substitute sliced bananas for the cantaloupe.

SUMMER BRUNCH FRUIT SALAD

Makes 3 cups: serves: 4 to 6

Someone gave me a bottle of Galiano back when Harvey Wallbangers were all the rage, sometime in the 1970s—it's still in my liqueur cabinet (and still almost full). However, when I was browsing through my liqueurs looking for an inspiration, there it was! It's a great and unusual flavor for this salad. If you don't have Galiano, or Benedictine, any fruit-flavored liqueur should be a suitable substitute.

1 cup diced cantaloupe
1 cup fresh raspberries
1 cup fresh blueberries
1 tablespoon Galiano or other liqueur (optional)

1. Place all the ingredients in a medium bowl and toss to combine. Let stand at least one hour for the flavors to meld.

COTTAGE CHEESE AND FRUIT SALAD

Makes: 3³⁄₄ cups; serves: 4 to 6

I love this salad for lunch during the summer. I prefer the fruits cut into ¹⁄₄-inch pieces, but, of course, if you prefer to use large chunks, do so.

2 cups cottage cheese
1 cup diced fruit (such as pineapple, orange, banana, cantaloupe, peaches, or nectarines)
½ cup chopped pecans
¼ cup golden raisins

1. Place all the ingredients in a medium bowl and toss to combine.

Variation: Use walnuts or toasted almonds instead of the pecans, and/or currants instead of the raisins.

DRESSINGS

Although most of the salads in this book include recipes for appropriate dressings, sometimes it's nice just to have some homemade dressing on hand to toss on any simple salad you throw together. With that thought in mind, these dressings are prepared in larger batches. Most of them will probably need to be shaken before serving. It's important to store these dressings in the refrigerator.

ITALIAN DRESSING

Makes: 3/4 cup; serves: 10 to 12

1/2 cup red wine vinegar
4 cloves garlic, halved
3 tablespoons extra virgin olive oil
2 tablespoons vegetable oil
1/8 teaspoon dried oregano
1/8 teaspoon dried thyme

1. Place all the ingredients into a container with a tight-fitting lid. Shake until completely combined; let stand at least 1 hour for the flavors to meld. Store in refrigerator between uses.

Variation: Substitute additional olive oil for the vegetable oil.

FRENCH VINAIGRETTE

Makes: 1 cup; serves: 24 to 30

1/4 cup red wine vinegar
1 tablespoon minced shallots
1 tablespoon Dijon mustard
1/2 cup vegetable oil
1/4 cup extra virgin olive oil

1. Place the vinegar, shallots, and mustard into a container with a tight-fitting lid. Shake until completely combined. Add the oils and shake until combined.

Variation: Use 1/2 teaspoon garlic, minced, instead of the shallots.

RUSSIAN DRESSING

Makes: 3/4 cup; serves: 12 to 24

1/2 cup mayonnaise
3 tablespoons ketchup
2 tablespoons sweet or India relish

1. In a medium bowl, stir together all the ingredients.

Variation: Add chopped fresh parsley to the dressing.

HERBED BUTTERMILK DRESSING

🔟

Makes: 1 scant cup; serves: 16

½ cup buttermilk
6 tablespoons mayonnaise
3 tablespoons sliced scallions (green and
    white parts)
3 tablespoons chopped fresh parsley
¼ teaspoon dried thyme

1. In a medium bowl, stir together all the ingredients.

Variations: Substitute chopped fresh basil for the parsley.

Substitute dried tarragon for the thyme.

TAHINI DRESSING

🔽

Makes: ⅔ cup; serves: 6 to 8

This dressing/sauce may thicken some as it stands. If it thickens too much, stir in extra water. You can double this recipe and use it as a dip with pita wedges.

⅓ cup tahini (sesame paste)
⅓ cup water
3 tablespoons fresh lemon juice
3 cloves garlic, minced
2 sprigs parsley

1. Place all ingredients in a blender. Cover and process until smooth.

Variation: Chop the parsley and stir together the ingredients instead of using a blender.

FETA DRESSING

🔽

Makes: 1¼ cups; serves: 6 to 8

This creamy, tangy dressing is especially well suited to bitter greens, such as watercress or arugula.

¾ cup crumbled feta cheese
½ cup unflavored yogurt
⅓ cup sour cream
½ clove garlic, minced
¼ teaspoon dried oregano
⅛ teaspoon pepper

1. Place the ingredients in a blender or food processor container fitted with a steel blade. Cover and process until smooth.

♥ **Variation:** For a lower-fat version, substitute additional yogurt for the sour cream.

Fresh Herb Balsamic Vinaigrette

— [V] —

Makes: 1 cup; serves: 12 to 20

Don't let the awful color of this dressing discourage you.

½ cup extra virgin olive oil
¼ cup balsamic vinegar
¼ cup lightly packed parsley leaves
¼ cup lightly packed basil leaves
1 teaspoon Dijon mustard
1 clove garlic, minced

1. Place the ingredients in a blender or food processor container fitted with a steel blade. Cover and process until smooth.

Variation: Substitute 1 to 2 shallots for the garlic.

BREADS

Quick Breads

Cranberry Bread   395

Zucchini Bread   395

Streusel-Topped Pumpkin Bread   396

Banana Bread   396

Orange-Pumpkin-Cranberry-Date Bread   397

Date-Nut Bread   397

Apple Biscuit Bread   398

Apricot-Prune Bread   398

Dried Fig–Cardamom Bread   399

Blue Cornmeal Bread   399

Blueberry Cornmeal Bread   400

Corn Pound Bread   400

Cheddar-Chili Cornbread   401

Cranberry-Fig Brown Bread   401

Untraditional Irish Soda Bread   402

Rye-rish Soda Bread   402

Biscuits and Scones

World's Best Whole Wheat Biscuits   403

Pecan-Orange Biscuits   403

Sweet Biscuits   404

Plantain Biscuits   404

Herbed Biscuits   405

Peppered Blue Cornmeal Biscuits   405

Parmesan Biscuits   406

Wheat Germ Drop Biscuits   406

Sourdough Drop Biscuits   407

Scones   407

Muffins

Basic Muffins   408

Struesel-Topped Muffins   408

Corn Muffins   409

Jam-Filled Muffins   409

Three-Grain Muffins   410

Date-Bran Muffins   410

Lemon–Poppy Seed Muffins   411

Cranberry-Oatmeal Muffins   411

Sweet Potato Meadow Muffins   412

Yeast Breads

Whole Wheat Bread   414

Cornmeal Bread   415

Semolina Bread   415

Rye Bread   416

Fresh Rosemary–Pepper Rye Bread   416

Pumpernickel   417

Wheat Berry Bread   417

Donna Mason's Dense and Chewy Whole Grain Bread   418

Five-Grain Bread   419

Russian Black Bread   420

Corn and Bran Bread   420

Anise Seed Bread   421

Challah   422

Swedish Limpa Bread   422

Anadama Bread   423

Garlic Knots   424

Focaccia   424

Basic Yeast Sourdough Starter   425

Sourdough French Bread   426

Flavored Breads and Toasts

Flavored Croutons   427

Crostini   427

Toasted Pitas   428

Butter Garlic Bread   428

Crackers

Nice and Crunchy, Crisp and Seedy Homemade Crackers   429

Parmesan Crackers   430

Garlic Pita Points   431

QUICK BREADS

CRANBERRY BREAD

Makes: one 9-inch loaf; serves: 16

This is one of my standby recipes for Thanksgiving dinner. But I also freeze cranberries each fall so that I can make this bread year-round.

2 cups chopped cranberries
½ cup sugar
1¼ cups all-purpose flour
¾ cup whole wheat flour
1½ teaspoons baking powder
1 teaspoon baking soda
1 teaspoon ground cardamom
½ teaspoon salt
¾ cup firmly packed light brown or dark brown sugar
½ cup vegetable oil
½ cup milk
2 eggs
2 teaspoons grated orange rind

1. Preheat the oven to 350°F. Grease and flour a 9 × 5 × 3-inch loaf pan.

2. In a medium bowl, stir together the cranberries and sugar; set aside.

3. In a large bowl, stir together both flours, the baking powder, baking soda, cardamom, and salt.

4. In a medium bowl, beat the brown sugar, oil, milk, eggs, and orange rind until combined. Stir the liquid mixture into the dry ingredients until combined. Stir in the reserved cranberries.

5. Spoon into the prepared pan and level off top. Bake 1 hour or until a wooden pick inserted in the center comes out clean. Let stand 20 minutes, then turn onto rack to cool completely.

Variations: Substitute cinnamon or pumpkin pie spice for the ground cardamom.

Walnut Cranberry Bread: Stir in 1½ cups chopped walnuts when you add the cranberries.

ZUCCHINI BREAD

Makes: two 8-inch loaves; serves: 24

A great bread to make in the summer when everyone is trying to get rid of their excess zucchini crop.

2 cups all-purpose flour
1 cup whole wheat flour
1 teaspoon baking powder
1 teaspoon baking soda
1 teaspoon salt
2 eggs
2 egg whites
2 cups sugar
1 cup vegetable oil
2 tablespoons fresh lemon juice
2 cups coarsely shredded zucchini
1 tablespoon grated lemon rind

1. Preheat the oven to 350°F. Grease and flour two 8½ × 3⅝ × 2⅝-inch loaf pans.

2. In a large bowl, stir together both flours, the baking powder, baking soda, and salt.

3. In a medium bowl, beat the eggs and egg whites until frothy, then beat in the sugar and oil. Beat in the lemon juice.

4. Stir the liquid ingredients into the dry ingredients until just combined; stir in the zucchini and lemon rind. Pour into prepared pan; bake 50 to 60 minutes or until a wooden pick inserted in the center comes out clean.

Variation: Omit the lemon rind and use 1 tablespoon ground cinnamon.

STREUSEL-TOPPED PUMPKIN BREAD

Makes: 1 loaf; serves: 16

Use canned pumpkin puree for this recipe so it can be prepared year-round.

Topping:
1/2 cup all-purpose flour
1/4 cup sugar
1/4 teaspoon ground cinnamon
1/4 cup (1/2 stick) unsalted butter or margarine

Bread:
1 cup all-purpose flour
1 cup whole wheat flour
2 teaspoons ground cinnamon
2 teaspoons baking powder
1 teaspoon baking soda
1/2 teaspoon ground nutmeg
1/2 teaspoon salt
1/2 cup (1 stick) unsalted butter or margarine
3/4 cup sugar
2 eggs
1 cup pumpkin puree
1/2 cup buttermilk
1/4 cup molasses
1 teaspoon vanilla

1. Preheat the oven to 325°F. Grease and flour a 9 × 5 × 3-inch loaf pan.

2. Prepare the topping by stirring together 1/2 cup flour, 1/4 cup sugar, and 1/4 teaspoon cinnamon in a medium bowl. Using a pastry cutter or two knives, cut in 1/4 cup butter or margarine until the mixture is crumbly and of a streusel texture; set aside.

3. To prepare the bread: In a large bowl or on a sheet of waxed paper, stir together 1 cup of both flours, 2 teaspoons cinnamon, the baking powder, baking soda, nutmeg, and salt.

4. In a large bowl, cream 1/2 cup butter. Beat in 3/4 cup sugar until light and fluffy. Beat in the eggs, pumpkin puree, buttermilk, molasses, and vanilla. Stir in the flour mixture until combined.

5. Spoon into prepared baking pan and even off the top. Sprinkle topping over batter.

6. Bake 1 hour 10 minutes or until a wooden pick inserted in the center comes out clean. Turn onto rack to cool.

Variation: Pecan-Streusel Pumpkin Bread: Stir 1 cup chopped pecans into batter and 1/3 cup chopped pecans into the streusel topping.

BANANA BREAD

Makes: 1 loaf; serves: 14 to 16

The bananas should be very ripe to have the necessary sweetness. Look for bananas with lots of small dark specks on the skin.

1 cup all-purpose flour
1 cup whole wheat flour
1 tablespoon baking powder
1 teaspoon baking soda
1 teaspoon salt
1/2 cup (1 stick) butter or margarine, softened
1/2 cup firmly packed light brown or dark brown sugar
2 eggs
1/3 cup honey
1 1/4 cups mashed ripe banana (about 3 to 4 medium bananas)

1. Preheat the oven to 350°F. Grease and flour a 9 × 5 × 2 3/4-inch loaf pan.

2. In a medium bowl or on a piece of waxed paper, stir together both flours, the baking powder, baking soda, and salt with a whisk.

3. In a large bowl, cream the butter or margarine and the sugar until light and fluffy. Beat in the eggs until thoroughly combined. Beat in the honey.

4. Beat in the banana alternately with the flour mixture. Spoon into prepared pan. Bake 50 minutes or until a wooden pick inserted in the center comes out clean. Remove from the oven and turn onto a wire rack to cool.

Variation: Add 1 cup chopped nuts to the batter.

Orange~Pumpkin~Cranberry~ Date Bread

Makes: one 9-inch loaf; serves: 14

Orange is the predominant flavor in this wonderful bread, which is very moist and not too sweet.

1 cup chopped cranberries
¼ cup sugar
1½ cups all-purpose flour
¾ cup whole wheat flour
1 tablespoon baking powder
1 teaspoon baking soda
½ teaspoon salt
1 cup chopped dates
2 eggs
¾ cup light brown or dark brown sugar
½ cup orange juice
⅓ cup vegetable oil
1 cup pureed pumpkin
2 teaspoons grated orange rind

1. Preheat the oven to 350°F. Grease and flour a 9 × 5 × 3-inch baking pan.

2. In a small bowl, toss together the cranberries and sugar; set aside.

3. In a large bowl, stir together both flours, the baking powder, baking soda, and salt. Toss in the dates.

4. In a medium bowl, beat the eggs; stir in the brown sugar, orange juice, and oil. Add the pumpkin and orange rind and stir until combined.

5. Stir the liquid ingredients into the dry ingredients until just combined; stir in the reserved cranberries. Pour into prepared pan; bake 55 minutes or until a wooden pick inserted in the center comes out clean.

Variation: Add 1 cup chopped pecans when you add the dates.

Date~Nut Bread

Makes: one 9-inch loaf; serves: 12 to 14

This bread is sweet with a walnut flavor, but no walnut pieces (since you are using ground walnuts). If you would like walnut pieces as well, stir in ½ to 1 cup of chopped walnuts in addition to the ground ones.

1 cup water
1 cup sugar
½ cup (1 stick) butter or margarine
1 cup chopped dates
1½ cups ground walnuts
1 cup all-purpose flour
1 cup whole wheat flour
1 tablespoon baking powder
½ teaspoon salt
2 eggs, beaten
1 teaspoon vanilla

1. Preheat the oven to 350°F. Grease and flour a 9 × 5 × 3-inch loaf pan.

2. In a small saucepan, stir together the water and sugar. Add the butter or margarine; cook, stirring, until sugar dissolves and butter has melted. Stir in dates and let cool 20 minutes.

3. In a large bowl, stir together the walnuts, both flours, the baking powder, and salt.

4. In a medium bowl, beat the eggs and vanilla.

5. Stir the eggs into the cooled liquid ingredients, then add to dry ingredients until just combined. Pour into prepared pan; bake 45 minutes or until a wooden pick inserted in the center comes out clean.

Variation: Substitute dried figs or apricots for the dates.

APPLE BISCUIT BREAD

Makes: one 9-inch loaf; serves: 14

This dense bread is made by the biscuit method and the result is a very thick batter. It bakes up just fine, but the top of the bread looks slightly lumpy.

1½ cups all-purpose flour
⅔ cup sugar
½ cup whole wheat flour
2 teaspoons ground cinnamon
2 teaspoons baking powder
1 teaspoon baking soda
½ teaspoon salt
⅓ cup butter or margarine
1½ cups coarsely chopped, peeled apples
1 cup buttermilk
1 egg, beaten
½ teaspoon vanilla

1. Preheat the oven to 350°F. Grease a 9 × 5 × 3-inch loaf pan.

2. In a large bowl, sift together the all-purpose flour, sugar, whole wheat flour, cinnamon, baking powder, baking soda, and salt. Cut in the butter or margarine until mixture resembles

coarse cornmeal. Fold in the apples until coated.

3. Stir together buttermilk, egg, and vanilla. Add to the dry ingredients, stirring until just moistened.

4. Spread into prepared pan and bake 50 to 60 minutes or until browned and a wooden pick inserted in the center comes out clean.

5. Cool in pan for 5 minutes. Turn onto a rack and cool completely before slicing.

Variation: Add ½ cup chopped walnuts when you add the apples.

APRICOT~PRUNE BREAD

Makes: 1 loaf; serves: 14

If you're not fond of prunes, just substitute extra apricots for them.

¾ cup chopped dried apricots
¾ cup chopped pitted prunes
1 tablespoon plus 1½ cups all-purpose flour
¾ cup whole wheat flour
1 tablespoon baking powder
1 teaspoon baking soda
½ teaspoon salt
½ cup (1 stick) butter or margarine
1 cup sugar
2 eggs
1 cup unflavored yogurt
2 teaspoons grated lemon rind

1. Preheat the oven to 350°F. Thoroughly grease and flour a 9 × 5 × 3-inch loaf pan.

2. On a piece of waxed paper, toss the apricots and prunes with 1 tablespoon all-purpose flour.

3. In a large bowl or on a piece of waxed paper, sift together 1½ cups all-purpose flour, the whole wheat flour, baking powder, baking soda, and salt.

4. In a large bowl, cream the butter or margarine with the sugar until light and fluffy. Add the eggs, one at a time, beating well after each addition. Beat in the yogurt and lemon rind.

5. Using a wooden spoon, stir in the flour mixture. Stir in the dried fruit.

6. Spoon into prepared pan. Bake 50 minutes to 1 hour or until a wooden pick inserted in the center comes out clean.

Variation: Substitute 1 cup of lemon yogurt for the unflavored.

DRIED FIG–CARDAMOM BREAD

Makes: one 9-inch loaf; serves: 10 to 14

I sometimes serve this bread as dessert; it's a perfect accompaniment to poached fruit.

1 1/2 cups all-purpose flour
1 cup sugar
3/4 cup whole wheat flour
2 teaspoons baking powder
1 1/2 teaspoons ground cardamom
1 teaspoon baking soda
1/2 teaspoon salt
1 1/2 cups chopped dried figs
2 eggs
1 1/3 cups buttermilk
1/3 cup butter or margarine, melted

1. Preheat the oven to 350°F. Grease and flour a 9 × 5 × 3-inch loaf pan.

2. In a large bowl, stir together the all-purpose flour, sugar, whole wheat flour, baking powder, cardamom, baking soda, and salt. Add the figs and toss.

3. In a medium bowl, beat the eggs; stir in the buttermilk and butter or margarine.

4. Stir the liquid ingredients into the dry ingredients until just combined. Pour into prepared pan; bake 50 minutes or until wooden pick inserted in the center comes out clean.

Variation: Substitute 1 1/2 teaspoons ground coriander or 1 tablespoon grated orange or lemon rind for the cardamom.

BLUE CORNMEAL BREAD

Makes: nine 3-inch squares; serves: 9

This very moist bread has a subtle corn taste. If you like cornbread very sweet, you may want to add up to 1/4 cup more sugar.

1 1/4 cups blue cornmeal
3/4 cup all-purpose flour
1/4 cup sugar
2 teaspoons baking powder
1 teaspoon baking soda
3/4 teaspoon salt, or to taste
2 eggs
1 1/2 cups buttermilk
1/4 cup (1/2 stick) melted butter or margarine

1. Preheat the oven to 400°F. Grease a 9-inch-square baking pan.

2. In a large bowl, stir together the cornmeal, flour, sugar, baking powder, baking soda, and salt.

3. In a medium bowl, beat the eggs. Add the buttermilk and butter or margarine and beat until completely combined.

4. Stir the liquid ingredients into the dry until the dry ingredients are moistened. Spread into prepared pan.

5. Bake 25 to 30 minutes or until a wooden pick inserted in the center comes out clean. Let cool and then cut into squares.

Variation: Cornbread: Use yellow or white cornmeal instead of the blue.

BLUEBERRY CORNMEAL BREAD

Makes: one 9-inch loaf; serves: 14 to 16

This is more of a quick bread than a traditional cornbread, and it's out of this world.

1½ cups all-purpose flour
¾ cup yellow cornmeal
2 teaspoons baking powder
½ teaspoon salt
½ cup shortening
¾ cup sugar
2 egg whites
1 egg
1 teaspoon vanilla extract
¾ cup milk
2 cups fresh or frozen blueberries (if using
    frozen, measure while frozen, then thaw)

1. Preheat the oven to 350°F. Grease and flour a 9 × 5 × 3-inch loaf pan.

2. In a large bowl or on a piece of waxed paper, stir together the flour, cornmeal, baking powder, and salt; set aside.

3. In a large bowl, cream the shortening. Add the sugar; cream until fluffy. Beat in the egg whites, egg, and vanilla. Beat in the dry ingredients alternately with the milk. Stir in the blueberries.

4. Spread into prepared pan; bake 1 hour or until a wooden pick inserted in the center comes out clean. Turn onto rack to cool.

Variation: Use chopped peaches, apples, or raisins instead of the blueberries.

CORN POUND BREAD

Makes: one 9-inch loaf cake; serves: 12

Somewhere between pound cake and cornbread, this very moist, corny-flavored bread is a great between-meal snack, breakfast cake, or even dessert.

One 8½-ounce can corn kernels, undrained
½ cup buttermilk
1⅓ cups all-purpose flour
⅔ cup cornmeal
2 teaspoons baking powder
1 teaspoon baking soda
½ teaspoon salt
½ cup (1 stick) butter or margarine, softened
1⅓ cups sugar
2 eggs
1 teaspoon vanilla

1. Preheat the oven to 350°F. Grease and flour a 9 × 5 × 3-inch loaf pan.

2. Place the corn and buttermilk into a blender or food processor container fitted with a steel blade. Cover and process until pureed.

3. In a large bowl or on a piece of waxed paper, stir together the flour, cornmeal, baking powder, baking soda, and salt with a whisk.

4. In a large bowl, cream the butter or margarine and sugar until completely combined. Beat in the eggs, one at a time, beating well after each addition. Beat in the vanilla.

5. Alternately beat in the dry ingredients with the corn puree. Beat until just combined. (The batter may look curdled.) Spoon into the prepared pan.

6. Bake 45 to 50 minutes or until a wooden pick inserted in the center comes out clean. Let cool in pan 10 minutes; turn onto a rack to cool completely.

Variation: Stir 1 cup additional corn into the batter before spreading into pan.

CHEDDAR~CHILI CORNBREAD

—————— 🔲 ——————

Makes: 9 squares; serves: 6 to 9

This is definitely a "heavy" bread. The chilies give it just a small kick. I like to serve this with jalapeño jelly or apple butter.

1 cup yellow cornmeal
1 cup all-purpose flour
1 tablespoon baking powder
½ teaspoon salt
1 cup milk
3 tablespoons melted butter or margarine
1 egg
1½ cups shredded Cheddar cheese
One 4-ounce can chopped green chilies, drained

1. Preheat the oven to 375°F. Grease an 8-inch-square baking pan.

2. In a medium bowl, stir together the cornmeal, flour, baking powder, and salt.

3. In a separate medium bowl, stir together the milk, butter or margarine, egg, cheese, and chilies. Add the liquid ingredients to the dry and stir until just combined. Spread into prepared pan.

4. Bake 35 minutes or until browned on top. Cut into 9 squares.

Variation: Stir in a drained 8-ounce can corn kernels.

CRANBERRY~FIG BROWN BREAD

—————— 🔲💙 ——————

Makes: 2 loaves; serves: 20 to 24
(10 to 12 per loaf)

This steamed bread is almost more like a steamed pudding dessert than most people's concept of

bread. But call it bread or call it pudding, I call it yummy!

¾ cup whole wheat flour
¾ cup rye flour
¾ cup cornmeal
1 teaspoon baking powder
1 teaspoon baking soda
½ teaspoon salt
1¾ cups buttermilk
1 cup molasses
2 tablespoons melted butter or margarine
1 cup chopped cranberries
1 cup chopped figs

1. Grease 2 empty coffee cans (or cans of similar size). Cut 4 circles of waxed paper the same diameter as the cans. Place one circle in the bottom of each can; grease and set aside.

2. In a large bowl or on waxed paper, stir together both flours, the cornmeal, baking powder, baking soda, and salt.

3. In a large bowl, combine the buttermilk, molasses, and butter or margarine. Add the dry ingredients to the buttermilk mixture and stir until combined. Stir in the cranberries and figs.

4. Spoon half the batter into each can. Grease the remaining circles of waxed paper and place, greased side down, onto the batter. Cover the top of the cans with a double thickness of aluminum foil. Fasten by tying with string or using a large rubber band.

5. Place the cans upright on a rack set in a large pot. Add water to reach halfway up the cans. Cover the pot and bring to a boil over high heat. Reduce heat and simmer 2 hours, or until the tops are puffed and a wooden pick inserted in the center comes out clean.

6. Remove loaves from cans, discard waxed paper, and cool on rack.

7. Cut into slices about ¼ inch thick.

Variation: Boston Brown Bread: Substitute 1½ cups dark raisins for the cranberries and figs.

UNTRADITIONAL IRISH SODA BREAD

Makes: 1 round loaf; serves: 8 to 12

I tried to duplicate a fabulous Irish soda bread served at the Landmark Tavern, a restaurant in New York City. This version uses whole wheat flour in addition to all-purpose flour. It's also sweet. If you find it hard to combine all the flour with the buttermilk, just turn any flour remaining in the bowl onto the floured board and knead it into the bread at that time.

1 ½ cups all-purpose flour
1 ½ cups whole wheat flour
⅓ cup sugar
2 teaspoons ground cinnamon
1 ½ teaspoons ground nutmeg
1 ½ teaspoons salt, or to taste
1 teaspoon baking powder
1 teaspoon baking soda
1 ½ cups buttermilk

1. Preheat the oven to 400°F.

2. In a large bowl, stir together both flours, the sugar, cinnamon, nutmeg, salt, baking powder, and baking soda.

3. Stir in the buttermilk until the mixture forms a ball. Knead on a lightly floured surface 3 minutes. Form into an 8-inch ball.

4. Place on a greased baking sheet. Cut an "X" in the top with a sharp knife.

5. Bake 30 to 40 minutes or until browned.

Variation: Stir 1½ cups raisins into the flour mixture before you add the buttermilk.

RYE-RISH SODA BREAD

Makes: 1 round loaf; serves: 8 to 12

In this version, rye flour replaces part of the all-purpose flour. It's a great bread and it's almost fat-free (most buttermilk is only 1% fat).

2 cups rye flour
2 cups all-purpose flour
1 ½ tablespoons caraway seeds
2 teaspoons salt, or to taste
1 teaspoon baking powder
1 teaspoon baking soda
1 ¾ cups buttermilk

1. Preheat the oven to 400°F.

2. In a large bowl, stir together both flours, the caraway seeds, salt, baking powder, and baking soda.

3. Stir in the buttermilk until the mixture forms a ball. Knead on a lightly floured surface 3 minutes. Form into an 8-inch ball.

4. Place on a greased baking sheet. Cut an "X" in the top with a sharp knife.

5. Bake 35 to 40 minutes or until browned.

Variation: Whole Wheat Irish Soda Bread: Substitute whole wheat flour for the rye.

BISCUITS AND SCONES

WORLD'S BEST WHOLE WHEAT BISCUITS

L

Makes: 12 to 14 biscuits; serves: 6 to 12

These are really easy to make since you don't have to cut in the shortening—just stir in the cream. I love them with raspberry jam, but they're fabulous even plain.

¾ cup all-purpose flour
½ cup whole wheat flour
1 tablespoon sugar
1 tablespoon baking powder
¾ teaspoon salt
1 cup heavy cream

1. Preheat the oven to 400°F. Grease a baking sheet.

2. In a large bowl, stir together both flours, the sugar, baking powder, and salt.

3. Using a fork, gradually stir in the cream until a soft dough is formed.

4. On a lightly floured board, knead the dough 10 to 12 times. Reflour board and pat into a circle or rectangle ½ inch thick. Using a 2½-inch biscuit cutter, cut into biscuits (or just cut into 2½-inch squares).

5. Place on prepared baking sheet and bake 15 to 18 minutes or until golden on top.

Variation: Add 1 teaspoon ground cinnamon and ¼ teaspoon ground nutmeg to the dry ingredients.

PECAN-ORANGE BISCUITS

V ♥

Makes: 12 biscuits; serves: 6 to 12

Serve this with honey or fruit-flavored butter.

1¼ cups all-purpose flour
¾ cup whole wheat flour
½ cup ground pecans
2 tablespoons sugar
1 tablespoon baking powder
½ teaspoon salt
3 tablespoons butter or margarine
¾ cup orange juice
1 tablespoon grated orange rind

1. Preheat the oven to 400°F. Grease a large baking sheet.

2. In a large bowl, stir together both flours, the pecans, sugar, baking powder, and salt.

3. Using a pastry blender or two knives, cut in the butter or margarine until mixture resembles coarse cornmeal.

4. Stir together the orange juice and orange rind. Add to the flour mixture and stir until juice is absorbed.

5. Knead in the bowl 10 to 12 times until dough forms a ball. Roll out dough between two pieces of waxed paper to ½-inch thickness. Using a 3-inch biscuit cutter, cut into rounds, rerolling dough scraps until all dough is used up. Place on prepared baking sheet.

6. Bake 18 to 20 minutes or until lightly browned on top.

Variation: Use walnuts instead of pecans.

SWEET BISCUITS

Makes: 14 to 18; serves: 7 to 9

These are not very sweet, but sweet enough to make them different from plain biscuits.

1¼ cups all-purpose flour
¾ cup whole wheat flour
⅓ cup sugar
1 tablespoon baking powder
¼ teaspoon salt
⅓ cup butter or margarine
1 cup milk

1. Preheat the oven to 425°F. Grease a baking sheet.

2. In a large bowl, combine both flours, the sugar, baking powder, and salt.

3. Using a pastry cutter or two knives, cut in the butter or margarine until mixture resembles coarse cornmeal.

4. Stir in enough milk until mixture forms a soft dough. Turn onto floured board and knead 10 to 12 times. Roll out dough to ³/₄-inch thickness. Using 2-inch biscuit cutter, cut into rounds. Place on prepared baking sheet.

5. Bake 15 minutes or until browned on top.

PLANTAIN BISCUITS

Makes: 16 biscuits; serves: 8 to 16

I tested these biscuits the same day that I made Butternut Squash Butter (page 492), then served the two together . . . it was a perfect match! Of course, these are also good with butter, jam, marmalade, or for a special treat, with jalapeño pepper jelly. They're also good just by themselves.

2 plantains, almost completely black
    (scant 1 pound)
1½ cups all-purpose flour
½ cup whole wheat flour
2 tablespoons sugar
1 tablespoon baking powder
1 teaspoon baking soda
1 teaspoon ground cardamom
½ teaspoon salt
1 cup heavy cream
3 tablespoons molasses
1 tablespoon fresh lime juice

1. Make a lengthwise slit in both plantain peels. Bake in a 350°F oven for 40 minutes or until tender. Cool and peel.

2. In a large bowl, stir together both flours, sugar, the baking powder, baking soda, cardamom, and salt.

3. Place the plantains, cream, and molasses into a blender or food processor container fitted with a steel blade. Cover and process until just pureed. Stir in the lime juice.

4. Stir plantain puree into dry ingredients until mixture forms a soft dough.

5. On a lightly floured board, knead the dough 8 times. Reflour board and pat into a circle or rectangle ¹/₂ inch thick. Using a 3-inch biscuit cutter, cut into biscuits (or just cut into 2¹/₂-inch squares).

6. Place on greased baking sheet and bake in preheated 350°F oven for 20 to 25 minutes or until golden on top.

HERBED BISCUITS

Ⓛ♥

Makes: 10 to 12 biscuits; serves: 5 to 12

These are great brunch or dinner biscuits.

1¼ cups all-purpose flour
¾ cup whole wheat flour
1 tablespoon baking powder
1 teaspoon dried basil
½ teaspoon baking soda
½ teaspoon salt
½ teaspoon dried thyme
¼ cup shortening
¾ cup buttermilk
½ cup chopped fresh parsley

1. Preheat the oven to 425°F. Grease a baking sheet.

2. In a large bowl, combine both flours, the baking powder, basil, baking soda, salt, and thyme.

3. Using a pastry cutter or two knives, cut in the shortening until mixture resembles coarse cornmeal.

4. Stir in the buttermilk and parsley until mixture forms a soft dough.

5. Turn onto floured board and knead 10 to 12 times. Roll out dough to ³/₄-inch thickness. Using a 2¹/₂-inch biscuit cutter, cut into rounds. Place on prepared baking sheet.

6. Bake 15 minutes or until browned on top.

Variation: Use dried herbs of choice, such as tarragon, oregano, savory, or dill, instead of basil and thyme.

PEPPERED BLUE CORNMEAL BISCUITS

Ⓛ

Makes: 12 to 14 biscuits; serves: 6 to 12

I didn't find these especially spicy, but then, it takes quite a fire for me to say something is really spicy. Judge for yourself. Without the pepper they make extremely good biscuits anyway.

1¼ cups all-purpose flour
¾ cup blue cornmeal
2 teaspoons baking powder
1 teaspoon baking soda
1 teaspoon salt, or to taste
1 teaspoon pepper
½ cup shortening
1 cup buttermilk

1. Preheat the oven to 400°F Grease a baking sheet.

2. In a large bowl, stir together the flour, cornmeal, baking powder, baking soda, salt, and pepper.

3. Using a pastry blender or two knives, cut in the shortening until mixture resembles coarse cornmeal. Stir in the buttermilk until mixture forms a dough.

4. On a well-floured board, knead the dough 10 times. Reflour board and pat into a circle or rectangle ¹/₂ inch thick. Using a 3-inch biscuit cutter, cut into biscuits (or just cut into 2¹/₂-inch squares).

5. Place on prepared baking sheet and bake 15 to 18 minutes or until golden on top.

Variations: Use white or yellow cornmeal instead of the blue.

For a milder biscuit, omit the pepper.

PARMESAN BISCUITS

Makes: 12 to 14 biscuits; serves: 6 to 14

These flavorful biscuits hold their own for any meal. I like to serve them with a soufflé or other egg dish for brunch. But I usually have a second type of bread available for anyone looking to spread something sweet on.

1 1/4 cups all-purpose flour
3/4 cup whole wheat flour
1 tablespoon baking powder
1/2 teaspoon salt
1/4 cup (1/2 stick) butter or margarine
1/2 cup grated Parmesan cheese
1 cup milk

1. Preheat the oven to 425°F. Grease a baking sheet.

2. In a large bowl, stir together both flours, the baking powder, and salt.

3. Using a pastry blender or two knives, cut in the butter or margarine until mixture resembles coarse cornmeal. Stir in the cheese and then the milk until mixture forms a dough.

4. On a lightly floured board, knead the dough 8 times. Reflour board and pat into a circle or rectangle 1/2 inch thick. Using a 2 1/2-inch biscuit cutter, cut into biscuits (or just cut into 2 1/2-inch squares).

5. Place on prepared baking sheet and bake 15 minutes or until golden on top.

Variation: Add 1 teaspoon dried oregano or basil when stirring in the cheese.

WHEAT GERM DROP BISCUITS

Makes: 12 to 15 biscuits; serves: 6 to 15

I like to make drop biscuits because you don't have to bother kneading, rolling, or cutting the biscuits— another example of my being a lazy cook.

1 cup all-purpose flour
1/2 cup whole wheat flour
1/2 cup honey-toasted wheat germ
1 tablespoon baking powder
3/4 teaspoon salt
1/2 teaspoon baking soda
1/2 cup shortening
1 cup buttermilk

1. Preheat the oven to 400°F. Grease a baking sheet.

2. In a large bowl, stir together both flours, the wheat germ, baking powder, salt, and baking soda.

3. Using a pastry blender or two knives, cut in the shortening until mixture resembles coarse cornmeal. Stir in the buttermilk until mixture forms a dough.

4. Drop dough by heaping tablespoons onto prepared baking sheet. Bake 18 to 20 minutes or until browned on peaks.

Variation: Stir in 1 teaspoon ground cinnamon and 1/4 teaspoon ground nutmeg when adding the flours.

SOURDOUGH DROP BISCUITS

[V]

Makes: 12 biscuits; serves: 6 to 12

I'm pleased with these biscuits, which use neither dairy products nor eggs—perfect for vegans. Some sourdoughs are quite thick (almost like batter), and some are thin (just slightly thicker than heavy cream). I used a thin sourdough for these biscuits; if yours is thick, just thin it with water.

1½ cups all-purpose flour
¾ cup spelt flour or whole wheat flour
2 tablespoons sugar
2 teaspoons baking powder
1 teaspoon baking soda
1¼ teaspoons salt, or to taste
½ cup shortening
1 cup sourdough starter (page 425)
¼ cup water

1. Preheat the oven to 400°F. Grease a baking sheet.

2. In a large bowl, stir together both flours, the sugar, baking powder, baking soda, and salt.

3. Using a pastry blender or two knives, cut in the shortening until mixture resembles coarse cornmeal. Stir in the sourdough and water until mixture forms a dough.

4. Drop dough by heaping tablespoons onto prepared baking sheet.

5. Bake 18 to 20 minutes or until browned on peaks.

Variation: For a more savory biscuit, stir in 1 teaspoon dried oregano when adding the flours.

SCONES

[LO]

Makes: 8 scones; serves: 8

The English tend to use currants rather than raisins in their scones, and you can, too. Serve these at afternoon "tea" with jam (although they are so delicious that they certainly don't need the jam).

1¼ cups all-purpose flour
¾ cup whole wheat flour
⅓ cup sugar
2 teaspoons baking powder
1 teaspoon baking soda
½ teaspoon salt
⅓ cup butter or margarine
1 cup dark raisins or currants
1 egg
¾ cup buttermilk
1 teaspoon vanilla

1. Preheat the oven to 400°F. Grease a baking sheet.

2. In a large bowl, combine both flours, the sugar, baking powder, baking soda, and salt.

3. Using a pastry cutter or two knives, cut in the butter or margarine until mixture resembles coarse cornmeal. Stir in the raisins.

4. In a medium bowl, beat the egg. Beat in the buttermilk and vanilla; stir into dry ingredients until mixture forms a soft dough.

5. Turn onto floured board and knead 10 to 12 times. On the prepared baking sheet, pat the dough into an 8-inch circle. Using a floured knife, cut into 8 wedges, but don't separate them.

6. Bake 18 to 20 minutes or until browned on top. Cool on rack. Separate the wedges when ready to serve.

Variation: Add chopped walnuts when you add the raisins. If you want to glaze these before baking, brush the top with heavy cream, then sprinkle lightly with sugar.

MUFFINS

BASIC MUFFINS

— 🔲 —

Makes: 12 muffins; serves: 6 to 12

These muffins rise high and are quite light for muffins made with any whole wheat flour.

1 ½ cups all-purpose flour
½ cup whole wheat flour
¼ cup sugar
1 tablespoon baking powder
1 teaspoon baking soda
½ teaspoon salt
1 egg
1 ½ cups buttermilk
3 tablespoons butter or margarine, melted

1. Preheat the oven to 400°F. Grease 12 2 ½-inch muffin cups.

2. In a large bowl, stir together both flours, the sugar, baking powder, baking soda, and salt.

3. In a medium bowl, lightly beat the egg. Beat in the buttermilk and the butter or margarine until completely combined.

4. Using a wooden spoon, stir liquid into dry ingredients until just moistened. Batter will be very thick. (Be careful not to overbeat or the muffins will have tunnels.)

5. Spoon 2 rounded tablespoons of the batter into each of the prepared muffin cups.

6. Bake 25 to 30 minutes or until lightly browned on top.

Variation: Blueberry Muffins: Add 1 cup blueberries to the batter.

STREUSEL-TOPPED MUFFINS

— 🔲 —

Makes: 12 muffins; serves: 6 to 12

⅓ cup whole wheat flour
2 tablespoons sugar
½ teaspoon cinnamon
1 ½ tablespoons butter or margarine, softened
1 recipe Basic Muffin batter, prepared (left)

1. Preheat the oven to 400°F. Grease 12 2 ½-inch muffin cups.

2. Prepare the topping by stirring together the flour, sugar, and cinnamon in a medium bowl. Cut in the butter or margarine until mixture is crumbly; set aside.

3. Spoon 2 rounded tablespoons of the batter into each of the prepared muffin cups.

4. Sprinkle the streusel topping over the muffins.

5. Bake 25 to 30 minutes or until lightly browned on top.

Variation: Add ½ cup chopped walnuts or pecans to the streusel topping.

CORN MUFFINS

Makes: 12 muffins; serves: 6 to 12

These don't rise very high, but they taste great.

1 cup cornmeal
1 cup all-purpose flour
1/2 cup sugar
2 teaspoons baking powder
1 teaspoon baking soda
1/2 teaspoon salt
1 egg
1 1/3 cups buttermilk
3 tablespoons butter or margarine, melted

1. Preheat the oven to 400°F. Grease 12 3-inch muffin cups.

2. In a large bowl, stir together the cornmeal, flour, sugar, baking powder, baking soda, and salt.

3. In a medium bowl, lightly beat the egg. Beat in the buttermilk and the butter or margarine until completely combined.

4. Using a wooden spoon, stir liquid into dry ingredients until just moistened. (Be careful not to overbeat or the muffins will have tunnels.)

5. Divide the batter evenly among the prepared muffin cups. Bake 18 to 22 minutes or until lightly browned on top.

Variation: Stir in 1 cup blueberries or chopped, sautéed apples.

JAM-FILLED MUFFINS

Makes: 12 muffins; serves: 6 to 12

1 recipe Basic Muffin batter, prepared (page 408)
1/4 cup jam, jelly, or preserves

1. Preheat the oven to 400°F. Grease 12 2 1/2-inch muffin cups.

2. Spoon 1 rounded tablespoon of the batter into each of the prepared muffin cups. Drop 1 teaspoon jam over the batter. Drop 1 more rounded tablespoon of batter to cover the jam.

3. Bake 25 to 30 minutes or until lightly browned on top.

Variation: Chocolate-Filled Muffins: Substitute 1 teaspoon mini chocolate morsels for the jam.

THREE-GRAIN MUFFINS

Makes: 12 muffins; serves: 6 to 12

These are dense but tasty.

1 cup all-purpose flour
½ cup oat bran
⅓ cup cornmeal
¼ cup wheat germ
¼ cup sugar
1 tablespoon baking powder
½ teaspoon baking soda
½ teaspoon salt
1 egg
¾ cup milk
3 tablespoons molasses
3 tablespoons vegetable oil

1. Preheat the oven to 400°F. Grease 12 2½-inch muffin cups.

2. In a large bowl, stir together the flour, oat bran, cornmeal, wheat germ, sugar, baking powder, baking soda, and salt.

3. In a medium bowl, lightly beat the egg. Beat in the milk, molasses, and oil until completely combined.

4. Using a wooden spoon, stir liquid into dry ingredients until just moistened. Batter will be very thick. (Be careful not to overbeat or the muffins will have tunnels.)

5. Spoon 2 rounded tablespoons of the batter into each of the prepared muffin cups.

6. Bake 18 to 20 minutes or until lightly browned on top.

Variation: Add ½ cup raisins to the batter.

DATE-BRAN MUFFINS

Makes: 12 muffins; serves: 6 to 12

If you're looking for a really delicious bran muffin, try these.

1⅓ cups buttermilk
¾ cup Bran Buds or All-Bran cereal
¾ cup all-purpose flour
¾ cup cornmeal
1 tablespoon baking powder
1 teaspoon baking soda
1 teaspoon salt
2 egg whites
¼ cup vegetable oil
¼ cup molasses
1 cup chopped dates

1. Preheat the oven to 425°F. Grease 12 2½-inch muffin cups.

2. In a medium bowl, combine the buttermilk and Bran Buds and let stand 5 minutes.

3. In a large bowl, stir together the flour, cornmeal, baking powder, baking soda, and salt.

4. Add the egg whites, oil, molasses, and dates to the bran mixture and stir until completely combined.

5. Using a wooden spoon, stir liquid into dry ingredients until just moistened. (Be careful not to overbeat or the muffins will have tunnels.)

6. Divide the batter evenly among the prepared muffin cups (they will be fairly full). Bake 12 to 15 minutes or until lightly browned on top.

Variation: Cornmeal Bran Muffins: Omit the chopped dates.

LEMON~POPPY SEED MUFFINS

Makes: 12 muffins; serves: 6 to 12

You can increase the lemony flavor by adding extra lemon rind.

1 ¼ cups all-purpose flour
¾ cup whole wheat flour
½ cup sugar
2 tablespoons poppy seeds
2 teaspoons baking powder
1 teaspoon baking soda
½ teaspoon salt
1 egg
¾ cup unflavored yogurt
¼ cup fresh lemon juice
3 tablespoons milk
1 tablespoon butter or margarine, melted
2 teaspoons grated lemon rind

1. Preheat the oven to 400°F. Grease 12 2 ½-inch muffin cups.

2. In a large bowl, stir together both flours, the sugar, poppy seeds, baking powder, baking soda, and salt.

3. In a medium bowl, lightly beat the egg. Beat in the yogurt, lemon juice, milk, butter or margarine, and lemon rind until completely combined.

4. Using a wooden spoon, stir liquid into dry ingredients until just moistened. Batter will be very thick. (Be careful not to overbeat or the muffins will have tunnels.)

5. Divide batter evenly into each of the prepared muffin cups.

6. Bake 18 to 22 minutes or until lightly browned on top.

Variation: Omit the poppy seeds.

CRANBERRY~OATMEAL MUFFINS

Makes: 12 muffins; serves: 6 to 12

¾ cup chopped cranberries
3 tablespoons sugar
1 ¼ cups all-purpose flour
½ cup quick-cooking oatmeal
2 tablespoons wheat germ
2 teaspoons baking powder
1 ½ teaspoons ground cinnamon
½ teaspoon baking soda
½ teaspoon salt
1 egg
¾ cup apple juice
½ cup buttermilk
¼ cup firmly packed light brown or dark brown sugar
3 tablespoons butter or margarine, melted

1. Preheat the oven to 400°F. Grease 12 3-inch muffin cups.

2. In a medium bowl, stir together the cranberries and sugar; let stand 10 minutes.

3. In a large bowl, stir together the flour, oatmeal, wheat germ, baking powder, cinnamon, baking soda, and salt.

4. In a medium bowl, lightly beat the egg. Beat in the apple juice, buttermilk, brown sugar, and butter or margarine until completely combined. Stir in the oatmeal mixture. Stir in the cranberries with any liquid that may be in the bowl.

5. Using a wooden spoon, stir liquid into dry ingredients until just moistened. (Be careful not to overbeat or the muffins will have tunnels.)

6. Divide the batter evenly among the prepared muffin cups (they will be fairly full). Bake 20 to 25 minutes or until lightly browned on top.

Variation: Substitute dried currants for the cranberries.

SWEET POTATO
MEADOW MUFFINS

—————— Ⓛ ——————

Makes: 12 muffins; serves: 6 to 12

*These are a cross between a biscuit and a muffin.
They're prepared in the method of a drop biscuit,
but have the sweetness and texture of a muffin,
and they look like golden meadow muffins. (For
those of you not familiar with the term "meadow
muffin" . . . just let me say it has something to do
with cows and meadows.)*

1²/₃ cups all-purpose flour
²/₃ cup whole wheat flour
1 tablespoon baking powder
1 teaspoon baking soda
½ teaspoon salt
½ teaspoon ground nutmeg
⅓ cup vegetable shortening
1¼ cups buttermilk
¾ cup mashed sweet potatoes (fresh,
    cooked; or canned)
⅓ cup firmly packed light brown or dark
    brown sugar

1. Preheat the oven to 400°F. Grease a large
baking sheet.

2. In a large bowl, stir together both flours, the
baking powder, baking soda, salt, and nutmeg.

3. Cut the shortening into the flour until the
mixture resembles coarse cornmeal.

4. In a medium bowl, stir together the buttermilk, sweet potatoes, and brown sugar until the
sugar is dissolved.

5. Stir buttermilk mixture into dry ingredients
until mixture forms a soft dough.

6. Drop 12 heaping soupspoonfuls onto the
prepared baking sheet.

7. Bake 20 to 25 minutes or until golden on top.
Cool 15 minutes on rack before serving.

Variation: Cinnamon Sweet Potato Biscuits:
Stir in 1 tablespoon ground cinnamon when
you stir together the dry ingredients. You can
leave in or omit the nutmeg.

YEAST BREADS

Working with Yeast

Yeast has a bad reputation as a temperamental ingredient. In fact, if treated properly, yeast will always work. The difference between success and failure is handling the yeast properly. Here are the keys to success.

Check the expiration date on the yeast package. Yeast, being a living thing, has a certain life expectancy, and all manufacturers print expiration dates on the yeast packages. If you are using the yeast after that date, it may not activate. You can prolong the shelf life of the yeast by storing it in the refrigerator or freezer.

Activate the yeast in the proper-temperature liquid and give it some food. Yeast activates best in water (or other liquids) that are 105° to 115°F. (If you don't have a thermometer to measure the temperature of the liquid, the liquid should feel quite warm, almost hot, to the touch.) Higher temperatures will kill off the yeast; at lower temperatures the yeast either will fail to awaken or will take much longer to rise. If you add a small amount of sugar to the water the yeast will activate more quickly.

Proof the yeast. Proofing verifies that the yeast has been activated. All you have to do is let the yeast and water mixture stand from about 5 minutes (if using sugar) to 15 minutes (if the water was not quite warm enough). At the end of that time $1/4$ inch of bubbly foam forms on top of the mixture. If this doesn't happen it means that the yeast has not been activated, so discard this batch and try again, double-checking the expiration date on the yeast package and the temperature of the water.

Activating and proofing the yeast in liquid are not essential to making yeast breads or cakes. Some recipes specify that you stir the yeast into the dry ingredients, then add the liquid and continue with the recipe. (Fleishmann's calls this method cool-rise.) I strongly prefer activating the yeast in liquid, then proofing, since you are assured in advance that the yeast is up and running before adding other ingredients. The cool-rise method doesn't guarantee that the yeast has been activated.

Choosing a recipe with some wheat flour will usually result in higher-rising breads. Yeast works by giving off gas that stretches the molecules in the dough. The amount of gluten in a flour will influence how elastic the dough is and, therefore, how high and how quickly it will rise. Wheat flour has the highest amount of gluten of all grains, which is why many breads contain at least some wheat flour. Rye, barley, and oats also contain gluten, but in lesser amounts (buckwheat, millet, amaranth, and quinoa may also contain some gluten).

Turn onto a well-floured board. This means placing between $1/4$ and $1/2$ cup flour onto the board before placing the dough on it.

Knead the dough thoroughly. Kneading develops the gluten into longer, stretchier strands. Here's how you knead dough: Form the dough into a ball. If the dough is sticky, coat it in flour. Also put some flour on the palms of your hands. Using your palms, push the dough down and away from you. Fold the dough in half and turn it $1/4$ turn, then push again. Continue pushing, folding, and turning for about 10 minutes, adding as much flour to the board and your hands as necessary so that the dough doesn't stick too badly.

The stickiness of the dough will determine the texture of the bread. Most recipes will say to add enough of the remaining flour until the dough is no longer sticky. If you are planning to make a free-form bread (one that is not baked in a pan to constrain its spreading), you will want to make a dough that is not sticky at all, because the moister (stickier) a dough is, the more inclined it is to spread over the baking sheet rather than to rise high. So, for a free-form loaf, knead in enough flour so that you can knead the dough at least six times without having to add more flour to the board.

If you are making Danish pastry or other products where you want a tender crumb, the dough may still be quite sticky after kneading. Breads that are baked in a pan may fall somewhere in between—not very sticky, but not too dry.

Let the dough rise until doubled in bulk. After kneading, place the dough in a large, greased bowl and cover the bowl lightly with greased plastic wrap. Place the bowl in a warm, draft-free spot for the dough to rise. The dough will rise more or less quickly depending on several factors: the type of flour used, the warmth of the spot it is in when rising, and the amount of salt in the dough (less salt will make dough rise faster). You can test to see if the dough has doubled in bulk by gently pressing the dough with your fingertip. If the slight indentation remains, the dough has doubled. If the dough springs back after pressing, it still has to rise more.

Whole Wheat Bread

Makes: 1 loaf; serves: 12 to 16

This is a slightly sweet, light, delicious bread.

1/2 cup very warm water (105°–115°F)
1/2 teaspoon sugar
1 package active dry yeast
2 cups whole wheat flour
1 to 1 1/2 cups all-purpose flour
2 teaspoons salt
1/2 cup water
2 tablespoons honey
2 tablespoons molasses
2 tablespoons vegetable oil

1. In a glass measuring cup, stir together the warm water and sugar. Stir in the yeast and let it proof (page 413).

2. In a large bowl, combine the whole wheat flour, 1/2 cup of the all-purpose flour, and the salt. Stir the yeast mixture, 1/2 cup water, the honey, molasses, and oil into the flour mixture. Stir in 1/2 cup more flour to make a dough that is firm enough to handle.

3. Turn dough onto a well-floured surface and knead in enough of the remaining flour to make a dough that is manageable and no longer sticky.

4. Place dough in a large, greased bowl and cover with greased plastic wrap. Set in a warm, draft-free spot until doubled in bulk.

5. Punch dough down and form into a loaf. Place in a greased 9 × 5 × 3-inch loaf pan. Cover with greased plastic wrap and let rise until doubled in bulk.

6. Preheat the oven to 350°F. Bake for 45 minutes or until loaf is browned on top and bottom and sounds hollow when tapped. Cool on wire rack.

CORNMEAL BREAD

— 🍞❤ —

Makes: 1 loaf; serves: 12 to 16

This is as close to white bread as you'll find in this book. It's light, in both texture and color, and very pleasant-tasting.

1 cup milk
²/₃ cup cornmeal
½ cup very warm water (105°–115°F)
½ teaspoon plus 2 tablespoons sugar
1 package active dry yeast
2 ³/₄ to 3 ½ cups all-purpose flour
2 teaspoons salt
3 tablespoons melted butter or margarine

1. In a medium bowl, stir together the milk and cornmeal; set aside.

2. In a glass measuring cup, stir together the warm water and ¹/₂ teaspoon of the sugar. Stir in the yeast and let it proof (page 413).

3. In a large bowl, stir together 1¹/₂ cups of the all-purpose flour, the remaining 2 table-spoons sugar, and the salt. Stir in the yeast mixture, cornmeal-milk mixture, and butter or margarine. Stir in 1 cup more of the remaining all-purpose flour.

4. Turn onto a well-floured surface and knead in enough of the remaining flour until dough is elastic and no longer sticky.

5. Place the dough in a large, greased bowl and cover with greased plastic wrap. Set in a warm, draft-free spot until doubled in bulk.

6. Punch dough down and form into a loaf. Place in a greased 9 × 5 × 3-inch loaf pan. Cover with greased plastic wrap and let rise until doubled in bulk.

7. Preheat the oven to 375°F. Bake for 45 to 55 minutes or until loaf is browned on top and bottom and sounds hollow when tapped. Cool on wire rack.

SEMOLINA BREAD

— Ⓥ —

Makes: 1 loaf; serves: 12 to 16

½ cup very warm water (105°–115°F.)
½ teaspoon sugar
2 packages active dry yeast
1½ to 2 cups all-purpose flour, divided
1½ cups semolina flour
2 teaspoons salt
³/₄ cup water
3 tablespoons olive oil
1 egg white (optional)
1 teaspoon water (optional)

1. In a glass measuring cup, stir together the warm water and sugar. Stir in the yeast and let it proof (page 413).

2. Combine 1 cup of the all-purpose flour, the semolina flour, salt, and ³/₄ cup water. Stir in the yeast mixture and oil. Stir in ¹/₄ cup more of the remaining all-purpose flour.

3. Turn onto a well-floured surface and knead in enough of the remaining flour until dough is elastic and no longer sticky.

4. Place dough in a large, greased bowl and cover with greased plastic wrap. Set in a warm, draft-free spot until doubled in bulk.

5. Punch dough down and form into a 6-inch round loaf. Place onto a greased baking sheet. Cover with greased plastic wrap and let rise until doubled in bulk.

6. Score the top of the bread using a very sharp knife. Beat the egg white with 1 teaspoon water and brush over the top of the bread, if desired.

7. Preheat the oven to 400°F. Bake for 40 to 45 minutes or until loaf is browned on top and bottom and sounds hollow when tapped. Cool on wire rack.

Ⓞ *Variation:* Sprinkle sesame seeds over the top after brushing with egg white.

RYE BREAD

Makes: 1 loaf; serves: 12 to 16

This makes a small, dense, chewy loaf of bread. You can make it with all rye flour and no all-purpose, but try to get "white" rye or light rye flour rather than whole grain rye flour, because the bread becomes extremely sour when made exclusively with whole grain rye.

½ cup very warm water (105°–115°F)
½ teaspoon sugar
2 packages active dry yeast
2 cups rye flour
2 teaspoons salt
½ cup mashed potatoes
½ cup water
1 to 1½ cups all-purpose flour

1. In a glass measuring cup, stir together the warm water and sugar. Stir in the yeast and let it proof (page 413).

2. In a large bowl, combine the rye flour and salt. Stir in the yeast mixture, potatoes, and ½ cup water. Stir in ¾ cup of the all-purpose flour to make a dough that is firm enough to handle.

3. Turn the dough onto a well-floured surface and knead in the remaining all-purpose flour.

4. Place the dough in a large, greased bowl and cover with greased plastic wrap. Set in a warm, draft-free spot until doubled in bulk.

5. Punch dough down and form into a loaf. Place in a greased 8½ × 3⅝ × 2⅝-inch loaf pan. Cover with greased plastic wrap and let rise until doubled in bulk.

6. Preheat the oven to 350°F. Bake for 1 hour or until loaf is lightly browned on top and bottom and sounds hollow when tapped. Cool on wire rack.

Variation: Add 1 tablespoon caraway seeds to the dough when you stir in the liquids.

FRESH ROSEMARY–PEPPER RYE BREAD

Makes: 1 loaf; serves: 16 to 20

If you don't have fresh rosemary, dried will do—use 1 tablespoon crumbled.

½ cup very warm water (105°–115°F)
½ teaspoon sugar
2 packages active dry yeast
2 cups rye flour
2¼ to 2¾ cups all-purpose flour
2 teaspoons salt
1½ teaspoons pepper
¾ cup water
¼ cup honey
¼ cup chopped fresh rosemary

1. In a glass measuring cup, stir together the warm water and sugar. Stir in the yeast and let it proof (page 413).

2. In a large bowl, combine the rye flour, 1 cup of the all-purpose flour, and the salt and pepper. Stir the yeast mixture into the flour mixture. Stir in ¾ cup water, the honey, and rosemary. Stir in 1 cup more of the all-purpose flour to make a dough that is firm enough to handle.

3. Turn dough onto a well-floured surface and knead in enough of the remaining flour to make a dough that is manageable and no longer sticky.

4. Place the dough in a large, greased bowl and cover with greased plastic wrap. Set in a warm, draft-free spot until doubled in bulk.

5. Punch dough down and form into a round loaf. Cover with greased plastic wrap and let rise until doubled in bulk. Using a sharp knife, cut 3 slashes into the top of the loaf.

6. Preheat the oven to 350°F. Bake for 40 minutes or until loaf is browned on top and bottom and sounds hollow when tapped. Cool on wire rack.

Variation: Omit the pepper for a milder flavor.

PUMPERNICKEL

Makes: 2 loaves; serves: 24

Pumpernickel is supposed to be a dense, heavy, ryelike bread. In that sense this version is a failure because it's actually light and moist. If you want a more traditional pumpernickel, follow the variation. You can use instant mashed potatoes if you don't want to start from scratch.

1 cup plus ½ cup very warm water (105°–115°F)
⅓ cup cornmeal
½ teaspoon sugar
2 packages active dry yeast
1 cup mashed potatoes
2 tablespoons molasses
2 tablespoons vegetable oil
2¾ to 3½ cups all-purpose flour
1¼ cups rye flour
2½ teaspoons salt

1. In a large bowl stir together 1 cup of the warm water and the cornmeal.

2. In a glass measuring cup, stir together the remaining ½ cup warm water and the sugar. Stir in the yeast and let it proof (page 413). Stir the proofed yeast, the potatoes, molasses, and oil into the cornmeal mixture.

3. Stir 1¼ cups of the all-purpose flour, the rye flour, and salt into the yeast-cornmeal mixture. Stir in ¾ cup more all-purpose flour to make a dough that is firm enough to handle.

4. Turn the dough onto a well-floured surface and knead in enough of the remaining flour to make a dough that is manageable and no longer sticky.

5. Place the dough in a large, greased bowl and cover with greased plastic wrap. Set in a warm, draft-free spot until doubled in bulk. Punch dough down and let rise again.

6. Punch dough down and form into a loaf. Place in two greased 8½ × 3⅝ × 2⅝-inch loaf pans. Cover with greased plastic wrap and let rise until doubled in bulk.

7. Preheat the oven to 375°F. Bake for 40 minutes or until loaf is browned on top and bottom and sounds hollow when tapped. Cool on wire rack.

Variation: Use 1 cup more rye flour and 1 cup less all-purpose flour. Add 1 tablespoon caraway seeds when you add the rye flour.

WHEAT BERRY BREAD

Makes: 1 loaf; serves: 12 to 16

Light and chewy, this bread is an excellent all-purpose bread. The drawback is that you must have cooked wheat berries on hand.

½ cup very warm water (105°–115°F)
½ teaspoon sugar
1 package active dry yeast
1½ cups whole wheat flour
1¼ to 2 cups all-purpose flour
2 teaspoons salt
½ cup water
¼ cup honey
2 tablespoons vegetable oil
1½ cups cooked wheat berries (whole grain wheat) (page 301)

1. In a glass measuring cup, stir together the warm water and sugar. Stir in the yeast and let it proof (page 413).

2. In a large bowl, combine the whole wheat flour, ¹/₂ cup of the all-purpose flour, and the salt. Stir the yeast mixture, ¹/₂ cup water, the honey, and oil into the flour mixture. Stir in the wheat berries and ³/₄ cup more all-purpose flour to make a dough that is firm enough to handle.

3. Turn dough onto a well-floured surface and knead in enough of the remaining flour to make a dough that is manageable and no longer sticky.

4. Place dough in a large, greased bowl and cover with greased plastic wrap. Set in a warm, draft-free spot until doubled in bulk.

5. Punch dough down and form into a loaf. Place in a greased 9 × 5 × 3-inch loaf pan. Cover with greased plastic wrap and let rise until doubled in bulk.

6. Preheat the oven to 350°F. Bake for 45 minutes or until loaf is browned on top and bottom and sounds hollow when tapped. Cool on wire rack.

Variation: Bulgur Bread: Use cooked bulgur instead of the wheat berries.

Donna Mason's Dense and Chewy Whole Grain Bread

— [V] —

Makes: one 9-inch loaf; serves: 14

I was a guest on the Donna Mason Show on WPTF-Radio in Raleigh, North Carolina (in fact, through the wonders of modern communication, I was not in Raleigh, but rather in my living room while we were on the air). During one of the station breaks, Donna mentioned that she was looking for a recipe for an old-fashioned dense and chewy bread to bake, so I volunteered to develop one for her—and here it is!

1¹/₃ cups water
¹/₃ cup cornmeal
¹/₄ cup bulgur
¹/₃ cup molasses
¹/₄ cup vegetable oil
1 cup whole wheat flour
1 cup Quaker Multigrain cereal or rolled oats
¹/₂ cup shelled, unsalted sunflower seeds
¹/₃ cup oat bran
¹/₄ cup wheat germ
2 teaspoons salt
¹/₂ cup very warm water (105°–115°F)
¹/₂ teaspoon sugar
2 packages active dry yeast
1 to 1¹/₂ cups all-purpose flour

1. In a 1-quart saucepan, stir together the 1¹/₃ cups water and the cornmeal. Bring to a boil over medium-high heat, stirring frequently. Stir in the bulgur. Cook 3 minutes, stirring; remove from heat. Stir in the molasses and oil; cool to lukewarm.

2. In a large bowl, stir together the whole wheat flour, Multigrain cereal, sunflower seeds, oat bran, wheat germ, and salt.

3. In a glass measuring cup, stir together the warm water and sugar. Stir in the yeast and let it proof (page 413).

4. Stir the cornmeal mixture into the bowl with the flour mixture. Add the proofed yeast and ¹/₂ cup of the all-purpose flour.

5. Turn onto a well-flour board and knead, using as much of the remaining flour as necessary, to form a dough that is slightly tacky but not sticky.

6. Place the dough in a large, greased bowl and cover with greased plastic wrap. Let rise in a warm, draft-free spot until doubled in bulk (about 1¹/₂ hours).

7. Grease a 9 × 5 × 3-inch loaf pan. Punch dough down, form into a loaf, and place in pan. Cover with greased plastic wrap and let rise until doubled in bulk (about 45 minutes).

8. Bake in a preheated 350°F oven, 1 hour or until the loaf sounds hollow when tapped.

Variation: Use chopped cashews or other nuts instead of the sunflower seeds.

FIVE-GRAIN BREAD

Makes: 1 loaf; serves: 12 to 16

The predominant flavor in this bread is the rye. Because the bread is prepared with a starter, you need 2 days to bake it. The first day you prepare the starter and the next day you make the bread.

1 cup plus ½ cup very warm water
　　(105°–115°F)
2 packages active dry yeast, divided
½ cup plus ½ cup rye flour
¼ cup cornmeal
½ teaspoon sugar
2 tablespoons molasses
1 tablespoon corn oil
1½ to 2 cups all-purpose flour
⅓ cup oat bran
¼ cup quick-cooking cream of rice cereal
2½ teaspoons salt

1. In a large bowl, stir together 1 cup of the warm water and 1 package of the yeast. Stir in ¹/₂ cup of the rye flour and the cornmeal. Cover lightly and let stand overnight.

2. In a glass measuring cup, stir together ¹/₂ cup warm water and the sugar. Stir in the other package of yeast and let it proof (page 413). Stir proofed yeast, molasses, and oil into the rye-cornmeal mixture.

3. Stir 1 cup of the all-purpose flour, the remaining ¹/₂ cup of the rye flour, the oat bran, cream of rice, and salt into the yeast-rye-cornmeal mixture. Stir in ¹/₂ cup more all-purpose flour to make a dough that is firm enough to handle.

4. Turn the dough onto a well-floured surface and knead in enough of the remaining flour to make a dough that is manageable and no longer sticky.

5. Place the dough in a large, greased bowl and cover with greased plastic wrap. Set in a warm, draft-free spot until doubled in bulk. Punch dough down and let rise again.

6. Punch dough down and form into a loaf. Place in a greased 9 × 5 × 3-inch loaf pan. Cover with greased plastic wrap and let rise until doubled in bulk.

7. Preheat the oven to 350°F. Bake for 50 minutes or until loaf is browned on top and bottom and sounds hollow when tapped. Cool on wire rack.

Variation: Add 1 tablespoon caraway seeds when you add the oat bran.

RUSSIAN BLACK BREAD

Makes: 1 loaf; serves: 12 to 16

This is the bread that many people mistake for pumpernickel because it's dark brown—real pumpernickel is the color of rye bread. The fennel seeds impart a lot of flavor, but if you're not fond of licorice, omit them.

1¼ cups milk
¼ cup cornmeal
¼ cup unsweetened cocoa powder
1 tablespoon instant coffee
¼ cup (½ stick) butter or margarine
½ cup water
½ cup molasses
2 tablespoons caraway seeds
1 tablespoon fennel seeds
½ cup very warm water (105°–115°F)
½ teaspoon sugar
2 packages active dry yeast
2 cups rye flour
2 cups whole wheat flour
1 tablespoon salt
1¼ to 2 cups all-purpose flour

1. In a 1½-cup saucepan scald the milk (heat until bubbles form around the edge of the pan). Remove from heat, stir in the cornmeal, cocoa powder, coffee, and butter or margarine until melted. Stir in ½ cup water, the molasses, caraway seeds, and fennel seeds; set aside.

2. In a glass measuring cup, stir together ½ cup warm water and the sugar. Stir in the yeast and let it proof (page 413).

3. In a large bowl, combine the rye and whole wheat flours and the salt. Stir the yeast mixture and the milk mixture into the flour mixture. Stir in 1 cup of the all-purpose flour to make a dough that is firm enough to handle.

4. Turn the dough onto a well-floured surface and knead in enough of the remaining all-purpose flour to make a dough that is manageable and no longer sticky.

5. Place the dough in a large, greased bowl and cover with greased plastic wrap. Set in a warm, draft-free spot until doubled in bulk.

6. Punch dough down and form into a loaf. Form into two 8-inch oval loaves and place on a greased baking sheet. Cover with greased plastic wrap and let rise until doubled in bulk.

7. Preheat the oven to 350°F. Bake for 50 minutes or until loaves are browned on top and bottom and sound hollow when tapped. Cool on wire rack.

Variation: Add 2 cups of raisins after you stir in the milk mixture.

CORN AND BRAN BREAD

Makes: 1 loaf; serves: 12 to 16

This is a moist and sweet and delicious bread.

1½ cups water
½ cup yellow or white cornmeal
½ cup Bran Buds or similar cereal
¼ cup molasses
½ cup very warm water (105°–115°F)
½ teaspoon sugar
2 packages active dry yeast
1½ cups whole wheat flour
1 tablespoon salt
¾ to 1½ cups all-purpose flour

1. In a 1-quart saucepan, bring 1½ cups water to a boil over high heat; remove from heat. Using a whisk, stir the cornmeal, Bran Buds, and molasses into the boiling water. Let stand 30 minutes, stirring occasionally, until warm but not hot.

2. In a glass measuring cup, stir together ¹/₂ cup warm water and the sugar. Stir in the yeast and let it proof (page 413).

3. In a large bowl, combine the whole wheat flour and salt. Stir the yeast mixture and the cornmeal mixture into the whole wheat flour. Stir in ³/₄ cup of the all-purpose flour to make a dough that is firm enough to handle.

4. Turn dough onto a well-floured surface and knead in enough of the remaining all-purpose flour to make a dough that is manageable, neither sticky nor dry. You should be able to knead the dough at least three times without its sticking to the board or your hands.

5. Place the dough in a large, greased bowl and cover with greased plastic wrap. Set in a warm, draft-free spot until doubled in bulk.

6. Punch dough down and form into a loaf. Place in a greased 9 × 5 × 3-inch loaf pan. Cover with greased plastic wrap and let rise until doubled in bulk.

7. Preheat the oven to 350°F. Bake for 45 to 50 minutes or until loaf is browned on top and bottom and sounds hollow when tapped. Cool on wire rack.

Variation: Raisin Corn Bran Bread: Add 1¹/₂ cups raisins to the dough when you stir in the corn-bran mixture.

ANISE SEED BREAD

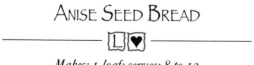

Makes: 1 loaf; serves: 8 to 12

The anise flavor in this bread is very strong. For a very nice, somewhat sweet bread with a milder flavor, see the variation.

¹/₂ cup very warm water (105°–115°F)
¹/₂ teaspoon sugar
1 package active dry yeast
1¹/₂ cups whole wheat flour
1 to 1³/₄ cups all-purpose flour
1¹/₂ teaspoons salt
¹/₂ cup milk or water
3 tablespoons butter or margarine, melted
¹/₄ cup firmly packed light brown or dark brown sugar
2 tablespoons molasses
1 tablespoon anise seeds

1. In a glass measuring cup, stir together the warm water and sugar. Stir in the yeast and let it proof (page 413).

2. In a large bowl, combine the whole wheat flour, ¹/₂ cup of the all-purpose flour, and the salt. In a medium bowl, stir together the milk, butter or margarine, brown sugar, molasses, and anise seeds. Add the milk mixture and the yeast mixture to the flour mixture. Stir in ¹/₂ cup more all-purpose flour to make a dough that is firm enough to handle.

3. Turn the dough onto a well-floured surface and knead in enough of the remaining all-purpose flour to make a dough that is manageable and no longer sticky.

4. Place the dough in a large, greased bowl and cover with greased plastic wrap. Set in a warm, draft-free spot until doubled in bulk.

5. Punch dough down and form into a loaf. Place in a greased 8¹/₂ × 3⁵/₈ × 2⁵/₈-inch pan. Cover with greased plastic wrap and let rise until doubled in bulk.

6. Preheat the oven to 350°F. Bake for 40 minutes or until loaf is lightly browned on top and bottom and sounds hollow when tapped. Cool on wire rack.

Variation: Decrease anise seeds to 1 or 1¹/₂ teaspoons or omit them completely.

CHALLAH

Makes: 1 loaf; serves: 12 to 16

Challah is the traditional braided bread served on Sabbath and most festive occasions in the Jewish religion. If there's any left over, it's great for French toast.

½ cup very warm water (105°–115°F)
3 tablespoons sugar, divided
2 packages active dry yeast
1¾ to 2¾ cups all-purpose flour
¾ cup whole wheat flour
2 teaspoons salt
2 eggs
⅓ cup milk
3 tablespoons butter or margarine, melted
1 egg white (optional)
Poppy seeds (optional)

1. In a glass measuring cup, stir together the warm water and ½ teaspoon of the sugar. Stir in the yeast and let it proof (page 413).

2. In a large bowl, combine ¾ cup of the all-purpose flour, the whole wheat flour, remaining sugar, and salt.

3. In a medium bowl, beat the eggs; beat in the milk, butter or margarine, and yeast mixture. Stir into the flour mixture. Stir in 1 cup more all-purpose flour to make a dough that is firm enough to handle.

4. Turn the dough onto a well-floured surface and knead in enough of the remaining all-purpose flour to make a dough that is manageable and no longer sticky.

5. Place the dough in a large, greased bowl and cover with greased plastic wrap. Set in a warm, draft-free spot until doubled in bulk.

6. Punch dough down; divide into thirds and form each into a 14-inch-long rope that is thinner at the ends and slightly thicker in the middle. Place the ropes on greased baking sheet. Braid the ropes very loosely, tucking the ends of the braid under the bread. Cover with greased plastic wrap and let rise until doubled in bulk. If desired, brush with egg white and sprinkle with poppy seeds.

7. Preheat the oven to 350°F. Bake for 35 to 40 minutes or until loaf is browned on top and bottom and sounds hollow when tapped. Remove from oven and cool 10 minutes; brush again with egg white, if desired, and bake 5 minutes longer or until glaze is set. Cool on wire rack.

Variation: Holiday Challah: Instead of dividing the dough into separate ropes to braid, roll the dough into one long rope, and coil it into a spiral shape, beginning from the center.

SWEDISH LIMPA BREAD

Makes: 1 loaf; serves: 12 to 16

I love this orange-flavored bread. It's traditionally prepared with anise seeds (as in the variation), but I prefer it without.

½ cup very warm water (105°–115°F)
½ teaspoon sugar
1 package active dry yeast
1½ cups rye flour
2 to 2¾ cups all-purpose flour
1½ teaspoons salt
¾ cup orange juice
¼ cup firmly packed light brown or dark brown sugar
3 tablespoons butter or margarine, melted
2 tablespoons honey
1 tablespoon grated orange rind

1. In a glass measuring cup, stir together the warm water and sugar. Stir in the yeast and let it proof (page 413).

2. In a large bowl, combine the rye flour, 1 1/4 cups of the all-purpose flour, and the salt. In a medium bowl, stir together the orange juice, brown sugar, butter or margarine, honey, and orange rind. Add the juice mixture and the yeast mixture to the flour mixture. Stir in 3/4 cup more all-purpose flour to make a dough that is firm enough to handle.

3. Turn the dough onto a well-floured surface and knead in enough of the remaining flour to make a dough that is manageable and no longer sticky.

4. Place the dough in a large, greased bowl and cover with greased plastic wrap. Set in a warm, draft-free spot until doubled in bulk.

5. Punch dough down and form into a 6-inch round loaf. Place on a greased baking sheet. Cover with greased plastic wrap and let rise until doubled in bulk.

6. Preheat the oven to 350°F. Bake for 50 minutes or until loaf is browned on top and bottom and sounds hollow when tapped. Cool on wire rack.

Variation: Add 1 1/2 teaspoons anise seeds when you add the orange juice.

ANADAMA BREAD

Makes: 1 loaf; serves: 8 to 12

The cornmeal and molasses are signature ingredients in this traditional New England bread. There are many stories about how it was named; what they all have in common is an angry farmer and his wife named Anna. Now you have the basic facts and can make up your own story.

1/2 cup very warm water (105°–115°F)
1/2 teaspoon sugar
1 package active dry yeast
1 cup whole wheat flour
1 1/4 to 1 3/4 cups all-purpose flour
1/2 cup yellow or white cornmeal
2 teaspoons salt
1/2 cup water
1/4 cup molasses
2 tablespoons vegetable oil

1. In a glass measuring cup, stir together 1/2 cup warm water and the sugar. Stir in the yeast and let it proof (page 413).

2. In a large bowl, combine the whole wheat flour, 3/4 cup of the all-purpose flour, the cornmeal, and salt. In a medium bowl, stir together the yeast mixture, 1/2 cup water, the molasses, and oil. Stir this mixture into the flour mixture. Stir in 1/2 cup more all-purpose flour to make a dough that is firm enough to handle.

3. Turn dough onto a well-floured surface and knead in enough of the remaining flour to make a dough that is manageable and no longer sticky.

4. Place the dough in a large, greased bowl and cover with greased plastic wrap. Set in a warm, draft-free spot until doubled in bulk.

5. Punch dough down and form into a loaf. Place in a greased 8 1/2 × 3 5/8 × 2 5/8-inch loaf pan. Cover with greased plastic wrap and let rise until doubled in bulk.

6. Preheat the oven to 350°F. Bake for 40 minutes or until loaf is browned on top and bottom and sounds hollow when tapped. Cool on wire rack.

🔲 *Variation:* Substitute milk for the 1/2 cup water in step 2.

GARLIC KNOTS

Makes: 24 knots; serves: 12 to 16

These tasty little rolls are a real hit with any garlic bread lover. If you don't feel like shaping these into rolls, you can just lay the ropes on the baking sheet and make garlic breadsticks.

¼ cup olive oil
4 cloves garlic, minced
½ cup very warm water (105°–115°F)
½ teaspoon plus 2 tablespoons sugar
2 packages active dry yeast
1½ cups whole wheat flour
1 to 1½ cups all-purpose flour
2 teaspoons salt
⅔ cup water
Garlic powder

1. Place the oil and garlic in a blender. Cover and blend until garlic is pureed.

2. In a glass measuring cup, stir together ½ cup warm water and ½ teaspoon of the sugar. Stir in the yeast and let it proof (page 413).

3. In a large bowl, combine the whole wheat flour, ½ cup of the all-purpose flour, the remaining 2 tablespoons sugar, and the salt. Add the yeast mixture, ⅔ cup water and 1 tablespoon of the garlic-oil to the flour mixture. Stir in ½ cup more all-purpose flour to make a dough that is firm enough to handle.

4. Turn the dough onto a well-floured surface and knead in enough of the remaining flour to make a dough that is manageable and no longer sticky.

5. Place the dough in a large, greased bowl and cover with greased plastic wrap. Set in a warm, draft-free spot until doubled in bulk.

6. Punch dough down and divide dough into 24 pieces. Roll pieces into ropes 7 inches long.

Tie each rope into a knot. Place knots onto 2 large greased baking sheets, leaving about 1½ inches between each knot. Cover with greased plastic wrap and let rise until doubled in bulk; brush with half of the remaining oil-garlic mixture.

7. Preheat the oven to 375°F. Bake for 20 to 25 minutes or until lightly browned. Remove knot rolls from the oven; brush immediately with the remaining oil-garlic mixture and sprinkle with garlic powder.

Variation: For an onion-garlic knot, sprinkle with minced onion before baking.

FOCACCIA

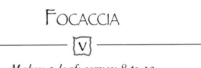

Makes: 1 loaf; serves: 8 to 12

It took five tries before the focaccia turned out the way I hoped, and that only happened by mistake because I hadn't been following my own directions. The result is a chewy bread with an open texture and crusty top and bottom. You can make focaccia like a cheeseless pizza with a soft top by spreading marinara sauce over the top before baking.

½ cup very warm water (105°–115°F)
½ teaspoon sugar
2 packages active dry yeast
1½ cups all-purpose flour
1 cup whole wheat flour
2 teaspoons salt
3 tablespoons olive oil
1 cup water
2 cups sliced onions
1 teaspoon chopped fresh rosemary, or
   ½ teaspoon dried rosemary, crumbled
Additional olive oil (optional)

1. In a glass measuring cup, stir together ½ cup warm water and the sugar. Stir in the yeast and let it proof (page 413).

2. In a large bowl, combine the all-purpose flour, whole wheat flour, and salt. Stir in the yeast mixture, 2 tablespoons of the oil, and 1 cup water.

3. Cover with greased plastic wrap. Set in a warm, draft-free spot until doubled in bulk.

4. While the dough is rising, heat the remaining 1 tablespoon oil in a saucepan over medium heat. Add the onions; cook, stirring, until softened, about 4 minutes. Stir in the rosemary.

5. Turn dough (which is very soft) onto a heavily floured board. Using floured hands, pat into a 9 × 13-inch rectangle. Place on a greased jelly roll pan (10 × 15 inches), cover with greased plastic wrap, and let rise 30 minutes. Create dimples in the dough by poking with floured fingertips every 2 inches or so. Sprinkle the onions on top. Drizzle with additional olive oil, if desired.

6. Bake in a preheated 425°F oven for 35 minutes or until loaf is lightly browned on top and bottom and sounds hollow when tapped. Cool on wire rack.

Variation: Spread 1 to 2 cups marinara sauce over the top of the bread after dimpling.

Sourdough

Besides the obvious reason that sourdough breads taste uniquely great, sourdough makes a perfect base for vegan pancakes, waffles, muffins, and biscuits.

BASIC YEAST SOURDOUGH STARTER

Makes: 1²/₃ cups

½ cup very warm water (105°–115°F)
½ teaspoon sugar
1 package active dry yeast
1 cup all-purpose flour
½ cup whole wheat flour
¾ cup water

1. In a glass measuring cup, stir together ½ cup warm water and the sugar. Stir in the yeast and let it proof (page 413).

2. In a large bowl combine the all-purpose flour and whole wheat flour. Add the yeast mixture and remaining ³/₄ cup water; stir until combined. Let stand, loosely covered, 2 days or until the liquid separates and floats on top.

3. Place the starter in a crock or other container with a loose-fitting cover. Store in the refrigerator until needed. Once a week, stir ¹/₃ cup water and ¹/₂ cup flour into the sourdough and let stand at room temperature 4 hours or overnight, then stir and return to refrigerator.

SOURDOUGH FRENCH BREAD

Makes: 4 baguettes or 1 round loaf;
serves: 12 to 16

¾ cup very warm water (105°–115°F)
2 teaspoons sugar
1 package dry active yeast
¾ cup whole wheat flour
2½ to 3 cups all-purpose flour
2 teaspoons salt
1 cup Sourdough Starter (page 425)

1. In a glass measuring cup, stir together the warm water and sugar. Stir in yeast and let it proof (page 413).

2. In a large bowl combine 1 cup of the all-purpose flour, the whole wheat flour, and salt.

3. Add yeast mixture and sourdough. Stir in ³/₄ cup more all-purpose flour to make a dough that is firm enough to handle.

4. Turn dough onto a well-floured surface and knead in enough of the remaining flour to make a dough that is manageable and no longer sticky.

5. Place the dough in a large, greased bowl and cover with greased plastic wrap. Set in a warm, draft-free spot until doubled in bulk. Punch down and let rise a second time.

6. Punch dough down and shape into a round; place on a greased baking sheet; cover with greased plastic wrap and let rise until doubled in bulk. If desired, cut slash marks into the top of the loaf.

5. Preheat the oven to 400°F. Bake for 25 to 30 minutes or until lightly browned. For a crispy crust, toss an ice cube into the oven during the first 10 minutes of baking, and a second ice cube during the next 10 minutes.

For baguettes: Divide the dough into four parts and roll each into ropes 12 inches long. Place onto 2 large greased baking sheets, leaving about 2 inches between each roll. Cover with greased plastic wrap and let rise until doubled in bulk. Bake as directed above.

FLAVORED BREADS AND TOASTS

FLAVORED CROUTONS

─────────── Ⓛ ───────────

Makes: 4 cups; serves: depends on use

Croutons are usually served on top of salads (especially Caesar salad) or soups (especially split pea soup), but they are also tasty just to snack on. You can use any kind of bread (fresh or stale) for croutons, although I usually use French or Italian. Also, you can cube the bread into any size cubes, although ¹/₂ inch is most common.

1 ¹/₂ tablespoons grated Parmesan cheese
¹/₂ teaspoon garlic powder
¹/₄ teaspoon dried oregano
¹/₄ teaspoon dried basil
¹/₄ teaspoon dried thyme
¹/₈ teaspoon pepper
Oil for frying
4 cups bread cubes

1. In a small bowl, combine the Parmesan, garlic powder, oregano, basil, thyme, and pepper.

2. In a 3-quart pot, heat ¹/₂ inch oil over medium-high heat, until the oil bubbles when a few crumbs of bread are dropped in. Add half the bread cubes and fry until golden on the bottom. Turn over and cook until second side browns. Lift from oil and drain on paper towels. Repeat with remaining bread cubes.

3. Place the croutons in a large bowl, sprinkle with the seasonings, and toss until coated.

Variations: Plain Croutons: Omit all the seasonings and simply fry the bread cubes.

Ⓥ Omit the cheese from the seasoning mixture.

CROSTINI

─────────── Ⓥ ───────────

Makes: 24 crostini; serves: 6 to 8

These toasts are excellent served with almost any spread or topping. Some people prepare these by frying, rather like croutons. I bake them and brush very lightly with oil, hoping that they are less greasy than the fried variety. I used fresh French bread to prepare these crostini; you can also make them with day-old bread, but the baking time may be shorter. Check for doneness at 10 minutes.

24 ¹/₂-inch-thick diagonal slices French bread
2 tablespoons olive oil

1. Preheat the oven to 350°F.

2. Lightly brush each side of the bread slices with the oil. Place on baking sheets in single layer. Bake 10 to 15 minutes per side or until crisped and browned.

Variation: Add garlic or herbs to the oil before brushing onto bread slices.

TOASTED PITAS

Makes: 2 toasted pita breads; serves: 2 to 4

These are really delicious—served warm they are rich and chewy; once cool, they crisp. I don't use the commercial pita breads that are smooth on the outside, but rather pocketless pitas or other types that tend to have a nubbly exterior.

Two 7-inch pita breads
1 tablespoon melted butter or margarine

1. Preheat the oven to 350°F.

2. Brush both sides of the pita breads generously with the butter or margarine. Place on a baking sheet and bake 5 minutes; turn once and bake 5 minutes longer. Cut into wedges to serve.

Variation: For a spicy version, add 1/8 teaspoon ground red pepper to the butter or margarine.

BUTTER GARLIC BREAD

Makes: 1 loaf; serves: 4 to 6

As far as I'm concerned, if there's garlic bread on the table and a nice green salad, I'm in heaven.

1/4 cup (1/2 stick) butter or margarine, softened
3 cloves garlic, pressed
1/4 teaspoon paprika or dried oregano (optional)
One 6½-ounce loaf Italian or French bread

1. Preheat the oven to 375°F.

2. Stir together the butter or margarine and the garlic. Stir in paprika, if desired.

3. Slice the bread in half lengthwise. Spread half of the butter or margarine on the cut side of each half of the bread. Wrap in aluminum foil.

4. Bake the bread 10 minutes or until heated through.

5. Increase the heat to broil. Unwrap the bread and open the foil so the buttered side is up. Broil 6 inches from heat until the butter or margarine is bubbly and the bread starts to brown but not burn, about 2 minutes.

Variation: Parmesan Garlic Bread: Sprinkle 1 to 2 tablespoons Parmesan cheese over the butter or margarine on each side of the bread.

CRACKERS

NICE AND CRUNCHY, CRISP AND SEEDY HOMEMADE CRACKERS

———————— V ————————

Makes 7 dozen crackers; serves 14 to 20

If you're a very observant reader of recipes, you will notice that these crackers bear an uncanny resemblance to Donna Mason's Dense and Chewy Whole Grain Bread (page 418). That's because this was my first recipe test for that bread. Early in the recipe test, it became clear that there was no way this dough would ever make a bread that would turn out moister than the Sahara Desert. But I had used all these excellent ingredients and was determined not to throw them away. So I tossed in lots of seeds and started rolling, and rolling, and rolling . . . (you get the picture) et voilà—great crackers, and lots of them!

½ cup water

¼ cup bulgur

1½ cups whole wheat flour

1 cup Quaker's Multigrain cereal or rolled oats

½ cup shelled, unsalted sunflower seeds

⅓ cup yellow or white cornmeal

⅓ cup oat bran

¼ cup wheat germ

2 tablespoons sesame seeds

1 tablespoon caraway seeds

1 tablespoon poppy seeds

2 teaspoons salt

¾ cup very warm water (105°–115°F)

½ teaspoon sugar

2 packages active dry yeast

⅓ cup molasses

¼ cup vegetable oil

½ cup all-purpose flour

1. In a 1-quart saucepan, bring the ½ cup water to a boil over medium-high heat. Stir in the bulgur. Simmer 5 minutes; remove from heat and cool to lukewarm.

2. In a large bowl, stir together the whole wheat flour, cereal, sunflower seeds, cornmeal, oat bran, wheat germ, sesame seeds, caraway seeds, poppy seeds, and salt.

3. In a glass measuring cup, stir together ¾ cup warm water and the sugar. Stir in the yeast and let it proof (page 413).

4. Stir the bulgur into the bowl with the flour mixture. Add in the proofed yeast, molasses, and oil.

5. Turn onto a well-floured board and knead in the all-purpose flour to form a dough that is very firm.

6. Divide the dough into 6 pieces. On a floured board, roll each piece into a rectangle that is ⅛ to ¹⁄₁₆ inch thick. Using a pastry cutter or sharp knife, cut rectangle into 1½-inch squares.

7. Bake squares on ungreased baking sheets in a preheated 350°F oven for 12 to 15 minutes or until browned around the edges. Cool on racks.

Variation: Leave out any or all of the seeds.

PARMESAN CRACKERS

Makes: 42; serves: 10 to 16

These are quite easy to make and the result is very pleasing. Rather than serve these as "crackers" per se I let people munch on them as hors d'oeuvres. Don't be alarmed by the amount of red pepper—they're really not too spicy. But if you prefer, you can use half the amount or use none at all.

1 cup grated Parmesan cheese
⅓ cup whole wheat flour
⅓ cup all-purpose flour
¼ teaspoon ground red pepper (optional)
6 tablespoons (¾ stick) butter or margarine
2 tablespoons water

1. In a large bowl, stir together the cheese and both flours. Stir in the pepper, if desired.

2. Using a pastry cutter or two knives, cut the butter or margarine into the flour mixture until it resembled coarse cornmeal. Sprinkle the water over the mixture and work into the dough with a fork.

3. Turn onto a lightly floured board and knead 12 times or until the dough just holds together.

4. Form into a log 8 inches long. Wrap in waxed paper and chill 2 hours.

5. Preheat the oven to 350°F.

6. Slice the log into rounds ⅛ inch thick. Place rounds on ungreased baking sheets. Bake 10 to 15 minutes or until browned. Cool on racks.

Variation: Stir in ¼ cup poppy seeds.

GARLIC PITA POINTS

[V]

Makes: 48 pita points; serves 6 to 12

*These are similar to Toasted Pitas (page 428)
except that I use the commercially available pita
with pockets for this version. These crispy crackers
are great for any Middle Eastern type of spread
or dip.*

⅓ cup olive oil
3 cloves garlic, pressed
¼ teaspoon dried thyme
¼ teaspoon dried oregano
One 12-ounce package pita breads

1. Preheat the oven to 350°F.

2. In a small bowl, stir together the oil, garlic,
thyme, and oregano.

3. Slice the top layer of each pita bread from
the bottom layer, creating two thin, round
pieces of bread. Brush the textured side
(previously the inside) of each pita half with the
oil mixture. Cut each round into eighths. Place
on baking sheets, oiled side up.

4. Bake 10 to 15 minutes or until pita points
are toasted and browned. Let cool.

Variation: Use whole wheat pitas instead of
plain.

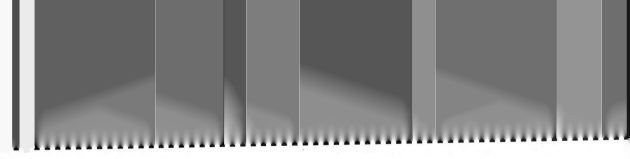

Pancakes

Buttermilk Pancakes   434

Wheat Germ–Honey
Pancakes   434

Lemon–Oat Bran
Pancakes   435

Sour Cream Pancakes   435

Gingerbread Pancakes   436

Cranberry-Orange
Pancakes   436

Light and Tangy Sourdough
Pancakes   437

Oatmeal Pancakes   437

Corn and Oat (No Wheat)
Pancakes   438

Low-Fat Pancakes   438

Banana Fritters   439

Waffles

Basic Waffles   439

Apple Pie Waffles   440

Banana–Poppy Seed
Waffles   440

Bran Waffles   441

Maple Waffles   441

French Toast

Cinnamon French
Toast   442

Maple French Toast   442

Orange French Toast   443

Garlic French Toast   443

Curried French Toast   444

Barbecue French Toast   444

Blintzes

Cheese Blintzes   445

Blueberry Blintzes   445

Spoon Bread   446

Cereal

Brown Sugar Granola   446

Eggs

Hash and Eggs   447

Scrambled Eggs with Cream
Cheese and Scallion   447

Hard-Cooked Eggs   448

Egg in Puff Pastry   448

Egg in a Muffin   448

Eggs Florentine   449

Huevos al Nido   449

Eggs Benedictish   450

Basic Omelet with
Filling   450

Spanish Omelet   451

Zucchini Omelet   451

Tofu–Soy Sprout Omelet with
Peanut Sauce   452

Vidalia Onion Omelet   452

Frittata   453

Piperade   453

Mexican Egg Enchilada   454

Grilled Vegetable
Piperade   454

Huevos Rancheros   455

Sandwiches

Spinach Egg Salad   456

Russian Egg Salad
Sandwich   457

Curried Egg Salad
Sandwich   457

Date-Nut Sandwich
Spread   458

Cream Cheese and Olive
Sandwich   458

Roasted Red Pepper–Caper
Sandwich   458

Roasted Pepper and
Mozzarella Sandwich   459

Brie Sandwich   459

Falafel   460

Grilled Cheese
Sandwich   460

Barbecue Tempeh on
a Bun   461

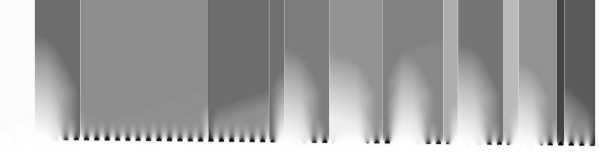

Barbecued Eggplant
Sandwiches   461

Sautéed Mushrooms
on Toast   461

Broiled Egg
Sandwiches   462

Welsh Rarebit   462

French Bread Pizza   463

Boboli and Vegetable
Melt   463

Quesadilla   464

Turnovers

Basic Knishes   465

Broccoli-Cheddar
Knishes   465

Kasha Knishes   465

Spinach Knishes   466

Sweet Potato–Squash
Knishes   466

Basic Empanadas   466

Vegetable Empanadas   467

Spinach Empanadas   467

Breakfast, it has been said, is the most important meal of the day. Unfortunately many
people choose to skip it. Brunch (the combination of breakfast and lunch, in case you've
never heard the term), on the other hand, is a
treasured tradition by many, especially on
weekends. For a Lacto-Ovo vegetarian, these
meals are easy to share with their meat-eating
friends since most people are happy to have
either eggs, pancakes, French toast, or waffles
for brunch. There are plenty of recipes for all
these brunch entrees in this chapter. For a
heartier brunch, you may want to look for
Quiches, Tarts, or Savory Puddings as well.

Egg Basics

If you want to serve plain eggs, but are not sure
how to cook them, you can find recipes as follows: Scrambled Eggs (see variation), page 447;
Fried Eggs (in step 5 of Hash and Eggs recipe),
page 447; Hard Cooked Eggs, page 448.
Here's how you poach them:

Poached Eggs: Bring 4 cups water, 1 tablespoon distilled white vinegar, and $\frac{1}{8}$ teaspoon
salt to a boil in a 2-quart saucepan. Break 6 eggs
(or less) into a medium bowl. Slip the eggs into
the water. Return to a boil and boil 2 minutes.
Lift eggs from water and drain. For softer
whites, cook less time; for harder yolks, cook
longer.

For more on Breakfast and Lunch, see
"Menu Planning" (pages 19–20).

PANCAKES

BUTTERMILK PANCAKES

———— 🔟 ————

Makes: 15 5-inch pancakes; serves: 4 to 6

Because these pancakes contain so much liquid, they have to cook slowly to ensure complete doneness without burning on the bottom.

1 1/2 cups all-purpose flour
1/2 cup whole wheat flour
1/4 cup sugar
2 teaspoons baking powder
2 teaspoons baking soda
1/4 teaspoon salt, or to taste
2 eggs
2 3/4 cups buttermilk
2 tablespoons melted butter or margarine
1/2 teaspoon vanilla extract
Butter, margarine, or oil for brushing

1. In a large bowl, stir together both flours, the sugar, baking powder, baking soda, and salt.

2. In a medium bowl, beat the eggs. Beat in the buttermilk, butter or margarine, and vanilla.

3. Add the milk mixture to the dry ingredients and stir until just combined. The batter may have some lumps.

4. Heat a skillet or griddle over medium heat until a drop of water dances across the surface of the pan before evaporating. Brush the skillet lightly with butter, margarine, or oil. For each pancake, drop 1/3 cup batter onto the skillet. Cook until one or two bubbles start to burst on the top; turn and cook until golden on the bottom.

Variations: Blueberry Pancakes: Add 1 cup blueberries to the batter.

Silver Dollars: Drop batter by 2 tablespoons at a time. Makes about 40.

WHEAT GERM–HONEY PANCAKES

———— 🔟 ————

Makes: 12 to 14 4 1/2-inch pancakes; serves: 4 to 6

These thick and very filling pancakes have a slightly crunchy texture from the wheat germ.

1 1/4 cups all-purpose flour
3/4 cup whole wheat flour
1/4 cup honey-crunch wheat germ
2 teaspoons baking powder
1 teaspoon baking soda
1/2 teaspoon salt, or to taste
3 eggs
1 1/2 cups milk
1/4 cup (1/2 stick) melted butter or margarine
1/4 cup honey
1/2 teaspoon vanilla
Butter, margarine, or oil for brushing

1. In a large bowl, stir together both flours, the wheat germ, baking powder, baking soda, and salt.

2. In a medium bowl, beat the eggs. Beat in the milk, butter or margarine, honey, and vanilla.

3. Add the milk mixture to the dry ingredients and stir until just combined. The batter may have some lumps.

4. Heat a skillet or griddle over medium-high heat until a drop of water dances across the surface of the pan before evaporating. Brush the skillet lightly with butter, margarine, or oil. For each pancake, drop 1/4 cup of batter onto the skillet. Cook until one or two bubbles start to burst on the top; turn and cook until golden on the bottom.

Variation: Substitute 1 tablespoon of molasses for one of the tablespoons of honey.

LEMON–OAT BRAN PANCAKES

Makes: 15 to 18 4¹/₂-inch pancakes; serves: 4 to 6

Unlike so many of my usual dense pancakes, these are pretty light.

1 ¹/₂ cups all-purpose flour
¹/₂ cup oat bran
3 tablespoons sugar
1 tablespoon baking powder
1 teaspoon baking soda
¹/₂ teaspoon salt, or to taste
2 eggs
3 tablespoons melted butter or margarine
2 tablespoons fresh lemon juice
2 teaspoons grated lemon rind
1 ³/₄ cups milk
Butter, margarine, or oil for brushing

1. In a large bowl, stir together the flour, oat bran, sugar, baking powder, baking soda, and salt.

2. In a medium bowl, beat the eggs. Beat in the butter or margarine, lemon juice, and lemon rind. Beat in the milk.

3. Add the milk mixture to the dry ingredients and stir until fairly smooth; let stand 5 minutes.

4. Heat a skillet or griddle over medium-high heat until a drop of water dances across the surface of the pan before evaporating. Brush skillet lightly with butter, margarine, or oil. For each pancake, drop ¹/₄ cup of batter onto the skillet. Cook until bubbles start to burst on the top; turn and cook until golden on the bottom.

Variation: Blueberry-Lemon Pancakes: Stir 1 cup blueberries into the batter.

SOUR CREAM PANCAKES

Makes: 12 3¹/₂-inch pancakes; serves: 3 to 4

This recipe makes 12 not-too-big, light, wonderful pancakes. Technically that serves 4, but if you have 4 pancake lovers you may want to double the recipe.

³/₄ cup all-purpose flour
¹/₂ cup whole wheat flour
3 tablespoons sugar
2 teaspoons baking powder
1 teaspoon baking soda
¹/₂ teaspoon salt
1 egg
1 cup milk
¹/₂ cup sour cream
1 ¹/₂ teaspoons vanilla
Butter, margarine, or oil for brushing

1. In a large bowl, stir together both flours, the sugar, baking powder, baking soda, and salt.

2. In a medium bowl, beat the egg. Stir in the milk, sour cream, and vanilla.

3. Add the milk mixture to the dry ingredients and stir until just combined. The batter may have some lumps.

4. Heat a skillet or griddle over medium heat until a drop of water dances across the surface of the pan before evaporating. Brush the skillet lightly with butter, margarine, or oil. For each pancake, drop 2 to 3 tablespoons of batter onto the skillet. Cook until one or two bubbles start to burst on the top; turn and cook until golden on the bottom.

Variation: Stir in ¹/₄ cup wheat germ for a crunchy texture and wheatier taste.

GINGERBREAD PANCAKES

Makes: 14 3¹/₂-inch pancakes; serves: 4 to 6

The gingerbread flavor is fairly mild here. If you like real snap, you may want to use extra ginger.

1¹/₄ cups all-purpose flour
³/₄ cup whole wheat flour
1 tablespoon baking powder
2 teaspoons ground ginger
1 teaspoon ground cinnamon
¹/₂ teaspoon salt, or to taste
¹/₈ teaspoon ground allspice
¹/₈ teaspoon ground cloves
2 eggs
1¹/₂ cups milk
3 tablespoons melted butter or margarine
2 tablespoons firmly packed light brown or dark brown sugar
1 tablespoon molasses
Butter, margarine, or oil for brushing

1. In a large bowl, stir together both flours, the baking powder, ginger, cinnamon, salt, allspice, and cloves.

2. In a medium bowl, beat the eggs. Beat in the milk, butter or margarine, brown sugar, and molasses.

3. Add the milk mixture to the dry ingredients and stir until just combined. The batter may have some lumps.

4. Heat a skillet or griddle over medium-high heat until a drop of water dances across the surface of the pan before evaporating. Brush the skillet lightly with butter, margarine, or oil. For each pancake, drop ¹/₄ cup of batter onto the skillet. Cook until one or two bubbles start to burst on the top; turn and cook until golden on the bottom.

Variation: Substitute 1 extra tablespoon brown sugar for the molasses.

CRANBERRY–ORANGE PANCAKES

Makes: 18 to 20 4¹/₂-inch pancakes; serves: 4 to 6

These make a great post-Thanksgiving breakfast.

³/₄ cup finely chopped fresh cranberries
¹/₃ cup sugar
2¹/₂ cups cake flour
1 cup oat bran
1 tablespoon baking powder
1 teaspoon baking soda
¹/₂ teaspoon salt, or to taste
1¹/₄ cups milk
1 cup orange juice
2 eggs, beaten
1 tablespoon melted butter or margarine
1 teaspoon grated orange rind
Butter, margarine, or oil for brushing

1. In a medium bowl, stir together the cranberries and sugar; let stand 5 minutes.

2. In a large bowl, stir together the flour, oat bran, baking powder, baking soda, and salt.

3. Add the milk, orange juice, eggs, butter or margarine, and orange rind to the cranberries.

4. Add the milk mixture to the dry ingredients and stir until fairly smooth; let stand 5 minutes.

5. Heat a skillet or griddle over medium-high heat until a drop of water dances across the surface of the pan before evaporating. Brush the skillet lightly with butter, margarine, or oil. For each pancake, drop a scant ¹/₄ cup of batter onto the skillet. Cook until bubbles start to burst on the top; turn and cook until golden on the bottom.

Variation: Omit the orange juice and rind; substitute additional milk for the orange juice.

LIGHT AND TANGY SOURDOUGH PANCAKES

Makes: 24 3¹/₂-inch pancakes; serves: 4 to 6

For the most part, breakfast foods such as pancakes and waffles contain eggs and/or milk. I was delighted to find that sourdough lends the right consistency and enough flavor to make these pancakes a winner. But, of course, the catch is that you have to have the starter on hand; otherwise you have to wait 2 days to prepare the starter. Even with the starter, you have to start the night before.

1 cup Basic Yeast Sourdough Starter
    (page 425)
1¹/₂ cups water
2 tablespoons light brown or dark brown
    sugar
1 tablespoon vegetable oil
1 cup all-purpose flour
¹/₂ cup whole wheat flour
¹/₂ cup wheat germ
2 teaspoons baking powder
1 teaspoon baking soda
¹/₂ teaspoon salt
Butter, margarine, or oil for brushing

1. Place the sourdough starter in a large bowl. Loosely cover and let stand overnight.

2. Stir in the water, brown sugar, and oil.

3. In a medium bowl or on waxed paper, stir together the two flours, the wheat germ, baking powder, baking soda, and salt.

4. Stir the flour mixture into the sourdough mixture until just combined.

5. Heat a skillet or griddle over medium heat until a drop of water dances across the surface before evaporating. Brush the skillet lightly with butter, margarine, or oil. For each pancake, drop 2 tablespoons of batter onto the skillet.

Cook until bubbles form and start to burst on top; turn and cook until golden on the bottom.

Variation: Stir chopped fruit into the batter before cooking.

OATMEAL PANCAKES

Makes: 10 3¹/₂-inch pancakes; serves: 3 to 4

Not surprisingly, these pancakes hint of oatmeal flavor, but don't worry—they're not as dense as a bowl of oatmeal.

1¹/₃ cups all-purpose flour
²/₃ cup quick-cooking oats
2 tablespoons sugar
2¹/₂ teaspoons baking powder
¹/₂ teaspoon salt, or to taste
1 egg
1¹/₃ cups milk
3 tablespoons melted butter or margarine
Butter, margarine, or oil for brushing

1. In a large bowl, stir together the flour, oats, sugar, baking powder, and salt.

2. In a medium bowl, beat the egg. Beat in the milk and butter or margarine.

3. Add the milk mixture to the dry ingredients and stir until just combined; let stand 5 minutes.

4. Heat a skillet or griddle over medium-high heat until a drop of water dances across the surface of the pan before evaporating. Brush the skillet lightly with butter, margarine, or oil. For each pancake, drop 3 tablespoons of batter onto the skillet. Cook until one or two bubbles start to burst on the top; turn and cook until golden on the bottom.

Variation: Stir in 1 teaspoon ground cinnamon when you add the baking powder.

CORN AND OAT (NO WHEAT) PANCAKES

— LO —

Makes: 12 pancakes; serves: 4

These pancakes have a great flavor with the familiar cornmeal texture. You can substitute whole wheat flour for the oat if you like.

1 cup cornmeal
¾ cup oat flour
3 tablespoons sugar
1 tablespoon baking powder
½ teaspoon salt
3 eggs
1 cup milk
3 tablespoons melted butter or margarine
Butter, margarine, or oil for brushing

1. In a large bowl, stir together the cornmeal, oat flour, sugar, baking powder, and salt.

2. In a medium bowl, beat the eggs. Stir in the milk and butter or margarine. Add the liquid ingredients to the dry ingredients and stir until combined.

3. Heat a skillet or griddle over medium heat until a drop of water dances across the surface of the pan before evaporating. Brush the skillet lightly with butter, margarine, or oil. For each pancake, drop 3 tablespoons of batter onto the skillet. Cook until one or two bubbles start to burst on the top; turn and cook until browned on the bottom.

Variation: Corn and Oat (No Wheat) Waffles: Heat a waffle iron. Use a generous cup of batter per batch. Makes eight 4-inch waffles.

LOW-FAT PANCAKES

— LO ♥ —

Makes: 16 4-inch pancakes; serves: 5 to 8

Moister and denser than "ordinary" pancakes, these do have a nice flavor, are very filling, and satisfy that pancake urge. They need to be cooked on medium heat so they have time to bake through.

1 cup all-purpose flour
⅓ cup whole wheat flour
⅓ cup cornmeal
2 teaspoons baking powder
1 teaspoon baking soda
½ teaspoon salt, or to taste
1¾ cups buttermilk
½ cup no-fat cottage cheese
¼ cup firmly packed dark brown or light brown sugar
3 egg whites
1 teaspoon vanilla
Butter, margarine, or oil for brushing (optional)

1. In a large bowl, stir together both flours, the cornmeal, baking powder, baking soda, and salt.

2. Put the buttermilk, cottage cheese, brown sugar, egg whites, and vanilla in a blender or food processor container fitted with a steel blade. Cover and process until smooth. Add the liquid ingredients to the dry ingredients and stir until combined.

3. Heat a nonstick skillet or griddle over medium heat until a drop of water dances across the surface of the pan before evaporating. (Or brush a skillet lightly with butter, margarine, or oil, if desired.) For each pancake, drop 3 tablespoons onto the skillet. Cook until one or two bubbles start to burst on the top; turn and cook until golden on the bottom.

BANANA FRITTERS

Makes: 14 5-inch pancakes; serves: 4 to 6

My grandmother would sauté up these heavenly treats for Sunday brunch. Sometimes she would use apples instead of bananas—I don't know which I loved more. Of course, Grandma never used whole wheat flour; that's my adaptation. Use a well-greased skillet for these, and use butter or margarine, not oil.

¾ cup all-purpose flour
½ cup whole wheat flour
3 tablespoons sugar
½ teaspoon baking powder
¼ teaspoon salt
2 egg whites
1 egg
1 cup milk
½ teaspoon vanilla extract
2 cups thinly sliced bananas
Butter or margarine for greasing

1. In a large bowl, stir together both flours, the sugar, baking powder, and salt.

2. In a medium bowl, beat the egg whites and egg. Stir in the milk and vanilla. Add the liquid ingredients to the dry ingredients and stir until fairly smooth. Stir in bananas.

3. Heat a skillet over medium-high heat until a drop of water dances across the surface of the pan before evaporating. For each fritter, drop ¼ cup of batter onto the skillet. Cook until browned on bottom and cooked almost completely through; turn and cook until browned on second side.

Variation: Blueberry Fritters: Use blueberries instead of bananas.

WAFFLES

Waffles are not too hard to prepare, but it's not uncommon for them to stick to the waffle iron (even a nonstick waffle iron). The reasons for sticking are that you didn't grease the iron, or, more likely, you didn't let the waffles cook long enough. Let them cook until they stop steaming completely. Once made, waffles freeze beautifully and can be reheated in the toaster.

BASIC WAFFLES

Makes: 10 4-inch waffles; serves: 4 to 6

They may be basic, but they're great. You can vary this recipe by tossing in fruit or nuts if you like.

1 cup all-purpose flour
1 cup whole wheat flour
⅓ cup sugar
1 tablespoon baking powder
1⅓ cups milk
⅓ cup vegetable oil
3 egg whites
½ teaspoon salt, or to taste
Butter, margarine, or oil for greasing

1. Preheat the waffle iron according to manufacturer's directions.

2. In a large bowl, stir together both flours, the sugar, and baking powder.

3. Stir the milk and oil into the dry ingredients until just combined; do not overmix. The batter should be lumpy.

4. In a medium bowl, beat the egg whites with the salt until stiff but not dry. Fold into the batter.

5. Grease the waffle iron and spread 1⅓ cup of batter onto it. Cook until the iron no longer steams, about 5 minutes. Repeat twice more with remaining batter.

Variation: Add 1 teaspoon ground cinnamon and ¼ teaspoon ground nutmeg.

APPLE PIE WAFFLES

Makes: 12 4-inch waffles; serves: 4 to 6

If you don't have pumpkin pie spice, you can substitute 1 teaspoon ground cinnamon and ¹/₄ teaspoon ground nutmeg.

1½ cups all-purpose flour
¾ cup whole wheat flour
¼ cup sugar
1 tablespoon baking powder
2 teaspoons ground pumpkin pie spice
¼ teaspoon salt, or to taste
2 eggs
2 cups milk
3 tablespoons melted butter or margarine
½ teaspoon vanilla
1½ cups chopped apples
Butter, margarine, or oil for greasing

1. Preheat the waffle iron according to manufacturer's directions.

2. In a large bowl, stir together both flours, the sugar, baking powder, pumpkin pie spice, and salt.

3. In a medium bowl, beat the eggs; beat in the milk, butter or margarine, and vanilla.

4. Stir the liquid ingredients into the dry ingredients until just combined. Stir in the apples.

5. Grease the waffle iron and spread 1¹/₄ cups of batter onto it. Cook until the iron no longer steams, about 5 minutes. Repeat twice more with remaining batter.

Variation: For a crunchy texture, add ¹/₃ cup ground pecans when you add the apples.

BANANA–POPPY SEED WAFFLES

Makes: 12 4-inch waffles; serves: 4 to 6

If you use ground poppy seeds (available in specialty shops), the poppy seed flavor will be much more pronounced.

1¼ cups all-purpose flour
¾ cup whole wheat flour
2 tablespoons poppy seeds
2 tablespoons sugar
2 teaspoons baking powder
1 teaspoon baking soda
½ teaspoon salt, or to taste
1¾ cups buttermilk
¾ cup mashed banana
3 eggs, separated
3 tablespoons melted butter or margarine
1 teaspoon vanilla
Butter, margarine, or oil for greasing

1. Preheat the waffle iron according to manufacturer's directions.

2. In a large bowl, stir together both flours, the poppy seeds, sugar, baking powder, baking soda, and salt.

3. In a medium bowl, stir together the buttermilk, banana, egg yolks, butter or margarine, and vanilla.

4. In a clean bowl, using clean beaters, beat the egg whites until stiff.

5. Stir the liquid ingredients into the dry ingredients until just combined. Fold in the egg whites.

6. Grease the waffle iron and spread 1¹/₄ cups of batter onto it. Cook until the iron no longer steams, about 5 minutes. Repeat twice more with remaining batter.

Variation: Omit the poppy seeds.

BRAN WAFFLES

🔲

Makes: 12 4-inch waffles; serves: 4 to 6

These are like bran muffins—but better.

1½ cups milk
1 cup bran cereal
½ cup all-purpose flour
½ cup whole wheat flour
2 teaspoons baking powder
¼ teaspoon salt, or to taste
3 eggs, separated
3 tablespoons melted butter or margarine
3 tablespoons molasses
1 teaspoon vanilla
Butter, margarine, or oil for greasing

1. Preheat the waffle iron according to manufacturer's directions.

2. In a 1-quart saucepan, heat the milk until scalded. Add the bran; let stand 10 minutes.

3. In a large bowl, stir together both flours, the baking powder, and salt. Stir the egg yolks, butter or margarine, molasses, and vanilla into the milk-bran mixture.

4. In a clean bowl, using clean beaters, beat the egg whites until stiff.

5. Stir the liquid ingredients into the dry ingredients until just combined. Fold in the egg whites.

6. Grease the waffle iron and spread 1½ cups of batter onto it. Cook until the iron no longer steams, about 5 minutes. Repeat twice more with remaining batter.

Variation: Add 1 tablespoon grated orange rind to the milk mixture.

MAPLE WAFFLES

🔲

Makes: 12 4-inch waffles; serves: 4 to 6

I used pure maple syrup, not pancake syrup, which is sweeter but would probably be okay in here anyway. Using the optional maple extract will add a more intense maple flavor.

1 cup all-purpose flour
¾ cup whole wheat flour
1 tablespoon baking powder
¼ teaspoon salt
1½ cups milk
⅓ cup pure maple syrup
⅓ cup vegetable oil
¼ teaspoon maple extract (optional)
3 egg whites
Butter, margarine, or oil for greasing

1. Preheat the waffle iron according to manufacturer's directions.

2. In a large bowl, stir together both flours, the baking powder, and salt.

3. In another bowl, beat together the milk, maple syrup, oil, and maple extract (if desired). Stir the maple mixture into the dry ingredients until well combined.

4. In a clean medium bowl, using clean beaters, beat the egg whites until stiff peaks form when the beaters are lifted. Fold the egg whites into the batter.

5. Grease the waffle iron and spread a generous cup of the batter onto it. Cook until the iron no longer steams, about 5 minutes or until the waffle is browned. Repeat with the remaining batter.

Variation: Add 2 teaspoons grated lemon rind when you add the syrup.

French Toast

Everyone has a different style of preparing French toast. I am a "quick dipper." I don't like my French toast soggy with egg mixture, so I do a quick dip into the batter on each side and I use firm bread that is not too spongelike. If you prefer well-soaked French toast, use squishy bread and let it stand in the egg mixture. You'll probably have a smaller yield if you soak the bread a lot.

I've presented two different types of French toast: sweet and savory. The sweet French toast recipes are more traditional. Serve the savory as brunch or lunch entrees, topped with cheese sauces instead of syrups.

Sweet French Toast

CINNAMON FRENCH TOAST

Makes: 10 to 12 slices; serves: 4 to 6

2 eggs
2 tablespoons sugar
1 teaspoon ground cinnamon
1/2 teaspoon vanilla
1/8 teaspoon salt, or to taste
3/4 cup milk
10 slices white or whole wheat bread
2 to 3 tablespoons butter or margarine, divided

1. In a shallow bowl, beat the eggs. Beat in the sugar, cinnamon, vanilla, and salt. Beat in the milk.

2. Dip each bread slice into the egg mixture until moistened on both sides.

3. In a large skillet, melt 1 tablespoon of the butter or margarine over medium-high heat. Add 4 slices of the soaked bread and cook until browned on the bottom. Turn and cook

until browned on the other side. Add as much butter or margarine as necessary to cook the second batch. Cook as for first 4 slices. Repeat once more with remaining 2 slices.

Variation: Traditional French Toast: Omit the cinnamon.

MAPLE FRENCH TOAST

Makes: 8 triangles; serves: 4

This French toast is so delicious you may not want to use anything on top, except maybe a dusting of confectioners' sugar. Or you may want to try a raspberry sauce (page 555) or orange sauce (page 552) instead of maple syrup. You'll need unsliced bread, which can be homemade or from the bakery.

Four 1 1/2-inch-thick slices white or whole wheat bread
4 eggs
3/4 cup half-and-half
2 tablespoons maple syrup
2 tablespoons sugar
1/2 teaspoon vanilla
1/8 teaspoon salt, or to taste
1/4 cup (1/2 stick) butter or margarine, divided

1. Remove the crusts from the bread; cut each slice in half diagonally to form 2 triangles.

2. In a medium bowl, beat the eggs. Beat in the half-and-half, syrup, sugar, vanilla, and salt until sugar is dissolved.

3. Dip each bread triangle in the egg mixture until soaked.

4. In a 10-inch skillet, melt 2 tablespoons of the butter or margarine over medium-high heat. Place half the triangles in the pan. Cook over medium heat until browned on the bottom. Turn and cook until browned on the other side. Remove from pan to serving platter (platter may be placed in warm oven to retain heat). Melt remaining butter or margarine and cook remaining bread. Serve immediately.

💙 *Variation:* For a lower-fat version, use skim milk instead of half-and-half; reduce butter or margarine to 1 tablespoon and cook in nonstick skillet.

ORANGE FRENCH TOAST

Makes: 10 slices; serves: 4 to 6

This is a great way to have French toast even if you're lactose-intolerant.

2 eggs
¾ cup orange juice
2 tablespoons orange liqueur or additional juice
2 tablespoons sugar
⅛ teaspoon salt, or to taste
10 slices white or whole wheat bread
2 to 3 tablespoons butter or margarine, divided

1. In a shallow bowl, beat the eggs. Beat in the orange juice, liqueur, sugar, and salt.

2. Dip each bread slice into the egg mixture until moistened on both sides.

3. In a large skillet, melt 1 tablespoon of the butter or margarine over medium-high heat. Add 4 slices of the soaked bread and cook until browned on the bottom. Turn and cook until browned on the other side. Add as much butter or margarine as necessary to cook the second batch. Cook as for first 4 slices. Repeat once more with remaining 2 slices.

Variations: Pineapple French Toast: Substitute pineapple juice for the orange juice.

💙 For a lower-cholesterol version, use 3 egg whites or an equivalent amount of egg substitute instead of the two whole eggs.

Savory French Toast

These are great brunch dishes. Serve them with cheese sauces instead of syrups—rather like Welsh rarebit.

GARLIC FRENCH TOAST

Makes: 8 to 10 slices; serves: 4 to 6

Serve this French toast with Swiss fondue (page 67) as a sauce.

2 eggs
½ cup milk
¼ cup beer or vegetable broth (pages 93–95)
2 cloves garlic, minced
⅛ teaspoon salt, or to taste
⅛ teaspoon pepper
8 slices rye bread, or 10 slices white or whole wheat bread
2 to 3 tablespoons butter or margarine, divided

1. In a shallow bowl, beat the eggs. Beat in the milk, beer or broth, garlic, salt, and pepper.

2. Dip each bread slice into the egg mixture until moistened on both sides.

3. In a large skillet, melt 1 tablespoon of the butter or margarine over medium-high heat. Add 4 slices of the soaked bread and cook until browned on the bottom. Turn and cook until browned on the other side. Add as much butter or margarine as necessary to cook second batch. Cook as for first 4 slices. Repeat once more with remaining 2 slices, if necessary.

Variation: Substitute broth or beer for the milk (if you're already using beer, use a beer-broth mixture, not more beer alone).

CURRIED FRENCH TOAST

Makes: 10 slices; serves: 4 to 6

Serve this French toast with any chutney (especially homemade), Chutney Sauce (page 483), or unflavored yogurt.

2 eggs
2 teaspoons curry powder
¼ teaspoon ground cinnamon
⅛ teaspoon ground ginger
⅛ teaspoon ground red pepper (optional)
½ cup vegetable broth (pages 93–95)
¼ cup beer, or ¼ cup additional vegetable broth
2 cloves garlic, minced
⅛ teaspoon salt, or to taste
⅛ teaspoon black pepper
10 slices whole wheat bread
2 to 3 tablespoons butter or margarine, divided

1. In a shallow bowl, beat the eggs. Beat in the curry powder, cinnamon, ginger, and red pepper. Stir in the broth, beer or additional broth, garlic, salt, and black pepper.

2. Dip each bread slice into the egg mixture until moistened on both sides.

3. In a large skillet, melt 1 tablespoon of the butter or margarine over medium-high heat. Add 4 slices of the soaked bread and cook until browned on the bottom. Turn and cook until browned on the other side. Add as much butter or margarine as necessary to cook second batch. Cook as for first 4 slices. Repeat once more with remaining 2 slices.

Variation: Add 1 tablespoon pureed chutney to the batter.

BARBECUE FRENCH TOAST

Makes: 8 to 10 slices; serves: 4 to 6

You can use any smooth (not chunky) barbecue sauce. I like Cattleman or Bullseye.

2 eggs
½ cup vegetable broth (pages 93–95)
¼ cup beer, or ¼ cup additional vegetable broth
3 tablespoons barbecue sauce
⅛ teaspoon pepper
8 slices rye bread, or 10 slices white or whole wheat bread
2 to 3 tablespoons butter or margarine, divided

1. In a shallow bowl, beat the eggs. Beat in the broth, beer or additional broth, barbecue sauce, and pepper.

2. Dip each bread slice into the egg mixture until moistened on both sides.

3. In a large skillet, melt 1 tablespoon of the butter or margarine over medium-high heat. Add 4 slices of the soaked bread and cook until browned on the bottom. Turn and cook until browned on the other side. Add as much butter or margarine as necessary to cook second batch. Cook as for first 4 slices. Repeat once more with remaining 2 slices, if necessary.

Variation: For a spicier version, add a few drops of Tabasco.

BLINTZES

CHEESE BLINTZES

Makes: 10 blintzes; serves: 3 to 4

Blintzes are a real favorite of mine, though I confess that, rather than make them, I usually buy them frozen in the supermarket. Cook them in a generous amount of butter or margarine to achieve a crispy outside.

1 egg
Two 7½-ounce packages farmer cheese
¼ cup sugar
2 teaspoons grated lemon rind (optional)
1 recipe Dessert Crepes (page 553)
Butter or margarine

1. In a medium bowl, beat the egg. Add the cheese, sugar, and lemon rind, if desired, and beat until combined.

2. Place 2 generous tablespoons of the cheese mixture in a 1-inch stripe down the center of a crepe.

3. Fold the top and bottom (1-inch borders) over the filling and fold one of the remaining sides over the filling.

4. Roll package over to close.

5. In a large skillet, melt the butter or margarine over medium-high heat. Add as many blintzes as will comfortably fit. Cook until browned on all sides. Repeat until all blintzes are cooked, using additional butter or margarine if necessary.

BLUEBERRY BLINTZES

Makes: 10 blintzes; serves: 3 to 4

Cook these in a generous amount of butter or margarine for a crispy outside. If you don't want to go through the bother of rolling up the blintzes, you can just serve the blueberry filling over the crepes as a sauce instead.

⅓ cup sugar
¼ cup water
2 tablespoons cornstarch
½ teaspoon grated lemon rind (optional)
2½ cups fresh or frozen blueberries
1 recipe Dessert Crepes (page 553)
Butter or margarine

1. In a 1½-quart saucepan, stir together the sugar, water, cornstarch, and lemon rind, if desired. Add the blueberries. Cook, stirring, until mixture comes to a boil and is thickened; cool.

2. Place 2 generous tablespoons of the blueberry mixture in a 1-inch stripe down the center of a crepe.

3. Fold the top and bottom (1-inch borders) over the filling and fold one of the remaining sides over the filling.

4. Roll package over to close.

5. In a large skillet, melt the butter or margarine over medium-high heat. Add as many blintzes as will comfortably fit. Cook until browned on all sides. Repeat until all blintzes are cooked, using additional butter or margarine if necessary.

Variation: Substitute orange rind for lemon.

SPOON BREAD

Makes: 4 cups; Serves: 4 to 6

Spoon bread is a Southern specialty that's just too good to stay regional. Some people like it smothered in butter or margarine with plenty of salt and pepper; others enjoy it with syrup or powdered sugar.

1 cup yellow cornmeal
1 tablespoon sugar
1/2 teaspoon salt, or to taste
2 1/2 cups milk, divided
3 tablespoons butter or margarine
3 eggs, separated
2 teaspoons baking powder

1. Preheat the oven to 350°F. Grease a 2-quart soufflé dish.

2. In 3-quart saucepan, stir together the cornmeal, sugar, and salt.

3. Gradually stir in 1 1/2 cups of the milk. Cook over low heat, stirring constantly, until mixture is very thick. Remove from heat; stir in butter or margarine until completely melted.

4. In a medium bowl, lightly beat the yolks; gradually beat in the remaining 1 cup milk.

5. Stir the baking powder and the yolk mixture into the cornmeal.

6. In a clean bowl with clean beaters, beat the whites until soft peaks hold. Stir 1/4 of whites into the cornmeal. Fold in remaining whites. Pour into prepared dish. Bake 40 to 50 minutes.

Variation: You can increase the sweetness by using 1/4 cup sugar instead of 1 tablespoon.

CEREAL

BROWN SUGAR GRANOLA

Makes: 4 cups; serves: 6 to 8

This is not as sweet as commercial granola. Use more raisins or any dried fruit or nut that you like.

3 tablespoons butter or margarine
1/3 cup firmly packed light brown or dark brown sugar
1 1/2 tablespoons apple or orange juice
2 cups rolled oats
1/3 cup sunflower seeds
3 tablespoons sesame seeds
1/2 cup wheat germ
1/4 cup oat bran
1/2 cup raisins

1. Preheat the oven to 350°F.

2. Place the butter or margarine in a 9 × 13-inch baking pan. Place in the oven for 3 to 5 minutes or until melted. Stir in the sugar until dissolved; stir in the juice.

3. Add the oats, sunflower seeds, and sesame seeds. Stir until coated with butter-sugar mixture. Bake 15 minutes, stirring once or twice.

4. Add the wheat germ and oat bran to the pan. Toss to combine. Bake 10 minutes longer, stirring once. Stir in the raisins.

Variation: Add chopped almonds when you add the wheat germ.

EGGS

HASH AND EGGS

Makes: 4 patties; serves: 2 to 4

Although traditionally made with corned beef or other leftover meat, these potato patties are perfectly delicious without the meat.

2 tablespoons oil, divided
¾ cup finely diced onions
¾ cup finely diced green bell peppers
3 large baked potatoes (page 280), chilled, peeled, and diced (about 5 cups)
½ teaspoon anchovy-free Worcestershire sauce
¼ teaspoon salt, or to taste
¼ teaspoon pepper
1 to 2 tablespoons milk
3 tablespoons butter or margarine, divided
4 eggs

1. In 10-inch skillet, heat 1 tablespoon of the oil over medium-high heat. Add the onions and green peppers; cook, stirring, until onions start to brown.

2. In medium bowl, combine the onion-pepper mixture, potatoes, Worcestershire sauce, salt, and pepper.

3. Stir in as much of the milk as necessary to help mixture hold together.

4. In 10-inch skillet, melt 1½ tablespoons butter or margarine with the remaining 1 tablespoon oil over medium-high heat. Form hash into 4 patties. Cook 10 to 15 minutes or until browned on the bottom. Turn and cook 15 minutes more or until browned on the other side.

5. Remove from the pan and drain on paper towels. In a clean 10-inch skillet, melt remaining 1½ tablespoons butter or margarine over medium-high heat. Add the eggs; cook until whites are set. Serve 1 egg on top of each hash patty.

Variation: Stir 2 to 3 tablespoons imitation bacon bits into the potato mixture before forming patties.

SCRAMBLED EGGS WITH CREAM CHEESE AND SCALLION

Makes: 1 cup; serves: 2

This is a very rich version of scrambled eggs. The melted cream cheese keeps the eggs quite moist.

4 eggs
2 tablespoons cream cheese, cut into small pieces
1 tablespoon chopped scallion (white and green parts)
⅛ teaspoon salt, or to taste
1 tablespoon butter or margarine
Fresh black pepper, for grinding

1. In a medium bowl, beat the eggs. Stir in the cream cheese, scallion, and salt.

2. In a large skillet, melt the butter or margarine over medium-high heat. Add the egg mixture; cook, stirring frequently, until eggs reach desired doneness. Grind the pepper on top, to taste.

Variations: Scrambled Eggs: Omit the cream cheese and scallion.

♥ For lower-fat scrambled eggs, use 2 whole eggs plus 4 egg whites and cook in a Teflon-lined pan using only 1 teaspoon butter.

HARD-COOKED EGGS

Makes: 8 perfectly cooked eggs; serves: 4 to 8

Everyone knows how to boil an egg, but as a food stylist, I learned (by asking my assistant to cook the eggs) that not everyone knows how to hard-cook an egg without getting the green ring around the yolk that indicates an overcooked egg.

8 eggs

1. Place the eggs in a 2-quart saucepan and add water to 1 inch above the eggs. Bring to a rolling boil over medium-high heat. Boil 2 minutes.

2. Remove from heat and let stand 15 minutes. Pour off hot water and add cold water to cover. Let cool; peel the eggs.

Variation: Easter eggs: Add food coloring and distilled white vinegar to the water before cooking the eggs.

EGG IN PUFF PASTRY

Makes: 4 eggs in pastry shells; serves: 2 to 4

Puff pastry shells made by Pepperidge Farms can generally be found in the freezer case of your local supermarket.

4 frozen puff pastry shells (patties)
4 poached eggs (page 433)
Freshly ground black pepper, to taste
¼ cup shredded mozzarella cheese
¼ cup shredded Cheddar cheese

1. Preheat the oven to 400°F.

2. Bake the pastry shells according to package directions.

3. Place 1 egg in each baked shell. Sprinkle a little pepper over each egg.

4. Toss both cheeses together. Top each egg with 2 tablespoons of cheese mixture. Bake 3 to 4 minutes or until cheese is melted.

Variation: Use all Cheddar cheese instead of the mozzarella.

EGG IN A MUFFIN

Makes: 4 sandwiches; serves: 2 to 4

This is my vegetarian version of an Egg McMuffin.

4 English muffins
2 tablespoons butter or margarine, divided
¼ cup mild or spicy taco sauce (optional)
4 slices American cheese
4 eggs
¼ teaspoon salt

1. Preheat the broiler.

2. Split the muffins in half; toast 4 halves. Spread each with 1 teaspoon butter or margarine. Toast remaining muffin halves; spread each with 1 tablespoon taco sauce, if desired. Top with 1 slice American cheese; set aside.

3. In a large skillet, melt remaining butter or margarine over medium-high heat. Add the eggs; sprinkle with salt. Cook to desired doneness.

4. Place one egg on top of each buttered muffin half.

5. Place the cheese-topped muffin halves under the broiler until cheese is melted. Close sandwiches. Serve immediately.

Variation: Use Cheddar cheese instead of American.

EGGS FLORENTINE

Makes: 8 poached eggs; serves: 4

Rich sauce with creamy spinach and perfectly poached eggs combine to make a dish that will please anyone. For a slightly less decadent version, substitute additional milk for the heavy cream.

3 tablespoons butter or margarine
1 clove garlic, minced
3 tablespoons all-purpose flour
1 1/4 cups milk
1/2 cup heavy cream
1 teaspoon Dijon mustard
1/4 teaspoon salt, or to taste
Pinch ground red pepper
1/4 cup grated Swiss cheese
1/4 cup plus 2 tablespoons grated Parmesan cheese
Two 10-ounce packages frozen chopped spinach, thawed and well drained
8 poached eggs (page 433)

1. Preheat the broiler.

2. In medium saucepan, melt the butter or margarine over medium heat. Stir in the garlic; cook 1 minute. Stir in the flour; cook 1 minute. Stir in the milk, cream, mustard, salt, and red pepper. Cook, stirring constantly, until mixture comes to boil. Cook 1 minute longer. Stir in the Swiss cheese and 1/4 cup of the Parmesan.

3. In a medium bowl, stir 1 cup of sauce into spinach. Spread spinach mixture over bottom of 8-inch-square pan.

5. Place eggs on top of spinach. Top with remaining sauce. Sprinkle with remaining Parmesan cheese.

6. Place under the broiler about 2 minutes, until top is browned.

Variation: Shortcut Eggs Florentine: Instead of making creamed spinach from scratch, use the store-bought variety (I love the one from Seabrook Farms).

HUEVOS AL NIDO

Makes: 4 tomatoes; serves: 2 to 4

This unusual egg dish—poached eggs on stuffed tomatoes—is great for brunch.

4 large ripe tomatoes
1 tablespoon oil
1/3 cup finely chopped onions
1/3 cup finely chopped green bell peppers
2 tablespoons unflavored bread crumbs
2 tablespoons grated Parmesan cheese
1/8 teaspoon salt, or to taste
1/8 teaspoon pepper
4 poached eggs (page 433)

1. Preheat the oven to 400°F.

2. Slice the tops off the tomatoes. Carefully scoop out the pulp; chop enough pulp to equal 1/4 cup and discard the rest.

3. In a medium skillet, heat oil over medium-high heat. Sauté the onions and peppers until onions are transparent, about 2 minutes. Stir in the bread crumbs, Parmesan, salt, pepper, and reserved tomato pulp.

4. Place 1/4 of mixture into each tomato. Bake 10 minutes.

5. Place 1 egg into each tomato. Serve immediately.

Variation: For a spicier version, add 2 teaspoons (or more) minced jalapeño peppers when you sauté the bell peppers.

EGGS BENEDICTISH

Makes: 8 English muffin halves; serves: 4

Roasted red pepper adds a big flavor dimension that you'd otherwise lose by leaving out the Canadian bacon used in "real" Eggs Benedict.

4 English muffins
8 roasted red pepper halves (page 276)
1 recipe Hollandaise Sauce (page 472)
8 poached eggs (page 433)

1. Split the muffins in half; toast.

2. Place one roasted red pepper on top of each toasted muffin half. Top each with one egg. Spoon Hollandaise Sauce over the eggs. Serve immediately.

Omelets

In the era of salmonella, most health officials are warning consumers to cook eggs "well." Previous to the health scare, recipes called for the top of the omelet to be left slightly soft. You can cook your omelets by Method A in the basic omelet recipe; this is the more traditional one but doesn't quite kill all the potential bacteria. As a compromise, you can also add the optional step that broils the top of the omelet to cook the egg. Or you can use Method B, which steams the top of the omelet while the bottom is cooking. The basic recipe makes two omelets. You can make the entire recipe in a large skillet, then cut the cooked omelet in half widthwise to serve two people, or you can use two medium skillets (or one medium skillet, twice) and make individual omelets.

If you're watching your cholesterol levels, you can use any of the frozen egg substitutes (such as Egg Beaters or Egg Scramblers) instead of fresh beaten eggs. Or you can substitute an extra egg white to replace a yolk. I suggest that you keep the proportions to at least 1 whole egg to 2 egg whites (for example, if the recipe calls for 4 eggs, you can use 2 whole eggs plus 4 whites) or the omelet loses too much flavor. You can also use cooking spray instead of butter.

Omelets are more brunchy than breakfasty, and also make perfectly fine dinners, too. In addition to the recipes given here, you can use most anything inside an omelet. If you have leftover vegetables, toss them in. Frittatas and piperades are first cousins to the omelet.

BASIC OMELET WITH FILLING

Makes: 2 omelets; serves: 4

You can prepare this with cheese filling, as suggested in the variation, or any other omelet filling you prefer.

4 eggs
2 egg whites
2 tablespoons water
¼ teaspoon salt, or to taste
2 tablespoons butter or margarine
Filling of choice (pages 451–52)

1. Beat the eggs and egg whites with the water and salt.

2. In a medium skillet, melt 1 tablespoon of the butter or margarine over medium-high heat. When hot, add half of egg mixture. Cook according to chosen method:

Method A: Cover the skillet and let the omelet cook until eggs are cooked through. If desired, cook top under preheated broiler for 2 minutes or until eggs are cooked through.

Method B: Lift the edges of the omelet with a spatula while tilting the skillet, letting the uncooked portion flow to the bottom.

3. Spoon half of desired filling onto half of the omelet.

4. Fold other half over the filling. Slide onto serving plate.

5. Melt remaining butter or margarine and repeat steps for second omelet.

Variations: Add fresh or dried herbs or spices (such as oregano, basil, parsley, and so on) to the beaten egg.

 Cheese Omelet: For each omelet, use ¹/₂ cup coarsely shredded hard cheese of choice (such as Cheddar, Swiss, Gouda, Edam, Fontina, Jarslberg, or Monterey Jack) as the filling.

SPANISH OMELET

Makes: 2 omelets; serves: 4

A perfect dish for unexpected company, a Spanish omelet is not only easy to make, but chances are you may have all the ingredients on hand.

2 tablespoons oil
3 cups sliced green bell peppers
1 ¹/₂ cups sliced onions
1 cup sliced celery
1 ¹/₂ cups chopped tomatoes
One 8-ounce can tomato sauce
2 tablespoons chopped fresh parsley
¹/₄ teaspoon salt, or to taste
¹/₄ teaspoon dried thyme
¹/₈ teaspoon ground red pepper
1 Basic Omelet recipe (page 450)

1. In a large skillet, heat the oil over medium-high heat. Sauté peppers, onions, and celery until onions are transparent, about 4 minutes. Add the tomatoes, tomato sauce, parsley, the thyme, and ground red pepper.

2. Cook, uncovered, 15 minutes or until vegetables are tender-crisp.

3. Follow Basic Omelet recipe to prepare the omelet and fill it.

Variation: Use red bell peppers instead of the green. Add herbs or spices such as oregano or cumin.

ZUCCHINI OMELET

Makes: 2 omelets; serves: 2

1 tablespoon vegetable oil
¹/₂ cup sliced onions
2 cups sliced zucchini
¹/₂ cup chopped red bell peppers
¹/₂ cup chopped mushrooms
2 tablespoons chopped fresh basil
¹/₈ teaspoon salt, or to taste
¹/₈ teaspoon pepper
1 Basic Omelet recipe (page 450)

1. In a large, oven-safe skillet, heat the oil over medium-high heat. Add the onions; cook, stirring, until transparent, about 2 minutes. Add the zucchini and peppers; cook, stirring, until tender-crisp, about 3 minutes. Add the mushrooms; cook, stirring, until softened, about 3 minutes. Stir in the basil, salt, and pepper.

2. Follow Basic Omelet recipe to prepare the omelet and fill it.

Variation: Lentils with Zucchini: Prepare filling as for omelet, and stir in 1 cup cooked lentils; serve as a side dish. Makes 3 cups.

TOFU–SOY SPROUT OMELET WITH PEANUT SAUCE

Makes: 1 omelet; serves: 2

This dish is very delicious but also very calorific.

Sauce:
1/3 cup water
2 tablespoons smooth peanut butter
2 tablespoons firmly packed light brown or dark brown sugar
1 tablespoon soy sauce
1 clove garlic, minced

Filling:
2 tablespoons water
1 1/2 teaspoons soy sauce
1 teaspoon sugar
1 teaspoon cornstarch
1 tablespoon vegetable oil
1 1/2 cups soybean sprouts
1/2 cup coarsely chopped snow peas
1/3 cup sliced scallions (1-inch pieces; green part only)
1 clove garlic, minced
1/2 cup (3 ounces) diced tofu (1/2-inch pieces)
1 Basic Omelet Recipe (page 450)

1. For the sauce: Place the water, peanut butter, brown sugar, soy sauce, and garlic in a small saucepan. Cook over medium heat, stirring constantly, until the mixture comes to a boil and thickens; set aside. (Makes 1/2 cup sauce.)

2. For the filling: In a small bowl, stir together the water, soy sauce, sugar, and cornstarch; set aside. In a medium skillet, heat the oil over high heat. Add the sprouts, snow peas, scallions, and garlic. Cook, stirring, until tender-crisp, about 3 minutes. Stir in the cornstarch mixture and tofu; cook, stirring, until the sauce is thickened, about 2 minutes; set aside.

3. Follow Basic Omelet recipe to prepare the omelet and fill it. Turn the omelet onto a serving plate and serve with the peanut sauce.

Ⓥ **Variation:** Skip the omelet and serve the vegetables and sauce over brown rice.

VIDALIA ONION OMELET

Makes: 2 omelets; serves: 4

There is nothing like a sweet, caramelized onion to enhance a dish.

2 tablespoons olive oil
4 cups sliced Vidalia onions
1/8 teaspoon pepper
1/8 teaspoon dried thyme
1 Basic Omelet recipe (page 450)

1. In a large skillet, heat the oil over medium-high heat. Sauté the onions until transparent, about 3 minutes. Add the pepper and thyme. Reduce heat to low and cook, covered, 30 minutes. Remove lid and cook, uncovered, 15 minutes longer.

2. Follow Basic Omelet recipe to prepare the omelet and fill it.

Variation: Caramelized Vidalias: Prepare the filling as for omelet. Serve with crackers as an hors d'oeuvre, use as a topping or filling for pizzas or breads, or use as a condiment.

Frittata

Makes: 1 omelet; serves 2 to 3

A frittata is an Italian open-face omelet. Use whatever vegetables you like instead of—or in addition to—the asparagus.

3 tablespoons butter or margarine, divided
1 cup chopped asparagus (1-inch pieces)
¾ cup chopped onions
1 cup shredded mozzarella cheese
1 teaspoon dried oregano
6 eggs
¼ teaspoon salt, or to taste
⅛ teaspoon pepper

1. Preheat the broiler.

2. In 10-inch skillet, melt 1 tablespoon of the butter or margarine over medium-high heat. Add the asparagus and onions; sauté until vegetables are softened, about 4 minutes.

3. In medium bowl, combine sautéed asparagus and onions with the cheese and oregano.

4. In medium bowl, beat together the eggs, salt, and pepper.

5. In a large, slope-sided pan, melt remaining 2 tablespoons butter or margarine over medium-high heat.

6. Pour the eggs into the skillet. Cook, stirring with a circular motion, until bottom of egg starts to set. Continue cooking until top is only slightly runny. Remove from heat; sprinkle with cheese mixture.

7. Place under the broiler 2 minutes or until cheese is melted.

Variation: Use any shredded cheese, such as Gouda or Swiss, instead of the mozzarella.

Piperade

Makes: 1 omelet: serves: 4

Piperade is not exactly an omelet and not exactly scrambled eggs, but the best of both.

1 tablespoon olive oil
1 cup chopped onions
1 clove garlic, minced
1 cup sliced green bell peppers
2½ cups chopped tomatoes
1½ teaspoons dried basil
½ teaspoon salt, or to taste
⅛ teaspoon pepper
6 eggs
1 tablespoon butter or margarine

1. In 10-inch skillet, heat the oil over medium-high heat. Add the onions and garlic; sauté until onions are transparent, about 2 minutes. Stir in the peppers; sauté until softened, about 3 minutes. Stir in the tomatoes, basil, and pepper. Cook, uncovered, stirring occasionally, 15 minutes or until vegetables have become saucelike.

2. Beat the eggs with the salt. Stir the butter or margarine into the vegetables; add the eggs. Cook, stirring gently, until eggs begin to set, about 3 minutes; continue cooking to desired doneness.

♥ *Variation:* For a lower-fat version, use half the oil and butter, and use 4 whole eggs plus 4 whites instead of 6 whole eggs.

MEXICAN EGG ENCHILADA

Makes: 6 enchiladas; serves: 3 to 4

Instead of filling tortillas to make the enchiladas, you can just serve this egg mixture as scrambled eggs, topped with a little salsa.

1 to 2 tablespoons vegetable oil
½ cup chopped onions
½ cup chopped green bell peppers
2 cloves garlic, minced
Six 5-inch corn tortillas
4 eggs
4 egg whites
¼ teaspoon salt, or to taste
One 4-ounce can chopped chilies, drained
2 tablespoons butter or margarine
½ to ¾ cup salsa, heated

1. In large skillet, heat 2 teaspoons of oil over medium-high heat. Add the onions, peppers, and garlic; cook, stirring, until tender-crisp, about 3 minutes. Remove from skillet, set aside.

2. Heat ½ teaspoon more oil. Add 1 tortilla; heat until softened, remove from skillet, and set aside. Repeat with each tortilla, using as much of the remaining oil as necessary.

3. Beat the eggs and egg whites with the salt. Stir in the cooked vegetables and chilies.

4. In 10-inch skillet, melt the butter or margarine over medium-high heat. Add the eggs; cook, stirring gently, until eggs begin to set, about 3 minutes. Continue cooking to desired doneness.

5. Place ⅓ cup of the egg mixture onto each tortilla; roll up to enclose. Place on individual plates and top each enchilada with about 2 tablespoons of sauce.

Variation: Substitute tostada shells for the tortillas; skip step 2.

GRILLED VEGETABLE PIPERADE

Makes: 1 omelet: serves: 2 to 3

I usually prepare this dish when I have some grilled vegetables left over from the night before. I like a combination of grilled eggplant, zucchini, onion, and bell peppers.

3 eggs
2 egg whites
½ teaspoon dried oregano
¼ teaspoon dried thyme
¼ teaspoon salt, or to taste
⅛ teaspoon pepper
1 cup chopped grilled vegetables (page 233)
1½ tablespoons butter or margarine

1. In a large bowl, beat the eggs and egg whites with the oregano, thyme, salt, and pepper. Stir in the vegetables.

2. In 10-inch skillet, melt the butter or margarine over medium-high heat. Add the egg-vegetable mixture. Cook, stirring gently, until eggs begin to set, about 3 minutes; continue cooking to desired doneness.

Variation: Substitute 2 tablespoons chopped fresh basil for the oregano.

HUEVOS RANCHEROS

Makes: 8 huevos rancheros; serves: 4

Make the sauce as hot or as mild as you like by varying the amount of ground red pepper. Or you can skip the sauce-making step and use store-bought salsa.

Salsa:
1 large ripe tomato, peeled, seeded, and cut into eighths

¼ small green bell pepper, cut in half

¼ small onion, cut in half

¼ teaspoon salt, or to taste

⅛ to ¼ teaspoon ground red pepper, or to taste

To finish the dish:
Eight 5-inch corn tortillas

1 tablespoon vegetable oil

3 tablespoons butter or margarine, divided

8 eggs, divided

1 small avocado, cut into eighths

1. Preheat the oven to 400°F.

2. For the salsa: Put the tomato, bell pepper, onion, salt, and red pepper into a blender or food processor container fitted with a steel blade. Cover and process until vegetables are finely minced or pureed.

3. Brush the tortillas lightly on each side with oil. Place on a large baking sheet and bake 7 to 10 minutes or until tortillas are crisp.

4. In a 10-inch slope-sided skillet, melt 1½ tablespoons of the butter or margarine over medium-high heat. Fry 4 of the eggs until whites are set. Place 1 egg on each of 4 tortillas. Place in oven to keep warm; cook remaining eggs in remaining butter or margarine.

5. Top each egg with 2 tablespoons of the vegetable puree and 2 slices of avocado.

Variation: For a quick version, use bottled salsa and/or packaged tostada shells.

SANDWICHES

You don't have to be a master chef to create a sandwich. Iceberg lettuce, sliced tomato, and mayo on toasted white bread happens to be one of my very favorite sandwiches. (Great as it is, I don't really think it merits a recipe.) But here are some sandwich-making suggestions.

How to Build a Sandwich

The Bottom Layer

If you don't have bread, you don't have a sandwich. The bread is always on the bottom, and usually on the top as well. One slice makes an open-face sandwich, two slices make a closed sandwich, and three slices make a club sandwich.

Any type of bread will do: Packaged sliced bread, homemade sliced bread, pita pockets, bagels, rolls, and even biscuits or muffins can be used.

The Second Layer

The second layer is usually the heartier part of the sandwich. This may be something very simple (such as sliced cheese) or may require more complicated recipes (such as spreads and/or salads). In addition to the recipes in this chapter, some good fillers are:

pâtés (pages 59–62)

hummus (pages 57–58)

cheese and vegetable spreads (pages 46–50, 51–56)

grilled vegetables (page 233)

roasted red peppers (page 276)

The Third Layer

Crunchers are vegetables that give bulk, texture, and flavor to complement the fillers. The most common topper is, of course, lettuce and tomato. But don't get stuck in that rut! Lots of other vegetables can add zest to your sandwich (you can also make a bunch of toppers into a sandwich filling):

sprouts

shredded vegetables: cabbage, carrots, beets, and other hard vegetables

sliced vegetables: cucumbers, celery, avocado, radishes, mushrooms, bell peppers, zucchini, yellow squash, jicama

grilled or roasted vegetables

sliced pickles

The Fourth Layer

Toppers make up the fourth layer. For a "melt," the topper is a slice of cheese that is then melted in the broiler or microwave oven. For a vegetable sandwich or one with lots of crunchers, the topping can be salad dressing.

More often the topper is the second slice of bread. The bottom side of the bread can be spread with a condiment to add flavor "zip" to make the sandwich really outstanding. There are many types of condiments that will enhance a sandwich:

Mustard: Mustard is a great fat-free, low-calorie choice. Most supermarkets carry an extensive array of mustards and gourmet stores have even more. Keep a variety on hand for sandwich making—yellow, brown, honey, Dijon, raspberry (page 471), coarse, country-style.

Mayonnaise: Whether homemade (page 471) or store-bought, mayo frequently "makes" the sandwich.

Ketchup: Ketchup is great for almost any occasion. Be adventurous—try your hand at homemade tomato ketchup (page 470) or raspberry ketchup (page 470).

Dressings: Russian (page 391) is always good on cheese sandwiches. Most creamy salad dressings are also good on sandwiches.

Flavored butters (page 489, 491–93)

Pesto (pages 476–77)

Relishes: prepared pickle relishes, such as India or sweet pickle relish.

Chutney (pages 486–88)

As you can gather, just about anything between two slices of bread that makes you happy is an excellent sandwich. Therefore I have not devoted many sandwich recipes to this chapter, but have given just a few basics to help out. For more sandwich ideas, check out the suggested menus (pages 456–64).

Egg Salad Sandwiches

Egg salads are a great staple for the brown bagger. For a lower-cholesterol version, you can use 6 hard-cooked eggs plus 8 hard-cooked egg whites, but be aware that the texture of the salad will be different from the original.

SPINACH EGG SALAD

Makes: 2³⁄₄ cups and 4 sandwiches; serves: 4

10 hard-cooked eggs
½ cup cooked, chopped spinach, drained
⅓ cup mayonnaise
3 tablespoons unflavored yogurt
2 teaspoons mustard
¼ teaspoon anchovy-free Worcestershire sauce.
¼ teaspoon salt, or to taste
4 Kaiser rolls
Fresh black pepper, for grinding
1 tomato, sliced
½ medium cucumber, sliced

1. In a medium bowl, chop the eggs.

2. In a small bowl, stir together the spinach, mayonnaise, yogurt, mustard, Worcestershire sauce, and salt. Add to the chopped eggs and stir until combined.

3. Cut the rolls in half, horizontally. Spread ¹/₄ of the egg salad onto each bottom half. Grind pepper on top. Top each with ¹/₄ of the tomato and cucumber slices. Close the sandwiches with the tops of the rolls.

Variation: Egg Salad: Omit the spinach (makes 2¹/₃ cups).

RUSSIAN EGG SALAD SANDWICH

------------------------- |O| -------------------------

Makes: 2¹/₂ cups and 4 sandwiches; serves: 4

A slightly snazzier egg salad.

10 hard-cooked eggs
¹/₄ cup mayonnaise
2 tablespoons chili sauce
1 tablespoon chopped fresh parsley
1 tablespoon Indian or sweet relish
¹/₄ teaspoon salt, or to taste
8 slices pumpernickel bread
Fresh black pepper, for grinding
1 tomato, sliced
¹/₂ medium cucumber, sliced

1. In a medium bowl, chop the eggs.

2. In a small bowl, stir together the mayonnaise, chili sauce, parsley, relish, and salt. Add to the chopped eggs and stir until combined.

3. Spread ¹/₄ of the egg salad onto each of 4 slices of bread. Grind pepper on top. Top each with ¹/₄ of the tomato and cucumber slices. Close the sandwiches with the remaining bread.

Variation: Use ketchup instead of chili sauce.

CURRIED EGG SALAD SANDWICH

------------------------- |O| -------------------------

Makes: 4 sandwiches; serves: 4

This salad has a nice combination of tangy (from the yogurt) and sweet (from the chutney).

12 hard-cooked eggs
¹/₄ cup unflavored yogurt
¹/₄ cup mayonnaise
2 tablespoons chutney, chopped
2 teaspoons curry powder
¹/₂ teaspoon salt, or to taste
¹/₈ teaspoon ground red pepper (optional)
8 slices pumpernickel bread
¹/₂ medium cucumber, sliced
1 cup alfalfa sprouts

1. In a medium bowl, chop the eggs coarsely. In small bowl, stir together the yogurt, mayonnaise, chutney, curry powder, salt, and red pepper. Stir the dressing into the chopped eggs.

2. Spread ¹/₄ of the egg salad onto each of 4 slices of bread. Top each with ¹/₄ of the cucumber slices and ¹/₄ cup alfalfa sprouts. Close the sandwiches with the remaining bread slices.

Variation: Stir in ¹/₂ cup frozen peas, thawed.

Cheese Sandwiches

DATE-NUT SANDWICH SPREAD

Makes: ³/₄ cup spread; serves: 2 to 3

This spread makes 2 very generous sandwiches or 3 average sandwiches. I like to serve it on a slightly sweet bread, such as Anadama (page 420), Russian Black Bread (page 423), or Swedish Limpa (page 422). It's even delicious on store-bought cinnamon-raisin bread.

½ cup pitted dates
²/₃ cup softened cream cheese or other
    spreadable cheese, or tofu cream cheese
⅓ cup walnuts
4 or 6 slices Anadama Bread

1. Place the dates in a food processor container fitted with a steel blade. Cover and process until coarsely chopped. Add the cheese and walnuts; process, with an on–off pulse, until ingredients are completely combined or as finely chopped as desired.

2. Spread equal amounts on 2 or 3 of the bread slices. Top with remaining bread.

Variation: You can alter the texture if you process until very smooth. You can also use pecans instead of walnuts.

CREAM CHEESE AND OLIVE SANDWICH

Makes: 3 or 4 sandwiches; serves: 3 or 4

When I was a kid, this was one of my favorite sandwiches. Mom never used parsley, and you don't have to either.

One 8-ounce package cream cheese,
    softened, or tofu cream cheese
²/₃ cup chopped pimiento-stuffed olives plus 2
    teaspoons liquid from the olives
2 tablespoons chopped fresh parsley
6 or 8 slices whole wheat or 7-grain bread

1. In a medium bowl, stir together the cream cheese, olives, olive juice, and parsley.

2. Spread ¼ or ⅓ of the mixture on each of 3 or 4 of the bread slices. Top with remaining bread.

Variation: Add 2 teaspoons minced onion to the mixture.

ROASTED RED PEPPER–CAPER SANDWICH

Makes: 3 or 4 sandwiches; serves: 3 or 4

The red pepper flavor is mild here; use extra roasted red peppers for a stronger flavor.

One 8-ounce package cream cheese,
    softened, or tofu cream cheese
1 roasted red pepper (homemade, page 276,
    or jarred, drained)
2 tablespoons sliced scallions (white and
    green parts)
1 tablespoon capers
6 or 8 slices pumpernickel bread

1. Place the cream cheese, red pepper, scallions, and capers in a food processor container fitted with a steel blade. Cover and process until combined.

2. Spread ¼ or ⅓ of the mixture on each of 3 or 4 of the bread slices. Top with remaining bread.

Variation: Puree the cream cheese with the scallions and capers. Top with whole roasted red peppers (you'll need 4).

ROASTED PEPPER AND MOZZARELLA SANDWICH

Makes: 2 sandwiches; serves: 2

Since the red peppers contribute so much to the flavor of this sandwich, I suggest making your own rather than using the jarred kind. Either fresh or smoked mozzarella is a great choice for this recipe.

2 teaspoons olive oil
2 cloves garlic, minced
Two 4-inch-long pieces French bread
Four ½-inch-thick slices mozzarella
4 roasted red pepper halves (homemade, page 276, or jarred, drained)
8 fresh basil leaves

1. In a bowl, stir together the olive oil and garlic.

2. Slice each bread piece in half lengthwise. Brush the garlic oil onto the cut side of the upper slice of bread.

3. Place 2 slices mozzarella onto the bottom half of each bread piece. (If desired, place bread with cheese under broiler or in microwave to melt the cheese.) Top the cheese with 2 red pepper halves, and place 4 basil leaves over the peppers. Cover each sandwich with the top piece of bread.

Variation: Tomato and Mozzarella Sandwich: Substitute 4 slices of ripe tomato for the roasted red pepper.

BRIE SANDWICH

Makes: 2 sandwiches; serves: 2

Arugula is called rocket in some parts of the country. If you're buying a wedge (rather than a whole round) of Brie, you can tell whether it's ripe by checking for a soft core—should be soft to the touch in the middle as well as around the edges. It's hard to call for an exact amount of Brie since the size of the cheese will determine the size of the slices. Just cut enough to make a ½-inch layer on the bread.

Two 4-inch-long pieces French bread
4 teaspoons sun-dried tomato pesto (page 477), or 6 oil-marinated sun-dried tomato halves
Four ½-inch-thick slices Brie
6 to 8 arugula leaves

1. Slice each bread piece in half lengthwise. Brush the pesto onto the cut side of the upper slice of bread, or place the tomato halves on the bottom slice.

2. Place the Brie slices on the bottom slice of each bread. Top the cheese with the arugula leaves. Cover each sandwich with the upper slice of bread.

Variation: Substitute romaine lettuce for the arugula, and/or add 4 roasted red pepper halves (homemade, page 276, or jarred).

Hot Sandwiches

FALAFEL

— V —

Makes: 4 falafels; serves: 4

This is a very popular meal in the Middle East. If you prefer, you can use 6 smaller pitas instead of the 4 full-size ones.

Falafel balls:
1½ cups cooked chickpeas (cooked from dry; or canned, drained)
¼ cup all-purpose flour
¼ cup loosely packed fresh parsley leaves
1 tablespoon fresh lemon juice
1 tablespoon minced onion
3 cloves garlic, minced
1 teaspoon ground cumin
¼ teaspoon salt, or to taste

To finish the dish:
Oil for deep frying
1½ cups shredded lettuce
¾ cup shredded red cabbage
½ cup chopped, seeded tomatoes
¼ cup very thinly sliced onions
4 pita breads
1 recipe tahini dressing (page 392)

1. Place the chickpeas, flour, parsley, lemon juice, onion, garlic, cumin, and salt in a food processor container fitted with a steel blade. Cover and process until smooth. Form the chickpea mixture into 1-inch-diameter balls.

2. Fill a 2-quart saucepan with oil 1½ inches deep. Heat over medium-high heat until bubbles form when a small bit of falafel is dropped in. Cook the falafel balls until browned all over. Remove from oil and drain.

3. In a medium bowl, toss together the lettuce, cabbage, tomatoes, and onions.

4. Make a slit along the top edge of each pita to form a large pocket. Place ¼ of the falafels into each pita. Top each with ¼ of the salad. Drizzle 1 to 2 tablespoons of the dressing over the salad.

Variation: Add chopped green bell peppers, radishes, cucumbers, or other vegetables to the salad part of this sandwich.

GRILLED CHEESE SANDWICH

— L —

Makes: 2 sandwiches; serves: 2

You can make this on a griddle or in a skillet; just don't make the heat too high or the bread will toast before the cheese melts. For a lower-fat sandwich, toast the bread in a toaster, place the cheese slices on the bread, and either broil or microwave the open-face sandwich, then close the sandwich.

4 slices white or whole wheat bread
4 to 6 slices American or Cheddar cheese
1 tablespoon butter or margarine, divided

1. On each of two slices of bread, place half of the cheese slices. Top with the remaining bread slices.

2. On a griddle or in a large skillet, melt 2 teaspoons of the butter or margarine over medium heat. Place the sandwiches in the pan and let cook until browned on the bottom. Melt the remaining 1 teaspoon butter or margarine and cook sandwiches on the second side until browned and the cheese has melted.

Variation: Place thin slices of tomato on sandwich before grilling (or spread ketchup on the bread—my personal favorite).

BARBECUE TEMPEH ON A BUN

Makes: 4 sandwiches; serves: 4

This is a fun way to serve tempeh that even kids may enjoy. If you don't have hot dog rolls around, you can fold a piece of white bread in half to form a boat for the sandwich.

1 recipe Tempeh Fingers (page 69)
4 hot dog buns
½ cup barbecue sauce, heated
¼ cup chopped onions

1. Place 5 to 6 tempeh fingers in each bun.

2. Spoon 2 tablespoons of barbecue sauce over the tempeh in each bun. Top with 1 tablespoon chopped onions.

Variation: Top with chili sauce instead of barbecue sauce.

BARBECUED EGGPLANT SANDWICHES

Makes: 2 pita sandwiches; serves: 2

If you have any leftover barbecued eggplant, this is a great way to use it up, but reheat it since it tastes much better warm. If you don't have leftover eggplant, this sandwich is tasty enough to warrant cooking it.

2 pita breads
4 slices barbecued eggplant (page 256)
Additional barbecue sauce (optional)

1. Cut a slit along the top edge of each pita bread.

2. Fill each with 2 slices barbecued eggplant; top with additional sauce, if desired.

Variation: Use hero bread and make into a hero sandwich.

SAUTÉED MUSHROOMS ON TOAST

Makes: 4 open-face sandwiches; serves: 4

You can also serve this topped with a cheese sauce. The cheese sauce from the Egg Sandwich (page 462) or the fondue recipe (page 67) would do fine.

3 tablespoons vegetable oil
1½ cups chopped onions
4 cups quartered white mushrooms (cap and stems)
¼ teaspoon salt, or to taste
4 slices white or whole wheat bread
Fresh black pepper, for grinding

1. In a large skillet, heat the oil over high heat. Add the onions; cook, stirring, until onions start to brown, about 5 minutes. Add the mushrooms; cook, stirring, until softened, about 4 minutes. Sprinkle with the salt.

2. While the mushrooms are cooking, toast the bread. Cut each slice of toast into 4 triangles. Arrange attractively on plate and top with the mushroom mixture. Grind pepper on top.

Variation: Use portobello, shiitake, or other wild mushrooms instead of some or all of the cultivated mushrooms.

BROILED EGG SANDWICHES

Makes: 4 open-face sandwiches; serves: 2 or 4

Hard-cooked eggs with a cheese sauce make this a very filling sandwich.

1 tablespoon butter or margarine
2 tablespoons all-purpose flour
½ cup milk
1 cup shredded Swiss cheese
4 slices bread, toasted
4 hard-cooked eggs, sliced (see page 448)

1. Preheat the broiler.

2. In a 1-quart saucepan, melt the butter or margarine over medium heat. Stir in the flour until absorbed.

3. Stir in the milk; cook, stirring, until mixture comes to a boil. Remove from heat and stir in the cheese.

4. Place the toast on a baking sheet. Top with slices of egg.

5. Pour ¼ of sauce over each toast slice. Place under the broiler and cook, 4 inches from heat, 2 minutes or until sauce is browned.

Variation: Use Cheddar or other hard cheese instead of the Swiss.

WELSH RAREBIT

Makes: 1½ cups; serves: 2 to 6

The name of this dish supposedly is derived from the idea that some stingy inhabitants of Wales served this cheese sauce instead of rabbit.

1 tablespoon butter or margarine
¼ cup beer
2 cups shredded Cheddar cheese
1 egg
½ teaspoon dry mustard
½ teaspoon paprika
½ teaspoon anchovy-free Worcestershire
   sauce
Pinch ground red pepper
4 to 6 slices toasted bread

1. In a 1½-quart, heavy-bottomed saucepan, melt the butter or margarine over medium heat. Add the beer and cook until warm. Add the cheese; cook, stirring, until cheese is melted.

2. In a medium bowl, beat the egg. Beat in the mustard, paprika, Worcestershire sauce, and red pepper. Beat ¼ cup of the cheese mixture into the egg mixture. Gradually pour the egg-cheese mixture into the melted cheese in the saucepan, stirring constantly over low heat. When mixture is hot (be sure not to let it come to a boil or the egg will coagulate), pour over the toast.

Variation: Add 2 tablespoons tomato paste when you add the egg.

Sandwich Pizzas

Occasionally there are times when making pizza from scratch (pages 200–203) is just too time-consuming. Of course, you can keep store-bought frozen pizzas on hand, but you might want to try making pizzas using various breads as the crusts, with prepared sauce and shredded cheeses on top.

FRENCH BREAD PIZZA

Makes: 2 French bread pizzas; serves: 4

If you like, you can sauté the vegetables in a little oil before placing them on the pizzas. Although I used mushrooms and bell peppers, you can use any veggies you prefer. You can also sprinkle oregano or red pepper flakes over the mozzarella.

One 7-ounce French bread, or 2 hero rolls
¼ cup marinara sauce (homemade, page 473, or store-bought)
1¼ cups shredded mozzarella cheese
½ cup sliced mushrooms
¼ cup diced green bell peppers

1. Preheat the oven to 400°F.

2. Slice the bread in half lengthwise. Spread 2 tablespoons sauce on the cut surface of each half. Top each half with ½ cup of the shredded mozzarella. Sprinkle half of the mushrooms and half of the peppers over each piece of bread. Sprinkle each piece with half of the remaining mozzarella.

3. Bake 10 minutes or until cheese has melted.

Variation: Pita Pizza: Substitute four 1-ounce pitas for the French bread.

BOBOLI AND VEGETABLE MELT

Makes: 2 pizzas; serves: 2 to 4

Boboli is a brand-name pizza crust sold in most supermarkets. If you can't find Boboli, use pita bread.

Two 4-ounce Boboli crusts (One 8-ounce package)
1 tablespoon olive oil
1 cup sliced mushrooms
½ cup sliced red or green bell peppers
½ cup sliced onions
½ cup sliced zucchini
¼ teaspoon oregano
¾ cup shredded Monterey Jack cheese

1. Preheat the oven to 425°F.

2. Place the Boboli on an ungreased baking sheet; bake 5 minutes.

3. In a large skillet, heat the oil over medium-high heat. Add the mushrooms, peppers, onions, zucchini, and oregano. Cook, stirring, until tender, about 5 minutes. Place half of the vegetable mixture over each Boboli. Top each with half of the Monterey Jack.

4. Return to the oven and bake 3 to 4 minutes longer or until cheese has melted.

Variation: Use shredded mozzarella or Cheddar cheese instead of the Monterey Jack.

QUESADILLA

Makes: 1 quesadilla; serves: 2

You can serve this topped with guacamole, salsa, and/or sour cream, if you like. If jalapeño peppers are too sharp for your taste, use chopped canned green chilies instead or omit the chilies completely.

1 cup shredded Monterey Jack cheese
2 large flour tortillas
1 seeded, marinated jalapeño pepper, thinly
    sliced
1 tablespoon vegetable oil

1. Sprinkle the cheese over one tortilla to within $1/2$ inch of the edge. Sprinkle the jalapeño pepper on top. Brush the edges of the tortilla with water. Place the second tortilla on top of the first, enclosing the cheese; press down around the edges of the tortilla to seal.

2. In a large skillet, heat the oil over medium-low heat. Add the tortilla; cook until softened on the bottom. Turn and cook on the second side until heated through and cheese has melted.

3. Cut into wedges to serve.

Variation: Spread salsa over bottom tortilla before sprinkling with cheese.

TURNOVERS

Knishes

Knishes make a great lunch entree. I use mashed potatoes as the base for all the knish fillings. You can use just plain mashed potatoes or anything of similar consistency, such as pureed beans. You can even use prepared instant mashed potatoes.

Since the dough recipe contains equal parts of butter or margarine, cheese, and each flour, you can easily increase the recipe to prepare more knishes: $1/2$ cup each for 4 knishes; or $2/3$ cup each for 6 knishes.

If you like your knishes with very thin crusts; roll the dough into an 18-inch square. Cut into six 6-inch squares. Prepare 2 cups of filling. I like the sweet potato knishes prepared with the thinner crust, and I tend to use the beaten egg on the thicker knishes, omitting it for the thinner ones.

If you're going to make Mini Knishes (page 465), you may want to double the recipe, because 12 Minis are going to be eaten in the blink of an eye.

BASIC KNISHES

Makes: 4; serves: 2 to 4

If you can't find pot cheese, use cottage cheese instead.

⅓ cup butter or margarine, softened
⅓ cup pot cheese (page 495), strained through a sieve
⅓ cup all-purpose flour
⅓ cup whole wheat flour
⅛ teaspoon salt, or to taste
1⅓ cups filling of choice
1 beaten egg (optional)

1. Preheat the oven to 350° F.

2. In a medium bowl, stir together the butter or margarine and cheese. Add both flours and salt. Stir until completely combined. Form into a 3 × 5-inch rectangle and wrap in plastic wrap. Chill 15 minutes.

3. Turn the dough onto a well-floured surface. Roll into a 12-inch square. Cut into 4 smaller squares (6 inches each).

4. Place ⅓ cup of filling in the center of each square. Brush edges of square with cold water or beaten egg, if desired. Lift the four corners to meet over the filling. Pinch top and seams together to seal. Press corners down and under to make a rounded knish. Repeat with remaining squares.

5. Place knishes seam sides down on a greased baking sheet. Brush with egg, if desired. Prick tops with fork to vent.

6. Bake for 40 minutes or until golden.

Variation: Mini Knishes: Roll the dough into a 12 × 9-inch rectangle and cut into 12 smaller 3-inch squares (instead of 6-inch squares). Fill each with about 2 tablespoons of the filling. Bake 30 to 40 minutes or until golden. Makes 12 mini knishes.

BROCCOLI~CHEDDAR KNISHES

Makes: 4 cups; serves: 2 to 4

1 cup chopped cooked broccoli
⅔ cup mashed potatoes (page 281)
½ cup shredded Cheddar cheese
1 recipe Basic Knishes (left)

1. Stir together all the filling ingredients.

2. Follow Basic Knishes recipe to prepare the knishes.

Variation: Add 2 tablespoons grated Parmesan cheese to the filling.

KASHA KNISHES

Makes: 4 cups; serves: 2 to 4

If you don't want to sauté the onion, you can just stir the oil and onion together in a small bowl, microwave on high for 45 seconds, then proceed with the recipe.

1 teaspoon vegetable oil
2 tablespoons minced onion
1½ cups cooked kasha (page 302)
½ cup mashed potatoes (page 281)
⅛ teaspoon salt, or to taste
⅛ teaspoon pepper
1 recipe Basic Knishes (left)

1. In a small skillet, heat the oil over medium-high heat. Add the onion; cook, stirring until softened, about 1 minute. Remove from heat; stir in the kasha, potatoes, salt, and pepper.

2. Follow Basic Knishes recipe to prepare the knishes.

Variation: Add ¼ cup snipped fresh dill when you stir in the kasha.

SPINACH KNISHES

Makes: 4 cups; serves: 2 to 4

¾ cup cooked, chopped fresh spinach,
    drained (or one 10-ounce package frozen
    spinach, thawed and squeezed dry)
1 cup mashed potatoes (page 281)
2 tablespoons grated Parmesan cheese
1 recipe Basic Knishes (page 465)

1. Stir together all the filling ingredients.

2. Follow Basic Knishes recipe to prepare the knishes.

Variation: Substitute ¼ cup shredded Swiss cheese for the grated Parmesan.

SWEET POTATO~SQUASH KNISHES

Makes: 4 cups; serves: 2 to 4

Unbelievably delicious, these knishes can be dessert.

⅔ cup mashed cooked sweet potatoes
⅔ cup mashed cooked butternut squash
1 tablespoon firmly packed light brown or
    dark brown sugar
1 tablespoon sour cream
¼ cup well-drained crushed pineapple
1 recipe Basic Knishes (page 465)

1. Stir together the potatoes, squash, sugar, and sour cream until well combined. Stir in the pineapple.

2. Follow Basic Knishes recipe to prepare the knishes.

Variation: Add ½ teaspoon ground cinnamon or ginger to the filling.

Empanadas

Traditionally, an empanada is a Spanish turnover with a spiced beef filling. Empanadas are usually fried, but they can be baked with good results, too.

In addition to the two fillings given here, Picadillo (page 225) can also be used. Prepared empanada dough can be purchased frozen in many Hispanic markets.

BASIC EMPANADAS

Makes: 10 empanadas; serves: 5

2 cups all-purpose flour
1 cup whole wheat flour
1 teaspoon salt, or to taste
1 cup shortening, divided
½ cup cold water
1 tablespoon distilled white vinegar
2 egg yolks
1¼ cups filling of choice
Oil for frying (optional)

1. In a large bowl, stir together both flours and the salt. Using a pastry cutter or two knives, cut in ⅔ cup of the shortening.

2. In a small bowl, stir together the water, vinegar, and egg yolks. Add to the flour and stir until mixture forms a ball. Chill 1 hour.

3. Roll the dough into a 10 × 15-inch rectangle. Spread the remaining ⅓ cup shortening over the dough. Fold the dough into thirds to form a book 5 × 10 inches. Roll the dough into a 10 × 15-inch rectangle again. Fold into a 5 × 10-inch book again, then roll into rectangle and refold one more time. Wrap in plastic wrap and refrigerate 2 hours.

4. Roll dough out into a 10 × 25-inch rectangle. Cut dough into ten 5-inch circles.

5. Place 2 to 3 tablespoons of filling in the center of each circle. Brush the edges of the dough with water. Fold dough in half over the filling and press the edges together with the tines of a fork to seal.

6. To fry: Pour ³⁄₄ inch oil into a large skillet. Heat over medium-high heat until oil bubbles when a small piece of dough is dropped in. Add the empanadas a few at a time. Fry until golden on the bottom. Turn and fry until golden on the second side. Drain. To bake: Prick the tops of the empanadas with the fork to vent. Place on greased baking sheet and bake at 400°F for 15 to 20 minutes or until browned.

VEGETABLE EMPANADAS

Makes: 2 cups filling; serves 5

½ cup diced carrots
1 tablespoon vegetable oil
½ cup chopped onions
½ cup chopped green bell peppers
2 cloves garlic, minced
½ teaspoon ground cumin
½ teaspoon paprika
¼ teaspoon salt, or to taste
⅛ teaspoon ground red pepper
½ cup chopped tomatoes
½ cup corn kernels (fresh, cooked; canned, drained; or frozen, thawed)
½ cup diced cooked potatoes (¼-inch pieces; page 280)
2 tablespoon chopped cilantro
1 recipe Basic Empanadas (page 466)

1. In a small saucepan, cook the carrots in boiling water until tender, about 5 minutes; drain.

2. In a medium skillet, heat the oil over medium-high heat. Add the onions, peppers, and garlic; cook until softened, about 2 minutes. Stir in the cumin, paprika, salt, and red

pepper until absorbed. Stir in the tomatoes, corn, potatoes, and cilantro. Cook, stirring, occasionally, 10 minutes.

3. Follow Basic Empanadas recipe to prepare the empanadas.

Variation: Substitute green peas for the corn.

SPINACH EMPANADAS

Makes: 1¹⁄₂ cups filling; serves: 5

1 tablespoon vegetable oil
⅓ cup chopped onions
2 cloves garlic, minced
1 tablespoon all-purpose flour
½ cup vegetable broth (pages 93–95)
One 10-ounce package frozen chopped spinach, thawed and well drained
⅓ cup chopped tomatoes
¼ cup sliced small pimiento-stuffed green olives
1 recipe Basic Empanadas (page 466)

1. In a medium skillet, heat the oil over medium-high heat. Add the onions and garlic; cook, stirring, until onions are softened, about 2 minutes. Stir in the flour until absorbed. Add the broth; cook, stirring, until mixture comes to a boil.

2. Stir in the spinach, tomatoes, and olives.

3. Follow Basic Empanadas recipe to prepare the empanadas.

Variation: Add 3 tablespoons toasted pine nuts when you add the olives.

CONDIMENTS, SAUCES, RELISHES, AND JAMS

Condiments

Ketchup   470

Raspberry Ketchup   470

Raspberry Vinegar   470

Raspberry Mustard   471

Food Processor
Mayonnaise   471

Tofu Mayonnaise   472

Blender Hollandaise   472

Sauces and Marinades

Garlic Tomato Sauce   473

Slow-Cooking Fresh Tomato
Marinara Sauce   473

Basil Marinara   474

Tomato–Red Pepper
Sauce   474

Tomato Sauce with
Vegetables   475

Red Pepper Coulis   475

Traditional Pesto   476

Cilantro Pesto   476

Spinach-Parsley Pesto   477

Sun-Dried Tomato
Pesto   477

Betty's Barbecue Sauce   477

Beer Barbecue Sauce   478

Orange-Flavored Barbecue
Sauce   478

Easy Salsa   479

Warm Salsa Sauce   479

Creamy Salsa   479

Salsa Verde   480

Salsa Ranchero   480

Cranberry Salsa   480

Fresh Pineapple Salsa   481

Sambal   481

Fried Crispy Onions   481

Nam Pla   482

Oriental Dipping Sauce   482

Hoisin-Soy Marinade   482

Southwest Marinade   482

Orange Glaze   483

Cilantro Chutney Sauce   483

Chutney Sauce   483

Relishes

Pico de Gallo   484

Cilantro–Two Onion
Relish   484

Sofrito   484

Green Tomato Relish   485

Beet-Horseradish
Sauce   485

Tomatillo-Corn Relish   485

Chutney

Mango Chutney   486

Tomato, Plum, and Dried
Fruit Chutney   486

Green Tomato–Pineapple
Chutney   487

Figs-Were-Cheap
Chutney   487

Blueberry-Mango
Chutney   487

Rhubarb-Walnut
Chutney   488

Nectarine Chutney   488

Flavored Butters, Jams, and Fruit and Vegetable Butters

Homemade Butter   489

Apricot Jam   490

Raspberry Jam   490

Damson Plum Jam   490

Apple-Pear-Plum Butter   491

Raspberry-Quince
Butter   491

Peach Butter   492

Butternut Squash
Butter   492

Prune Butter (Lekvar)   493

Apricot Lekvar   493

Lemon Curd   494

Miscellaneous Stuff

Ghee   494

Paneer   495

Pot Cheese (Topfen)   495

Yogurt Cheese   496

Raita   496

Tomato Raita   496

Homemade Coconut
Milk   497

Easy Coconut Milk   497

Most of the recipes in this chapter are suitable for preserving but I'm not a "canner." I prepare enough to last a week or two in the refrigerator or maybe to give away a jar or two (and tell my friends to refrigerate it and use it soon). If you prefer to preserve food by canning for a longer shelf life, be sure to read up on proper canning techniques before you get started. A good source for this information is the *Ball Blue Book: The Guide to Home Canning and Freezing*. You can obtain a copy at a modest price from Alltrista Corporation, Consumer Products Company, Consumer Affairs Department, P.O. Box 2729, Muncie, Indiana 47307-0729.

CONDIMENTS

KETCHUP

Makes: 3 cups

This is a little thinner than Heinz, but a good use of your tomato crop.

12 cups ripe tomato wedges (about
     4 1/2 pounds)
2 cups onion wedges
1/2 cup lightly packed celery leaves
1/2 cup distilled white vinegar
1/3 cup sugar
1 teaspoon salt, or to taste
1 bay leaf
1/4 teaspoon ground clove
1/8 teaspoon ground allspice

1. In a 6-quart pot, combine all the ingredients. Bring to a boil over high heat. Reduce heat to low and simmer, uncovered, 3 hours or until very thick. Discard the bay leaf.

2. Place 1/4 of the sauce in a blender or food processor container fitted with a steel blade. Cover and process until smooth. Pour the puree through a fine sieve to remove any tomato skins. Repeat with remaining sauce.

RASPBERRY KETCHUP

Makes: 1 cup

I like to use this just as I would use tomato ketchup—as a sandwich spread or as a base for barbecue sauce. It adds an unexpected dimension to recipes.

2 cups raspberries
1/2 cup chopped, peeled apple
1/2 cup chopped red onions
1/3 cup sugar
1/4 cup water
3 tablespoons distilled white vinegar
1 small clove garlic, minced
1/2 teaspoon salt

1. Place all the ingredients in a 2-quart saucepan. Bring to a boil over medium heat. Reduce heat to low and simmer, uncovered, 40 minutes.

2. Place in a food processor container fitted with a steel blade. Cover and process until smooth. Pour the puree through a sieve to remove the seeds.

Variation: Strawberry Ketchup: Use sliced strawberries instead of the raspberries; don't bother to sieve the ketchup.

RASPBERRY VINEGAR

Makes: 1 1/4 cups

Homemade raspberry vinegar is the color of cranberry juice, with a sweet bouquet; use it to dress up any salad. Rice vinegar (available in Asian groceries or the Asian section of your supermarket) has a mild, sweetish flavor. It's worth the effort to find it; if you can't, use distilled white vinegar and stir in a teaspoon or two of sugar. Don't throw out the raspberries after you've prepared the vinegar—use them to make Raspberry Mustard (page 471).

1 1/3 cups fresh raspberries
1 cup rice vinegar
2 tablespoons red wine vinegar

1. Combine the raspberries and both vinegars. Let stand at room temperature 3 days.

2. Strain vinegar into a jar and press any vinegar from the raspberries. Discard raspberries or save for other uses.

Variations: For a sweeter taste, use all rice vinegar.

Blueberry Vinegar: Use slightly crushed blueberries instead of raspberries (you can also make Blackberry Vinegar the same way).

RASPBERRY MUSTARD

V ♥

Makes 1³/₄ cup

This is ideal for raspberries that you've used to make raspberry vinegars. This mustard is slightly fruity, very tangy, and slightly salty—perfect for perking up dreary sandwiches.

1 cup Dijon mustard
½ cup raspberries left over from Raspberry Vinegar (page 470)
¼ cup honey

1. Stir together all the ingredients.

Variation: Fresh Raspberry Mustard: Use ¼ cup fresh raspberries instead of the vinegar raspberries and only 2 tablespoons honey.

Emulsions and Mayonnaise

FOOD PROCESSOR MAYONNAISE

Makes: 1¹/₄ cups

Have all the ingredients at room temperature before preparing the mayonnaise. If your mayonnaise has separated or curdled, try this: in a clean bowl, beat an egg yolk, then gradually beat in the curdled mayonnaise. If you want your mayonnaise a little thicker, let the food processor run a little longer after you've finished adding the oil.
Warning: *Raw eggs can be hazardous to your health. Use only the freshest and best-quality eggs, but even these can have salmonella.*

1 egg
1½ teaspoons fresh lemon juice
1½ teaspoons distilled white vinegar
¼ teaspoon dry mustard
⅛ teaspoon salt
1 cup vegetable oil, divided

1. Place the egg, lemon juice, vinegar, mustard, salt, and ¹/₄ cup of the oil in a food processor container fitted with a plastic or steel blade. Cover and process until thoroughly combined.

2. With the motor running, drizzle the remaining oil slowly through the chute. Store covered in the refrigerator for no more than 7 to 10 days.

Variations: Use different flavored vinegars (such as tarragon, red or white wine, raspberry, etc.) and different oils to vary the flavors of the mayonnaise. Stir in herbs or mustard to flavor the mayonnaise as well.

TOFU MAYONNAISE

— v —

Makes: ¹/₂ cup

In order for this "mayonnaise" to be smooth without grittiness and similar in texture to "regular" mayonnaise, you must use "soft" tofu, which can be found packaged in water in the refrigerator case of the supermarket or health food stores. (If you use firm tofu, the mayonnaise is gritty and requires extra oil; if you use silken, it comes out more saucelike.) I keep it only about 5 days in the refrigerator, so I make fairly small batches.

½ cup cubed soft tofu
2 tablespoons vegetable oil
2 teaspoons fresh lemon juice
¼ teaspoon sugar
⅛ teaspoon salt, or to taste

1. Place all the ingredients in a blender container (a blender is preferable to a food processor for this purpose). Cover and blend until smooth.

Variations: Add tarragon, parsley, or other herbs to the mayonnaise.

Lemon Tofu Mayonnaise: Increase lemon juice to 1 tablespoon and add ¹/₂ teaspoon grated lemon rind.

BLENDER HOLLANDAISE

— LO —

Makes: 1 cup; serves: 6 to 12 (depending on use)

I find this the easiest way to be assured of a successful hollandaise. The secret to no-fail sauce is to be sure to drizzle the butter very slowly into the egg mixture. To facilitate this, I drop the butter from a teaspoon, rather than pouring from the saucepan. Use butter, not margarine. **Warning:** *Raw eggs can be hazardous to your health. Use only the freshest and best-quality eggs, but even these can have samonella. Do not store this sauce in the refrigerator for more than 3 days.*

3 egg yolks
1 tablespoon fresh lemon juice
2 teaspoons dry sherry
¼ teaspoon dry mustard
⅛ teaspoon salt, or to taste
Pinch ground red pepper
¾ cup (1½ sticks) unsalted butter, melted
Water, if necessary

1. In a blender container, combine the egg yolks, lemon juice, sherry, mustard, salt, and red pepper. Cover and blend until combined.

2. With the motor running, add the butter to the egg mixture one drop at a time. As the sauce thickens, you can increase the flow of butter to the blender. If sauce is too thick, add water to thin to desired consistency.

SAUCES AND MARINADES

Aren't marinades items you use for meat? Yes, but they are also delicious for brushing such foods as mushrooms, onions, eggplant, and tofu, or any kebab before grilling, broiling, or baking.

GARLIC TOMATO SAUCE

Makes: 4 cups; serves: 6 to 8

There's nothing shy about the flavor of this tomato sauce. It starts with fresh tomatoes and a fairly amazing amount of garlic and ends as a wonderful sauce.

1/4 cup olive oil
1/3 cup paper-thin slices garlic
8 cups tomato chunks (about 3 pounds)
1/4 cup tomato paste
1/4 teaspoon salt, or to taste

1. In a 4-quart pot, heat the oil over medium-high heat. Add the garlic; cook, stirring, until softened, about 30 seconds.

2. Add the tomatoes; cook until the tomatoes give off enough liquid so that most of the pieces are submerged. Stir in the tomato paste. Bring to a boil. Reduce heat to medium and cook, uncovered, 50 minutes or until thickened. Stir in the salt.

Variation: Stir in chopped fresh basil or parsley, or stir in such dried herbs as basil, thyme, or oregano.

SLOW-COOKING FRESH TOMATO MARINARA SAUCE

V ♥

Makes: 5²/₃ cups; serves: 8 to 10

My dad thought this recipe tasted good, but he couldn't understand why anyone would want to make homemade sauce when you can buy stuff in a jar. For one thing, this is a great way to use up an overabundance of ripe tomatoes. A second reason, I like to think, is that this one really does taste better than the jarred variety.

3 tablespoons olive oil
3 cups chopped onions (about ¾ pound)
2 tablespoons minced garlic (about 12 cloves)
5 pounds ripe tomatoes, cut into chunks (12 to 14 cups)
1 cup chopped fresh parsley
1 cup chopped fresh basil
¾ teaspoon dried thyme
1½ teaspoons salt
¼ teaspoon pepper

1. In a 6-quart pot, heat the oil over medium-high heat. Add the onions and garlic; cook, stirring, until softened, about 3 minutes.

2. Add the tomatoes; cook until tomatoes give off enough liquid so that most of the pieces are submerged. Bring to a boil. Stir in parsley, basil, thyme, salt, and pepper. Reduce heat to low and simmer, uncovered, 5 hours or until sauce is thickened.

3. Put the sauce in a blender or food processor container fitted with a steel blade. Cover and process until fairly smooth (you will probably have to do this in a few batches).

Variation: Chunky Marinara Sauce: Peel the tomatoes before cutting them into chunks, then don't puree the mixture after cooking.

BASIL MARINARA

[V][♥]

Makes: 5¹/₂ cups; serves: 8 to 10

This is an interesting sauce for lasagna or manicotti.

3 tablespoons olive oil
1¹/₂ cups chopped onions
4 cloves garlic, minced
One 28-ounce can whole tomatoes in thick puree, undrained
1 cup water
One 6-ounce can tomato paste
³/₄ cup chopped fresh basil
¹/₂ cup chopped parsley
1 teaspoon sugar
¹/₂ teaspoon salt, or to taste

1. In a 3-quart saucepan, heat the oil over medium-high heat. Add the onions and garlic; cook, stirring, until onions are transparent, about 2 minutes.

2. Add the tomatoes with puree and break them up with the back of a spoon. Stir in the remaining ingredients. Bring to a boil. Reduce heat and simmer, uncovered, 40 minutes.

TOMATO–RED PEPPER SAUCE

[V][♥]

Makes: 2¹/₄ cups; serves: 3 to 5

This sauce is almost a coulis (see page 475) or maybe it is a coulis—I'll leave that up to you. It's a slightly sweet sauce that is much better when prepared with homemade roasted red peppers. Serve it over cheese ravioli or with timbales. If your tomatoes are not very juicy, you may want to add the 2 to 3 tablespoons of water to the recipe.

1 tablespoon olive oil
1 cup chopped onions
3 cloves garlic, minced
2 cups chopped tomatoes
1 teaspoon sugar
1 cup roasted red bell peppers (page 276)
¹/₄ teaspoon salt, or to taste
¹/₈ teaspoon ground red pepper
2 to 3 tablespoons water (optional)

1. In a 1¹/₂-quart saucepan, heat the oil over medium-high heat. Add the onions and garlic; cook, stirring, until onions are transparent, about 2 minutes. Add the tomatoes and sugar; bring to a boil. Reduce heat to low and simmer, uncovered, 15 minutes.

2. Place the peppers, tomato mixture, salt, and red pepper in a blender or food processor container fitted with a steel blade. Cover and process until smooth.

Variation: Curried Tomato–Red Pepper Sauce: Add 2 teaspoons curry powder before you add the tomatoes.

Tomato Sauce with Vegetables

Makes: 5¹/₂ cups; serves: 8 to 10

3 tablespoons olive oil
1 cup finely chopped onions
1 cup finely chopped celery
1 cup finely chopped carrots
4 cloves garlic, minced
One 28-ounce can whole tomatoes in thick puree, undrained
1¾ cups water
One 6-ounce can tomato paste
¼ teaspoon salt, or to taste

1. Heat the oil in a 4-quart pot over medium-high heat. Add the onions, celery, carrots, and garlic; cook, stirring, until vegetables are tender, about 4 minutes.

2. Add the tomatoes with puree and break them up with the back of a spoon. Stir in the water, tomato paste, and salt. Bring to a boil. Reduce heat and simmer, uncovered, 50 minutes or until thickened.

Variation: Add broccoli florets, chopped or sliced zucchini or yellow squash, cut green beans, or other vegetables to the sauce 5 to 10 minutes before it is finished cooking.

Coulis

I was always impressed when I saw that one of the choices in an elegant restaurant was served with a coulis. It took me a while to realize that coulis, as used in '90s jargon, is simply a pureed sauce. Historically, *coulis* was the term applied to sauces in general, and more specifically for *au jus*—the juices released from cooking meat. Clearly that's not our definition.

Red Pepper Coulis

Makes: 1 cup; serves: 4 or more (depending on use)

This smooth and wonderfully flavorful sauce enhances any slightly bland dish. Serve it as a dip for crudités or appetizers, such as zucchini sticks (page 68).

3 medium roasted red bell peppers (page 276)
12 oil-marinated sun-dried tomato halves

1. Place the peppers and tomatoes in a blender or food processor container fitted with a steel blade. Cover and process until smooth.

Variation: Use orange or yellow peppers instead of the red.

Pesto

Pesto is usually considered a sauce, but I use it just as often as a seasoning or spread. That's the reason for the variety of types of pesto presented here.

Try stirring a little pesto into unflavored cooked grain, such as rice, couscous, or bulgur. A little pesto will spark up any dish: Add some to salad dressing, spread it on a sandwich (instead of mayo or mustard), stir it into mayonnaise or yogurt to create a dip, or add some to anything that seems a little bland to you.

Traditionally pesto is a raw basil-garlic-oil-pignoli sauce, but the term has broadened and seems to include almost anything you want to puree with oil and garlic. If I don't use up all my prepared pesto, I like to put a tablespoon or two of it into each compartment of an ice cube tray and freeze it. I then empty the frozen cubes into a plastic freezer bag to be used at a future date.

TRADITIONAL PESTO

—  —

Makes: 1 cup

I can never walk past a bunch of basil without having to buy it; consequently many of the recipes in this book call for fresh chopped basil. However, my favorite use is still pesto sauce. I think the secret to my really outstanding pesto is that I don't puree the ingredients, but chop each finely and then just stir them together. I even mince the garlic by hand—I don't use a garlic press for this recipe.

2 cups packed basil leaves
⅓ cup pine nuts (pignoli)
⅔ cup extra virgin olive oil
1 tablespoon garlic, minced
¼ teaspoon salt, or to taste

1. Place the basil in a food processor container fitted with a steel blade (a blender will not work for this purpose). Cover and process until finely chopped. Empty into a medium bowl.

2. Place the pine nuts in the food processor container; cover and process until finely chopped. Empty into the medium bowl.

3. Stir in the oil, garlic, and salt.

Variations: Substitute parsley for half of the basil.

 Stir in ½ cup grated Parmesan cheese.

CILANTRO PESTO

—  —

Makes: ⅔ cup

I like to use this pesto on rice rather than pasta, although it tastes just fine on pasta.

2 cups packed cilantro leaves
2 cloves garlic
⅓ cup extra virgin olive oil
⅛ teaspoon salt, or to taste

1. Place the cilantro and garlic in a food processor container fitted with a steel blade (a blender will not work for this purpose). Cover and process until finely chopped.

2. Add the oil and salt to the processor. Cover and process until fairly smooth.

Variation: Substitute 1 cup packed parsley leaves for 1 cup of the cilantro.

SPINACH~PARSLEY PESTO

[V]

Makes: 1 cup

Unlike Traditional Pesto (page 476), I do puree this really delicious pesto in the food processor. It's great when fresh basil is not available.

2 cups packed spinach leaves
½ cup packed parsley leaves
½ cup walnuts
3 cloves garlic
½ cup extra virgin olive oil
¼ teaspoon salt, or to taste

1. Place the spinach, parsley, walnuts, and garlic in a food processor container fitted with a steel blade (a blender will not work for this purpose). Cover and process until finely chopped.

2. While the motor is running, gradually pour the olive oil into the processor. Add the salt; process until combined.

Variation: Substitute pine nuts for the walnuts.

SUN~DRIED TOMATO PESTO

[V]

Makes: ³/₄ cup

I use this pesto most frequently as a sandwich spread because it makes any ordinary sandwich into something extraordinary. Start with dried— not oil-marinated—sun-dried tomatoes.

½ cup lightly packed sun-dried tomatoes
⅔ cup boiling water
½ cup extra virgin olive oil
4 cloves garlic

1. In a medium bowl, combine the tomatoes and water. Let stand 10 minutes; drain.

2. Place the tomatoes, oil, and garlic in a food processor container fitted with a steel blade (a blender will not work for this purpose). Cover and process until fairly smooth.

Variation: Add fresh basil leaves.

BETTY'S BARBECUE SAUCE

[V][♥]

Makes: ³/₄ cup

Betty Boldt Rosenbaum makes this incredibly simple, delicious barbecue sauce. Of course, Betty uses it on spare ribs. I use it for vegetable kebabs, especially onion kebabs.

¼ cup ketchup
¼ cup honey
¼ cup soy sauce

1. In a medium bowl, stir together all the ingredients.

Variation: For a spicier version, add some chili oil to taste.

BEER BARBECUE SAUCE

☑ ♥

Makes: 1³/₄ cups

This sauce is fairly chunky from all the vegetables. If you prefer a more traditionally smooth barbecue sauce, you can puree it.

1 tablespoon vegetable oil
½ cup finely chopped onions
½ cup finely chopped green bell peppers
3 cloves garlic, minced
One 8-ounce can stewed tomatoes
½ cup beer
¼ cup tomato paste
¼ cup firmly packed light brown or dark brown sugar
1½ tablespoons distilled white vinegar
2 teaspoons anchovy-free Worcestershire sauce
1 teaspoon Dijon mustard
¼ teaspoon Tabasco (optional)
⅛ teaspoon salt, or to taste

1. In a 1-quart saucepan, heat the oil over medium-high heat. Add the onions, peppers, and garlic; cook, stirring, until softened, about 3 minutes. Add the tomatoes and break them up with the back of a spoon. Stir in the remaining ingredients.

2. Bring to a boil; reduce heat and simmer, uncovered, 40 minutes or until thickened.

3. For a smooth sauce, place cooled sauce in a blender container. Cover and process until smooth.

Variation: You can use water instead of beer, but then it's just barbecue sauce.

ORANGE-FLAVORED BARBECUE SAUCE

☑ ♥

Makes: 2 cups

The orange flavor is subtle after cooking, but the end result is a very delicious and slightly unusual barbecue sauce.

2 tablespoons vegetable oil
1 cup chopped onions
2 cloves garlic, minced
¾ cup orange juice
One 8-ounce can tomato sauce
⅓ cup firmly packed light brown or dark brown sugar
¼ cup ketchup
2 tablespoons tomato paste
1 tablespoon steak sauce (A-1)
2 teaspoons cider vinegar
1 teaspoon anchovy-free Worcestershire sauce
¼ teaspoon salt, or to taste

1. In a 1½-quart saucepan, heat the oil over medium-high heat. Add the onions and garlic; cook, stirring, until onions are transparent, about 2 minutes. Stir in the remaining ingredients. Bring to a boil.

2. Reduce heat and simmer, uncovered, 15 minutes, stirring occasionally.

Variation: For a spicier version, stir in ground red pepper to taste.

EASY SALSA

Makes: 2²/₃ cups; serves: 12 to 16

Not quite as easy, but even better, is to start with 2 cups finely chopped fresh tomatoes instead of the canned.

One 14½-ounce can whole peeled tomatoes, undrained

One 4-ounce can chopped green chilies, undrained

½ cup sliced scallions (white and green parts)

½ cup chopped onions

¼ cup chopped fresh cilantro

2 tablespoons fresh lime juice

2 cloves garlic, minced

¼ teaspoon ground cumin

¼ teaspoon sugar

¼ teaspoon salt, or to taste

½ cup chopped fresh tomatoes

1. Place all the ingredients except the chopped tomatoes in a blender or food processor container fitted with a steel blade. Cover and process until finely chopped.

2. Transfer to a bowl and stir in the chopped tomatoes. Let stand at least one hour for the flavors to meld.

Variation: Omit the canned chopped chilies and substitute 1 or 2 seeded fresh jalapeño peppers.

WARM SALSA SAUCE

Makes: 1½ cups; serves: 6 to 10

This cooked salsa is milder than most and is excellent to serve as a sauce over such dishes as omelets, patties, and loaves.

1 tablespoon olive oil

½ cup sofrito (homemade, page 484, or store-bought)

1 cup stewed tomatoes (homemade, page 296, or one 8-ounce can)

⅛ teaspoon salt, or to taste

1. In a 1½-quart saucepan, heat the oil over medium-high heat. Add the sofrito; cook, stirring, until just barely softened, about 30 seconds.

2. Add the tomatoes and salt; bring to a boil. Serve warm or cool.

Variation: For a spicier version, add ⅛ to ¼ teaspoon ground red pepper.

CREAMY SALSA

Makes: 1 cup

This creamy sauce is tangy from the salsa. Use it instead of yogurt or sour cream on top of chili or as a dip for vegetables (I especially like Belgian endive or celery with this).

½ cup unflavored yogurt

¼ cup sour cream

¼ cup chopped scallions (white and green parts)

3 tablespoons salsa (red or green)

2 tablespoons mayonnaise

¼ teaspoon ground cumin

1. In a medium bowl, stir together all the ingredients.

Variation: Add chopped chilies to taste.

SALSA VERDE

Makes: 1¹/₂ cups; serves: 8 to 12

For a truly wonderful flavor, I make this with fresh tomatillos (also known as Mexican green tomatoes), but you can use canned ones if that's all that's available in your area.

10 to 12 medium tomatillos (1 pound)
¹/₃ cup chopped onions
¹/₄ cup lightly packed fresh cilantro leaves
1 jalapeño pepper (or more or less
    to taste), seeded and chopped
2 cloves garlic, minced
¹/₂ teaspoon sugar
¹/₄ teaspoon salt, or to taste

1. Place the tomatillos in a 2-quart saucepan, covered with water. Bring to a boil. Reduce heat and simmer 10 minutes or until tender when pierced with a fork; drain.

2. Place the cooked tomatillos in a food processor container fitted with a steel blade. Cover and process until not quite smooth. Add the remaining ingredients and pulse on and off, often enough to combine the ingredients but to leave the texture coarse.

SALSA RANCHERO

Makes: 2¹/₄ cups; serves: depends on the use

This sauce is incredibly wonderful with anything. Serve it as a dip with chips, with tacos or tostadas, on chili, or stir it into bean soups. For a thicker dip, use less enchilada sauce. Or use more enchilada sauce, to taste. This salsa improves as it ages and the flavors meld.

¹/₃ cup mild or hot store-bought enchilada
    sauce
1 cup finely chopped tomatoes
¹/₂ cup finely chopped onions
¹/₄ cup finely chopped green bell peppers
¹/₄ cup finely chopped red bell peppers

1. Heat the enchilada sauce to boiling. Remove from heat and stir in the remaining ingredients. Cool.

Variation: Stir in ¹/₄ cup chopped fresh cilantro.

CRANBERRY SALSA

Makes: 1²/₃ cups; serves: 8 to 12

Fruity, spicy, and tart, this salsa is almost like fresh cranberry relish with a bang. Use it to jazz up bean or rice dishes.

1 cup coarsely chopped tomatoes
¹/₂ cup cranberries
¹/₂ cup coarsely chopped apple
¹/₃ cup coarsely chopped onions
¹/₄ cup coarsely chopped orange (with rind)
2 tablespoons chopped, seeded jalapeño
    peppers
2 cloves garlic, minced
¹/₂ teaspoon salt, or to taste

1. Place all the ingredients in a food processor container fitted with a steel blade. Cover and process until finely chopped.

Variation: Use fewer or more jalapeño peppers to taste. If fresh jalapeños are not available, use ¹/₄ teaspoon ground red pepper, or to taste.

FRESH PINEAPPLE SALSA

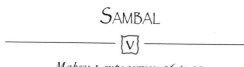

Makes: 1²/₃ cups; serves: 8 to 12

Be sure to use ripe pineapple (slightly overripe is okay too) in this incredibly wonderful salsa.

2 cups fresh pineapple chunks
1/3 cup coarsely chopped onions
1/3 cup chopped fresh cilantro
1 tablespoon chopped, seeded jalapeño pepper
1/2 teaspoon salt, or to taste

1. Place all the ingredients in a food processor container fitted with a steel blade. Cover and process until finely chopped.

Variation: Use less or more jalapeño to taste. If fresh jalapeños are not available, use 1/4 teaspoon ground red pepper, or to taste.

SAMBAL

[V]

Makes: 1 cup; serves: 16 to 32

Sambals are Indonesian condiments served with the traditional rijstaffel (literally, rice table), a banquet of many, many dishes eaten with rice. Sambals can be as simple as chopped peanuts or shredded coconut. Prepared sambals tend to be spicy relishes . . . and I do mean spicy! Only the bravest of the brave will use much.

1 cup minced, seeded tomatoes
3 tablespoons minced shallots
1 tablespoon fresh green jalapeño peppers, seeded and minced
1 tablespoon fresh red jalapeño peppers, seeded and minced
1 tablespoon lime juice

1 teaspoon grated lime rind
1/4 teaspoon salt, or to taste

1. Combine all the ingredients in a medium bowl. Let stand at least one hour, preferably overnight.

Variation: Use only green or only red jalapeño peppers.

FRIED CRISPY ONIONS

[V]

Makes: ¹/₃ cup

This is one of the simple sambals, which you sprinkle on top of dishes. It's also divine stirred into mashed potatoes.

Oil for frying
1 cup very thinly sliced onions

1. Pour oil 1 inch deep into a 1¹/₂-quart saucepan. Heat over medium-high until oil bubbles when a slice of onion is dropped in. Add 1/2 of the onions to the pan. Cook until very well browned.

2. Remove from pot with slotted spoon. Drain on paper towels. Repeat with remaining onions.

NAM PLA

Makes: 2 cups

This is a basic ingredient in almost all Thai and Indonesian cooking. Unfortunately, it's generally made with anchovies—which excludes its use in vegetarian dishes. Although you could use un-flavored soy sauce, this vegetarian version is pretty close to the real thing. Store it in the refrigerator.

1 1/3 cups water
2/3 cup soy sauce
Six 1 1/2-inch pieces kelp
1 sun-dried tomato (dry—not oil-marinated)

1. In a 1-quart saucepan, combine all the ingredients. Bring to a boil over medium heat. Strain.

ORIENTAL DIPPING SAUCE

Makes: generous 1/3 cup

This is the sauce that you serve with steamed or fried dumplings and tempura.

3 tablespoons water
2 tablespoons soy sauce
2 teaspoons mirin (rice wine) or dry sherry
1 teaspoon thinly sliced scallion
1 teaspoon minced fresh ginger
1 teaspoon sugar
1 clove garlic, minced

1. In a small bowl, stir together all the ingredients. Let stand 1 hour for the flavors to meld.

HOISIN-SOY MARINADE

Makes: 1/2 cup

I brushed this marinade on eggplant before I broiled it. I liked the flavor of the marinade, though I was not crazy about it on the eggplant—but my guests loved it.

1/4 cup light soy sauce
2 tablespoons mirin (rice wine) or dry sherry
1 tablespoon honey
1 tablespoon hoisin or plum sauce
2 cloves garlic, minced
1 teaspoon sesame oil
1 teaspoon minced ginger

1. In a medium bowl, stir together all the ingredients.

SOUTHWEST MARINADE

Makes: 1/2 cup; serves: enough to glaze 4 to 6 skewers

This is a tangy, almost barbecue type of sauce.

3 tablespoons vegetable oil
1 teaspoon chili powder
1/2 teaspoon paprika
1/4 teaspoon ground cumin
1/8 teaspoon ground red pepper
3 tablespoons fresh lime juice
2 tablespoons water
2 tablespoons chopped fresh cilantro
2 tablespoons tomato paste
1 1/2 teaspoons honey
2 cloves garlic, minced
1/8 teaspoon salt, or to taste

1. In a medium bowl, stir together the oil, chili powder, paprika, cumin, and red pepper.

2. Add the remaining ingredients; stir until smooth.

Variation: Add extra ground red pepper for a spicier version.

ORANGE GLAZE

Makes: ¹/₂ cup; serves: enough to glaze 6 skewers

This glaze is especially good for sweet potato or onion kebabs.

¼ cup mirin (rice wine) or dry sherry
¼ cup orange juice concentrate
1 tablespoon soy sauce
1 teaspoon grated orange rind
1 clove garlic

1. In a medium bowl, stir together all the ingredients.

Variation: Add 1 tablespoon minced fresh ginger.

CILANTRO CHUTNEY SAUCE

Makes: ¹/₂ cup; serves: 4 to 8

This is really more of a dipping sauce (like the Oriental Dipping Sauce on page 482) than an actual chutney. Serve this with Samosas (page 74) or a curry.

½ cup lightly packed fresh cilantro leaves
¼ cup lightly packed fresh mint leaves
1 small scallion, cut into pieces
⅓ cup unflavored yogurt
2 jalapeño peppers, halved and seeded
1 tablespoon fresh lemon juice
1 clove garlic, minced
¼ teaspoon salt, or to taste

1. Place all the ingredients in a blender container. Cover and blend until pureed.

CHUTNEY SAUCE

Makes: ²/₃ cup; serves: 4 to 8

This sauce is nice to serve with curries instead of raita or unflavored chutney. You can use any chutney that you like for this recipe (there are some delicious chutneys on pages 486–88) or you can use any store-bought chutney.

⅓ cup chutney
⅓ cup unflavored yogurt

1. Place the chutney in a blender or food processor container fitted with a steel blade. Cover and process until fairly smooth.

2. In a medium bowl, stir together the puree and yogurt.

Variation: Substitute sour cream for the yogurt.

RELISHES

PICO DE GALLO

Makes: 2¹/₃ cups

This simple raw relish is great to sprinkle on top of anything that can use a little perking up. Make this relish as spicy as you like (as written, it's fairly mild) by playing around with the amount of jalapeño pepper.

1½ cups finely chopped fresh tomatoes
½ cup finely chopped onions
⅓ cup finely chopped green peppers
¼ cup finely chopped red peppers
¼ cup chopped fresh cilantro or parsley
1 teaspoon finely chopped fresh jalapeño peppers, or to taste
½ teaspoon salt, or to taste

1. In a medium bowl, stir together all the ingredients.

CILANTRO–TWO ONION RELISH

Makes: 1¹/₄ cups

I love to sprinkle this on top of most bean dishes, stir it into yogurt, add it to soups, or toss it on anything that needs a bit of zip.

½ cup finely chopped onions
¼ cup chopped fresh parsley
¼ cup chopped fresh cilantro
¼ cup chopped scallions (white and green parts)

1. In a small bowl, stir together all the ingredients.

Variation: Omit the cilantro and increase the amount of parsley.

SOFRITO

Makes: 2¹/₃ cups

This is the base for many Spanish/Caribbean and Italian dishes.

2 medium green bell peppers, seeded and cut into eighths
1 large onion, cut into eighths
½ cup slightly packed cilantro leaves
2 tablespoons cider vinegar
6 cloves garlic
3 jalapeño peppers, halved and seeded
¼ teaspoon dried oregano
¼ teaspoon salt, or to taste

1. Place all the ingredients in a food processor container fitted with a steel blade. Cover and process until vegetables are finely chopped.

2. Place into a blender; cover and process until pureed. For a less smooth puree you can just continue to use the food processor instead of tranferring to the blender.

Variation: Cooked Sofrito: In a 2-quart saucepan, heat 3 tablespoons olive oil over medium-high heat. Add the sofrito; cook, stirring, until peppers taste cooked, about 5 minutes.

GREEN TOMATO RELISH

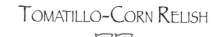

Makes: 5 cups

It's amazing how much influence a few slices of lemon can have on a whole batch of relish—be sure you don't omit them.

6 cups diced green tomato (¼-inch pieces; about 3 pounds)
3 cups chopped onion
1 cup distilled white vinegar
¾ cup sugar
2 tablespoons seeded, minced jalapeño peppers
4 slices lemon
1¼ teaspoons celery seed
1 teaspoon salt, or to taste

1. In a 6-quart pot, stir together all the ingredients. Bring to a boil over high heat. Reduce heat and simmer, uncovered, 1 hour.

BEET~HORSERADISH SAUCE

Makes: about 1 cup

I use bottled horseradish for this recipe. If you choose freshly grated horseradish, use significantly less (to taste).

One 8¼-ounce can sliced beets, drained
¼ cup grated white horseradish
2 tablespoons chopped onions
1 tablespoon distilled white vinegar
2 teaspoons sugar

1. Place all the ingredients in a food processor container fitted with a steel blade. Cover and process until finely chopped or smooth, whichever you prefer.

Variation: Use only one tablespoon horseradish for a mild sauce. Use ⅓ cup or more horseradish for a hotter version.

TOMATILLO~CORN RELISH

Makes: 1¼ cups

I'm not sure whether to call this a relish or a salsa. Either way, it's great as a condiment or as a dip with tortilla chips.

1 tablespoon vegetable oil
¼ cup chopped onions
¼ cup chopped green bell peppers
2 cloves garlic, minced
1 cup chopped tomatillos (papery outer shell removed)
1 tablespoon fresh lime juice
1 teaspoon cider vinegar
½ teaspoon dill seed
½ teaspoon sugar
¼ teaspoon ground cumin
¼ teaspoon salt, or to taste
¼ teaspoon ground red pepper
1 cup corn kernels (fresh; canned, drained; or frozen)
2 tablespoons chopped fresh cilantro

1. In a 1½-quart saucepan, heat the oil over medium heat. Add the onion, peppers, and garlic; cook, stirring, until softened, about 2 minutes.

2. Add the tomatillos, lime juice, vinegar, dill seed, sugar, cumin, salt, and red pepper. Bring to a boil; reduce heat and simmer, covered, 10 minutes, stirring occasionally. Stir in the corn; return to a boil. Reduce heat and simmer, uncovered, 10 minutes, stirring occasionally. Stir in the cilantro. Cool.

Variation: For a more colorful relish, use red bell peppers instead of the green.

CHUTNEY

Chutneys are most frequently associated with Indian cooking, although they are used in Indonesian, Pakistani, and other cuisines throughout Southeast Asia. Major Grey's mango chutney is probably the most commonly known prepared chutney in this country. Most chutneys are sweet and slightly or very spicy. They are great eaten as a relish, or they can be used in many dishes as a flavoring agent, or even as a condiment for a sandwich instead of mustard, mayo, or ketchup.

MANGO CHUTNEY

Makes: 4³/₄ cups

After a day or two in the refrigerator, the pepper in this chutney seems to disappear, but just wait— it attacks later. This recipe makes a rather large amount, but I like to share it with friends. You can easily halve the recipe for a smaller yield.

4 cups chopped ripe mangos
1 cup chopped dried apricots
1 cup chopped walnuts
½ cup golden or dark raisins
½ cup sugar
¼ cup chopped onions
¼ cup water
2 tablespoons cider vinegar
2 tablespoons chopped fresh ginger
2 teaspoons ground turmeric
¼ teaspoon ground red pepper
1 clove garlic, minced

1. Combine all the ingredients in a 3-quart saucepan. Bring to a boil over medium-high heat, stirring constantly.

2. Reduce heat and simmer, uncovered, 20 minutes, stirring occasionally, until thickened.

Variations: Omit the ground red pepper and use 2 tablespoons minced fresh jalapeño peppers instead.

For a really fiery chutney, use both the ground red pepper and the jalapeño.

TOMATO, PLUM, AND DRIED FRUIT CHUTNEY

Makes: 5 cups

The dried papaya is very important to the result of this recipe, so be sure to include it.

3 cups chopped ripe tomatoes
2 cups chopped fresh plums
1½ cups golden or dark raisins
1 cup chopped dried papaya
1 cup chopped dried peaches
One 6-ounce container frozen apple juice concentrate
1 tablespoon plus 1 teaspoon minced fresh ginger
½ teaspoon ground allspice
¼ teaspoon crushed red pepper

1. Place all the ingredients in a 3-quart saucepan. Bring to a boil over medium heat. Reduce heat and simmer 20 to 30 minutes, stirring frequently, until most of the liquid is absorbed. Cool.

Variations: You can substitute dried apricots or nectarines for the dried peaches.

You can also stir in 1 to 2 cups chopped walnuts for texture.

GREEN TOMATO~ PINEAPPLE CHUTNEY

— [V][♥] —

Makes: 2²/₃ cups

The jalapeño pepper adds just a little "kick" to this chutney—for a really hot chutney, add more.

2 cups chopped green tomatoes
1 ½ cups chopped fresh pineapple
1 cup chopped dried apricots
½ cup golden or dark raisins
½ cup frozen apple juice concentrate
1 tablespoon minced fresh ginger
1 teaspoon minced jalapeño peppers
    (optional)
1 teaspoon coriander seeds, cracked
¼ teaspoon salt, or to taste

1. Place all the ingredients in a 2-quart sauce-pan. Bring to a boil over medium heat. Cook, stirring frequently, 15 minutes or until most of the liquid is absorbed. Cool.

Variation: Use chopped dried apples or peaches instead of the apricots.

FIGS~WERE~CHEAP CHUTNEY

— [V][♥] —

Makes: 3 cups

I brought this chutney (and Marble Cheesecake, page 530) as my contribution to a surprise party for Randy Kraft. The chutney was a great hit (so was the party). When one of the guests asked how had I come up with an idea to make fig chutney, I answered, "Figs were cheap"—hence the title.

2 cups quartered fresh figs
1 cup chopped walnuts
¾ cup chopped dried pears
½ cup chopped apples
½ cup dark or golden raisins
½ cup sugar
¼ cup water
¼ cup chopped fresh cilantro
2 tablespoons fresh lime juice
1 tablespoon minced ginger
¼ teaspoon ground red pepper

1. Place all the ingredients in a 2-quart sauce-pan. Bring to a boil over medium heat. Cook, stirring frequently, 15 minutes or until most of the liquid is absorbed. Cool.

Variation: Omit the chopped cilantro and use chopped pear instead of apple.

BLUEBERRY~MANGO CHUTNEY

— [V][♥] —

Makes: 2³/₄ cups

This is one of those I'll-just-eat-it-with-a-spoon-while-I-stand-in-front-of-the-refrigerator chutneys.

2 cups blueberries
1 cup chopped mango
1 cup finely chopped dried peaches or
    apricots
⅔ cup sugar
½ cup finely chopped dried pears
¼ cup water
2 tablespoons minced fresh ginger
2 tablespoons minced fresh jalapeño peppers
1 teaspoon ground turmeric
¼ teaspoon ground cloves

1. Place all the ingredients in a 2-quart sauce-pan. Bring to a boil over high heat. Reduce heat and simmer, uncovered, 5 to 10 minutes, or until slightly thickened, with some blueberries still whole.

Variation: Blueberry-Nectarine Chutney: Use nectarines instead of mangoes.

RHUBARB-WALNUT CHUTNEY

Makes: 2 1/2 cups

Great on top of ice cream or just by itself.

3 cups diced rhubarb (1/2-inch pieces), divided
2/3 cup sugar
2/3 cup apple juice
2 tablespoons distilled white vinegar
3 cloves garlic, minced
1/4 teaspoon ground allspice
1/4 teaspoon ground cloves
1/4 teaspoon ground red pepper
1 cup chopped walnuts
1/4 cup golden raisins
1/8 teaspoon salt, or to taste

1. In a 2-quart saucepan over high heat, bring 2 cups of the rhubarb, the sugar, apple juice, vinegar, garlic, allspice, cloves, and red pepper to a boil. Reduce heat and simmer, uncovered, 20 minutes.

2. Add the remaining 1 cup rhubarb, the walnuts, and raisins. Bring to a boil. Reduce heat and simmer, 15 minutes or until the mixture is thickened. Stir in the salt.

Variation: Use any other spices you prefer; for example, use a cinnamon stick or star anise instead of the allspice.

NECTARINE CHUTNEY

Makes: 1 1/2 cups

You can substitute fresh peaches for the nectarines.

1/2 cup coarsely chopped dried apricots
1/2 cup orange juice
1 cup peeled, cubed nectarines
1/4 cup sugar
1/4 cup raisins (golden or dark)
1/4 cup chopped walnuts
1 tablespoon distilled white vinegar
1 tablespoon fresh lemon juice
2 teaspoons minced ginger
1/8 teaspoon salt, or to taste
1/8 teaspoon ground red pepper

1. In a 1 1/2-quart saucepan, combine the apricots with the orange juice; let stand 10 minutes. Stir in the remaining ingredients.

2. Bring to a boil. Reduce heat and simmer, uncovered, stirring frequently, 10 minutes or until thickened.

Variation: Substitute water for the orange juice and increase the sugar to 1/3 cup.

FLAVORED BUTTERS, JAMS, AND FRUIT AND VEGETABLE BUTTERS

Flavored Butters

Use flavored butter as a spread, for seasoning in cooking, or in sauces. You can make flavored butter by stirring seasonings into softened butter. Following are some suggestions, but you can stir just about anything into butter. Use as much as you like; the amounts in parentheses are just suggestions for each $1/2$ cup butter:

chopped fresh herbs, such as parsley or basil leaves (or a combination of the two) or dill (3 tablespoons)

dried herbs, such as thyme, rosemary, basil, marjoram, or any combination thereof (1 tablespoon)

garlic, put through a garlic press (3 cloves)

minced shallots (1 tablespoon)

chopped scallions (2 tablespoons; white and green parts)

ripe Stilton or other blue cheese ($1/4$ cup)

curry powder (1 tablespoon)

chopped chutney (2 tablespoons)

honey (1 tablespoon)

jam or preserves (2 tablespoons)

Although homemade butter is great, you can just as successfully make any of the flavored butters listed above with softened store-bought butter.

HOMEMADE BUTTER

Makes: $1/2$ cup

This is best made from unpasteurized heavy (whipping) cream, if you can find it.

1 cup heavy cream
Ice water
Salt (optional)

1. Place the cream in a medium-deep bowl. Beat with an electric mixer on high speed until the butter separates from the water. Drain off any water.

2. Fill the bowl with ice water and pour the butter, water, and ice into a strainer to drain. Replace butter in bowl and repeat until water is no longer cloudy. While rinsing the butter, stir/knead with wooden spoon to work butter into a pliable ball. Stir in salt, if desired. Pack into container and store, covered, in refrigerator.

Variation: Stir any of the suggested flavorings into the butter while it is still softened (before placing in refrigerator). All flavoring quantities are given for $1/2$ cup butter.

APRICOT JAM

Makes: 3 cups

This is one of my favorite flavors.

4 cups coarsely chopped apricots
2½ cups sugar

1. Place the apricots into a 3-quart saucepan. Add the sugar. Cook, stirring, until the sugar liquifies and the mixture comes to a boil. Boil on medium-high 10 minutes or until the mixture is slightly thickened.

Variation: Ginger-Apricot Jam: Add 2 tablespoons minced ginger when you add the apricots.

RASPBERRY JAM

Makes: 2 cups

Fresh raspberry jam is tart and better than most or possibly all commercially available raspberry jam, and it's so easy to make.

4 cups fresh raspberries
1½ cups sugar

1. In a 3-quart saucepan, crush the raspberries. Stir in the sugar. Cook over medium heat until the sugar dissolves and the berries give off liquid.

2. Increase heat to medium-high and cook, stirring frequently, until thickened, about 7 minutes.

Variation: Substitute either strawberries or blackberries for the raspberries.

DAMSON PLUM JAM

Makes: 2 cups

Like so many of the "sweets" that I prepare, this one is very tart, just the way I like it.

1 pound Damson plums or other ripe plums
1½ cups sugar

1. Halve the plums and remove the pit. Cut the halves in half.

2. Place the plums in a 3-quart saucepan. Add the sugar; cook, stirring, until the sugar liquifies and mixture comes to a boil. Cook on medium-high 10 minutes or until the mixture is slightly thickened.

Variation: Plum and Strawberry Jam: Use only ½ pound plums and 2 cups of hulled, halved strawberries.

Fruit and Vegetable Butters

Fruit butters are great spreads. Unlike jams, they are not loaded with sugar, and unlike butters, they are not high in fat—in fact, they don't have any fat. In addition to using these as spreads for breads, muffins, biscuits, or scones, they are also great as fillings for mini turnovers or cookies.

Fruit butters will keep two weeks, covered, in the refrigerator. If you preserve them (according to proper preserving techniques, which you can find in the *Ball Blue Book* or other books on preserving), they can be stored at room temperature. I usually keep one jar of butter for myself and give the rest to friends. That way I don't have to bother canning. (Don't forget to tell your friends to store the fruit butter in the refrigerator, and to use it in the appropriate amount of time.)

APPLE-PEAR-PLUM BUTTER

Makes: 2³/4 cups

6 cups peeled apple chunks
3 cups peeled pear chunks
1 cup diced plums
1/4 cup water
1/4 cup sugar
1/2 teaspoon ground allspice
1/4 teaspoon ground cloves
1/8 teaspoon ground mace

1. Place all the ingredients in a 3-quart pot. Bring to a boil over high heat. Reduce heat and simmer, covered, 15 minutes. Uncover and simmer 2 to 2¹/2 hours longer, stirring occasionally, or until mixture is thick enough to leave a path on the bottom of the pan when a wooden spoon is dragged through it.

2. For a smooth butter, place the mixture in a blender or food processor container fitted with

a steel blade. Cover and process until smooth. Chill.

Variation: Old-Fashioned Apple Butter: Replace the 3 cups pear chunks with apple chunks; omit the plum. Add 1 teaspoon ground cinnamon, or to taste.

RASPBERRY-QUINCE BUTTER

Makes: 4 cups

Quinces are very hard fruit that somewhat resemble pears. They're available in the fall and have a flavor similar to a pear and pineapple mix. Unlike pears, they don't give off very much liquid when cooking, nor do they dissolve during cooking.

2¹/2 cups water
3/4 cup sugar
8 cups cubed, peeled quinces
3/4 cup fresh or frozen (unsweetened) raspberries

1. In a 4-quart pot, bring the water and sugar to a boil over high heat, stirring occasionally. Add the quinces and return to a boil.

2. Reduce heat and simmer, uncovered, 1 hour. Add the raspberries; return to a boil. Reduce heat and simmer ¹/2 hour longer, stirring occasionally.

3. Place fruit and any liquid in a blender or food processor container fitted with a steel blade. Cover and process until smooth.

4. Return to pot and cook on low heat 15 minutes longer, stirring frequently, until mixture is thick and retains its shape when dropped from a spoon.

Variations: Quince Butter: Omit the raspberries.

Stewed Quinces: Omit the raspberries. Remove the quinces from heat when quite tender, after about 45 minutes of cooking; chill.

PEACH BUTTER

Makes: 1 cup

If you are using very juicy peaches, you will not need the water at all. Judge it by seeing if the peaches have given off enough liquid to cover the fruit chunks when you first bring the fruit to a boil. If not, add just enough of the water to cover the peaches. Similarly, if your peaches are quite sweet, you may want to add the lemon juice to adjust the flavor to your taste.

4 cups peeled peach chunks
1/3 cup firmly packed light brown or dark brown sugar
1/4 cup water, if necessary
Lemon juice, to taste

1. Place the peaches and sugar in a 2-quart saucepan. Bring to a boil over medium-high heat. Add water, if necessary. Reduce heat and simmer, uncovered, 1 3/4 to 2 hours, stirring occasionally, or until mixture is thick enough to leave a path on the bottom of the pan when a wooden spoon is dragged through it. Taste the mixture and add lemon juice if too sweet.

2. For a smooth butter, place mixture in a blender or food processor container fitted with a steel blade. Cover and process until smooth. Chill.

Variation: Add 1/2 teaspoon or more ground cinnamon when you start cooking.

BUTTERNUT SQUASH BUTTER

Makes: 2 1/2 cups

Cardamom and coriander are not spices that everyone has on hand, but they are worth the investment (and I'll be honest—they are expensive) because they make this butter very different from the usual cinnamon-clove flavors generally associated with more common fruit butters.

6 cups cubed, peeled butternut squash
3/4 cup firmly packed light brown or dark brown sugar
1/2 cup water
2 teaspoons ground cinnamon
1 teaspoon ground coriander
1 teaspoon ground cardamom
1/2 teaspoon ground ginger

1. Place all the ingredients in a 3-quart pot. Bring to a boil over high heat. Reduce heat and simmer, covered, 15 minutes. Uncover and simmer 1 to 1 1/2 hours longer, stirring occasionally and mashing the pieces of squash, until mixture is thick enough to leave a path on the bottom of the pan when a wooden spoon is dragged through it.

2. For a smooth butter, place the mixture in a blender or food processor container fitted with a steel blade. Cover and process until smooth. Chill.

Variation: Use whatever variety of ground spices you have on hand—cloves, nutmeg, allspice, and so on.

PRUNE BUTTER (LEKVAR)

V ♥

Makes: 1 1/2 cups

In many Eastern European stores, you can buy this prepared "by the barrel"—scooped out of a barrel. It's also sold as pie filling by Solo. Lekvar is a popular cookie filling for such treats as Hamentashen (triangular cookies with fruit filling, page 537) and Danish pastry.

One 12-ounce package pitted prunes
3/4 cup water
1/4 cup sugar

1. Place the prunes, water, and sugar in a 2-quart saucepan. Bring to a boil; reduce heat and simmer, uncovered, 20 minutes or until thick.

2. Place the mixture in a food processor container fitted with a steel blade. Cover and process until smooth.

Variations: Lemon-scented Lekvar: Replace 1 tablespoon of the water with lemon juice and add 2 teaspoons grated lemon rind. Increase sugar to 1/3 cup.

Orange-scented Lekvar: Replace 1/4 cup of the water with orange juice and add 1 tablespoon grated orange rind.

APRICOT LEKVAR

V ♥

Makes: 1 1/3 cups

This lekvar is quite tart and thick. You may want to use 2/3 cup sugar instead of the 1/2 cup that I prefer. If you want a thinner lekvar, you can add 1 or 2 tablespoons of water or orange juice as you puree it.

One 8-ounce package dried apricots
2/3 cup water
1/2 cup sugar

1. Place the ingredients in a 2-quart saucepan. Bring to a boil; reduce heat and simmer, uncovered, 20 minutes or until thick.

2. Place the mixture in a food processor container fitted with a steel blade. Cover and process until smooth.

Variation: Add 1 to 2 tablespoons orange liqueur or anisette to the cooking water.

LEMON CURD

Makes: 2²/₃ cups

I think that lemon curd, sometimes called lemon butter, is the most delicious spread in the world, especially heavenly on a croissant. It also makes the most divine filling for lemon meringue pie (or tarts, page 526). Use butter—don't substitute margarine in this recipe.

2 eggs
2 egg yolks
1 cup sugar
½ cup lemon juice
2 tablespoons grated lemon rind
1 cup (2 sticks) unsalted butter, cut into
    1-inch-thick pats

1. Place the eggs and yolks in the top of a double boiler. Using a whisk, beat lightly. Whisk in the sugar, then the lemon juice and rind. Stir in the butter pats.

2. Place over simmering water. Cook, stirring with a wooden spoon, until mixture thickens (do not allow to boil), enough to thickly coat a spoon.

3. Pour into jars and let chill. (Lemon curd will thicken further upon chilling.) Store in the refrigerator.

Variation: Lime Curd: Substitute lime juice and rind for lemon.

MISCELLANEOUS STUFF

GHEE

Makes: 14 tablespoons

This is the Indian version of clarified butter— butter that has all the milk solids removed. Because there is no milk to spoil, ghee can be stored, covered, at room temperature without spoiling for a few months. The difference between clarified butter and ghee is that ghee is cooked until the milk solids brown, thereby imparting a deeper golden color to the butter.

1 cup (2 sticks) unsalted butter

1. Place the butter in a heavy 1-quart saucepan. Cook over medium-low heat until the butter starts to boil; continue cooking, uncovered, until the sizzling sounds stop and the solids on the bottom turn brown (about 8 minutes).

2. Remove from heat and let stand 10 minutes. Strain through a fine sieve to remove any milk solids.

Variation: Clarified Butter: Melt the butter over low heat until it just starts to bubble. Skim off any foam from the top. Pour the clear liquid into a small bowl; discard white milky part. Makes ³/₄ cup.

PANEER

Makes: 1 1/2 cups; serves: 4 or more

This is a fresh cheese frequently used in Indian cooking. It's really easy to make and very pleasant tasting.

2 quarts milk
1 teaspoon salt
1/4 cup fresh lemon juice

1. In a 4-quart saucepan, bring the milk and salt to a boil over medium-high heat. Stir in the lemon juice until mixture forms curds. Remove from heat.

2. Pour mixture through a strainer or colander lined with three layers of cheesecloth. Lift the corners of the cheesecloth and form a package with the cheese enclosed in the cheesecloth. Twist the cheesecloth to squeeze as much excess liquid as possible from the cheese.

3. Tie the corners of the cheesecloth to the handle of a wooden spoon or similar utensil. Place over a deep bowl or pot, so that the cheese is hanging suspended over a container that will catch the liquid that drips. Let drain in this manner for 1 hour.

4. Remove the cheese from the cheesecloth and wrap in waxed paper or plastic wrap. Place under a heavy weight (such as a heavy book or a brick) and let stand 1/2 hour to compress the cheese. Keeps up to 5 days in the refrigerator.

POT CHEESE (TOPFEN)

Makes: 2 1/2 cups; serves: 4 to 6

When making cheese or other temperature-specific foods, I am always concerned that I follow instructions to the letter. In this instance, I was rather cavalier about following directions. The recipe suggested cooking the curd to 120°–130°F, stirring once or twice. I then forgot about the mixture until I smelled it on the stove. By then the temperature was 170°F. I went ahead and followed the directions from there, and the pot cheese was just fine. So, don't get too nervous if you've missed the exact temperatures suggested.

1 cup buttermilk
2 quarts milk

1. In a large bowl, let buttermilk come to room temperature.

2. Place milk in 3-quart saucepan. Over low heat, bring milk to between 85°F and 90°F, stirring frequently. This should make the milk lukewarm, not hot. Stir into the buttermilk.

3. Let stand in warm place until curd is formed (about 24 hours on a warm day, more on a cooler one) or until it tastes slightly sour. The consistency will be anywhere from thick yogurt to soft tofu. Transfer to a double boiler. Cook over (not in) simmering water until mixture registers 120°F to 130°F, stirring once or twice. Cook, at a constant temperature, between 120° and 130°F, stirring occasionally, until the curds start to separate from whey. Let cool.

4. Drain through a colander lined with cheesecloth, trying to keep the curds as intact as possible. When drained, tie the cheesecloth over the handle of a wooden spoon and let hang over a deep bowl or pot. Let stand 6 hours or overnight (I do this in the refrigerator). Pack into storage container and chill. Keeps up to 5 days in the refrigerator.

YOGURT CHEESE

Makes: ¹/₂ cup; serves: 2 to 6

Prepare this using any unflavored yogurt, from whole milk to low-fat to nonfat.

1 cup unflavored yogurt

1. Place the yogurt into a strainer lined with 3 layers of cheesecloth. Place the strainer over a bowl and refrigerate overnight. Keeps up to 5 days in the refrigerator.

Variation: Stir in herbs and/or garlic to flavor the cheese.

RAITA

Makes: 1²/₃ cups; serves: 6 to 8

This is the perfect condiment to serve with curries, especially very spicy ones, since it helps to put the fire out.

1 cup unflavored yogurt
1 cup chopped cucumber
1 small clove garlic, minced
1 tablespoon chopped fresh cilantro

1. In a medium bowl, stir together all the in-gredients. Let stand at least 20 minutes for the flavors to meld.

Variation: Add ¹/₄ cup chopped red pepper.

TOMATO RAITA

Makes: 1 cup; serves: 4 to 6

Although raita is traditionally made with just yogurt, this one uses sour cream as well.

¹/₃ cup unflavored yogurt
¹/₄ cup sour cream
¹/₂ small clove garlic, minced
¹/₈ teaspoon ground cumin
²/₃ cup finely chopped tomatoes
3 tablespoons chopped cilantro

1. In a medium bowl, stir together the yogurt, sour cream, garlic, and cumin.

2. Add the tomatoes and cilantro; stir until combined.

♥ *Variation:* For an even lower-fat version, substitute additional unflavored yogurt for the sour cream.

Coconut Milk

Many people mistakenly believe that the liquid in the coconut is coconut milk. It is, in fact, coconut water, and is not the ingredient called for in the recipes in this book. You can purchase canned coconut milk (unsweetened) in many Asian groceries, or make either of the following recipes at home.

Just to confuse the issue, coconut milk is also available sweetened. It's usually called cream of coconut and put out with brand names such as Coco Lopez or Coco Casa. The sweetened milk is not interchangeable with unsweetened coconut milk. If you are using a recipe that calls for sweetened coconut milk and you can't locate any, sweetened condensed milk would be an adequate substitute (but, of course, it won't have the coconut flavor, just the right sweetness and consistency).

HOMEMADE COCONUT MILK

Makes: 1³/₄ cups

Instead of the 2 cups water, you can substitute some or all of the coconut water for an equal amount of unflavored water.

1 fresh coconut
2 cups boiling water

1. Using a large nail, hammer holes into all three of the "eyes" of the coconut. Rest the coconut, "eyes" down, over a bowl. Allow all of the coconut water to drain into the bowl. Discard the water or use it for part of the boiling water called for here.

2. Crack the coconut into pieces with the hammer. Remove the coconut meat from the shell. (If you're finding this hard to do, baking the coconut for 10 minutes at 350°F will make the job easier.) Remove the brown skin from the coconut flesh. Coarsely chop the coconut.

3. Place half of the coconut into a blender container with half of the water. Cover and blend on high speed until finely ground (about 1 minute). Pour through a strainer lined with a double layer of cheesecloth. Lift the edges of the cheesecloth and wring out as much of the liquid as possible from the coconut. Repeat with remaining coconut and water.

Variation: You can do a second "pressing" to get a more diluted coconut milk by returning the coconut to the blender and adding more boiling water.

EASY COCONUT MILK

Makes: 1 cup

This method is not as easy as buying canned coconut milk, but at least you don't have to crack and peel the coconut. Be sure to use unsweetened coconut (usually available in health food stores), not the sweetened stuff you find in the baking section of the supermarket.

1¹/₂ cups water
1 cup unsweetened shredded coconut

1. In a 1¹/₂-quart saucepan, bring the water and coconut to a boil.

2. Place the mixture in a blender container. Cover and blend on high speed until finely ground (about 1 minute). Pour through a strainer lined with a double layer of cheesecloth. Lift the edges of the cheesecloth and wring out as much of the liquid as possible from the coconut.

DESSERTS

Yeast-Based Desserts

Danish Pastry Dough   500

Danish Pastry   501

Sweet Yeast Dough   501

Sticky Buns   502

Walnut Stollen   503

Cakes and Tortes

Strawberry Shortcake   503

Chocolate Cherry Loaf   504

Fresh Peach Cake   504

Walnut Torte   505

Peanut Butter Cake   505

Blueberry Coffeecake   506

Plum Upside Down Cake   506

Raspberry–Cream Cheese Cake   507

Sweet Potato–Apple Cake   508

"Vedding" Cake   508

Dried Apricot Cake   509

Carrot Cake   510

Coconut-Pineapple Cake   510

Apple Gingerbread   511

Coconut Parsnip Layer Cake   511

Buttermilk Mocha Cake   512

Pecan-Squash Cake   513

Banana–Whipped Cream Refrigerator Cake   513

Lemon-Scented Angel Food Cake   514

Icings, Fillings, and Frostings

Light Chocolate Frosting   515

Mocha Buttercream Frosting   515

Coffee-Rum Buttercream Frosting   515

Chocolate–Sour Cream Frosting   516

Butter–Cream Cheese Frosting   516

Cream Cheese Frosting   516

Ganache   517

Confectioners' Sugar Glaze   517

Pies and Tarts

Oil Crust   517

Flaky Pastry   518

Citrus Crust   518

Tartlet Shells   519

Food Processor Farmer-Cheese Pastry Dough   519

Apple Pie   520

Lattice-Top Peach Pie   520

Sour Cherry Pie   521

Strawberry-Rhubarb Tart with Oat Streusel Topping   521

Cranberry-Pear Chutney Tart   522

Apricot-Raspberry Tart   522

Fresh Raspberry Tart with Blueberry Filling   523

Easy Apple Tart   523

Apple-Strawberry Tart   524

Cheese Tart   524

Frozen Piña Colada Mousse Tarts   524

Honey Apple-Fig Tart   525

Fruit Tartlets   525

Lemon Meringue Tartlets   526

Walnut Fudge Tartlets   526

Whipped Cream Tartlets   527

Filled Pastries   527

Little Apple Turnovers   527

Strudel

Basic Strudel   528

Apple Strudel Filling   529

Sweet Cherry Strudel Filling   529

Cheese Strudel Filling   529

Fresh Raspberry Strudel
Filling   529

Pineapple Strudel
Filling   530

Walnut Strudel Filling   530

Cheesecakes

Marble Cheesecake   530

Raspberry Swirl
Cheesecake   531

Pumpkin Cheesecake   532

Cookies

Oatmeal Raisin
Cookies   532

Oatmeal Bar Cookies   533

Cornmeal Sandies   533

Peanut Butter Cookies   534

Poppy Seed Cookies   534

Gingerbread Cookies   535

Mom's Hard-Boiled Egg
Cookies   535

Raspberry Roll-Ups   536

Pecan–Wheat Germ
Cookies   536

Hamantashen   537

Wonton Cookies   537

Lemon Squares   538

Coconutty Cookies   538

Apricot Meringue
Squares   539

Apple Squares   539

Lady Brownies   540

Fruit Desserts

Strawberry-Raspberry
Strada   540

Apple Brown Betty   541

Bourbon Broiled
Pineapple   541

Stewed Peaches and
Cherries   542

Orange-Basted
Bananas   542

Strawberries with
Zabaglione   542

Fresh Orange Slices in
Liqueur   543

Apple-Pear Sauce   543

Poached Pears in Fruit
Juice   544

Poached Pears in Wine and
Lime   544

Sickle Pears on a
Pillow   545

Spiced Sickle Pears   545

Apple Crisp   546

Chocolate-Dipped Straw-
berries   546

Caramelized Grapes   547

Mousses, Puddings, and Custards

Leftover Coconut Rice
Pudding   547

Raisin Bread Pudding   548

Cranberry Bread
Pudding   548

Orange Polenta
Pudding   549

Honey Couscous
Pudding   549

Rum Flan   550

Sorbets

Anisette Raspberry
Sorbet   550

Port Wine–Plum Sorbet   551

Grapefruit Sorbet   551

Kiwi-Pineapple Sorbet   552

Crepes and Sauces

Crepes Suzette   552

Dessert Crepes   553

Orange Crepes   553

Creme Anglaise   554

Chocolate Sauce   554

Raspberry Sauce   555

Sugar is an important ingredient in most desserts. In addition to being a sweetener, it also acts as a tenderizer in baked goods, prevents crystallization in ice creams, and serves as a preservative in condensed milk. Sugar comes in many forms, most of which are not interchangeable.

Granulated sugar, usually referred to simply as "sugar," is also called table sugar. It is highly refined sugar and can be used interchangeably with superfine.

Brown sugar is sugar that has not been completely refined—some of the molasses is left in. The difference between light brown and dark brown sugar is the amount of molasses that has been extracted: The dark brown has a more intense "molasses" flavor. Light brown and dark brown sugar can be used interchangeably. Both should be measured by packing the sugar firmly into the measuring cup.

Superfine sugar, also called extra fine or bar sugar, is granulated sugar that has been more finely ground. Its advantage over granulated sugar is that it dissolves more quickly. It is interchangeable with granulated.

Confectioners' sugar is the most finely ground sugar and has been mixed with cornstarch to prevent clumping. It is not interchangeable with any other sugar. It should not be sifted before measuring.

Cinnamon-sugar can be bought already prepared in the sugar or spice department of the supermarket. You can prepare it at home by stirring together ground cinnamon and granulated sugar to taste.

Yeast-Based Desserts

Danish Pastry Dough

Makes: about 1 1/2 pounds of dough

This dough bakes up to be very light and tender. Don't be concerned if you still see small butter chunks in the dough after you've finished rolling it.

1 cup (2 sticks) butter or margarine
1/3 cup very warm water (105°–115°F)
1/2 teaspoon plus 2 tablespoons sugar, divided
1 package active dry yeast
1 egg
1/4 cup milk
3/4 cup whole wheat flour
1 1/2 to 2 cups all-purpose flour
1 teaspoon salt

1. Slice the butter or margarine into 1/2-inch pieces; place in refrigerator until needed.

2. In a glass measuring cup, stir together the warm water and the 1/2 teaspoon sugar. Stir in the yeast and let stand about 10 minutes to proof (page 413).

3. In a large bowl, combine the yeast mixture, egg, milk, and remaining 2 tablespoons sugar. Beat in the whole wheat flour and 1/2 cup of the all-purpose flour, until a sticky dough is formed. Cover with greased plastic wrap and let stand 2 hours in a warm, draft-free spot.

4. In a large bowl, stir together 1 cup all-purpose flour and the salt. Using a pastry cutter or two knives, cut in the butter until it is the size of peas. (If the yeast mixture is not ready, refrigerate the flour mixture until it is.) Add the yeast mixture to the flour mixture and stir until combined (don't be concerned about trying to form into a uniform dough).

5. Turn the dough onto a well-floured board and pat and shape dough into a 4 × 6-inch rectangle. Using a floured rolling pin, roll dough into a 10 × 14-inch rectangle, adding flour to the board and rolling pin as necessary.

6. Fold dough into a "book" by folding the one short edge of the dough over ⅓ of the dough to form a piece of dough that is ½ double thickness and ½ single thickness. Fold the single thickness over the double thickness to form a closed "letter" that will measure 10 × 4¾ inches. If patches of butter are exposed, pat them with flour. Cover in plastic wrap and let rest in refrigerator 20 minutes.

7. Repeat rolling and resting 3 more times. Cover and refrigerate at least one hour. You can also let this rest up to one day, or freeze for future use. At this point, continue with recipes calling for Danish pastry.

DANISH PASTRY

Makes: 16 Danish; serves: 8 to 16

You can use any of the strudel fillings for the pastries (you'll probably have to double to recipe), or canned pie fillings (such as cherry, or blueberry), or dried fruit butters (page 493).

1 recipe Danish Pastry Dough (page 500)
1¾ cups filling
Honey for brushing

1. Cut dough in half (to about a 5-inch square). Using a floured rolling pin on a lightly floured board, roll the dough into a 8 × 16-inch rectangle. Cut into eight 4-inch squares.

2. Place a rounded tablespoon of filling into the center of the dough.

3. Fold one corner over the filling. Lift the opposite corner and fold it over the first fold, then pinch dough to seal. For a Danish square,

lift all four corners and pinch to seal; pinch the seams to seal.

4. Place Danish on a greased baking sheet. Cover with greased plastic wrap and let double in bulk. Repeat with remaining dough and filling.

5. When the Danish have doubled in bulk, bake in 375°F oven for 18 minutes or until browned. Remove from oven and brush lightly with honey. Return to oven and bake 3 minutes longer. Remove from oven; let cool on rack.

Variation: Omit the honey; dust with confectioners' sugar or drizzle with Confectioners' Sugar Glaze (page 517).

SWEET YEAST DOUGH

Makes: about 2 pounds

I use oil instead of flour on the board and rolling pin to roll out the sweet dough; that way the dough can be rolled out even though it is still quite sticky. I also knead the dough differently from bread doughs: I oil the board and my hands, then I push the dough back and forth, turn the dough over, and rotate it. By not pressing the dough into the board, you avoid its sticking. This dough should remain light and moist, so try to use the minimum amount of flour.

½ cup very warm water (105°F)
2 packages active dry yeast
2 cups all-purpose flour, divided
1½ cups whole wheat flour
½ cup sugar
½ teaspoon salt
½ cup milk
½ cup (1 stick) softened butter or margarine
2 eggs, beaten

1. In a glass measuring cup, stir together the warm water and the yeast and let it proof (page 413).

2. In a large bowl, combine 1 cup of the all-purpose flour, the whole wheat flour, sugar, and salt. Add the yeast mixture, milk, butter, and eggs. Using an electric mixer, beat until a sticky dough is formed. Using a wooden spoon, stir in $^{1}/_{2}$ cup more of the all-purpose flour. Stir in the remaining $^{1}/_{2}$ cup flour.

3. Turn the dough onto a greased board and knead, as described above, about 4 to 5 minutes. The dough will still be sticky. Place in a greased bowl and cover with greased plastic wrap. Let stand in a warm, draft-free spot until doubled in bulk. Punch dough down and use as required in recipes calling for sweet dough.

STICKY BUNS

Makes: two 9-inch round "cakes" or 20 buns; serves: 16 to 20

I think these buns originated in Pennsylvania, and if only for that alone we are grateful to the descendants of William Penn. Be sure to let the buns sit in the pan a few minutes before turning them out or the topping will run over everything. These buns do not make such wonderful leftovers, so plan to make only as many as you need. You can halve the recipe easily to serve 8 to 10 people.

Topping:

$^{1}/_{4}$ cup ($^{1}/_{2}$ stick) butter or margarine
$^{3}/_{4}$ cup firmly packed light brown or dark brown sugar
1 tablespoon water
2 tablespoons light or dark corn syrup
$^{1}/_{2}$ teaspoon vanilla
1 $^{1}/_{2}$ cups chopped pecans

Filling:

1 cup firmly packed light brown or dark brown sugar
1 tablespoon ground cinnamon
1 cup dark raisins

To finish the dish:

1 recipe Sweet Yeast Dough (page 501)
2 tablespoons butter or margarine, melted

1. Preheat the oven to 375°F. Grease two 9-inch round pans.

2. To prepare the topping, melt $^{1}/_{4}$ cup butter or margarine in a 1$^{1}/_{2}$ quart saucepan. Stir in $^{3}/_{4}$ cup brown sugar, the water, corn syrup, and vanilla. Bring to a boil. Cook 30 seconds. Pour half of the syrup into each prepared baking pan. Sprinkle $^{3}/_{4}$ cup of the pecans over the syrup in each pan; set aside.

3. To prepare filling, toss together 1 cup brown sugar and the cinnamon in a medium bowl; add the raisins and toss.

4. On a floured surface, roll half the dough into an 8 × 14-inch rectangle. Brush with 1 tablespoon of the melted butter or margarine and sprinkle with half of the sugar mixture to within $^{1}/_{2}$ inch of the dough edges.

5. Roll from the long side into a log. Seal the edges by pinching. Slice into 10 pieces.

6. Place the slices of pastry, cut side down, onto the topping in one of the pans.

7. Repeat with remaining dough and sugar mixture. Cover pans of dough with greased plastic wrap and let stand until doubled in bulk.

8. Bake 20 to 25 minutes or until browned. Let stand 3 minutes, then turn onto serving plates.

Variation: Omit the topping and bake the buns until browned. Cool on wire rack and top with Confectioners' Sugar Glaze (page 517).

WALNUT STOLLEN

Makes: 18 slices; serves: 18

Stollen, a traditional German holiday cake, is usually filled with candied fruits, but I like this walnut filling much better.

1½ cups ground walnuts
½ sugar
2 tablespoons melted butter or margarine
⅓ cup golden raisins
2 teaspoons fresh lemon juice
1 teaspoon grated lemon rind
½ recipe Sweet Yeast Dough (page 501)
1 egg, beaten (optional)
Confectioners' Sugar Glaze (page 517; optional)

1. Preheat the oven to 375°F. Grease a large baking sheet.

2. In a medium bowl, combine the walnuts, sugar, and butter or margarine. Add the raisins, lemon juice, and lemon rind; toss to combine; set aside.

3. On an oiled surface, roll the dough into a 16 × 7-inch rectangle. Place the filling down the length of the center of the pastry in a 2-inch-wide, flattened log.

4. Lift the two sides over the filling and pinch to seal seam.

5. Transfer to a baking sheet, seam side down. Cover with greased plastic wrap and let stand until doubled in bulk. If desired, brush with beaten egg for a shiny finish.

6. Bake 20 to 25 minutes or until browned. Let cool on wire rack. If desired, drizzle with Confectioners' Sugar Glaze. Cut into slices to serve.

Variation: Substitute ½ cup ground hazelnuts for ½ cup of the walnuts.

CAKES AND TORTES

STRAWBERRY SHORTCAKE

Makes: one 9-inch cake; serves: 8 to 10

This is a traditional shortcake made with a biscuit dough, which makes very dense cake layers, not the type one thinks of as birthday cake. Instead of making cake layers, you can just bake biscuits and turn them into individual shortcakes.

1 recipe Sweet Biscuit dough (page 404)
1 cup heavy cream
2 tablespoons confectioners' sugar
1½ cups sliced fresh strawberries
Whole strawberries for garnish

1. Preheat the oven to 425°F. Grease a 9-inch round cake pan.

2. Prepare dough according to biscuit recipe. Instead of rolling out, pat into pan. Bake 25 minutes or until browned on top.

3. Remove from the oven and cool on rack. Slice horizontally to form two layers.

4. In a medium bowl, beat the cream and confectioners' sugar until stiff peaks form.

5. Spread half the cream onto the cut side of the bottom layer of the cake. Top with sliced strawberries. Top with second layer, cut side down.

6. Spread remaining whipped cream over the top layer. Arrange whole berries decoratively.

Variation: Use any fruit for the top and filling.

CHOCOLATE CHERRY LOAF

Makes: one 9-inch tube cake; serves: 10 to 14

My guests absolutely loved this cake, but be warned—it got that old familiar compliment: "It's not too sweet." The cherries are quite tart and were mistaken for cranberries. If you can't find dried cherries, use 1¹⁄₂ cups canned, drained bing cherries (pitted, of course); omit the port wine; and skip step 2 entirely.

¾ cup dried cherries
⅓ cup port wine or apple juice
2 tablespoons plus 1 cup sugar, divided
¾ cup sifted all-purpose flour
¼ cup whole wheat flour
1 teaspoon baking powder
½ teaspoon baking soda
½ cup (1 stick) butter or margarine
2 eggs
Three 1-ounce squares unsweetened chocolate, melted
1 teaspoon vanilla
¾ cup milk

1. Preheat the oven to 375°F. Thoroughly grease and flour a 9-inch tube pan (8- to 10-cup capacity).

2. In a small saucepan, bring the cherries, port, and two tablespoons of the sugar to a boil over medium heat. Remove from heat and let stand to cool.

3. In a large bowl or on a piece of waxed paper, sift together both flours, the baking powder, and baking soda.

4. In a large bowl, cream the butter or margarine with the remaining 1 cup sugar until light and fluffy. Add the eggs, one at a time, beating well after each addition. Stir in the chocolate, vanilla, and cherries with port or apple juice.

5. Add the flour mixture alternately with the milk, ¼ cup at a time, beating until smooth after each addition.

6. Spoon into prepared pan. Bake 50 minutes or until a wooden pick inserted in the center comes out clean.

Variation: Chocolate-Glazed Chocolate Cherry Cake: Prepare 1 recipe Ganache (page 517) and spoon it over the cake to glaze. Chill until firmed. Remove from refrigerator at least 30 minutes before serving time to bring to room temperature.

FRESH PEACH CAKE

Makes: nine 2¹⁄₂-inch squares; serves: 9

This pretty-easy-to-bake cake can be made with a variety of fruits, such as plums, apples, or apricots. You can also use frozen (unsweetened) peach slices. Just measure them frozen, then thaw.

3 cups peeled, sliced peaches
1 tablespoon melted butter or margarine
¼ cup firmly packed light brown or dark brown sugar
½ cup all-purpose flour
¼ cup whole wheat flour
1 teaspoon baking powder
¼ teaspoon salt
1 egg
½ cup sugar
¼ cup vegetable oil
1 teaspoon vanilla
1½ cups granola cereal

1. Preheat the oven to 350°F. Grease and flour an 8-inch-square baking pan.

2. In a medium bowl, toss together the peaches, butter or margarine, and brown sugar. Let stand while you prepare the batter.

3. In a medium bowl or on a piece of waxed paper, stir together both flours, the baking powder, and salt.

4. In a large bowl, beat the egg. Add the sugar, oil, and vanilla and beat until combined.

5. Stir the flour mixture into the egg mixture. Spread into the prepared pan. Sprinkle the peaches on top. Top the peaches with the granola.

6. Bake 45 minutes or until a wooden pick inserted in the center comes out clean. Cool on rack. Cut into 9 squares.

Variation: Spiced Apple Cake: Substitute apples for the peaches. Add 1 teaspoon ground cinnamon and 1/4 teaspoon ground nutmeg to the apple mixture when you add the brown sugar.

3. In a large bowl, beat the egg yolks with the sugar until thick. Beat in the rum.

4. In a separate bowl, beat the egg whites with the salt until stiff peaks form. Fold beaten whites into the yolk mixture. Fold in 1/3 of the walnut mixture at a time.

5. Spread into prepared pan and bake 45 to 50 minutes or until top springs back when lightly touched. Let cool in pan 15 minutes. Run knife around edge of pan and release springform. Cool completely.

6. Split cake into 2 layers horizontally. Spread 1 cup frosting on cut half of bottom layer. Place top layer, cut side down, over the filling and frost top and sides with remaining frosting.

Variation: Substitute ground hazelnuts for half the walnuts.

WALNUT TORTE

Makes: one 9-inch cake; serves: 8 to 10

I like to frost and fill this cake with Coffee-Rum Buttercream Frosting (page 515) or whipped cream. You can also fill with apricot jam and frost with one of the other frostings.

1 tablespoon plus 1/2 cup unflavored bread crumbs
1 1/2 cups finely grated walnuts
6 eggs, separated
1 cup sugar
2 tablespoons rum
1/2 teaspoon salt
2 1/2 cups frosting and filling of choice

1. Preheat the oven to 325°F. Grease a 9-inch springform pan; dust with 1 tablespoon of the bread crumbs.

2. In a medium bowl or on a piece of waxed paper, combine the remaining 1/2 cup bread crumbs and the walnuts.

PEANUT BUTTER CAKE

Makes: one 8-inch 4-layer cake; serves: 8 to 12

Finish this cake with the Light Chocolate Frosting (page 515), the Chocolate–Sour Cream Frosting (page 516), or the Butter–Cream Cheese Frosting (page 516).

1 1/2 cups all-purpose flour
3/4 cup whole wheat flour
2 teaspoons baking powder
3/4 cup smooth peanut butter
3/4 cup (1 1/2 sticks) butter or margarine
1 cup sugar
3/4 cup firmly packed light brown or dark brown sugar
3 eggs
1 cup milk
Frosting and filling of choice

1. Preheat the oven to 350°F. Grease and flour two 8-inch round baking pans.

2. In a large bowl or on a piece of waxed paper, stir together both flours and the baking powder.

3. In a large bowl, cream the peanut butter, butter or margarine, and both sugars until light and fluffy. Beat in the eggs one at a time. Add the dry ingredients alternately with the milk, beating well after each addition.

4. Spread into prepared baking pans. Bake 40 minutes or until a wooden pick inserted in the center comes out clean and cake has pulled away from the edge of the pan. Turn onto rack to cool.

5. Cut each layer in half horizontally to form 4 layers. Frost and fill with your desired frosting.

Variation: Stir in 1 cup of mini chocolate morsels.

BLUEBERRY COFFEECAKE

Makes: 12 3 × 2-inch pieces; serves: 12

You can use any fruit in this coffeecake. Chopped peaches, raspberries, chopped apples, or chopped plums would be especially good.

1 ¼ cups all-purpose flour

½ cup whole wheat flour

1 cup sugar

2 teaspoons baking powder

1 teaspoon baking soda

¼ teaspoon salt, or to taste

2 cups blueberries (fresh, or one 12-ounce bag frozen unsweetened blueberries, thawed and drained)

1 egg

⅔ cup milk

7 tablespoons butter or margarine, melted

1 tablespoon fresh lemon juice

1 teaspoon grated lemon rind

1. Preheat the oven to 375°F. Grease and flour a 9-inch-square baking pan.

2. In a large bowl, stir together both flours, the sugar, baking powder, baking soda, and salt. Toss in the blueberries.

3. In a large bowl, beat the egg. Beat in the milk, butter or margarine, lemon juice, and lemon rind. Stir into the dry ingredients until combined.

4. Spread into the prepared pan. Bake 50 minutes or until a wooden pick inserted in the center comes out clean and cake has pulled away from the edges of the pan. Cut into pieces.

Variation: Streusel-Topped Blueberry Coffeecake: To prepare the streusel, in a medium bowl, stir together ⅓ cup all-purpose flour, ⅓ cup whole wheat flour, ½ cup sugar, and ½ teaspoon cinnamon. Using a pastry blender or two knives, cut ⅓ cup butter or margarine into the flour until mixture resembles coarse meal. Sprinkle over batter before baking.

PLUM UPSIDE DOWN CAKE

Makes: nine 2½-inch squares; serves: 9

Italian plums are the small oval ones (sometimes called prunes). If you can't find them, use 6 to 8 larger plums but cut them into sixths or eighths instead of quarters. If you want to gild the lily, you can serve this delicious cake with a scoop of vanilla ice cream on the side.

Topping:

½ cup firmly packed dark or light brown sugar

⅓ cup butter or margarine, melted

12 to 14 Italian plums, quartered

Cake:

¾ cup all-purpose flour

½ cup whole wheat flour

2 teaspoons baking powder

½ teaspoon salt, or to taste

⅓ cup butter or margarine

¾ cup sugar

2 eggs

⅓ cup firmly packed almond paste

½ cup milk

1. Preheat the oven to 375°F.

2. Prepare the topping by stirring together the brown sugar and melted butter or margarine. Pour into an 8-inch-square baking pan. Arrange the plum wedges over the sugar mixture; set aside.

3. In a large bowl or on a piece of waxed paper, stir together both flours, the baking powder, and salt.

4. In a large bowl, cream ⅓ cup butter or margarine and sugar until light and fluffy. Beat in the eggs. Beat in the almond paste until smooth. Add the dry ingredients alternately with the milk, beating well after each addition.

5. Spread into the prepared baking pan. Bake 50 to 60 minutes or until a wooden pick inserted in the center comes out clean and cake has pulled away from the edge of the pan. Let stand 3 minutes. Invert onto serving platter. Cut into squares.

Variation: Use any type of fresh fruit on top, such as peaches, apricots, pineapple, or regular plums.

RASPBERRY–CREAM CHEESE CAKE

Makes: one 9-inch loaf; serves: 10 to 12

This cake is really delicious, but the looks are less than perfect. The top of the loaf is rough and flat instead of smooth and mounded. Slice the cake and no one will notice anything but the flavor. You can leave out the fruit and serve this as a unflavored poundcake.

1½ cups all-purpose flour

½ cup whole wheat flour

2 teaspoons baking powder

½ teaspoon baking soda

½ teaspoon salt

One 8-ounce package cream cheese, softened

½ cup (1 stick) butter or margarine, softened

1½ cups sugar

3 eggs

1½ teaspoons vanilla

1 cup fresh raspberries

1. Preheat the oven to 350°F. Heavily grease and flour a 9 × 5 × 3-inch loaf pan.

2. In a medium bowl or on a piece of waxed paper, stir together both flours, the baking powder, baking soda, and salt.

3. In a large bowl, cream the cream cheese with the butter or margarine; add the sugar and beat until fluffy. Beat in the eggs one at a time. Beat in the vanilla. Stir in the flour until completely combined. Gently fold in the raspberries (because the batter is thick, they will fall apart somewhat).

4. Bake 1 hour or until a wooden pick inserted in the center comes out clean. Turn onto rack to cool.

Variation: Use blueberries instead of raspberries.

SWEET POTATO–APPLE CAKE

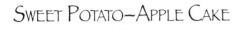

Makes: 12 3 × 2-inch pieces; serves: 12

This ideal coffee cake is not too sweet, but very moist and light.

1½ cups all-purpose flour
½ cup whole wheat flour
2 teaspoons baking powder
1½ teaspoons ground cinnamon
1 teaspoon baking soda
½ teaspoon salt
¼ teaspoon ground nutmeg
½ cup (1 stick) butter or margarine
½ cup firmly packed light brown or dark
    brown sugar
⅓ cup sugar
2 eggs
1 cup mashed baked sweet potatoes
1 cup buttermilk
2 cups chopped, peeled apples
Cinnamon-Sugar (page 500)

1. Preheat the oven to 350°F. Grease and flour a 9-inch-square baking pan.

2. In a large bowl or on a piece of waxed paper, stir together both flours, the baking powder, cinnamon, baking soda, salt, and nutmeg.

3. In a large bowl, cream the butter or margarine; add both sugars and beat until fluffy. Beat in the eggs, one at a time. Beat in the sweet potatoes, then the buttermilk.

4. Stir in the dry ingredients until combined. Stir in the chopped apples.

5. Spread into the prepared baking pan. Sprinkle top generously with Cinnamon-Sugar. Bake 1 hour or until a wooden pick inserted in the center comes out clean and cake has pulled away from the edges of the pan. Cut into pieces.

Variation: Substitute well-drained canned pineapple chunks for the apple.

"VEDDING" CAKE

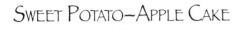

Makes: one 10-inch bundt cake; serves: 16 to 20

My Aunt Emma vas a vonderful Viennese baker. Her Vedding Cake vas always a family favorite, although I've never figured out who serves pound cake for their wedding. Slice this tender cake with a serrated knife.

1 cup golden raisins
1 tablespoon plus 1¾ cups sifted all-purpose
    flour, divided
1 cup sifted whole wheat flour
¼ teaspoon salt
¼ teaspoon baking soda
1 cup (2 sticks) unsalted butter or margarine,
    softened
2 cups sugar
3 eggs
3 egg whites
2 tablespoons fresh lemon juice
2 teaspoons grated lemon rind
1 teaspoon vanilla
One 8-ounce container sour cream
Confectioners' sugar

1. Preheat the oven to 350°F. Thoroughly grease and flour a 10-inch bundt or tube pan.

2. In a large bowl, or on a piece of waxed paper toss together the raisins and 1 tablespoon of the all-purpose flour until the raisins are coated.

3. In a large bowl, or on a piece of waxed paper, combine the remaining all-purpose flour, the whole wheat flour, salt, and baking soda.

4. In a large bowl, cream the butter or margarine with the sugar until light and fluffy. Beat in the eggs and egg whites, one at a time, beating well after each addition. Beat in the lemon juice, lemon rind, and vanilla.

5. Add the flour mixture alternately with the sour cream, beating until smooth after each addition. Stir in the coated raisins.

6. Spoon into prepared pan. Bake 1 hour to 1 hour 15 minutes or until a wooden pick inserted in the center comes out clean. Turn onto rack to cool. Sprinkle the top with confectioners' sugar before serving.

Variation: Omit the raisins, and/or substitute 1 tablespoon grated orange rind for the lemon rind (but use the lemon juice anyway).

DRIED APRICOT CAKE

Makes: one 9-inch loaf; serves: 10 to 12

Everyone always asks for the recipe of this very moist, dense, flavorful loaf.

1 ⅓ cups all-purpose flour, divided
½ cup whole wheat flour
2 teaspoons baking powder
1 teaspoon baking soda
½ teaspoon salt
2 cups chopped dried apricots
½ cup orange juice
⅓ cup buttermilk
2 tablespoons honey
1 tablespoon grated orange rind
1 teaspoon grated fresh ginger, or
    ½ teaspoon ground ginger
½ cup (1 stick) butter or margarine
⅔ cup sugar
2 eggs

1. Preheat the oven to 350°F. Heavily grease and flour a 9 × 5 × 3-inch loaf pan.

2. In a medium bowl or on a piece of waxed paper, stir together 1 cup of the all-purpose flour, the whole wheat flour, baking powder, baking soda, and salt.

3. On a piece of waxed paper, toss the apricots in the remaining ⅓ cup all-purpose flour to coat; set aside.

4. In a medium bowl, beat the orange juice, buttermilk, honey, orange rind, and ginger.

5. In a large bowl, cream the butter or margarine with the sugar and beat until fluffy. Beat in the eggs (the mixture will look curdled).

6. Beat in the dry ingredients alternately with the juice-buttermilk mixture. Stir in the apricots and any flour that remains on the paper. Spread into the baking pan.

7. Bake 45 to 50 minutes or until a wooden pick inserted in the center comes out clean. Turn onto rack to cool.

Variation: Substitute chopped prunes for the apricots.

CARROT CAKE

Makes: one 9 × 13-inch cake; serves: 20

This delicious carrot cake is very versatile. Serve it as is (unflavored), or sprinkle with powdered sugar. Or top it with Cream Cheese Frosting (page 516). It's an ideal base for a birthday cake. Just prepare the cake according to recipe and then follow directions in the variation for a layer cake.

2 cups all-purpose flour
1 cup wheat germ
¾ cup whole wheat flour
1 tablespoon baking powder
2 teaspoons baking soda
½ teaspoon salt
1½ cups chopped walnuts
1 cup golden raisins
1 cup firmly packed light brown or dark
    brown sugar
¾ cup honey
¾ cup vegetable oil
¾ cup buttermilk
3 eggs
3 cups coarsely shredded carrots
1 cup lightly packed, shredded sweetened
    coconut
2 teaspoons vanilla extract

1. Preheat the oven to 350°F. Grease and flour a 9 × 13-inch baking pan.

2. In a large bowl, using a wire whisk, stir together the all-purpose flour, wheat germ, whole wheat flour, baking powder, baking soda, and salt. Stir in the walnuts and raisins.

3. In a separate large bowl, beat together the brown sugar, honey, oil, buttermilk, and eggs. Stir in the carrots, coconut, and vanilla.

4. Stir the carrot mixture into the flour mixture until thoroughly combined. Pour into prepared pan.

5. Bake 1 hour or until a wooden pick inserted into the center comes out clean. Remove from the oven and let stand 20 minutes. Turn onto rack to cool completely. Cut into 2-inch squares.

Variations: Omit the coconut.

Carrot Layer Cake: Slice the cake horizontally into two layers. Prepare a double recipe of Cream Cheese Frosting (page 516); fill and frost cake.

COCONUT~PINEAPPLE CAKE

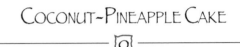

Makes: 16 squares; serves: 16

This super-moist cake was a favorite of many of the guests at a dessert tasting.

1 cup all-purpose flour
¾ cup whole wheat flour
1½ teaspoons baking powder
½ teaspoon baking soda
¼ teaspoon salt
½ cup (1 stick) butter or margarine, softened
1 cup sugar
½ cup unsweetened coconut milk (page 497)
3 eggs
1½ cups sweetened shredded coconut,
    divided
One 8-ounce can crushed pineapple in
    unsweetened juice, undrained
3 tablespoons raspberry preserves

1. Preheat the oven to 350°F. Grease and flour a 9-inch-square baking pan.

2. In a medium bowl or on a piece of waxed paper, stir together both flours, the baking powder, baking soda, and salt.

3. In a large bowl, cream the butter with the sugar. Beat in the coconut milk and eggs (the mixture will looked curdled). Stir in 1 cup of the coconut and the pineapple with juice. Stir in the flour mixture.

4. Spread the batter into the prepared pan. Dollop the top of cake with raspberry preserves, $1/2$ teaspoon at a time. Sprinkle with remaining $1/2$ cup coconut.

5. Bake 45 to 55 minutes or until a wooden pick inserted in the center comes out clean. Cut into squares.

Variation: Substitute sieved apricot preserves for the raspberry.

APPLE GINGERBREAD

Makes: one 8-inch cake; serves: 9

For a nice topping, sprinkle additional sugar, or Cinnamon-Sugar (page 500), over the batter before baking.

1 cup all-purpose flour
$1/2$ cup whole wheat flour
2 teaspoons ground ginger
1 teaspoon baking powder
1 teaspoon baking soda
1 teaspoon ground cinnamon
$1/4$ teaspoon ground nutmeg
$1/8$ teaspoon ground allspice
$1/3$ cup vegetable oil
1 egg
$2/3$ cup sugar
3 tablespoons molasses
$1/2$ cup unflavored yogurt
$1 1/2$ cups chopped, peeled apples

1. Preheat the oven to 350°F. Grease and flour an 8-inch-square baking pan.

2. In a medium bowl, or on waxed paper, stir together both flours, the ginger, baking powder, baking soda, cinnamon, nutmeg, and allspice.

3. In a large bowl, beat the oil and egg until combined. Add the sugar and molasses and beat until combined. Beat in the flour mixture alternately with the yogurt. Stir in the apples.

4. Spoon into the baking pan. Bake 40 minutes or until a wooden pick inserted in the center comes out clean. Cool in pan; cut into 9 squares.

Variation: Add 1 cup raisins or currants when you add the apples.

COCONUT PARSNIP LAYER CAKE

Makes: two 9-inch cake layers; serves: 10 to 14

Don't tell your guests there's parsnip in this moist and dense layer cake until after they've tasted it and started to rave about how incredibly delicious it is. I like to frost it with Butter–Cream Cheese Frosting (page 516), but it also goes well with whipped cream or any vanilla or spice frosting.

$1 1/4$ cups all-purpose flour
$3/4$ cup whole wheat flour
2 teaspoons ground cinnamon
2 teaspoons baking powder
1 teaspoon baking soda
$1/2$ teaspoon salt
1 cup chopped walnuts
2 eggs
$3/4$ cup sugar
$1/2$ cup sweetened cream of coconut (such as Coco Casa or Coco Lopez)
$1/2$ cup vegetable oil
1 teaspoon vanilla
$1 1/2$ cups finely shredded parsnips
One 8-ounce can juice-packed, crushed pineapple, undrained
1 cup shredded sweetened coconut

1. Preheat the oven to 350°F. Heavily grease and flour two 9-inch round cake pans.

2. In a medium bowl or on a sheet of waxed paper, stir together both flours, the cinnamon, baking powder, baking soda, and salt. Add the walnuts and toss to coat.

3. In a large bowl, beat the eggs. Add the sugar and beat until thick. Beat in the cream of coconut, vegetable oil, and vanilla. Stir in the parsnips and pineapple.

4. Stir in the flour mixture until completely combined. Stir in the shredded coconut. Pour into prepared pans. Bake 25 to 35 minutes or until a wooden pick inserted in the center comes out clean.

Variation: Substitute carrots for the parsnips.

BUTTERMILK MOCHA CAKE

Makes: one 9-inch 2-layer cake; serves: 8

You don't necessarily get too much mocha flavor in the cake itself (if you didn't know it was mocha you would probably guess it was chocolate), but it complements the frosting.

1 ¼ cups buttermilk
1 ½ tablespoons instant coffee powder or
    granules
1 ½ cups all-purpose flour
²⁄₃ cup unsweetened cocoa
½ cup whole wheat flour
2 teaspoons baking powder
1 teaspoon baking soda
¼ teaspoon salt
¾ cup (1 ½ sticks) butter or margarine,
    softened
1 ½ cups sugar
3 eggs
1 teaspoon vanilla extract
1 recipe Mocha Buttercream Frosting
    (page 515)

1. Preheat the oven to 350°F. Heavily grease two 9-inch round cake pans. Cut two 9-inch circles of waxed paper and place one in each pan. Grease the waxed papers then dust with flour.

2. In a small bowl, stir together the buttermilk and coffee powder until dissolved.

3. In a large bowl or on a piece of waxed paper, sift together all-purpose flour, cocoa, whole wheat flour, baking powder, baking soda, and salt.

4. In a large bowl, cream the butter or margarine. Add the sugar and beat until light and fluffy. Beat in the eggs, one at a time.

5. Beat in the flour mixture alternately with the coffee-buttermilk mixture. Stir in the vanilla. Spread half the batter into each prepared pan.

6. Bake 35 to 40 minutes or until wooden pick inserted in the center comes out clean. Cool 20 minutes in pan. Turn onto rack, remove waxed paper, and cool completely. Fill and frost with Mocha Buttercream Frosting.

Variation: Use Ganache (page 517) to fill and frost cake.

PECAN~SQUASH CAKE

Makes: one 10-inch bundt cake; serves: 16 to 20

A bit sweeter than a zucchini bread, this cake is just chock-full of raisins and nuts. And it's perfect for anyone with a sensitivity to dairy products.

2 cups all-purpose flour
1 cup whole wheat flour
½ cup wheat germ
1 tablespoon ground cinnamon
2 teaspoons baking powder
1 teaspoon baking soda
½ teaspoon salt
2 cups light or dark raisins
3 eggs
2 cups sugar
1½ cups vegetable oil
1 teaspoon vanilla
3 cups coarsely shredded yellow squash
2 cups chopped pecans

1. Preheat the oven to 350°F. Heavily grease and flour a 10-inch bundt pan.

2. In a medium bowl or on a sheet of waxed paper, stir together both flours, the wheat germ, cinnamon, baking powder, baking soda, and salt. Add the raisins; toss lightly to coat.

3. In a large bowl, beat the eggs. Add the sugar and beat until thick. Beat in the oil and vanilla, then the squash.

4. Stir in the flour mixture until completely combined. Stir in the nuts. Pour into prepared pan. Bake 1 hour 10 minutes or until a wooden pick inserted in the center comes out clean. Turn onto rack to cool.

Variation: Zucchini-Walnut Cake: Substitute zucchini for the squash, and walnuts for the pecans

BANANA~WHIPPED CREAM REFRIGERATOR CAKE

Makes: one 9-inch cake; serves: 6 to 10

You may not need all the cookies in the box—just as many are necessary to create the specified number of layers. Be sure your bananas are quite ripe for this recipe.

2 cups heavy cream
⅓ cup confectioners' sugar
3 cups chopped ripe bananas
One 1-pound box gingersnaps

1. In a large bowl, beat the cream with the sugar until stiff peaks form. Fold in the bananas.

2. Place a layer of gingersnap cookies in a 9-inch springform pan.

3. Spread ½ of the banana mixture over the cookies.

4. Top with another layer of cookies and spread remaining banana mixture over the cookies. Top with another layer of cookies. Cover with plastic wrap and place in the refrigerator at least 6 hours or overnight. Release side of pan to serve.

Variation: Add 2 tablespoons orange liqueur to the cream before beating.

LEMON-SCENTED ANGEL FOOD CAKE

Makes: one 10-inch cake; serves: 12 to 16

The lemon flavor (and the orange in the variation) is subtle. For a stronger fruit flavor, add 1/4 teaspoon lemon (or orange) extract when you fold in the rind. Whole wheat pastry flour is available in health food stores. If you can't find it, just triple-sift regular whole wheat flour before measuring.

1 2/3 cups sugar, divided
1 cup sifted cake flour
1/3 cup sifted whole wheat pastry flour
1 1/2 cups egg whites, room temperature (about 12 egg whites)
1 1/2 teaspoons cream of tartar
1/2 teaspoon salt
1 tablespoon grated lemon rind
1 teaspoon vanilla extract

1. Preheat the oven to 350°F.

2. In a medium bowl or on a sheet of waxed paper, sift together 2/3 cup of the sugar with both flours. Sift three more times; set aside.

3. In a large bowl, beat the egg whites, on high speed, with the cream of tartar and salt until soft peaks form. Beat in the remaining 1 cup of sugar two tablespoons at a time.

4. Sift 1/4 of the flour mixture over the egg whites. Using a rubber spatula, fold in the flour until none of the flour shows. Continue sifting and folding in 1/4 of the flour mixture at a time until all has been incorporated into the egg whites. Fold in the lemon rind and vanilla.

5. Using the spatula, spread the batter into an ungreased, 10-inch tube pan with a removable bottom.

6. Bake 45 to 50 minutes or until a pick inserted in the center comes out clean. Invert pan to cool, 2 hours.

7. To remove cake from pan, run a thin, sharp knife around the outer edge and around the tube in the center. Press the bottom forward; loosen cake from the bottom by running a knife between the cake and the pan.

Variations: Orange-Scented Angel Food Cake: Use grated orange rind instead of the lemon.

Angel Food Cake: Omit the lemon rind. If desired, stir in 1/4 teaspoon almond extract.

ICINGS, FILLINGS, AND FROSTINGS

LIGHT CHOCOLATE FROSTING

Makes: 3 cups, enough to fill and frost a 9-inch 3-layer cake

This frosting is light in color and has a mild chocolate flavor.

One 8-ounce package cream cheese, softened
½ cup (1 stick) butter or margarine, softened
Four 1-ounce squares semisweet chocolate, melted
3 cups confectioners' sugar

1. In a medium bowl, beat the cream cheese and butter or margarine until fluffy.

2. Beat in the melted chocolate, then beat in the confectioners' sugar ¼ cup at a time until mixture is fluffy.

MOCHA BUTTERCREAM FROSTING

Makes: 2 cups, enough to fill and frost an 8-inch round 2-layer cake

Mocha is a hard flavor to pin down—not quite chocolate and not quite coffee. I think this frosting has a good balance between the two flavors. If you prefer mocha with a strong coffee flavor, halve the cocoa; for a more chocolatey flavor, use less coffee and 1 tablespoon more cocoa.

1 tablespoon hot water
1½ teaspoons instant coffee granules
½ cup (1 stick) butter or margarine, softened
¼ cup unsweetened cocoa
3 tablespoons sour cream
3½ cups sifted confectioners' sugar

1. In a small bowl, stir together the water and coffee until the coffee is dissolved.

2. In a large bowl, beat the butter or margarine until light and fluffy. Beat in the cocoa until completely combined. Beat in the coffee and sour cream.

3. Beat in the confectioners' sugar one cup at a time until all the sugar has been incorporated.

Variation: Chocolate Buttercream Frosting: Omit the instant coffee and water and use 2 tablespoons milk instead.

COFFEE-RUM BUTTERCREAM FROSTING

Makes: 2¾ cups, enough to fill and frost a 9-inch 2-layer or 3-layer cake

This is a very sweet and rich frosting. I use superfine sugar to avoid a graininess from granulated sugar.

2 tablespoons rum
1 tablespoon instant coffee granules
¾ cup superfine sugar
4 egg yolks
1 cup (2 sticks) butter or margarine, softened

1. In a small bowl, stir together the rum and instant coffee; let stand to allow the coffee to dissolve.

2. Place the sugar and egg yolks in the top of a double boiler over simmering water. Using an electric mixer on high speed, beat until thick.

3. Remove top of double boiler from heat; beat in the rum-coffee mixture. Beat in the butter or margarine 1 tablespoon at a time. Let chill in the refrigerator for 40 minutes.

4. Beat until light and fluffy.

Variation: Orange Buttercream: Substitute 2 tablespoons orange juice concentrate for the rum and 1 tablespoon grated orange rind for the coffee.

CHOCOLATE–SOUR CREAM FROSTING

Makes: 1 ²/₃ cups, enough to fill and frost an 8-inch or 9-inch 2-layer cake

The sour cream gives this velvety frosting a nicely tart undertone.

8 ounces semisweet chocolate
1 cup sour cream
¼ cup confectioners' sugar

1. Melt the chocolate in the top of a double boiler over simmering water.

2. Add the sour cream and sugar and stir until smooth.

Variation: Omit the sugar for a more "bitter" sweet.

BUTTER–CREAM CHEESE FROSTING

Makes: 2 ¹/₄ cups, enough to fill and frost a 9-inch 2-layer cake.

A cross between cream cheese frosting and buttercream, this is my favorite white frosting.

One 8-ounce package cream cheese, softened
¼ cup (½ stick) butter or margarine, softened
2 cups confectioners' sugar
1 teaspoon vanilla extract

1. In a medium bowl, beat the cream cheese and butter or margarine until fluffy.

2. Beat in the confectioners' sugar ¼ cup at a time until mixture is fluffy. Beat in the vanilla.

Variation: Ginger Butter–Cream Cheese Frosting: Stir in 1 to 2 teaspoons ground ginger (or to taste) when you add the vanilla.

CREAM CHEESE FROSTING

Makes: 2¹/₂ cups, enough to fill and frost an 8-inch or 9-inch round 2-layer cake.

This is the traditional frosting for carrot cake and similar desserts.

Two 8-ounce packages cream cheese, softened
1 cup confectioners' sugar

1. Beat the cream cheese and confectioners' sugar until light and fluffy.

Variation: Orange–Cream Cheese Frosting: Stir 1 tablespoon grated orange rind into the cream cheese frosting.

GANACHE

L

*Makes: 1 ³/₄ cups, enough to fill and frost a
9-inch 2-layer cake*

*This smooth, rich glaze is thicker than an actual
glaze but thinner than a frosting.*

8 ounces semisweet chocolate
1 cup heavy cream

1. In a small heavy saucepan, melt the chocolate with the cream. Let cool slightly until of
desired thickness for glazing.

Variations: Substitute 2 tablespoons of your
favorite liqueur for 2 tablespoons of cream.

Truffles: Reduce cream to ³/₄ cup and add
¹/₄ teaspoon almond extract. Let the ganache
chill completely, then form into 1-inch balls and
roll in unsweetened cocoa or sprinkles.

CONFECTIONERS' SUGAR GLAZE

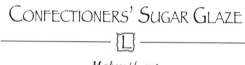

L

Makes: ¹/₃ cup

*Drizzle this over baked goods to dress up any plain
loaves or bundt cakes, buns, turnovers, or Danish.*

1 cup sifted confectioners' sugar
1 tablespoon milk

1. In a medium bowl, stir together confectioners' sugar and milk until smooth. Cover with
plastic wrap if not using immediately.

Ⓥ **Variations:** Substitute juice or water for
the milk.

Decorative Icing: Add 2 to 3 extra tablespoons
of confectioners' sugar to the glaze. Divide into
2 bowls and add desired food color. Using a
pastry bag fitted with a very small, round tip,
pipe onto cookies or cakes.

PIES AND TARTS

OIL CRUST

V

*Makes: enough for two 9-inch crusts or
4¹/₂–5 dozen tartlets*

*I find oil crusts easier to make than those with
shortening or butter, because you get to skip the
first step of cutting in the shortening.*

1³/₄ cups all-purpose flour
³/₄ cup whole wheat flour
1 teaspoon salt
¹/₂ cup vegetable oil
¹/₃ to ¹/₂ cup ice water

1. In a large bowl, stir together both flours and
the salt. Stir in the oil and 3 tablespoons of the
water; add as much of the remaining water as
necessary to form a stiff dough. Chill.

2. Divide the dough in half and roll out as
directed in specific recipes.

Variation: Use olive oil for savory dishes.

FLAKY PASTRY

[V]

*Makes: enough dough for two 9-inch pie crusts
(about 1 pound)*

To my mind, all-butter pastry makes the best-tasting crust and all-shortening pastry makes the flakiest. I use a combination of both to get a flaky-tasty crust.

1¼ cups all-purpose flour
¾ cup whole wheat flour
1 teaspoon salt, or to taste
½ cup (1 stick) cold butter or margarine
¼ cup shortening
4 to 5 tablespoons ice water

1. In a large bowl, stir together both flours and the salt. Using a pastry cutter or two knives, cut in the butter or margarine and shortening until the mixture resembles coarse cornmeal.

2. Pour 1 tablespoon of the water over one section of the flour. Using a fork, work the dough until combined, then continue with remaining water. Form into a ball.

3. Divide the dough in half and roll out as directed in specific recipes.

Variations: All-Shortening Crust: Substitute ½ cup shortening for the butter or margarine.

All-Butter Crust: Substitute ¼ cup butter for the shortening.

CITRUS CRUST

[V]

Makes: enough dough for two 9-inch pie crusts

The lemon flavor in this crust is just superb. It makes a perfect complement for sweet or fruity fillings.

1½ cups all-purpose flour
½ cup whole wheat flour
3 tablespoons sugar
¼ teaspoon salt
⅔ cup butter or margarine
¼ cup fresh lemon juice
2 teaspoons grated lemon rind
1 tablespoon cold water, if necessary

1. In a large bowl, stir together both flours, the sugar, and salt. Using a pastry cutter or two knives, cut in the butter or margarine until the mixture resembles coarse cornmeal.

2. Stir together the lemon juice and lemon rind. Pour 1 tablespoon of the lemon juice over one section of the flour. Using a fork, work the dough until combined, then continue with remaining lemon juice. If all the flour is not moist and the dough cannot be formed into a ball after you've added all the juice, use the water.

3. Divide the dough in half and roll out as directed in specific recipes.

Variation: Use orange rind instead of the lemon rind.

TARTLET SHELLS

— V —

Makes: 3–4 dozen (depending on how thin dough is rolled); serves: 16 to 20

You want to roll the dough very thin for this recipe or else the tarts will be too doughy and you'll lose the flavor of the fillings. I like the flavor of the Citrus Crust for tartlets, but you can make them with any recipe for one-crust pastry (or halve the recipe for a two-pastry crust). You can gather the scraps and reroll the dough once for extra tartlets, but don't roll the scraps more than once or the tart shells will be too tough.

½ recipe Flaky Pastry dough or Citrus Crust (page 518)

1. Preheat the oven to 400°F.

2. Prepare crust according to directions.

3. Roll dough thin, ⅛ to ¹⁄₁₆ inch thick (thin enough to see the tabletop or work surface through it).

4. Using a 2½-inch round biscuit cutter, cut into circles.

5. Fit each circle of dough into a mini muffin cup. Weigh down with pie weights or dried beans.

6. Bake 10 to 12 minutes or until lightly browned.

7. Remove from pans; cool on racks. Discard beans, if used.

FOOD PROCESSOR FARMER-CHEESE PASTRY DOUGH

— L —

Makes: 26 ounces of dough

Using the food processor makes this pastry very easy to prepare. However, if you don't have a food processor, you can still prepare the dough by putting the farmer cheese through a fine strainer, then stirring in the butter, then flours, and salt.

One 7½-ounce package farmer cheese
1 cup (2 sticks) salted butter or margarine, softened
¾ cup whole wheat flour
½ teaspoons salt
1¼ cups all-purpose flour

1. Place the farmer cheese in a food processor container fitted with a steel blade. Cover and process until smooth. With the motor running, add the butter or margarine, 2 tablespoons at a time, through the chute.

2. Add the whole wheat flour and salt. Cover and process until combined. Add all the all-purpose flour and process, using the on–off pulse, until dough forms a ball.

3. Wrap in plastic wrap and chill 1 to 2 hours.

4. Roll out as called for in recipes.

Variation: Sweetened Farmer-Cheese Pastry: Add ¼ cup sugar when you add the whole wheat flour.

APPLE PIE

[V]

Makes: one 9-inch pie; serves: 6 to 8

This is the American favorite, for good reason.

⅔ cup sugar

3 tablespoons all-purpose flour

1 teaspoon ground cinnamon

¼ teaspoon ground nutmeg

⅛ teaspoon salt, or to taste

6 cups sliced, peeled McIntosh apples

2 tablespoons fresh lemon juice

¼ cup firmly packed light brown or dark brown sugar

1 recipe Flaky Pastry (page 518)

2 tablespoons butter or margarine

1 egg, beaten (optional)

1. Preheat the oven to 425°F.

2. In a small bowl or on a piece of waxed paper, stir together the sugar, flour, cinnamon, nutmeg, and salt. In a large bowl, toss the apples with the lemon juice until completely coated. Add the flour mixture and brown sugar to the apples; toss to combine completely.

3. Roll out half the pastry into a 12-inch circle. Place in a 9-inch pie plate. Spoon the filling into the pie plate. Dot with butter.

4. Roll the second half of the pastry into an 11-inch circle. Place on top of filling. Press edges of both crusts to seal, then crimp. For a shiny crust, brush with egg, if desired. Prick with fork to vent.

5. Bake 45 to 50 minutes or until crust is browned and filling is bubbly. Cool on rack.

Variation: Add ⅓ cup currants and ½ cup chopped walnuts.

LATTICE-TOP PEACH PIE

[V]

Makes: one 9-inch pie; serves: 6 to 8

The best peach pie is always made with great, ripe, delicious, peaches. Underripe, overripe, or tasteless peaches make a less perfect pie (but still not too shabby).

⅓ cup sugar

3 tablespoons all-purpose flour

1 teaspoon cinnamon

8 cups peeled peach wedges (7 large peaches)

½ cup firmly packed dark brown sugar

2 tablespoons fresh lemon juice

¼ teaspoon salt, or to taste

Pastry for a 2-crust pie (pages 517–18)

1. Preheat the oven to 400°F.

2. In a large bowl, stir together the sugar, flour, and cinnamon. Add the peaches, brown sugar, lemon juice, and salt; toss until peaches are completely coated with the sugar mixture.

3. Roll out half the pastry into a 12-inch circle. Place in a 9-inch pie plate. Spoon the filling into the pie plate.

4. Roll the second half of the pastry into a 10-inch circle. Cut into ³/₄-inch-thick strips. Place pastry strips in a lattice pattern on top of pie. Press edges of both crusts to seal, then crimp.

5. Bake 45 to 55 minutes or until crust is browned and filling is bubbly. Cool on rack.

[L] **Variation:** For a richer filling, dot top of filling with 1 tablespoon butter before topping with pastry.

SOUR CHERRY PIE

[V]

Makes: one 9-inch pie; serves: 6 to 8

Sour cherries are the "real" thing when it comes to pie making; unfortunately, they're only in season for a short time. Don't expect your pie filling to come out bright red like the cherries in the can— sour cherries are bright red on the outside but yellow on the inside, so the filling is a much more subtle pink. Measure out the cherries before you pit them. The pie thickens upon cooling, so if you're planning on serving it warm, you may need a little extra cornstarch.

1 1/2 cups sugar
3 1/2 tablespoons cornstarch
5 cups fresh sour cherries, pitted
1/4 teaspoon almond extract
Pastry for 2-crust pie (pages 517–18)

1. Preheat the oven to 400°F.

2. In a large bowl, stir together the sugar and cornstarch. Add the cherries and almond extract; toss until cherries are completely coated with the sugar mixture.

3. Roll out half the pastry into a 12-inch circle. Place in a 9-inch pie plate. Spoon the filling into the pie plate.

4. Roll the second half of the pastry into an 11-inch circle. Place on top of pie. Press edges of both crusts to seal, then crimp. Cut a hole in the top or prick with a fork to vent.

5. Bake 45 to 55 minutes or until crust is browned and filling is bubbly. Cool on rack.

Variation: Use three 16-ounce cans sour cherries, drained, instead of the fresh.

STRAWBERRY~RHUBARB TART WITH OAT STREUSEL TOPPING

[V]

Makes: one 10-inch tart; serves: 6 to 8

If you serve this tart warm, use extra cornstarch, since the filling thickens as it cools.

Filling:
1 1/4 cups sugar
3 tablespoons cornstarch
1/4 teaspoon ground mace or nutmeg
3 cups quartered strawberries
1 1/2 cups diced rhubarb (1/2-inch pieces)

The shell:
1 prebaked 10-inch tart shell (pages 517–19)

Topping:
1/3 cup all-purpose flour
1/4 cup whole wheat flour
1/4 cup sugar
1/4 teaspoon pumpkin pie spice or ground cinnamon
3 tablespoons butter or margarine, melted
1/2 cup quick-cooking oats

1. Preheat the oven to 375°F.

2. For filling, in a large bowl, stir together 1 1/4 cups sugar, the cornstarch, and mace. Add the strawberries and rhubarb. Stir until combined; let stand 5 minutes.

3. Spoon the fruit (and any syrup) into the tart shell.

4. For the topping, in a medium bowl, stir together both flours, 1/4 cup sugar, and the spice. Add the butter or margarine and stir until the mixture makes fine crumbs. Stir in the oats. Sprinkle over the berry mixture.

5. Bake 40 minutes or until topping is browned and filling is bubbly.

Variation: Add 3/4 cup chopped nuts to the topping.

CRANBERRY~PEAR CHUTNEY TART

Makes: one 10-inch tart; serves: 8

This tart started out as a chutney recipe, but the texture was too fruity, almost like apple saucey—not great for chutney, but stupendous nevertheless. So, being the sometimes frugal person that I am, I refused to give up on the recipe and ... voilà!

1½ cups fresh whole cranberries
1¼ cups chopped dried pears
1¼ cups water
¾ cup chopped walnuts
½ cup dark or golden raisins
½ cup plus 3 tablespoons sugar, divided
1 teaspoon ground coriander
½ teaspoon ground allspice
¼ teaspoon ground red pepper
1 fully baked 10-inch tart shell (pages 517–19)
2 fresh pears, cored and sliced very thin

1. In a 2-quart saucepan, stir together the cranberries, dried pears, water, walnuts, raisins, ½ cup of the sugar, coriander, allspice, and red pepper. Bring to a boil over high heat. Reduce heat and simmer 30 minutes or until thickened. Spread into prepared shell.

2. Preheat the broiler.

3. Arrange the fresh pear slices in concentric circles on top of the chutney mixture. Sprinkle with the remaining 3 tablespoons sugar. Broil 5 to 7 minutes or until the pears are browned on the edges. (You may want to cover the pastry with aluminum foil to prevent it from browning too much.)

Variation: Use thinly sliced apple instead of pear on top.

APRICOT~RASPBERRY TART

Makes: one 9-inch tart; serves: 6 to 8

This is a genuinely tart tart. My tasters were divided; half said, "This tart is great—it's not too sweet," but the others thought it tasted great but needed more sugar. If you like your tarts sweet, add sugar to taste.

Pastry for 2-crust pie (pages 517–18)
¾ cup sugar
2 tablespoons cornstarch
3 cups sliced fresh apricots
1 cup fresh raspberries

1. Preheat the oven to 375°F.

2. Roll out half the pastry into an 11-inch circle. Place in a 9-inch tart pan. Weigh the pastry down with pie weights or beans. Bake 15 minutes. Remove from oven; remove weights and cool.

3. In a large bowl, stir together the sugar and cornstarch. Add the apricots and raspberries; toss to combine.

4. Spoon into the tart shell.

5. Roll the remaining pastry into a 10-inch circle. Cut into strips and arrange in a lattice over the filling. Press the edges of the strips into the edge of the crust to seal.

6. Bake 40 to 45 minutes or until crust is browned and fruit is bubbly.

Variation: Raspberry-Apricot Tart: Use 3 cups raspberries to 1 cup apricot slices.

FRESH RASPBERRY TART WITH BLUEBERRY FILLING

—— [V] ——

Makes: one 9-inch tart; serves: 4 to 6

You can use frozen blueberries instead of the fresh for the filling—just measure them while still frozen. If fresh raspberries are not available or are too costly, you can use strawberries or any other fresh berries.

¾ cup apple juice
2 tablespoons sugar
2½ tablespoons cornstarch
1½ cups blueberries
1 fully baked 10-inch tart shell (pages 517–19)
1½ cups raspberries

1. In a 1½-quart saucepan, stir together the apple juice, sugar, and cornstarch. Stir in the blueberries. Bring to a boil, stirring constantly. Pour into prebaked shell. Chill.

2. Top with fresh raspberries.

Variation: Orange-Blueberry Tart: Substitute orange juice for the apple juice; add 1 teaspoon grated orange rind and 2 additional tablespoons sugar when cooking the blueberries. Top with additional blueberries instead of the raspberries.

EASY APPLE TART

—— [V] ——

Makes: 1 tart; serves: 4 to 6

I think this tart is more attractive when you leave the skin on the apples, but it's probably easier to eat if you peel them. It's up to you.

1½ cups apples, cored and sliced very thin
1 tablespoon lemon juice
1 sheet Pepperidge Farm prepared puff pastry
2 tablespoons sieved apricot jam
1 tablespoon sugar

1. Preheat the oven to 400°F.

2. In a medium bowl, toss the apple slices with the lemon juice.

3. On a lightly floured surface, roll the pastry into a 10 × 12-inch rectangle.

4. Cut 5 strips (each ¾ × 12 inches) from one side of the puff pastry. Place the pastry on an ungreased baking sheet.

5. Brush the pastry with some of the jam. Make a border of pastry by placing 2 of the strips onto the long outer edges of the pastry. Cut 1 of the remaining strips in half and place each half between the other strips along each of the shorter edges. (The apricot jam should act as glue to hold the strips in place.)

6. Arrange the apple slices attractively within the pastry-strip borders. Brush the apples with the remaining jam.

7. Arrange the remaining 3 pastry strips decoratively over the apples. Sprinkle with sugar.

8. Bake 15 to 20 minutes or until puffed and browned.

Variation: Use a combination of apple and pear slices.

APPLE-STRAWBERRY TART

Makes: two 14-inch tarts; serves: 8 to 12

This is slightly tart, almost like a strawberry-rhubarb mixture. It uses a puff pastry base instead of the usual pastry crust.

2 cups peeled, chopped apples
2 cups hulled, halved strawberries
1/4 cup sugar
1 sheet Pepperidge Farm prepared puff pastry

1. Preheat the oven to 375°F. Grease a baking sheet.

2. Place the apples, strawberries, and sugar in a 2-quart saucepan. Bring to a boil over medium-high heat or until strawberries have given off enough liquid to dissolve the sugar. Cook 10 to 15 minutes, stirring occasionally. Mash with a fork until the largest chunks are broken; cool (makes 2 cups sauce).

3. Roll the pastry into a 12 × 14-inch sheet. Cut sheet in half, forming 2 pieces each 6 × 14 inches. Cut 1/2-inch strips from each edge of each piece of pastry. Place pastry sheets on prepared baking sheet; brush edges of each pastry with water. Place strips along the edges of each of the pastries (the strips will puff up to form the border crust).

4. Spread 1/2 of the filling in each of the pastries, being careful not to touch or cover the border pastry strips.

5. Bake 25 to 30 minutes or until pastry is puffed and golden.

Variation: Use any prepared pie filling instead of the apple-strawberry mixture.

CHEESE TART

Makes: one 9-inch tart; serves: 8

If you haven't made pot cheese, use ricotta cheese.

Pastry for a 9-inch tart (pages 517–19)
2 eggs
1/2 cup sugar
1/3 cup sour cream
1 tablespoon fresh lemon juice
1 teaspoon grated lemon rind
2 cups pot cheese (page 495)
1 tablespoon sieved apricot preserves

1. Preheat the oven to 350°F.

2. Line a 9-inch tart pan with the pastry. Weigh down with beans or pie weights; bake 15 minutes. Remove weights.

3. In a medium bowl, beat the eggs lightly. Beat in the sugar, sour cream, lemon juice, and lemon rind. Stir in the cheese.

4. Brush the pastry with the apricot preserves. Pour in the cheese mixture. Bake 45 minutes or until slightly puffy all over.

Variation: Use 1 tablespoon orange juice and 2 teaspoons orange rind instead of the lemon juice and lemon rind.

FROZEN PIÑA COLADA MOUSSE TARTS

Makes: 12 tarts (3 cups mousse); serves: 6 to 12

Prepared tart shells are usually available in the baking goods section of the supermarket. If you can't find them, you can line individual tart pans with graham cracker crumb crust (page 532).

One 8-ounce can juice-packed crushed
   pineapple, drained
¾ cup sweetened cream of coconut (such as
   Coco Casa or Coco Lopez)
1 cup heavy cream
12 prepared individual graham cracker–
   crumb-crust tart shells

1. Place the pineapple and cream of coconut in a blender container. Cover and blend until smooth.

2. In a large bowl, beat the cream until stiff peaks form. Fold in the pineapple mixture. Spoon into tart shells. Freeze until firm.

Variations: Fold in 1 cup shredded sweetened coconut.

Frozen Piña Colada Mousse: Fill 6 to 8 dessert cups or glasses with the Piña Colada Mousse. Freeze.

HONEY APPLE-FIG TART

Makes: one 9-inch tart; serves: 6

½ recipe Citrus Crust (page 518)
1½ cups chopped, peeled McIntosh apples
1½ cups finely chopped dried figs (about 24
   small figs, chopped)
1 cup chopped walnuts
¼ cup honey

1. Preheat the oven to 425°F.

2. Roll the dough into a 10-inch circle and place it in a 9-inch tart pan.

3. In a medium bowl, toss together the apples, figs, walnuts, and honey. Spoon into the crust.

4. Bake 40 minutes or until browned on top.

Variation: Honey Pear-Fig Tart: Use 1½ cups chopped, peeled pears instead of apples.

Tartlets

I prefer to entertain larger numbers of guests with "single-subject" foods. That means either "cocktails," where I serve a variety of appetizers, dips, and cheeses, or "dessert," which is a large assortment of finger foods plus coffee, tea, and wine or liqueurs. Tartlets are terrific for parties—they're easy to prepare in advance (you can even freeze them). This way you have time to socialize at your own party.

FRUIT TARTLETS

Makes: 36 tartlets; serves: 8 to 12

Some good fruit choices are sliced strawberries, peaches, kiwis, bananas, and apricots; whole berries or grapes; or canned mandarin oranges.

¾ cup milk
1 egg yolk
2 tablespoons sugar
2 tablespoons all-purpose flour
1 teaspoon orange liqueur, optional
¼ teaspoon vanilla
36 baked Tartlet Shells (page 519)
1 to 2 cups fruit or berries

1. In a 1-quart saucepan, heat the milk until bubbles form around the edges; set aside.

2. In a medium bowl, using a whisk, beat the egg yolk with the sugar until light yellow. Whisk in the flour until smooth. Gradually stir in the heated milk. Return to the saucepan and cook over medium heat, stirring constantly, until thick and smooth. Stir in the orange liqueur and vanilla.

3. Place about 1 teaspoon filling in each shell. Top with fruit. Refrigerate until serving time.

Variation: Brush tops of tarts with strained, warmed apricot preserves.

LEMON MERINGUE TARTLETS

Makes: 36 tartlets; serves: 8 to 12

Of course, homemade curd is far superior to store-bought, but either way, these tarts are going to be a real success.

36 baked Tartlet Shells (page 519)
¾ cup lemon curd (homemade, page 494, or store-bought)
2 egg whites
⅛ teaspoon cream of tartar
⅓ cup sugar

1. Preheat the oven to 400°F.

2. Place the tartlet shells on a large baking sheet. Fill each half full with lemon curd (about 1 slightly rounded teaspoon per shell).

3. In a medium bowl, combine the egg whites and cream of tartar. Beat on high speed until stiff but not dry. Add the sugar 1 tablespoon at a time, beating well after each addition.

4. Place the meringue mixture into a pastry bag fitted with a star tip. Pipe a generous star of meringue on top of the curd in each shell.

5. Bake 4 to 5 minutes or until browned on the ridges of the stars.

Variations: Use lime curd (page 494) instead of lemon.

Lemon Meringue Tart: Bake a 9-inch tart shell, add full recipe of lemon curd (page 494), double the amount of meringue (use 4 egg whites), spread on top of tart, and continue according to recipe.

WALNUT FUDGE TARTLETS

Makes: 4 dozen; serves: 12 to 16

Because these tartlets are very tiny, they dry out quickly—which is not too terrible, because then they taste like cakey brownies. To keep the fudgy consistency, cover them with plastic wrap or keep them stored in plastic baggies.

2 squares unsweetened chocolate
2 tablespoons butter or margarine
½ cup sweetened condensed milk
2 tablespoons dark brown sugar
2 egg yolks
½ cup chopped walnuts
1 teaspoon vanilla
48 baked Tartlet Shells (page 519)
Confectioners' sugar

1. Preheat the oven to 350°F.

2. In a saucepan, melt the chocolate over low heat. Remove from heat and stir in the butter or margarine until melted. Stir in the condensed milk and brown sugar. Stir in the egg yolks until combined. Stir in the walnuts and vanilla.

3. Spoon about 1 rounded teaspoon of the fudge mixture into each baked pastry cup.

4. Bake 12 to 15 minutes, or until puffy. Cool on rack. Sprinkle with confectioners' sugar.

Variation: Use pecans instead of walnuts.

WHIPPED CREAM TARTLETS

Makes: 36 tarts; serves: 8 to 12

Sieve the jam before measuring. I used orange liqueur, but raspberry or cherry would also be nice.

36 baked Tartlet Shells (page 519)
6 tablespoons sieved jam
1 cup heavy cream
2 tablespoons confectioners' sugar
1 tablespoon fruit-flavored liqueur

1. Arrange the shells on a serving platter. Fill each with ¹/₂ teaspoon jam.

2. In a medium bowl, beat the cream with the sugar and liqueur until stiff peaks hold. Place a large dollop of cream over the jam.

Variation: Use fudge sauce instead of jam.

FILLED PASTRIES

Makes: 45; serves: 12 to 15

If you bake these until lightly browned, they will be soft; richer brown will yield a crispier crust.

1 recipe farmer-cheese pastry (page 519)
1 cup Lekvar (prune or apricot butter; homemade, page 493, or store-bought)

1. Preheat the oven to 375°F.

2. Divide the dough into thirds. Roll out each third until quite thin, ¹/₈ to ¹/₁₆ inch thick. Using a 3-inch biscuit cutter, cut dough into rounds. Place 1 teaspoon filling in the center of each circle. Dampen edge of pastry with water. Fold in half; press edges with tines of fork to seal. Prick top with fork to vent.

3. Place on ungreased baking sheet and bake 20 minutes or until nicely browned. Cool on rack.

Variation: Use any variety of homemade or store-bought fillings; fruit butters (pages 491–92) are especially good.

LITTLE APPLE TURNOVERS

Makes: 9; serves: 9

Most turnovers are too big for a single serving. These are just right.

3 cups chopped, peeled apples
1 tablespoon fresh lemon juice
¹/₃ cup sugar
2 tablespoons currants
1 sheet Pepperidge Farm prepared puff pastry
Confectioners' sugar

1. In a 2-quart saucepan, stir together the apples, lemon juice, and sugar. Cook over medium heat, stirring frequently, 10 minutes or until softened. Stir in currants. Cool.

2. Preheat the oven to 375°F.

3. Thaw pastry according to package directions. Roll out to 12-inch square. Cut into 9 squares. Place 1¹/₂ tablespoons filling in the center of each square. Brush edges of pastry with water and fold over into triangle. Press lightly to seal. Prick top with fork for ventilation.

4. Place on ungreased baking sheets. Bake 20 to 25 minutes or until puffed and golden; cool. Sprinkle with confectioners' sugar.

Variation: Use any prepared pie filling instead of the apple mixture.

STRUDEL

My grandmother used to make her own strudel leaves (paper-thin sheets of dough), a time-consuming and exacting task. Today you can buy phyllo leaves (which are almost identical to strudel leaves) in the freezer compartment of most supermarkets. How the leaves have been handled will affect the ease of preparing your strudel. If, during transport from manufacturer to supermarket or from supermarket to home, the leaves are defrosted and then refrozen, they may be almost impossible to separate when you want to use them. Unfortunately, there is no way to correct this except to buy another box (preferably from a different market).

Strudel leaves can be fussy. In addition to sticking together when improperly stored, they dry out very quickly because they are so thin. When you are making your strudels, keep the unused leaves under plastic wrap or a slightly damp towel (not too damp or the leaves will stick together). Leaves with a small tear here or there are okay for the inner layers, but try to get an intact leaf for the outer layer (the first leaf you use).

You can embellish strudels by adding ground nuts to the crumbs separating the layers. Or use graham cracker crumbs, or make any of your favorite cold breakfast cereals into crumbs and use them between the layers instead of the cornflake or bread crumbs suggested.

Strudels do not have to be limited to dessert items. They also make delicious entrees (pages 177–78) or appetizers (page 74). Strudels are best the day you bake them, when the leaves are crispy, but you can reheat them if they should become soggy.

BASIC STRUDEL

V

Makes: 1 strudel; serves: 6

6 phyllo sheets (12 × 17 inches each), thawed according to package directions

2 to 3 tablespoons melted butter or margarine, or vegetable oil

5 tablespoons cornflake crumbs or unflavored bread crumbs, divided

1½ to 2 cups filling of choice (pages 529–30)

1. Preheat the oven to 350°F.

2. Remove the thawed phyllo sheets from the package. (Reseal the package tightly so that remaining sheets won't dry out.) Place 1 sheet on a work surface, with the long edge parallel to the edge of the work surface. Brush lightly with the butter or margarine and sprinkle lightly with some of the crumbs.

3. Place the next phyllo sheet on top of the first and brush with butter and sprinkle with crumbs, as before. Repeat with the third, fourth, and fifth sheets. Place the last sheet of phyllo on top of the stack.

4. Spoon the filling onto the phyllo, forming a 2 × 12-inch log, 2 inches from the edge of one long border. Fold the short edges over the filling. Starting with the long edge closest to the filling, fold the phyllo up over the filling, encasing it, and then roll up the rest of the phyllo stack (but not too tightly so the strudel doesn't burst). The completed strudel should look like a neat log.

5. Place the strudel, seam side down, on a greased baking sheet and brush the top with any remaining butter or margarine.

6. Bake 30 to 40 minutes, or until golden. Cut into thick slices to serve.

Reheating: If there are any leftovers, they should be refrigerated. They will become noticeably soggy, but will crisp up again when heated in a 350°F oven for 20 to 25 minutes.

APPLE STRUDEL FILLING

— [V] —

Makes: filling for 1 strudel; serves: 6

1 1/2 cups shredded, peeled apples
3 tablespoons sugar
2 tablespoons cornflake crumbs
1 tablespoon melted butter or margarine
1/2 teaspoon ground cinnamon

1. Mix all the ingredients together in a medium bowl.

Variation: Add 1 to 2 tablespoons of dried currants.

SWEET CHERRY STRUDEL FILLING

— [V] —

Makes: filling for 1 strudel; serves: 6

One 16-ounce can pitted dark sweet cherries, drained, juice reserved
1/4 cup sugar
1 teaspoon fresh lemon juice
1/4 teaspoon grated lemon rind
2 tablespoons cornstarch
1 tablespoon kirsch (cherry liqueur) or port wine

1. In a 1-quart saucepan, stir together the drained cherries, the sugar, lemon juice, and lemon rind.

2. In a small bowl, stir together the cornstarch, kirsch, and 2 tablespoons of the cherry juice. Add to cherry mixture in saucepan. Cook, stirring, over medium heat until mixture becomes clear and thickens. Let cool 15 minutes.

Variation: Substitute additional cherry juice for the kirsch.

CHEESE STRUDEL FILLING

— [LO] —

Makes: filling for 1 strudel; serves: 6

1 egg
One 7 1/2-ounce package farmer cheese
2 tablespoons softened cream cheese
1 1/4 teaspoons grated lemon rind
1/4 cup sugar
1 tablespoon all-purpose flour
1/4 cup golden raisins

1. In a medium bowl, beat the egg. Add the farmer cheese, cream cheese, and lemon rind; stir until combined.

2. In a small bowl, stir together the sugar and flour; stir into cheese mixture. Stir in the raisins.

Variation: Substitute grated orange rind for the lemon rind.

FRESH RASPBERRY STRUDEL FILLING

— [V] —

Makes: filling for 1 strudel; serves: 6

1 1/4 cups fresh raspberries
1/3 cup sugar
1 1/2 tablespoons cornstarch
1 tablespoon water

1. In a 1 1/2-quart saucepan, stir together the raspberries and sugar.

2. In a small bowl, stir together the cornstarch and water. Add to raspberries in saucepan. Cook, stirring very gently so that some raspberries stay intact, over medium heat until mixture is very thick and looses opaqueness. Let stand until cool before using in strudel.

Variation: Use cranberry juice cocktail instead of water.

PINEAPPLE STRUDEL FILLING

— V —

Makes: filling for 1 strudel; serves: 6

One 8-ounce can crushed pineapple packed in unsweetened juice, drained, juice reserved
¼ cup sugar
¼ cup orange juice
2 tablespoons cornstarch
1 teaspoon grated orange rind

1. In a 1½-quart saucepan, stir together the drained pineapple and sugar.

2. In a small bowl, stir together the reserved pineapple juice, the orange juice, cornstarch, and orange rind. Add to pineapple in saucepan. Cook, stirring, over medium heat until mixture is very thick and looses opaqueness. Let stand 20 minutes before using.

Variation: Substitute orange liqueur for part of the orange juice.

WALNUT STRUDEL FILLING

— L —

Makes: filling for 1 strudel; serves: 6

1 cup ground walnuts
¼ cup sugar
¼ cup golden raisins
¼ cup sour cream
1 tablespoon melted butter or margarine
1 teaspoon ground lemon rind
¼ teaspoon ground cinnamon

1. In a medium bowl, stir together all the ingredients.

Variation: Substitute ½ cup ground, toasted hazelnuts for ½ cup of the walnuts.

CHEESECAKES

MARBLE CHEESECAKE

— LO —

Makes: one 8½-inch cheesecake; serves: 12 to 16

Although I usually use chocolate cookies for this crust, you can use graham crackers, vanilla wafers, or any other cookie crumbs just as well.

Crust:
17 chocolate wafer cookies, or 1⅓ cups chocolate goldfish cookies
3 tablespoons melted butter or margarine
1 tablespoon sugar

Filling:
Four 8-ounce packages cream cheese, softened
1¼ cups sugar
4 eggs
½ cup Tia Maria, Kahlua, or other liqueur
6 squares semisweet chocolate
½ cup sour cream

1. Preheat the oven to 350°F. Grease a 9-inch springform pan.

2. For the crust, crumble the cookies and place in a blender or food processor container fitted with a steel blade. Cover and process until finely crumbed (you should have 1 cup). Pour into a medium bowl; stir in butter or margarine and 1 tablespoon sugar. Press into the bottom of prepared pan. Bake 8 minutes. Remove from oven and cool.

3. For the filling, in a bowl, beat the cream cheese with 1¼ cups sugar until well combined. Beat in the eggs one at a time until just combined. Beat in the liqueur until just combined. Pour all but ½ cup batter into the pan.

4. In a 1-quart saucepan, melt the chocolate over very low heat. Stir in the sour cream, then the reserved batter.

5. Drop the saucepan batter by large spoonfuls over the batter in the pan. Run a knife back and forth through the batter a few times to distribute the chocolate, being careful not to disturb the bottom crust.

6. Place the springform pan into a larger pan filled with 1¹/₂ inches of very hot water. Bake 1 hour 15 minutes or until puffy and lightly browned on top (the center may still be slightly soft; it will firm up on chilling). Remove from oven to cool to room temperature, then chill until 1 hour before serving.

Variation: Orange Marble Cheesecake: Use an orange-flavored liqueur and 1 tablespoon grated orange rind in the nonchocolate half of the batter.

RASPBERRY SWIRL CHEESECAKE

Makes: one 9-inch cheesecake; serves: 10 to 12

My testers loved this cheesecake. The only complaint was that there were seeds in the raspberries. I tried pureeing, then straining the raspberries, but the cheesecake wasn't as good.

Crust:
1 cup chocolate cookie crumbs (page 532)
2 tablespoons sugar
3 tablespoons melted butter or margarine

Filling:
Three 8-ounce packages cream cheese, softened
¹/₂ cup sour cream
2 eggs
1 cup sugar, divided
One 10-ounce package frozen raspberries in light syrup, thawed

1. Preheat the oven to 350°F. Grease a 9-inch springform pan.

2. Prepare the crust by stirring together the crumbs and 2 tablespoons sugar. Add the melted butter or margarine and stir until combined. Press into prepared pan. Bake 10 minutes; set aside.

3. Prepare the filling. In a medium bowl, beat the cream cheese until fluffy. Beat in the sour cream, then the eggs and all but 2 tablespoons of the 1 cup sugar.

4. Stir together the raspberries in syrup with the remaining 2 tablespoons sugar. Pour over the cheese mixture.

5. Using a large spoon, ladle the cheese mixture (scooping from the bottom, so that the cheese filling becomes somewhat mixed with the raspberries and sauce) into the pan.

6. Place the springform pan into larger pan filled with 1¹/₂ inches of very hot water. Bake 1 hour to 1 hour 15 minutes or until browned on top (the center may still be slightly soft; it will firm up on chilling). Cool to room temperature, then chill.

Variation: Strawberry Swirl Cheesecake: Use one 10-ounce package frozen strawberries in light syrup, thawed; instead of the raspberries.

PUMPKIN CHEESECAKE

Makes: one 8¹/₂-inch cheesecake; serves: 10 to 12

This makes a nice change from pumpkin pie for Thanksgiving.

Crust:
1 cup graham cracker crumbs
3 tablespoons melted butter or margarine
2 tablespoons sugar

Filling:
Three 8-ounce packages cream cheese, softened
1¹/₂ cups sugar
4 eggs
1 cup pumpkin puree (canned)
1 teaspoon ground cinnamon
³/₄ teaspoon ground ginger

1. Preheat the oven to 325°F. Grease an 8¹/₂- or 9-inch springform pan.

2. For the crust, in a medium bowl, stir together the graham cracker crumbs, butter or margarine, and 2 tablespoons sugar. Press into the bottom of the springform pan. Bake 8 minutes. Remove from oven and cool.

3. For the filling, in a large bowl, beat the cream cheese with 1¹/₂ cups sugar until well combined. Beat in the eggs one at a time until just combined. Beat in the pumpkin, cinnamon, and ginger until just combined. Pour all batter into the pan.

4. Place the springform pan into a larger pan filled with 1¹/₂ inches of very hot water. Bake 1 hour 30 to 40 minutes (add 15 minutes extra if you're using an 8¹/₂-inch pan) or until puffy and lightly browned on top (the center may still be slightly soft; it will firm up on chilling). Remove from oven to cool to room temperature, then chill until 1 hour before serving.

Variation: Use chocolate cookie crumbs instead of the graham cracker crumbs.

COOKIES

OATMEAL RAISIN COOKIES

Makes: 2 to 2¹/₂ dozen; serves: 8 to 12

These cookies have lots of raisins—too many, according to some of my testers. You may want to use fewer.

¹/₂ cup whole wheat flour
¹/₂ teaspoon ground cinnamon
¹/₂ teaspoon baking soda
¹/₂ teaspoon salt (optional)
2 cups rolled oats (old-fashioned oatmeal)
1 cup raisins
¹/₂ cup (1 stick) butter or margarine, softened
1 cup sugar
1 egg
2 tablespoons water
1 teaspoon vanilla extract

1. Preheat the oven to 350°F. Thoroughly grease 2 large baking sheets.

2. In a medium bowl, stir together the flour, cinnamon, baking soda, and salt. Stir in the oats and raisins; set aside.

3. In a large bowl, cream the butter or margarine. Add the sugar and beat until light and fluffy. Beat in the egg, water, and vanilla. Beat in the dry ingredients until completely combined.

4. Drop by rounded tablespoons, leaving about 1¹/₂ inches between cookies. Press with fork to flatten slightly.

5. Bake 12 to 15 minutes, or until browned on bottom. Cool on racks.

Variation: For crispier cookies, reduce water to 1 tablespoon and use quick-cooking oats (not instant) instead of the rolled oats.

OATMEAL BAR COOKIES

[V]

Makes: 48 bars or 24 squares; serves: 8 to 12

These are a good after-school snack or lunchbox filler.

1 cup (2 sticks) butter or margarine, softened
1 cup firmly packed light brown or dark brown sugar
2½ cups rolled oats (old-fashioned oatmeal)
1 cup all-purpose flour
2 teaspoons ground cinnamon
1 teaspoon vanilla
1 cup dark or golden raisins
1 cup chopped walnuts

1. Preheat the oven to 350°F. Grease a 9 × 13-inch baking pan.

2. In a large bowl, cream the butter or margarine with the brown sugar until light and fluffy.

3. Beat in the oats, flour, cinnamon, and vanilla.

4. Stir in the raisins and walnuts.

5. Pat into prepared pan. Bake 35 minutes or until the top is golden. Cool completely in pan. Cut into 1 × 2-inch bars or 2-inch squares.

Variation: Use chopped dried apricots instead of raisins.

CORNMEAL SANDIES

[O]

Makes: 6½ dozen; serves: 16 to 20

These are very delicate-tasting cookies and the cornmeal really does give them a "sandy" feel. I like to make the dough ahead of time and freeze it in logs. Then, when unexpected company arrives (or, more likely, when I'm running too late to make a "real" dessert from scratch), I pull out a log or two and bake them up.

2 cups all-purpose flour
1 cup cornmeal
½ teaspoon salt
1 cup (2 sticks) butter or margarine
½ cup sugar
1 egg
1 teaspoon vanilla
Additional sugar

1. In a medium bowl or on a piece of waxed paper, stir together the flour, cornmeal, and salt. In a large bowl, cream the butter or margarine with the ½ cup sugar until light and fluffy. Beat in the egg and vanilla. Beat in the cornmeal mixture.

2. Divide the dough in half and form into two 10-inch logs. Cover each in waxed paper or plastic wrap; chill 1 hour or until firm (or freeze for later use).

3. Preheat the oven to 350°F.

4. Slice the logs into pieces ³/₁₆ inch thick. Place on ungreased baking sheets. Bake 15 to 18 minutes or until slightly browned on the bottom.

5. While the cookies are still warm, roll in additional sugar to coat. Cool on racks.

Variation: Blue Sandies: Use blue cornmeal for a more exotic-looking cookie (it will taste the same).

PEANUT BUTTER COOKIES

Makes: 56 cookies; serves: 12 to 24

If you want chunky peanut cookies, don't use chunky peanut butter instead of smooth, but rather add chopped peanuts to the dough as suggested in the variation.

1 cup all-purpose flour
2/3 cup whole wheat flour
1/2 teaspoon baking powder
1/2 teaspoon baking soda
1/4 teaspoon salt
1 cup creamy peanut butter
1/2 cup (1 stick) butter or margarine, softened
2/3 cup firmly packed brown sugar
1/2 cup sugar
2 eggs

1. Preheat the oven to 375°F.

2. In a large bowl or on a piece of waxed paper, stir together both flours, the baking powder, baking soda, and salt.

3. In a large bowl, cream the peanut butter and butter or margarine with both sugars. Beat in the eggs. Stir in the dry ingredients.

4. Form the dough into 1 1/2-inch balls. Place the balls on ungreased baking sheets, 2 inches apart. Press with the floured tines of a fork to make a cross-hatched design in the top of the cookies.

5. Bake 12 to 14 minutes. Remove from pan and cool on racks.

Variation: Add 2/3 cup chopped cocktail peanuts (salted or unsalted) to the dough after you stir in the dry ingredients.

POPPY SEED COOKIES

Makes: 90; serves: 20 to 30

I think there are plenty of poppy seeds in these, but you may want to add an extra tablespoon. Like with Cornmeal Sandies (page 533), you can shape the dough into logs, then freeze the dough for later use.

1 1/2 cups all-purpose flour
1 cup whole wheat flour
1/2 teaspoon salt (optional)
3 tablespoons poppy seeds
1 cup (2 sticks) butter or margarine, softened
1 cup sugar
2 egg yolks
1 egg
1 teaspoon vanilla extract

1. In a medium bowl or on a piece of waxed paper, stir together both flours and the salt. Stir in the poppy seeds.

2. In a large bowl, cream the butter or margarine with the sugar; beat in the yolks, egg, and vanilla.

3. Beat in the flour–poppy seed mixture. Divide dough into thirds and form each into an 8-inch log. Roll each log in waxed paper and chill until firm, about 2 hours.

4. Preheat the oven to 325°F. Slice the cookies into 1/4-inch-thick rounds. Bake 15 to 18 minutes or until the edges of the cookies are lightly browned. Cool on racks.

Variation: Pine Nut Cookies: Substitute 1 1/3 cups of chopped pine nuts for the poppy seeds (you need lots more pine nuts for flavor).

GINGERBREAD COOKIES

*Makes: 16 to 18 5-inch gingerbread men;
serves: 16 to 18*

*I can't resist making gingerbread men from this
dough, but you can cut any shape you like. The
cookies can be decorated with Confectioners' Sugar
Glaze (page 517).*

2 cups all-purpose flour
2 cups whole wheat flour
1 1/2 tablespoons ground ginger
1 teaspoon ground cinnamon
1 teaspoon baking soda
1/4 teaspoon ground cloves
1/4 teaspoon salt
1/2 cup (1 stick) butter or margarine, softened
1/2 cup firmly packed light brown or dark
   brown sugar
1/2 cup molasses
1/2 cup water

1. In a medium bowl or on a piece of waxed
paper, stir together both flours, the ginger, cinnamon, baking soda, cloves, and salt.

2. In a large bowl, cream the butter or margarine with the brown sugar until combined. Beat
in the molasses and water (the mixture will look
very curdled). Beat in the flour mixture. Form
into a ball and wrap in waxed paper. Chill at
least 1 hour.

3. Preheat the oven to 350°F.

4. Using a floured rolling pin on a floured
surface, roll out the dough (1/2 at a time) until
1/4 inch thick. Cut into cookies with cookie
cutters of desired shape.

5. Place on an ungreased baking sheet; bake
10 to 12 minutes or until the cookies do not
leave an indentation when lightly touched. Let
cool on rack.

Variation: Spice Cookies: Add 1/3 cup dried
currants and 1/2 teaspoon pepper to the dry
ingredients and 1/4 cup more brown sugar
when you cream the butter. Beat 2 eggs into
the butter-sugar mixture before adding the
molasses. Drop by heaping teaspoons onto
greased baking sheets. Bake 10 to 12 minutes at 350°F. Makes 4 dozen.

MOM'S HARD-BOILED EGG COOKIES

Makes: 8 dozen; serves: 20 to 30

*I love these cookies, maybe because they're the only
cookies Mommy ever baked. She is a sensational
cook but never a baker—she left that to my
grandmother, who was a great baker. (It goes
without saying that mom never used whole wheat
flour in her version!)*

6 hard-cooked egg yolks
1 1/2 cups all-purpose flour
3/4 cup whole wheat flour
1/2 teaspoon salt
1 cup (2 sticks) butter or margarine, softened
1 cup sugar
1 teaspoon vanilla

1. Preheat the oven to 350°F.

2. Put the yolks through a fine sieve; set aside.

3. In a medium bowl or on waxed paper, stir
together both flours and the salt.

4. In a large bowl, cream the butter or margarine with the sugar. Beat in the sieved egg
yolks, then the vanilla.

5. Beat in the flour. Place dough in a cookie
press and press into desired shapes on
ungreased cookie sheets. Bake 8 to 10 minutes
or until edges are lightly browned.

Raspberry Roll-Ups

Makes: 48 cookies; serves: 8 to 12

Instead of using the jam filling, you can use just the cinnamon-sugar filling and add raisins or chocolate chips.

½ pound cottage cheese
1 cup (1 stick) butter or margarine, softened
2 cups all-purpose flour
2 tablespoons melted butter or margarine
½ cup seedless raspberry jam, melted
⅔ cup firmly packed dark brown sugar
½ teaspoon ground cinnamon
¾ cup chopped walnuts
1 egg, beaten (optional)
1 tablespoon water (optional)

1. Preheat the oven to 350°F.

2. Put the cottage cheese through a sieve.

3. In a large bowl, beat the cottage cheese and butter or margarine until combined. Stir in the flour to make a smooth pastry. Divide dough into 3 equal parts. If dough is too soft to roll out, refrigerate until it reaches rolling consistency.

4. On a well-floured surface, roll each part of the dough into a 10-inch circle. Brush each circle with melted butter or margarine, then with jam.

5. In a small bowl, combine the brown sugar and cinnamon. Sprinkle each circle with the cinnamon mixture and then with the walnuts. Cut the circles into 16 pie-shaped wedges of equal size. Beginning at the wide end, roll up each wedge. Arrange roll-ups on greased cookie sheets, with seams down. If you desire a shiny finish, beat together egg and water in a small bowl and brush over each roll-up.

6. Bake 30 to 35 minutes or until pastry is browned. Remove from baking sheet and cool on racks.

Variation: Use sieved apricot jam instead of raspberry.

Pecan-Wheat Germ Cookies

Makes: 5 to 6 dozen cookies (depending on shape); serves: 20 to 30

I made these cookies for my "park" friends (the people I meet every morning when I walk my dog), so it was only fitting that I used a cookie cutter in the shape of a dog bone. Because of the brown, textured look, they really did resemble dog biscuits!

1½ cups finely ground pecans
1 cup all-purpose flour
¾ cup whole wheat flour
½ cup honey-toasted wheat germ
¼ teaspoon salt
¾ cup (1½ sticks) butter or margarine, softened
1 cup sugar
1 egg
1 teaspoon vanilla

1. In a medium bowl or on a piece of waxed paper, stir together the pecans, both flours, the wheat germ, and salt.

2. In a large bowl, cream the butter or margarine; add the sugar and beat until combined. Beat in the egg and vanilla. Using a spoon, mix in the pecan-flour mixture. Form into a ball and wrap in waxed paper. Chill 30 minutes.

3. Preheat the oven to 350°F.

4. Using a lightly floured rolling pin on a lightly floured surface, roll out the dough (½ at a time) until ¼ inch thick. Cut into cookies with cookie cutters of desired shape.

5. Place on ungreased baking sheet; bake 12 minutes or until lightly browned.

HAMANTASHEN

Makes: about 20; serves: 5 to 8

Traditionally prepared to celebrate the Jewish holiday of Purim, these cookies represent the three-cornered hat worn by the villain Haman, who tried to murder the entire Jewish population of Persia.

1 ¼ cups all-purpose flour
¾ cup whole wheat flour
¼ teaspoon salt
⅔ cup butter or margarine, softened
⅓ cup sugar
1 egg
3 tablespoons milk
1 teaspoon grated lemon rind
1 teaspoon vanilla extract
1 cup Lekvar (prune or apricot butter; homemade, page 493, or store-bought)

1. In a medium bowl or on a piece of waxed paper, stir together both flours and the salt.

2. In a large bowl, cream the butter or margarine with the sugar. Beat in the egg, milk, lemon rind, and vanilla. Beat in the flour mixture. Flatten dough into two 4 × 6-inch rectangles; cover with waxed paper and chill 1 hour or until fairly firm.

3. Preheat the oven to 350°F. Grease 2 large cookie sheets.

4. Using a floured rolling pin on a well-floured board, roll 1 of the chilled dough rectangles to ¼-inch thickness. Cut the dough into circles with a 3-inch round cookie cutter.

5. Place 1 rounded teaspoon Lekvar in the center of each cookie. Brush the edges of the dough with water. Lift the sides of the dough so that it forms a triangle where the filling shows through the center; pinch the edges of the dough to seal. Place on prepared cookie sheets. Reroll any dough left after cutting out the circles; cut out additional circles to make cookies. Fill and fold as described. Repeat with remaining chilled dough.

6. Bake 15 to 20 minutes or until browned on the bottom.

Variation: Use poppy seed pie filling (available in cans) instead of the Lekvar.

WONTON COOKIES

Makes: 60 cookies; serves: 10 to 15

These crispy cinnamon-sugar cookies are ideal to serve with creamy desserts or fruit salads. You can buy frozen wonton skins, which are thin squares of dough, in Asian markets.

¼ cup sugar
1 teaspoon ground cinnamon
15 frozen wonton skins, thawed
Oil for deep frying

1. In a small bowl, stir together the sugar and cinnamon.

2. Quarter the wonton skins into triangles.

3. In a 3-quart pot, heat the oil until it bubbles when a small piece of wonton skin is dropped in. Add the wonton triangles a few at a time. Cook until browned on both sides, turning if necessary. Lift from oil with a slotted spoon; drain on paper towels. Sprinkle with cinnamon-sugar. Continue until all wonton triangles are cooked.

Variation: Tortilla Cookies: Substitute 8 flour tortillas, cut into eighths, for the wontons.

LEMON SQUARES

Makes: 24; serves: 8 to 12 (or 4 cookie monsters)

Crust:
½ cup all-purpose flour
¼ cup whole wheat flour
½ teaspoon baking powder
¼ teaspoon salt
¾ cup (1½ sticks) butter or margarine, softened
⅓ cup sugar
1 egg

Topping:
4 eggs
½ cup fresh lemon juice
2 teaspoons grated lemon rind
¾ cup sugar
¼ cup all-purpose flour
½ teaspoon baking powder
¼ teaspoon salt
Confectioners' sugar

1. Preheat the oven to 350°F. Grease a 9 × 13 × 2-inch baking pan.

2. Prepare the crust by stirring together both flours, ½ teaspoon baking powder, and ¼ teaspoon salt.

3. In a medium bowl, cream the butter with ⅓ cup sugar. Beat in 1 egg, then the dry ingredients. Spread into prepared pan. Bake 20 minutes or until lightly browned.

4. While the crust is baking, prepare topping. In a medium bowl, beat 4 eggs, the lemon juice, and lemon rind until combined.

5. Stir together ¾ cup sugar, ¼ cup flour, ½ teaspoon baking powder, and ¼ teaspoon salt. Add to lemon mixture and beat until combined. Pour over baked crust. Return to oven and bake 20 minutes longer.

6. Cool in pan. Sprinkle generously with confectioners' sugar. Cut into 2-inch squares.

Variation: Lime Squares: Substitute ⅓ cup lime juice and 1 tablespoon lime rind for the lemon juice and rind.

COCONUTTY COOKIES

Makes: 4 dozen; serves: 12 to 15

You can dress up these cookies by rolling them in additional coconut before baking. Oat flour is available in health food stores.

1¼ cups all-purpose flour
1 cup oat flour or whole wheat flour
1 teaspoon baking powder
¼ teaspoon salt
1 cup (2 sticks) butter or margarine, softened
¾ cup sugar
1 egg
One 7-ounce package sweetened shredded coconut
1 teaspoon vanilla extract

1. Preheat the oven to 325°F.

2. In a medium bowl or on a piece of waxed paper, stir together both flours, the baking powder, and salt.

3. In a large bowl, cream the butter or margarine with the sugar until light and fluffy. Beat in the egg; then the flour mixture. Beat in the coconut and vanilla.

4. Roll into balls about 1½ inches in diameter. Place on ungreased baking sheets.

5. Bake 20 to 25 minutes or until slightly browned. Cool on rack.

Variation: Porcupines: Before placing cookies on baking sheet, roll them in additional coconut.

APRICOT MERINGUE SQUARES

—— O ——

Makes: 35 squares; serves: 12 to 18

You can use prepared apricot pie filling (a thick puree marketed by Solo brand) or Lekvar, but not fruity pie filling, jam, or preserves.

Crust:
1 cup (2 sticks) butter or margarine, softened
$\frac{1}{2}$ cup sugar
2 egg yolks
1 teaspoon vanilla
$\frac{3}{4}$ cup all-purpose flour
$\frac{1}{4}$ cup whole wheat flour
$\frac{1}{2}$ teaspoon baking powder
$\frac{1}{4}$ teaspoon baking soda

Filling:
1$\frac{1}{2}$ cups apricot pie filling or apricot Lekvar
(homemade, page 493, or store-bought)

Topping:
3 egg whites
$\frac{1}{2}$ cup sugar

1. Preheat the oven to 350°F.

2. For the crust, in a medium bowl, cream the butter or margarine and $\frac{1}{2}$ cup sugar. Beat in the egg yolks and vanilla.

3. In a medium bowl or on waxed paper, stir together both flours, the baking powder, and baking soda. Add to the butter mixture. Beat until combined.

4. Spread the dough into an ungreased jelly roll pan ($10\frac{1}{2} \times 15 \times 1$). Spread the apricot filling on the dough.

5. In a medium bowl, using clean beaters, beat the egg whites until frothy. Gradually beat in $\frac{1}{2}$ cup sugar until whites hold firm peaks. Spread the meringue over the apricot filling.

6. Bake 40 minutes or until top starts to brown. Cut into 35 squares.

Variation: Use prune Lekvar instead of the apricot.

APPLE SQUARES

—— V ——

Makes: 15 3 × 2$\frac{1}{2}$-inch squares; serves: 15

I'm not sure if these actually qualify as cookies or as pastry, but either way, with their old-world flavor, they qualify as superb.

Filling:
6 cups sliced, peeled McIntosh apples
$\frac{1}{2}$ cup sugar
$\frac{1}{4}$ cup water
3 tablespoons sieved apricot jam

Dough:
2 cups all-purpose flour
1 cup whole wheat flour
$\frac{1}{2}$ cup sugar
1$\frac{1}{2}$ cups (3 sticks) butter or margarine, very soft
2 tablespoons lemon juice
1 tablespoon grated lemon rind

1. For the filling, place the apples, $\frac{1}{2}$ cup sugar, and the water in a 3-quart saucepan. Cook over medium heat, uncovered, 25 minutes or until apples are very soft, stirring often during the last five minutes of cooking. Remove from heat; stir in apricot jam; set aside.

2. For the dough, combine both flours and $\frac{1}{2}$ cup sugar. Cut in the butter or margarine until mixture resembles cornmeal. Stir in the lemon juice and lemon rind.

3. Preheat the oven to 325°F. Grease a 9 × 13-inch baking pan.

4. Divide dough into 2 balls, one slightly larger than the other. Spread or pat the larger portion of the dough into the bottom of prepared pan. Bake 15 minutes.

5. Gently spread the apple filling over the crust, close to, but not touching, the edges of the pan.

6. Break the remaining dough into pieces. Roll into ropes and form a lattice top. Bake 1 hour

15 minutes or until apple filling is lightly browned around the edge of the pan. Cool in pan. Cut into 15 squares.

Variation: Instead of preparing the applesauce for the filling, use 6 cups store-bought applesauce; drain 15 minutes through cheesecloth, then stir in the apricot preserves. Proceed with recipe.

LADY BROWNIES

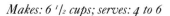

Makes: 24 brownies; serves: 8 to 12

This is basically my sister's recipe for brownies, but I've substituted whole wheat flour for half of the all-purpose flour.

1 cup (2 sticks) butter or margarine
Four 1-ounce squares unsweetened chocolate
2 cups sugar
4 eggs
½ cup whole wheat flour
½ cup all-purpose flour
1 teaspoon vanilla

1. Preheat the oven to 350°F. Grease and flour a 9 × 13-inch baking pan.

2. In a 2-quart saucepan, melt the butter or margarine and the chocolate; set aside.

3. In a large bowl, using an electric mixer, beat the sugar and eggs until thick. On low speed, beat in the melted chocolate, then both flours and the vanilla until just combined.

4. Pour into prepared baking pan. Bake 35 minutes; cool. Cut into 2-inch squares.

Variation: In addition to or instead of nuts, stir in 1 cup of raisins or chocolate chips.

Gentleman Brownies: Stir in 1 cup chopped walnuts when you add the vanilla.

FRUIT DESSERTS

In addition to these delicious meal finishers, you may want to turn to the salad chapter for fruit salads, some of which make excellent desserts.

STRAWBERRY-RASPBERRY STRADA

Makes: 6 ½ cups; serves: 4 to 6

I like to use a glass bowl so you can see the pretty layers. It's great served with vanilla ice cream.

3 cups sliced fresh strawberries
2 cups raspberries (fresh; or unsweetened, frozen)
⅓ cup sugar
2 tablespoons orange liqueur
6 cups cubed pound cake, sponge cake, lady fingers, or similar 1-inch pieces

1. In a 2-quart saucepan, stir together the berries, sugar, and liqueur. Cook, stirring, over medium heat until the sugar is dissolved.

2. Place ⅓ of the cake cubes into a 1½-quart glass dish. Top with ½ of the berry mixture. Press down slightly with the back of a large spoon. Top with ½ of the remaining cake cubes. Pour remaining fruit and syrup over the cubes. Press down slightly with the back of a large spoon. Top with remaining cubes.

3. Chill, covered with plastic wrap, 4 hours or more.

APPLE BROWN BETTY

[V]

Makes: 4 cups; serves: 4

You can add extra raisins if you like more than those just in the raisin bread.

6 slices raisin bread, cubed
¼ cup (½ stick) butter or margarine, melted
4 cups cored, peeled, and thinly sliced apples (about 4)
½ cup firmly packed light brown or dark brown sugar
⅓ cup water
1 tablespoon fresh lemon juice
½ teaspoon cinnamon
¼ teaspoon salt

1. Preheat the oven to 400°F. Heavily grease a 2-quart baking dish.

2. In a medium bowl, toss together the bread cubes and butter or margarine.

3. In a large bowl, combine the apples, brown sugar, water, lemon juice, cinnamon, and salt.

4. Place ½ of the bread cubes in the bottom of the baking dish. Top with the apples (reserving the liquid from the bottom of the apple mixture), then top with remaining bread cubes. Pour the apple liquid over the bread cubes.

5. Bake, covered, 30 minutes. Uncover and bake 15 minutes longer.

Variation: Use white or whole wheat bread instead of raisin bread.

BOURBON BROILED PINEAPPLE

[V] [♥]

Makes: 8 slices; serves: 4

Serve this dish as dessert or even as an appetizer at brunch.

2 tablespoons light brown or dark brown sugar
1 tablespoon butter or margarine
1 tablespoon bourbon
8 slices fresh pineapple (about ½ inch thick)

1. Preheat the broiler.

2. In a small bowl, stir together the brown sugar, butter or margarine, and bourbon.

3. Place the pineapple slices in one layer on a baking sheet. Brush with ½ of the sugar mixture. Broil 6 inches from heat for 5 minutes.

4. Turn the slices and brush with remaining sugar mixture. Broil 5 minutes longer.

Variations: For a nonalcoholic version, use orange juice instead of liquor.

Rum Broiled Pineapple: Use rum instead of bourbon.

STEWED PEACHES AND CHERRIES

Makes: 5 cups; serves: 6 to 10

If you're very conscientious, you'll pit the cherries and peel the peaches before you cook them. A not-too-expensive gadget makes the cherry-pitting job pretty fast. Faster still is leaving the pits in, but remember to warn your family and friends before they bite down on them. As for the peach skin, I kind of like eating it—or maybe that's just my excuse for not peeling.

5 cups sliced peaches
2 cups Bing or Queen Anne cherries
3 cups water
⅓ cup sugar

1. Place all the ingredients in a 4-quart sauce-pan. Bring to a boil over high heat. Reduce heat and simmer uncovered 30 minutes.

Variation: Sugarless Stewed Peaches and Cherries: Omit the sugar and stir in artificial sweetener to taste after the fruit has finished cooking.

ORANGE-BASTED BANANAS

Makes: 8 banana halves; serves: 4

The bananas should be ripe but not overly so. Use bananas with completely yellow skin, with only a few light brown spots; any riper and the bananas may become too mushy when sautéed. This dessert is great as is, but served with vanilla ice cream it becomes celestial.

1½ tablespoons butter or margarine
4 bananas, peeled and halved lengthwise
⅓ cup orange juice
2 tablespoons orange liqueur, or 2 additional tablespoons orange juice plus 1 additional teaspoon sugar
1 tablespoon sugar
1 teaspoon grated orange rind

1. In a large skillet, melt the butter or margarine over medium-high heat.

2. Add the bananas; cook, turning once, until browned on both sides. Remove to serving platter.

3. Add the orange juice, liqueur, sugar, and orange rind to the skillet. Cook over high heat until syrupy and slightly thickened.

4. Return the bananas to the skillet; cook, basting with orange sauce until glazed. Return to platter to serve.

Variation: Serve topped with chopped toasted pecans or walnuts.

STRAWBERRIES WITH ZABAGLIONE

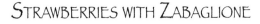

Makes: 2 cups; serves: 4

This sauce cannot be prepared in advance of serving time.

1 egg yolk
1 tablespoon sugar
¼ cup Madeira wine
2 cups strawberries, hulled and rinsed (sliced, if desired)

1. In the top of a double boiler, combine the egg yolk, sugar, and Madeira. Using an electric mixer, beat 5 minutes on high speed. Place over simmering water and beat until thickened, or about the consistency of very soft whipped cream.

2. Place berries into serving cups. Top with zabaglione. Serve immediately.

Variation: Use any berry or combination of berries instead of the strawberries.

FRESH ORANGE SLICES IN LIQUEUR

Makes: 2¹/₂ cups; serves: 4 to 6

Add some fresh raspberries for a colorful presentation.

4 small navel oranges
1 cup water
3 tablespoons sugar
3 tablespoons orange liqueur

1. Grate 2 teaspoons orange rind from one of the oranges. Peel the oranges, removing all the skin and pith. Slice into ¹/₄-inch-thick rounds.

2. In a 2-quart nonreactive saucepan, bring the water, sugar, liqueur, and grated orange rind to a boil over medium-high heat. Let boil 2 minutes.

3. Add the orange slices and bring to a boil; reduce heat and simmer 2 minutes. Remove from heat and let cool in cooking liquid.

Variation: Substitute orange juice for the orange liqueur.

APPLE-PEAR SAUCE

Makes: 4¹/₂ cups; serves: 8 to 12

To peel or not to peel, that is the question. If you are going to make smooth apple-pear sauce using a Foley food mill (a hand-cranked machine that purees foods), you can leave the skins on and they will be separated out in the food mill (and if you are using red apples, you'll have a nice pink sauce). Otherwise, peel before cooking.

6 cups apple chunks (1-inch pieces, peeled or unpeeled)
3 cups pear chunks (1-inch pieces, peeled or unpeeled)
¹/₂ cup sugar
¹/₃ cup water
1 slice lemon

1. Place all the ingredients in a 4-quart pot. Bring to a boil over high heat. Reduce heat and simmer, 30 to 45 minutes, stirring occasionally, or until fruits are very soft (the cooking time will vary depending on the ripeness of the pears). Discard the lemon slice.

2. For chunky sauce: Stir the fruit with a whisk until it is of desired consistency. For smooth sauce: Put fruit through a Foley food mill, or puree in a food processor.

Variation: Old-Fashioned Apple Sauce: Replace the 3 cups pear chunks with apple chunks; omit the lemon. If desired, stir in cinnamon to taste.

POACHED PEARS IN FRUIT JUICE

Makes: 3 cups; serves: 4 to 8

You can poach many different fruits or a combination of fruits (such as peaches, nectarines, grapes, Asian apple-pears, cherries, and blueberries) in this mixture. I especially like the poached pears with grapes.

4 small ripe pears
2 small oranges
1⅓ cups apple juice
¼ cup orange juice
¼ cup sugar
3 tablespoons pineapple juice
½ cup green or red seedless grapes

1. Peel, halve, and core pears. Peel and slice the oranges.

2. In a 2-quart saucepan, combine the apple juice, orange juice, sugar, and pineapple juice. Add the pears, oranges, and grapes. Bring to a boil over medium heat. Reduce heat and simmer, uncovered, 20 minutes.

3. Let fruit cool in syrup; chill.

Variation: Poach peaches, nectarines, or other fruits of choice.

POACHED PEARS IN WINE AND LIME

Makes: 16 pear halves; serves: 6 to 8

It doesn't matter what type of pear you use for this recipe. What will determine poaching time is the ripeness. If the pears are ripe they will finish poaching in 30 minutes. Very underripe pears will require considerably more time, and may need extra sugar.

2 cups white wine (medium dry or fruity)
2 cups water
½ cup sugar
¼ cup fresh lime juice
1 teaspoon grated lime rind
8 ripe pears

1. In a 6-quart pot, stir together the wine, water, sugar, lime juice, and lime rind.

2. Peel, halve, and core the pears. Add to the pot. Bring to a boil over medium-high heat. Reduce heat and simmer 30 minutes or until pears are tender and translucent. Cool.

Variation: Poached Pears with Raspberry Sauce: Prepare Raspberry Sauce (page 555). Pour ⅓ cup on each dessert plate. Drain 1 or 2 poached pear halves per person. Slice thinly; fan the slices and place in the sauce. Garnish with mint leaves.

SICKLE PEARS ON A PILLOW

— V —

Makes: 8 pastries; serves: 8

These pears started out as dumplings, but the pastry wouldn't stay up around the pears as they baked. The taste, however, was great and the pears looked cute on the pastry, so they became pears on a pillow. Use large sickle pears so they don't look too insignificant on a large pastry bed.

1/4 cup sieved raspberry, blackberry, or boysenberry jam
1 teaspoon cornstarch
2 tablespoons sugar
One 17 1/4-ounce package frozen puff pastry sheets, thawed
Additional sugar
8 sickle pears, peeled

1. Preheat the oven to 350°F. Grease a large baking sheet.

2. In a small bowl, stir together the jam and cornstarch; stir in the 2 tablespoons sugar.

3. Unfold the first pastry sheet. Sprinkle the work surface with sugar. Roll the pastry into a 10-inch square. Cut into four 5-inch squares.

4. Place one pear in the center of each pastry square. Spoon 1/8 (about 1 scant tablespoon) of the jam mixture over the pear. Brush the edges of the pastry with water. Pull up the four corners of the pastry to the top of the pear (if you've left the stem on, it should peek out of the pastry) to encase the pear; pinch the edges together to seal. Repeat with remaining pastry sheet, pears, and jam.

5. Place on baking sheet and bake 30 minutes or until pastry is golden and puffed and looks like a pear sitting on a pillow of pastry.

Variation: Pear Turnover: Substitute 1/2 sliced, peeled Bartlett, Anjou, or Bosc pear for the sickle pears. Place on pastry square, drizzle with jam, fold in half, and seal edges of pastry; prick with fork to vent. Bake as above.

SPICED SICKLE PEARS

— V ♥ —

Makes: 30 small pears; serves: 8 to 10

I was torn between placing this recipe here or in the relish chapter. These pears taste great and make lovely gifts when packed in jars. Feel free to double the recipe if you're making it for gift giving.

1 1/2 quarts water
1 1/2 cups sugar
1/2 cup red wine
2 tablespoons red wine vinegar
3 cinnamon sticks
8 whole allspice
6 juniper berries, or 2 teaspoons gin
2 star anise
1 1/2 teaspoons grated lemon rind
30 small sickle pears

1. In a 6-quart pot, combine the water, sugar, wine, vinegar, cinnamon, allspice, juniper, anise, and lemon rind. Bring to a boil. Reduce heat and simmer, uncovered, 15 minutes.

2. Add the pears. Simmer 40 minutes or until tender. Cool; refrigerate overnight for the flavors to meld.

3. Pack in jars (for long-term storage, follow proper canning techniques found in any book on preserving).

Variation: Substitute cranberry juice for the wine.

APPLE CRISP

Makes: 4¹/₂ cups; serves: 4 to 6

This all-American dessert is really excellent served warm with a scoop of vanilla ice cream.

Filling:
6 cups sliced, peeled apples
1 teaspoon fresh lemon juice
¹/₂ cup sugar
1¹/₂ teaspoons ground cinnamon

Topping:
¹/₄ cup all-purpose flour
¹/₄ cup whole wheat flour
3 tablespoons sugar
3 tablespoons butter or margarine
¹/₂ cup quick-cooking oatmeal

1. Preheat the oven to 350°F. Grease a 2-quart casserole.

2. For the filling, toss the apples with lemon juice in the casserole. Add ¹/₂ cup sugar and the cinnamon; toss to combine.

3. For the topping, in a medium bowl, stir together both flours and 3 tablespoons sugar. Using a pastry blender or two knives, cut the butter into the flour mixture until crumbly. Stir in the oatmeal. Sprinkle over the apples in the casserole.

4. Bake 1 hour or until topping is slightly browned.

Variation: Add ¹/₂ cup chopped walnuts to the topping.

CHOCOLATE-DIPPED STRAWBERRIES

Makes: 15 to 24 strawberries; serves: 5 to 8

Not only are these delicious, but they are extremely easy to prepare. You can also use this chocolate mixture as a fondue—just melt the ingredients together and let guests dip for themselves.

¹/₂ cup semisweet chocolate chips
¹/₂ ounce unsweetened chocolate
3 tablespoons heavy cream
15 extra-large strawberries (or 24 small)

1. In a small pot, melt both chocolates and the cream.

2. Dip the strawberries. Place on tray lined with aluminum foil to cool. Chill until serving time.

Variation: Use dried apricots instead of strawberries.

CARAMELIZED GRAPES

Makes: 12 to 15 clusters; serves: 4 to 6

I first tasted these in Vienna, where they were sold on skewers from an open-air stand. They have to be made just a few hours before serving time or the caramel glaze starts to melt. Although I prefer green grapes for this use, you can use either red or green—just be sure they're seedless. I find it easier to dip small clusters of grapes than skewered grapes. Be sure to keep your fingers away from the hot sugar syrup.

12 to 15 clusters of 2 to 3 grapes each
¼ cup water
½ cup sugar

1. Rinse the grapes well in advance of the time you want to use them so they are completely dried before dipping.

2. Line a baking sheet with foil; grease the foil.

3. Put the water in a 1-quart saucepan. Add the sugar. Cook, stirring, over high heat until the mixture comes to a boil. Let boil 3 minutes without stirring.

4. Stir until syrup starts to turn a light gold; remove from heat. Dip the grapes and place on prepared sheet.

MOUSSES, PUDDINGS, AND CUSTARDS

LEFTOVER COCONUT RICE PUDDING

Makes: 4 cups; serves: 6 to 8

This is not rice pudding that is left over, but rather rice pudding made from leftover rice. I devised it as something to do with all that extra white rice from my take-out Chinese food. The pudding will look very thick and pasty after cooking in the cornstarch. Don't worry; it thins and gets creamy as it cools.

3 cups water
1½ cups cooked rice
⅔ cup sweetened condensed milk
1 cup chopped sweetened coconut
1 teaspoon vanilla
¼ teaspoon salt
2 tablespoons cornstarch
2 tablespoons water
1 egg

1. In a 2-quart saucepan, stir together the water, rice, and condensed milk. Bring to a boil over medium-high heat. Reduce heat and simmer, uncovered, 40 minutes or until the rice is very soft and swollen.

2. Stir in the coconut, vanilla, and salt; simmer 5 minutes longer.

3. In a medium bowl, stir together the cornstarch and water. Add the egg and beat until combined. Gradually stir in 1 cup of the rice mixture. Return to pot and continue cooking, stirring constantly, until mixture just comes to a boil.

Variation: Coconutty Rice Pudding: For a more intense coconut flavor, substitute sweetened cream of coconut (such as Coco Casa or Coco Lopez) for the sweetened condensed milk.

RAISIN BREAD PUDDING

🔲

Makes: 4 cups; serves: 4

This dessert is delicious just as is, but it is also super-duper when served with a custard sauce or Creme Anglaise (page 554).

4 slices raisin bread, cubed
2 tablespoons butter or margarine, melted
2 eggs
1/3 cup sugar
1/4 teaspoon ground cinnamon
1/4 teaspoon ground nutmeg
1/4 teaspoon salt
1 1/3 cups very warm milk
1 teaspoon vanilla

1. Preheat the oven to 350°F. Grease a 1 1/2-quart casserole.

2. Put the bread in prepared casserole. Toss with the melted butter or margarine.

3. In a medium bowl, beat the eggs; add the sugar, cinnamon, nutmeg, and salt. Beat until combined.

4. Gradually stir in the milk (try not to create too much foam). Stir in the vanilla. Pour over the bread.

5. Bake 45 to 50 minutes, or until a knife inserted in the center comes out clean. Serve warm or chilled.

Variation: Use plain white or whole wheat bread.

CRANBERRY BREAD PUDDING

🔲 ♥

Makes: 5 cups; serves: 6 to 8

You can use fruit other than the cranberries, but you will want to reduce the sugar to 1/3 cup.

2 eggs
2 cups milk
1/2 cup sugar
1 teaspoon vanilla
1/4 teaspoon ground nutmeg
3 cups whole wheat bread cubes
1 cup chopped cranberries

1. Preheat the oven to 350°F. Grease a 2-quart casserole.

2. In a large bowl, beat the eggs. Add the milk, sugar, vanilla, and nutmeg. Add the bread cubes and cranberries and let stand 30 minutes. Pour into prepared casserole.

3. Place casserole in a larger pan and fill that with enough boiling water to come 1 inch up the side of the casserole. Bake 50 minutes or until a wooden pick inserted in the center comes out clean.

Variation: Use 1 teaspoon cinnamon instead of the nutmeg.

ORANGE POLENTA PUDDING

[O]

Makes: 2 3/4 cups; serves: 4 to 6

This is basically a dessert spoonbread. Serve it with Raspberry Sauce (page 555) or Orange Sauce (page 552, step 1) for extra flavor. You can make the polenta from scratch or use instant polenta.

1 cup orange juice
3 eggs, separated
1/2 cup sugar
3 tablespoons melted butter or margarine
2 tablespoons orange liqueur or additional
    orange juice
1 tablespoon grated orange rind
1 1/2 cups cooked polenta (page 307)

1. Preheat the oven to 350°F. Grease a 2-quart casserole or soufflé dish.

2. In a large bowl, beat the orange juice, egg yolks, sugar, butter or margarine, liqueur, and orange rind until thoroughly combined. Beat in the polenta until smooth.

3. In a separate bowl, beat the egg whites until stiff but not dry. Fold into the orange mixture. Pour into prepared pan.

4. Bake 55 minutes or until a knife inserted in the center comes out clean.

Variation: Add 1 teaspoon ground ginger when you add the orange rind.

HONEY COUSCOUS PUDDING

[L ♥]

Makes: 4 1/2 cups; serves: 6 to 8

You may want to add extra honey for a sweeter pudding. If you like rose water, substitute it to taste for the ground cardamom.

1 quart milk
1/3 cup honey
3/4 cup couscous
1/2 cup golden raisins
1/4 teaspoon ground cardamom
1/8 teaspoon salt, or to taste

1. In the top of a double boiler, stir together the milk and honey. Place over simmering water. Stir in the couscous, raisins, cardamom, and salt.

2. Cook, uncovered, 30 to 35 minutes or until thickened, stirring occasionally.

Variation: For a richer pudding, substitute light cream or half-and-half for part of the milk.

Rum Flan

Makes: 1 ring; serves: 4 to 6

This flan has a very distinct rum flavor; for a milder version use only half the rum and replace the remaining half with additional milk. It's important to let the flan stand (refrigerated) overnight to allow the caramel to melt into a sauce.

1/3 cup water
2/3 cup sugar, divided
3 eggs
1 cup milk
1/4 cup light or dark rum
1 teaspoon vanilla

1. Preheat the oven to 350°F. Grease a 4-cup ring mold.

2. In a 1-quart saucepan, stir together the water and 1/3 cup of the sugar. Bring to a boil over high heat, stirring until the sugar is dissolved. Continue to boil until the syrup starts to darken and turn amber, about 5 to 6 minutes. Pour into the mold.

3. In a medium bowl, beat the eggs; add the milk, the remaining 1/3 cup sugar, the rum, and vanilla. Mix until just combined (try not to create too much foam). Pour over the sugar in the mold.

4. Place the mold into a larger container and fill that with enough boiling water to come 1 inch up the ring mold. Bake 35 minutes or until a knife inserted in the center comes out clean. Chill overnight. Unmold onto serving plate.

Variation: For a nonalcoholic version, substitute milk for the rum.

Sorbets

Anisette Raspberry Sorbet

Makes: 2 1/2 cups; serves: 8

The licorice flavor of the anisette complements the raspberries beautifully. If you are not a licorice fan, substitute a fruit-flavored liqueur for the anisette. Because of the high alcohol content, allow 24 hours for the sorbet to freeze completely.

4 cups raspberries
1/2 cup sugar
1/2 cup water
1/4 cup anisette liqueur

1. Place all the ingredients in a 2-quart saucepan. Bring to a boil over medium-high heat. Reduce heat and simmer, uncovered, 5 minutes. Cool to room temperature.

2. Strain through a coarse strainer, mashing to obtain as much pulp but as few seeds as possible.

3. Pour into a metal bowl and place in the freezer for 2 hours.

4. Beat the sorbet with an electric mixer until the texture is uniform; return to the freezer.

5. Repeat step 4 every couple of hours until sorbet is completely frozen.

6. For a fluffy consistency, about 1 hour before serving put the frozen sorbet in a food processor container fitted with a steel blade. Cover and process until the ice crystals are broken up.

7. Return to the freezer until serving time.

Variation: Substitute orange, raspberry, or cherry liqueur for the anisette.

Port Wine–Plum Sorbet

[V]

Makes: 3 cups; serves: 4 to 6

You may have to adjust the amount of sugar to your own taste. Plums come in many varieties, which will affect the sweetness of the fruit (as will its ripeness). I used fairly tart plums when I tested this recipe. Start with half the sugar called for and then taste until you get the flavor you prefer. Bear in mind that freezing lessens the sweetness of the puree. Because of the high alcohol content, allow 24 hours for the sorbet to freeze completely.

2 cups quartered ripe plums
³⁄₄ cup water
¹⁄₂ cup sugar
¹⁄₃ cup port wine
¹⁄₈ teaspoon ground nutmeg

1. Place all the ingredients in a 1¹⁄₂-quart saucepan. Bring to a boil. Reduce heat and simmer 5 minutes or until fruit is tender. Remove from heat and cool to room temperature.

2. Place the mixture in a blender or food processor container fitted with a steel blade. Cover and process until smooth.

3. Pour into a metal bowl and place in the freezer for 2 hours.

4. Beat the sorbet with an electric mixer until the texture is uniform; return to the freezer.

5. Repeat step 4 every couple of hours until sorbet is completely frozen.

6. For a fluffy consistency, about 1 hour before serving put the frozen sorbet in a food processor container fitted with a steel blade. Cover and process until the ice crystals are broken up.

7. Return to the freezer until serving time.

Variation: For a nonalcoholic version, use apple juice instead of wine.

Grapefruit Sorbet

[V] [♥]

Makes: 3 cups; serves: 6 to 8

This is one of my favorite sorbets to serve as intermezzo (a small sorbet served between courses to cleanse the palate). You may have to fiddle with the ingredients. The grapefruits I used were quite sweet, so I used ¹⁄₄ cup sugar and added lemon juice for tartness. You may need more sugar and less lemon juice if your grapefruits are extremely tart.

2 cups fresh grapefruit juice
1 cup water
¹⁄₄ cup sugar
1 tablespoon fresh lemon juice
1 tablespoon grated grapefruit rind

1. In a 2-quart saucepan, stir together all the ingredients. Bring to a boil; reduce heat and simmer, uncovered, 5 minutes. Cool to room temperature.

2. Pour into a metal bowl and place in the freezer for 2 hours.

3. Beat the sorbet with an electric mixer until the texture is uniform; return to the freezer 1 to 2 hours longer.

4. Repeat step 3 until sorbet is completely frozen.

5. For a fluffy consistency, about 1 hour before serving put the frozen sorbet in a food processor container fitted with a steel blade. Cover and process until the ice crystals are broken up.

6. Return to the freezer until serving time.

Variation: Mint Grapefruit Sorbet: When the sorbet has finished cooking, add ¹⁄₂ cup lightly packed mint leaves, then place in a blender or food processor container fitted with a steel blade. Cover and process until the mint is finely chopped. Cool and proceed according to directions.

KIWI~PINEAPPLE SORBET

Ⓥ ♥

Makes: 3¹/₂ cups; serves: 4 to 6

The kiwifruit gives this sorbet a tart undertone—and an exquisite color. Because of the high alcohol content, allow 24 hours for the sorbet to freeze completely.

2 cups peeled, cubed kiwifruit (4 large or
    6 small)
1¹/₂ cups unsweetened pineapple juice
¹/₃ cup sugar
¹/₄ cup orange liqueur
1 teaspoon grated lime rind

1. Place all the ingredients in a 1¹/₂-quart saucepan. Bring to a boil. Remove from heat and cool to room temperature.

2. Pour into a blender or food processor container fitted with a steel blade. Cover and process until smooth.

3. Pour into a metal bowl and place in the freezer for 2 hours.

4. Beat the sorbet with an electric mixer until the texture is uniform; return to the freezer.

5. Repeat step 4 every couple of hours until sorbet is completely frozen.

6. For a fluffy consistency, about 1 hour before serving put the frozen sorbet in a food processor container fitted with a steel blade. Cover and process until the ice crystals are broken up.

7. Return to the freezer until serving time.

Variation: For a nonalcoholic version, use orange juice instead of liqueur.

CREPES AND SAUCES

Crepes are very delicate pancakes. It's important for the pan to be hot or the crepes will stick. You can turn the crepes with a spatula, or by just flipping them in the pan.

CREPES SUZETTE

ⓁⓄ

Makes: 12 crepes; serves: 4 to 6

I use freshly squeezed orange juice to get the very best flavor for this recipe. Don't forget—to avoid singed eyebrows, keep your head back when you flambé the crepes.

¹/₄ cup (¹/₂ stick) butter or margarine
³/₄ cup orange juice
1¹/₂ teaspoons grated orange rind
1 tablespoon sugar
3 tablespoons orange liqueur
12 Dessert Crepes (page 553) or Orange
    Crepes (page 553)
3 tablespoons brandy
Confectioners' sugar

1. In a large skillet (preferably nonaluminum), melt the butter or margarine over medium-high heat. Stir in the orange juice, orange rind, and sugar. Bring to a boil; remove from heat.

2. Stir in the orange liqueur. Place over low heat. Dip each crepe in the orange sauce until coated; fold into quarters and place on a heat-proof platter.

3. In a small saucepan, heat the brandy over low heat. Ignite it (preferably using a long match or straw) and pour over the crepes. After the flames subside, sprinkle with confectioners' sugar.

DESSERT CREPES

Makes: 10 to 12 7½-inch crepes; serves: 4 to 5

Crepes are versatile items. You can roll preserves or prepared pie fillings in the crepes and serve them as dessert or brunch. You can use crepes as wrappers for sweet blintzes, or just serve them folded with fruit or chocolate sauce.

1⅓ cups milk
½ cup all-purpose flour
½ cup whole wheat flour
2 eggs
3 tablespoons melted butter or margarine
3 tablespoons sugar
1 teaspoon vanilla extract
½ teaspoon salt

1. Place all the ingredients in a blender or food processor container fitted with a steel blade. Cover and process until smooth. Let stand 30 minutes.

2. Heat a medium slope-sided skillet (10 inches across the top, 7½ inches across the bottom) over medium heat until a drop of water dances across the surface before evaporating. Brush lightly with oil, butter, or margarine.

3. Pour a scant ¼ cup batter into the pan and tilt, rotating the pan, so that the batter spreads over the bottom.

4. Cook until the top of the crepe is no longer shiny and the bottom is browned. Gently turn the crepe and cook second side until browned in spots.

Variation: Use ¼ teaspoon almond extract instead of the teaspoon of vanilla extract.

ORANGE CREPES

Makes: 10 to 12 crepes; serves: 4 to 5

Use these for Crepes Suzette (page 552).

¾ cup orange juice
⅔ cup milk
½ cup all-purpose flour
½ cup whole wheat flour
2 eggs
3 tablespoons melted butter or margarine
2 tablespoons sugar
1 teaspoon grated orange rind
½ teaspoon salt

1. Place all the ingredients in a blender or food processor container fitted with a steel blade. Cover and process until smooth. Let stand 30 minutes.

2. Heat a medium slope-sided skillet (10 inches across the top, 7½ inches across the bottom) over medium heat until a drop of water dances across the surface before evaporating. Brush lightly with oil, butter, or margarine.

3. Pour a scant ¼ cup batter into the pan and tilt, rotating the pan, so that the batter spreads over the bottom.

4. Cook until the top of the crepe is no longer shiny and the bottom is browned. Gently turn the crepe, and cook second side until browned in spots.

Variation: Substitute 1 teaspoon lemon rind for the orange rind.

CRÈME ANGLAISE

— LO —

Makes: 1 cup; serves: 4 to 6

This is a delicious custard sauce that you can serve over bread puddings, with poached pears, or with anything that you'd like to spruce up.

1 cup milk
3 egg yolks
¼ cup sugar
½ teaspoon vanilla extract

1. In a 1½-quart saucepan, bring the milk to a simmer.

2. While the milk is heating, using a whisk, beat the yolks with the sugar until light and lemon colored.

3. Gradually whisk in ½ of the milk. Stir the yolk mixture into the remaining milk in the saucepan.

4. Over low heat, cook the custard, stirring constantly with a wooden spoon, until the mixture comes to a simmer (it must not boil or the mixture will curdle). The sauce is finished when it is thick enough to coat the back of a spoon.

CHOCOLATE SAUCE

— L —

Makes: 1 ½ cups; serves: 6 to 12

This is a pretty versatile sauce. When chilled, it's quite thick, rather like creamy chocolate pudding. When warm, it's very thin and makes a fine dipping sauce for fruits, especially bananas, kiwis, or strawberries.

⅓ cup water
½ cup sugar
Two 1-ounce squares unsweetened chocolate
One 1-ounce square semisweet chocolate
½ cup heavy cream
1 tablespoon Frangelico or other liqueur (optional)

1. Place the water in a 1½-quart saucepan; stir in the sugar. Cook on medium-high heat until mixture comes to a boil, stirring frequently until sugar is dissolved.

2. In a 1-quart saucepan, melt both chocolates with the heavy cream. Stir in sugar syrup and, if desired, liqueur.

3. Serve warm, at room temperature, or chilled. Store in refrigerator if not using all at once.

Variations: For a bittersweet sauce, substitute extra unsweetened chocolate for the semisweet.

Chocolate Mousse: Whip 1 cup heavy cream; fold in 1 recipe room-temperature chocolate sauce. Chill. Makes 2½ cups

RASPBERRY SAUCE

Makes: 1 cup; serves: 6 to 8

*Use this sauce drizzled on crepes or serve it with
poached fruit or as a dip.*

One 10-ounce package frozen raspberries in
    light syrup, thawed
2 tablespoons sugar
1 tablespoon raspberry or orange liqueur
    (optional)
1 teaspoon cornstarch

1. Place the raspberries and syrup in a blender
container. Cover and process until pureed.
Sieve to remove the seeds.

2. Place the raspberry puree, sugar, liqueur,
and cornstarch in a 1-quart saucepan. Stir until
completely combined. Cook over medium
heat, stirring, until mixture comes to a boil.
Cool.

⎣ ***Variation:*** Peach Melba: Top canned
peach halves with vanilla ice cream and
drizzle with raspberry sauce.

Coffee

Berliner   557

After-Dinner Coffee   558

Tea

Fresh Mint Tea   558

Fresh Ginger Tea   558

Hot Apple Tea   559

Fruit Drinks

Limeade   559

Mulled Cider   560

Dominican Pineapple Cider   560

Blender Fruit Shakes

Lasso   561

Banana-Blueberry Smoothie   561

Persimmon-Pineapple Thick Shake   561

Pineapple-Banana Thick Shake   562

Frozen Fruit Shake   562

Raspberry-Watermelon Cooler   562

Orange Not Quite Julius   563

Fresh Piña Colada   563

Meetz   564

Party Drinks

Virgin Mary Mix   564

Party Punch   564

Sangria   565

Pink Champagne Punch   565

Heavenly Eggnog   565

Homemade Mocha Cream Liqueur   566

Malted Milk   566

Chocolate Egg Cream   566

Coffee

I think that coffee tastes vary so widely that a basic recipe for perfect coffee would be presumptuous on my part (especially since my preference is for fairly weak coffee—far from perfect for many people). However, once you've prepared your perfect cup of coffee, there are many terrific things you can do with it. Following are two of my favorites.

Berliner
L

Makes: 4 glasses; serves: 4

My father introduced the family to this treat, whose origins go to Berlin. A clever trick of my mother's is to freeze leftover coffee into ice cubes so that when making Berliners or even plain iced coffee, the ice cubes don't dilute the flavor as they melt.

16 ice cubes
4 cups iced coffee
Cream or milk (optional)
Sugar or sweetener (optional)
4 scoops vanilla ice cream

1. Place 4 of the ice cubes in each of 4 tall glasses. Pour 1 cup of coffee into each glass.

2. Flavor with cream and sugar to taste, if desired. Top each glass with 1 scoop of ice cream.

Variation: Substitute coffee or chocolate ice cream for the vanilla.

AFTER-DINNER COFFEE

Makes: 4 cups; serves: 4

Depending on which liqueurs you prefer, there are a host of different coffees you can make. Some of my favorite liqueurs are Kahlua (coffee-flavored), Tia Maria (chocolate-flavored), Amaretto (almond-flavored), and Frangelica (hazelnut-flavored).

½ cup heavy cream
1 tablespoon sugar
3 cups hot coffee (regular or decaffeinated)
½ cup liqueur of choice
Sweetener, to taste

1. In a medium bowl, beat the cream with the sugar until stiff peaks form.

2. In a pitcher or coffee pot, stir together the coffee and liqueur, and additional sweetener, if desired. Pour into 4 coffee cups. Top each with a generous dollop of the whipped cream.

Variations: Vanilla Whipped Cream: Add 1 teaspoon vanilla to the cream before beating.

Chocolate Whipped Cream: Add 2 tablespoons cocoa plus an additional 2 tablespoons sugar to the cream before beating.

Coffee Whipped Cream: Add 2 teaspoons instant coffee plus an additional 1 tablespoon sugar to the cream before beating.

TEA

FRESH MINT TEA

Makes: scant 3 cups; serves: 3 to 4

Refreshing is the right word for mint tea. It's also good to sip if you have a slightly upset stomach.

3 cups water
3 cups lightly packed mint leaves
Fresh lime or lemon wedges (optional)
Sweetener (optional)

1. In a 1½-quart saucepan, bring the water to a boil over high heat; remove from heat. Stir in the mint leaves; let steep 10 to 15 minutes or until leaves lose their bright green color and start to sink to the bottom of the pot.

2. Strain the tea; discard the leaves. If desired, squeeze in the lime and drop in the squeezed wedges; add sweetener.

Variation: Iced Mint Tea: Chill and serve over ice cubes.

FRESH GINGER TEA

Makes: ½ cup; serves: 1

Since ginger is a known stomach settler, I use this tea medicinally. I also find it excellent when you're fighting off a cough. As an extra bonus, it's got a great taste.

1 teaspoon freshly grated ginger root
½ cup boiling water
Sweetener, to taste
1 lemon wedge

1. Place the ginger in a cup. Pour in the boiling water; sweeten as desired.

2. Strain out the ginger after 5 minutes (or leave it in and enjoy the pulpy texture). Squeeze in the lemon and drop in the squeezed wedge.

Variation: Use a lime wedge instead of lemon.

HOT APPLE TEA

Makes: 5 cups; serves: 6 to 8

When I have a cold I get very tired of drinking plain tea, so I mix up a batch of fruit tea (apple or orange). You can stir the ingredients together, then just heat one cup at a time as you need it. If you're so inclined, a little rum doesn't hurt this mixture at all.

3 cups steeped tea
2 cups apple juice
1 tablespoon fresh lemon juice
Sweetener, to taste

1. In a 1½-quart saucepan, stir together the tea and both juices. Add sweetener, if desired.

2. Heat over medium heat until warmed.

Variation: Substitute orange juice for the apple.

FRUIT DRINKS

LIMEADE

Makes: 1 quart; serves: 4 to 6

Summer and country and lemonade are almost as American as apple pie. Lemonade or limeade—they're both just perfect when the weather's steamy.

2 ¾ cups cold water
1 cup fresh lime juice
⅔ cup sugar
¼ teaspoon grated lime rind
Ice

1. In a pitcher or other container, stir together the water, lime juice, sugar, and rind until sugar dissolves. Chill.

2. Serve over ice.

Variation: Lemonade: Use lemon juice and rind instead of lime.

MULLED CIDER

Ⓥ♥

Makes: 4¹/₄ cups; serves: 4 to 6

This is a perfect beverage for a cool autumn evening.

1 quart apple cider
¼ cup firmly packed light brown or dark
    brown sugar
2 cinnamon sticks
8 whole cloves
8 whole allspice
4 juniper berries

1. Place all the ingredients in a 1¹/₂-quart saucepan. Bring to a simmer. Simmer, uncovered, 15 minutes.

Variation: Add rum to taste.

DOMINICAN PINEAPPLE CIDER

Ⓥ♥

Makes: 4¹/₂ cups; serves: 4 to 6

My friend Mario Alvarez said his family in the Dominican Republic makes this all the time. It's certainly a good use for pineapple skin, which usually gets thrown out. I found this cider just a hair too sweet, but Mario assures me that it was just right and that he drinks this even sweeter.

Rind and cores from 1 pineapple
4 cups water
¾ cup firmly packed light brown or dark
    brown sugar

1. Rinse the rind thoroughly. Cut into quarters (if not already quartered). Cut each quarter into thirds. Place in a large bowl. Add the water, sugar, and any available pineapple scraps to the bowl.

2. Cover lightly with waxed paper; let stand 3 days, stirring occasionally, or until a thin white film forms on top. Stir film into cider.

3. Strain the juice into a pitcher; chill.

Variation: Use granulated sugar instead of brown.

BLENDER FRUIT SHAKES

These are great snacks that you won't have to twist anyone's arm to drink. Because they're made with fresh fruit, they're loaded with vitamins. Preparing the drinks in the blender means that all the fiber remains in the drink. The variations include adult versions of these drinks.

LASSO

Makes: 1 ¼ cups; serves: 1 to 2

This refreshing Indian beverage can be made with other soft-fleshed fruits, such as papaya, peaches, or nectarines.

½ cup unflavored yogurt
⅓ cup mango cubes
¼ cup orange juice
2 ice cubes
2 teaspoons sugar, or to taste

1. Place all the ingredients in a blender container. Cover and blend until smooth.

Variation: Add ½ teaspoon fresh minced ginger, or ¼ teaspoon ground ginger.

BANANA~BLUEBERRY SMOOTHIE

Makes: 2 ⅓ cups; serves: 3 to 4

1 cup blueberries
¾ cup banana chunks
¾ cup apple juice
3 ice cubes

1. Place all the ingredients in a blender container. Cover and blend until smooth.

Variations: Use orange or pineapple juice instead of the apple.

For an alcoholic version, add blackberry brandy or orange liqueur, to taste.

PERSIMMON~PINEAPPLE THICK SHAKE

Makes: 2 ½ cups; serves: 3 to 4

It's very important that the persimmon be very ripe because an underripe persimmon will feel like a wad of cotton in your mouth.

2 cups fresh pineapple cubes
¾ cup very ripe persimmon cubes
3 ice cubes

1. Place all the ingredients in a blender container. Cover and blend until smooth.

Variation: Add peach schnapps, to taste.

PINEAPPLE-BANANA THICK SHAKE

Makes: 2 ¹/₂ cups; serves: 3 to 4

2 cups fresh pineapple cubes
¾ cup banana chunks
½ cup orange juice
3 ice cubes

1. Place all the ingredients in a blender container. Cover and blend until smooth.

Variations: Use cranberry cocktail instead of orange juice.

For an alcoholic version, add rum, to taste.

FROZEN FRUIT SHAKE

Makes: 2 cups; serves: 2 to 3

You can use banana slices, blueberries, peaches, raspberries, strawberries, or any combination thereof as the frozen fruit.

1 cup unsweetened frozen fruit
1 cup milk
Sweetener, to taste (optional)

1. Place all the ingredients in a blender container. Cover and blend until smooth.

Variation: Add ¹/₄ teaspoon vanilla extract to the blender.

RASPBERRY-WATERMELON COOLER

Makes: 1 quart; serves: 4 to 6

You may want to add some sweetener, depending on your own taste and/or the sweetness of the watermelon. If you don't want the raspberry seeds, strain the fruits before adding the soda.

3 cups cubed, pitted watermelon, divided
One 10-ounce package frozen raspberries in
   light syrup
1 cup club soda or seltzer
Sugar, to taste (optional)

1. Place 1¹/₂ cups of the watermelon in a blender container. Add the frozen raspberries, breaking the block into smaller pieces. Cover and blend until smooth (strain if desired). Pour into a 1-quart (or larger) pitcher.

2. Add remaining 1¹/₂ cups watermelon to blender container. Cover and blend until smooth. Add to the pitcher. Stir in the soda; add sugar, if desired.

Variation: Add 1 cup blueberries when you add the second 1¹/₂ cups of watermelon to the blender.

ORANGE NOT QUITE JULIUS

[L]

Makes: 1 1/2 cups; serves: 2 to 3

When I was in college at New York University there was an Orange Julius stand on 8th Street. I loved the flavor of these shakes, which at that time came with or without a raw egg. This is as close as I can come to that fondly remembered beverage. Be sure to use cream of coconut—which is a sweetened product available canned—not the unsweetened coconut milk (page 497).

1 cup orange juice
3 tablespoons cream of coconut (such as Coco Casa or Coco Lopez)
2 tablespoons nonfat dry milk powder
2 ice cubes
1/2 teaspoon vanilla extract

1. Place all the ingredients in a blender container. Cover and blend until smooth.

FRESH PIÑA COLADA

[L]

Makes: 1 2/3 cups; serves: 2 to 3

Most piña coladas are made with pineapple juice, but I use fresh pineapple for a truly divine treat. Be sure to use cream of coconut—which is a sweetened product available canned—not the unsweetened coconut milk (page 497).

1 cup chopped fresh pineapple
1/3 cup cream of coconut (such as Coco Casa or Coco Lopez)
2 to 3 tablespoons rum
2 tablespoons milk
2 ice cubes

1. Place all the ingredients in a blender container. Cover and blend until smooth.

Variation: Omit the rum and reduce the cream of coconut to 1/4 cup.

MEETZ

Makes: 2 quarts (8 cups); serves: 12 to 16

Meetz means "juice" in Hebrew. But it's quite thick and sweet—really much more like fruit nectar than juice. It's nice with seltzer or club soda as well as plain. If you have a Foley food mill you can just cut the fruit in chunks and then put it through the mill to remove the skin and seeds. Otherwise, peel and core the fruit before cooking and skip the food-mill step.

6 cups chopped (unpeeled) overripe pears or
    other fruit
6 cups water
½ cup sugar
3 tablespoons lemon juice

1. In a 4-quart pot, stir together the pears, water, and sugar. Bring to a boil. Reduce heat and simmer 45 minutes. Run the pears through a Foley food mill to remove the skin and pits.
2. Place ¼ of the pears with liquid in a blender or food processor container fitted with a steel blade. Add the lemon juice. Cover and puree. Repeat with remaining pears. Chill.

Variation: Spiced Meetz: Add 2 cinnamon sticks and 10 cloves to the water before cooking. Remove the spices before pureeing.

PARTY DRINKS

VIRGIN MARY MIX

Makes: 6⅓ cups; serves: 6 to 8

I like to keep this around the house as a great waker-upper.

One 46-ounce can tomato juice
⅓ cup fresh lemon or lime juice
½ teaspoon anchovy-free Worcestershire
    sauce
½ teaspoon Tabasco

1. Combine all the ingredients in a large pitcher. Chill.

Variation: Bloody Mary: Add vodka or gin to taste and 3 tablespoons prepared horseradish.

PARTY PUNCH

Makes: 8¼ cups; serves: 12 to 16

Serve this punch topped with thin orange slices for garnish. If you want a little fizz in your punch, stir in a liter of ginger ale or 7-Up.

2 cups brewed tea, chilled
2 cups pineapple juice
2 cups lemonade (homemade, page 559, or
    store-bought)
2 cups orange juice
¼ cup honey

1. In a large bowl, stir together the tea, pineapple juice, lemonade, and orange juice.
2. Stir in the honey until dissolved.

Variation: Stir in rum, to taste. Float 1 to 2 pints lemon sherbet and/or orange sherbet on top.

SANGRIA

Makes 5 cups; serves: 6 to 8

Serve this in a large pitcher with a wooden spoon to lift out the fruit slices.

1 bottle (750 ml) red or white wine
⅓ cup sugar
⅓ cup orange liqueur
1 orange, sliced thin
1 apple, sliced thin

1. Place all the ingredients in a large pitcher. Stir until sugar dissolves. Chill.

Variation: Add any of the following fruits in addition to or instead of the orange and apple: sliced peach, nectarine, pear, or plum; or whole berries.

PINK CHAMPAGNE PUNCH

Makes: 9 ½ cups; serves: 6 to 18

You can float sherbet in this punch, or you can make a frozen "wreath" by freezing juice and fruit in a ring mold.

2 cups chilled cranberry juice
⅓ cup lemon juice
⅓ cup sugar
½ cup orange liqueur
2 bottles (750 ml each) chilled champagne

1. In a large bowl, stir together the cranberry juice, lemon juice, and sugar until sugar is dissolved. Stir in the liqueur.

2. Stir in the champagne just before serving.

Variation: Use orange juice instead of cranberry or use half orange and half cranberry.

HEAVENLY EGGNOG

Makes: 8 cups; serves: 12 to 15

Definitely not a beverage for the health-conscious, this is a devilishly unforgettable treat once or twice a year. (I make it every year for New Year's Eve.) In the unlikely event you have any left over, you can keep it in the refrigerator for 3 to 4 days—just stir before serving. (I have been known to have it for breakfast on January 1.) **Warning:** *Raw eggs can be hazardous to your health. Use only the freshest and best-quality eggs.*

4 eggs, separated
½ cup sugar
2 cups milk
¼ cup whiskey or bourbon
¼ cup rum
3 tablespoons Amaretto or Kahlua
1 cup heavy cream
Freshly grated nutmeg (optional)

1. In a large bowl, beat the egg yolks with the sugar until thick and light yellow. Beat in the milk, whiskey, rum, and Amaretto.

2. In a medium bowl, using clean beaters, beat the egg whites until stiff but not dry.

3. In a separate bowl, beat the cream until stiff peaks form.

4. Fold the egg whites and whipped cream into the mixture from step 1.

Variation: Substitute Morgan's Spiced Rum for the whiskey.

HOMEMADE MOCHA CREAM LIQUEUR

[L]

Makes: 3 ¹/₂ cups; serves: 8 to 12

I make this unbelievably rich concoction to give as a much-appreciated gift. You can store it in the refrigerator up to 2 weeks.

¹/₃ cup sugar
¹/₄ cup water
1¹/₂ tablespoons cocoa
2 teaspoons instant coffee
One 14-ounce can sweetened condensed milk
1 cup heavy cream
1 cup vodka
2 teaspoons vanilla

1. In a 2-quart saucepan, stir together the sugar, water, cocoa, and instant coffee. Cook, stirring, over medium heat until all the ingredients have dissolved. Stir until combined. Remove from heat.
2. Stir in the condensed milk, the cream, vodka, and vanilla. Chill.

Variations: Coffee Liqueur: Omit the cocoa and increase the instant coffee to 2 tablespoons.

Chocolate Liqueur: Omit the coffee and increase the cocoa to ¹/₄ cup.

MALTED MILK

[L]

Makes: 1 ¹/₄ cups; serves: 1 to 2

I always used to drink malted milk shakes with hamburgers; now I like them before bed with graham crackers.

1 cup vanilla ice cream
¹/₂ cup milk
1 tablespoon malt powder
¹/₂ teaspoon vanilla extract

1. Place all the ingredients in a blender container. Cover and blend until smooth.

Variations: Chocolate Malted: Substitute chocolate ice cream for the vanilla and add 2 tablespoons chocolate syrup.

Thick Shake: Use extra ice cream for desired thickness.

CHOCOLATE EGG CREAM

[L]

Makes: 1 cup; serves: 1

There is no egg and traditionally no cream in this New York favorite. However, I find that cream is delicious in this egg cream. Fox's U-Bet is the chocolate syrup of choice for this beverage.

3 tablespoons heavy cream
2 tablespoons chocolate syrup
²/₃ cup chilled seltzer or club soda

1. In a tall glass, stir together the cream and chocolate syrup. Add the seltzer, stirring all the time.

Variation: For a traditional egg cream, use milk instead of cream.

INDEX

A

After-Dinner Coffee, 558
All-Butter Crust, 518
All-Shortening Crust, 518
Almond(s). *See Also* Nuts
  Broccoli with Orange and, 243
  Ding Vegetables, 180–181
  Fennel and Celery with Water
    Chestnuts and Toasted,
    Sautéed, 258
  Millet, Orange-, 312
  Mole, 88
  Salad, Boston Lettuce with
    Jícama, Oranges, and, 371,
  Soup, Jerusalem Artichoke–, 120
  Wild Rice with Apples and, 323
Anadama Bread, 423
Angel Food Cake, 514
Angel Food Cake, Lemon-
    Scented, 514
Angel Food Cake, Orange-
    Scented, 514
Anise Seed Bread, 421
Anisette Raspberry Sorbet, 550
Antipasto Salad, 341
Appetizers Listings, 44–45
Apple. *See Also* Fruit
  Acorn Squash, -Stuffed, 292
  Bread, Biscuit, 398
  Brown Betty, 541
  Butter, Old-Fashioned, 491
  Butter, -Pear, -Plum, 491
  Cake, Spiced, 504–505
  Cake, Sweet Potato, 508
  Cider, Mulled, 560
  Crisp, 546
  Gingerbread, 511
  Kasha with Jícama and, 306
  Pie, 520
  Red Cabbage with,
    Braised, 247

Salad
  Brown Rice, Cantaloupe
    and, 378
  Bulgur- 374
  Cabbage and, Red, 366
  Fennel-, -Gouda, 370
  Slaw, -Carrot, 366
  Waldorf, 365
  Wild Rice with, and
    Walnuts, 378
  Winter, 388
Sauce, Noodles with Sour
    Cream and, 331
Sauce, Old-Fashioned, 543
Sauce, -Pear, 543
Sauerkraut with, and
    Caraway Seeds,
    246–247
Soup, Squash and, 120
Squares, 539–540
Strudel Filling, 529
Tart, Easy, 523
Tart, Honey, -Fig, 525
Tart, -Strawberry, 524
Tea, Hot, 559
and Turnip, 298–299
Turnovers, Little, 527
Waffles, Pie, 440
Wild Rice with, and
    Almonds, 323
Apricot(s)
  Bread, -Prune, 398–399
  Cake, Dried, 509
  Jam, 490
  Jam, Gingered, 489–490
  Lekvar, 493
  Rice, -Pineapple, Brown,
    320–321
  Squares, Meringue, 539
  Tart, Raspberry, 522
Arranged Tomato-Mozzarella
    Salad, 350

Artichoke(s)
  About, 234
  with Curried Mayonnaise, 83
  Dip, and Parmesan, 66
  Hearts, Chickpea and Grilled
    Vegetable Salad, 386
  Hearts, Pasta Salad, 381
  Hearts, Risotto with
    Gorgonzola and, 156–157
  with Lemon-Garlic
    Mayonnaise, 84
  Microwaved, 235
  with Raspberry Vinaigrette, 84–85
  Steamed, 235
  Stuffed, Italian-Style, 84
Arugula Salad with Fresh Figs
    and Feta Cheese, 367
Arugula Salad with Fruit and
    Lime-Ginger Dressing, 367
Arugula, Salad, Honeydew, and
    Raspberries, with Honey-
    Mustard Dressing, 367
Asian Millet Salad, 380
Asian Pear Salad, Shredded Red
    Cabbage and, 366
Asparagus
  About, 236
  Croustades, 78–79
  Frittata, 453
  with Honey-Mustard Sauce, 64
  with Lemon Butter, 236
  Pasta, Springtime, 191
  Quiche, Dilled, 212
  Salad, and Hearts of Palm, 353
  Salad, Sautéed Summer
    Vegetable 237
  Sautéed, Tomatoes, and Red
    Onion, 236–237
  Sesame, 237
  Soup, Chilled Creamy
    Cauliflower-, 110–111
  Soup, Cream of, 116

Asparagus *(cont.)*
  Soup, Creamy Cauliflower-,
    110–111
  Spicy Sesame, 237
  Szechuan, with Water
    Chestnuts, 238
  with Walnuts and Browned
    Butter, 236
Atakilt Acilch'a, 163
Autumn Brussels Sprouts, 245
Autumn Brown Rice, 320
Avgolemono Soup, 103
Avocado
  Dip, Yogurt, 64
  Guacamole, 56
  Nachos Grande, 68
  Salad
    Black Bean and Tomato, 385
    Bulgur Salad with Sofrito
      Dressing, 374–375
    Chunky, 349
    Romaine, and Cucumber, 343
    Tomato-, 351
  Soup, Rich and Creamy, 133

B

Baba Ganoujh, 54
Baby Limas and Barley, 150
Baby Spinach Salad, 345
Baked
  Beans, 332–333
  Brie and Sun-Dried
    Tomatoes, 76
  Eggplant, 255
  Eggplant, and Zucchini,
    Mozzarella, 170
  Goat Cheese, Salad Greens
    with, 346
  Onions, Stuffed 272
  Plantains, 278
  Potatoes, 280
  Potatoes, Stuffed, 283
  Spaghetti, 216
  Squash, Whole, 292
  Tomatoes, Basil Stuffed, 296
  Ziti, 199

Bali Vegetables, 249
Balsamic Vinegar, About, 18–19
Banana
  Bread, 396–397
  Cake, –Whipped Cream
    Refrigerator, 513
  Fried Sweet, 279
  Fritters, 439
  Orange-Basted, 542
  Salad, Blueberry-Nectarine,
    388
  Salad, Calypso-Berry, 389
  Salad, Papaya-, -Orange, 389
  Smoothie, -Blueberry, 561
  Thick Shake, Pineapple-, 562
  Waffles, -Poppyseed, 440
Barbecue(ed)
  Beans, 332
  Eggplant, 256
  French Toast, 444
  Oven Fries, 283
  Rice with Beans and
    Corn, 319
  Sandwiches, Eggplant, 461
  Sauce, 332
  Sauce, Beer, 478
  Sauce, Betty's, 477
  Sauce, Orange-Flavored, 478
  Tempeh on a Bun, 461
  Tofu and Beans, Spanish-, 222
  Tofu and Rice with Black
    Beans, Very Quick, 221
  Vegetables, 233
Barley
  About, 301, 302, 304
  Baby Limas and, 150
  Fran's Great Grain Dish, 152
  with Mushrooms, 304
  Mushrooms and, Spicy Cheesy,
    160–161
  with Rutabaga and Carrots, 305
  Soup, Mushroom-, 126
  Soup, Split Pea and, 123
  with Spinach, 305
  -Stuffed Peppers, 161
  with Vegetables, 161
  Zucchini 304–305

Basic
  Empanadas, 466–467
  Knishes, 465
  Muffins, 408
  Omelet with Filling, 450–451
  Polenta, 307
  Sourdough Starter, 425
  Strudel, 528
  Waffles, 439–440
Basil
  Beans with Tomato and,
    White, 335
  Lasagna, Green and White, 197
  Marinara, 474
  Pasta with Creamy, Sauce, 194
  Pesto Sauce for Pizza, 202–203
  Pesto, Traditional, 476
  Pesto Vegetables, 291
  Risotto, Tomato and, 158
  Salad, -Mint Cucumber, and
    Pea, 356
  Salad, Pesto Cauliflower, 358–359
  Salad, Tomato-Mozzarella, 350
  Soup, -Cauliflower, 111
  Spaghetti Squash, -Garlic, 294
  Tart, Squash and, 215
  Tomatoes, -Stuffed Baked, 296
Batter-Fried Cauliflower, 251
Bean(s). *See Also* Bean Sprouts,
    Black Beans, Chick Peas,
    Lentils, Kidney Beans,
    Seitan, Soy Beans, Tempeh,
    Tofu, Textured Vegetable
    Protein
  About, 7–8, 13–14, 331
  Baked, 332–333
  Caponata, Beany, 56
  Cooking Table, 13–14
  Cranberry, Creamy Swiss Chard
    with, 263
  Creole Red, and Rice, 142
  Eggplant with Butter, and
    Plums, 146
  Escarole and, 263
  Frijoles, 331
  Lima, with Dill, Buttered,
    334–335

Limas and Barley, Baby, 150
Pâté, Carrot, 61
Pâté, Tricolor Curried, 62
Refried, 332
Salad
  Olive and Vegetable
    Salad, 356
  Pigeon, and Corn, 386
  Sautéed Portobello
    Mushrooma and Pinto,
    382–383
  Small White, with Wheat
    Berries, 150
  Stuffed Olive and
    Roman, 382
  Three-, 385
  Tomato-, 350
  Wild Rice and Rice, 379
Soup
  Collard and Black-Eyed
    Pea, 122
  Escarole-, 127
  Kitchen Sink, 121
  Split Pea and Black-Eyed
    Pea, 124
  Three-, Vegetable, 125
Spaghetti Squash with Curried
  Carrots and, 144–145
Squash, Curried with, 144
Stew, Rattlesnake, 139
Strudel, Spinach-Mushroom
  Filling, 177
Succotash, 334
Vegetables with Kamut
  and, 148
White, with Tomatoes and
  Basil, 335
Yellow, Green, and Spaghetti
  Squash with, 144
Bean Curd. See Tofu
Bean Sprouts
  About, 238
  Hoisin, with Cloud Ears, 239
  Omelet with Peanut Sauce,
    Tofu-Soy, 452
  Salad, and Watercress,
    Wilted, 362

Seitan with, and Mushrooms, 227
Stir-Fried Mung, 238
Beer Barbecue Sauce, 478
Beet(s)
  About, 240
  Baked Root Vegetables,
    Ginger-, 299
  with Cranberries, 240
  in Red Wine and Honey, 240
  Salad and Pear, with Honey-
    Yogurt Dressing, 370
  Sauce, -Horseradish, 485
  Soup, Borscht, 131
  Soup, Borscht with Spring
    Salad, 131
  Sweet and Sour, 240
Belgian Endive Salad
  Blackberry-, 368
  Cucumber, and Radish
    with Creamy Mustard
    Dressing, 355
  Farmer's Market, 342
  with Graeta Olive Dressing,
    Julienned, 346
  and Radicchio, with Fresh
    Raspberries, 368
  Red, White, and Green, with
    Balsamic Vinegar, 348
  with Roasted Red Pepper and
    Boursin Dressing, 347
  Strawberry-, 368
  Tomato, and Hearts of
    Palm, 351
Bell Pepper(s)
  About 276
  Broccoli Rabe with Yellow, and
    Carrots, 243
  Eggplant with Red, and
    Shiitake Mushrooms, 169
  Eggs Benedictish, 450
  Millet with, Chili, 311
  Omelet, Spanish, 541
  Pico de Gallo, 484
  Rice, Wild with Orzo and
    Three-Color, 322
  Rice, Wild and White, with
    Three-Color, 322

Rice with Three, 277
Rice with Onion and Red,
  Brown, 320
Roasted Red, 276–277
  Coulis, 475
  Dip, and Sun-Dried Tomato,
    64–65
  Lasagna with, Cream
    Sauce, 198
  Salad, Cardoon with, 358
  Salad, Endive, with, and
    Boursin Dressing, 347
  Salad, and Leeks Vinai-
    grette, 80
  Salad, and Potato, 365
  Sandwich, and Mozzarella,
    459
  Sandwich, –Caper, 458–459
  Sauce, Tomato-, 474
  Sauce, Tomato-, Curried, 474
  Soup, -Tomato, 98
  Tart, Roasted Eggplant
    and, 214
  Ziti with, and Grilled
    Eggplant, 192
Roasted Yellow or Orange,
  276–277
Salad, 357
Salad, Black Bean, 357
Salad, Pineapple, and
  Celery, 370
Sautéed, a Trio of, 277
Snow Peas, Cauliflower, and
  Red, 274
Snow Peas, Cauliflower, and
  Red, Oriental, 274
Sofrito, 484
Sofrito, Cooked, 484
Soup, -Celery, 102
Soup, Curried Yellow, 103
Soup, Gazpacho, 130
Stuffed, Barley-, 161
Stuffed, Wildly, 160
Berliner, 557
Berry Berry Berry Good Fruit
  Salad, 389
Betty's Barbecue Sauce, 477

Beverage Listings, 556
Bird's Nest, 180
Biscuit(s)
  Bread, Apple, 398
  Cinnamon Sweet Potato, 412
  Cornmeal, Peppered Blue, 405
  Herbed, 405
  Parmesan, 406
  Pecan-Orange, 403
  Plantain, 404
  Sourdough Drop, 407
  Sweet, 404
  Wheat Germ Drop, 406
  Whole Wheat, World's
    Best, 403
Bitter Greens with Pears and
    Stilton Dressing, 369
Black Beans
  About, 7–8, 13–14
  Broccoli with, and Garlic, 143
  Burritos, Brown Rice and, 154
  with Celery, 333
  and Celery, Sautéed, 333
  Chili, 155
  Dip, 153
  Dip, Southwest Corn and, 66
  Hummus, 58
  Jerusalem Artichokes with, 265
  Mooros y Christianos, 141
  Picadillo, 225
  -Polenta Pie, 155
  and Rice, 141
  Rice and, Cilantro, 141
  Rice and, Parsley, 141
  Salad, –Bell Pepper, 357
  Salad, Corn and, 384
  Salad, and Olive, 384–385
  Salad, and Tomato, 385
  Sauce, Soysprouts in, 239
  Soup, 122
  Spread, 58
  Stew, Cauliflower and, 140
  Stew, Southwestern, 140
  Tofu and Rice with, Very Quick
    Barbecue, 221
  Tostadas, 153
Blackberry-Endive Salad, 368

Blender Hollandaise, 472
Blintzes, Blueberry, 445
Blintzes, Cheese, 445
Bloody Mary, 564
Blue Cornmeal Bread, 399
Blue Sandies, 533
Blueberry(ies). *See Also* Fruit
  Blintzes, 445
  Bread, Cornmeal, 400
  Chutney, -Mango, 487–488
  Chutney, -Nectarine, 487–488
  Coffeecake, 506
  Fritters, 439
  Muffins, 408
  Pancakes, 434
  Pancakes, -Lemon, 435
  Salad
    Berry Berry Berry Good, 389
    Calypso-Berry, 389
    Cantaloupe-, 390
    Fruit, Summer Brunch, 390
    -Nectarine, 388
  Smoothie, Banana-, 561
  Tart, Fresh Raspberry with,
    Filling, 523
  Tart, -Orange, 523
  Vinegar, 471
Boboli and Vegetable Melt, 463
Boiled Cabbage, 246
Boiled Potatoes, 281
Bok Choy, About, 241
Bok Choy with Spaghetti
    Squash, 295
Bok Choy, Stir-Fried, 241
Borscht, 131
Borscht with Spring Salad, 131
Boston Brown Bread, 401
Boston Lettuce with Jícama,
    Oranges, and Almonds, 371
Bourbon Broiled Pineapple, 541
Braised
  Brussels Sprouts, 244
  Celery, 258
  Celery with Wild Mushrooms,
    252
  Fennel, 258
  Red Cabbage with Apples, 247

Bran
  Bread, Corn and, 420–421
  Bread, Raisin Corn, 420–421
  Muffins, Cornmeal, 410
  Muffins, Date, 410
  Pancakes, Oat, Lemon-, 435
  Waffles, 441
Brandied Candied Sweet
    Potatoes, 286
Brandied Mushroom Spread, 60
Bread Listings, 394
Bread
  Crostini, 427
  Croutons, Flavored, 427
  Garlic, Butter, 428
  Garlic, Parmesan, 428
  Pitas, Toasted, 428
  Pudding, Cranberry, 548
  Pudding, Raisin, 548
  Pudding, Savory Mushroom,
    210
  Pudding, Savory, Spinach and
    Dill, 210
  Soufflé, Easy Faux, 209
  Salad, Grilled Vegetable and, 352
Breakfast, About, 19, 433
Breakfast Listings, 432
Brie Sandwich, 459
Broccoflower, About, 241
Broccoflower, Puree of, 241
Broccoli. *See Also* Broccoflower,
    Broccoli Rabe
  About, 242
  with Black Beans and
    Garlic, 143
  Burmese Crispy Vegetables
    with Yellow Pea Curry, 146
  in Cheese Sauce, 250–251
  Creamy Parmesan, 260–261
  Knishes, -Cheddar, 465
  Noodles with, and Cabbage,
    204–205
  with Orange and Almonds, 243
  with Oyster Mushrooms, 242
  Pasta with, and Garlic, 189
  Quiche, -Cheddar, 213
  Salad, 357

Salad, -Potato, 364
Sautéed, with Garlic, 242
with Sautéed Vegetables, 273
Sautéed, and Zucchini, 242–243
Soufflé, 208–209
Soup, Buttermilk, 119
Soup, Crunchy, Cheddar-, 118
-Stuffed Tomatoes, 297
Szechuan, 179
Timbales, Herb, 288–289
Ziti with, and Rosemary, 195
Broccoli Rabe, About, 243
Broccoli Rabe with Rice
    Noodles, 206
Broccoli Rabe Sautéed, with
    Chestnuts, 244
Broccoli Rabe with Yellow
    Peppers and Carrots, 243
Broiled. *See Also* Grilled
  Eggplant, 255
  Pineapple, Bourbon, 541
  Pineapple, Rum, 541
  Sandwiches, Egg, 462
  Tomatoes, 295
  Tomatoes, Cheesy, 295
  Vegetables, Basic, 233
Broth About, 8, 93–94
Broth, Mighty Vegetable, 94
Broth, Mushroom, 95
Broth, Vegetable Juice, 95
Brown Baggin It, 19–20
Brown Betty, Apple, 541
Brown Bread, Boston, 401
Brown Bread, Cranberry-Fig, 401
Brown Rice. *See* Rice, Brown
Brown Sugar Granola, 446
Brownies, 540
Brunch Listings, 432
Brussels Sprouts, About, 244
Brussels Sprouts Autumn, 245
Brussels Sprouts Braised, 244
Brussels Sprouts, Winter
    Vegetables for a Crowd, 245
Buckwheat. *See* Kasha
Bulgur
  About, 302, 324
  Bread, 417–418

Bread, Donna Mason's Dense
    and Chewy Whole Grain,
    418–419
with Celery, 325
Salad, Apple-, 374
Salad, S-D-T , 374
Salad with Sofrito Dressing,
    374–375
Spaghetti Squash with,
    Marinara Sauce, 165
with Squash, Carrots, and
    Collards, 325
-Stuffed Eggplant, 167
with Summer Sqaush, 324
Tabouli, 373
with Tofu and Cauliflower, 221
Tomato, with Eggplant, 324
Buns, Sticky, 502
Burgers, Lentil, 162
Burmese Crispy Vegetables
    with Yellow Pea Curry,
    146
Burritos, Brown Rice and Black
    Bean, 154
Butter(ed)
  Beans, Eggplant with, and
    Plums, 146
  Clarified, 494
  Flavored, 489
  Frosting, –Cream Cheese, 516
  Frosting, Ginger, –Cream
    Cheese, 516
  Fruit
    About, 491
    Apple, Old-Fashioned, 491
    Apple-Pear-Plum, 491
    Apricot, 393
    Butternut Squash, 492
    Lemon Curd, 494
    Lime Curd, 494
    Peach, 492
    Prune, 493
    Quince, 491
    Raspberry-Quince, 491
  Garlic Bread, 428
  Ghee, 494
  Homemade, 489

Lima Beans with Dill, 334–335
Sweet Potatoes, Rum, 286
Buttercream Frosting,
    Chocolate, 515
Buttercream Frosting, Coffee-
    Rum, 515–516
Buttercream Frosting,
    Mocha, 515
Buttercream Frosting,
    Orange, 516
Buttermilk Broccoli Soup, 119
Buttermilk Pancakes, 434
Buttermilk Mocha Cake, 512
Butternut. *See Also* Squash
Butternut Squash Butter, 492
Butternut Squash with Curried
    Millet Filling, 166
Button Mushrooms Persiller, 268

C

Cabbage. *See Also* Chinese
    Cabbage
About, 246
Atakilt Acilch'a, 163
Boiled, Spiced, 246
Cavetelli with, and Caramel-
    ized Onions, 193
Colcannon, 282
Coleslaw, 360–361
Coleslaw, Tricolor, 361
Coleslaw, Zucchini, 361
Curry, and Mushroom, 182
Gado Gado, 224
Moo Shu Vegetables, 219
Noodles with Broccoli and,
    204–205
Red
  Braised with Apples, 247
  Salad, and Apple, 366
  Salad, with Ketchup
    Dresssing, 362
  Salad, Shredded, and Asian
    Pear, 366
  Sautéed with Balsamic
    Vinegar, 247
Salad, and Cashew, 362

Cabbage *(cont.)*
Salad, Health , 358
Sauerkraut with Apples and
Caraway Seeds, 246–247
Sautéed, with Snow Peas, 246
Soup Portugese Vegetable, 105
Soup, Saint Patrick's Day, 105
Soup, Sweet and Sour, 109
Strudel Filling, Kasha, 178
Stuffed, Sweet and Sour,
166–167
Wheat Berries with Calabaza
and, 328–329
Caesar Salad, 340
Cake. *See Also* Cheesecake
Angel Food, 514
Angel Food, Lemon-
Scented, 514
Angel Food, Orange-
Scented, 514
Apple, Spiced, 504–505
Apricot, Dried, 509
Carrot, 510
Chocolate Cherry Loaf, 504
Chocolate Cherry, Chocolate-
Glazed, 504
Coconut-Pineapple, 510–511
Coffeecake, Blueberry, 506
Coffeecake, Streusel-Topped
Blueberry, 506
Cream Cheese, Raspberry-, 507
Gingerbread, Apple, 511
Layer, Carrot, 510
Layer, Coconut Parsnip,
511–512
Mocha, Buttermilk, 512
Peach, Fresh, 504–505
Peanut Butter, 505–506
Pecan-Squash, 513
Refrigerator, Banana–Whipped
Cream, 513
Strawberry Shortcake, 503
Sweet Potato–Apple, 508
Upside Down, Plum, 506–507
"Vedding," 508–509
Walnut Torte, 505
Zucchini-Walnut, 513

Calypso-Berry Salad, 389
Candied Sweet Potatoes,
Brandied, 286
Cannellini Bean Soup,
Escarole–, 127
Cantaloupe
Salad, -Blueberry, 390
Salad, Brown Rice and
Apple 378
Salad, Summer Brunch
Fruit, 390
Soup, Ginger-, 134
Soup, Yin and Yang, 134
Caponata, 55
Caponata, Beany, 56
Cardoon Salad with Roasted Red
Peppers, 358
Cardoon, Wheat Berries
with, 329
Caramelized Grapes, 547
Caramelized Onion and Sun-
Dried Tomato Dip, 65
Caramelized Vidalias, 452
Caribbean Carrot Soup, 113
Carrot(s)
About, 248
Ataklit Acilch'a, 163
Baked Root Vegetables,
Ginger-, 299
Bali Vegetables, 249
Barley with Rutabaga
and, 305
Broccoli Rabe with Yellow
Peppers and, 243
Bulgur with Squash, and
Collards, 325
Cake, 510
Jalapeño, 248
Orange-Sautéed Rutabaga
and, 300
Parslied, 248
Pâté, 61
Pâté, Tricolor Curried, 62
Puree, Gingered, 249
Salad, Moroccan, 360
Salad, Shredded, and
Jícama, 359

Salad, Shredded, and Yellow
Turnip, with Cardamom
Dressing, 60
Sesame, 248
Slaw, Apple-, 366
Soup, Carribean, 113
Soup, -Cauliflower, 111
Soup, Celeriac, 112
Soup, Parsnip-, 112
Spaghetti Squash with Curried,
and Beans, 144–145
Tzimmes, 287
Cashew, Salad, Cabbage and, 362
Cashews, Wheat Berries
with, 328
Cauliflower
About 250
Bulgur with Tofu, 221
in Cheese Sauce, 250–251
Couscous with Diced
Vegetables, Spiced, 327
Fried, Batter-, 251
Kasha with Tofu, 221
with Parsley and Lemon, 250
Pâté, Tricolor Curried, 62
Polanaise, 250
Salad, Pesto, 358–359
Sautéed Peppers, Onions,
and, 277
Snow Peas, and Red Bell
Peppers, 274
Snow Peas, and Red Bell
Peppers, Oriental, 274
Soup
-Asparagus, Creamy, 110–111
Basil-, 111
Carrot-, 111
Cream of, 116
Curried, 112
Lentil-, 128
Stew, and Black Bean, 140
Vegetables for a Crowd,
Winter, 245
Cavetelli with Cabbage and
Carmelized Onions, 193
Caviar, Olive, 52
Caviar, Poor Man's, 53

Caviar, Zuccchini-Olive, 52
Celeriac
  About, 251
  Baked, Parmesan ,266
  Saute, Julienned, and
    Celery, 251
  Soup, Root Vegetable and Split
    Pea, 124
  Vegetables, Bali, 249
Celery
  About, 252
  with, Black Beans, 333
  Braised, 258
  Braised with Wild
    Mushrooms, 252
  Bulgur with, 325
  au Gratin, 258–259
  Salad, Pineapple, Red Pepper,
    and, 370
  Sautéed, Black Beans and, 333
  Sautéed Celeriac and,
    Julienned, 251
  Sautéed Fennel and, with
    Water Chestnuts and
    Toasted Almonds, 258
  Soup, Bell Pepper–, 102
  Soup, Cheesy, 102
  Stuffed, 46
Challah, 422
Chayote, Sweet Potato
    Stuffed, 293
Cheddar Cheese Soup,
    Tomato–, 100
Cheddar Chili Cornbread, 401
Cheese. See Also Cheesecake,
    Cream Cheese, Feta
    Cheese, Goat Cheese,
    Mozzarella, Parmesan
  Baked Brie and Sun-Dried
    Tomatoes, 76
  Balls, Rice-Spinach-, 75
  Blintzes, 445
  Bread, Cheddar-Chili Corn, 401
  Cake, Raspberry–Cream, 507
  Celery au Gratin, 258–259
  Chili Rellenos, 215
  Dip, Chili con Queso, 66

Dip, Stilton, 369
Dressing, Bitter Greens with
    Pears and Stilton, 369
Dressing, Endive Salad with
    Roasted Red Peppers and
    Boursin, 347
Dressing, Watercress and
    Romaine with Roquefort,
    348
Eggplant Rollatini, 172
Eggs, Scrambled with Cream
    and Scallion, 447
Fennel au Gratin, 258–259
Fondue, 67
Gnocchi with Butter and, 204
Gnocchi, Spinach and
    Ricotta, 204
Grits with, 308
Knishes, Broccoli-, 465
Lasagna with Bell
    Pepper Cream Sauce,
    Mushroom, 198
Lasagna, Green and White, 196
Lasagna, Vegetable, 197
Macaroni and, Good Old, 216
Macaroni and, Three, 216
Manicotti, 188–189
Melt, Boboli and
    Vegetable, 463
Melt, Zucchini-Leek, 159
Millet with, Chili, 311
Mushrooms and Barley, Spicy,
    160–161
Nachos, 67
Nachos Grande, 68
Noodle Pudding, 330
Noodle Pudding, Savory, 330
Omelet, 450–451
Pancakes, Low-Fat, 438
Paneer, 495
Pasta Torte, 199
Pastry Dough, Food Processor
    Farmer-, 519
Pastry Dough, Sweetened
    Farmer-, 519
Pizza, White, 203
Pot, 495

Potatoes au Gratin, 284
Potatoes au Gratin, Stilton, 284
Quesadilla, 464
Quiche, Broccoli-Cheddar, 213
Quiche, Dilled Asparagus, 212
Quiche, Vidalia Onion, 211
Risotto with Gorgonzola and
    Artichoke Hearts, 156–157
Saag Paneer, 182
Salad, Cottage, and Fruit, 390
Salad, Fennel-Apple-
    Gouda, 370
Sandwich, Brie, 459
Sandwich, Grilled, 460
Sauce, Broccoli in, 250–251
Sauce, Cauliflower in, 250–251
Sauce, Polenta with
    Gorgonzola, 81
Soufflé, 208–209
Soufflé, Easy Faux, 209
Soufflé, Roquefort, 208
Soup, Cheesy Celery, 102
Soup, Crunchy Broccoli-
    Cheddar, 118
Soup, French Onion, 102
Soup, Tomato Cheddar, 100
Spaghetti, Baked, 216
Spread(s)
  About, 46
  Garlic-Herb, 46
  Greek Cucumber Salad, 50
  Log, Party, 49
  Schmear Kaese, 47
  Stilton Marscapone, 50
Strudel Filling, 529
Stuffed Mushrooms, 82
Stuffed Shells, Escarole
    and, 188
Tart, 524
Tart, Gorgonzola, Leek, and
    Fennel, 213
Tomatoes, Broiled , 295
Tomatoes, Scalloped, 297
Topfen, 495
Welsh Rarebit, 462
Winter Vegetables for a
    Crowd, 245

Cheese (cont.)
Yogurt, 495
Ziti Baked, 199
Cheesecake
Marble, 530–531
Marble, Orange, 530–531
Pesto, 47
Pumpkin, 532
Raspberty Swirl, 531
Roquefort, 48
Strawberry Swirl, 531
Sun-Dried Tomato, 47
Vegetable Savory, 48
Cheesy Broiled Tomatoes, 295
Cheesy Celery Soup, 102
Cherry(ies)
Loaf, Chocolate, 504
Pie, Sour, 521
Stewed Peaches and, 542
Stewed Peaches and,
Sugarless, 542
Strudel Filling, Sweet, 529
Chestnuts Broccoli Rabe,
Sautéed with, 244
Chestnuts, Brussels Sprouts,
Autumn, 245
Chestnuts, Roasted, 89
Chevre, Herbed, 49
Chickeny Croquettes, 225–226
Chickpea(s). See Also Bean(s)
Couscous with Vegetable Sauce
and, 152–153
Falafel, 460
with Escarole, Garbanzo
Beans, 333
Green Beans with, in
Groundnut Sauce, 262
Hummus, 57
Hummus, Vegetable, 57
and Kale, Curried, 147
Salad
Antipasto, 341
and Grilled Vegetable, 386
Marinated, 386
Pasta, 382
Three Bean, 385
and Sprouted-Pea, 387

Soup, Vegetable, 129
Spread, Beany Caponata, 56
Stewed Garbanzo Beans with
Zuc-Quinoa, 151
Wafers, 86
Zucchini and Yellow Squash
with, 143
Chili, 154
About Oil, 17
Black Bean, 155
Cornbread, Cheddar, 401
Fried Okra, 269
Millet with Cheese, 311
Millet with Peppers, 311
Peanuts, 87
Popcorn, 90
con Queso, 66
Rellenos, 215
Rice with Tomatillos, 317
Chilled Cauliflower Soup,
110–111
Chilled Cucumber Soup, 132
Chilled Parsley Root and Parsnip
Soup, 113
Chilled Strawberry Soup, 135
Chinese Cabbage
About, 246
Moo Shu Vegetables, 219
Noodles with Seitan, 226
and Oriental Vegetables, 179
Soup, 108
Soup, and Noodle, 108
Chips, Potato, 87
Chips, Sweet Potato, 87
Chips, Tortilla, Homemade,
86–87
Chocolate
Brownies, 540
Cake, Glazed Chocolate
Cherry, 504
Cheesecake, Marble, 530–531
Cheesecake, Orange Marble,
530–531
-Dipped Strawberries, 546
Egg Cream, 566
Frosting, Buttercream, 515
Frosting, Light, 515

Frosting, Sour Cream, 516
Ganache, 516–517
Liqueur, 566
Loaf, Cherry, 504
Malted, 566
Mousse, 554
Muffins, -Filled, 409
Sauce, 554
Tartlets, Walnut Fudge, 526
Truffles, 516–517
Whipped Cream, 558
Cholesterol, 4–6
Cholesterol in Foods, Table, 6
Chopped Tomato and Olive
Spread, 51
Chowder, Corn, 110
Chowder, Manhattan-Style
Vegetable, 109
Chunky Salad, 349
Chunky Marinara Sauce, 473
Chutney
About, 486
Blueberry-Mango, 487–488
Blueberry-Nectarine, 487–488
Dip, 64
Figs-Were-Cheap, 487
Green Tomato–Pineapple, 487
Mango, 486
Nectarine, 488
Rhubarb-Walnut, 488
Sauce, 483
Sauce, Cilantro, 483
Tart, Cranberry-Pear, 522
Tomato, Plum, and Dried
Fruit, 486
Cider Dominican Pineapple, 560
Cider, Mulled, 560
Cilantro
Chutney Sauce, 483
Cucumber Salad, 354–355
Pesto, 476
Relish, –Two Onion, 484
Rice and Black Beans, 141
Cinnamon Biscuits, Sweet
Potato, 412
Cinnamon French Toast, 442
Citrus Crust, 518

Clarified Butter, 494
Cloud Ears, Hoisin Sprouts
    with, 239
Coconut
    Cake, Carrot, 510
    Cake, Parsnip Layer,
        511–512
    Cake, -Pineapple, 510–511
    Cookies, Coconutty, 538
    Milk, About, 497
    Milk, Easy, 497
    Milk, Homemade, 497
    Mousse, Frozen Piña Colada,
        524–525
    Piña Colada, Fresh, 563
    Rice, 315
    Rice Pudding, Coconutty,
        547–548
    Rice Pudding, Leftover,
        547–548
    Rice, Sweetened, 315
    Salad, Curried Rice, 377
    Tarts, Frozen Piña Colada
        Mousse, 524–525
Codes, Vegetarian, 4
Codes, Heart Healthy, 43
Coffee
    After-Dinner, 558
    Berliner, 557
    Frosting, -Rum Buttercream,
        515
    Liqueur, 566
    Whipped Cream, 558
Coffeecake. See Cake
Colcannon, 282
Cold Marinated Szechuan Green
        Beans, 261
Coleslaw, 360–361
Coleslaw, Tricolor, 361
Coleslaw, Zucchini, 361
Collard and Black-Eyed Pea
        Soup, 122
Collards. See Greens
Condiments Listings, 468
Confectioners' Sugar Glaze, 517
Continental Fried Rice, 318–319
Cooked Sofrito, 484

Cookies
    Blue Sandies, 533
    Brownies, Lady, 540
    Brownies, Gentleman, 540
    Coconutty, 538
    Cornmeal Sandies, 533
    Gingerbread, 535
    Hamantashen, 537
    Hard-Boiled Egg, Mom's, 535
    Oatmeal, Bar, 533
    Oatmeal Raisin, 532
    Peanut Butter, 534
    Pecan–Wheat Germ, 536
    Pine Nut, 534
    Poppy Seed, 534
    Porcupines, 538
    Roll-Ups, Raspberry, 536
    Spice, 535
    Squares, Apple, 539–540
    Squares, Apricot Meringue, 539
    Squares, Lemon, 538
    Squares, Lime, 538
    Tortilla, 537
    Wonton, 537
Cooking from Scratch, 7
Cooking times
    Beans, 14
    Processed grains, 302
    Rice, 303
    Whole grains, 301
Corn. See Also Cornmeal, Polenta
    About, 252
    Boiled, 252
    Bread, Pound, 400
    Chowder, 110
    Creamed, 254
    Dip, and Black Bean,
        Southwest, 66
    Fritters, 254
    Latkes, 71
    Microwaved, 252–253
    and Millet Casserole, 162
    Okra with, Creole, 269
    Potato Pancakes, and
        Scallion-, 71
    Pudding, 253
    Pudding, Tex-Mex, 253

Quinoa with Mixed
        Vegetables, 313
    Relish, Tomatillo, 485
    Rice with Beans and,
        Barbecue, 319
    Rizcous, and Beans, 323
    Salad, and Black Bean, 384
    Salad, Pigeon Bean and, 386
    Salad, Wheat Berry–, 372–373
    Salad, Wild Rice and, 322
    Soup, Cream of, 116
    Soup, Southwest Salsa, 97
    Soup, and Spinach, Tomato, 99
    Stew, Mexicali, 142
    Stew, Rattlesnake, 139
    Stew Southwestern, 140
    Stuffed Yellow Squash, 291
    Succotash, 334
    Wild Rice and, 322
Cornmeal. See Also Corn, Grits,
        Polenta
    About, 307
    Biscuits, Peppered Blue, 405
    Bread, 399, 415
        Anadama, 423
        Blue, 399
        Blueberry, 400
        and Bran, 420–421
        and Bran, Raisin, 420–421
        Cheddar-Chili, 401
        Corn Pound, 400
        Donna Mason's Dense and
            Chewy, 418–419
    Chili Rellenos, 215
    Cookies, Blue Sandies, 533
    Cookies, Sandies, 533
    Fritters, 254
    Hush Puppies, 308
    Muffins, 409
    Muffins, Bran, 410
    Muffins, Date-Bran, 410
    Muffins, Three Grain, 410
    Pancakes, and Oat
        (No Wheat), 438
    Polenta with Gorgonzola,
        Sauce, 81
    Polenta Pie, Black Bean, 155

Cornmeal *(cont.)*
  Spoon Bread, 446
  Tamale Pie, 223
  Waffles, Corn and Oat
    (No Wheat), 438
Cottage Cheese. *See* Cheese
Coulis, Red Pepper, 475
Coulis, Tomato-Leek, 99
Couscous
  About, 302, 325
  with Dates
  with Diced Vegetables,
    Spiced, 327
  with Eggplant, 326–327
  with Golden Fruits and
    Vegetables, 326
  Morrocan Vegetables with, 145
  Pudding, Honey, 549
  Salad, Creamy, 375
  Salad, Fruited, 375
  Salad with Oranges, 376
  -Stuffed Grape Leaves, 73
  -Stuffed Papaya, 326
  with Vegetable Sauce and
    Chickpeas, 152–153
Crackers Pita Points,
    Garlic, 431
Crackers, Nice and
    Crunchy, Crisp and Seedy
    Homemade, 429
Crackers Parmesan, 430
Cranberry(ies)
  Beets with, 240
  Bread, 395
  Bread, -Fig Brown, 401
  Bread, Orange-Pumpkin-,
    -Date, 397
  Muffins, -Oatmeal, 411
  Pancakes, -Orange, 436
  Pudding, Bread, 548
  Rice, Brown Autumn, 320
  Salsa, 480
  Tart, -Pear, 522
Cream(ed)(y). *See also* Cream
    Cheese, Salad Dressing
  Baked Eggplant and Zucchini, 170
  Broccoli, Parmesan, 260–261

Corn, 254
  Dressing, Cucumber, Endive
    and Radish Salad with,
    Mustard, 355
  Green Beans, Parmesan,
    260–261
  Liqueur, Chocolate, 566
  Liqueur, Coffee, 566
  Liqueur, Mocha, 566
  Pâté, Mushroom, 59
  Peas, 275
  Polenta, 307
  Salad, Couscous, 375
  Salsa, 479
  Soup
    of Asparagus, 116
    Avocado, Rich and, 133
    Cauliflower-Asparagus,
      110–111
    Cauliflower-Asparagus,
      Chilled, 110–111
    of Corn, 116
    of Crudite, 117
    French Lentil, 128
    Garlic, Roasted, 115
    of Mushroom, 117
    of Parsley Root and
      Parsnip, 113
    Potato, 114
    Spinach, Fresh, 118
    Tomato and Leek, 99
  Spinach, 288
  Swiss Chard with Cranberry
    Beans, 263
Cream Cheese
  Cake, Raspberry, 507
  Frosting, 516
  Frosting, –Butter, 516
  Frosting, Ginger Butter, 516
  Frosting, Orange Butter, 516
  Spread, Date Nut, 455
  Spread, and Olive, 458
  Spread, Roasted Red Pepper–
    Caper, 458–459
Creme Anglaise, 554
Creole Okra with Corn, 269
Creole Red Beans and Rice, 142

Crepes, Dessert, 553
Crepes, Orange, 553
Crepes Suzette, 552
Crimini Mushroom and Green
    Bean Soup, 107
Crisp, Apple, 546
Crispy Noodles, 85
Croquettes, Chickeny, 225–226
Crostini, 427
Croustade Cups, 78
Croustades, Asparagus, 79
Croustades, Mushroom, 78
Croutons, Flavored, 427
Croutons, Plain, 427
Croutons, Tempeh, 69
Crudite Soup, Cream of, 117
Crunchy Broccoli-Cheddar
    Soup, 118
Crust. *See* Pastry
Cucumber
  About, 255
  Escarole and Sliced, 264
  Raita, 496
  Salad
    Basil-Mint, and Pea, 356
    Cilantro, 354–355
    Dilled, 356
    Endive, and Radish
      with Creamy Mustard
      Dressing, 355
    Fennel, 354
    Greek, 50, 355
    Romaine, Avocado, and, 343
    South of the Border, 348–349
    Watercress, and Onion,
      with Creamy Pepper
      Dressing, 347
    Wilted, 354
  Sautéed, with Tarragon, 255
  Soup, Chilled, 132
  Soup, Gazpacho, 130
Curry(ied)(ies)
  Burmese Crispy Vegetables
    with Yellow Pea, 146
  Cabbage and Mushroom, 182
  Carrots and Beans, Spaghetti
    Squash with, 144–145

Chickpeas and Kale, 147
French Toast, 444
Mayonnaise, Artichokes
    with, 83
Millet, 310
Millet Filling, Butternut
    Squash with, 166
Mixed Vegetable, 181
Okra with Green Beans, 270
Okra, Plantain, and Sweet
    Potato, 183
Pâté, Tricolor, 62
Rice, Fried, 318
Saag Paneer, 182
Salad, Coconut Rice, 377
Salad, Millet, 380–381
Sandwich, Egg Salad, 457
Sauce, Red Pepper, 270–271
Sauce, Tomato–Red
    Pepper, 474
Soup
    Cauliflower, 112
    Mulligatawny, 103
    Senegalese, 104
    Spinach and Tomato, 98
    Sweet Potato–Mango, 115
    Tomato, 98
    Yellow Pepper, 103
Squash with Beans, 144
Zucchini and Fennel, 290

D

Dairy Products, About, 14
Dal, Split Pea, 123
Damson Plum Jam, 490
Danish Pastry, 501
Danish Pastry Dough, 500–501
Date-Bran Muffins, 410
Date Bread, Orange-Pumpkin-
    Cranberry-, 397
Date-Nut Bread, 397–398
Date-Nut Sandwich Spread, 458
Decadent Baked Stuffed
    Potatoes, 283
Decorating Icing, 517
Dessert Crepes, 553

Desserts Listings, 498–499
Dill(ed)
    Cucumber Salad, 356
    Lima Beans, Pureed with,
        334–335
    Peas, 275
    Potatoes, 281
    Quiche, Asparagus, 212
    Rice and Pea Salad, 376
    Wheat Berries with Brown
        Rice, 329
Dipping Sauce, Oriental, 482
Dips, About, 63
Dips Listings, 44
Dolmas, 72–73
Dominican Pineapple Cider, 560
Donna Mason's Dense and
    Chewy Whole Grain Bread,
    418–419
Dough. See Also Pastry
    Danish Pastry, 500–501
    Semolina, 185
    Spinach, 186
    Tomato, 185
    Yeast, Sweet, 501–502
Dressing. See Salad Dressing
Dried Apricot Cake, 509
Dried Fig–Cardamom Bread, 399
Dumplings, Mini Vegetable, 76
Dumplings, Mushroom
    Paprikash with, 174

E

Easter Eggs, 448
Easy
    Coconut Milk, 497
    Faux Soufflé, 209
    Salsa, 479
    Sauce, Fresh Marinara, 191
    Tart, Apple, 523
Egg(s). See Also Omelet
    About, 15, 433
    Benedictish, 480
    Cholesterol and fat in, 5–6
    Cookies, Mom's Hard-Boiled,
        535

Cream, Chocolate, 566
Easter, 448
Eggnog Heavenly, 565
Enchilada, Mexican, 454
Florentine, 449
Florentine, Shortcut, 449
Frittata, 453
Hard-Cooked, 448
Hash and, 447
Huevos al Nido, 449
Huevos Rancheros, 455
in a Muffin, 448
Piperade, 453
Piperade, Grilled Vegetable,
    454
Poached, 433
in Puff Pastry, 448
Quiche, Broccoli-Cheddar, 213
Quiche, Dilled Asparagus, 212
Quiche, Vidalia Onion, 211
Rolls 77
Salad, 457
Salad, Spinach, 456–457
Sandwich, Curried, Salad, 457
Sandwich, Russian, Salad, 457
Sandwiches, Broiled, 462
Sauce, Hollandaise, 472
Scrambled, 447
Scrambled, with Cream Cheese
    and Scallion, 447
Soufflé, Broccoli, 208–209
Soufflé Roquefort, 208
Stuffed, 85
Timbales, Broccoli Herb, 288–
    289
Timbales, Onion, 270–271
Timbales, Spinach-Herb, 288–
    289
Zabaglione, Strawberries with,
    542–543
Eggplant
    About 255–256
    Baked, 255
    Baked, and Zucchini, Creamy,
        170
    Barbecued, 256
    Broiled, 255

Eggplant *(cont.)*
Bulgur with, Tomato, 324
with Butter Beans and
Plums, 146
Couscous with, 326–327
Grilled Vegetable
Parmesan, 170
Mediterranean, 169
Microwaved, 255–256
Moussaka, 149
Mozzarella Baked, and
Zucchini, 170
Parmigiana, 171
Pasta with Tomato and,
Sauce, 190
Ratatouille, 257
with Red Peppers and Shiitake
Mushrooms, 169
Rollatini, 172
Sandwiches, Barbecue, 461
Sautéed with Tomatoes,
Capers, and Garlic, 256
Spread
Baba Ganoujh, 54
with Balsamic Vinegar
Caponata, 55
Caponata, Beany, 56
Grilled, 53
Olive Caviar, 52
Poor Man's Caviar, 53
Ratatouille, 55
Sue Levy's, 53
Stuffed, Bulgur-, 167
Stuffed, Quinoa-, 168
Stuffed, Turkish, 168
Stuffed Young, 256–257
Tart, Roasted, and Red
Pepper, 214
and Tofu with Plum Sauce,
220–221
Wheat Berries with Gingered,
328
Wheat Berries Provencal, 327
Ziti with Roasted Red Pepper
and Grilled, 192
Empanadas, About, 466
Empanadas Basic, 466–467

Empanadas, Spinach, 467
Empanadas Vegetable, 467
Enchilada Mexican Egg, 454
Endive. *See* Belgian Endive
Entree Listings, 136–138
Escarole. *See Also* Greens
and Beans, 263
and Cucumber, Sliced, 264
Garbanzo Beans with, 333
Kamut with Sautéed, and
Yellow Squash, 309
with Mushrooms, 264
Risotto with, 157
Sautéed, 263
Soup, -Bean, 127
Soup, Lentil-, 127
Stuffed Shells, and Cheese, 188
Ethiopian Vegetable Stew, 163

F

Fajitas, 163
Falafel, 460
Farmer-Cheese Pastry Dough,
Food Processor, 519
Farmer's Market Salad, 342
Fat, About, 4–6
Fat Content Codes, 43
Fats in Food, Table, 6
Fennel
About, 258
Braised, 258
Curried Zucchini and, 290
au Gratin, 258–259
Green Beans, Italian-Style, 260
Quinoa with Jerusalem
Artichokes and, 314
Salad, Apple-Gouda-, 370
Salad, Cucumber, 354
Salad, Grilled, and Orange, 371
Sautéed, and Celery with Water
Chestnuts and Toasted
Almonds, 258
Soup, Curried Yellow Pepper, 103
Soup, Peppery Potato-, 114
Spaghetti Squash with, 294
Tart, Gorgonzola, Leek, and, 213

Feta Cheese
Dressing, 392
Eggplant, Mediterranean, 169
Potato Pancakes, Greek, 70
Salad
Arugula, with Fresh Figs
and, 367
Cucumber, Greek 50
Greek, 341
Potato, Greek, 363
Tomato and, 351
Warm Lentil with Balsamic
Dressing, 383
Spanakopita, 176
Tart, Tomato–, 212
Fiddlehead Ferns with Wild
Rice, 321
Fig(s)
Bread, -Cardamom,
Dried, 399
Bread, Cranberry-, 401
Tart, Honey Apple–, 525
Salad, Arugula with Fresh,
and Feta Cheese, 367
Chutney, -Were-Cheap, 487
Filled Pastries, 527
Five-Grain Bread, 419
Flaky Pastry, 518
Flan, Rum, 550
Flavored Butter, 489
Flavored Croutons, 427
Flavored Oils, About, 17
Flour, About, 302
Focaccia, 424–425
Fondue, German, 67
Fondue, Swiss Cheese, 67
Food Processor Farmer-Cheese
Pastry Dough, 519
Food Processor Mayonnaise, 471
Fran's Great Grain Dish, 152
French
Bread, Sourdough, 426
Pizza, Bread, 463
Salad, Lentil, with Hearts of
Palm, 384
Soup, Lentil-Vegetable, 129
Soup, Onion, 102

Toast
  About, 442
  Barbecue, 444
  Cinnamon, 442
  Curried, 444
  Garlic, 443
  Maple, 442–443
  Orange, 443
  Pineapple, 443
  Traditional, 442
  Vinaigrette, 391
Fresh
  Bread, Rosemary-Pepper Rye, 416–417
  Cake, Peach, 504–505
  Mustard, Raspberry, 471
  Orange Slices in Liqueur, 543
  Piña Colada, 563
  Salsa, Pineapple, 481
  Soup, Spinach Cream, 118
  Soup, Tomato, 97
  Strudel Filling, Raspberry, 529
  Tart, Raspberry, with Blueberry Filling, 523
  Tea, Ginger, 558–559
  Tea, Mint, 558
  Vinaigrette, Herb Balsamic, 393
Fried
  Bananas, Sweet, 279
  Cauliflower, Batter, 251
  Mozzarella, 68
  Okra, 269
  Onion, Crispy, 481
  Onion Rings, 271
  Plantains, Green, 279
  Polenta, 307
  Rice, 318
  Rice, Continental, 318–319
  Rice, Curried, 318
  Zucchini Sticks, 68–69
Frijoles, 331
Frittata, 453
Fritters, Banana, 439
Fritters, Blueberry, 439
Fritters, Corn, 254

Frosting
  Buttercream, Coffee–Rum, 515–516
  Butter–Cream Cheese, 516
  Buttercream, Mocha, 515
  Chocolate, Light, 515
  Chocolate, Sour Cream, 516
  Cream Cheese, 516
  Ganache, 517
Frozen Piña Colada Mousse, 524–525
Frozen Piña Colada Mousse Tarts, 524–525
Frozen Fruit Shake, 562
Fruit(ed). *See Also* Individual Listings
  About, 15
  Couscous with Golden, and Vegetables, 326
  Millet with Dried, 312
  Salad
    About, 387
    Berry Berry Berry Good, 389
    Calypso-Berry, 389
    Cottage Cheese and, 390
    Couscous, 375
    Shredded Red Cabbage and Asian Pear, 366
    Summer Brunch, 390
    Tropical Wheat Berry, 373
    Waldorf, 365
    Winter, 388
  Shake, Frozen, 562
  Soup, Yin and Yang, 133
  Tartlets, 525–526
Fudge Tartlets, Walnut, 526

G

Gado Gado, 224
Ganache, 517
Garbanzo Beans. *See* Chickpea(s)
Garden Tomato Soup, 100
Garden Vegetable Salad, 349
Garlic(ky)
  Bread, Butter, 428
  Broccoli with Black Beans and, 143

Dip, Roasted, 63
French Toast, 443
Green Beans, 259
Green Beans, Orange-Glazed, 259
Knots, 424
Olives, Spicy, 86
Pasta with Broccoli and, 189
Pasta with Olive Oil and, 189
Pasta with Olives, and Pine Nuts, 189
Pea Puree, 58
Pita Points, 431
Roasted, 51
Sauce, Tomato, 473
Sautéed, Broccoli with, 242
Sautéed Escarole, 263
Sautéed Eggplant with Tomatoes, Capers, and Garlic, 256
Sautéed, Spinach, 263
Soup, Creamy Roasted Garlic, 115
Spaghetti Squash, Basil, 294
Spread, -Herb, 46
Stuffed Mushrooms, Parmesan, 83
Yellow Poatoes with Red Swiss Chard, Rosemary, and, 285
Gazpacho, 130
Gazpacho, Green, 130
Gazpacho, Yellow, 130
Gelles Family Salad, 339
German Fondue, 67
Ghee, 494
Ginger(ed)
  -Baked Root Vegetables, 299
  Carrot Puree, 249
  Cookies, Gingerbread, 535
  Dressing, Arugula Salad with Fruit and Lime-, 367
  Frosting, Butter–Cream Cheese, 516
  Gingerbread, Apple, 511
  Glaze, Confectioners' Sugar, 517
  Glaze, Orange, 483
  Jam, Apricot, 490

Ginger(ed) *(cont.)*
Pancakes, Gingerbread, 436
Snow Peas with Scallions and, 274
Soup, -Cantaloupe, 134
Tea, Fresh, 558–559
Wheat Berries with, Eggplant, 328
Glaze, Confectioners' Sugar, 517
Gnocchi
with Butter and Cheese, 204
di Patate, 203
Spinach, 203
Spinach and Ricotta, 204
with Wild Mushroom Sauce, 195
Goat Cheese
Baked, Salad Greens with, 346
Dressing, Spinach Salad with, 344
Ravioli Filling, 187
Salad, Greens with Baked, 346
Salad, Wheat Berry with Tomatoes and, 372
on Sliced Baguette, Sun-Dried Tomato and, 49
Spread, Chevre, Herbed, 49
Spread, Garlic-Herb, 46
Spread, Goat, on Sliced Baguette,
Spread, Sun-Dried Tomato and, 49
Good Old Macaroni and Cheese, 216
Gorgonzola Cheese Sauce, Polenta with, 81
Gorgonzola, Leek, and Fennel Tart, 213
Gorgonzola, Risotto with, and Artichoke Hearts, 156–157
Grain Dish, Fran's Great, 152
Grains. *See Also* Individual Grains
Grains Cooking Tables, 301, 302
Grains, About, 7, 8, 9,10, 11, 300–302
Granola, Brown Sugar, 446
Grape Leaves, Stuffed, 72–73

Grapefruit Salad, -Kiwi, 388
Grapefruit Sorbet, 551
Grapefruit Sorbet, Mint, 551
Grapes, Caramelized, 547
Grapes, Sautéed Jícama with, Lime-, 265
Greek
Potato Pancakes, 70
Salad, 341
Salad, Cucumber, 50, 355
Salad, Potato, 363
Green Bean(s)
About, 259
Atakilt Acilch'a, 163
Creamy Parmesan, 260–261
Curried Chickpeas and Kale, 147
Curried Okra with, 270
Curry, Mixed Vegetable, 181
Gado Gado, 224
Garlic, 259
Italian-Style and Fennel 260
with Lemon Butter, 236
Marinated Szechuan, Cold, 261
Orange-Glazed Garlic, 259
Salad with Creamy Mustard Dressing, 357
Salad, Three Bean, 385
Sesame, 237
Soup, Crimini Mushroom and, 107
Stew, Indonesian Vegetable, 164
Szechuan, 261
with Chickpeas in Groundnut Sauce, 262
with Shallots, Spicy, 260
Green Gazpacho, 130
Green Potato Salad, 363
Green Tomato–Pineapple Chutney, 487
Green Tomato Relish, 485
Green and White Lasagna, 196
Greens. *See Also* Escarole
About, 262
Collards, 263
Collards, Bulgur with Squash, Carrots, and, 325

Collards, Zucchini, and Tomatoes, 262
with Grilled Mushrooms, Mixed, 343
Kale, Curried Chickpeas and, 147
Salad, Mixed, Vegetable Threads, 342–434
Soup, Collard and Black-Eyed Pea, 122
Soup, Sorrel, 131
Swiss Chard with Cranberry Beans, Creamy, 263
Swiss Chard with Rosemary and Garlic Yellow Potatoes, 285
with Vegetable Threads, Mixed 342–343
Grilled
Parmesan, Vegetable, 170
Piperade, Vegetable, 454
Salad, Chickpea and, Vegetable, 386
Salad, Fennel and Orange, 371
Salad, Vegetable and Bread, 352
Sandwich, Cheese, 460
Spread, Eggplant, 53
Teriyaki, Vegetables, 234
Vegetables, Basic, 233
Grits, About, 308
Grits with Cheese, 308
Guacamole, 56
Gumbo Soup, 101

H

Hamantashen, 537
Hard Boiled Egg Cookies, Mom's, 535
Hard Cooked Eggs, 448
Hash and Eggs, 447
Hazelnut Praline, Mashed Sweet Potatoes with, 285
Health, About, 4–7
Health Salad, 358
Hearts of Palm French Lentil Salad with, 384

Hearts of Palm Salad,
    Asparagus, 353
Hearts of Palm Salad, Tomato,
    Endive and, 351
Heavenly Eggnog, 565
Herb(s)(ed). *See Also* Basil,
    Cilantro, Dill, Parsley
    About, 15–16
    Biscuits, 405
    Chèvre, 49
    Dressing, Buttermilk 392
    Soup, Tomato, 97
    Stuffed Mushrooms, 82
    Vinaigrette, Fresh,
        Balsamic, 393
Hoisin-Soy Marinade, 482
Hoisin Sprouts with Cloud
    Ears, 239
Hoisin Walnuts, 88
Holiday Challah, 422
Hollandaise, Blender, 472
Homemade Butter, 489
Homemade Coconut Milk, 497
Homemade Mocha Liqueur, 566
Homemade Tortilla Chips, 86–87
Honey
    Beets in Red Wine and, 240
    Dip, -Mustard, 64
    Dressing, -Mustard,
        Arugula, Honeydew, and
        Raspberries, 367
    Dressing, -Yogurt, Beet and
        Pear Salad, with 370
    Pancakes, Wheat Germ, 434
    Plantains, -Lemon Glazed, 279
    Pudding, Couscous, 549
    Tart, Apple-Fig, 525
Honeydew and Raspberries,
    Arugula Salad with, 367
Honeydew Soup, Minted, 133
Honeydew Soup, Kiwi-, 133
Honeydew Soup, Yin and
    Yang, 134
Horseradish Dip, Yogurt-, 65
Horseradish Sauce, Beet-, 485
Hot Apple Tea, 559
Hot and Sour Soup, 108–109

Huevos al Nido, 449
Huevos Rancheros, 455
Hummus, 57
Humus, Black Bean, 58
Hummus, Vegetable, 57
Hush Puppies, 308

I

Iced Mint Tea, 558
Icing, Decorative, 517
Indian Rice, Yellow, 316
Indonesian Vegetable Stew, 164
Ingredients, About, 13–19
Ingredients, Shopping for, 12–13
Irish Soda Bread, Untraditional, 402
Israeli Salad, 356
Italian Dressing, 391
Italian Popcorn, 91
Italian Stuffed Tomato, 298
Italian-Style Green Beans and
    Fennel, 260

J

Jalapeño Carrots, 248
Jalapeño Jícama, 248
Jam
    Apricot, 490
    Apricot, Ginger, 490
    Muffins, -Filled, 409
    Plum, Damson, 490
    Plum and Strawberry, 490
    Raspberry, 490
Jamaican Kiwi-Strawberry
    Salad, 387
Jerusalem Artichoke, About, 265
Jerusalem Artichoke–Almond
    Soup, 120
Jerusalem Artichokes with Black
    Beans, 265
Jerusalem Artichokes and
    Fennel, Quinoa with, 314
Jícama
    About, 265
    Jalapeño, 248
    Kasha with, and Apples, 306

Salad, Boston Lettuce with,
    Oranges, and Almonds, 371
Salad, Chickpea and Sprouted-
    Pea, 387
Salad, Kasha, and Mandarin
    Orange, 380
Salad, Shredded Carrot
    and, 359
Salad, Tropical Wheat
    Berry, 373
Sautéed, -with Grapes,
    Lime, 265
Julienned Endive Salad with
    Graeta Olive Dressing, 346
Julienned Vegetables,
    Sautéed, 80

K

Kamut, About, 301, 309
Kamut and Beans, Vegetables
    with, 148
Kamut, Thanksgiving, 309
Kamut with Sautéed Escarole
    and Yellow Squash, 309
Kasha
    About, 302,306
    Basic Cooking, 303
    with Jícama and Apples, 306
    Knishes, 465
    Salad, Jícama, and Mandarin
        Orange, 380
    Strudel Filling, Cabbage, 178
    Stuffed Cabbage, Sweet and
        Sour, 166–167
    with Tofu and Cauliflower, 221
    Varniskas, 306
Kebabs, Vegetable, 233
Ketchup, 470
    Raspberry, 470
    Strawberry, 470
Kidney Bean(s)
    Barbecue, 332
    Chili, 154
    Grain Dish, Fran's Great,
        152
    Minestrone, 96

Kidney Bean(s) *(cont.)*
  Rice with, and Corn,
    Barbecue, 319
  Rice, and Tofu, Madrid, 222
  Rizcous, Corn, and, 323
  Salad, Macaroni and, 382
  Salad, Three Bean, 385
  Stew, Mexicali, 142
  Tamale Pie, 223
  Tofu and, Spanish-, Barbecue, 222
Kitchen Sink Soup, 121
Kiwi Fruit Salad, Grapefruit-, 388
Kiwi-Honeydew Soup, 133
Kiwi-Pineapple Sorbet, 552
Kiwi-Strawberry Salad,
    Jamaican, 387
Knishes
  About, 464
  Basic, 465
  Broccoli-Cheddar, 465
  Kasha, 465
  Mini, 464
  Spinach, 466
  Sweet Potato–Squash, 466
Kohlrabi, About, 266
Kohlrabi, Parmesan Baked, 266

L

Lasagna, Green and White, 197
Lasagna Mushroom, with Bell
    Pepper Cream Sauce, 198
Lasagna, Vegetable, 196
Lasso, 561
Latkes. *See Also* Potato Pancakes
Latkes, 70
Latkes, Corn, 71
Latkes, Traditional, 70
Lattice-Top Peach Pie, 520
Leek(s)
  About, 266
  Coulis, Tomato, 99
  Melt, Zucchini-, 159
  Provencal, 266–267
  Soup
    Potato, 114
    Tomato and, Cream, 99

Vichyssoise, 114
  and Wild Rice, 126
  Zucchini-, 106
Tart, Gorgonzola, and
    Fennel, 213
Tart, Mushroom, 214
Vinaigrette, and Roasted Red
    Peppers, 80
Leftover Coconut Rice Pudding,
    547–548
Lekvar, Apricot, 393
Lekvar, 393
Lekvar, Orange-Scented, 493
Lekvar, Lemon-Scented, 493
Lemon
  Butter, Asparagus with, 236
  Butter, Green Beans with, 236
  Cake, -Scented Angel
    Food, 514
  Cauliflower with Parsley
    and, 250
  Crust, Citrus, 518
  Curd, 494
  Dressing, -Scented Balsamic,
    345
  Lekvar, Scented, 493
  Lemonade, 559
  Mayonnaise, Artichokes with,
    -Garlic, 84
  Mayonnaise, Tofu, 472
  Muffins, Poppy Seed, 411
  Pancakes, Blueberry-, 435
  Pancakes, –Oat Bran, 435
  Plantains, Honey-, Glazed, 279
  Rice, Wild and White, 321
  Soup, Avgolemono, 103
  Squares, 538
  Tart, Meringue, 526
  Tartlets, Meringue, 526
Lentil(s)
  Burgers, 162
  Moussaka, 149
  Pasta with Vegetables and,
    Randy Kraft's, 192
  Salad, Brown Rice and, 377
  Salad, French, with Hearts of
    Palm, 384

Salad, and Mushroom, 383
Salad, Warm, with Balsamic
    Dressing, 383
Shepherd's Pie, 147
Soup, -Cauliflower, 128
Soup, Creamy French, 128
Soup, -Escarole, 127
Soup, French, -Vegetable, 129
Stew, and Mushroom, 148
in Tomato Sauce, 334
with Zuchini 451
Lettuce and Pea Soup, 106
Light and Tangy Sourdough
    Pancakes, 437
Light Chocolate Frosting, 515
Lima Beans. *See* Beans
Lime
  Curd, 494
  Dressing, Arugula Salad with,
    -Ginger, 367
  Limeade, 559
  Poached Pears in Wine and, 544
  -Sautéed Jícama with
    Grapes, 265
  Squares, 538
Liptauer, 47
Little Apple Turnovers, 527
Lo Mein, 206
Low-Fat Pancakes, 438
Lunch, About, 19–20
Lunch Listings, 432

M

Macaroni and Bean Salad, 382
Macaroni and Cheese, Good
    Old, 216
Macaroni and Three
    Cheeses, 216
Madrid Rice, Beans, and
    Tofu, 222
Mail Order Sources, 43
Malted Milk, 566
Mandarin Quinoa Salad, 381
Mandarin Soup, 107
Mango
  Chutney, 486

Soup, Curried Sweet
    Potato-, 115
Salad, Calypso Berry, 389
Salad, -Strawberry, 389
Manhattan-Style Vegetable
    Chowder, 109
Manicotti, 188–189
Maple French Toast, 442–443
Maple Waffles, 441
Marble Cheesecake, 530–531
Marble Cheesecake, Orange,
    530–531
Marinade Hoisin-Soy, 482
Marinade, Orange Glaze, 483
Marinade Southwest, 482–483
Marinara Sauce
    Basil, 474
    Chunky 473
    Easy Fresh, 191
    Slow-Cooking Fresh
        Tomato, 473
    Spaghetti Squash with
        Bulgur, 165
Marinated Chickpea Salad, 386
Marinated Szechuan Green
    Beans, Cold, 261
Mashed. *See Also* Pureed
    Potatoes, Perfect, 281
    Potatoes, Ruthie's
        Thanksgiving Chive, 282
    Rutabaga, 299
    Sweet Potatoes with Hazelnut
        Praline, 285
    Sweet Potatoes, Pecan, 286
Mayonnaise
    Curried, Artichokes with ,83
    Food Processor, 471
    Lemon-Garlic, Artichokes
        with, 84
    Tofu, 472
    Tofu, Lemon, 472
Meals in Minutes, 7
Mediterranean Eggplant, 169
Mee Grob, 207
Meetz, 564
Meetz, Spiced, 564
Menu Planning, 20–42

Caribbean-Spanish-African
    Cuisine, 24–25
Chinese Cuisine, 25–26
Company's Coming, 21–22
Eastern European Cuisine, 27–28
Elegant Dinner to Impress the
    Boss, 22–24
French Cuisine, 28–30
Greek Cuisine, 30–31
Hearty Meals, 39–40
Indian Cuisine, 31–32
Italian Cuisine, 32–34
Japanese Cuisine, 34–35
Last-Minute Meals, 40–42
Mexican and Southwest
    Cuisine, 35–37
Middle Eastern Cuisine, 37–38
Timing, 20–21
Mexicali Stew, 142
Mexican Egg Enchilada, 454
Mexican Millet, 311
Microwaved(ing)
    Artichokes, 235
    Baked Potatoes, 280
    Eggplant, 255
    Squash, 292
    Vegetables, 232
Mighty Vegetable Broth, 94
Millet
    About, 310
    Basic Cooking, 301
    Butternut Squash with Curried,
        Filling, 166
    Casserole, Corn and, 162
    Chili, with Cheese, 311
    Chili, with Peppers, 311
    Curried, 310
    with Dried Fruits, 312
    Mexican, 311
    Orange-Almond, 312
    Salad, Asian, 380
    Salad, Curried, 380–381
Minestrone, 96
Mini Egg Rolls, 77
Mini Vegetable Dumplings, 76
Mint(ed)
    Peas, 275

Salad, Basil-, Cucumber,
    and Pea, 356 ·
Sorbet, Grapefruit, 551
Soup, Honeydew, 133
Soup, Lettuce and Pea, 106
Soup, Pea, 124
Tea, Fresh, 558
Miso Soup, 121
Mixed Greens with Grilled
    Mushrooms, 343
Mixed Greens with Vegetable
    Threads, 342–343
Mixed Vegetable Curry, 181
Mocha Buttercream Frosting, 515
Mocha Cake, Buttermilk, 512
Mocha Cream Liqueur, Home-
    made, 566
Mole Almonds, 88
Mom's Hard-Boiled Egg
    Cookies, 535
Moo Shu Vegetables, 219
Mooros y Christianos, 141
Moroccan Carrot Salad, 360
Moroccan Vegetables with
    Couscous, 145
Moussaka, 149
Mousse, Chocolate, 554
Mousse, Frozen Piña Colada,
    524–525
Mozzarella
    Baked Eggplant and
        Zucchini, 170
    Bites, 68
    en Carrozza, 69
    Fried, 68–69
    Parmesan, Grilled Vegetable,
        170
    Parmigiana, Eggplant, 171
    Parmigiana, Stuffed Shells, 188
    Salad, 68
    Salad, Tomato-, 350
    Sandwich, Roasted Pepper
        and, 459
    Sandwich, Tomatoes and, 459
Muffin(s)
    Basic, 408
    Blueberry, 408

Muffin(s)
  Basic, 408
  Blueberry, 408
  Chocolate-Filled, 409
  Corn, 409
  Cornmeal Bran, 410
  Cranberry-Oatmeal, 411
  Date-Bran, 410
  Egg in a, 448
  Jam-Filled, 409
  Lemon-Poppy Seed, 411
  Streusel-Topped, 408
  Sweet Potato Meadow, 412
  Three-Grain, 410
Mulled Cider, 560
Mulligatawny Soup, 104
Mushroom(s)
  About, 267
  Barley with, 304
  Braised Celery with Wild, 252
  Bread Pudding, Savory, 210
  Broth, 95
  Burgers, Lentil, 162
  Croustades, 78
  Curry, Cabbage and, 182
  Eggplant with Red Peppers
    and Shiitake, 169
  Escarole with, 264
  Greens with Grilled, Mixed,
    343
  Lasagna with Bell Pepper
    Cream Sauce, 198
  Oyster, Broccoli with, 242
  Paprikash with Dumplings, 174
  Pâté, Creamy, 59
  Persiller, Button, 268
  Ragout of Wild, 173
  Ravioli Filling, Rosemary, 187
  Risotto, Rosemary-, 158–159
  Salad
    Lentil and, 383
    Mixed Greens with
      Grilled, 343
    Sautéed Portobello, and Pinto
      Bean, 382–383
    Spinach and, I, 344
    Spinach and, II, 345

Sauce, Gnocchi with Wild, 195
Sautéed Snow Peas, Peas,
    and, 273
Sautéed on Toast, 461
Sautéed, with Water
    Chestnuts, 267
Sautéed Wild, and Peas, 268
Seitan with Bean Sprouts
    and, 227
Soup, -Barley, 126
Soup, Cream of, 117
Soup, Crimini, and Green
    Bean, 107
Spread, Brandied, 60
Spread, –Water Chestnut, 60
Stew, Lentil and, 148
Stir-Fried Vegetables with, on a
    Bird's Nest, 180
Stroganoff, 173
Strudel Filling, Spinach-, 177
Strudel Filling, Wild Rice–, 178
Stuffed
  Cheese, 83
  Garlicky Parmesan, 83
  Herb, 82
  Old-Fashioned, 82
  Peppers, Wildly, 160
  Stilton, 82
Tart, -Leek, 214
Tartlets, 59
Torta di Funghi e Patate,
    Tuscan, 175
Tortellini with Wild, Sauce, 195
Zucchini with Shiitake, 290–291
Mustard Dip, Honey-,64
Mustard, Fresh Raspberry, 471
Mustard, Raspberry, 471

N

Nachos, 67
Nachos Grande, 68
Nam Pla, 482
Nectarine Chutney, 488
Nectarine Chutney, Blueberry-,
    487–488
Nectarine Salad, Blueberry-, 388

Nectarine Salad, Spinach,
    Strawberry and, 369
Nice and Crunchy, Crisp and
    Seedy Homemade Crackers,
    429
Noodle(s)
  About, 330
  with Broccoli and Cabbage,
    204–205
  Crispy, 85
  Lo Mein, 206
  Mee Grob, 207
  with Peanut Sauce, 205
  Pudding, 330
  Pudding, Savory, 330
  Rice, Broccoli Rabe with, 206
  with Seitan, 226
  with Sesame Sauce, 205
  Soup, Chinese Cabbage
    with, 108
  with Sour Cream and Apple
    Sauce, 331
Nut(s). See Individual Listings

O

Oat Grain Dish, Fran's Great, 152
Oatmeal
  Bread, Donna Mason's Dense
    and Chewy Whole Grain,
    418–419
  Cookies, Bar, 533
  Cookies, Raisin, 532
  Muffins, Cranberry, 411
  Pancakes, 437
  Pancakes, Corn and,
    (No Wheat), 438
  Waffles, Corn and,
    (No Wheat), 438
Oil, About, 5, 16–17
Oil Crust, 517
Okra
  About, 269
  Creole, with Corn, 269
  Curried, with Green Beans, 270
  Curry, Plaintain, and Sweet
    Potato, 183

Fried, 269
Fried, Chili, 269
Soup, Gumbo, 101
Old-Fashioned Apple Butter, 491
Old-Fashioned Apple Sauce, 543
Old-Fashioned Stuffed
    Mushrooms, 82
Olive(s)
  About Oil, 16–17
  Caviar, 52
  Caviar, Zucchini-, 52
  Dressing, Julienned Endive
      Salad with Graeta, 346
  Garlicky, Spicy, 86
  Leeks Provencal, 266–267
  Millet, Mexican, 311
  Pasta with, Garlic, and Pine
      Nuts, 189
  Pasta Puttanesca, 190–191
  Picadillo, Black Bean, 225
  Salad
    Bean, and Vegetable, 356
    Black Bean and, 384–385
    Chickpea, Marinated, 386
    Greek, 341
    Pasta, 381
    Potato, Greek, 363
    Rice, Picadillo, 376–377
    Rice and Roman Bean,
        Stuffed, 382
    Rice, Spanish, 376–377
    South of the Border, 348–349
  Sandwich, Cream Cheese
      and, 458
  Spread, Chopped Tomato
      and, 51
Omelet. See Also Eggs
  About, 450
  Basic, with Filling, 450–451
  Cheese, 450–451
  Spanish, 451
  Tofu-Soy Sprout, with Peanut
      Sauce, 452
  Zucchini, 451
  Onion, Vidalia, 452
Onion
  About, 270

Caramelized Vidalias, 452
Cavetelli with Cabbage and
    Caramelized, 193
Dip, Caramelized, and
    Sun-Dried Tomato, 65
Fried Crispy, 481
Fried, Rings, 271
Omelet, Vidalia, 452
Quiche, Vidalia, 211
Relish, Cilantro-Two, 484
Rice with, and Red Bell
    Pepper, Brown, 320
Salad, Watercress, Cucumber,
    and, with Creamy Pepper
    Dressing, 347
Sautéed Peppers, and
    Cauliflower, 277
Sautéed Red, Asparagus,
    Tomatoes, and, 236–237
Soup, 101
Soup, French, 102
Soup, Sherried, 101
Stuffed, Baked, 272
Sweet and Sour Pearl, 271
Timbales, 270–271
Orange
  Bananas, -Basted, 542
  Biscuits, Pecan-, 403
  Bread, -Pumpkin-Cranberry-
      Date, 397
  Bread, Swedish Limpa,
      422–423
  Broccoli with, and
      Almonds, 243
  Cake, -Scented Angel
      Food, 514
  Cheesecake, Marble, 530–531
  Crepes, 553
  French Toast, 443
  Frosting, Buttercream, 516
  Frosting, Cream Cheese, 516
  Glaze, 483
  Green Beans,-Glazed
      Garlic, 259
  Julius, Not Quite, 563
  Lekvar, Scented, 493
  Millet, -Almond, 312

Pancakes, Cranberry-, 436
Parsnip, -Glazed, 272
Pudding, Polenta, 549
Rutabaga and Carrots, -
    Sautéed, 300
Salad
  Boston Lettuce with Jícama,
      and Almonds, 371
  Calypso Berry, 389
  Couscous with, 376
  Grilled Fennel and, 371
  Kasha, Jícama, and
      Mandarin, 380
  Mandarin Quinoa, 381
  Papaya-Banana-, 389
  Winter, 388
Sauce, -Flavored Barbecue, 478
Slices in Liqueur, Fresh, 543
Sweet Potatoes, Mashed, 286
Tart-Blueberry, 523
Oriental Dipping Sauce, 482
Oriental Snow Peas, Cauliflower,
    and Red Pepper, 274
Orzo Stuffed Tomatoes, 298
Orzo Wild Rice with and Three-
    Color Peppers, 322
Oven Fries, 283

P

Pancake(s)
  Blueberry, 434
  Blueberry-Lemon, 435
  Buttermilk, 434
  Corn and Oat (No Wheat), 438
  Cranberry-Orange, 436
  Gingerbread, 436
  Lemon-Oat Bran, 435
  Low-Fat, 438
  Oatmeal, 437
  Silver Dollar, 434
  Sour Cream, 435
  Sourdough, Light and
      Tangy, 437
  Wheat Germ-Honey, 434
Paneer, 495
Pantry, Stocking, 9–11

Papaya-Banana-Orange
   Salad, 389
Papaya, Couscous-Stuffed, 326
Paprika with Dumplings,
   Mushrooms, 174
Paprikash Rice, 316
Parmesan
   Biscuits, 406
   Bread, Garlic, 428
   Broccoli, Creamy, 260–261
   Celeriac, Baked, 266
   Crackers, 430
   Dip, Artichoke and, 66
   Green Beans, Creamy,
      260–261
   Grilled Vegetable, 170
   Kohlrabi, Baked, 266
Parmigiana, Eggplant, 171
Parmigiana, Stuffed Shells, 188
Parsley(ied)
   Carrots, 248
   Cauliflower with, and
      Lemon, 250
   Mushrooms Persiller,
      Button, 268
   Pesto, Spinach-, 477
   Potatoes, Boiling, 281
   Rice, 315
   Rice and Black Beans, 141
   Salad, 344
   Salad, Green Potato, 363
   Soup, Cream of, Root and
      Parsnip, 113
   Soup, Cream of, Root and
      Parsnip, Chilled, 113
Parsnip
   About, 272
   Cake, Coconut Layer,
      511–512
   Orange-Glazed, 272
   Soup, -Carrot, 112
   Soup, Cream of Parsley Root
      and, 113
   Soup, Cream of, Root and
      Parsnip, Chilled, 113
Party Cheese Log, 49
Party Punch, 564

Pasta. *See Also* Lasagna, Sauce(s)
   About, 184
   with Broccoli and Garlic, 189
   Cavetelli with Cabbage and
      Caramelized Onions, 193
   with Creamy Basil Sauce, 194
   Dough, Semolina, 185
   Dough, Spinach, 186
   Dough, Tomato, 185
   Kasha Varniskas, 306
   Macaroni and Cheese, Good
      Old, 216
   Macaroni and Cheese, Three
      Cheese, 216
   Manicotti, 188–189
   Minestrone, 96
   with Olive Oil and Garlic, 189
   with Olives, Garlic, and Pine
      Nuts, 189
   Penne Primavera with Creamy
      Tomato Sauce, 193
   Penne with Vodka Sauce, 194
   Puttanesca, 190–191
   Salad, 381
   Salad, Macaroni and Bean,
      382
   Soup, Escarole and Bean, 127
   Spaghetti, Baked, 216
   Springtime, 191
   Stuffed Peppers, Wildly, 160
   Stuffed Shells, Escarole and
      Cheese, 188
   Stuffed Shells Parmigiana,
      Escarole and Cheese, 188
   Stuffed Tomatoes, Orzo, 298
   Technique, 184–185
   with Tomato and Eggplant
      Sauce, 190
   Torte, 199
   Tortellini with Wild Mushroom
      Sauce, 195
   with Vegetables and Lentils,
      Randy Kraft's, 192
   Wild Rice with Orzo and
      Three-Color Peppers, 322
   with Yellow Tomato Sauce,
      191

Ziti, Baked, 199
Ziti with Broccoli and
   Rosemary, 195
Ziti with Roasted Red Pepper
   and Grilled Eggplant, 192
Pastry(ies). *See Also* Turnovers
   Crust, All-Butter, 518
   Crust, All-Shortening, 518
   Crust, Citrus, 518
   Crust, Oil, 517
   Danish, 501
   Dough, Danish, 500–501
   Dough, Sweet Yeast, 501
   Empanada, 466–467
   Farmer-Cheese, Dough, Food
      Processor, 519
   Farmer-Cheese,
      Sweetened, 519
   Filled, 527
   Flaky, 518
   Tartlet Shells, 519
Pâté
   Carrot, 61
   Mushroom, Creamy, 59
   Mushroom Spread,
      Brandied, 60
   Mushroom–Water Chestnut
      Spread, 60
   Tricolor Curried, 62
Pea(s). *See Also* Pea Pods, Split
   Peas
   About, 275
   Creamed, 275
   Creamed, Lower-Fat, 275
   Creamed, Richer, 275
   Dilled, 275
   Minted, 275
   Pureed, 276
   Pureed, Garlic, 58
   Risi e Bisi, 159
   Salad, Chickpea and
      Sprouted, 387
   Salad, Dilled Rice and, 376
   Salad, Basil-Mint Cucumber
      and, 356
   Sautéed Snow, and Wild
      Mushrooms, 273

Sautéed Wild Mushrooms
and, 268
Soup, Lettuce and, 106
Soup, Minted Lettuce, 106
Soup, Sherried, 124
Spelt and, 310
Pea Pods. *See Also* Pea(s)
About, 273
Snap Pea Salad,–Tomato, 352
Snow Peas
Cauliflower, and Red Bell
Pepper, 274
Cauliflower, and Red Bell
Pepper, Oriental, 274
Rice, Fried, 318
Sautéed Cabbage with, 246
Sautéed, Peas, and Wild
Mushrooms, 273
with Scallions and Ginger,
274
Sautéed, and Wild
Mushrooms, 273
Sugar Snap Saute, 273
Peach(es)
Butter, 492
Cake, Fresh, 504–505
Melba, 555
Pie, Lattice-Top, 520
Salad, and Strawberry, 388
Stewed, and Cherries, 542
Stewed, and Cherries,
Sugarless, 542
Peanut(s)
Cake, Butter, 505–506
Chili, 87
Cookies, Butter, 534
Rice, Curried Fried, 318
Sauce, Green Beans
with Chickpeas in
Groundnut, 262
Sauce, Noodles with, 205
Sauce, Tofu–Soy Sprout
Omelet with, 452
Sauce, Tempeh with Sate,
226
Soup, 119
Trailmix, 89

Pear(s)
Butter, Apple-, -Plum, 491
on a Pillow, Sickle, 545
Poached in Fruit Juice, 544
Poached in Wine and
Lime, 544
Pureed with Winter
Squash, 293
with Raspberry Sauce, 544
Salad, Beet and,with Honey-
Yogurt Dressing, 370
Salad, Bitter Greens with, and
Stilton Dressing, 369
Salad, Grapefruit-Kiwi, 388
Sauce, Apple-, 543
Spiced Sickle, 545
Tart, -Cranberry, 522
Turnover, 545
Pecan
Biscuits, -Orange, 403
Bread, Date-, 397–398
Bread, -Streusel Pumpkin, 396
Cake, Squash, 513
Cookies, –Wheat Germ, 536
Mashed Sweet Potatoes, 286
Sticky Buns, 502
Penne Primavera with Creamy
Tomato Sauce, 193
Penne with Vodka Sauce, 194
Peppered Blue Cornmeal
Biscuits, 405
Peppers. *See* Bell Peppers
Peppery Potato–Fennel
Soup, 114
Perfect Mashed Potatoes, 281
Persimmon-Pineapple Thick
Shake, 561
Pesto
About, 476
Cheesecake, 47
Cilantro, 476
Salad, Cauliflower, 358–359
Sauce for Pizza, 202–203
Spinach-Parsley, 477
Sun-Dried Tomato, 477
Traditional, 476
Vegetables, 291

Picadillo, Black Bean, 225
Picadillo Rice Salad, 376–377
Pico de Gallo, 484
Pie. *See Also* Tart, Tartlet
Pie, Apple, 520
Pie, Peach, Lattice-Top, 520
Pie Sour Cherry, 521
Pigeon Bean and Corn Salad, 386
Pignoli (Pine Nut) Cookies, 534
Pignoli Ravioli Filling,
Spinach-, 187
Pignoli, Pasta with Olives, Garlic,
and, 189
Pilaf, Quinoa, 313
Piña Colada, Fresh, 562
Piña Colada Mousse, Frozen,
524–525
Piña Colada Mousse Tarts,
Frozen, 524–525
Pine Nut. *See* Pignoli
Pineapple
Broiled, Bourbon, 541
Broiled, Rum, 541
Cake, -Coconut, 510–511
Cake, Coconut Parsnip Layer,
511–512
Chutney, Green Tomato–, 487
Cider, Dominican, 560
French Toast, 443
Piña Colada, Fresh, 563
Punch, Party, 564
Rice, Apricot-, Brown , 320–321
Salad, Couscous, Creamy, 375
Salad, Red Pepper, and
Celery, 370
Salad, Winter, 388
Salsa, Fresh, 481
Sorbet, -Kiwi, 552
Strudel Filling, 530
Sweet and Sour Bean Curd, 220
Tarts, Frozen Piña Colada
Mousse, 524–525
Thick Shake, -Banana, 562
Thick Shake, Persimmon-, 561
Pink Champagne Punch, 565
Piperade, 453
Piperade, Grilled Vegetable, 454

Pita Points, Garlic, 431
Pitas, Toasted, 428
Pizza
  About, 200–201
  Boboli and Vegetable Melt, 463
  Crust, Semolina, 202
  Crust, Whole Wheat, 201
  French Bread, 463
  Sauce, Pesto, for, 202–203
  Sauce, Tomato, for, 202
  Technique 200–201
  White, 203
Plain Croutons, 417
Plaintain(s)
  About, 278
  Baked, 278
  Biscuits, 404
  Curry, Okra, and Sweet Potato,
    183
  Fried Sweet Bananas, 279
  Glazed, Honey-Lemon, 279
  Loaf, and Sweet Potato, 278
  Tostones, 279
Plum
  Butter, Apple-Pear-, 491
  Cake, Upside Down, 506–507
  Chutney, Tomato, and Dried
    Fruit, 486
  Eggplant with Butter Beans
    and, 146
  Jam, Damson, 490
  Jam, and Strawberry, 490
  Sauce, Eggplant and Tofu with,
    220–221
  Sorbet, Port Wine–, 551
Poached Eggs, 433
Poached Pears in Fruit Juice, 544
Poached Pears with Raspberry
    Sauce, 544
Poached Pears in Wine and
    Lime, 544
Polenta. See Also Cornmeal
  Basic, 307
  Creamy, 307
  Fried, 307
  with Gorgonzola Cheese
    Sauce, 81

Pie, Black Bean–, 155
  Pudding, Orange, 549
Poor Man's Caviar, 53
Popcorn, 90–91
Popcorn, Chili, 90
Popcorn, Italian, 91
Popcorn, Spicy Seasoned, 90
Poppy Seed Cookies, 534
Poppy Seed Muffins,
    -Lemon, 411
Poppy Seed Waffles, Banana, 440
Porcupines, 538
Port Wine–Plum Sorbet, 551
Portuguese Vegetable Soup, 105
Pot Cheese, 495
Potato(es). See Also Sweet
    Potatoes
  About, 280
  Baked, 280
  Barbecue Oven Fries, 283
  Boiled, 281
  Chips, 87
  Colcannon, 282
  Dilled, 281
  Empanadas, Vegetable, 467
  Gnocchi di Patate, 203
  au Gratin, 284
  au Gratin, Stilton, 284
  Hash, Eggs and, 447
  Mashed, Perfect, 281
  Mashed, Ruthie's
    Thanksgiving Chive, 282
  Microwaved Baked, 280
  Oven Fries, 283
  Pancakes, 70
  Pancakes, Corn and
    Scallion-, 71
  Pancakes, Greek, 70
  Parslied Boiling, 281
  Peppery, -Fennel, 114
  Salad, 363
    Broccoli-, 364
    Greek, 363
    Green, 363
    Roasted Red Pepper and, 365
    Vegetable and, 364
  Samosas, 74–75

Soup, Leek, 114
Soup, Vichyssoise, 114
Strudel Filling, Vegetable-, 177
Stuffed Baked, 283
Stuffed, Decadent Baked, 283
Torta di Funghi e Patate,
    Tuscan, 175
Yellow, with Red Swiss Chard,
    Rosemary, and Garlic, 285
Prune Bread, Apricot-, 398–399
Prune Butter, 493
Pudding
  Bread, Cranberry, 548
  Bread, Raisin, 548
  Corn, 253
  Corn, Tex-Mex 253
  Couscous, Honey, 549
  Noodle, 330
  Noodle, Savory, 330
  Polenta, Orange, 549
  Rice, Leftover Coconut,
    547–548
  Rice, Coconutty, 547–548
Puff Pastry, Egg in, 448
Pumpernickel, 417
Pumpkin Bread, Orange-,
    Cranberry-Date, 397
Pumpkin Bread, Pecan-Streusel
    Bread, 396
Pumpkin Bread, Streusel-
    Topped, 396
Pumpkin Cheesecake, 532
Punch, Pink Champagne, 565
Punch, Party, 564
Puree(d)
  of Broccoflower, 241
  Carrots, Gingered, 249,
  Lima Beans with Dill, 334–335
  Peas, 276
  Winter Squash with Pear, 293

Q

Quesadilla, 464
Quiche. See Also Tart
Quiche, Asparagus, Dilled, 212
Quiche Broccoli-Cheddar, 213

Quiche Onion, Vidalia, 211
Quick Cooking Grains, 7
Quince Butter, 491
Quinces, Stewed, 491–492
Quinoa
  About, 301, 313
  Italiano, 314
  with Jerusalem Artichokes and
    Fennel, 314
  with Mixed Vegetables, 313
  Pilaf, 313
  Salad, Mandarin, 381
  with Shredded Vegetables, 313
  Stewed Garbanzo Beans with
    Zuc-, 151
  -Stuffed Eggplant, 168

R

Radicchio Salad, Endive and,
    with Fresh Raspberries, 368
Radish Salad, Cucumber,
    Endive, and, with Creamy
    Mustard Dressing, 355
Radish Salad, Red, 353
Ragout of Wild Mushrooms, 173
Raisin Bread Pudding, 548
Raisin Corn Bran Bread,
    420–421
Raita, 495
Raita, Tomato, 495
Randy Kraft's Pasta with
    Vegetables and Lentils, 192
Randy's Vegetable Soup, 96–97
Raspberry(ies)
  Butter, -Quince, 491
  Cake, –Cream Cheese, 507
  Cheesecake, Swirl, 531
  Cooler, -Watermelon, 562
  Jam, 490
  Ketchup, 470
  Mustard, 471
  Mustard, Fresh, 471
  Peach Melba, 555
  Roll-Ups, 536
  Salad, Arugula, Honeydew, and,
    with Honey-Mustard, 367

Salad, Berry Berry Berry
    Good, 389
Salad, Endive and Radiccio
    with Fresh, 368
Salad, Summer Brunch
    Fruit, 390
Sauce, 555
Sauce, Pears with, 544
Sorbet, Anisette, 550
Strada, Strawberry-, 540
Strudel Filling, Fresh, 529
Tart, -Apricot, 522
Tart, with Blueberry Filling,
    Fresh, 523
Vinaigrette, Artichokes with,
    84–85
Vinegar, 470–471
Ratatouille, 257
Ratatouille Spread, 55
Rattlesnake Stew, 139
Ravioli Filling, Goat Cheese,
    187
Ravioli Filling, Rosemary-
    Mushroom, 187
Ravioli Filling, Spinach-
    Pignoli, 187
Ravioli Technique, 186
Red Cabbage Salad with
    Ketchup Dressing, 362
Red Pepper. *See* Bell Pepper(s)
Red Radish Salad, 353
Red, White, and Green Salad
    with Balsamic Vinegar, 348
Refried Beans, 332
Refrigerator Cake, Banana–
    Whipped Cream, 513
Relish(es) Listings, 468–469
Rhubard Tart, Strawberry-, with
    Oat Streusel Topping, 521
Rhubarb-Walnut Chutney, 488
Rice. *See Also* Risotto, Rizcous,
    Wild Rice
  About, 301, 315
  Basic Cooking, 303–304
  Brown
    Apricot-Pineapple, 320–321
    Autumn, 320

Burritos, and Black Bean,
    154
  Kamut, Thanksgiving, 309
  with Onion and Red Bell
    Pepper, 320
  Salad, Cantaloupe and
    Apple, 378
  Salad, and Lentil, 377
  Spinach, 319
  Stuffed Eggplant,
    Turkish, 168
  Wheat Berries with,
    Dilled, 329
White
  Barbecue, with Beans and
    Corn, 319
  Barbecue Tofu and,
    with Black Beans, Very
    Quick, 221
  and Black Beans, 141
  and Black Beans,
    Cilantro, 141
  and Black Beans, Parsley, 141
  -Cheese Balls, Spinach-, 75
  Chili, with Tomatillos, 317
  Coconut, 315
  Coconut, Sweetened, 315
  Creole Red Beans and, 142
  Fried, 318
  Fried, Continental, 318–319
  Fried, Curried, 318
  Lemon, Wild and, 321
  Madrid, Beans, and Tofu, 222
  Paprikash, 316
  Parslied, 315
  Pudding, Coconutty,
    547–548
  Pudding, Leftover Coconut,
    547–548
  Saffron, 315
  Salad
    and Pea, Dilled, 376
    Curried Coconut, 377
    Picadillo, 376–377
    Spanish, 376–377
    Stuffed Olive and Roman
    Bean, 382

Rice *(cont.)*
    Wild Rice and, 379
    Spanish, 317
    Short Grain, Basic, 304
    with Three Peppers, 277
    Wild, and, with Lemon, 321
    Wild, and, with Three Color
        Peppers, 322
    Yellow Indian Rice, 316
Rich and Creamy Avocado
    Soup, 133
Risi e Bisi, 159
Risotto. *See Also* Rice, Wild Rice
  About, 156
  with Escarole, 157
  with Gorgonzola and Artichoke
    Hearts, 156–157
  alla Milanese, 156
  Risi e Bisi, 159
  Rosemary-Mushroom, 158–159
  Spinach, 157
  Tomato and Basil, 158
Rizcous, About, 323
Rizcous, Corn, and Beans, 323
Roasted. *See Also* Bell Peppers
Roasted Chestnuts, 89
Roasted Garlic, 51
Roasted Garlic Dip, 63
Roasted Garlic Soup,
    Creamy, 115
Romaine, Avocado, and
    Cucumber Salad, 343
Romaine, Watercress and,
    with Roquefort Dressing,
    348
Root Vegetable and Split Pea
    Soup, 124
Roquefort Cheesecake, 48
Roquefort Dressing,
    Watercress and Romaine
    with, 348
Roquefort Soufflé, 208
Rosemary-Mushroom Ravioli
    Filling, 187
Rosemary-Mushroom Risotto,
    158–159
Rum Broiled Pineapple, 541

Rum Flan, 550
Russian Black Bread, 420
Russian Dressing, 391
Russian Egg Salad Sandwich, 457
Rutabaga
  About, 298
  Baked Root Vegetables,
    Ginger-, 299
  Barley with, and Carrots, 305
  Mashed, 298
  Quinoa with Shredded
    Vegetables, 313
  Sautéed, and Carrots,
    Orange-, 300
  Turnip, Salad, Shredded Carrot
    and Yellow with Cardamom
    Ruthie's Thanksgiving
    Chive Mashed Potatoes, 282
Rye Bread, 416
  Five Grain, 419
  Pumpernickel, 417
  -rish Soda, 402
  Rosemary-Pepper, Fresh,
    416–417
  Russian Black, 420
  Swedish Limpa, 422–423

S

Saag Paneer, 182
Saffron Rice, 315
Saint Patrick's Day Soup, 105
Salad, About, 339
Salad Listings, 336–338
Salad Dressing
  About, 391
  Balsamic, Warm Lentil,
    with, 383
  Boursin, Endive with Roasted
    Red Pepper and, 347
  Cardamom, Shredded Carrot
    and Yellow Turnip with,
  Creamy Mustard, Cucumber,
    Endive and Radish
    Salad, 355
  Creamy Mustard, Green Bean
    Salad with, 357

  Creamy Pepper, Watercress,
    Cucumber, and Onion, 347
  Feta, 392
  French Vinaigrette, 391
  Fresh Herb Balsamic
    Vinaigrette, 393
  Goat Cheese, Spinach,
    with, 344
  Graeta Olive, Julienned Endive
    Salad, 346
  Herbed Buttermilk, 392
  Honey-Mustard,
    Arugula, Honeydew, and
    Raspberries, 367
  Honey-Yogurt, Beet and Pear,
    with, 370
  Italian, 391
  Ketchup, Red Cabbage
    with, 362
  Lemon-Scented Balsamic
    Dressing, 345
  Lime-Ginger, Arugula Salad
    with Fruit and, 367
  Roquefort, Watercress and
    Romaine with, 348
  Russian, 391
  Sofrito, Bulgur Salad with,
    374–375
  Stilton, Bitter Greens and with
    Pears and, 369
  Tahini, 392
  Vinaigrette, Artichokes with
    Raspberry, 84–85
  Vinaigrette, Roasted Red
    Pepper and Leek, 80
Salad Greens with Baked Goat
    Cheese, 346
Salsa
  Cranberry, 480
  Creamy 479
  Easy, 479
  Huevos Rancheros, 455
  Pineapple, Fresh, 481
  Ranchero, 480
  Sauce, Warm, 479
  Soup, Southwest, 97
  Verde, 480

Salt. *See* Sodium
Sambal, 481
Samosas, 74–75
Sandwich. *See Also* Pizza
  About, 19–20, 455–456
  Brie, 459
  Cream Cheese and Olive, 458
  Date-Nut Spread, 458
  Egg, Broiled, 462
  Egg Salad, 456
  Egg Salad, Curried, 457
  Egg Salad, Russian, 457
  Egg Salad, Spinach, 456–457
  Eggplant, Barbeuce, 461
  Falafel, 460
  Grilled Cheese, 460
  Mushrooms on Toast,
    Sautéed, 461
  Quesadilla, 464
  Roasted Red Pepper–Caper,
    458–459
  Roasted Pepper and
    Mozzarella, 459
  Tempeh on a Bun,
    Barbecue, 461
  Welsh Rarebit, 462
Sangria, 565
Sauce(s). *See Also* Barbecue,
    Marinades, Pesto, Salsa
  Beet-Horseradish, 485
  Bell Pepper Cream, Mushroom
    Lasagna with, 198
  Black Bean, Soybean Sprouts
    in, 239
  Brown, Tofu in, 218
  Cheese, Broccoli in, 250–251
  Cheese, Cauliflower in,
    250–251
  Chutney, 483
  Cilantro Chutney, 483
  Coulis, Red Pepper, 475
  Coulis, Tomato-Leek, 99
  Creamy Basil, Pasta with, 194
  Creamy Tomato, Penne
    Primavera with, 193
  Dessert
    Chocolate, 554

Creme Anglaise, 554
  Raspberry, 555
  Raspberry, Pears with, 544
Gorgonzola Cheese, Polenta
  with, 81
Groundnut, Green Beans with
  Chickpeas in, 262
Hollandaise, Blender, 472
Honey-Mustard, Asparagus
  with, 64
Mushroom, Gnocchi with
  Wild, 195
Mushroom, Tortellini with
  Wild, 195
Nam Pla, 482
Oriental Dipping, 482
Peanut, Noodles with, 205
Peanut, Tofu–Soy Sprout
  with, 452
Plum, Eggplant and Tofu
  with, 220–221
Puttanesca, Pasta, 190–191
Red Pepper, Curried, 270–271
Sambal, 481
Sate, Tempeh with, 226
Sesame, Noodles with, 205
Tomato
  and Eggplant, Pasta with, 190
  Garlic, 473
  Marinara, Basil, 474
  Marinara, Chunky, 473
  Marinara, Easy Fresh, 191
  Marinara, Slow-Cooking
    Fresh Tomato, 473
  Pasta with, Yellow, 191
  for Pizza 202
  –Red Pepper, 474
  –Red Pepper, Curried, 474
  with Vegetables, 475
Vegetable, Couscous with, and
  Chickpeas, 152–153
Vodka, Penne with, 194
Sauerkraut with Apples and
  Caraway Seeds, 246–247
Sauté(ed)
  Asparagus, Tomatoes, and Red
    Onion, 236–237

Black Beans and Celery, 333
  Broccoli with Garlic, 242
  Broccoli and Zucchini, 242–243
  Broccoli Rabe with
    Chestnuts, 244
  Cabbage with Snow Peas, 246
  Cucumbers with Tarragon, 255
  Eggplant with Tomatoes,
    Capers, and Garlic, 256
  Escarole, 263
  Fennel and Celery with Water
    Chestnuts and Toasted
    Almonds, 258
  Jícama with Grapes, Lime, 265
  Mushrooms and Peas, Wild, 268
  Mushrooms with Water
    Chestnuts, 267
  Mushrooms on Toast, 461
  Peppers, Onions, and
    Cauliflower, 277
  Peppers, A Trio of, 277
  Red Cabbage with Balsamic
    Vinegar, 247
  Rutabaga and Carrots,
    Orange-, 300
  Salad, Portobello Mushroom
    and Pinto Bean, 382–383
  Salad, Summer Vegetable, 237
  Snow Peas, Peas, and Wild
    Mushrooms, 273
  Spinach, 263
  Sugar Snap, 273
  Tomatoes, 296
  Vegetables, Broccoli with, 273
  Vegetables, Julienned, 80
  Vegetables, Summer, 236–237
  Zucchini, Young, 289
Savory Mushroom Bread
    Pudding, 210
Scalloped Tomatoes, 297
Schav, 131
Schmear Kaese, 47
Scones, 407
Scrambled Eggs, 447
Scrambled Eggs with Cream
    Cheese and Scallion, 447
Seasoned Popcorn, Spicy, 90

Seitan, About, 217
Seitan with Bean Sprouts and
    Mushrooms, 227
Seitan Noodles with, 226
Semolina Bread, 415
Semolina Pasta Dough, 185
Semolina Pizza Crust, 202
Senegalese Soup, 104
Sesame
    About, Oil, 17
    Asparagus, 237
    Asparagus, Spicy, 237
    Green Beans, 237
    Sauce, Noodles with, 205
Shepherd's Pie, Lentil, 147
Sherried Onion Soup, 101
Sherried Pea Soup, 124
Shopping List for Ingredients,
    12–14
Shortcake, Strawberry, 503
Shortcut Eggs Florentine,
    449
Shredded Carrot and Jícama
    Salad, 359
Shredded Carrot and Yellow
    Turnip with Cardamom
    Dressing, 360
Shredded Red Cabbage and
    Asian Pear Salad, 366
Shredded Turnip with Chopped
    Vegetables, 359
Sickle Pears on a Pillow, 545
Side Dishes, About, 231
Side Dish Listings, 228–231
Silver Dollar Pancakes, 434
Slow-Cooking Fresh Tomato
    Marinara Sauce, 473
Small White Beans with Wheat
    Berries, 150
Snap Peas See Pea Pods
Snow Peas. See Pea Pods
Soda Bread, Irish, 402
Soda Bread, Rye-rish, 402
Sodium, About, 17
Sodium in Foods, Table, 6
Sofrito, 484
Sofrito, Cooked, 484

Sofrito Dressing, Bulgur Salad
    with, 374–375
Sorbet
    Anisette Raspberry, 550
    Grapefruit, 551
    Kiwi-Pineapple, 552
    Mint Grapefruit, 551
    Port Wine–Plum, 551
Soufflé, Broccoli, 208–9
Soufflé, Easy Faux, 209
Soufflé, Roquefort, 208
Soup Listings, 92–93
Sour Cream, Chocolate–
    Frosting, 516
Sour Cream Pancakes, 435
Sour Cherry Pie, 521
Sourdough
    About, 425
    Biscuits, Drop, 407
    Bread, French, 426
    Pancakes, Light and Tangy,
        437
    Starter, Basic, 425
Sourgrass Soup, 131
South of the Border Salad,
    348–349
Southwest Corn and Black Bean
    Dip, 66
Southwest Marinade, 482–483
Southwest Salsa Soup, 97
Southwestern Stew, 140
Soybean(s). See Also Tempeh,
    Tofu, Textured Vegetable
    Protein
Soybean Curd. See Tofu
Soybean Products, About, 17–18
Soybean Soup, Miso, 121
Soybean Sprouts in Black Bean
    Sauce, 239
Spaghetti Squash
    About, 164, 292
    Basil-Garlic, 294
    with Beans, Yellow, Green,
        and, 144
    with Bok Choy, 295
    with Bulgur Marinara
        Sauce, 165

with Curried Carrots and
    Beans, 144–145
with Fennel, 294
Provencal, 165
Spasta, 164
and Tomato Sauce, 164
Spaghetti. See Pasta
Spanakopita, 176
Spanish
    Omelet, 451
    Rice, 317
    Salad, Restaurant, 340
    Salad, Rice, 376–377
    Tofu and Beans, -Barbecue, 222
Spasta, 164
Spelt, About, 301, 309
Spelt and Peas, 310
Spice(d)
    Cabbage, Boiled, 246
    Cake, Apple, 504–505
    Cookies, 535
    Couscous with Diced
        Vegetables, 327
    Meetz, 564
    Pears, Sickle, 545
Spicy
    Asparagus, Sesame, 237
    Green Beans with Shallots, 260
    Mushrooms and Barley, Cheesy,
        160–161
    Olives, Garlicky, 86
    Popcorn, Seasoned, 90
    Wafers, Chickpea, 86
Spinach
    About, 287
    with Barley, 305
    Barley with Vegetables, 161
    Bread Pudding, and Dill
        Savory, 210
    Creamed, 288
    Creamy, 288
    Dumplings, Mini Vegetable 76
    Egg Salad, 456–457
    Eggs Florentine, 449
    Eggs Florentine, Shortcut, 449
    Empanadas, 467
    Gnocchi, 203

Gnocchi, and Ricotta, 204
Knishes, 466
Lasagna, Green and White, 197
Pancakes, Greek Potato, 70
Pasta Dough, 186
Pâté, Tricolor Curried, 62
Pesto, Parsley-, 476
Ravioli Filling, -Pignoli, 187
Rice, Brown, 319
-Rice-Cheese- Balls, 75
Risotto, 157
Saag Paneer, 182
Salad
  Baby, 345
  with Goat Cheese
    Dressing, 344
  and Mushroom I, 344
  and Mushroom II, 345
  Strawberry, and
    Nectarine, 369
Sautéed, 263
Soup
  Avgolemono, 103
  Cream, Fresh, 118
  Portuguese Vegetable, 105
  Tomato, Corn, and, 99
  and Tomato, Curried, 98
Spanakopita, 176
Strudel Filling,
  -Mushroom, 177
Timbales, -Herb, 288–289
Split Pea
  Curry, Burmese
    Crispy Vegetables with
    Yellow, 146
  Puree, Garlic, 58
  Puree, Yellow, 59
  Soup
    and Barley, 123
    and Black-Eyed Pea, 125
    Dal, 123
    Minted, 124
    Root Vegetable and, 124
    Sherried, 124
Spoon Bread, 446
Spread(s) Listings, 44
Spread(s), About, 46

Spring Salad, Borscht with,
  131
Spring Vegetable Soup, 96
Springtime Pasta, 191
Sprout(s) Soy, Tofu–, Omelet
  with Peanut Sauce, 452
Sprouted-Pea Salad,
  Chickpea, 387
Squash. See Also Pumpkin,
  Spaghetti Squash
  About, 289, 292
  Bulgur with Summer, 321
  Grilled Vegetable
    Parmesan, 170
  Pesto Vegetables, 291
  Spasta, 164
  Tart, and Basil, 215
  Winter
    Acorn, Apple-Stuffed, 292
    Baked Whole, 292
    Bulgur with, Carrots, and
      Collard, 325
    Butter, Butternut, 492
    Butternut, with Curried
      Millet Filling, 166
    Chayote, Sweet–Potato
      Stuffed, 293
    Cheesecake, Pumpkin, 532
    Couscous with Golden Fruit
      and Vegetables, 326
    Curried with Beans, 144
    Knishes, Sweet Potato–, 466
    Microwaved, 292
    Pureed, with Pear, 293
    Rice, Autumn Brown, 320
    Soup, and Apple, 120
    Wheat Berries with Calabaza
      and Cabbage, 328–329
  Yellow
    with Beans, Green, and
      Spaghetti, 144
    Bulgur with, 324
    Cake, Pecan, 513
    with Chickpeas, 143
    Kamut with Sautéed Escarole
      and, 309
    Stuffed, 291

Zucchini
  Barley, 304–305
  Bread, 395
  Cake, -Walnut, 513
  Caviar, -Olive, 52
  with Chickpeas, and
    Yellow, 143
  Coleslaw, 361
  Collards, and Tomatoes, 262
  Curried, and Fennel, 290
  Italian-Style, 290
  Lentils with, 451
  Melt, -Leek, 159
  Mozzarella Baked Eggplant
    and, 170
  Omelet, 451
  Ratatouille, 257
  Salad, 352–353
  Sautéed Broccoli and,
    242–243
  Sautéed Young, 289
  Soup, -Leek, 106
  Stewed Garbanzo Beans with
    -Quinoa, 152
  Sticks, Fried, 68–69
  with Shiitake Mushrooms,
    290–291
Steamed Artichokes, 235
Steaming Vegetables, 232
Stewed Garbanzo Beans with
  Zuc-Quinoa, 151
Stewed Peaches and
  Cherries, 542
Stewed Quinces, 491–492
Stewed Tomatoes, 296
Sticky Buns, 502
Stilton Dip, 369
Stilton Marscapone, 50
Stilton Potatoes au Gratin, 284
Stilton Stuffed Mushrooms,
  82
Stir-Fried Bok Choy, 241
Stir-Fried Mung Bean
  Sprouts, 238
Stir-Fried Vegetables with
  Mushrooms on a Bird's
  Nest, 180

Stollen, Walnut, 503
Strada, Strawberry and
      Raspberry, 540
Strawberry(ies)
   Cheesecake, Swirl, 531
   Chocolate-Dipped, 546
   Jam, Plum and, 490
   Ketchup, 470
   Salad
      –Belgian Endive, 368
      Berry Berry Berry Good,
         389
      Calypso-Berry, 389
      Jamaican Kiwi-Strawberry,
         387
   Kasha, Jícama, and Mandarin
      Orange, 380
      Mango-, 389
      and Peach, 388
      Spinach, and Nectarine, 369
      Wheat Berry, Tropical, 373
   Shortcake, 503
   Soup, Chilled, 135
   Strada, -Raspberry, 540
   Tart, Apple-, 524
   Tart with Oat Streusel Topping,
      -Rhubarb, 521
   with Zabaglione, 542–543
Streusel-Topped Blueberry
      Coffeecake, 506
Streusel-Topped Muffins, 408
Streusel-Topped Pumpkin
      Bread, 396
Streusel Topping, Strawberry-
      Rhubarb Tart with Oat, 521
Stroganoff, Mushrooms, 173
Strudel
   About, 528
   Apple Filling, 529
   Basic Technique, 528
   Bites, 74
   Cabbage Kasha Filling, 178
   Cheese Filling, 529
   Cherry Filling, Sweet, 529
   Pineapple Filling, 530
   Raspberry Filling, Fresh,
      529

Spinach-Mushroom,
      Filling, 177
Vegetable-Potato,
      Filling, 177
Walnut Filling, 530
Wild Rice–Mushroom,
      Filling, 178
Stuffed
   Artichokes, Italian Style, 84
   Cabbage, Sweet and Sour,
      166–167
   Celery, 46
   Eggplant, Bulgur-, 167
   Eggplant, Quinoa-, 168
   Eggplant, Turkish, 168
   Eggplant, Young, 256–257
   Eggs, 85
   Grape Leaves, 72–73
   Mushrooms
      Cheese, 83
      Garlicky Parmesan, 83
      Herb, 82
      Old-Fashioned, 82
      Stilton, 82–83
   Onion, Baked, 272
   Papaya, Couscous-, 326
   Potatoes, Baked, 283
   Potatoes, Decadent, Baked, 283
   Salad, Olive, Rice and Roman
      Bean, 382
   Shells, Escarole and
      Cheese, 188
   Squash, Acorn, Apple-, 292
   Squash, Yellow, 291
   Tomatoes, Basil-, Baked, 296
   Tomatoes, Broccoli-, 297
Succotash, 334
Sue Levy's Eggplant Spread, 53
Sugar, About, 500
Sugar Snaps. See Pea Pods
Sugarless Stewed Peaches and
      Cherries, 542
Sukiyaki, 218
Summer Brunch Fruit Salad, 390
Sun-Dried Tomato(es)
   Baked Brie and, 76
   Cheesecake, 47

Coulis, Red Pepper, 475
Dip, Caramelized Onion
      and, 65
Dip, Red Pepper and, 64–65
and Goat Cheese on Sliced
      Baguette, 49
Pasta Puttanesca, 190–191
Pasta, Springtime, 191
Pesto, 477
Salad, Bulgur S-D-T, 374
Salad, Brown Rice and
      Lentil, 377
Ziti, Baked, 199
Swedish Limpa Bread, 422–423
Sweet Biscuits, 404
Sweet Cherry Strudel
      Filling, 529
Sweet and Sour
   Bean Curd, 220
   Beets, 240
   Onions, Pearl, 271
   Soup, Cabbage, 109
   Stuffed Cabbage, 166–167
Sweet Potato(es). See Also
      Potato(es)
   Butter Rum, 286
   Cake, -Apple, 508
   Candied, Brandied, 286
   Chips, 87
   Curry, Okra, Plantain, and, 183
   Knishes, –Squash, 466
   Loaf, Plantain and, 278
   Mashed with Hazelnut
      Praline, 285
   Mashed, Orange, 286
   Mashed, Pecan, 286
   Muffins, Meadow, 412
   Pancakes, 72
   Soup, Curried, –Mango, 115
   –Stuffed Chayote, 293
   Tzimmes, 287
Sweet Yeast Dough, 501–502
Sweetened Coconut Rice, 315
Sweetened Farmer-Cheese
      Pastry, 519
Swiss Cheese, French Onion
      Soup, 102

Swiss Cheese Fondue, 67
Swiss Chard. *See* Greens
Szechuan
  Asparagus with Water
    Chestnuts, 238
  Broccoli, 179
  Green Beans, 261
  Green Beans, Cold
    Marinated, 261
  Shredded Vegetables with
    Pressed Tofu, 217

T

Tables
  Bean Cooking, 14
  Fat Content of Foods, 6
  Cooking, Processed Grains, 302
  Cooking, Rice, 303
  Cooking, Whole Grains, 301
  Shopping Guide, 12–13
Tabouli, 373
Tahini Dressing, 392
Tamale Pie, 223
Tart(s). *See Also* Pie(s), Tartlets
  Apple, Easy, 523
  Apple-Strawberry, 524
  Apricot-Raspberry, 522
  Blueberry-Orange, 523
  Cheese, 524
  Cranberry-Pear Chutney, 522
  Eggplant and Red Pepper,
    Roasted, 214
  Gorgonzola, Leek, and
    Fennel, 213
  Honey Apple-Fig, 525
  Lemon Meringue, 526
  Mousse, Frozen Piña Colada,
    524–525
  Mushroom-Leek, 214
  Raspberry-Apricot, 522
  Raspberry, with Blueberry
    Filling, Fresh, 523
  Squash and Basil, 215
  Strawberry-Rhubarb with Oat
    Streusel Topping, 521

Tomato-Feta, 212
  Wild Mushroom, Leek, 214
Tartlets. See Also Croustade(s),
    Pie(s), Tart(s)
  Fruit, 525–526
  Lemon Meringue, 526
  Mushrooms, 59
  Shells, 519
  Walnut Fudge, 526
  Whipped Cream, 527
Tea Apple, Hot, 559
Tea Fresh Mint, 558
Tea, Ginger, Fresh, 558–559
Tea, Iced Mint, 558
Tempeh
  About, 217
  Barbecue, on a Bun, 461
  Croutons, 69
  Fingers, 69
  with Sate Sauce, 226
Tempura, 181
Teriyaki Grilled Vegetables, 234
Tex-Mex Corn Pudding, 253
Textured Vegetable Protein
    (TVP)
  About, 217
  Chili, Black Bean, 155
  Croquettes, Chickeny
  Picadillo, Black Bean, 225
Thanksgiving Kamut, 309
Thanksgiving Mashed Potatoes,
    Ruthie's Chive, 282
Thick Shake, 566
Three-Bean Salad, 385
Three-Bean Vegetable Soup,
    125
Three Cheese Macaroni and
    Cheese, 216
Three-Grain Muffins, 410
Timbales, Broccoli Herb,
    288–289
Timbales, Onion, 270–271
Timbales, Spinach-Herb,
    288–289
Toasted Pitas, 428
Tofu
  About, 217

Barbecue, and Beans,
    Spanish, 222
Barbecue, and Rice with Black
    Beans, Very Quick, 221
in Brown Sauce, 218
Bulgur with, and
    Cauliflower, 221
Egg Rolls, 77
Gado Gado, 224
Kasha with Cauliflower, 221
Mayonnaise, 472
Mayonnaise, Lemon, 472
Mee Grob, 207
Moo Shu Vegetables, 219
Omelet, –Soy Sprout with
    Peanut Sauce, 452
with Plum Sauce, Eggplant
    and, 220–221
Rice, Beans, and, Madrid, 222
Soup, Miso, 121
Sukiyaki, 218
Sweet and Sour Bean Curd, 220
Tamale Pie, 223
Vegetables with Pressed,
    Szechuan Shredded, 217
Tomatillo Relish, Corn, 485
Tomatillos, Chili Rice with, 317
Tomatillos, Salsa Verde, 480
Tomato(es). *See Also* Sun-Dried
    Tomatoes
  About, 295
  Broiled, 295
  Broiled, Cheesy, 295
  Bulgur with Eggplant, 324
  Chutney, –Pineapple,
    Green, 487
  Chutney, Plum, and Dried
    Fruit, 486
  Collards, Zucchini, and, 262
  Coulis, -Leek, 99
  Eggplant, Mediterrean, 169
  Juice, Bloody Mary, 564
  Juice, Virgin Mary Mix, 564
  Ketchup, 470
  Pasta Dough, 185
  Pico de Gallo, 484
  Piperade, 453

Tomato(es) *(cont.)*
Raita, 496
Relish, Green, 485
Risotto, and Basil, 158
Salad
  -Avocado, 351
  -Bean, 350
  Black Bean and, 385
  Bread, Grilled Vegetable, 352
  Endive, and Hearts of
    Palm, 351
  and Feta Cheese, 351
  -Mozzarella, 350
  Sautéed Summer
    Vegetable, 237
  -Scallion, 350
  Snap Pea-, 352
  Warm, 350
  Wheat Berry with, and Goat
    Cheese, 372
Salsa, Easy, 479
Salsa Ranchero, 480
Salsa Sauce, Warm, 479
Sambal, 481
Sandwich, and Mozzarella,
  459
Sauce
  Curried, Red Pepper, 474
  and Eggplant, Pasta with, 190
  Garlic, 473
  Lentils in, 334
  Marinara, Basil, 474
  Marinara, Chunky, 473
  Marinara, Easy Fresh, 191
  Marinara, Slow-Cooking
    Fresh, 473
  Penne Primavera with
    Creamy, 193
  for Pizza, 202
  Puttanesca, Pasta, 190–191
  –Red Pepper, 474
  Spaghetti Squash and, 164
  with Vegetables, 475
  Yellow, Pasta with, 191
Sautéed, 296
Sautéed Asparagus, and Red
  Onion, 236–237

Sautéed Eggplant with, Capers,
  and Garlic, 256
Scalloped, 297
Soup
  –Cheddar Cheese, 100
  Corn, and Spinach, 99
  Curried, 98
  Curried Spinach, 98
  Fresh, 97
  Garden, 100
  Gumbo, 101
  Herbed, 7
  and Leek, Creamy, 99
  Red Pepper–, 98
  Southwest Salsa, 97
  Tortilla, 100–101
Spread, Chopped, and Olive, 51
Stewed, 296
Stuffed Baked, Basil-, 296
Stuffed, Broccoli-, 297
Stuffed, Italian, 298
Stuffed, Orzo-, 298
Tart, Feta-, 212
White Beans with, and
  Basil, 335
Topfen, 495
Torte, Walnut, 505
Tortellini with Wild Mushroom
  Sauce, 195
Tortilla(s)
  Chips, Homemade, 86–87
  Cookies, 537
  Enchilada, Mexican Egg, 454
  Fajitas, 163
  Huevos Rancheros, 455
  Nachos, 67
  Nachos Grand, 68
  Quesadilla, 464
  Soup, 100–101
  Tostadas, Black Bean, 153
Tostadas, Black Bean, 153
Tostones, 279
Traditional French Toast, 442
Traditional Latkes, 70
Traditional Pesto, 476
Trail Mix, 89
Tricolor Coleslaw, 361

Tricolor Curried Pâté, 62
A Trio of Sautéed Peppers, 277
Tropical Wheat Berry Salad, 373
Truffles, 516–517
Turkish Stuffed Eggplant, 168
Turnip(s). *See Also* Rutabaga
  (Yellow Turnip)
Turnip About, 298
Turnip and Apples, 298–299
Turnip Salad, Shredded, with
  Chopped Vegetables, 359
Turnover(s),
  Apple, Little, 527
  Empanadas Basic, 466–467
  Empanadas, Spinach, 467
  Empanadas Vegetable, 467
  Knishes
    Basic, 465
    Broccoli-Cheddar, 465
    Kasha, 465
    Mini, 464
    Spinach, 466
    Sweet Potato-Squash, 466
  Pear, 545
  Samosa, 74–75
Tuscan Torta di Funghi
  e Patate, 175
TVP. *See* Textured Vegetable
  Protein
Tzimmes, 287

U

Upside Down Cake, Plum,
  506–507
Untraditional Irish Soda
  Bread, 402

V

Vanilla Whipped Cream, 558
"Vedding" Cake, 508–509
Vegetable(s). *See Also* Individual
  Vegetables
  About, 12–13, 15, 232–233
  Almond Ding, 180–181
  Bali, 249

Barbecued, 233
Barley with, 161
Broiled, 233
Broth, Juice, 95
Broth, Mighty, 94
Burmese Crispy, with Yellow
    Pea Curry, 146
Cheesecake, Savory, 48
Chinese Cabbage and
    Oriental, 179
Couscous with Diced,
    Spiced, 327
Couscous with Golden Fruit
    and, 326
Curry, Mixed, 181
for a Crowd, Winter, 245
Dumplings, Mini, 76
Empanadas, 467
Grilled, Basic, 233
Grilled, Teriyaki, 234
Grilling, 232–3
Hummus, 57
with Kamut and Beans, 148
Kebabs, 233
Lasagna, 196
Melt, Boboli and, 463
Microwaving, 232
Moo Shu, 219
Moroccan, with Couscous,
    145
Parmesan, Grilled, 170
Pasta with, and Lentils, Randy
    Kraft's, 192
Pesto, 291
Piperade, Grilled, 454
Quinoa with Mixed, 313
Quinoa with Shredded, 313
Root, Ginger-Baked, 299
Salad
  Bean, Olive and, 356
  Chickpea and Grilled, 386
  Garden, 349
  Grilled, and Bread, 352
  Mixed Greens with,
    Threads, 342
  and Potato, 364
  Sautéed Summer, 237

Shredded Turnip with
    Chopped Vegetables, 359
  Wheat Berry–, 372
Sauce and Chickpeas,
    Couscous with, 152–153
Sauce, Tomato with, 475
Sautéed, Broccoli with, 273
Sautéed Julienned, 80
Sautéed Summer, 256–257
Shredded, with Pressed Tofu,
    Szechuan, 217
Soup
  Chickpea, 129
  Chowder, Manhattan-
    Style, 109
  Lentil-, French, 129
  Portuguese, 105
  Randy's, 96–97
  Root, and Split Pea, 124
  Three-Bean, 125
Steaming, 232
Stew, Ethiopian, 163
Stew, Indonesian, 164
Stir-Fried with Mushrooms on a
    Bird's Nest, 180
Strudel Filling, -Potato, 177
Tempura, 181
Threads, Mixed Greens with,
    342–343
Vegetarian Codes, 4
Vegetarians, Types of, 3
Vegetarians and Health, 4–6
Very Quick Barbecue Tofu and
    Rice with Black Beans, 221
Very Rich Broccoli-Cheddar
    Soup, 118
Vichyssoise, 114
Vidalia Onion Omelet, 452
Vidalia Onion Quiche, 211
Vidalias Caramelized, 452
Vinaigrette. *See* Salad Dressing
Vinegar, About, 18–19
Vinegar, Blueberry, 471
Vinegar, Raspberry, 470–471
Virgin Mary Mix, 564
Vitamins and Minerals, 4
Vodka Sauce, Penne with, 194

W

Wafers, Spicy Chickpea, 86
Waffles
  About, 439
  Apple Pie, 440
  Banana-Poppyseed, 440
  Basic, 439–440
  Bran, 441
  Corn and Oat (No Wheat),
    438
  Maple, 441
Waldorf Salad, 365
Walnut. *See Also* Nut
  Asparagus with, and Browned
    Butter, 236
  Bread, Cranberry, 395
  Bread, Date-, 397–398
  Cake, Zucchini-, 513
  Chutney, Rhubarb-, 488
  Hoisin, 88
  Salad, Wild Rice with Apple
    and, 378
  Sandwich Spread, Date-, 458
  Stollen, 503
  Strudel Filling, 530
  Tartlets, Fudge, 526
  Torte, 505
Warm Lentil Salad with Balsamic
    Dressing, 383
Warm Tomato Salad, 350
Warm Salsa Sauce, 479
Water Chestnuts Sautéed Fennel
    and Celery with Toasted
    Almonds, 258
Water Chestnuts Sautéed
    Mushrooms with, 267
Water Chestnut Spread,
    Mushroom-, 60
Water Chestnuts, Szechuan
    Asparagus with, 238
Watercress, Cucumber, and
    Onion Salad with Creamy
    Pepper Dressing, 347
Watercress and Romaine with
    Roquefort Dressing, 348

Watercress Salad, Wilted
   Sprout, 362
Watermelon Cooler,
   Raspberry-, 562
Welsh Rarebit, 462
Wheat. *See Also* Bulgur,
   Couscous, Noodles,
   Semolina
About, 324
Berry(ies)
   Bread, 417–418
   with Brown Rice, Dilled, 329
   with Calabaza and Cabbage,
      328–329
   with Cardoon, 329
   with Cashews, 328
   with Gingered Eggplant, 328
   Provençal, 327
   Salad, Corn-, 372–373
   Salad, with Tomatoes and
      Goat Cheese, 372
   Salad, Tropical, 373
   Salad, -Vegetable, 372
   with, Small White Beans,
      150
   Bread, Whole, 414
   Germ Cookies, Pecan-, 536
   Germ Drop Biscuits, 406
   Germ-Honey Pancakes, 434
   Grain Dish, Fran's Great, 152
Whipped Cream, Chocolate, 558
Whipped Cream, Coffee, 558
Whipped Cream Tartlets, 527
Whipped Cream, Vanilla, 558
White Beans. *See* Bean(s)
White Pizza, 203
Whole Wheat Pizza Crust, 201
Whole Wheat Bread, 414

Wild Mushroom and Leek
   Tart, 214
Wild Rice. *See Also* Rice, Risotto
About, 301, 303
   with Apples and Almonds, 323
   and Corn, 322
   Fiddlehead Ferns with, 321
   Lemon, and White, 321
   with Orzo and Three-Color
      Peppers, 322
   Salad with Apples and
      Walnuts, 378
   Salad, and Corn, 322
   Salad, and Rice Bean, 379
   Salad, and White, 379
   Soup, Leek and, 126
   Strudel Filling,
      -Mushroom, 178
   Stuffed Peppers, Wildly, 160
   and White Rice with Three-
      Color Peppers, 322
Wildly Stuffed Peppers, 160
Wilted Cucumber Salad, 354
Wilted Sprout and Watercress
   Salad, 362
Winter Salad, 388
Winter Vegetables for a
   Crowd, 245
Wonton Cookies, 537
World's Best Whole Wheat
   Biscuits, 403

Y

Yeast, About, 413–414
Yeast Dough, Danish Pastry,
   501–502

Yeast Dough, Sweet,
   501–502
Yeast Sourdough Starter, Basic, 425
Yellow Gazpacho, 130
Yellow, Green, and Spaghetti
   Squash with Beans, 144
Yellow Indian Rice, 316
Yellow Pepper Soup, Curried,
   103
Yellow Split Pea Puree, 59
Yellow Tomato Sauce, Pasta
   with, 191
Yields, About, 6–7
Yin and Yang Soup, 133
Yogurt
   Cheese, 495
   Dip, Avocado, 64
   Dip, Chutney, 64
   Dip, Honey Mustard, 64
   Dip, -Horseradish, 65
   Lassi, 561
   Raita, 495
   Raita, Tomato, 495
   Salsa, Creamy, 479
   Sauce, Chutney, 483

Z

Zabaglione, Strawberries with,
   542–543
Ziti Baked, 199
Ziti with Broccoli and
   Rosemary, 195
Ziti with Roasted Red Pepper
   and Grilled Eggplant, 192
Zucchini. *See* Squash